WEALTH INDICES OF INVESTMENTS
IN THE U.S. CAPITAL MARKETS
Year-End 1925 = $1.00

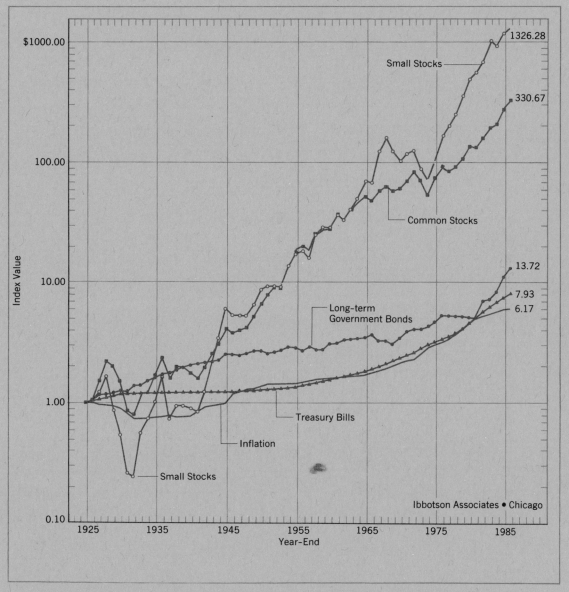

Source: Roger G. Ibbotson and Rex A. Sinquefield, *Stocks, Bonds, Bills, and Inflation* (SSBI), 1982, updated in *SSBI 1987 Yearbook,* Ibbotson Associates, Chicago, 1987, p. 9. Reprinted by permission.

INVESTMENTS:
ANALYSIS AND
MANAGEMENT

INVESTMENTS:
ANALYSIS AND
MANAGEMENT

Second Edition

Charles P. Jones

North Carolina State University

John Wiley & Sons

New York   Chichester   Brisbane   Toronto   Singapore

Cover Design by Carolyn Joseph
Cover Art by Marjory Dressler

Library of Congress Cataloging in Publication Data:

Jones, Charles Parker, 1943–
    Investments: analysis and management

    Includes index.
    1. Investments. 2. Investment analysis. I. Title.

HG4521.J663 1988   332.6   87-23153
ISBN 0-471-85284-8

Printed in the United States of America

10 9 8 7 6 5 4 3 2 1

To Kay and Kathryn
and
To Helen

PREFACE

This book endeavors to give its readers a good understanding of investments while stimulating their interest in the subject. This understanding and interest can be very valuable because each of us must make various investment decisions during our lifetime—definitely as individuals and possibly as managers. Upon completing this book, the reader will be able to appreciate what is involved in making investment decisions, what the opportunities are, and where the problems can arise.

Students are provided with an adequate background in a clear and concise manner. Since the book is designed for the first course in investments, descriptive material must be—and is—thoroughly covered. Furthermore, the analytics of investments are presented throughout the book in order that students can learn to reason these issues out for themselves and be better prepared when the investing decisions of the real world are confronted.

The book was written for juniors and seniors in four-year colleges and universities. Standard prerequisites for most students taking this course include accounting and economics, and possibly financial management. A course in statistics is useful but not essential. I have sought to minimize formulas and to simplify difficult material, consistent with the presentation of investments from a thoroughly up-to-date standpoint. Relevant, state-of-the-art material has been simplified and structured specifically for the benefit of the beginning student.

Organization of the Book

This book is divided into seven parts. Part One provides a background for students before they encounter the specifics of security analysis and portfolio management. Chapter 1 establishes a framework for the entire book by outlining the factors involved in investments. It is very important for beginners to obtain an overall idea of what investing is all about at the outset. Chapter 2 describes the wide range of financial asset alternatives available with primary emphasis on marketable securities. Chapter 3 analyzes financial markets, focusing both on the actual operations and functioning of markets and the changing structure of the marketplace. Sources of information available to investors, both published and computerized, are discussed in Chapter 4. Finally, Chapter 5, by describing the risk–return concepts that underlie all investment analysis, establishes a risk–return framework for the remainder of the book.

Parts Two and Three focus on the basic approach to security analysis by presenting the "how-to" tools and techniques. Part Two discusses the calculation and management of bonds, a logical starting point in learning to value all securities. Part Three builds on these concepts in discussing the valuation (security analysis) of common stocks. Chapters 6 and 8 provide the necessary information about bonds and common stocks, while Chapters 7 and 9 discuss their valuation. Appendix 7–A, covering preferred stocks, makes a good transition between Parts Two and Three.

Given the basis for analyzing and valuing common stocks established in Part Three, Parts Four and Five proceed to the three strategies typically discussed in the selection of common stocks. Part Four covers fundamental analysis, the heart of security analysis. Because of its scope and complexity, Chapters 10, 11 and 12 are required to adequately cover the fundamental approach. The order of these chapters—market, industry, and company—reflects the recommended order of procedure in doing fundamental analysis.

Part Five discusses the other two approaches to common stock selection—technical analysis and the efficient markets approach. Technical analysis, discussed in Chapter 13, remains a controversial subject. The reason for this is explained in Chapter 14, which describes the efficient-market hypothesis. As explained in Chapter 1, investors should be aware of and carefully consider this hypothesis; however, it need not dominate the entire book. For example, Chapter 14 discusses current market "anomalies," which deserve careful investor consideration.

Parts Three, Four, and Five are devoted to common stocks, a reasonable allocation given investor interest in common stock. Part Six discusses the other major securities available to investors. Chapter 15 analyzes options (puts and calls), a popular investment alternative in recent years. Stock index options are also covered. Chapter 16 continues the analysis of equity-derivative securities by focusing on warrants and convertibles. Chapter 17 is devoted to financial futures, an important new topic in investments. Finally, Chapter 18 analyzes the investor's alternative of indirect investing—buying shares in an investment company and thereby indirectly owning a portfolio of securities.

Part Seven is concerned with portfolio management and portfolio performance measurement. Chapter 19 contains a complete discussion of modern portfolio concepts, with primary emphasis on the essentials of Markowitz portfolio theory and the single-index model. Chapter 20 discusses capital market theory, which contains material necessary for the understanding of today's investing environment. Chapter 21 concludes the text with a discussion on how to measure portfolio performance. This is a logical conclusion to both Part Seven and the entire book because all investors are keenly interested in how well their investments have performed. Mutual funds are used as examples of how to apply these portfolio performance measures (and of the problems in interpretation that can result).

Special Features

This text offers several important features, some of which are unique. First, the sequence of chapters has been carefully structured and coordinated as a package, reflecting considerable experimentation and careful thought. While other arrangements are workable, I find this one to be the most satisfactory in a beginning investments course. Starting with background material and progressing through an analysis of various securities to a discussion of portfolio management, the book proceeds from easier to more difficult concepts, and from fewer to more numerous equations.

Second, I have diligently sought to hold the text to a length that is manageable for the average student. Instructors may choose to omit chapters, depending on preferences and constraints. Although it requires a tight schedule, the entire text can be covered in a one semester course, including the use of supplementary material such as articles, questions and problems from the end of chapters, or microcomputer problems and illustrations.

Third, each chapter features several items specifically designed for the student's benefit. Key words appear in boldface, and are defined in the glossary. Other important words are italicized. Each chapter contains a thorough and detailed summary to help the student review the material. Each chapter also contains an extensive set of questions and problems that are keyed specifically to the chapter material and which are designed to thoroughly review the concepts in each chapter. In addition, some chapters have "Extended Problems with Examples," which provide the student with even more practice. These problems are self-contained in that they guide students through the problem by showing them some of the solutions. The extensive set of problems presented in this book helps to fill a gap that has existed in investments texts.

Another distinctive feature of this book is the use of boxed inserts. These inserts provide timely and interesting material from the popular press, enabling the student to see the real-world side to issues and concepts discussed in the text. These boxed inserts have been rigorously culled from the potentially large number outstanding on the basis of their likely interest to the reader, their relevance in illustrating important concepts, and their timeliness.

Second Edition Changes

The second edition has been thoroughly updated using the latest information and numbers available. Several chapters have been streamlined in approach and content. For example, Chapter 1 has been redone following the suggestions of reviewers. As another example, Chapter 3 has been restructured to provide better organization and flow. The use of the market model has been decreased in Chapter 8. Several appendixes have been eliminated, and in some cases this material has been integrated directly into the chapter—for example, the Black–Scholes model is now a part of Chapter 15. The selected references at the end of chapters have been thoroughly updated.

Every effort has been made to include the important new concepts being discussed in investments, consistent with the constraint on the total length of the text and a commitment to keep the material understandable and interesting to beginners. Portfolio insurance, program trading, and junk bonds are good examples of new or often-heard terms that are included somewhere in the text, either in the chapter material itself or in boxed inserts. On the other hand, some current events, such as the unfolding insider-trading scandals, are probably best handled by the instructor using specific, current incidents.

Acknowledgments

A number of individuals helped me with this project. I particularly thank Jack W. Wilson, North Carolina State, who read the original manuscript and offered many useful comments, provided material for some of the appendixes, and worked out many of the problems (including the extended problems) for the text. He has continued his valuable assistance in the second edition.

Several reviewers have provided excellent comments and suggestions for improvements throughout the preparation of this manuscript. Exercising patience, and no doubt restraint, they caught many of my mistakes and omissions, and tolerated my preferences for handling particular subjects. I am most appreciative of their efforts, especially those of Randall Billingsley, Virginia Polytechnic Institute and State University; Pat Hess, Ohio State University; Richard DeMong, University of Virginia; Keith Broman, University of Nebraska; Ron Braswell, Florida State University; Donald Puglisi, University of Delaware; Howard VanAuken, Iowa State University; James Buck, East Carolina University; and Malcolm Torgerson, Western Illinois University. In-depth reviews for this edition were provided by Eugene Furtado, Kansas State University; William B. Gillespie, St. Louis University; and Edward Saunders, Northeastern University. Their advice and recommendations led to several significant improvements. The reviewers' work has been invaluable to me.

In addition to the above, a number of users have responded to the first edition and offered useful comments and opinions. This list includes P. R. Chandy, North Texas State University; D. Monath, University of Louisville; Larry J. Johnson, University of Tulsa; Stan Atkinson, University of Central Florida; Howard W. Bohnen, St. Cloud State University; James M. Tipton, Baylor University; William P. Dukes, Texas Tech University; A. Bhattacharya, University of Cincinnati; and Christopher Ma, University of Toledo. I wish to thank in particular two users, John Groth of Texas A&M University and Seth Anderson of The University of Alabama at Birmingham, who supplied me with detailed comments, suggestions, and corrections in the course of using the text.

I would also like to thank my former editor at Wiley, Rich Esposito, for his confidence in me. He provided the original support and guidance I needed to complete a difficult task on a tight schedule. The current editor, Joe Dougherty, has been very helpful in planning and preparing this revised edition. The other Wiley professionals with whom I have worked on this project have been excellent.

Finally, I would like to thank my family, who shared this burden fully and magnificently. Without their support, a project such as this would have been difficult at best. I thank my wife who helped me tremendously in the preparation of the manuscript and without whose help I would have been unable to finish on schedule.

Charles P. Jones

CONTENTS

PART ONE

BACKGROUND

CHAPTER 1

A BACKGROUND FOR UNDERSTANDING INVESTMENTS

For four of the six years from 1980 to 1986, professional portfolio managers failed to perform as well as the overall stock market. Why?

Is it possible to have earned 40% or more investing in default-free Treasury bonds in only one year?

Why did the price of Texas Instruments stock fall 32% ($50.75 per share) in only two days (a total drop in market value of $1.2 billion)?

How can futures contracts, with a reputation for being extremely risky, be used to reduce an investor's risk?

What is the average annual rate of return on common stocks? What can an investor reasonably expect to earn from stocks in the future?

The objective of this text is to help you understand the investments field as it is currently understood, discussed, and practiced so that you can intelligently answer questions such as the preceding ones. To accomplish this objective, key concepts are presented to provide an appreciation of the theory and practice of investments.

Both descriptive and quantitative materials about investing are readily available. Some of this material is very enlightening; much of it is debatable because there are many controversies in investments and some of it is worthless. This text seeks to cover what is particularly useful and relevant for today's investment climate. It offers some ideas about what you can reasonably expect to accomplish by using what you learn and, therefore, what you can realistically expect to achieve as an investor in today's investment world. *In fact, learning to avoid the many pitfalls awaiting you as an investor by clearly understanding what you can reasonably expect from investing your money may be the single most important benefit to be derived from this text.* In support of this statement, see Box 1–1.

BOX 1–1   THE HUSTLER'S BEST FRIEND: YOU

Should investing be much different now that the arbs are tranquilized? Not very. Sure, Boesky and most of the Princes of Greed are no longer around to cut a slice out of investors' hides. But the major dangers that investors face haven't changed. It's still a jungle out there.

The worst menace, as old as markets, is right in your own bosom: greed, the lure of big bucks made easily. The arbs made megamillions in takeovers, but they have hurt individual investors much less than that army of hustlers relying on slick merchandising. Your own greed is the hustler's best friend.

"Come grow with us," the catchy phrase of Robert Brennan's First Jersey Securities, took out thousands of investors while making large fortunes for Brennan and some of his merry band, as *Forbes* senior editor Dick Stern detailed in both the July 16, 1984 and Dec. 29, 1986 issues. First Jersey's pitch was probably too blatant for most *Forbes* readers, but there are other, more sophisticated ones to steer clear of.

Among the most important are the claims made by brokers and money and mutual fund managers about their sensational records. A classic example is Fred Alger, one of the legendary "Freds" of the go-go markets of the Sixties. His major fund rocketed up in the speculative bubble of 1967–68, only to go down in flames when the go-go market collapsed. Alger says he did not solely manage the fund in the crash, and thus does not debit this disaster to his performance record. That's kind of like playing golf and counting only your good shots.

A current multimillion-dollar media blitz blithely displaying Fred's handsome face alongside a jerry-built record of selected accounts claims that he has beat the S&P's 500 10-to-1 on average annually since 1965. Had you put $10,000 with Alger back in 1965, the advertisements blare, it would be worth $651,228 today. (The fine print states that he had only one account back then and does not indicate whether he has kept it.)

The only thing I would personally take as written in granite in this record is the last part of the small print: "Past results do not guarantee future performance." They sure don't, especially when the record seems to be deliberately selective.

Questionable claims are not the only menace. Some of the Brahmins of the investment business are excellent marketers and not too proud to cash in on the latest speculative fad. So when a salesman tries to talk you into buying, say, the latest new variety of mutual fund, thank him politely and hang up the phone.

As for hot-performing funds, some firms

run hatcheries in sizzling investment areas. The process is simple. A number of funds are started in-house in a fast-paced area, with only those chalking up spectacular records eventually being sold to the public. The new fund hits an eager public with an excellent record. Those funds with poorer results quietly sink to the bottom of the pond.

If you haven't already, make a resolution this year to curb your own greed and thus make life a little tougher for those with doubtful merchandise to peddle. Here are a few antigreed rules: Avoid hot stories. Investigate before you buy. Searching a record is time-consuming but worth its weight in gold. (It's amazing that people spend dozens of hours shopping for television sets, cars or dishwashers but invest tens of thousands of dollars on the basis of only a two- or three-minute sales talk.)

If your questions get a reply like "It's moving up, and we're only allotting you stock because we want you as a client," run, do not walk, to the nearest exit. If a performance record has numerous caveats and gives itself wide benefits of the doubt in measurements, again beat a retreat.

The point is, if it looks too easy, it probably is. Avoid it.

Source: Adapted from David Dreman's column, by permission of *Forbes* magazine, January 26, 1987. © Forbes Inc., 1987.

The Nature of Investments

Some Definitions

The term *investing* can cover a wide range of activities. It often refers to investing money in certificates of deposit, bonds, common stocks, or mutual funds. More knowledgeable investors would include other financial assets such as warrants, puts and calls, futures contracts, and convertible securities. Investing encompasses very conservative positions and aggressive speculation.

An **investment** can be defined as the commitment of funds to one or more assets that will be held over some future time period. **Investments,** therefore, is the study of the investment process. Basically, investments is concerned with the management of an investor's wealth, which is the sum of current income and the present value of all future income. (Therefore, present value and compound interest concepts have an important role in the investing process.) The field of investments encompasses many aspects; however, as the title of this book suggests, it can be thought of in terms of two functions: analysis and management.

The term *investments*, in this text, refers in general to financial assets and in particular to marketable securities. **Financial assets** are pieces of paper evidencing a financial claim on some issuer, such as the federal government or a corporation; on the other hand, **real assets** are tangible assets such as gold, silver, diamonds, art, and real estate. **Marketable securities** are financial assets that are easily and cheaply tradable in organized markets. Technically, investments includes both financial and real assets, and both marketable and nonmarketable assets. Because of the vast scope of investment opportunities available to investors, however, we do not include a direct, detailed study of real assets, and only briefly mention nonmarketable assets.[1]

Why Do We Invest?

We invest to make money! Although everyone would agree with this statement, we need to be more precise (after all, this is a college textbook). We invest to improve our welfare, which for our purposes can be defined as monetary wealth, both current and future.[2] We will assume that investors are interested only in the monetary benefits to be obtained from investing as opposed to such factors as the psychic income to be derived from impressing your friends with your financial prowess.

Funds to be invested come from assets already owned, borrowed money, and savings or foregone consumption. By foregoing consumption today and investing the savings, investors expect to enhance their future consumption possibilities; that is, they are interested in increasing their wealth. Investors also seek to manage their wealth effectively, obtaining the most from it while protecting it from inflation, taxes, and other factors. In order to accomplish both objectives, people invest.

The Importance of Studying Investments

It is important to remember that all individuals have wealth of some kind—if nothing else, the value of their services in the marketplace. Most individuals must make investment decisions sometime in their lives. Some workers, for example, can decide if their retirement funds are to be invested in stocks or bonds. Others may wish to maximize the return from their "savings account" funds by investing in alternatives to insured savings accounts.

A good example of how a typical individual may be faced with investment decisions, and the critical importance of making good investment decisions, is the Individual Retirement Account (IRA), available to many income earners despite the landmark Tax Reform Act of 1986. IRA funds can be invested in a wide range of assets, ranging from the very safe to the quite speculative. IRA owners are allowed to have self-directed brokerage accounts, which offer a wide range of investment opportunities. As these funds may be invested for as long as 40 or more years, good investment decisions are critical, as shown by the examples in Table 1–1. Over many years of investing, the differences in results that investors realize, due solely to the investment returns earned, can be staggering.

---

[1] Most of the principles and techniques discussed in this text are applicable to real assets.

[2] An excellent discussion of the wealth problem for investors can be found in Charles A. D'Ambrosio, *Principles of Modern Investments* (Chicago: SRA, 1976), Chapter 3.

TABLE 1–1 Possible Payoffs from Long-Term Investing

Amount Invested per Year ($)	Number of Years	Final Wealth if Funds Are Invested at		
		5%	10%	15%
		—Total Number of Dollars ($)—		
2000	20	66,132	114,550	204,880
2000	30	132,878	328,980	869,480
2000	40	241,600	885,180	3,558,000

As noted, investments involves the enhancement of one's economic welfare through the sound management of present and future monetary wealth. This wealth, which is in the form of various assets, should be evaluated and managed as a unified whole, that is, within a **portfolio** context (the term *portfolio* designates the asset holdings of an investor). A careful study of investment analysis and portfolio management principles can provide a sound framework for both managing and increasing wealth.

In the final analysis, we study investments in the hope of earning better returns in relation to the risk we assume when we invest. Furthermore, we would like to avoid as many pitfalls as possible, such as those illustrated in Box 1–1—and the many more that await you.

A Perspective on Investing

The investment of funds in various assets is only part of the overall financial decisionmaking and planning that most individuals must do. Before investing, each individual should develop an overall financial plan. Such a plan will typically include the decision of whether to purchase a house, a major investment for most individuals. Also, decisions must be made about insurance of various types—life, health, disability, and protection of business and property. Finally, many individuals provide for emergency reserve funds.[3]

It is assumed in this text that investors have an overall financial plan and are now interested in managing and enhancing their wealth by investing in an optimal combination of financial assets.

Understanding the Investment Process

To view the investment process in an organized manner involves an analysis of the basic nature of investment decisions, the division of activities in the decision process, and the major factors in the investors' operating environment that affect their investment decisions.

---

[3] Personal financial decisions of this type are discussed in detail in personal finance texts. See, for example, Lawrence Gitman and Michael Joehnk, *Personal Financial Planning, Fourth Edition* (New York: Dryden Press, 1987).

Common stocks have, on average, produced larger returns over the years than savings accounts or bonds, so why did all investors not invest in common stocks and realize these larger returns? The answer to this question is that in order to pursue these higher returns investors must assume larger risks. Underlying all investment decisions is the trade-off between return and risk. Therefore, we will first consider these two basic parameters that are of critical importance to all investors and the trade-off that exists between them.

Given the foundation for making investment decisions—the trade-off between expected return and risk—we can consider the decision process in investments as it is typically practiced today. Although numerous separate decisions must be made, for organizational purposes this decision process has traditionally been divided into a two-step process: security analysis and portfolio management. The former involves the valuation of securities, whereas the latter involves the management of an investor's investment selections as a portfolio (unit), with its own unique characteristics.

Finally, we will consider some external factors that affect the decision process. These factors, which influence investor actions and always should be kept in mind in considering the investment process, include the uncertain future, the investment environment, and the question of market efficiency.

The Basic Nature of the Investment Decision

Why invest? Stated at its simplest, investors wish to earn a return on their money. Cash has an opportunity cost: by holding cash you miss the opportunity to earn a return on that cash. Furthermore, in an inflationary environment the purchasing power of cash diminishes, with high rates of inflation (such as in 1980) bringing a relatively rapid decline in purchasing power.

Investors buy, hold, and sell financial assets in order to earn returns on them. Within the spectrum of financial assets, why do some people buy common stocks instead of safely depositing their money in an insured savings account? The answer, surely, is that they are trying to earn returns larger than those available from such safer (and lower yielding) assets as savings accounts and Treasury bills. They know they will be taking a greater risk of losing some of their money by buying common stocks, but they expect to earn a greater return. Investors would like the returns to be as large as possible; however, this objective is subject to constraints, primarily risk.[4]

A great year for the stock market was 1982, with total returns in excess of 20% on a broad cross-section of common stocks. Nevertheless, several

---

[4] Although risk is the most important constraint on investors, other constraints clearly exist. Taxes and transaction costs are often viewed as constraints. Some investors may face legal constraints on the types of securities they can purchase or the amount they can hold.

professionally managed funds managed to lose money that year. As this example shows, marketable securities offering variable returns across time are risky! The investment decision must, therefore, always be considered in terms of both risk and return. The two are inseparable.

There are different types, and therefore different definitions, of risk. We will define **risk** as the chance that the actual return on an investment will be different from its expected return.[5] Using the term *risk* in this manner, we can say that the nominal return on a Treasury bill has no practical risk because there is no reasonable chance that the U.S. government will fail to redeem these obligations as they mature in 13 or 26 weeks. On the other hand, there is some risk, however small, that Exxon or General Electric will be unable to redeem an issue of 30-year bonds when they mature. And there is a very substantial risk of not realizing the expected return on any particular common stock over some future holding period such as a year, six months, one month, or even one day.

In economics in general, and investments in particular, we assume that investors are rational. Rational investors prefer certainty to uncertainty. They dislike risk or, more precisely, they are risk averse. A **risk averse investor** is one who will not assume risk simply for its own sake and will not incur any given level of risk unless there is an expectation of adequate compensation for having done so. The fact that investors want to earn as large returns as possible while being risk averse creates the basic nature of the investing process: a trade-off between return and risk. Investors cannot reasonably expect to earn larger returns without assuming larger risks.

Within the realm of financial assets investors can achieve virtually any position on an expected return–risk spectrum such as that depicted in Figure 1–1. The line *RF* to *B* is the assumed trade-off between expected return and risk that exists for all investors interested in financial assets. This trade-off always slopes upward because the vertical axis is **expected return** (the anticipated return for some future period), and rational investors will not assume more risk unless they *expect* to be compensated for doing so. The expected return should be large enough to compensate for taking the additional risk; however, there is no guarantee that the additional returns will be realized. In investments, it is critical to distinguish between an expected return and a **realized return** (i.e., the actual return over some past period).

RF in Figure 1–1 is the return on a riskless asset such as Treasury bills. This position has zero risk and an expected return equal to the current rate of return available on riskless assets such as Treasury bills. This **risk-free rate of return,** which is available to all investors, will be designated as *RF* throughout the text.

---

[5] As we shall see in Chapter 5, expected return is a precise statistical term, not simply the return the investor expects. As indicated in our definition, risk involves chances, or probabilities, which will also be discussed in Chapter 5 along with measures of the dispersion in the expected return.

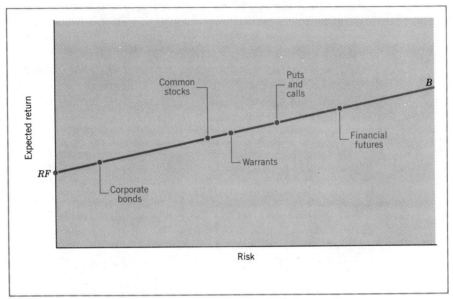

FIGURE 1–1   **The expected return–risk trade-off available to investors.**

Figure 1–1 shows approximate relative positions for some of the financial assets that will be discussed in Chapter 2. As we move from riskless Treasury securities to more risky corporate bonds, equities, and so forth, we assume more risk in the expectation of earning a larger return. Common stocks are quite risky, in relation to bonds, but they are not as risky as an unhedged purchase of options (puts and calls) or futures contracts (all of these terms will be defined in the next chapter). Obviously, Figure 1–1 depicts broad categories. Within a particular category, such as common stocks, a wide range of expected return and risk opportunities exists at any time.

An important point in Figure 1–1 is the trade-off between expected return and risk that should prevail in a rational environment. Investors unwilling to assume risk must be satisfied with the risk-free rate of return, *RF*. If they wish to try to earn a larger rate of return, they must be willing to assume a larger risk as represented by moving up the expected return–risk trade-off into the wide range of financial assets available to investors. Although all rational investors like returns and dislike risk, they are satisfied by quite different levels of expected return and risk; or, put differently, investors have different limits on the amount of risk they are willing to assume and, therefore, the amount of return that can realistically be expected. In the field of economics, the explanation of these differences in preferences is that rational investors strive to maximize their utility, the perception of which varies among investors.[6]

Always remember that the risk–return trade-off depicted in Figure 1–1 is **ex ante,** meaning "before the fact"; that is, before the investment is actually made the investor expects higher returns from assets that have a higher risk. This is the only sensible expectation for risk-averse investors, who are assumed to constitute the majority of all investors. **Ex post** (meaning "after the fact" or when we know what has occurred), for a given period of time such as a month or a year or even longer, the trade-off may turn out to be flat, or even negative. Such is the nature of risky investments!

The Decision Process

Investors have a wide range of securities from which to choose. They invest in an attempt to maximize the expected returns from these opportunities, but they face constraints, the most pervasive of which is risk. Traditionally, investors have analyzed and managed securities using a broad two-step process: security analysis and portfolio management.

Security Analysis

The first part of the investment decision process involves the valuation and analysis of individual securities, which is referred to as **security analysis.** Those people whose profession it is to do this are called security analysts and are usually employed by institutional investors. Of course, there are millions of amateur security analysts in the form of individual investors.

The valuation of securities is a time-consuming and difficult job. First of all, it is necessary to understand the details of the various securities and the factors that affect them. Second, a valuation model is applied to these securities to estimate their price, or value. Value is a function of the future returns on a security and the risk attached thereto. Both of these parameters must be estimated and then brought together in a model.

In the case of bonds, the valuation process is relatively easy because the returns are known and the risk can be approximated from currently available data. This does not mean, however, that all the problems of bond analysis are easily resolved. Suffice it to say that interest rates are the primary factor

---

[6] Utility theory is a very complex subject; however, for our purposes we can equate maximization of utility with the maximization of welfare. Because welfare is a function of present and future wealth, and wealth in turn is a function of current and future income discounted (reduced) for the amount of risk involved, in effect investors maximize their welfare by optimizing the expected return–risk trade-off. In the final analysis, expected return and risk are the foundation of all investment decisions.

affecting bond prices, but no one can consistently forecast changes in interest rates.

The valuation process is much more difficult for common stocks than for bonds. The investor must deal with the overall economy, the industry, and the individual company. Both the expected return and risk of common stocks must be estimated.

After completing the formal valuation process just outlined, at least one significant question remains to be answered—the issue of market efficiency, which has implications for the valuation and selection of stocks. Sufficient creditable evidence exists to make intelligent investors consider this concept carefully, as will be explained later in the chapter.

Portfolio Management

The second major component of the decision process is **portfolio management.** After securities have been evaluated, a portfolio should be selected. Concepts on why, and how, to build a portfolio are well known. Much of the work in this area is in the form of mathematical and statistical models, which have had a profound effect on the study of investments in this country in the last 30 years.

Having built a portfolio, the astute investor must consider how, and when, to revise it. This raises a number of important questions. Portfolios must be managed, regardless of whether an investor is active or passive. Questions to be considered include taxes, transaction costs, maintenance of the desired risk level, and so on.

Finally, all investors are interested in how well their portfolio performs. This is the bottom line of investments. Measuring portfolio performance is an inexact procedure, even today, and needs to be carefully considered.

External Factors Affecting the Decision Process

The investment decision process as just described can be lengthy and involved. Intelligent investors should be aware of this. Regardless of what each individual does, however, certain factors in today's investment environment affect all investors. These factors should be constantly kept in mind as investors work through the investment decision process.

The Great Unknown

The first, and paramount, factor that all investors must come to grips with is the uncertainty. Investors buy financial assets expecting to earn returns over some future holding period. These returns, with few exceptions, can only be expected and may not be realized. The simple fact that dominates investing, although many investors never seem to fully appreciate it, is that the realized return on an asset with any risk attached to it may be different from what was expected—sometimes, quite different.

Estimates are imprecise, at best; at worst, they are completely wrong. All that investors can do is make the most informed return and risk estimates they can, act on them, and be prepared for shifting circumstances. They may—and very often do—use past data to make their estimates. Quite often the past must be modified to incorporate what investors believe is most likely to happen. Regardless of how careful and informed we are, the future is unknown, and mistakes will be made. This will always be true for risky assets.

Some investors try to handle uncertainty by building elaborate quantitative models, and others simply keep it in the back of their mind. All investors, however, are affected by it. What is important to remember is that basing investment decisions solely on the past is going to lead to errors. A 10% average return on all stocks for the last 10 years does not in any way guarantee a 10% return for the next year, or even an average 10% return for the next 10 years.

Someone can always tell you what you should have bought or sold last year. What they cannot do is guarantee you a successful portfolio for next year. Unanticipated events will affect the stock market, and, in turn, most individual stocks. Interest rates, the major factor affecting bonds, cannot be predicted with any significant degree of consistency.

Although uncertainty is always present, all is not lost. It is often possible to make reasonable and informed judgments about the outcomes of many investment opportunities; it is not possible, however, to consistently make totally accurate forecasts about risky securities.

Investment decisions are both an art and a science. To succeed in investing, we must think in terms of *what is expected to happen*. We already know what has happened, but the past may or may not repeat itself. Although the future is uncertain, it is manageable, and a thorough understanding of the basic principles of investing will allow investors to cope intelligently with the situation.

The Investments Environment

Consider the following quote from a "Capital Markets" column of *Forbes*, a popular investment magazine.

> Giants tread Wall Street these days. How is a small investor to compete with them? After all, . . . [they] have access to information the little guy doesn't have.[7]

There are two broad categories of investors—individual investors and **institutional investors.** The latter group includes bank trust departments, pension funds, mutual funds, and insurance companies. Although individuals are the indirect beneficiaries of these institutional investors because

---

[7]See Ben Weberman, "Pebbles on the Beach," *Forbes*, January 16, 1984, p. 127.

they indirectly own or benefit from these institutions' portfolios, on a daily basis they are "competing" with these institutions. Both groups are trying to make intelligent trading decisions about securities. Can individual investors hope to compete fairly with institutions, and how is their decision process affected by these large portfolios?

It is true that the institutional investors are the "professional" investors, with vast resources at their command. Does the average investor have a reasonable chance in the market? Yes—in the sense that he or she can expect generally to earn a fair return for the risk taken. Furthermore, individual investors with a well thought-out strategy can often avoid some of the big mistakes made by the pros—see Box 1–2.

On average, the individual investor will probably do just as well as the big institutional investors because markets are usually quite efficient and securities fairly priced. And some investors will do better. Consider a continuation of the previous quote from *Forbes*.

BOX 1–2 INDIVIDUAL INVESTORS CAN AVOID SOME MISTAKES MADE BY THE PROS

If you have a well-thoughtout investment plan that puts a fixed percentage into mutual funds, stocks, bonds and other financial vehicles, stick to it. People who tamper with long-term goals all too often change them at precisely the wrong time.

Learn a lesson from the mistakes of the nation's major pension funds. The tremendous bull market from the 1950s to the early 1970s was accompanied by a dismal bond market. Assuming that pattern was forever, pension funds deemphasized bonds and increased their holdings of stocks from under 40% of assets in 1958 to 74% by 1972. *Institutional Investor* magazine put a dinosaur on the cover of its February 1969 issue with the caption "Can the Bond Market Survive?" The article went on to say: "In the long run, the public market for straight debt might become obsolete."

Sad to say, the largest part of the equity buildup and the switch away from debt came near the top of the stock market.

The dinosaur picked itself up and began to roar. From 1973 to 1980 bonds sharply outperformed stocks. What happened next? You guessed it. The large pension fund managers did a flip-flop, reducing stocks and increasing their bond portfolios dramatically. Soon only about 15% of their massive flows of new money was directed to equities, against 100% a decade earlier. Again, brilliant timing. There followed the largest rise in stock prices in two decades.

Moral: Adopt a sound investment posture and stick to it; don't shift with the prevailing winds. If you are in good stocks, stay there.

Source: Adapted from David Dreman's column, by permission of *Forbes* magazine, September 8, 1986. © Forbes Inc., 1986.

Never mind. A lot of individuals do all right. One way they do so is to look for pockets in the market so small that mega-institutions can't be bothered with them—imperfections in the market that smart investors can take advantage of.[8]

These possible imperfections in the market relate to market efficiency, which we will consider next.

The Question of Market Efficiency

One of the most profound ideas to affect the investment decision process and, indeed, all of finance is the idea that the securities markets, particularly the equity markets, are efficient. This means that in the United States (at least) we appear to have efficiently priced markets in which the prices of securities do not depart for any length of time from the justified economic values calculated for them. Economic values for securities are determined by investor expectations about earnings, risks, and so on, as investors grapple with the uncertain future. If the market price of a security does depart from its estimated economic value, in an efficient market investors will act to bring the two values together. Thus, as new information arrives in an efficient marketplace, causing a revision in the estimated economic value of a security, its price adjusts quickly and, on balance, correctly to this information. In other words, securities are efficiently priced on a continuous basis. We will discuss the full implications of this statement in Chapter 14.

An efficient market does not have to be perfectly efficient to have a profound impact on investors. All that is required is that the market be economically efficient, meaning that after acting upon information to trade securities and subtracting *all* costs (transaction costs, taxes, to name two), the investor would have been as well off with a simple buy-and-hold strategy. If the market is economically efficient, securities could depart somewhat from their economic (justified) values, but it would not pay investors to take advantage of these small discrepancies.

Obviously, the possibility that the stock market is efficient has significant implications for investors. In fact, one's knowledge of and belief in this idea, known as the **Efficient Market Hypothesis** (EMH), will directly affect how one views the investment process and makes investment decisions. Those who are strong believers in the EMH may adopt, to varying degrees, a passive investment strategy because of the likelihood that they will not be able to find underpriced securities. These investors will seek to minimize transaction cost and taxes and the time and resources devoted to analyzing securities which should, if the EMH is correct, be correctly priced to begin with.

Investors who do not accept the EMH will continue to seek out undervalued securities, believing that they can identify such securities and that

---

[8] Ibid. Both quotes by permission of *Forbes*.

lags exist in the market's adjustment of these securities' prices to new (better) information. These investors will generate more search costs (both in time and money) and more transaction costs, but they believe that the marginal benefit will outweigh the marginal costs incurred.

It is important for all investors at the outset of their study of investments at least to be aware of this idea and its potential implications. A tremendous amount of research has been done on the EMH over the last 20 years, and much evidence has accumulated. Very impressive evidence exists that the market is quite efficient. Certainly, the idea cannot be dismissed out of hand. However, more evidence of market inefficiencies has been accumulating recently. Possibilities for astute investors appear to exist and have been documented. In the final analysis, the issue remains open.

The point to keep in mind at this stage is that investors should learn as fully and carefully as possible about the actual environment that exists in today's investment world. Although startling, the EMH hypothesis cannot be quickly dismissed. The intelligent course of action is to understand the situation, employ what is useful and disregard or use sparingly the remainder, and make the best decisions possible. Only by understanding the investment process and the issues involved in the efficient markets controversy can one hope to answer the question, "How efficient is the market?"

Organizing the Text

The presentation in the following chapters is organized around the previously discussed decision process involved in investments—security analysis and portfolio management. The investments business has traditionally been divided into these two broad areas, each of which encompasses a wide spectrum of activities.

Four chapters of background material follow this introductory chapter. We will consider, in turn, the assets available to investors and the markets in which they trade. We will then examine the sources of information available to investors. Finally, we will examine return and risk in some detail since these two parameters underlie all investment decisions.

Thirteen chapters of the book are devoted to evaluating alternative investment opportunities and explaining the basics of security analysis. We will begin with a study of bonds because the valuation process can be learned more quickly by studying bonds. We will then examine common stocks. In the case of both of these assets we will consider the basics in one chapter, followed by a separate chapter on valuation techniques.

Because of the complexity of common stocks, three additional chapters are needed to describe the basics of fundamental analysis, the most popular method for analyzing stocks. These chapters are purposefully sequenced from market to industry to company analysis. A discussion of technical analysis follows this sequence on fundamental analysis, and in turn is logically followed by a discussion of efficient markets.

An in-depth analysis of alternative investment opportunities follows the material on common stocks. Separate chapters cover options, warrants and convertibles, and futures. Finally, indirect investing in the form of investment companies is considered.

The text concludes with three chapters on portfolio management. The basics of portfolio theory and management are examined first, followed by a discussion of capital market theory. The logical capstone to a study of investments, the measurement of portfolio performance, is analyzed last.

Summary

This introductory chapter serves as a basis for the remainder of this text, providing an overview of what investments is all about.

An investment is the commitment of funds to one or more assets that will be held over some future period. Investments is the study of the investment process. The investment opportunities considered in this text consist of a wide array of financial assets (primarily marketable securities), which are paper claims on some issuer.

We invest in order to improve our welfare, defined here as monetary wealth. The basic element of all investment decisions is the trade-off between expected return and risk. Financial assets are arrayed along an upward sloping expected return–risk trade-off, with the risk-free rate of return as the vertical axis intercept. Investors seek to maximize expected returns subject to constraints, primarily risk. Expected return and risk are directly related; the greater (smaller) the expected return, the greater (smaller) the risk.

Risk is defined as the chance that the actual return on an investment will differ from its expected return. Rational investors are risk averse, meaning that they are unwilling to assume risk unless they expect to be adequately compensated.

For organizational purposes, the investment decision process has traditionally been divided into two broad steps: security analysis and portfolio management. The former is concerned with the valuation of securities. Valuation, in turn, is a function of expected return and risk. Portfolio management encompasses building an optimal portfolio for an investor. Considerations include initial portfolio construction, revision, and the measurement of performance.

Major factors affecting the decision process include uncertainty in investment decisions, the investments environment, and the efficiency of the market. These factors should be considered carefully by investors as they study investments, evaluate information and claims, and make decisions.

Key Words

Efficient Market Hypothesis (EMH)	Marketable securities
Ex ante	Portfolio
Expected return	Portfolio management
Ex post	Real assets
Financial assets	Realized return
Institutional investors	Risk
Investment	Risk averse investor
Investments	Risk-free rate of return
	Security analysis

QUESTIONS AND PROBLEMS

1. Define investments.
2. Describe the broad two-step process involved in making investment decisions.
3. Why is the study of investments important to many individuals?
4. Distinguish between a financial asset and a real asset.
5. Carefully describe the risk–return trade-off faced by all investors.
6. In terms of Figure 1–1, when would an investor expect to earn the risk-free rate of return?
7. Define risk.
8. Summarize the basic nature of the investment decision in one sentence.
9. Distinguish between expected return and realized return.
10. Give a general definition for risk. How many specific types can you think of?
11. What other constraints besides risk do investors face?
12. Are all rational investors risk averse? Do they all have the same degree of risk aversion?
13. What external factors affect the decision process? Which do you think is the most important?
14. What are institutional investors? How are individual investors likely to be affected by institutional investors?
15. What is meant by the expression "efficient market"?
16. Of what significance is an efficient market to investors?

17. Why should the required rate of return be different for a corporate bond and a Treasury bond?

Selected References

D'Ambrosio, Charles A. *Principles of Modern Investments*. Chicago: SRA, Inc., 1976.

Ellis, Charles D. *Investment Policy: How to Win the Loser's Game*. Homewood, Ill.: Dow Jones-Irwin, 1985.

Gipson, James. *Winning the Investment Game*. New York: McGraw-Hill, 1985.

Gitman, Lawrence J., and Joehnk, Michael D. *Personal Financial Planning, Fourth Edition*. New York: Dryden Press, 1987.

Irwin, Robert. *How to Prepare for Tomorrow While Living Well Today*. Glenview, Ill.: Scott Foresman, 1986.

Jones, Charles P., Tuttle, Donald L., and Heaton, Cherrill P. *Essentials of Modern Investments*. New York: Ronald Press, 1977.

Nelson, Wayne F. *Extraordinary Investments for Ordinary Investors*. New York: G. P. Putnam, 1984.

CHAPTER 2

TYPES OF SECURITIES

This chapter surveys the major types of securities available to investors. Each will be discussed briefly, in order to introduce the reader to the types of securities available in the money and capital markets. Later chapters will present additional details about these securities, allowing the reader to concentrate specifically on a particular security.

Our discussion is as current as possible; however, rapid changes make it necessary for all investors to keep up. New securities have appeared recently, and others undoubtedly will be offered in the coming months and years. The financial markets in the United States are dynamic, with new securities being developed to meet the changing needs and preferences of investors.

The emphasis in this chapter (and text) is on financial assets, which are pieces of paper representing financial claims on the issuers of the securities. In particular, the emphasis is on marketable securities, which are claims that are negotiable, or salable, in various marketplaces, as discussed later in Chapter 3. Although the emphasis is on marketable securities, investors quite often own some nonmarketable financial assets. These assets are widely known and used and, at the very least, represent an alternative to the types of securities discussed in this text. These assets are discussed at the beginning of the chapter.

Marketable securities may be classified as either money market or capital market instruments. They can also be classified as either fixed-income or equity securities. Money market instruments will be discussed first. Capital market instruments, which are more important to most investors, will be separated into fixed-income instruments and equity instruments (common stocks), and then the other types of securities, which with one exception are options on common stock, will be discussed.

Finally, indirect investing will be examined. Rather than invest directly in securities, investors can invest indirectly by purchasing the shares of an investment company, which, in turn, invests in securities of various types. Thus, investors can indirectly own part of a portfolio of securities by owning shares in an intermediary which, in turn, owns the securities. This is a very important alternative for all investors to consider.

Figure 2–1 organizes the types of financial assets to be analyzed in this text. The organization is based on the classifications discussed earlier. Thus, investors have two broad alternatives: direct investing or indirect investing (or a combination of the two). Investing directly, beyond nonmarketable assets, investors can choose money market securities or capital market securities; the latter consist of fixed-income securities and equity securities. Other types of securities include various claims on common stocks (both corporate-created and investor-created) and financial futures contracts. Most, or all, of these assets are also available to investors through indirect investing. In summary:

INVESTORS CAN

Invest Directly in	*Invest Indirectly in*
Money market securities	Money market securities
Capital market securities	Capital market securities
Other types of securities	Other types of securities

Use a Combination of Direct and Indirect Investing

Nonmarketable Financial Assets

We begin the discussion with a brief review of savings deposits and other well known savings vehicles. Such investment alternatives are not marketable; rather, the investor must transact with the issuer (or its representative).

Savings Deposits

Savings accounts are undoubtedly the best known type of investment in the United States. Many individuals have one sometime in their lifetime. These accounts are held at commercial banks or "thrift" institutions such as savings and loan associations and credit unions. (The distinctions between

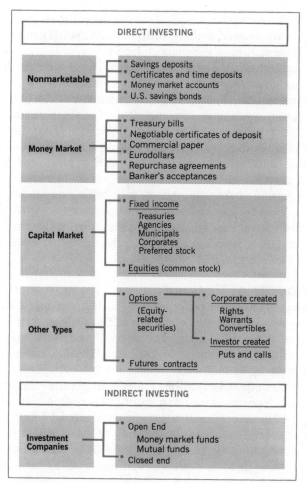

DIRECT INVESTING

Nonmarketable
- Savings deposits
- Certificates and time deposits
- Money market accounts
- U.S. savings bonds

Money Market
- Treasury bills
- Negotiable certificates of deposit
- Commercial paper
- Eurodollars
- Repurchase agreements
- Banker's acceptances

Capital Market
- Fixed income
  - Treasuries
  - Agencies
  - Municipals
  - Corporates
  - Preferred stock
- Equities (common stock)

Other Types
- Options
  (Equity-related securities)
  - Corporate created
    - Rights
    - Warrants
    - Convertibles
  - Investor created
    - Puts and calls
- Futures contracts

INDIRECT INVESTING

Investment Companies
- Open End
  - Money market funds
  - Mutual funds
- Closed end

FIGURE 2–1 **Major types of financial assets.**

banks and thrifts have decreased since the deregulation of the banking industry in the early 1980s. The trend is toward individual institutions offering a wide range of financial services.)

Savings accounts in insured institutions (and your money should not be in a noninsured institution) offer a high degree of safety on both the principal and the return on that principal. At most commercial banks, accounts are insured by the Federal Deposit Insurance Corporation (FDIC).[1] Liquidity is taken for granted and, together with the safety feature, probably accounts substantially for the popularity of savings accounts. (**Liquidity** can be

---

[1] At savings and loan associations and credit unions, accounts are insured by the Federal Savings and Loan Insurance Corporation and the National Credit Union Administration respectively.

defined as the ease with which an asset can be converted to cash—an asset is liquid if it can be sold quickly with, at most, small price changes, assuming no new information in the marketplace.)

Historically, the rate of interest paid on these accounts has been regulated by various government agencies. For example, in the early 1980s federal regulations permitted banks to pay a maximum of 5¼% in interest on regular savings (compounding at some institutions could increase the effective rate), while thrifts could pay a maximum of 5½%.[2] This low return helped to spawn the rise of competitors for the savings dollar. In particular, money market funds (discussed later in the chapter) were created and have enjoyed phenomenal growth.

As of April 1, 1986, the interest rate ceiling on all deposit accounts was removed. Few banks raised their rates, however, apparently believing that "passbook" savers are insensitive to the rates being paid on these accounts (otherwise, they would have moved the funds to alternative, and higher yielding, investments).[3]

Certificates of Deposit

Commercial banks and other institutions offer a variety of savings certificates known as **certificates of deposit** (CDs). These certificates are available for various maturities, with higher rates offered as maturity increases (larger deposits may also command higher rates, holding maturity constant). They are insurable up to $100,000.

Legislation effective October 1, 1983, lifted interest rate restrictions on all new time deposits with a maturity exceeding 31 days; additionally, minimum-balance requirements were eliminated.[4] In effect, institutions are free to set their own rates and terms on most CDs. (Although reduced, however, penalties for early withdrawal of funds remain in effect.) Investors, therefore, need to evaluate their alternatives carefully.

Money Market Deposit Accounts

In 1982, federal regulators allowed financial institutions to offer **money market deposit accounts** (MMDAs) with no interest rate ceilings; this means that these accounts can pay rates competitive with money market funds (i.e., rates currently available on money market instruments) and compete directly with such funds for investors' business.

---

[2] As of January 1, 1984, federal regulations were changed to allow banks to pay a maximum of 5½% on regular savings.

[3] Since April 1, 1986, some institutions have opted to pay less than the 5½% on savings accounts typically offered. Competition has occurred in the form of tiered savings accounts, whereby the larger the balance maintained, the higher the rate of interest paid. Since the average savings account balance is less than $1500, this approach is not likely to have much effect.

[4] Financial institutions often impose minimum deposit requirements.

A typical bank offers a money market "investment" account, which pays competitive money market rates and is insured up to $100,000 by the FDIC. A minimum deposit may be required by the institution (often $1000) to open this type of account.[5] As long as the balance remains above this minimum, interest is paid daily during the statement period at the money market rate.[6] If the balance falls below the minimum required, the interest rate drops to the current rate being paid on savings accounts.

Federal regulations restrict the number of transactions allowed each month. Six preauthorized or automatic transfers are allowed each month, up to three of which can be by check. As many withdrawals as desired can be made in person, and there are no limitations on the number of deposits.

The typical bank also offers a money market checking account, or **"Super NOW" account** (introduced in January 1983). As many checks and transfers as desired can be made from this type of account.[7] The rate earned will be slightly lower than on the "investment" account.

U.S. Government Savings Bonds

One final nonmarketable asset commonly owned by individuals is the non-marketable debt of the U.S. government in the form of savings bonds. Following this discussion, all references to government securities will be to marketable issues—Treasury bills, notes, and bonds.

Savings bonds are nonmarketable, nontransferable, nonnegotiable, and cannot be used for collateral. They are purchased from the Treasury, most often through payroll deduction plans and banks and savings institutions. Series EE bonds are sold at 50% of face value, which ranges from $50 to $10,000. Investors receive interest on these bonds in a lump sum at redemption. The rate of interest is calculated twice a year at 85% of the average yield on five-year Treasury securities. A guaranteed minimum rate is offered if the bonds are held for at least five years. Therefore, depending upon how long the bond is held and the prevailing interest rates, investors receive more or less than the face amount at redemption. Federal tax can be deferred until the bond is redeemed, and the interest is exempt from state and local taxes.

Traditionally, savings bonds were considered a poor investment because of a maximum fixed interest rate that was noncompetitive during periods of high inflation. In 1982, the floating rate and a minimum 7.5% rate were instituted, and savings bonds became competitive. By 1985–86 they were attractive and popular investment opportunities because of falling interest rates (the current rate paid is based on the average Treasury yield for the preceding six months). Although the Treasury lowered the guaranteed

---

[5] As of January 1, 1986, federal regulations on the minimum denomination required for MMDAs were eliminated.

[6] The minimum balance may be stated as an average daily balance.

[7] A monthly maintenance charge may be imposed as well as a charge for each debit on the account.

minimum rate to 6% on November 1, 1986, because of the low level of interest rates at that time, the amount of savings bonds outstanding had reached a record level of $93 billion by early 1987.

Money Market Securities

Money market securities are short-term debt instruments sold by governments, financial institutions, and corporations to investors with temporary excess funds to invest. The size of the transactions in the money market typically is large ($100,000 or more). The maturities of money market instruments range from one day to one year, and are often less than 90 days.

This market is dominated by financial institutions—particularly banks—and governments. Some of these instruments are negotiable and actively traded, and some are not. Investors may invest directly in some of these securities, but more often they do so indirectly through money market mutual funds, which are investment companies organized to own and manage a portfolio of securities and which in turn are owned by investors. Thus, many individual investors own shares in money market funds that, in turn, own one or more of these money market certificates; therefore, investors should be aware of these securities.

Another reason a knowledge of these securities is important is the use of the **Treasury bill** (T-bill) as a benchmark asset. Although in some pure sense there is no such thing as a risk-free financial asset, on a practical basis the Treasury bill is risk free. There is no practical risk of default by the U.S. government. The Treasury bill rate will be used throughout the text as a proxy for the risk-free rate of return available to investors (i.e., the *RF* shown and discussed in Figure 1–1).

In summary, money market instruments are characterized as short-term, liquid investments, with an extremely low probability of default. The minimum investment is generally large. These debt securities are typically owned by individual investors indirectly in money market mutual funds. Table 2–1 describes the major money market securities.

TABLE 2–1 Major Money Market Securities

1. **Treasury Bills.** The premier money market instrument, a fully guaranteed, very liquid IOU from the U.S. Treasury. They are sold on an auction basis every week at a discount from face value in denominations of $10,000 to $1 million; therefore, the discount determines the yield. The greater the discount at time of purchase, the higher the return earned by investors. Typical maturities are 13 and 26 weeks. New bills can be purchased by investors on a competitive or noncompetitive bid basis. Outstanding (i.e., already issued) bills can be purchased and sold in the secondary market, an extremely efficient market where government securities dealers stand ready to buy and sell these securities.

TABLE 2-1 (*Continued*)

2. **Negotiable Certificates of Deposit (CD).** Issued in exchange for a deposit of funds by most American banks, the CD is a marketable deposit liability of the issuer, who usually stands ready to sell new CDs on demand. The deposit is maintained in the bank until maturity, at which time the holder receives the deposit plus interest. However, these CDs are negotiable, meaning that they can be sold in the open market before maturity. Dealers make a market in these unmatured CDs. Maturities typically range from 14 days (the minimum maturity permitted) to one year. The minimum deposit is $100,000.

3. **Commercial Paper.** A short-term, unsecured promissory note issued by large, well-known and financially strong corporations (including finance companies). Denominations start at $100,000, with a maturity of 270 days or less. Commercial paper is usually sold at a discount either directly by the issuer or indirectly through a dealer, with rates comparable to CDs. Although a secondary market exists for commercial paper, it is weak and most of it is held to maturity. Commercial paper is rated by a rating service as to quality (relative probability of default by the issuer).

4. **Eurodollars.** Dollar-denominated deposits held in foreign banks or in offices of U.S. banks located abroad. Although this market originally developed in Europe, dollar-denominated deposits can now be made in many countries, such as those of Asia. Eurodollar deposits consist of both time deposits and CDs, with the latter constituting the largest component of the Eurodollar market. Maturities are mostly short-term, often less than six months. The Eurodollar market is primarily a wholesale market, with large deposits and large loans. Major international banks transact among themselves with other participants including multinational corporations and governments. Although relatively safe, Eurodollar yields exceed that of other money market assets because of the lesser regulation for Eurodollar banks.

5. **Repurchase Agreement (RPs).** An agreement between a borrower and a lender (typically institutions) to buy and repurchase U.S. government securities. The borrower initiates an RP by contracting to sell securities to a lender and agreeing to repurchase these securities at a prespecified price on a stated date. The effective interest rate is given by the difference between the purchase price and the sale price. The maturity of RPs is generally very short, from 3 to 14 days, and sometimes overnight. The minimum denomination is typically $100,000.

6. **Banker's Acceptance.** A time draft drawn on a bank by a customer, whereby the bank agrees to pay a particular amount at a specified future date. Banker's acceptances are negotiable instruments because the holder can sell them for less than face value (i.e., discount them) in the money market. They are normally used in international trade. Banker's acceptances are traded on a discount basis, with a minimum denomination of $100,000. Maturities typically range from 30 to 180 days, with 90 days being the most common.

Capital Market Securities

The **capital market** encompasses instruments with maturities greater than one year. Risk is much higher than in the money market because of the time to maturity and the financial soundness of some of the issuers. Marketability is poorer in some cases. The capital market includes both debt and equity instruments, with the latter having no maturity date.[8]

Fixed-Income Securities

We will begin our review of the principal types of investment opportunities available with **fixed-income securities.** All of these securities have a *specified payment schedule.* In most cases—such as with a traditional bond—they promise to pay stated amounts at stated times; that is, the amount of the payment and the date of payment are known in advance. Some of these securities carry a risk that the indicated payment will not materialize according to the specified conditions for reasons other than default (for example, income bonds and preferred stocks). Although some of the newer securities in this area deviate from the traditional-bond format, they still have a specified payment schedule.

Fixed-income investment opportunities in the capital markets have traditionally consisted primarily of bonds, which are contracts for the borrowing of money. With a traditional bond, the borrower (who issues the bonds) agrees to repay the principal at a specified maturity date and interest at specified intervals in the interim. All details are specified in the contract, and failure to meet a specified condition can result in default.

We will discuss the four major types of bonds in the United States. Within each major type there are variations, such as mortgage-backed securities, which will be briefly described. Finally, preferred stock will be classified as a fixed-income security because of the fixed nature of its dividends. Preferred stock will be discussed last in this section since it is part debt security and part equity, and logically can be placed between the two.

Federal government securities The U.S. government, in the course of financing its operations, issues numerous notes and bonds with maturities greater than one year.[9] The U.S. government is considered the ultimate creditor; therefore, for practical purposes investors do not consider the possibility of risk of default for these securities. An investor purchases these

---

[8]For a detailed discussion of the capital markets, see Herbert E. Dougall and Jack E. Gaumnitz, *Capital Markets and Institutions: Fifth Edition* (Englewood Cliffs, N.J.: Prentice-Hall, 1986).

[9]Through 1982, Treasury securities were sold in bearer form, meaning they belong to the bearer (whoever possesses them). Most federal, state and local, and corporate bonds issued after January 1, 1983, must be registered in the owner's name (unless the maturity is one year or less).

securities with the expectation of earning a steady stream of interest payments and with full assurance of receiving the par value of the bonds when they mature.

Treasury bonds generally have maturities from 10 to 30 years, although a bond can be issued with any maturity.[10] Like Treasury bills, they are sold in competitive auctions. Unlike bills, they are sold at face value, with investors submitting bids on yields.

Interest payments (coupons) are paid semiannually. Face value denominations are $1000, $5000, $10,000, $100,000, $500,000, and $1 million.

Federal agency securities Since the 1920s, the federal government has created various federal agencies designed to help certain sectors of the economy, through either direct loans or guarantee of private loans. These federal credit agencies compete in the marketplace for funds by selling **federal agency securities.**

There are two types of federal credit agencies. Legally, "federal agencies" are part of the federal government. These agencies borrow from the Federal Financing Bank (FFB), which, in turn, borrows from the Treasury. Although some of these securities remain available to investors as a result of sales before the creation of the FFB in 1973, it is likely that in the future all federal agency debt will be FFB securities. These securities are fully guaranteed by the federal government.[11]

In contrast to federal agencies that are officially a part of the government, "government-sponsored agencies" are quasi-private institutions that sell their own securities in the marketplace in order to raise funds for their specific purposes. Although these agencies have the right to draw upon Treasury funds up to some approved amount, their securities are not guaranteed by the government as to principal or interest. Nevertheless, the rapidly growing agency market is dominated by the government-sponsored agencies, which include the Federal National Mortgage Association, the Federal Home Loan Mortgage Corporation, the Federal Home Loan Banks, and the Farm Credit Banks; the latter now issues securities replacing those previously issued by the Federal Land Banks, the Federal Intermediate Credit Banks, and the Banks for Cooperatives.

Perhaps the best known of these agencies is the Federal National Mortgage Association (FNMA), which is designed to help the mortgage markets. The FNMA and its issues are known by the name *Fannie Mae*. Although government sponsored, it is now a privately owned corporation. A variety of Fannie Mae issues are available, with maturities ranging from short-term to

---

[10] U.S. securities with maturities of 1 to 10 years are technically referred to as Treasury notes.

[11] Federal agencies include the Government National Mortgage Association (GNMA, and referred to as "Ginnie Mae"), the Export–Import Bank, Tennessee Valley Authority, U.S. Postal Service, Federal Housing Administration, and Farmers Home Administration.

25 years. This agency also issues and guarantees securities backed by conventional mortgages bought from lenders. These securities are part of the rapidly growing market of fixed-income securities known as **mortgage-backed securities,** which are securities representing an investment in an underlying pool of mortgages. Over $250 billion of these securities had been issued by 1986, primarily by FNMA and two other agencies, the Government National Mortgage Association and the Federal Home Loan Mortgage Corporation.

Another well known investment to many investors is the *Ginnie Mae* issues of the Government National Mortgage Association (GNMA). This wholly owned government agency issues fully backed securities (i.e., they are full faith and credit obligations of the U.S. government) in support of the mortgage market.[12] The GNMA Pass-Through Certificates have attracted considerable attention in recent years because the principal and interest payments on the underlying mortgages used to collateralize them are "passed through" to the bondholder monthly as the mortgages are repaid. Although the stated maturity can be as long as 40 years, the average life of these pass-throughs to date has been less than 12 years. Pass-throughs present investors with uncertainty because they can receive varying amounts of monthly payments depending upon how quickly homeowners pay off their mortgages. These certificates originate in minimum denominations of $25,000 but are available from brokerage firms in the form of investment trust units for about $1000 each.

Agency securities usually have short- to medium-term (10 years) maturities, with denominations ranging from $1000 for a longer-term issue to $10,000 or more for the shorter-term notes. Interest payment provisions may range from monthly to annually, and some are exempt from state and local taxes whereas others are not.

Federal agency securities can be thought of as an alternative to U.S. Treasury securities from the investor's standpoint. The feeling in the marketplace seems to be that the Treasury would not stand by and permit a government-sponsored agency to default; however, they have to be viewed as having slightly greater default risk. Longer-term issues may trade less frequently than comparable Treasury bonds. These two factors together cause these securities to carry slightly higher yields.

Municipal securities Bonds sold by states, counties, cities, and other political entities (e.g., airport authorities, school districts) other than the federal government and its agencies are called **municipals.** There are roughly 50,000 different issuers with almost 2 million different issues outstanding, with credit ratings ranging from very good to very suspect. Thus, risk varies

---

[12] A related mortgage-backed security is "Freddie Mac," issued by the Federal Home Loan Mortgage Corporation. This is a participation security paying a monthly return. Unlike Ginnie Mae, Freddie Mac is not guaranteed by the U.S. government itself.

widely, as does marketability. A well-publicized failure occurred in 1983 with the Washington Public Power Supply System's $2.25 billion default on its Nos. 4 and 5 nuclear power plants, the largest municipal bond default in U.S. history. Roughly 80,000 investors received a rude shock when the utility announced that it could not pay the approximately $185 million of annual interest payments on these bonds.[13] Overall, however, the default experience on municipal bonds has been quite favorable.

Two basic types of municipals are *general obligation bonds,* which are backed by the "full faith and credit" of the issuer, and *revenue bonds,* which are repaid from the revenues generated by the project they were sold to finance (e.g., a toll road or airport improvement).[14] In the former case, the issuer can tax residents to pay for the bond interest and principal. In the latter case, the project must generate enough revenue to service the issue. Most long-term municipals are sold as *serial bonds,* which means that a specified number of the original issues mature each year until the final maturity date. For example, a 10-year serial issue of the municipals might have 10% of the issue maturing each year for the next 10 years.

The distinguishing feature of most municipals is their exemption from federal taxes.[15] Because of this, the stated rate on these bonds will be lower than that on comparable nonexempt bonds. Any capital gains on these bonds are still subject to taxes. The higher an investor's tax bracket, the more attractive municipals become. A taxable equivalent yield can be calculated for any municipal bond return and any marginal tax bracket using the following formula:

$$\text{Taxable equivalent yield} = \frac{\text{Tax-exempt municipal yield}}{1 - \text{Marginal tax rate}} \qquad (2\text{--}1)$$

Thus, an investor in the 28% marginal tax bracket who invests in a 10% municipal bond would have to receive

$$0.10/(1 - 0.280) = 13.89\%$$

from a comparable taxable bond to be as well off.

As a result of tax reform, municipal bonds used to finance nonessential

---

[13] See Lynn Asinorf, "WPPSS Begins to Cause Pain for Investors," *The Wall Street Journal,* December 28, 1983, p. 15.

[14] Municipalities also issue short-term obligations. Some of these qualify for money market investments because they are short-term and of high quality. Bonds backed by the general revenues of the political entities can be for maturities as short as one year. Notes are also issued, typically with a maturity of less than one year. These notes may be of the tax anticipation or the revenue anticipation form. The former are issued against anticipated tax revenues, whereas the latter are issued against other anticipated revenues (e.g., payments from the federal government).

[15] In some cases, the municipal bondholder can also escape state and/or local taxes. For example, a North Carolina resident purchasing a bond issued by the state of North Carolina would escape all taxes on the interest received.

government functions are now taxable—specifically, private-purpose municipal bonds issued after August 7, 1986. Some of these bonds are fully taxable to all investors, while others are taxable only to investors subject to the alternative minimum tax.

Corporates Most of the larger corporations, several thousand in total, issue **corporate bonds** to help finance their operations. Many of these firms have more than one issue outstanding. Philadelphia Electric, for example, had 19 different issues of bonds listed on the "New York Exchange Bonds" page of *The Wall Street Journal* in 1986. Although an investor can find a wide range of maturities, coupons, and special features available from corporates, the typical corporate bond matures in 20 to 40 years, pays semiannual interest, is callable, carries a sinking fund, and is sold originally at a price close to par value, which is almost always $1000.[16]

There are numerous types of corporate bonds. A *debenture* is an unsecured bond, although the holders usually have first call on the earnings (or assets) of the issuer. Bonds that are "secured" by a legal claim to specific assets of the issuer in case of liquidation are called *mortgage bonds. Income bonds* pay interest only if the corporation earns the required payment amount by a specified date. These bonds are an exception to the rule that bond issuers must pay the interest payments and repay the principal payments when due or risk default and possible bankruptcy. Finally, a *convertible bond* can be converted into a specified number of shares of the common stock of the issuer. All of these features will be discussed in Chapter 6.

Corporate bonds, unlike Treasury securities, carry the risk of default by the issuer. Two rating agencies, Standard & Poor's and Moody's, provide a relative safety rating for each major bond, and bond buyers usually check these ratings carefully. (These ratings are explained in Chapter 6.)

New fixed-income securities Our money and capital markets are constantly adapting to meet new requirements and conditions. The result is new types of securities not previously available. We will now consider some of these newer securities.

Zero coupon bonds represent a radical departure from bonds of the past (CDs can also be issued in zero coupon form, but for convenience we will discuss bonds). As their name implies, these bonds are issued with no coupons, or interest, to be paid during the life of the bond. The purchaser pays less than par value for zero coupons and receives par value at maturity. The difference in these two amounts generates an effective interest rate, or rate of return. As in the case of Treasury bills, the lower the price paid for the bond, the higher the effective return.

---

[16]There are various exceptions to this generalization, of course, including bonds with warrants attached, mortgage-backed bonds, collateral trust bonds (which are backed by financial assets), and zero coupon bonds.

BOX 2–1 ANIMAL HOUSE—TIGRS, COLTS, OPOSSMS, AND MORE

Blame it all on Merrill Lynch & Co.

The firm's TIGRs—Treasury investment growth receipts—were successful enough to spawn a slew of imitators. Salomon Brothers Inc. soon followed with CATS, or certificates of accrual on Treasury securities. Now, more than animals are running amok on Wall Street.

How About a Test Drive?

Salomon is selling securities backed by auto loans called CARs, or certificates of automobile receivables. Drexel Burnham Lambert Inc. calls its version of the same thing FASTBACs, or first automotive short-term bonds and certificates.

One type of securities can be bought, depending on the firm, as STARS, or short-term auction-rate stock; DARTS, or Dutch-auction-rate transferable securities; MAPS, market-auction preferred stock; AMPS, auction-market preferred stock; and CAMPS, cumulative auction-market preferred stock.

Shearson Lehman Brothers Inc. recently tagged a floating-rate mortgage-backed security with one of Wall Street's most popular words: FIRSTS, or floating-interest-rate short-term securities.

Merrill Lynch, knowing no boundaries, added COLTS, or continuously offered long-term securities, and OPOSSMS, options to purchase or sell specific mortgage-backed securities. Salomon bolstered its lineup with HOMES, or homeowner-mortgage Eurosecurities, and CARDs, certificates for amortizing revolving debts, backed by credit-card receivables.

A Salomon spokeswoman gives one explanation for the practice: "Names without acronyms can be tongue-twisting and hard to remember." A Merrill official offers another: "It's one-upmanship."

Some officials say the trend has gotten out of hand. Wesley Jones, head of product development at First Boston Corp., says if an acronym "sounds like an animal, it won't describe what you've got."

ZCCBs and SLOBs

Likewise, by the time a name has been massaged to produce an acronym, it may tell little of the product. For example, Merrill Lynch offers LYONs, or liquid-yield option notes; these are really zero-coupon convertible bonds, but calling them ZCCBs wouldn't sound nearly as good for these companions of TIGRs.

Of course, the uncontrived names of some securities actually form acronyms, but these rarely make useful marketing tools. First Boston, for instance, once underwrote an offering of secured-lease obligation bonds. It used the full name.

Source: Ann Monroe, "LYONs and TIGRs, No BEARs, Oh, My! LYONs and TIGRs, No . . .", *The Wall Street Journal,* February 18, 1987, p. 29. Reprinted by permission of *The Wall Street Journal,* © Dow Jones & Company, Inc. (1987). All Rights Reserved.

Corporate zero coupon bonds flooded the bond market in 1981 and 1982. Issuers included McDonald's, JC Penney, GMAC, and Bank America. Zero coupon Treasury bonds are also available; however, they are created by investment banker-dealers who take a regular coupon bond and "strip" it into the principal and a series of short-maturity zeros representing specific interest payments every six months for the life of the bond. For example, a 20-year Treasury bond becomes 40 separate securities maturing every six months plus a zero coupon claim on the principal for a total of 41 claims. A good illustration of these receipts are the Treasury Investment Growth Receipts (TIGRs or tigers) issued by Merrill Lynch, a large stock brokerage firm (another institution's similar issues are referred to as CATS). For example, in 1982 Merrill Lynch sold an issue of these receipts representing claims on $500 million of principal and over $2 billion of interest on 14% U.S. Treasury bonds maturing in 2011. Maturities on these receipts range from three months to 29 years. Investors buy the receipts at a discount and receive the particular interest or principal payment when it comes due. A custodian bank holds the U.S. government bonds, and Merrill Lynch pays off the receipts with the proceeds from the bonds. The backing of the U.S. government virtually eliminates the risk of default on these receipts.

Merrill Lynch has also sold LYONS, zero coupon corporate notes that can be converted into the common stock of the issuer. Zero coupon municipals are also available, and with the signing of the 1986 tax act stripped municipal bonds began to be marketed.

Adv / Disadv

Tigers, and similar securities, appeal to investors for several reasons. First, they can purchase only the receipts that fit their particular requirements, such as a child's educational needs 15 years from time of purchase. More important, these receipts can lock in a fixed rate of return for a long period, thereby eliminating reinvestment risk. Zero coupons are not popular with high tax bracket investors because the taxes must be paid each year as though interest were earned. They can be suitable for investors who do not pay taxes, such as pension funds or individual IRA or Keogh accounts. Zero coupon bonds minimize callability risks for an investor; furthermore, for those investors who wish to speculate on changes in interest rates, these bonds offer maximum price volatility.

In the area of mortgage-backed securities, collateralized mortgage obligations (CMOs) have been created to offer investors an even flow of funds instead of the varying payoffs received from pass-through certificates. Four series were offered with different maturities, and principal payments retire each one in consecutive order. Interest is paid semiannually, with rates slightly higher than comparable-maturity Treasury issues.

The 1986 tax act created a new structure for mortgage-backed securities called "Remics" (real estate mortgage investment conduits). The tax problems that had arisen with attempts to make mortgage-backed securities more like corporate bonds by issuing CMOs have been eliminated by Remics. Under this structure, cash flows from a pool of mortgages can be rearranged in many different ways without encountering tax problems. This will undoubtedly lead to new securities that have been rearranged from mortgages.

Preferred stock   Although technically an equity security, **preferred stock** is known as a hybrid security because it resembles both fixed-income and equity instruments. As an equity security, preferred stock has an infinite life; the corporate issuer is never obligated to redeem it. However, most preferred stocks issued today are callable and therefore may not remain outstanding forever. Also, like equity securities, it pays dividends. Preferred stock resembles fixed-income securities in that the dividend is specified and known in advance and is fixed in amount; in effect, preferred stock can provide a stream of income very similar to that of a bond. The difference is that the stream continues forever, unless the issue is called, or otherwise retired. Because of its stipulated payments, preferred stock is treated by most investors as a fixed-income security and is therefore considered at this point. However, in discussing preferred stock as a fixed-income security it is worthwhile to remember that the price fluctuations in preferreds often exceed those in bonds.

Preferred stock dividends are often stated as a percentage of **par value** (i.e., the stated or face value for a security); therefore, a preferred stock's par value is meaningful and important to know. A $100 par value preferred paying a 10% dividend would pay $10 per year, for example, whereas the same rate on a $50 par value preferred would yield only $5 per year. Many preferred stock dividends are stated in annual dollar amounts, such as $10 or $5 in the examples given here.

Preferred stock dividends are not legally binding but must be voted on each period by a corporation's board of directors. If the issuer fails to pay the dividend in any year, the unpaid dividend(s) will have to be paid in the future before common stock dividends can be paid if the issue is cumulative (if noncumulative, dividends in arrears do not have to be paid). In the event of omitted dividends, preferred stock owners may be allowed to vote for the directors of the corporation.

More than one-third of the preferred stock sold in recent years is convertible into common stock at the owner's option. Convertibility will be discussed in Chapter 16.

Preferred stock occupies a middle position between bonds and common stock both in terms of priority of payment of income and in case the corporation is liquidated. Preferred stockholders are paid after the bondholders, but before the common stockholders.

Equity Securities

Unlike fixed-income securities, **equity securities** represent an ownership interest. The holder of equities is one of the owners of a corporation, with a residual claim on the assets and income of the corporation. Equity securities have no maturity date, and in the case of common stock no specified return that has to be paid, now or ever.[17] Thus, equity securities involve substantial risk.

---

[17] Again, preferred stock is technically an equity security, but most investors think of it as a fixed income security. It was, therefore, covered in the previous section.

Common stock represents the ownership of corporations. As a purchaser of 100 shares of common stock, an investor owns $100/n\%$ of the corporation (where n is the number of shares of common stock outstanding). As owners, the holders of common stock are entitled to elect the directors of the corporation and vote on major issues. Each owner is usually allowed to cast votes equal to the number of shares owned for each director being elected. Such votes occur at the annual meeting of the corporation, which each shareholder is allowed to attend.[18]

If a firm's shares are held by only a few individuals, it is referred to as a "closely held" firm. The company that publishes *Reader's Digest* is an example of a large company that is closely held. By being closely held, a company can avoid public disclosures of financial information. Most companies choose to "go public," meaning that common stock is sold to the general public. This is done primarily to enable the company to raise additional capital more easily.

If a corporation meets certain requirements, it may, if the corporation chooses, be listed on one or more exchanges. Otherwise, it will be traded in the over-the-counter market to be discussed in Chapter 3. The stock would be referred to as a listed security, in the first case, and an unlisted security in the second case. For large corporations, the regulatory difference between being listed and unlisted is small.

The common stockholder is the residual claimant on both the income and the assets of the corporation, receiving what remains after both the creditors and the preferred stockholders have been paid. In some cases, nothing is left, whereas in others such a claim can be worth a substantial amount of money. Note that the common stockholder has no specific promises to receive any cash from the corporation since the stock never matures, and dividends do not have to be paid. Dividends are declared by the board of directors, who can raise and lower (or eliminate) them as they see fit. Thus, the dividend can be doubled or eliminated. Common stock dividends, if declared, are paid quarterly.

Other Types of Securities

Equity-Derivative Securities

Equity-derivative securities are securities with a claim on the common stock of a corporation. The owner of such a security has the right, under specified conditions, to either make delivery on, or take delivery of, a specified amount of common stock. These securities are marketable and trade on

---

[18] Most shareholders do not attend, often allowing management to vote their proxy. Therefore, although technically more than 50% of the outstanding shares are needed for control of a firm, effective control can often be exercised with considerably less because not all of the shares are voted.

secondary markets. Rather than own the stock itself, investors can own a marketable claim on that stock. They need never own the stock to participate in the benefits that accrue if the corporation does well and the price of its stock rises. Equity-derivative securities can be created by corporations or investors (both individuals and institutions).

Corporate-created securities Perhaps the most basic claims on equity created by a corporation are *rights,* which permit current stockholders, for a very short-term period (up to 10 weeks), to have the first right to purchase new shares of stock being sold by the corporation at a specified price. Recipients of the rights may exercise them, let them expire, or sell them in the marketplace. They have a small market value (price) because they permit the holder to purchase the shares at a discount from current market prices.

Warrants are long-term rights to purchase common stock from the corporation, with maturities typically in years. A holder of warrants can turn the warrants in to the corporation anytime before they expire, together with a stipulated amount of money, and obtain a stipulated number of shares of common stock (all terms of the warrant are specified by the issuer when the warrants are issued). Warrants are often attached to the bonds or the preferred stock being sold by a corporation in order to make the issue more attractive. Like rights, warrants are traded on exchanges. In effect, warrants are a substitute for the underlying common stock, with both advantages and disadvantages.

Convertible securities (i.e., convertible bonds and convertible preferred stock) have a built-in conversion feature. The holders of the bonds or preferred have the option to convert whenever they choose. Typically, no money is involved—the bonds or preferred stock are turned in to the corporation for a specified number of common shares. Convertibles are two securities simultaneously: a fixed-income security paying a specified interest or dividend payment and a claim on the common stock that will become increasingly valuable as the price of the underlying common stock rises. Thus, the prices of convertibles may fluctuate over a fairly wide range, depending on whether they are currently trading like other fixed-income securities or currently reflect movements in the price of the underlying common stock.

Investor-created securities In today's investing world the word **options** refers to **puts** and **calls.** These are created not by corporations but by investors wishing to trade in claims on a particular common stock. A call (put) option gives the buyer the right to purchase (sell) 100 shares of a particular stock at a specified exercise price within a specified time. Maturities on new puts and calls are available up to nine months away. Several exercise prices are created for each underlying common stock, so that investors have a choice in both the maturity and the price they will pay or receive.

Buyers of calls are betting that the price of the underlying common stock will rise, making the call option more valuable. Put buyers are betting that the price of the underlying common stock will decline, making the put option more valuable. Both put and call options are written (created) by investors who are betting the opposite of their respective purchasers. The sellers (writers) receive an option premium for selling each new contract and the buyer pays this option premium. Once the option is created and the writer receives the premium from the buyer, it can be traded as much as investors desire in the secondary market. Its premium will then be the market price of the contract as determined by investors. The price will fluctuate constantly, just as the price of the underlying common stock changes. This makes sense, because the option is affected directly by the price of the stock that gives it value. In addition, the option's value is affected by the time remaining to maturity, current interest rates, the volatility of the stock, and the price at which the option can be exercised.

Thus, puts and calls allow both buyers and sellers (writers) to speculate on the short-term movements of certain common stocks. Buyers are able to obtain an option on the common stock for a small, known premium, which is the maximum that the buyer can lose. If the buyer is correct about the price movements on the common, gains are magnified in relation to having bought (or sold short) the common because a smaller investment is required; however, the buyer has only a short time in which to be correct. Writers (sellers) are able to earn the premium as income, based upon their beliefs about a stock; they will win or lose, depending on whether their beliefs are correct or incorrect.

Futures Contracts

Futures contracts have been available on commodities such as corn and wheat for a long time; recently, they have become available on several financial instruments. Futures can be purchased on stock market indexes, currencies, Treasury bills, Treasury bonds, bank certificates of deposit, and GNMA's. Futures are marketable; trading occurs on organized markets such as the Chicago Board of Trade.

A futures contract is an agreement providing for the future exchange of a particular asset between a buyer and a seller. The seller contracts to deliver the asset at a specified delivery date in exchange for a specified amount of cash from the buyer. Although the cash is not required until the delivery date, a "good faith deposit" is required to reduce the chance of default by either party; such a deposit is called the "margin." The margin is small compared to the value of the contract.

Most futures contracts are not exercised; rather, they are "offset" by taking a position opposite to the one initially undertaken. For example, a purchaser of a May Treasury bill futures contract can close out the position by selling an identical May contract before the delivery date; a seller can close out the same position by purchasing that contract.

Most participants in futures are either *hedgers* or *speculators*. The former seeks to reduce price uncertainty over some future period. For example, by purchasing a futures contract, a hedger can lock in a specific price for the asset and be protected from adverse price movements. Sellers, likewise, can protect themselves from downward price movements. Speculators, on the other hand, seek to profit from the uncertainty that will occur in the future. If prices are expected to rise (fall), contracts will be purchased (sold). Correct anticipations can result in very large profits because only a small margin is required.

One of the newest innovations in financial markets is options on futures. Calls on futures give the buyer the right, but not the obligation, to assume the futures position.

The Investor's Alternative—Indirect Investing

The discussion to this point has involved the types of securities that can be bought and traded in various markets. Such instruments as common and preferred stocks, puts and calls, and savings deposits are within reach of almost all investors. They can also buy Treasury bills with a $10,000 minimum, or purchase Treasury, municipal, or corporate bonds if they choose (and are willing to accept the lower liquidity of municipals and corporates). Although many investors will never deal in negotiable CDs or banker's acceptances, they are bought and sold by some investors, including institutions. Repurchase agreements, however, are a specialized item, not designed for individual investors.

Investors always have an alternative to direct investing—**indirect investing,** which refers here to the buying and selling of the shares of investment companies, which, in turn, purchase and hold portfolios of securities. **Investment companies** are organized for the purpose of investing in securities of various kinds. Each has specific objectives, such as capital gains, maximum current income, or tax-free income. Investors purchasing shares of a particular investment company are purchasing an ownership interest in its portfolio of securities and are entitled to a pro rata share of the dividends, interest, and capital gains. Owners also must pay a pro rata share of the company's expenses and its management fee; however, this is a very reasonable amount and should not discourage purchase of investment company shares if such a purchase is otherwise justified.

Open-End Investment Companies (Mutual Funds)

Investors purchase most investment company shares directly from the company itself and sell their shares back to the company (which is obligated to redeem them). Such investment companies are called **open-end investment companies** and are popularly referred to as mutual funds. The companies sell as many shares as investors demand, investing the proceeds in additional securities in accordance with that company's investment objectives. The company stands ready to repurchase shares from investors wishing to sell, resulting in a shrinkage in the fund's size.

All sales and purchases of open-end investment companies are made at the net asset value per share (a sales charge may also be included), which reflects what the company's portfolio is actually valued at on the day of the transaction.[19] Thus, if one buys shares of a mutual fund that holds the 30 Dow Jones Industrial stocks and the prices of these 30 stocks rise strongly for several days, the 30 stocks will be worth more and therefore the shares of the fund holding these 30 stocks will be worth more.

One of the two major types of open-end investment companies is the **money market mutual fund,** which specializes in money market instruments. The more traditional type, the mutual funds (and their close relation, the closed-end funds), invest primarily in capital market instruments. As in the earlier discussion of money market instruments and those available in the capital market, money market funds will be discussed first and then mutual funds.

Money market mutual funds   In response to new trends that emerged in the 1970s, the investment company industry created money market funds to invest in the short-term, highly liquid, low-risk money market instruments discussed earlier in this chapter. The money market funds own portfolios of Treasury bills, negotiable CDs, prime commercial paper, and so forth. Investors can buy into these funds for an initial investment of around $2500 to $3000, with some funds requiring as little as $1000. Interest is earned and declared daily and investors can sell their shares anytime they choose. The expenses of the fund are very low. Check-writing privileges are available, usually in amounts of $500 or more. Until the checks are cleared, investors continue to earn interest on their funds.

Money market funds provide investors with an alternative not otherwise available to many. They can participate in the ownership of money market instruments that are liquid and of very low risk and short maturity, earning the competitive rates being paid on these instruments that otherwise might not be available to them.

Mutual funds   These investment companies invest in capital market securities, primarily stocks and bonds. Each fund has a stated objective, which it must adhere to, such as income, growth, or maximum capital gains. Therefore, investors know the general nature of the portfolio when they invest. In addition, some funds specialize in particular industries or technologies, providing investors with specific choices. Most funds are very broadly diversi-

---

[19] Specifically, the net asset value per share of an investment company is found by totaling the market value of all the securities in its portfolio, subtracting out any liabilities that may exist, and dividing by the number of shares of the investment company's stock that is outstanding.

fied, providing a real service to many investors who could not otherwise achieve adequate diversification. Some funds known as index funds attempt to duplicate a market average such as the Standard & Poor's 500. In effect, this allows the investor to purchase shares in "the market" itself, with no input from the fund's management. In contrast, most funds argue that one of their services to investors is providing the expertise of their portfolio managers.

Closed-End Investment Companies

The alternative form of investment company, accounting for a much smaller percentage of total investment company assets, is the **closed-end investment company,** whose shares are traded on exchanges exactly like any other shares of stock. Closed-end companies have a fixed number of shares of their stock outstanding and investors use their brokers to buy and sell these shares, paying their regular brokerage fees. With this exception, closed-end companies operate in a manner similar to open-end companies. However, unlike mutual funds, closed-end companies can sell for less (at a discount) or more (at a premium) than their net asset values.

Conclusion

An investment company is a clear alternative for an investor seeking to own stocks and bonds. Rather than purchase and manage a portfolio, investors can, in effect, turn their money over to an investment company and allow it to do all the work and make all the decisions (for a fee, of course). This is an important issue that all investors should think about carefully. There are possible advantages and disadvantages to each alternative. In Chapter 18 this issue will be considered in more detail.

Ownership of Financial Assets

Having reviewed the basic types of securities available to investors, we will now *briefly* assess the ownership of the various assets available for investment. It is not always possible to obtain exact figures on each of the assets discussed, but a number of useful observations can be made.

Amounts of Financial Assets Outstanding

Large amounts of short-term (18 months or less) U.S. government securities are available to investors, and large denomination time deposits constitute a big part of the money market. Other money market instruments would likely be owned by individual investors indirectly through money market funds.

As for capital market instruments, the total marketable U.S. government debt is second only to mortgages, and exceeds by one-third the total of state and local, corporate, and foreign bonds. The total market value of all corporate equities fluctuates widely over time. For example, the market value of all equity securities *increased* some $250 billion in the first two weeks of January 1987 alone (obviously, it could lose that much just as quickly).

Household Ownership of Financial Assets

Roughly one-fourth of households' total financial assets in 1986 were in the form of deposits, including demand deposits, small time and savings deposits, money market mutual fund shares, and large time deposits. Small time and savings deposits constituted a large proportion of this one-fourth because they are a familiar and popular method of providing liquidity and safety. Money market fund shares grew rapidly in the early 1980s as investors sought to earn the higher money market rates of recent years. From a base of less than $4 billion in 1977, this investment had grown to $236 billion by early 1987. However, the creation of money market deposit accounts (MMDAs) in December 1982 and "Super NOW" accounts in January 1983 lessened the appeal of money market shares because financial institutions could pay money market rates on these accounts, and the Super NOWs can be used as a checking account. MMDAs went from $0 in November 1982 to over $550 billion by mid-1987.

As for the marketable securities owned by households, probably less than 10% of their total financial assets was held in the four major debt securities discussed: U.S. government securities, agency issues, municipals, and corporates. Municipal bonds was the largest of these four positions. The mid-January 1987 market value of the U.S. equity market was $2.75 trillion. Individual investors owned a substantial amount of this directly or indirectly through institutional investors.

Households own an increasingly large amount of pension fund reserves. Much of this amount is being invested by pension funds, on behalf of households, in fixed-income and equity securities. Many of those affected will have some say in whether their pension fund dollars are invested in fixed-income or equity securities. Thus, a study of investments can be useful for many people.

Institutional Ownership of Common Stocks

A resurgence in the number of individuals owning shares of stock occurred between 1975 and 1985, with the number exceeding 47 million by 1985.[20] Survey data indicate that in 1985 one in four adults owned common stocks. Nevertheless, individual investors have been net sellers of stocks (purchases of stocks less sales, including equity mutual funds) for many years. If individuals are selling, who is buying?

---

[20] This includes both corporate shares and stock mutual funds.

As of 1980, available data showed that institutional investors owned 35% of the market value of all New York Stock Exchange-listed stock. This percentage remained constant during 1975 to 1980, although it had been rising steadily before that time. If omitted institutional investors in common stocks such as bank-administered personal trust funds, private hedge funds, and nonbank trusts were included, the total institutional holdings would probably have amounted to about 50% of the entire market value of all stocks on the NYSE. Pension funds are the largest single institutional owner of common stocks.

The large percentage of common stocks owned by institutions is an important factor in U.S. equity markets. These investors purchase and sell thousands of shares per transaction; furthermore, because of legal and practical considerations, they tend to concentrate on a select list of the largest U.S. corporations. Both of these factors can have implications for various stocks. For example, look at the list of most actively traded stocks on the New York Stock Exchange for a given day (as shown in *The Wall Street Journal*). Many of the same stocks, which are institutional favorites, tend to show up day after day. This institutional presence also is related to the question of market efficiency, a subject that will be discussed in Chapter 14.

Summary

This chapter has described the major types of securities available to investors. Major categories include nonmarketable securities, money market instruments, capital market securities (divided into fixed-income and equity securities), other securities, and indirect investments in the form of investment company shares.

Nonmarketable securities are widely owned by investors, perhaps as the "first" investment they make. Savings deposits are well known and commonly used. Substantial amounts of certificates of deposit also are owned, each with its own characteristics. Money market accounts, including the Super NOW checking accounts, offer competitive money market rates. U.S. savings bonds have enjoyed a resurgence in popularity with investors.

Money market investments include Treasury bills, negotiable certificates of deposit (CDs), commercial paper, Eurodollars, repurchase agreements, and banker's acceptances. The first three are obligations (IOUs) of the federal government, banks and corporations, respectively. Money market instruments are characterized as short-term, highly liquid, very safe investments. Treasury bills are the premier money market investment, widely known and purchased.

Capital market investments have maturities in excess of one year. Fixed-income securities, one of the two principal types of capital market securities, have a specified payment schedule. They include four types of bonds: U.S. governments, federal agencies, municipals, and corporates. All of these bonds represent a promise on the part of the issuer to pay a stated rate of interest and to repay the principal at a stated maturity date. The mortgage-backed securities of some of the federal agencies are becoming an important opportunity for investors.

Preferred stock, while technically an equity security, is regarded by investors as a fixed-income security because of its stated (and fixed) dividend. Preferred has no maturity date but may be retired by call or other means.

Common stock (equity) represents the ownership of the corporation. The stockholder is the residual claimant in terms of both income and assets. Stockholders may receive no dividend, or any amount of dividends, depending on the board of directors.

Other types of securities include several forms of equity-derivative securities, and futures contracts. Equity-derivative securities derive all or part of their value from the underlying common stock and can be divided into two categories: corporate-created and investor-created. The former includes rights, which enable existing stockholders to purchase newly issued shares of common stock for a short time. Warrants are long-term claims on common stock, with the holder able to trade warrants in the same manner as the common. Convertible bonds and preferred enable the owner to enjoy the privileges of either a bond or a preferred stock while having a claim on the common stock of the same issuer.

Investor-created equity derivative securities are called options. These calls (puts) are multiple-month (up to nine) rights to purchase (sell) a common stock at a specified price. These options allow both buyers and sellers (writers) to speculate on the price movements of stocks for which these claims are available. Options are also available on several stock market indexes as well as fixed-income securities.

Futures contracts provide for the future exchange of a particular asset between a buyer and a seller. A small margin can control a contract, most of which are closed out and not exercised. A recent innovation is options on futures.

All investors have an alternative to purchasing these financial assets of indirect investing. This involves the purchase of shares of an investment company, which is in business to hold a particular portfolio of securities. Investors can buy shares in funds specializing in either the money market or the capital market. Investment companies are classified as either open-end (which includes both money market funds and mutual funds) or closed-end, depending upon whether their own capitalization (number of shares outstanding) is constantly changing or fixed.

Large amounts of financial assets are outstanding, particularly U.S. government securities and equity securities. Institutional investors own a substantial amount of NYSE stocks and account for a very large percentage of the daily trading in these stocks.

Key Words

Calls	Money market deposit accounts
Capital market	Money market mutual fund
Certificates of deposit	Mortgage-backed securities
Closed-end investment companies	Municipal securities
Convertible securities	Open-end investment company
Corporate bonds	Options
Equity securities	Par value
Equity-derivative securities	Preferred stock
Federal agency securities	Puts
Fixed-income securities	Super NOW account
Futures contracts	Treasury bill
Indirect investing	Treasury bond
Investment company	Warrant
Liquidity	Zero coupon bond
Money market	

QUESTIONS AND PROBLEMS

1. Outline the classification scheme for marketable securities used in the chapter. Explain each of the terms involved.
2. What is the difference between a savings deposit and a certificate of deposit?
3. How do money market accounts at banks and thrifts differ from their other investment opportunities?
4. What does it mean for Treasury bills to be sold at discount?
5. Distinguish between a negotiable certificate of deposit and the certificates of deposit discussed in the section "Nonmarketable Securities."
6. Name the four issuers of bonds discussed in this chapter. Which do you think would be most risky as a general proposition?
7. How can an investor distinguish between Fannie Mae and Ginnie Mae?
8. Name and explain the difference between the two types of municipal securities.
9. Assuming an investor is in the 15% tax bracket, what taxable equivalent must be earned on a security to equal a municipal bond yield of 9.5%?
10. What are the advantages and disadvantages of zero coupon bonds?
11. Is there any relationship between a "tiger" and a zero coupon bond?
12. Why is preferred stock referred to as a "hybrid" security?

13. Why is preferred stock classified in this chapter as a fixed-income security?
14. Why is the common stockholder referred to as a "residual claimant"?
15. Do all common stocks pay dividends? Who decides?
16. What is meant by the term equity-derivative security? Distinguish between those that are corporate-created and those that are investor-created.
17. What are two differences between a warrant and a call?
18. How are puts and calls created?
19. On which financial instruments can futures contracts be purchased?
20. What is meant by "indirect" investing?
21. What is an investment company? Distinguish between an open-end and a closed-end company.
22. What is a money market fund? Why would it appeal to investors?
23. What is an index fund?
24. Do households own more equity securities or long-term debt securities?
25. How do individual investors and institutional investors compare in the ownership of common stocks?
26. Distinguish between a serial bond and a term bond.
27. How is a Series EE government savings bond like a zero coupon bond?
28. Explain why the par value on a preferred stock may be an important item to know.

Selected References

Board of Governors of the Federal Reserve System, *Federal Reserve Statistical Release,* issued weekly.

Board of Governors of the Federal Reserve System, *Flow of Funds Accounts,* quarterly.

Cook, Timothy Q. *Investments of the Money Market.* Federal Reserve Bank of Richmond, 1981.

Dougall, Herbert E., and Gaumnitz, Jack E. *Capital Markets and Institutions,* 5th ed. Englewood Cliffs, N.J.: Prentice-Hall, 1986.

Fabozzi, Frank J., editor. *Readings in Investment Management.* Homewood, Ill.: Richard D. Irwin, 1983.

Gup, Benton E. *The Basics of Investing,* 3rd ed. New York: John Wiley, 1987.

Kidwell, David S., and Peterson, Richard L. *Financial Institutions, Markets, and Money,* 3rd ed. Chicago: Dryden Press, 1987.

Nelson, Wayne F. *How to Buy Money.* New York: McGraw-Hill, 1981.

Poindexter, J. C., and Jones, C. P. *Money, Financial Markets and the Economy.* St. Paul, Minn.: West Publishing, 1980.

Smith, Milton. *Money Today More Tomorrow.* Cambridge, Mass.: Winthrop, 1981.

Tucker, James F. *Buying Treasury Securities at Federal Reserve Banks.* Richmond, Va.: Federal Reserve Bank of Richmond, 1980.

Weston, J. Fred, and Copeland, Thomas E. *Managerial Finance,* 8th ed. Hinsdale, Ill.: Dryden Press, 1986.

CHAPTER 3

SECURITIES MARKETS

The purpose of this chapter is to outline the structure of the securities markets in the United States and to describe how securities are traded. The emphasis is primarily on stocks, and to a lesser extent bonds, because these are the securities that investors will most often buy and sell. The mechanics of trading puts and calls and warrants are very similar to those of common stocks. And, as noted in the last chapter, most investment company shares are bought from and sold to the investment company itself. The factors involving these other securities will be discussed in those chapters dealing specifically with each security.

The structure and operating mechanisms of the security markets in the United States have changed drastically in the last 10 to 15 years. Accordingly, this chapter concludes with a look at some of these changes and a discussion of what the future may hold.

The discussion will be organized around the two basic types of markets that exist—the primary and secondary. **Primary markets** involve the sale of new securities, whereas **secondary markets** provide a forum for the trading of securities after their initial sale. Before considering these two types of markets, however, we will examine their importance to the economy.

The Importance of Financial Markets

Business firms need tremendous amounts of capital to finance their operations. In order to grow and expand, they must invest capital in amounts beyond their capacity to save in any reasonable period of time. Similarly, governments must borrow large amounts of money to provide the goods and services demanded of them by the populace. The financial markets permit both business and government to raise the needed funds by selling securities. Simultaneously, investors with excess funds are able to invest and earn a return, enhancing their welfare.[1]

Primary markets are absolutely vital to capitalistic economies if they are to function properly, since they serve to channel funds from savers to borrowers. Furthermore, they provide an important allocative function by channeling the funds to those who can make the best use of them—presumably, the most productive. In fact, the primary function of a capital market is to allocate resources optimally. A securities market with this characteristic is said to be *allocationally efficient*. An *operationally efficient* market, on the other hand, is one with the lowest possible prices for transactions services.

Primary markets would not function well without secondary markets. Savers would be reluctant to invest in new securities if they had to hold these securities to maturity or incur large search costs in finding a seller when they were ready to sell. The existence of well-functioning secondary markets, where investors come together to trade existing securities, assures the purchasers of primary securities that they can quickly sell their securities if the need arises. Of course, such sales may involve a loss, because there are no guarantees in the financial markets. A loss, however, may be very preferable to no cash at all if the securities could not be sold readily.

In summary, secondary markets are indispensable in the United States to the proper functioning of the primary markets. The latter, in turn, are indispensable to the proper functioning of the economy.

The Primary Markets

As noted, a primary market is one in which a borrower issues new securities in exchange for cash from an investor (buyer). New sales of Treasury bills, or IBM stock, or North Carolina bonds all take place in the primary markets. The issuers of these securities—the U.S. government, IBM, and the state of North Carolina, respectively—receive cash from the buyers of these new securities, who in turn receive financial claims that previously did not exist. Note that in these three examples some amount of these securities is outstanding before the new sales occur. In other cases the issuer is selling securities for the first time. Regardless, once securities are sold by the original purchasers, they trade in secondary markets. New securities may trade 1000 times in the secondary market, but the original issuers will be

---

[1] For a discussion of these issues, see J. C. Poindexter and C. P. Jones, *Money, Financial Markets and the Economy* (St. Paul, Minn.: West Publishing, 1980), Chapter 10.

unaffected in the sense that they receive no additional cash from these transactions.

The Investment Banker

Since most issuers of securities do not raise long-term capital frequently, they usually lack the expertise needed to do the best job possible; furthermore, suppliers of capital are widely dispersed, and efficiently reaching all of them requires organization. In the course of selling new securities, therefore, issuers often rely upon an investment banking firm. Along with performing activities such as helping corporations in mergers and acquisitions, these firms specialize in the design and sale of securities in the primary market.

Investment bankers act as intermediaries between issuers and investors. They provide important services to business firms seeking to raise long-term funds. Specifically, the investment banker provides the following functions, each of which will be discussed: the advisory function, the underwriting function, and the marketing function.

Investment banking functions Because of their expertise in selling securities on a continual basis, investment bankers can provide their clients with advisory services during the planning stage preceding the issuance of new securities. This advice includes the type of security to be sold, the features to be offered with the security, the price, and the timing of the sale. Such advisory work occurs in a "negotiated" bid arrangement, whereby the issuer has chosen the investment banker at the initiation of the process and the two negotiate and work together thereafter.[2]

The **underwriting** function consists of the investment banker's purchasing the securities (once the details of the issue have been negotiated) and subsequently reselling them to investors.[3] Investment bankers provide a valuable service to the issuers at this stage because the bankers assume the risk of price declines in the securities. The issuer receives its check and can spend the proceeds for the purposes for which the funds are being raised. The investment bankers own the securities until they are resold. The term *underwriting* refers to the fact that the investment banker assumes the risk of selling the securities.

Investment bankers bear risk in the underwriting stage. Although many issues are sold out quickly (i.e., the first day they are offered to the public),

---

[2] An alternative arrangement is a competitive bid, whereby the firm decides beforehand the details of the sale, solicits bids from investment bankers, and accepts the best offer. This arrangement is usually required of most public utilities. However, most corporate stock and bond offerings are sold on a negotiated basis rather than a competitive bid basis.

[3] Corporate offerings are classified as either "seasoned" issues or "initial" public offerings. The former refers to new securities sold by companies with existing public markets for their securities; the latter indicates the initial sale of securities by a company.

others may require days or even weeks. A price decline in the securities during this time could result in a loss for the investment bankers. However, most issues are sold successfully, with the price approximating that agreed on during the planning stage before the sale. Investment bankers are compensated by a "spread," which is the difference between what they pay the issuer for the securities and what they sell them for to the public (i.e., the securities are purchased from the issuer for a discount).

In addition to having expertise in these matters and closely scrutinizing any potential issue of securities, investment bankers can protect themselves by forming a **syndicate,** or group of investment bankers. This allows them to diversify their risk. One investment banker acts as the managing underwriter, overseeing the underwriting syndicate. This syndicate becomes part of a larger group that sells the securities.

The third function mentioned for investment bankers is marketing. Securities have typically been sold through a selling group consisting of the sales division of the underwriting syndicate and selected retail brokerage houses. The selling group functions under a selling group agreement which specifies the operating conditions, such as how the spread will be split among the various parties and how long the group will operate.

Figure 3–1 illustrates a primary offering of securities through investment bankers, a process referred to as a **syndicated offering.** The issuer (seller) of the securities works with the originating investment banker in designing the specific details of the sale. Documents are prepared to satisfy federal laws. In particular, the issuer files a registration statement with the Securities & Exchange Commission (SEC) containing financial and other information about the company and issues a **prospectus,** which summarizes this information, to officially offer the securities for sale.

The underwriter forms a syndicate of underwriters willing to undertake the sale of these securities. The selling group consists of the syndicate members plus, if necessary, other firms affiliated with the syndicate. The selling group cannot begin its sales efforts until the legal requirements have been met. In particular, new issues must be registered with the SEC at least 20 days before being publicly offered.[4] Upon approval from the SEC, the selling group begins selling the securities to the public. The issue may be fully subscribed (sold out) quickly, or it may require several days (or longer) to sell. During this time the underwriting manager can legally elect to stabilize the market by placing purchase orders for the security at a fixed price. Underwriters feel that such stabilization is sometimes needed to provide for an orderly sale (thereby helping the issuer) and reduce their risk (thereby helping themselves).

---

[4] However, the selling group can send out a preliminary prospectus to investors describing the new issue. No offering date or price is shown and the prospectus is identified clearly as an informational sheet and not a solicitation to sell the securities; for this reason, the preliminary prospectus is often referred to as a "red herring."

Investment banking function very important
Glass Steagal
Today banks + investment banks moving together

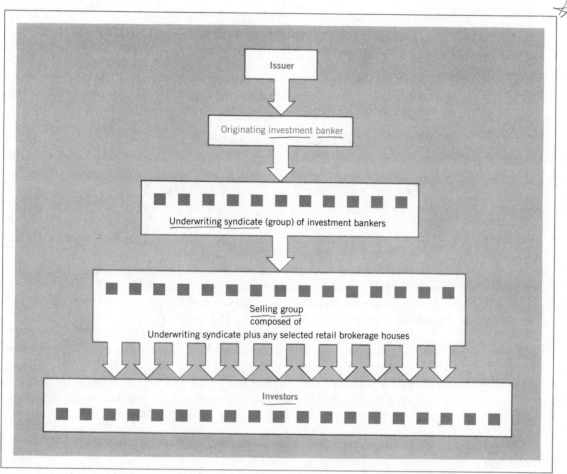

FIGURE 3—1 The issuance process for new securities in the primary market.

New trends in investment banking Securities and Exchange Rule 415 (the **shelf rule**), effective in 1982, permits qualified companies to file a "short form registration" and "place on the shelf" securities to be sold. The issuing company can sell the new securities over time by auctioning pieces of the issue to the lowest cost bidder, providing flexibility and savings. This rule, along with the general deregulation of the financial services industry, may have a significant impact on investment bankers, shifting their emphasis away from underwriting.

Another significant development in investment banking is the "unsyndicated stock offering," whereby the corporation distributes the entire stock issue directly to institutional investors; that is, the securities are not syndicated through the normal retail distribution network to individual investors. The issuers save the fees paid for a normal syndicated offering, which can be substantial; furthermore, the issuing process may be streamlined because the issuer is dealing with a small number of presumably sophisticated buyers. The underwriters handling these unsyndicated offerings may earn a larger net return, although total fees are lower, because they do not have to share the fees with the underwriting syndicate. In the early 1980s, only 1 to 2% of all common stock issued was unsyndicated, whereas by the mid-1980s as much as one third was sold in this manner.

Public and Private Placements

There has been a trend in recent years for more corporations to place their new securities issues privately rather than publicly. This means that the securities are sold directly to financial institutions, such as life insurance companies and pension funds, bypassing the open market. Debt securities are most commonly privately placed.

The advantages of **private placement** include not having to register the issue with the SEC, saving both time and money. Investment bankers' fees are also saved because they are not typically used in private placements; even if they are used, the underwriting spread is saved.[5] The savings in time can sometimes be important, as market conditions can change rapidly between the time an issue is registered and sold.

The disadvantages of private placements include a higher interest cost (or dividend cost), because the financial institutions usually charge more than would be offered in a public subscription, and possible restrictive provisions on the activities of the borrower. Also, a lack of marketability exists because the issue is unregistered; therefore, the buyer may demand additional compensation, in the form of a higher yield, from the lender.

Secondary Markets: Structure

Once new securities have been sold in the primary market, an efficient mechanism must exist for their resale if investors are to view securities as attractive opportunities. Secondary markets provide the means for investors to trade securities among themselves.[6]

Secondary markets exist for the trading of common and preferred stock, warrants, bonds, and puts and calls. The structure of each of these markets is discussed in this section and the mechanics of trading in secondary markets in the following section. Figure 3–2 diagrams the structure of the secondary markets.

---

[5] Investment bankers in this situation are paid a finder's fee. The bankers have many contacts, which may be helpful, and they provide information to the issuer in evaluating the buyer's offer.

[6] Again, this does not directly effect the issuer, who sells new securities in the primary market in order to raise funds.

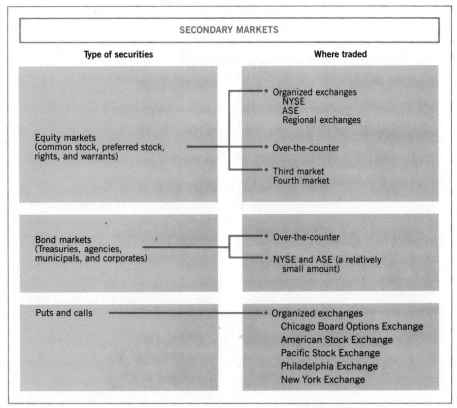

SECONDARY MARKETS	
Type of securities	**Where traded**

Equity markets (common stock, preferred stock, rights, and warrants)	• Organized exchanges
	   NYSE
	   ASE
	   Regional exchanges
	
	• Over-the-counter
	
	• Third market
	   Fourth market

Bond markets (Treasuries, agencies, municipals, and corporates)	• Over-the-counter • NYSE and ASE (a relatively small amount)

Puts and calls	• Organized exchanges
	   Chicago Board Options Exchange
	   American Stock Exchange
	   Pacific Stock Exchange
	   Philadelphia Exchange
	   New York Exchange

FIGURE 3–2   The structure of the secondary markets in the United States.

Equity Markets

Common stocks, preferred stocks, and warrants are traded in the equity markets. As is the case for all secondary markets, equity markets can be classified as either **auction markets** or **negotiated markets.** The former involve an auction (bidding) process in a specific physical location, with **brokers** representing investors. Brokers are intermediaries who represent both buyers and sellers and attempt to obtain the best price possible for either in a transaction. Brokers collect commissions for their efforts and have no vested interest in whether a customer buys or sells or in what is bought or sold.

Negotiated markets involve a network of **dealers** who make a market by standing ready to buy and sell securities at specified prices. Unlike brokers, dealers have a vested interest in the transaction because the securities are bought from them and sold to them, and they earn a profit in these trades by the spread, or difference between the two prices.

The auction markets include the New York Stock Exchange, the American Stock Exchange, and the regional exchanges. Negotiated markets involve the over-the-counter market.

New York Stock Exchange Founded in 1792, the New York Stock Exchange (NYSE) is the oldest and most prominent secondary market in the United States, if not the world. It is a not-for-profit corporation with 1474 members as of 1986, 1366 of whom own a "seat."[7] Most of the members are partners or directors of stockbrokerage houses.[8] Members may transfer seats, subject to the approval of the Exchange. The price of a seat has varied sharply over the years, ranging from less than $100,000 in the mid-1970s to a record $1.1 million by April 1987.

Most members of the NYSE act as brokers for customers, buying and selling securities for them. They are called **commission brokers** and are members of brokerage houses. Floor brokers, on the other hand, are brokers acting as free lancers who handle overflows for various commission brokers and share in their commissions. Floor traders trade for their own account, paying no commissions.[9]

Specialists, who own roughly 25% of all the seats on the NYSE, are assigned to each of the trading posts on the floor of the NYSE where they handle one or more of the stocks traded at that post. Specialists act as both brokers and dealers. As a broker, they maintain the *limit book,* in which is recorded all limit orders or orders that have been placed by investors to buy or sell a security at a specific price (or better) and will not be executed until that price is reached. The commission brokers leave the limit orders with the specialist to be filled when possible; therefore, the specialist receives part of the broker's fee.

Specialists also act as dealers, buying and selling shares of their assigned stock(s) so as to maintain an orderly market. The stock exchanges function essentially as a continuous market, assuring investors that they can almost always buy and sell a particular security at some price. Assuming that public orders do not arrive at the same time so that they can be matched, the specialist will buy from commission brokers with orders to sell and sell to those with orders to buy, hoping to profit by a favorable spread between the two sides.

Specialists are required by the NYSE to maintain a continuous, orderly market in their assigned stocks. In order to provide this continuous market, specialists must often go "against the market," which requires adequate capital. The NYSE requires specialists to be able to assume a position of 5000 shares in their assigned stocks.[10]

---

[7] The other 108 individuals paid an annual fee to have access to the trading floor.

[8] For example, Merrill Lynch, the largest retail stockbrokerage firm, owns over 20 seats.

[9] Such traders are speculating on their own behalf, sometimes buying and selling on the same day ("day-trading"). Their activities have decreased over the years.

[10] Specialists must be approved by the Board of Governors of the NYSE and have experience, ability as a dealer, and specified minimum capital.

BOX 3–1 COLD-CALL COWBOYS

We are looking for individuals with a deep desire to earn a great deal of money," says David Barrus, a district manager for Blinder, Robinson & Co. He's preaching to a class of 30 eager would-be stockbrokers gathered at the penny stock firm's Madison Avenue office in New York. "Last year our rookie of the year, a former truck driver in Chicago, earned in excess of $130,000."

The attendees straighten up in their seats. "This is a chance to get involved in the most exciting thing anybody can do," Barrus tells them. "I know. I am a broker with 1200 clients, and I am 32 years old. Eight years ago I worked at McDonald's. Now I manage millions of dollars and earn in excess of $400,000 a year."

The chance of a lifetime? Nearly 50,000 people became registered to sell stocks, bonds and packaged securities last year alone. In all, there are 404,000 people registered to sell securities of one kind or another. No wonder you get so many calls and letters.

For the stoutest hearts, big money could be there. According to the Securities Industry Association, the average broker earned $80,000 last year. But don't let that average mislead you. It includes superbrokers who gross over $1 million in commissions a year. "A good slug of brokers earn half the average," says SIA General Manager Adrian Banky. "In a bear market a broker oriented toward selling stocks and bonds can see his business drop 30% or 40%." Small wonder only 41% of all brokers remain in the business more than three years.

Still, there is no shortage of applicants, who have two roads to travel. The high road is with a major brokerage firm. But getting hired can seem as hard as getting into medical school. "In 1986 we trained 800 new brokers, but we had 70,000 applicants," says Joel Margolies, head of retail branches at Shearson Lehman Brothers.

Only one new broker in five starts out with one of the major firms, which provide a base salary for up to 16 months, training and name recognition. After that, brokers keep 25% to 50% of their gross commissions.

"Dean Witter has been awesome for me," says 25-year-old Eric J. Shames, who passed up law school in 1984 to become a broker and grossed $385,000 in 1986. "Besides the name, they back me with everything—research, a beautiful office. All I have to do is put in the time."

Merrill Lynch's 17-week training program includes three weeks at its campus-like complex in Princeton, N.J., which features high-tech simulation drills, jacuzzis to cool out in, and fine dining. Merrill says it spends $30,000 to $50,000 per trainee.

The vast majority of potential brokers, however, have to take the low road and get no such coddling. Their training with a small firm usually consists of a few product lectures and the chance to watch an established salesman at work. Then they're given a desk, a phone and a telephone directory. Sometimes the atmosphere is a bit rough. "As soon as I walked in the door I knew I was hired because I was dressed better than the president," says Dominic Smorra, who left a small o-t-c firm in New Jersey last year to join Merrill Lynch. "I was working with ex-auto mechanics and construction workers. The secretaries were abused, foul language was rampant. I couldn't stomach it."

All new brokers must become registered with the National Association of Securities Dealers, of course. The six-hour, 250-

question General Securities exam used to be child's play. Until last June the pass rate for the exam hovered around 65%. The test is now tougher; less than 60% pass.

There is no proven formula for becoming a successful broker. Rich friends and a gift of gab help. A sales background usually is a big plus, too. But advanced degrees can work against you. Says Barrus at Blinder, Robinson, "I hate Harvard M.B.A.s—they think too much. I need doers."

Self-confidence is a must. Says Barrus: "All I need is a name and number to be successful. I don't care if they are qualified investors. I'll take names off of subway cars."

Rookies and pros alike are constantly on the prowl for new clients, spending upwards of 70 hours a week cold-calling, often using the same directories. Others concentrate on mailings, seminars and teaching night classes to woo customers. Some women brokers find they have an advantage selling to women professionals, but others find they are more successful with male clients. "A lot of men enjoy my 'intuitive ability,'" quips a woman broker in New York.

"The level of rejection is incredible, but there can be no lapse in your mental attitude," says one ex-broker, who admits he couldn't hack it and now does odd jobs for a living. "One day you can be the best guy in the world, the next you can rattle off 150 calls, and no one wants to talk to you."

According to Bill Meyer, a psychologist at Rohrer, Hibler & Replogle, the most successful brokers seem to be driven almost solely by money and profit. They tend not to make other sacrifices and, as a result, have a higher tendency toward divorce. "These people find this pressure to earn very exciting," Meyer says. "They are driven."

Source: Matthew Schifrin, "Cold-call Cowboys," *Forbes,* February 23, 1987, pp. 140–141. Reprinted by permission. *Forbes* magazine, February 23, 1987, © Forbes, Inc., 1987.

The New York Stock Exchange has specific listing requirements that companies must meet in order to be listed (i.e., accepted for trading), as shown in Table 3–1. Initial as well as continuing listing requirements must be met; otherwise, a firm could be delisted from the exchange. The NYSE can suspend or delist a firm whenever it believes that continued trading would not be advisable. A record 135 companies were added to the NYSE in 1986, bringing the total to 1575 companies accounting for some 2300 stocks (because some companies have listed both common stock and one or more issues of preferred stock).[11]

The NYSE had a 1986 share volume of over 35 billion shares, which was almost 50% of the total equities trading in domestic securities markets. By dollar volume the figure was even higher, almost 70%. Daily trading volume averaged 141 million shares in 1986, compared to less than 40 million shares daily in 1979. In January, 1987, for the first time in its history, trading

---

[11] The 135 number refers to original new common stocks—because of removals, the net change for 1986 was 33.

NYSE "club" that all people can't join

TABLE 3–1 *Minimum* **Listing Requirements for the New York Stock Exchange**

1. Demonstrated earning power consisting of a minimum level of profitability for the preceding three years. *brand new co. couldn't list, co. who didn't do well*

2. Net tangible assets of $18 million, but greater emphasis on aggregate market value of the common stock. *size limitation*

3. Market value of publicly held shares within a range of $9 to $18 million. The $18 million figure was applicable at the end of 1986. *small co's couldn't join*

4. A total of 1,100,000 common shares held by the public. *size limitation*

5. Either 2000 holders of at least 100 shares or 2200 total stockholders together with recent average monthly trading volume of 100,000 shares. *size limitation + close held corp limit*

Source: Fact Book 1987, New York Stock Exchange, Inc., 1987, p. 21. With permission.

---

volume exceeded one billion shares in one week and over 300 million shares in one day.

American Stock Exchange   The American Stock Exchange (AMEX) is the only other national organized exchange. Its organization and procedures resemble those of the NYSE, except that it is smaller (approximately 650 seats) and fewer companies are listed there (796 in 1986). The listing requirements for stocks on the AMEX are less stringent than those of the NYSE. Many companies that grow and prosper eventually move their listing to the NYSE. Since 1976 dual listing of stocks on both the NYSE and the AMEX has been permitted.

The AMEX accounted for 4% of the total 1986 share volume; furthermore, in dollar volume, it accounted for less than 3%.

Regional exchanges   Several regional exchanges exist, including the Midwest Stock Exchange, the Pacific Stock Exchange, the Boston Stock Exchange, the Philadelphia Stock Exchange, and the Cincinnati Stock Exchange. Although these exchanges are patterned after the NYSE, the listing requirements are considerably more lenient.

Regional exchanges list small companies that may have limited geographic interest. They also engage in dual listing—that is, they list securities that are also listed on the NYSE and the AMEX; in fact, most of the securities traded are also traded on the NYSE or the AMEX. This allows local brokerage firms that are not members of a national exchange to purchase a seat on a regional exchange and trade in dual-listed securities. By offering lower commissions on such stocks, regional exchanges have attracted business that otherwise would go to the larger exchanges.

The over-the-counter market   In contrast to auction markets, the **over-the-counter (OTC) market** is a negotiated market. Transactions not handled on an organized exchange are handled in this market; that is, this market essen-

Other exchanges similar rules but less severe

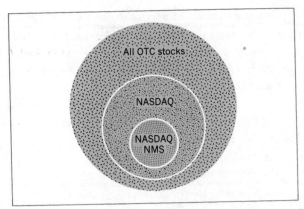

FIGURE 3–3 The structure of the over-the-counter market.

tially handles **unlisted securities,** defined as securities not listed on a stock exchange. The OTC market has become a major player in the securities markets and in all likelihood will continue to gain in importance.

The OTC market is not a place; it has no central location but is, rather, a way of doing business. It consists of a network of dealers linked together by communications devices, including the latest technological equipment. These dealers can deal directly with each other and with customers. In fact, in many respects the OTC market represents the market of the future, as we will discuss later.

The **National Association of Security Dealers (NASD)** is a self-regulating body of brokers and dealers that oversees OTC practices, much as the NYSE does for its members. NASD licenses brokers when they successfully complete a qualifying examination. Violation of the fair practices prescribed by the NASD are grounds for censure, fine, suspension, or expulsion. The self-regulating function of the NASD serves to protect the public as well as the interest of its members.

The over-the-counter market can best be described by thinking of smaller and smaller parts, as illustrated in Figure 3–3. The entire OTC market consists of more than 10,000 stocks.[12] However, many of these stocks are quite small and often inactively traded. Although by this criterion it is the largest securities market in the world, in terms of the total dollar value of transactions the OTC is much smaller than the NYSE.

In 1971 the NASD initiated a computerized communications network called **NASDAQ** (an acronym for the NASD Automated Quotation System) that offers current (up-to-the-minute) bid–ask prices for thousands of OTC

---

[12] OTC stocks that meet certain requirements are quoted daily in *The Wall Street Journal.* For those not carried, quotes can be obtained from the National Quotation Bureau, which reports daily prices on several thousand OTC securities.

stocks. Interested investors can obtain the current bid and ask prices from all the market makers for a security, assuring them of receiving the best price. Before the advent of NASDAQ, investors had to rely on their brokers placing calls to various dealers to obtain quotes, an inexact process at best. Price spreads on NASDAQ-carried stocks have narrowed even more since 1980 when NASDAQ began releasing the highest bids and lowest asks rather than representative quotations.

NASDAQ-traded stocks are the key component of the OTC market. NASDAQ continues to expand and reached a total of 4417 companies by the end of 1986. Almost 29 billion shares were traded in 1986, accounting for almost 40% of all equities trading in that year.

A significant development occurred on April 1, 1982, with the start-up of the **NASDAQ National Market System (NASDAQ/NMS),** a component of the NASDAQ market. The NMS is a combination of the competing market makers in OTC stocks and the up-to-the-minute reporting of trades, using data identical to that shown for the NYSE and AMEX (i.e., high, low, and last prices, as well as the net change from one day to the next). There are an average of 10 market makers per security. By 1986, 2613 securities traded on NASDAQ/NMS, accounting for 69% of all NASDAQ volume.[13]

In summary, the common stock issues traded in the OTC market vary widely in size, price, quality, and trading activity. Many are small, struggling speculative companies, often not far removed from having obtained public financing in a primary offer. Others are comparable to NYSE stocks and could, if they chose, be listed there. In fact, more and more OTC companies are choosing to remain OTC companies rather than move on to the AMEX or NYSE.[14] For example, in 1982 more than 1500 OTC companies qualified for these exchanges but remained OTC.

Table 3–2 shows share and dollar volume for all equities trading in domestic markets in 1986. The NYSE continues to dominate in both categories. However, NASDAQ share volume has increased dramatically since 1975 relative to both the NYSE and the AMEX, as shown in Figure 3–4.

The third and fourth markets   All off-exchange transactions in securities listed on the organized exchanges take place in the so-called **third market.** This market was created to serve the needs of large institutional investors who did not want to pay full brokerage costs on large transactions. These large buyers and sellers were brought together by brokers who were not members of organized exchanges, and therefore were not required to charge the high commissions required on the exchanges. With the elimination of

---

[13] This discussion is based on the *NASDAQ 1986 Fact Book,* Washington, D.C.: The National Association of Securities Dealers, Inc., p. 2.

[14] This discussion is based on "The Institutionalization of NASDAQ," *Forbes,* November 8, 1982, p. 127.

TABLE 3–2   Share of Equity Markets Trading in 1986—All Exchanges and NASDAQ

	Share Volume (millions)		Dollar Value (millions)	
NYSE	35,680	47.7%	$1,374,350	67.1%
AMEX	2,979	4.0	44,453	2.2
Regionals	6,088	8.1	200,770	9.8
NASDAQ	28,737	38.4	378,216	18.5
NASDAQ/OTC Trading in Listed Securities	1,326	1.8	48,649	2.4
Totals	74,810	100.0%	$2,046,438	100.0%

Source: 1987 Fact Book: NASD, National Association of Securities Dealers, Inc., Washington, D.C., 1987. Reprinted by permission.

fixed commissions in 1975, activity in the third market declined significantly. Less than 2% of share volume in all domestic markets occurs in this market.

Today, a few third market brokers provide investors with the flexibility to trade when the NYSE is closed. For example, Jeffries & Co., a leading third market broker in Los Angeles, specializes in trading big blocks off the floor of major exchanges, particularly when the NYSE is not open. Generally it makes a market in a stock by matching buyers and sellers (and collecting commissions), but Jeffries often takes positions in stocks in order to facilitate trading.

The **fourth market** refers to transactions made directly between large institutions (and wealthy individuals), bypassing brokers and dealers. Several different privately owned automated systems exist to provide current information on specific securities that the participants are willing to buy or

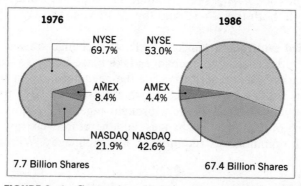

FIGURE 3–4   Comparison of share volume: NYSE, AMEX, and NASDAQ, 1976 and 1986.

Source: National Association of Securities Dealers, Inc., 1987 *Fact Book,* p. 14. Reprinted by permission.

sell. Essentially, the fourth market is a communications network among investors interested in trading large blocks of stock. Because their trades do not have to be reported, little is known about their activities in this market.

Bond Markets

Just as stockholders need good secondary markets to be able to trade stocks and thus preserve their flexibility, bondholders need a viable market in order to sell before maturity. Otherwise, many investors would be reluctant to tie up their funds for up to 30 years. At the very least, they would demand higher initial yields on bonds, which would hinder raising funds by those who wish to invest productively.

Investors can purchase either new bonds being issued in the primary market or existing bonds outstanding in the secondary market. Yields for the two must be in equilibrium. If IBM's bonds are trading in the secondary market to yield 12% over a 20-year period, for example, comparable new IBM bonds will be sold with approximately the same yield.

Some bonds are traded on the NYSE (about 3600 in 1986) and very few on the AMEX, and their prices can be seen daily in *The Wall Street Journal*. However, the secondary bond market is primarily an OTC market, with a large network of dealers making markets in the various bonds. The volume of bond trading in the OTC market dwarfs that of all the exchanges combined.

Investors can buy and sell bonds through their brokers, who in turn trade with bond dealers. Certain features of the bond markets should be noted.

Treasury bonds U.S. Treasury notes and bonds are widely purchased and held and widely traded. The Federal Reserve conducts open market operations with Treasury securities, and institutions such as commercial banks deal in very large quantities. The result is a broad and deep market with a volume of transactions exceeding that of any other security.

The Treasury bond market consists of selected market makers who trade with the open market desk of the Federal Reserve Bank of New York. These large dealers include the bond departments of several banks and this network has widely spread branches and dealers. In addition, many large banks act as dealers (make markets) in particular issues. Although larger investors can transact directly with these dealers, most investors use their banks, brokers, and so on and pay commissions on the order of $30 to $50 per purchase or sale. Small amounts of Treasury bonds can be traded on the American Stock Exchange for a small charge per $1000 of securities.

Federal agency bonds Federal agency securities trade in good secondary markets with basically the same dealer market and procedures used as in the case of Treasury securities. Larger issues are more easily traded than smaller issues, and recently issued securities are usually more actively traded than those outstanding for some time.

Municipal bonds Municipal securities often have a relatively thin market with only moderate activity in the secondary market. This is because most bonds are held to maturity and therefore traded infrequently.

Probably fewer than 5% of all securities firms maintain an active municipal bond operation. Some specialize in particular types of issues, but most trade across the spectrum. Of course, an investor's broker can contact and transact with these dealers.

Individual investors can be important in this market. One estimate is that in 1982 individual purchases accounted for as much as 75% of new issues. However, when the individual is ready to sell, it may be difficult to find a buyer for just a few bonds unless significant price concessions are made. Some market professionals believe that investors with less than $50,000 to put into municipals would do better by buying a unit investment trust, an indirect investing method.[15]

Corporate bonds Although a substantial number of corporate bonds are listed on the exchanges with numerous small trades being executed there, exchange trading in corporate bonds is only a very small part of this market. For example, on a typical day some two-thirds of the roughly 3000 issues on the NYSE's bond board do not trade at all, and a typical trade is less than 15 bonds. Liquidity is not always good for these small transactions, with delays occurring in the trade; furthermore, price concessions often have to be made. Investors should be careful in trading small amounts of corporate bonds and be prepared for delays and costs. The price that appears in newspapers for these exchange-traded bonds may vary significantly from the actual price at which the bond trades.

Most corporate bonds are traded off the exchanges by institutions dealing in round lots of at least 250 bonds, and often larger amounts. This institutional market behaves independently of the bond trading on the exchanges, where a computer collects bids to buy and offers to sell from around the country and executes a trade when a match is made. At times, prices between the two markets can differ by several points.[16]

Put and Call Market

Options trading on organized exchanges began in 1973. There are now five option exchanges that have standardized the terms of trade for these securities, thereby increasing their liquidity. The original option buyer or seller (writer) can easily close out a position by making an opposite transaction in one of these markets.

Each of these exchanges has a physical location with a trading floor and designated areas for the options of each stock listed on the exchange to be

---

[15] These are fixed, diversified portfolios of bonds sold in multiples of $1000 each (with a sales charge of about 4%) that pay interest monthly.

[16] See David Henry, "Patience Rewarded," *Forbes,* May 19, 1986, p. 82.

traded. Members of each exchange buy and sell directly on the floor, with nonmembers using floor brokers to execute orders. Some exchanges use market makers, who are members of the exchange, to perform a dealer function, while other exchanges use specialists. Market makers compete with each other to buy and sell options assigned to them, whereas specialists are charged with maintaining a fair and orderly market in their assigned options. Both market makers and specialists are regulated by their respective exchanges as to what they can do in setting bid–ask spreads and in the sequence of prices at which their options trade.

Regulation of the Securities Markets

Much of the legislation governing the securities markets and industry was enacted during the Great Depression. Many fraudulent and undesirable practices occurred in the 1920s and the markets as a whole were shattered in the Crash of 1929. Congress subsequently sought to improve the stability and viability of the securities markets, enacting the basis of all securities regulation in the 1930s. Additional acts have been legislated over the last 50 years. Table 3–3 contains a brief description of the major legislation affecting securities markets.

The Securities and Exchange Commission

The **Securities and Exchange Commission** was created in 1934 as an independent, quasi-judicial agency of the U.S. government.[17] Its mission is to administer laws in the securities field and to protect investors and the public in securities transactions. The Commission consists of five members appointed by the president for five year terms. Its staff consists of lawyers, accountants, security analysts, and others divided into divisions and offices (including nine regional offices).

In general, the SEC administers the securities laws previously mentioned (as well as others not mentioned). Thus, under the Securities Act of 1933, the SEC sees that new securities being offered for public sale are registered with the commission and under the 1934 act it sees that the same is done for securities trading on national exchanges. It is important to note that the registration of securities in no way ensures that investors purchasing them will not lose money. Registration means only that adequate disclosure has been made by the issuer. In fact, the Securities and Exchange Commission (SEC) has no power to disapprove securities for lack of merit.

The Securities Acts Amendments of 1964 directs the SEC to apply reporting provisions to most OTC stocks. Under the two acts of 1940, investment companies and investment advisors must register with the SEC and disclose

---

[17] For a good discussion of the SEC, see "Securities and Exchange Commission," reprinted in *The C.F.A. Study Guide I*, Charlottesville, Va.: The Institute of Chartered Financial Analysts, 1982.

TABLE 3–3 Major Legislation Regulating the Securities Markets

1. The Securities Act of 1933 (the "Securities Act") deals primarily with new issues of securities. The intent was to protect potential investors in new securities by requiring issuers to register an issue with full disclosure of information. False information is subject to criminal penalties and lawsuits by purchasers to recover lost funds.

2. The Securities Exchange Act of 1934 (SEA) extended the disclosure requirements to the secondary market and established the SEC to oversee registration and disclosure requirements. Organized exchanges are required to register with the SEC and agree to be governed by existing legislation.

3. The Maloney Act of 1936 extended SEC control to the OTC market. It provides for the self-regulation of OTC dealers through the National Association of Securities Dealers (NASD), which licenses and regulates members of OTC firms. The SEC has authority over the NASD, which must report all its rules to the SEC.

4. The Investment Company Act requires investment companies to register with the SEC and provides a regulatory framework within which they must operate. Investment companies are required to disclose considerable information and to follow procedures designed to protect their shareholders. This industry is heavily regulated.

5. The Investment Advisors Act of 1940 requires individuals or firms who sell advice about investments to register with the SEC. Again, registration connotes only compliance with the law. Almost anyone can become an investment advisor because the SEC cannot deny anyone the right to sell investment advice unless it can demonstrate dishonesty or fraud.

6. The Securities Investor Protection Act of 1970 established the Securities Investor Protection Corporation (SIPC) to act as an insurance company in protecting investors from brokerage firms that fail. Assessments are made against brokerage firms to provide the funds with backup government support available.

7. The Securities Acts Amendments of 1975 was a far-reaching piece of legislation, calling for the SEC to move toward the establishment of a national market. This act abolished fixed brokerage commissions.

certain information; in effect, the SEC ensures that these two groups will meet the requirements of the laws affecting them.

The SEC is required to investigate complaints or indications of violations in securities transactions. A good example is "insider trading," which has been a primary enforcement emphasis of the SEC. "Insiders" (officers and directors of corporations) are prohibited from misusing (i.e., trading on) corporate information not generally available to the public and required to file reports with the SEC showing their equity holdings.

Insider-trading "scandals" were prominent in 1986. Dennis Levine, a key member of the mergers and acquisitions department of Drexel Burnham Lambert Inc., was charged with insider trading in a major case with many repercussions. A well-known arbitrageur, Ivan Boesky, was fined $100 million by the SEC in a highly publicized insider-trading case.

Secondary Markets: The Mechanics of Trading

Opening a Brokerage Account

In general, it is quite easy for any responsible person to open a brokerage account. An investor selects a broker or brokerage house by personal contact, referral, reputation, and so forth. Member firms of the NYSE are supposed to learn certain basic facts about potential customers, but only minimum information is normally required; in fact, personal contact between broker and customer sometimes does not occur, with transactions carried out by telephone or in writing.

The most basic type of account is the **cash account,** whereby the customer pays the brokerage house the full price for any securities purchased. Many customers open a **margin account,** which allows the customer to borrow from the brokerage firm to purchase securities. (Margin is explained in some detail later.) The NYSE requires a minimum margin deposit of $2000 to open this type of account (regardless of the transaction contemplated).

In 1977, Merrill Lynch, the largest retail brokerage firm in the United States, started a new type of account, which it called the cash management account (CMA). This account, which requires a minimum balance to open and the payment of an annual fee, automatically reinvests the account holders' free credit balances in shares of a money market fund chosen by the investor. Account holders are issued bank checks and a Visa credit card. Checks can be written against the account's assets, both cash and securities.[18] In addition, instant loans based on the marginable securities in the account can be obtained for virtually any purpose, not just securities transactions, at the current broker's call money rate plus ¾% to 2¼%. Each month the customer receives a comprehensive summary statement.

The CMA account was phenomenally successful and by 1982 perhaps a dozen other brokerage firms were offering similar accounts.

The Securities Investor Protection Corporation (SIPC), a quasi-government agency, insures each customer account of about 12,000 member brokers against brokerage firm failure. Each account is covered for as much as $500,000 (coverage of cash is limited to $100,000). From 1970 through 1985, SIPC paid out in excess of $180 million in helping some 190,000 inves-

---

[18] The checks are actually drawn on Bank One of Columbus, N.A., Columbus, Ohio. This bank pays and clears the check and notifies Merrill Lynch.

tors recover over $700 million from 189 failed brokers with SIPC insurance (would you want a broker without such insurance?).[19]

How Orders Work

On the organized exchanges *Traditionally,* a typical order from an investor for 100 shares of IBM might be handled as follows. The investor phones his or her broker, or registered representative, and asks how IBM is doing. The broker can punch a few buttons on an electronic console and immediately see the last trade for IBM, as well as other information such as the high and low for the day and the number of shares traded. Assuming that the investor is willing to pay the last trade price for IBM, or a price close to that, the broker can be instructed to buy 100 shares of IBM "at the market." This order will be transmitted to the broker's New York office and then to the member partner on the exchange floor (or the broker may work through some other exchange member). The representative on the floor will go to the trading post for IBM, where the specialist handling IBM is located, and ask "How's IBM?"

The specialist is charged with maintaining a fair and orderly market in IBM. The specialist knows the current quotes for IBM because he or she keeps a record of all limit orders for the stock. Assuming no other member partner has come to the post to sell IBM, the specialist will quote a current bid and ask price for 100 shares. The partner then indicates that there is a purchase order to be filled (at the asking price). A confirmation is relayed back to the investor's broker, who notifies the investor. The trade will appear on the NYSE consolidated tape, which since June 1975 has reported transactions for all NYSE-listed securities; in 1986 this involved five stock exchanges (in addition to the NYSE) and two over-the-counter markets.[20] Daily papers such as *The Wall Street Journal* report the high and low prices for each stock wherever they occur.[21] Share volume shown on the tape increased to a record 42.5 billion shares by 1986 with the NYSE accounting for over 84% of consolidated volume.

In actuality, the NYSE has become highly automated.[22] An electronic system matches buy and sell orders entered before the market opens, setting the opening price of a stock. The NYSE has SuperDOT, an electronic order-routing system for NYSE-listed securities.[23] Member firms send orders directly to the post where the securities are traded and confirmation of trading

---

[19] See Brenton R. Schlender, "If a Broker Fails, Settling Claims Can Take Time," *The Wall Street Journal,* February 3, 1986, p. 23.

[20] In 1986 there were no dually-listed issues with the American Stock Exchange.

[21] An investor needs to realize that a limit order placed to sell a stock at, say 101½, may not have been executed although the quotes from yesterday's trading in today's paper show a price of 101½ as the high. This will happen if the investor's broker placed the order on the NYSE, but the stock's high was reached on the Pacific Stock Exchange, for example.

[22] The same is true for the AMEX.

[23] This discussion is taken from the *New York Stock Exchange Fact Book 1987,* New York: New York Stock Exchange, p. 16.

is returned directly to the member firm over the same system. As a part of SuperDOT, the Opening Automated Report Service (OARS) automatically and continuously pans member firms' pre-opening buy and sell orders, presenting the imbalance to the specialist up to the opening of a stock. OARS handles market orders of up to 5099 shares. SuperDOT also includes a post-opening market order system designed to accept post-opening market orders of up to 2099 shares.

In the over-the-counter market Dealers in the OTC market arrive at the prices of securities by both negotiating with customers specifically and by making competitive bids. Dealers match the forces of supply and demand with each dealer making a market in certain securities. They do this by standing ready to buy a particular security from a seller or sell it to a buyer. Dealers quote bid and ask prices for each security; the **bid price** is the highest price offered by the dealer, and the **ask price** is the lowest price at which the dealer is willing to sell. The dealer profits from the "spread" between these two prices. Actively traded stocks on the OTC market have as many as 10 to 20 market makers (dealers) competing, which helps to keep the spread small. In effect, the OTC dealer functions much as the specialist does for an exchange-listed stock.

As of 1985, the Small Order Execution System (SOES) included all NASDAQ issues. All SOES trades are automatically executed at the best price available in NASDAQ, as automatically reported to NASDAQ.[24]

Types of Orders

Three basic types of orders are used by investors: market orders, limit orders, and stop orders. Each of these orders is explained in Table 3–4.

Investors can enter limit or stop orders as *day orders,* which are effective for only one day, or as *good-until-canceled orders,* which remain in effect for six months unless canceled or renewed.

A standard order is a round lot, which is 100 or a multiple of 100 shares; an odd lot is any number of shares between 1 and 99. Odd lots have traditionally cost the transactor an extra ⅛ or ¼ of a point. Odd lots are now executed by the NYSE directly by computer. Some large brokerage firms now handle their own odd lots, and most investors who transact in odd lots are actually transacting with a dealer.

Clearing Procedures

Most securities are sold on a *regular way* basis, meaning the *settlement date* is five *business* days after the trade date.[25] On the settlement date the customer becomes the legal owner of any securities bought, or gives them up if

---

[24] A 5000 share limit for NASDAQ and a 1000 share limit for NASDAQ/NMS was in effect in 1985.

[25] A sale could be made as a "cash" transaction, which requires delivery and settlement the same day.

TABLE 3–4 Types of Orders Used by Investors

1. **Market orders,** the most common type of order, instruct the broker to buy or sell the securities immediately at the best price available. As a representative of the buyer or seller, it is incumbent upon the broker to obtain the best price possible. A market order ensures that the transaction will be carried out, but the exact price at which it will occur is not known until its execution and subsequent confirmation to the customer.

2. **Limit orders** specify a particular price to be met or bettered. They may result in the customer obtaining a better price than with a market order or in no purchase or sale occurring because the market price never reaches the specified limit. The purchase or sale will occur only if the broker obtains that price, or betters it (lower for a purchase, higher for a sale). Limit orders can be tried immediately or left with the broker for a specific time or indefinitely. In turn, the broker leaves the order with the specialist who enters it in the limit book.

   EXAMPLE: Assume the current market price of a stock is $50. An investor might enter a buy limit order at $47; if the stock declines in price to $47, this limit order, which is on the specialist's book, will be executed at $47 or less. Similarly, another investor might enter a sell limit order for this stock at $55; if the price of this stock rises to $55, this investor's shares will be sold.

3. **Stop orders** specify a certain price at which a market order takes effect. For example, a stop order to sell at $50 becomes a market order to sell as soon as the market price reaches (declines to) $50. However, the order may not be filled exactly at $50 because the closest price at which the stock trades may be $49⅞. The exact price specified in the stop order is therefore not guaranteed and may not be realized.

   EXAMPLE 1: A sell stop order can be used to protect a profit in the case of a price decline. Assume, for example, that a stock bought at $32 currently trades at $50. The investor does not want to limit additional gains, but may wish to protect against a price decline. To lock in most of the profit, a sell stop order could be placed at $47.

   EXAMPLE 2: A buy stop order could be used to protect a profit from a short sale. Assume an investor sold short at $50, and the current market price of the stock is $32. A buy stop order placed at, say, $36 would protect most of the profit from the short sale.

sold, and must settle with the brokerage firm by that time.[26] Most customers allow their brokerage firm to keep their securities in a **street name,** that is, the name of the brokerage firm. The customer receives a monthly statement showing his or her position as to cash, securities held, any funds borrowed from the broker, and so on.

---

[26]The purchaser of securities typically will not be able to take physical delivery of the securities on the settlement date because they will not be available by then.

Brokerage houses must settle all transactions with the other party to the transaction, either another brokerage house or the specialist. A clearing house facilitates this process by taking the records of all transactions made by its members during a day, verifying both sides of the trades, and netting out the securities and money due or to be paid each member. Members of clearing houses include brokerage houses, banks, and others involved with securities. The National Securities Clearing Corporation operates such a central clearing house for trades on the New York and American stock exchanges and in the OTC markets.

Use of stock certificates as part of the settlement is dying out in the United States. The Depository Trust Company (DTC) has helped to eliminate their use by placing these transactions on computers. Members (brokers and dealers) who own certificates (in street name) deposit them in an account and can then deliver securities to each other in the form of a bookkeeping entry.

This **book-entry system,** as opposed to the actual physical possession of securities in either registered or "bearer" form, is essential to minimize the tremendous amount of paperwork that would otherwise occur with stock certificates. At the beginning of 1986, almost two-thirds of all outstanding corporate bonds and over one half of all NYSE common stocks and all outstanding municipal bonds had been "immobilized" by deposit in DTC vaults.[27] As of August 1986 all marketable Treasury securities are issued in book-entry form only.

Commissions

For most of its long history, the New York Stock Exchange required its members to charge fixed (and minimum) commissions.[28] Although this was a source of bitter contention and gave rise to the third market, as discussed earlier, little changed until 1975 when Congress, as part of the Securities Acts Amendments of 1975, eliminated all fixed commissions. Fees are supposed to be negotiated, with each firm free to act independently.

Investors can attempt to negotiate with their brokers, and different brokers charge different commissions. The overall competition in the industry presumably has an effect on the rates that are set. Customers are free to shop around, and smart ones do so. In practice, however, the larger retail brokerage houses have set commissions at specified rates for the typical small investor. In contrast, negotiated rates are the norm for institutional customers who deal in large blocks of stock. The rates charged institutional investors have declined drastically, from an average of 25 cents a share in 1975 to an average of 7.2 cents a share by the end of 1986. This appeared to

---

[27] See Ben Weberman, "Book-entry blues," *Forbes,* May 5, 1986, p. 104.

[28] Technically this is price fixing and therefore illegal, but the NYSE was exempted from prosecution under the antitrust laws.

TABLE 3–5 Representative Brokerage Commission Schedule

Shares Bought or Sold	Price per Share	Representative Full-Commission Broker	Representative Discount Broker
100	$60	$ 98	$ 49
500	15	181	85
3000	25	879	209

represent a leveling off in the decline because the average was virtually unchanged from the year before.[29]

One significant result of the "May Day" change insofar as brokerage commissions are concerned is the birth and growth of the **discount brokers.** These brokerage houses concentrate on executing orders and charge only for this service. In contrast, a full-service brokerage house offers a variety of services, in particular advice and research recommendations. The result of the change in 1975 was to *unbundle* brokerage services so that customers pay only for the services they really want. The discount houses are the ultimate in unbundling, essentially offering only execution services at rates 30 to 70% lower than the full-service houses. By the mid-1980s they had about 20% of the retail market. Table 3–5 illustrates some "representative" brokerage commissions for both a full-service brokerage firm and a discount broker (obviously, exact rates will vary between firms).

Margin

As previously noted, accounts at brokerage houses can be either cash accounts or margin accounts. With a margin account the customer can pay part of the total amount due and borrow the remainder from the broker, who in turn typically borrows from a bank to finance customers.[30] The bank charges the broker the broker loan rate, and the broker in turn charges the customer this rate plus approximately 1–1½% more.

The Board of Governors of the Federal Reserve System (Fed) has the authority to specify the *initial margin,* which is used as a policy device to influence the economy. Historically, initial margin for stocks has ranged between 40 and 100%, with a current level of 50% for a number of years. Exchanges and brokerage houses can require more initial margin than that set by the Fed if they choose. Furthermore, all exchanges and brokers require a *maintenance margin* below which the actual margin cannot go. The NYSE requires an investor to maintain an equity of 25% of the market value of any securities held (and in practice brokers usually require 30% or more) on long positions; maintenance margins on short positions are higher.

---

[29] See George Anders, "Institutional Stock Market Commissions Seem to Be Leveling Off After Long Fall," *The Wall Street Journal,* December 31, 1986, p. 20.

[30] In order to do this, a customer must sign a hypothecation agreement allowing the broker to use the securities as collateral with the bank.

Margin is that part of a transaction's value that a customer must pay to initiate the transaction; that is, it is that part of the total value of the transaction that cannot be borrowed from the broker. If the initial margin requirement is 50% on a $10,000 transaction (100 shares at $100 per share), the customer must put up $5000, borrowing $5000 from the broker.[31] Subsequently, the actual margin must be calculated.

If the actual margin exceeds the initial margin, the excess margin could be withdrawn from the account or more stock could be purchased without additional cash. Conversely, if the actual margin declines below the initial margin, problems can arise, depending on the amount of the decline. Assume that the maintenance margin is 40%, with a 50% initial margin, and that the price of the stock declines from $100 to $90 per share. Equation 3–1 is used to calculate actual margin.[32]

$$\text{Actual margin} = \frac{\text{Market value of securities} - \text{Amount borrowed}}{\text{Market value of securities}}$$

$$44.44\% = \frac{\$9000 - \$5000}{\$9000} \tag{3–1}$$

The actual margin is now between the initial margin of 50% and the maintenance margin of 40%. This would result in a restricted account, meaning that additional margin purchases are prohibited, although no additional equity (cash) has to be put into the account by the customer.

A **margin call** is issued when the actual margin declines below the maintenance margin. If additional cash (or securities) is not advanced, the securities can be sold by the broker. Brokerage houses calculate the actual margin in their customers' accounts daily to determine if a margin call is required. This is known as having the brokerage accounts *marked to market*.

Assume in the previous example that the maintenance margin is 25%. If the price of the stock drops to $80, the actual margin will be 37.5% [($8000 − $5000)/$8000]. Because this is above the maintenance margin, there is no margin call. However, if the price of the stock declines to $66.66, the actual margin will be 25% [($6666 − $5000)/$6666].

Any additional decline in price will result in a margin call, given a maintenance margin of 25%. Assume the price declines to $60. The amount of the margin call will be

$$\$6000 \times 25\% = \$1500 \quad \text{the equity required}$$
$$\$6000 - \$5000 \text{ (the amount borrowed)} = \underline{\$1000} \quad \text{current equity}$$
$$\$\ 500 \quad \text{margin call}$$

---

[31] With a 60% requirement, the customer must initially put up $6000.

[32] The difference between the market value of the securities and the amount borrowed is the investor's equity.

Although the margin requirement for common stocks and convertible bonds is 50%, it is only 30% for "acceptable" municipal and corporate bonds. U.S. government securities require only 8–15% margin. Long positions in puts and calls are not marginable; therefore, option buyers must put up 100% cash when taking long positions. Uncovered short positions in puts and calls require margin from the investor. Thus, an investor with $2000 equity in an option account who writes (sells) call contracts may have to post additional margin.[33]

The appeal of margin trading to investors is that it magnifies any gains on a transaction by the reciprocal of the margin requirement (i.e., 1/margin percentage; for example, with a margin of 40%, the magnification is 1/0.4 = 2.50). Unfortunately, it also magnifies any losses. And regardless of what happens, the margin trader must pay the interest costs on the margin account. An investor considering a margined stock purchase should remember that the stock price can go up, remain the same, or go down. In two of these three cases, the investor loses; furthermore, even if the stock goes up, the breakeven point is now higher by the amount of the interest charges.

Short Sales

The purchase of a security technically results in the investor being "long" the security; that is, the security is bought, and owned, because the investor believes the price is likely to rise. But what if the investor thinks that a security will decline in price? If he or she owns it, it might be wise to sell. If the security is not owned, the investor wishing to profit from the expected decline in price can sell the security short. **Short sales** are a normal part of market transactions.

How can an investor sell short; that is, sell something not owned? Not owning the security to begin with, it will have to be borrowed from a third party. The broker, on being instructed to sell short, will make these arrangements for this investor by borrowing the security from those held in street-name margin accounts, and, in effect, lending it to the short seller.[34]

The short seller's broker sells the borrowed security in the open market, exactly like any other sale, to some investor wishing to own it. The short seller expects the price of the security to decline. Assume that it does. The short seller instructs the broker to repurchase the security at the currently lower price and cancel the short position (by replacing the borrowed security). The investor profits by the difference between the price at which the borrowed stock was sold and the price at which it was repurchased.

---

[33] The margin requirements have to be calculated on an individual basis. These requirements are exchange-imposed minimums, and some brokerage houses may have stricter requirements.

[34] The securities could be borrowed from another broker. Also, individuals sometimes agree to lend securities to short sellers in exchange for interest-free loans equal to the collateral value of the securities sold short. Collateral value equals the amount of funds borrowed in a margin transaction.

As an example, assume an investor named Helen believes that the price of General Motors (GM) will decline over the next few months, perhaps because of foreign competition or high interest rates, both of which discourage domestic car purchases. Helen does not currently own GM shares, but wants to profit if her assessment is correct. She calls her broker with instructions to sell 100 shares of GM short at its current market price of $50 per share. The broker borrows 100 shares of GM from Kellie, who has a brokerage account with the firm and currently owns GM ("long"). The broker sells the 100 shares at $50 per share, crediting the $5000 proceeds (less commissions, which we will ignore for this example) to Helen's account. Note that Kellie knows nothing about this transaction, nor is she really affected. Kellie receives a monthly statement from the broker showing ownership of 100 shares of GM.[35]

Assume that six months later the price of GM has declined, as predicted by Helen, and is now $38 per share. Helen, satisfied with this drop in the price of GM, instructs the broker to purchase 100 shares of GM and close out the short position. Her profit is $5000 − $3800, or $1200 (again, ignoring commissions). The broker replaces Kellie's missing stock with the just-purchased 100 shares and the transaction is complete. Notice that two trades are required to complete a transaction or "round trip." Investors who purchase securities plan to sell them eventually. Investors who sell short plan to buy back eventually—they have simply reversed the normal buy–sell procedure by selling and then buying.

Several technicalities are involved in a short sale. These are outlined in Table 3–6.

How popular are short sales? In 1986, 3.1 billion shares (in round lots) were sold short on the NYSE, which was 8.7% of all reported sales. NYSE members accounted for almost 80% of short sales on the NYSE, with specialists, who often sell short to meet public buy orders, accounting for about half of this total. The public accounted for the remainder (about 750 million shares). Although investors have often bypassed short selling in the OTC market, this is changing (see Box 3–2).

The Changing Securities Markets

For the last 10 to 15 years the securities markets have been changing rapidly, with many more changes expected over the coming years. This is significant for at least two reasons. First, securities markets in the United States under-

---

[35] Should Kellie wish to sell the GM stock while Helen is short, the broker will simply borrow 100 shares from Elizabeth, a third investor who deals with this firm and owns GM stock, to cover the sale. It is important to note that all of these transactions are book entries and do not typically involve the actual stock certificates.

TABLE 3–6 The Details of Short Selling

---

1. Dividends declared on any stock sold short must be covered by the short seller. After all, the person from whom the shares were borrowed still owns the stock and expects all dividends paid on it.

2. Short sellers must have a margin account to sell short and must put up margin as if they had gone long. The margin can consist of cash or any unrestricted securities held long.

3. The net proceeds from a short sale, plus the required margin, are held by the broker; thus, no funds are immediately received by the short seller. The lender must be fully protected. To do this, the account is marked-to-the-market (as mentioned earlier in connection with margin accounts). If the price of the stock declines as expected by the short seller, he or she can draw out the difference between the sale price and the current market price. If the price of the stock rises, however, the short seller will have to put up more funds.

4. There is no time limit on a short sale. Short sellers can remain short indefinitely. The only problem arises when the lender of the securities wants them back. In most cases the broker can borrow elsewhere, but in some situations, such as a thinly capitalized stock, this may not be possible.

5. Short sales are permitted only on rising prices, or an uptick. A short seller can sell short at the last trade price only if that price exceeded the last different price before it. Otherwise, they must wait for an uptick. Although the order to the broker can be placed at any time, it will not be executed until an uptick occurs.

BOX 3–2 SHORT SELLING FOR THE SMALL INVESTOR

Short selling in the over-the-counter market has long been regarded as too risky for most individuals.

It *is* risky; a wrong guess can mean a loss that exceeds the original investment. But short selling in the OTC market has become more accessible to individual investors—and market professionals think that individuals who know what they're doing should take the plunge.

"It should be as easy for a person to sell short as go long" (that is, buy a stock), says Charles R. Schwab, chairman and chief executive officer of discount broker Charles Schwab & Co. "You make money in different ways in different markets," he says.

"There is a time to short and a time to go long."

Adds John Pinto, head of the National Association of Securities Dealers' surveillance department, "It's a legitimate method of investing."

In a classic short sale, an investor sells borrowed shares in anticipation of a price decline. The idea is to profit by buying shares later at a lower price to cover the transaction. The danger, of course, is that the price of the stock will rise instead.

The Put Option Option

It's also possible to short by buying a put option, a contract that gives an investor the right to sell a stock at a predetermined price within a specified time. If within that time the market price of the stock falls below the specified price, the investor sells the put at a profit. If the price rises, the investor lets the put expire.

In a typical short sale, brokers require investors to deposit 50% of the market value of the shares borrowed in a margin, or credit, account to cover potential losses. If the stock's price rises, investors will get "margin calls" to put in more money whenever the deposit falls below a certain percentage of the stock's market value.

In the past, only some brokers allowed individual investors to short OTC stocks. Over the last two years, however, the Federal Reserve Board has made many Nasdaq stocks—including all 2600 in the National Market System—eligible for purchase on margin, or credit.

Among other things, this has increased the supply of stocks purchased on margin and available to be shorted. Brokerage firms can lend their own shares or shares that customers have bought on margin and left on deposit.

"Short selling is more easily facilitated now that NMS securities are marginable," says Barry Snowbarger, senior vice president in charge of trading at Schwab. So most big brokers, including discounters, have begun to permit investors to short OTC stocks through margin accounts.

Prudent short sellers set a loss limit, but this isn't as easy in the OTC market as it is with a stock traded on the New York Stock Exchange. With a Big Board issue, an investor can place an order to close out the short position by buying shares if the market price rises to a certain level. In the OTC market, however, most brokers won't take the responsibility.

There is another potential hazard if the shares used in the short sale are shares that were bought on margin by another investor. If that investor decides to sell them, and the broker can't find replacement shares, the short seller could be forced to close out his position at a loss.

The least risky way to short is to use put options. But the exchanges that offer option contracts do so for only the 45 of the most actively traded securities.

Investors must decide whether the benefits of shorting make the risks and costs worthwhile. Say an investor wanted to sell short 100 shares of a $15 stock through Broker Securities Inc., a national discount broker based in Norfolk, Va. The investor would pay the firm's standard minimum commission of $35 when the borrowed shares were sold and a second $35 commission when the shares to cover the transaction were bought in the market.

Forgone Interest

The investor would forgo interest on the $750 deposit needed to meet the standard 50% margin requirement, if the money was paid in cash. But the investor could make the deposit in Treasury bills and continue to earn interest on them.

The short seller would also be responsible for any dividends paid on the borrowed securities, although few of the stocks investors are likely to short pay dividends.

As a result, the cost to short 100 shares of the $15 stock could be no more than the cost to buy and sell the same 100 shares: two $35 commission fees. That would mean that the stock would have to drop only 70 cents a share to $14.30 before the investor could begin to make a profit. If the stock dropped to $10 a share, the investor would clear $430.

The costs would rise if the investor had guessed wrong, and the stock's price went up. Suppose, for instance, that the $15 stock rose to $20 and that the investor, worried that things could only get worse, closed out the short position. The investor would be out the two $35 commissions plus an additional $500 to purchase the 100 shares needed to cover the short sale at the higher market price: a total of $570.

Instead of selling short, the hypothetical investor could have bought a put option—paying a commission of $35 plus the "premium," or price of the put, in this case about $200. If the stock price dropped below $15, the investor would pay another $35 to exercise the contract.

Thus, the stock price would have to drop $2.70 a share to $12.30 before the investor would make any profit. Were it to drop to $10 a share, the investor would clear $280 on the 100 share contract.

On the other hand, if the stock price rose to $20, the investor would simply let the put expire and be out $235—one $35 commission plus the premium.

Source: Priscilla Ann Smith, "Short Selling For the Small Investor," *The Wall Street Journal,* October 31, 1986, p. 37. Reprinted by permission of *The Wall Street Journal,* © Dow Jones & Company, Inc. (1987). All Rights Reserved.

went relatively few changes for many years. The New York Stock Exchange enjoyed a monopoly position, which it defended vigorously. Second, investors need to understand how the markets are changing, and why. In all likelihood, the procedures and mechanics of trading used in the future will be very different from those of the past.

The Stimulus for Market Changes

At least two reasons account for markets undergoing such rapid changes.

1. The emerging role of the institutional investors in the marketplace.
2. The passage of the Securities Acts Amendments of 1975.

Institutional investors are very different from individual investors for whom the securities exchanges were primarily designed. They have different requirements and different views, and their emergence as the dominant force in the market has necessitated significant changes in how markets are structured and operated.

The role of the institutional investors can be appreciated by considering some statistics. Individual investors have been net sellers of stocks for a number of years, with the institutions absorbing these shares. The institutions owned about 35% of all NYSE-listed stocks in 1980 and accounted for half the value of all shares traded on the NYSE in that year.

Institutional investors often trade in large "blocks," which are defined as transactions involving at least 10,000 shares. Large block activity on the NYSE is an indicator of institutional participation. The average size of a trade on the NYSE has grown sharply over the years, doubling between 1974 and 1981. Block trades on the NYSE have increased year after year and in 1986 an average of 2631 blocks changed hands each day, accounting for one half NYSE reported volume.[36]

The growth of institutional trading that occurred in the 1960s and 1970s clashed head-on with a basic NYSE rule requiring all members to charge a minimum fixed commission. This commission structure was designed with relatively small orders in mind and made no provision for the large institutional orders that were becoming more and more common. Substantial economies of scale exist in executing large orders because a large element of fixed costs is involved in every trade, regardless of size. Brokerage firms were receiving excess returns on large orders. Knowing this, institutions sought changes in the minimum fixed commissions. The rise of the third market is a good example of changes occurring to accommodate the institutional investors. Negotiated commissions were the end result of the activity by institutions to obtain a change in the commission structure.

The second factor stimulating a change in our markets was the passage of the Securities Acts Amendments in 1975, the most far-reaching securities legislation since the 1930s. The purpose of this act is to promote a fully competitive national system of securities trading. The act called for a **national market system** (NMS) but left its final form undefined. The result was the evolution toward some type of national market, but its final form is not mandated and remains unknown.

The Form for a National Market

Given the congressional mandate for an NMS, and the changes that have occurred to date, what lies ahead? Although no one knows the exact form an NMS will take when fully developed, certain procedures and trends are emerging.

To achieve the goals of the 1975 act, the SEC has suggested four basic parts of an NMS foundation:

1. Abolish minimum fixed brokerage commissions.
2. Have a central reporting mechanism for price quotations and transactions.
3. Have a central order routing system.
4. Provide for a national protection of limit orders.

The first of these was accomplished by the SEC in 1975. The second is operational and is a necessary ingredient in reducing market fragmentation because it provides investors with the best trading data available.

The purpose of a central order routing system is to obtain the best executions possible for investors. This is accomplished by electronically routing orders to whatever market is offering the best price to a buyer or a seller.

---

[36] *New York Stock Exchange Fact Book 1987*, New York: New York Stock Exchange, p. 12.

Such a system promotes competition and should lower spreads, because the dealers with the most attractive prices would automatically receive the orders. This system is progressing slowly, as the SEC experiments to find the most satisfactory procedure. Brokerage houses, in particular Merrill Lynch, now have electronic systems that search out the best market for a customer's order and send the order to that market quickly.

One alternative for a routing system is the **Intermarket Trading System** (ITS), a network of electronic terminals linking together eight markets.[37] The ITS allows the brokers, specialists, and market makers (trading for their own accounts) on any one of the eight markets to interact with their counterparts on any of the other exchanges. These participants would use the nationwide composite quotation system to check for a better price. However, the ITS system does not guarantee that the orders will be routed because NYSE brokers can ignore better quotes on other exchanges. It is the system favored by the NYSE.

Like other recent developments in the marketplace, ITS started slowly but has grown rapidly. Starting with 11 stocks on two exchanges in April 1978, it had expanded to 1278 issues, with volume of 1.8 billion shares, by year-end 1986.[38]

The fourth item, national protection of limit orders, would provide for limit orders from all markets to be brought together with execution priority depending only on price and time priority. Thus, orders would be filled on whichever exchange a limit price is reached, whereas now a limit order may execute on the NYSE although a different price is reached on other exchanges.

This part of a proposed NMS, known as a central limit order book (CLOB), has made the least progress. No nationwide system exists. The NYSE does have a limit order system as part of its SuperDOT electronic order-routing system. This system electronically files limit orders up to 30,099 shares.

Where do we go from here? Congress continues to press the SEC for an NMS and the SEC in turn has stepped up the pressure on the industry. More changes will occur, but the final structure of the securities market cannot yet be predicted. An important development that will influence the direction and form of securities markets in the future is the emerging NASDAQ National Market System discussed earlier. This system of trading OTC stocks with competitive multiple market makers reporting last-sale data continuously (i.e., real-time trade reporting) has made a significant impact in the relatively short time it has existed. Both individual and institutional investors are attracted by the increased visibility of the securities traded in this manner.

---

[37] The eight are the New York, American, Boston, Cincinnati, Midwest, Pacific, and Philadelphia exchanges, and the NASD.

[38] The 1278 eligible stocks at the end of 1986 represented most of the stocks traded on more than one exchange; 1083 were listed on the NYSE and 195 on the ASE.

The NASDAQ NMS combines the continuous reporting of trades found on the organized exchanges with the system of competitive multiple market makers found in the OTC market. Perhaps this is the best combination of existing practices, and the path that the national market system for all securities will follow.

By 1985 U.S. equities exchanges were seeking electronic linkages with foreign markets. Barriers to international trading were starting to fall. For example, the "Big Bang" occurred in October, 1986 when the London Stock Exchange eliminated fixed commissions and barriers to competition among brokers, market makers, and underwriters that had existed for many years. The deregulation of the third largest stock exchange in the world (after New York and Tokyo) will have important implications for global trading. Furthermore, NASDAQ now carries quotations on some London Stock Exchange issues, with the London Exchange doing the same.

Summary

Financial markets are of crucial importance to the U.S. economy. They include primary markets, where new securities are sold, and secondary markets, where existing securities are traded. Both are indispensable.

Primary markets involve investment bankers who specialize in selling new securities. They offer the issuer several functions, including advisory, underwriting, and marketing. After meeting certain requirements, securities are sold through a selling group. Alternatives to the traditional public placements include private placements and unsyndicated offerings.

Secondary markets exist for the various securities. The equity markets consist of auction markets (exchanges) and negotiated markets (over-the-counter, or OTC, market). Brokers act as intermediaries, representing both buyers and sellers; dealers make markets in securities, buying and selling for their own account.

The New York Stock Exchange (NYSE) is the premier secondary market. Its members—commission brokers, floor traders and floor brokers, and specialists—act in various capacities to provide a continuous market for NYSE stocks. Certain listing requirements must be met for a stock to trade on either the NYSE or the American Stock Exchange (AMEX). The AMEX, on which fewer and generally smaller stocks trade, resembles the NYSE in its operations. Finally, several regional exchanges around the country list small companies of limited interest as well as securities traded on the NYSE and AMEX.

The OTC market is a network of dealers making markets in unlisted securities. The National Association of Security Dealers (NASDAQ) oversees OTC practices. NASDAQ, an automated quotation system, provides current bid–ask prices for over 4000 stocks, enhancing OTC trading. A new subcomponent of NASDAQ, the NASDAQ National Market System

(NMS), offers multiple market makers and up-to-the-minute price information in the format used on the organized exchanges.

An offshoot of the OTC market is the third market, in which listed securities trade with the assistance of an intermediary (broker). In the fourth market, transactions occur directly among large institutions.

Although some bonds are traded on the NYSE (and to a lesser extent on the AMEX), most bond trading occurs in the OTC market. While Treasury bonds and federal agency bonds enjoy broad markets, the markets for municipal bonds and corporate bonds are often less liquid. Small investors may suffer delays and extra transaction costs in the municipal and corporate markets.

Puts and calls are traded on five option exchanges under standardized terms of trade. Warrants are traded on the same markets as equities.

Much of the regulation for the U.S. securities markets was written in the 1930s and 1940s. The Securities and Exchange Commission administers the securities laws, investigating complaints or violations.

Opening a brokerage account is easy. With a cash account, the customer pays in full on the settlement date; with a margin account money can be borrowed from the broker to finance purchases. Most orders sent to the exchanges involve a specialist and are now highly automated. Specialists, acting as brokers and dealers, maintain an orderly market for a particular security, often going against the market.

Market orders are executed at the best price available, whereas limit orders specify a particular price to be met or bettered. Stop orders specify a certain price at which a market order is to take over.

Most securities are left with brokers in street names. Stock certificates are dying out with records maintained on computers. Brokerage commissions are now negotiable. Full-line brokerage houses charge more than discount brokers, but offer recommendations.

Margin is the equity an investor has in a transaction. The Federal Reserve sets an initial margin, but all exchanges and brokers require a maintenance margin. An insufficient amount can result in a margin call.

An investor sells short if a security's price is expected to decline. The investor borrows the securities sold short from the broker, hoping to replace them through a later purchase at a lower price.

The securities markets are changing rapidly, stimulated by the demands of the institutional investors and by the mandate of the Securities Acts Amendments of 1975 to create a national market. To finish creating a national market system (NMS), given the existence of negotiated commissions and a central reporting mechanism for price quotations and transactions, a central routing system is needed. The Intermarket Trading System of the NYSE fulfills some of the requirements of such a system, but there is no guarantee that the best price will be realized. The other item needed for an NMS is national protection of limit orders, which has made the least progress.

An important development in the future of the markets is the NASDAQ National Market System, perhaps a prototype for the future. Although the exact form the NMS will take remains unknown, rapid changes in the securities markets will continue to occur.

Key Words

Ask price
Auction market
Bid price
Book-entry system
Broker
Cash account
Commission broker
Dealer
Discount broker
Fourth market
Intermarket Trading System
Investment banker
Limit orders
Margin
Margin account
Margin call
Market order
NASDAQ
NASDAQ National Market System
National Association of Security
   Dealers (NASD)

National market system
Negotiated market
Over-the-counter market
Primary market
Private placement
Prospectus
Secondary market
Securities and Exchange
   Commission (SEC)
Shelf rule
Short sale
Specialist
Stop order
Street name
Syndicate
Syndicated offering
Third market
Underwriting
Unlisted security

QUESTIONS AND PROBLEMS

1. Discuss the importance of the financial markets to the U.S. economy. Can primary markets exist without secondary markets?
2. Discuss the functions of an investment banker.
3. Outline the process for a primary offering of securities involving investment bankers.

4. Outline the structure of equity markets in the United States. Distinguish between auction markets and negotiated markets.

5. Distinguish between a floor broker and a commission broker. What is a floor trader?

6. Explain the role of the specialists, describing the two roles they perform. How do they act to maintain an orderly market?

7. Do you think that specialists should be closely monitored and regulated because of their limit books?

8. Is there any similarity between an over-the-counter dealer and a specialist on an exchange?

9. Explain the difference between NASD and NASDAQ.

10. Distinguish between the third market and the fourth market.

11. Identify the legislative act which:
    a. initiated the regulation of securities markets by the federal government
    b. extended disclosure requirements to secondary issues
    c. established the Securities and Exchange Commission
    d. called for the creation of a national market system (NMS).

12. Discuss the advantages and disadvantages of a limit order versus a market order. How does a stop order differ from a limit order?

13. What is meant by selling securities on a "regular way" basis?

14. What are the advantages and disadvantages of using a street name?

15. Explain the margin process, distinguishing between initial margin and maintenance margin. Who sets these margins?

16. What conditions result in an account being "restricted"? What prompts a margin call?

17. How can an investor sell a security not currently owned?

18. What conditions must be met for an investor to sell short?

19. What are two primary factors accounting for the rapid changes in U.S. securities markets?

20. Name at least four recent changes in securities markets and trading procedures.

21. List the four basic parts of a national market system as suggested by the Securities and Exchange Commission. What is the current status of these four items?

22. Why do you think the New York Stock Exchange favors the Intermarket Trading System (ITS)?

23. Discuss recent international developments that relate to U.S. financial markets.

24. How does the NASDAQ differ from the conventional OTC market? What are its implications for the future?

25. Consider an investor who purchased a stock at $100 per share and the current market price is $125. At what price would a limit order be placed to assure a profit of $30 per share? What type of stop order would be placed to assure a profit of at least $20 per share?

26. Explain the difference, relative to the current market price of a stock, between the following types of orders: sell-limit, buy-limit, buy-stop, and sell-stop.

27. Assume an investor sells short 200 shares of stock at $75 per share. At what price must the investor cover the short sale in order to realize a gross profit of $5000? $1000?

28. Assume that an investor buys 100 shares of stock at $50 per share and the stock rises to $60 per share. What is the gross profit assuming an initial margin requirement of 50%? 40%? 60%?

29. Assume an initial margin requirement of 50% and a maintenance margin of 30%. As investor buys 100 shares of stock on margin at $60 per share. The price of the stock subsequently drops to $50.
    a. What is the actual margin at $50?
    b. The price now rises to $55—is the account restricted?
    c. If the price declines to $49, is there a margin call?
    d. Assume that the price declines to $45—what is the amount of the margin call? At $35?

30. What is the margin requirement for U.S. government securities?

Selected References

Batten, William M. "The National Market System." *The Wall Street Journal*, June 18, 1982, p. 29.

Dougall, Herbert E., and Jack E. Gaumnitz. *Capital Markets and Institutions*, 5th ed. Englewood Cliffs, N.J.: Prentice-Hall, 1986.

Kidwell, David S., and Peterson, Richard L. *Financial Institutions, Markets, and Money*, 3rd ed. Chicago: Dryden Press, 1987.

Klemkosky, Robert C., and Wright, David J. "The Changing Structure of the Stock Market: The National Market System." *Business Horizons* (July/August, 1981), pp. 10–20.

Malkiel, B. G. *A Random Walk Down Wall Street*. New York: Norton, 1975.

NASD Fact Book. Annual. Washington, D.C. National Association of Securities Dealers, Inc.

New York Stock Exchange, *Fact Book*. Annual. New York: New York Stock Exchange, Inc.

Poindexter, J. C., and Jones, C. P. *Money, Financial Markets and the Economy*, St. Paul, Minn.: West Publishing, 1980.

Teweles, Richard J., and Edward S. Bradley. *The Stock Market*, 4th ed. New York: John Wiley, 1982.

Tinic, Seha M., and West, Richard R. *Investing in Securities: An Efficient Markets Approach*. Reading, Mass.: Addison-Wesley, 1979.

Van Horne, James C. *Financial Market Rates and Flows*, 2nd ed. Englewood Cliffs, N.J.: Prentice-Hall, 1984.

CHAPTER 4

SOURCES OF INVESTMENT INFORMATION

Investments is an information-oriented subject. Investors make their investment decisions on the basis of their expectations for the future. The fact that a particular common stock rose or fell 50 (or 150) points last year is of little current value to prospective buyers or sellers. What matters is its prospects for the coming year, and to assess these prospects investors need information about securities.

The problem that most investors face is not obtaining information, but selectively choosing among a bewildering number of sources and an almost endless flow of facts and figures. The United States is an information-oriented society, in which there is a proliferation of printed and computer-accessible data that have no end in sight. How, then, can the investor cope? The answer involves recognizing one's own needs, knowing what is available, and proceeding from there in a reasonable manner.

Before reviewing the sources of investment information, it is worthwhile to evaluate the use of the information.

Users of Investment Information

Chapter 1 discussed some external factors affecting the investment decision process. One of these factors is the environment in which investors find themselves. Two broad categories of investors are playing the investments game, individual and institutional investors. Although both groups have the same basic objectives, they go about their investment process somewhat differently. When it comes to information, each has its own needs and uses for information. In the case of investment information, we can begin to appreciate why this distinction was made in Chapter 1.

Individual Investors

The average investor in securities is a part-timer, with neither the ability nor the time to evaluate a large (and often complex) flow of information. Most individual investors have a job, and a life, apart from investing. Individuals have an opportunity cost in obtaining investment information, such as reading publications, tracking stock prices, and building files (printed or computerized) on securities. This opportunity cost is the time and resources foregone that could have been used in other endeavors.

There is also a question of efficiency. What can most investors expect to collect or learn in the way of basic information (as opposed to "insights") that is not already known by the market as a whole? Unless they are particularly diligent or insightful, chances are that the information has been collected and is available, if only they know where to look.

Where does this leave individual investors who need information to make investment decisions? What information should be sought? The astute investor needs to understand the valuation process and the basics of portfolio management, both of which constitute the remainder of this book. As will be seen in the following chapters, investors should follow certain procedures in analyzing various securities. A knowledge of these procedures will suggest the primary types of information of interest to investors.

After learning about the valuation and management of bonds, for example, investors will quickly appreciate the necessity of knowing about the level of and movements in interest rates, which affect all bonds (and, indeed, all securities); therefore, they should be aware of the general state of the economy, particularly government actions in the form of monetary and fiscal policies. Government publications will be helpful here, as will certain analyses of the economy regularly published by banks and brokerage houses.

In the case of equities, a three-step valuation process will be described in Chapter 9. This involves analyzing, first, the overall economy and state of the stock market, then industries, and finally companies. Individual investors need to obtain information that will help them to make intelligent appraisals of each of these three steps, and information is available on all three.

In the final analysis, most individuals who invest can do only so much in the way of obtaining and evaluating information. They need to recognize fully their constraints and limitations. All investors must have information in order to invest intelligently—the question is what and how much.

Institutional Investors

At the other end of the scale are the institutional investors whose full-time job is to value securities and manage portfolios. These institutions have staffs that specialize by type of job, such as security analyst or portfolio manager; area, such as common stock analyst versus bond analyst; and other designations, such as a computer industry analyst or an automobile industry analyst.

Institutional investors have economists, accountants, computer specialists, and others on whom to rely. They have massive computer facilities and information banks. They can purchase information from other specialists or build their own unique data bases. In short, institutional investors can do what needs to be done in collecting and managing information.

What does all of this mean? First of all, it is reasonable to assume that institutional investors have access to, and use, a wide variety of information in making their investment decisions. Individual investors should assume that, if information is potentially useful, manageable, and obtainable on a reasonable basis, some institutional investor has it. Second, it means that for most information, it is more efficient to let the institutions and advisory organizations collect and distribute it. Individual investors cannot reasonably expect to duplicate the thorough, ongoing efforts of institutions whose job it is to collect the information and use it and, in the process, make it known.

As discussed in Chapter 1, the disparity between the resources and abilities of the two groups does not mean that individual investors are severely disadvantaged. Individual investors may be able to interpret the same information used by institutional investors more insightfully, thereby deriving additional benefit from it. To do this, however, the investor must know something about the sources of investment information available, to which we now turn.

A Users' Guide to Investment Information

This discussion is organized into two major parts, published information and computerized information. In the next section, the major sources of published information available to individual investors will be discussed *roughly* in order of their general availability and use by investors. The objective in this chapter is to provide a concise view of what is available that is likely to be of use to different investors, depending on their needs and abilities. This information will be expanded on at appropriate places throughout the remainder of the book.

Next, computerized sources of information are considered. Although traditionally computer information has been of little direct use to the typical individual investor, institutions use it extensively and investors can obtain some or all of the results from them. Furthermore, the dramatic rise of the microcomputer is radically changing the accessibility of computerized investment information.

Published Sources of Information

The Financial Press

Virtually all investors have access to, and read, the general financial press on a daily or weekly basis because of its widespread availability and timeliness. This information may appear daily and weekly, in the case of newspapers, or weekly or biweekly, in the case of magazines such as *Business Week* and *Forbes*, respectively.

Newspapers Perhaps the most popular and best known source of daily financial information is *The Wall Street Journal* (WSJ).[1] It provides detailed coverage of financial and business-related news, on both a national and world level. Daily quotations from the principal bond, option, and stock markets are a well-known feature of the WSJ. Of particular interest to many investors is earnings information on various corporations, on both a reported basis in the form of quarterly and annual earnings reports and a prospective basis in the form of news reports concerning expected earnings. The WSJ carries several columns that may be of interest to investors, including "Heard on the Street," "Abreast of the Market," "Bond Markets," and "Dividend News."

Barron's, published by the same publisher (Dow Jones Company, Inc.), is a weekly newspaper with more detailed articles on general business topics and particular companies. It carries weekly price and volume quotations for all financial markets.[2] *Barron's* also includes regular columns on weekly activities in the stock market, the bond market, the options market, commodities, the international situation, and dividend news.

The *M/G Financial Weekly* is a weekly newspaper delivered on Monday. It carries detailed information (e.g., earnings, dividends, prices, and volume) for roughly 3400 securities, separated into industry groups.[3] Each week the performance of these industry groups is shown for the current week and the last 4, 13, and 52 weeks. Numerous charts and tables are provided on the market indices, dividend yields, P/E ratios, volume, and so forth. Regular columns include fixed-income securities, the "market week," selected research reports, and other items of current interest.

---

[1] An alternative source is *The New York Times*, a daily newspaper known for its large business and financial coverage. Much of this information parallels that contained in the *WSJ*.

[2] Another weekly, *The Commercial and Financial Chronicle*, has daily prices for the leading exchanges and weekly prices for regional exchanges and the OTC market.

[3] The Media General carries every common stock listed on the NYSE and AMEX, plus some 700 OTC stocks.

Magazines A wide variety of financial magazines exist. This discussion outlines some of the better known general magazines. Specialized magazines include *Pension and Investment Age,* intended for those people involved in managing or overseeing pension fund assets, and the *OTC Review,* obviously focusing on the OTC market. The latter is a source of earnings reports for OTC stocks as well as statistics on OTC trading.

Turning to the general magazines or "popular press," *Forbes* is a biweekly magazine offering articles on various companies and investments topics, as well as columnists with opinions on particular market segments and activities. *Forbes* publishes an index that measures U.S. economic activity, including graphs of its eight components (industrial production, orders, housing starts, etc.). It also publishes a graph of the Dow Jones and Wilshire 5000 stock market indices, as well as tables comparing six market indices for the last 4 weeks and 52 weeks and showing stock performance based on "five key investor yardsticks."

The first issue of *Forbes* in January of each year contains the "Annual Report on American Industry," which shows how the 1000+ largest U.S. public companies compare in profitability, growth, and stock market performance for five year periods and the latest 12 months. One issue each year evaluates the performance of mutual funds.

Business Week covers the major developments occurring in business during the week. It contains articles about specific companies and industries. Regular features include marketing, labor, finance, and other subjects. The "Business Outlook" column analyzes the business environment and developing changes in it.

Fortune is a biweekly magazine with articles on general business trends, written with an emphasis on the perspective of corporate managers. A well-known regular feature of *Fortune* is "Personal Investing."[4]

Corporate Reports

An important source of information is the corporation itself. Owners of common stock will receive the annual reports issued by each company and nonshareholders can obtain the annual report from the company or their broker.

Annual reports highlight the most recent fiscal year. Extended discussions of activities, problems, and prospects are often part of the report. In addition, the annual report contains audited financial information. The balance sheet, income statement, and statement of changes in financial position are shown, usually for at least the current and preceding years. A summary of accounting policies may be included, as well as detailed notes to the financial statements. Such information can aid diligent investors in better assessing the current and future condition of the company.

---

[4] Additional publications of a similar nature to the three discussed here include *Dun's Review* and *Financial World*. These publications typically carry more detailed articles.

Brokerage Firms

Most investors have access to investment information in the form of oral and written information from their brokers. The typical brokerage house has a research department that provides a steady flow of reports for consumption by all investors, whether individuals or institutions. In addition, these firms subscribe to well-known investment information sources that can be used by their customers.

Brokerage houses have their own research staffs of economists and analysts. They make recommendations to buy, hold, or sell securities. Some brokerage houses deal primarily with institutional investors, whereas others, known as "retail" brokerage houses, deal primarily with individuals. Major retail brokerage houses include, among others, Merrill Lynch, Pierce Fenner & Smith (Merrill Lynch), Hutton, Dean Witter Reynolds, Prudential Bache, Shearson Lehman Brothers, Smith Barney, Harris Upham, and A. G. Edwards.

Each brokerage house puts out a number of pamphlets for investors. These reports cover the economy, the stock and bond markets, options, industries, and specific companies. Merrill Lynch, for example, has "Investments for a Changing Economy," "Interest Rates," "Investment Strategy," and "Taxable Bond Indices," among others.

The traditional full-service brokerage firms provide most of this information "free" to their customers; however, the cost of providing this service is presumably built into the commissions paid by their customers. Discount brokers do not provide such information. They are selling execution capability, and the investor makes his or her own decisions. Thus, investors have a choice and should choose brokers according to the types of services needed (and the ability of brokerage houses to deliver cost-effective services).

Brokerage houses are a source of both information and recommendations. The emphasis, however, is on recommendations because brokers earn commissions based on the amount of trading that investors do. Furthermore, most recommendations are "buy" recommendations as opposed to "sell" recommendations.

Investment Information Services

A large amount of information is available to investors from companies that specialize in providing investment information and advice. Investors can subscribe to these services, several of which offer a variety of products, or they can read at least some of them free of charge at their library or at the offices of their broker. Although some of these services offer both information and investment advice, for *organizational purposes* they will be separated into information services (this section), and advisory (recommendation) services (next section). Remember, however, the same service can provide both information and recommendations.

Investors can access financial information and data from a variety of investment information services. These include such services as Dun &

BOX 4–1 FOLLOW THE WINOS' LEAD

Who has more continual access to tidy investment tidbits, stockbrokers or hobos? The hobos, it seems. As a kid I used to hang out in the San Francisco Business Library—just blocks from the brokers. All winter long the hobos and winos flooded in to keep warm, but there was rarely a broker in sight. For top investment results, try following the winos' lead.

From Seattle to Tampa, from Boston to Los Angeles, without doubt, there are better research facilities in any medium-size or larger city library than in most brokerage firms. Of course, you have to be willing to spend time and effort at it, but the information is there to make you an informed investor.

And it's free. Many folks are unfamiliar with the dandy tools they could use if only they would hang out with the winos and bums. I have never met an unhelpful librarian, so ask for aid. But, to get started, here are some of my favorite gizmos.

Standard & Poor's Corporation Records is a must. I couldn't last two days without it. Its seven huge volumes have a ton of basic knowledge on almost every publicly traded stock. When readers write for the address of some obscure stock I have mentioned, I do them a favor by insisting they learn how to look it up themselves in the *S&P's*. It might not have enough data for you to decide to buy a stock, but it often has enough to convince you to avoid one. *Standard & Poor's Stock Guide* gives you recent pricing information, including price/earnings ratios, dividends, yields, etc.

The F&S Index is the best-kept secret since the $64 question. It's like a customized reader's guide to everything in print about a company or industry. In minutes you can track down years of magazine and newspaper articles on a stock—and dig more deeply than most stock buyers and sellers ever take time for. It covers publications ranging from the big financial press to obscure industrial trade journals (available through interlibrary loan if your library doesn't carry them).

By the same publisher (God bless them) as the above is *Predicasts F&S Index of Corporate Change*. It will pilot you through years of organizational gyrations, such as joint ventures, bankruptcies, liquidations, reorganizations, name changes and subsidiary changes. For instance, I like the seemingly fruitless but at times rewarding search for bargains among bankrupt companies. That would be ever so much harder without this source. *The Wall Street Journal Index* covers what the *WSJ* has run by company, industry, topic or whatever. Pick a subject. Quick as a wink, you could check out anything they had printed—either on the subject or specific companies.

The Wall Street Transcript is a great source of what The Street is thinking, feeling and doing. It covers brokerage firm research reports, publishes text from newsletters, has regular interviews with a host of security analysts and money managers. Best of all, it indexes all mentions of stocks from previous issues. If a stock isn't here, it probably isn't in Wall Street's eye (and by contrarian logic might be a good buy). When a stock is mentioned, you can get a quick and dirty assessment of what The Street thinks of it.

Ward's Directory lists—by Zip Code—almost every corporation, so you can check them out regionally. There was a paragraph on *Ward's* in my Dec. 3, 1984 column, but it is so useful, it's worth a second tout and more than a second of your time.

How would you feel about a stock where the insiders bailed out? The SEC's *Official Summary of Insider Transactions* gives a monthly breakdown on officers and directors who have been buying and selling their own stock. Do you need a quick scan on recent articles about a business, person or subject—maybe Texaco, John Templeton or tender offers? *The Business Index* from Information Access Corp. covers articles from over 800 publications.

There's too much at the library to do all of it justice here. Maybe you blow a boodle on newsletters. Try reading them at the library. Did you get 300 shares of American Widget when Uncle Morris died? Do you need its price on the date of his death for estate taxes? Try Standard & Poor's *Daily Stock Price Record*. You need to know about all the publications in a certain field, like chemical processing; you can learn about them from *Cahners*.

Source: Adopted from Kenneth L. Fisher, "Follow the Winos' Lead," *Forbes*, April 22, 1985, p. 168. Reprinted by permission. *Forbes* magazine, April 22, 1985, © Forbes, Inc., 1985.

Bradstreet, Inc., the widely known credit reporting company. But the two best known sources of a wide variety of investment information are Standard & Poor's Corporation (S&P) (a subsidiary of McGraw-Hill) and Moody's Investor Services, Inc. (owned by Dun & Bradstreet), both New York-based. These two services issue a systematic, continuous flow of reports on a daily, weekly, and monthly basis. Investors can subscribe to only those parts that are of interest to them, such as the common stock service or the bond service. Both sources are commonly available in larger public and college libraries.

Both services issue basic reference volumes covering corporations in some detail. For example, Moody's *Industrial Manual* devotes several pages, in very small print, to each company covered. Moody's also issues the *OTC Industrial Manual, The Public Utility Manual,* the *Bank & Finance Manual,* the *Transportation Manual,* the *Municipal & Government Manual,* and the *International Manual.* All of these manuals are updated in separate binders every Tuesday and Friday.[5]

The comparable series for Standard & Poor's is their six volume *Corporation Records.* These are in alphabetical order and are issued regularly, with daily updates in a seventh volume called *Daily News.* Unlike Moody's, this coverage is not separated by areas such as transportation or public utilities.

Both of these services issue separate information sets for overall economic conditions, stocks, bonds, convertibles, and so on. For example, Standard & Poor's *Outlook,* issued weekly, assesses the stock market in the previous week and has "The Current Outlook" as well as a section entitled "Forecast and Policy." Particular industries and stocks are usually recommended in each issue. Moody's issues a similar weekly publication called the *Stock Survey.*

[5]The *Transportation Manual* is updated every Friday and the *International Manual* biweekly on Fridays.

Often of special interest to investors seeking information about a particular company are the short (two page) reports on companies put out by each service. Standard and Poor's *Stock Reports* are divided into New York Stock Exchange, American Stock Exchange, and Over the Counter and Regional Exchanges, each in four volumes. Figure 4–1 shows S&P *Stock Reports* for a NYSE firm, EG&G. The comparable Moody's service, *Investors Fact Sheets,* is likewise separated by exchanges. These sources are less detailed than those discussed previously but offer the investor both a compact source of current information and a historical balance sheet, income statement, and market data (10 years for Standard & Poor's, 7 for Moody's).

Investors can use an even briefer source of information on stocks of interest from Moody's *Handbook of Common Stocks* or Standard & Poor's *Stock Guide.* The former is issued in spring, summer, fall, and winter editions, and contains one page of write-up and data for each covered stock. Figure 4–2 shows an excerpt for EG&G from Moody's *Handbook.* The *Stock Guide,* issued monthly, contains brief information on several thousand listed and unlisted stocks.

As for bonds, Standard & Poor publishes a *Bond Outlook,* containing such information as changes in bond ratings, convertibles of interest, new issues, and data about the bond markets themselves. The comparable Moody's publication is the *Bond Survey,* issued weekly. Each issue is a thick, detailed coverage of virtually everything happening currently in the bond market with regard to recent issues, prospective issues, bond averages, and so forth. All types of issues are covered—Treasuries, agencies, corporates, and municipals.

Standard & Poor's also issues the *Bond Guide,* a monthly publication providing concise information for a large number of companies, both domestic and foreign. Figure 4–3 shows a page from the *Bond Guide.*

Investment Advisory Services and Market Letters

A wide variety of investment advisory services and market letters are available to investors. Many offer a combination of analyses and projections along with stock recommendations. Investment advisory services may specialize in particular selection techniques or in particular assets (e.g., options) or areas (e.g., new issues). The larger services may offer several different products for investors. Most investment advisory services offer trial subscriptions, allowing investors to sample what is available.[6]

Because of the wide variety of services and letters available to investors, we will describe only one in detail. We will then briefly mention others that are well known among many investors.

Value Line *The Value Line Investment Survey (VL)* is the largest (by number of subscribers) and probably best known investment advisory service in

---

[6]A good source of trial subscriptions is *Barron's.*

EG&G Inc.

789

NYSE Symbol EGG   Options on Phila (Mar-Jun-Sep-Dec)   In S&P 500

Price	Range	P-E Ratio	Dividend	Yield	S&P Ranking	Beta
Dec. 29'86 28¾	1986 43–27⅝	16	0.56	1.9%	A	1.14

Summary

EG&G provides a variety of specialized scientific products and services to government and industrial customers for technical applications. Following more than a decade of uninterrupted growth, earnings are expected to decline in 1986 due to weakness at its commercial instruments and components operations. A recovery is forecast for 1987.

Current Outlook

Earnings for 1987 are likely to approximate $2.00 a share, up from the $1.65 expected for 1986.

A modest increase in the $0.13 quarterly dividend is likely in 1987.

Revenues are anticipated to increase more than 5% in 1987. The gain should be led by a rebound in components sales, which should benefit from a projected recovery in the electronics industry. Increased services provided to the Government should also assist growth. Because the company's activities focus on research and development, it should not be significantly affected by recent reductions in the increase in defense and other Government spending. Continued lackluster capital spending will likely restrain the rebound in the instrument segment. Margins should benefit from recent cost reductions, the absence of nonrecurring charges and plant relocation costs, and a lower tax rate. Aggressive efforts to increase business with the Government should aid long-term results.

Net Sales (Million $)

13 Weeks:	1986	1985	1984	1983
Mar.	276	276	247	207
Jun.	281	285	268	227
Sep.	287	289	270	238
Dec.	---	305	287	232
	---	1,155	1,072	904

Revenues for the nine months ended September 28, 1986 declined 0.6%, year to year. Primarily due to sharply lower earnings of the components and instruments segments, pretax income was 12% lower. After taxes at 37.9%, versus 36.0%, net income decreased 15%, to $1.23 a share from $1.47.

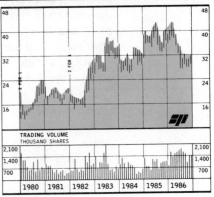

Common Share Earnings ($)

13 Weeks:	1986	1985	1984	1983
Mar.	0.48	0.47	0.46	0.35
Jun.	0.43	0.50	0.45	0.39
Sep.	0.33	0.50	0.47	0.40
Dec.	E0.41	0.60	0.50	0.42
	E1.65	2.07	1.88	1.56

Important Developments

Dec. '86—EGG said that the decline in orders for components and instrumentation had bottomed out. It also noted that its Government business remained strong. Earlier, EGG reported that the U.S. Department of Energy renewed one of its contracts for an additional five years with an estimated value of $1.3 billion.

Next earnings report due in late January.

Per Share Data ($) Yr. End Dec. 31	1985	1984	¹1983	1982	1981	¹1980	1979	1978	¹1977	¹1976
Book Value	6.50	4.97	7.13	5.93	4.86	3.97	3.89	2.44	2.49	2.15
Earnings	2.07	²1.88	²1.56	²1.38	²1.21	²0.97	²0.79	²0.62	0.42	0.34
Dividends	0.48	0.40	0.36	0.32	0.25	0.20	0.15	0.10½	0.09	0.04
Payout Ratio	23%	20%	23%	24%	21%	21%	15%	17%	22%	12%
Prices—High	43	36⅛	38⅛	30⅝	22	24⅜	12⅜	8⅜	5½	4⅞
Low	31¼	26⅛	26	14½	16⅛	11⅜	6½	4¼	4	3½
P/E Ratio—	21–15	19–14	24–17	22–11	18–13	25–12	16–8	13–7	13–10	14–10

Data as orig. reptd. Adj. for stk. div(s). of 100% Feb. 1982, 100% Feb. 1980. 1. Reflects merger or acquisition. 2. Ful. dil.: 1.85 in 1984, 1.53 in 1983, 1.33 in 1982, 1.17 in 1981, 0.93 in 1980, 0.76 in 1979, 0.59 in 1978. E-Estimated.

Standard NYSE Stock Reports
Vol. 54/No. 3/Sec. 14

January 7, 1987

Standard & Poor's Corp.
25 Broadway, NY, NY 10004

FIGURE 4–1   A coverage of one NYSE company from Standard & Poor's *Stock Reports*.

Source: Standard & Poor's *Stock Reports*, New York, Standard & Poor's Corporation, January 7, 1987, p. 789. Reprinted by permission of Standard & Poor's Corporation.

EG&G, Inc.

Income Data (Million $)

Year Ended Dec. 31	Revs.	Oper. Inc.	% Oper. Inc. of Revs.	Cap. Exp.	Depr.	Int. Exp.	Net Bef. Taxes	Eff. Tax Rate	Net Inc.	% Net Inc. of Revs.
1985	1,155	97.1	8.4%	17.3	15.1	11.5	³88.6	37.1%	55.7	4.8%
1984	1,072	85.6	8.0%	13.5	13.0	7.0	³85.0	37.0%	53.5	5.0%
¹1983	904	68.6	7.6%	11.4	9.9	2.0	³77.7	40.0%	46.6	5.2%
1982	801	62.5	7.8%	9.6	9.0	2.0	³66.5	39.6%	40.2	5.0%
1981	704	59.9	8.5%	10.4	7.8	1.5	³60.9	44.0%	²34.1	4.8%
¹1980	613	51.5	8.4%	11.4	6.3	1.3	48.4	45.6%	26.3	4.3%
1979	522	40.3	7.7%	6.8	5.6	1.1	38.0	45.6%	20.6	4.0%
1978	441	31.6	7.2%	4.7	4.5	1.3	31.3	46.5%	16.7	3.8%
¹1977	376	27.4	7.3%	4.3	4.6	1.3	25.1	48.0%	13.1	3.5%
¹1976	251	22.8	9.1%	11.0	5.0	1.1	³17.8	46.1%	9.6	3.8%

Balance Sheet Data (Million $)

Dec. 31	Cash	Current Assets	Current Liab.	Ratio	Total Assets	Ret. on Assets	Long Term Debt	Common Equity	Total Cap.	% LT Debt of Cap.	Ret. on Equity
1985	17.4	268	184	1.5	430	13.5%	15.8	203	237	6.6%	31.3%
1984	18.3	245	205	1.2	387	15.6%	15.3	150	178	8.6%	31.4%
1983	93.5	257	103	2.5	339	15.2%	11.3	215	231	4.9%	23.7%
1982	70.3	213	74	2.9	270	15.9%	12.2	175	193	6.3%	25.2%
1981	52.2	188	68	2.8	225	15.9%	10.8	138	155	7.0%	27.3%
1980	40.3	167	71	2.3	199	12.8%	12.4	109	125	10.0%	24.4%
1979	18.3	135	64	2.1	161	15.5%	11.0	82	95	11.6%	31.1%
1978	10.0	108	53	2.1	130	13.8%	11.4	64	77	14.8%	26.0%
1977	26.8	111	40	2.7	135	10.3%	12.1	79	93	12.9%	17.8%
1976	15.2	82	28	2.9	107	9.3%	12.4	61	78	16.0%	16.1%

Data as orig. reptd. **1.** Reflects merger or acquisition. **2.** Reflects acctg. change. **3.** Incl. equity in earns. of nonconsol. subs.

Business Summary

EG&G is a diversified company that manufactures electronic instruments and components, and provides technical services. Industry segment contributions in 1985:

	Sales	Profits
Instruments	10%	10%
Components	27%	31%
Environmental & biomedical services	4%	9%
Custom services & systems	27%	22%
Department of Energy support	31%	15%
Investments	1%	13%

Foreign operations accounted for 5.6% of revenues and 10% of pretax income in 1985.

Components work includes the production of electro-optic components used to generate and measure light, electromechanical products for dealing with problems of heat transfer from the heart of dense electronics, and specialized mechanical products used for sealing rotating shafts.

As prime contractor to the DOE and other government agencies, EG&G is involved in the space-shuttle, nuclear power and weapons develop-

ment, testing and maintenance. Custom support services, mainly research, are also provided.

The instrumentation operations consist of high-technology products in the nuclear, electronic, optical, energy, and environmental fields.

A number of small subsidiaries provide environmental control monitoring services and biomedical research services.

Dividend Data

Dividends have been paid since 1965. A dividend reinvestment plan is available.

Amt. of Divd. $	Date Decl.	Ex-divd. Date	Stock of Record	Payment Date
0.13	Mar. 26	Apr. 14	Apr. 18	May 9'86
0.13	May 28	Jul. 14	Jul. 18	Aug. 8'86
0.13	Sep. 24	Oct. 10	Oct. 17	Nov. 7'86
0.14	Nov. 25	Jan. 16	Jan. 23	Feb. 10'87

Next dividend meeting: late Mar. '87.

Capitalization

Long Term Debt: $7,217,000, incl. $497,000 of 3½% debs. conv. into com. at $11.56 a sh.

Common Stock: 27,312,000 shs. ($1 par).
Institutions hold about 48%.
Shareholders of record: 17,625.

Office—45 William St., Wellesley, Mass. 02181. **Tel**—(617) 237-5100. **Chrmn & CEO**—D. W. Freed. **Pres & COO**—J. M. Kucharski. **Treas**—P. A. Broadbent. **Investor Contact**—P. F. Chapski. **Dirs**—D. W. Freed, R. F. Goldhammer, J. B. Gray, K. F. Hansen, J. M. Kucharski, R. M. MacDougall, B. J. O'Keefe, W. F. Pounds, J. F. Thompson, G. R. Tod, J. F. Turley. **Transfer Agent**—First National Bank of Boston. **Incorporated** in Massachusetts in 1947.

EG & G, INC.

LISTED	SYM.	LTPS◆	STPS◆	IND. DIV.	REC. PRICE	RANGE (52-WKS.)	YLD.
NYSE	EGG	99.3	78.6	$0.52*	28	43 - 29	1.9%

UPPER MEDIUM GRADE. A PROMINENT CONSULTANT IN THE ENERGY AND ENVIRONMENTAL FIELDS, RESEARCH LED TO NUMEROUS PROPRIETARY PRODUCTS.

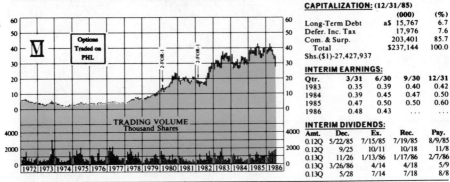

CAPITALIZATION: (12/31/85)

	(000)	(%)
Long-Term Debt	a$ 15,767	6.7
Defer. Inc. Tax	17,976	7.6
Com. & Surp.	203,401	85.7
Total	$237,144	100.0

Shs.($1)-27,427,937

INTERIM EARNINGS:

Qtr.	3/31	6/30	9/30	12/31
1983	0.35	0.39	0.40	0.42
1984	0.39	0.45	0.47	0.50
1985	0.47	0.50	0.50	0.60
1986	0.48	0.43	...	...

INTERIM DIVIDENDS:

Amt.	Dec.	Ex.	Rec.	Pay.
0.12Q	5/22/85	7/15/85	7/19/85	8/9/85
0.12Q	9/25	10/11	10/18	11/8
0.13Q	11/26	1/13/86	1/17/86	2/7/86
0.13Q	3/26/86	4/14	4/18	5/9
0.13Q	5/28	7/14	7/18	8/8

BACKGROUND:

EG&G provides technical and scientific products and services to commercial, industrial, and governmental customers. It designs and produces sophisticated electronic and nuclear equipment; manufactures mechanical, electro-mechanical, and electro-optic products and components; conducts environmental studies and surveys; performs research in cancer, drugs, and birth control. It is active in physics and space research, and nuclear and nonnuclear energy-development programs. In 1985, instruments contributed 9.4% of revenues (13.4% operating income); components 27.4% (41.6%); environmental products 3.8% (12.1%); custom services 27.0% (29.2%); department of energy support and other 32.4% (36.7%).

RECENT DEVELOPMENTS:

For the quarter ended 6/30/86, net income fell to $11.7 million from $13.4 million a year ago. Earnings declined reflecting the slowdown in demand in the commercial markets for instruments, electronic and mechanical compounds. Results continue to benefit from strong earnings from the government and investment segments. Sales dipped to $286.5 million from $288.8 million. For the six months net income declined 5% to $24.7 million from $25.9 million last year. Sales rose to $573.9 million from $568.1 million.

PROSPECTS:

Near-term sales and earnings are expected to be mixed. Possible reduction in new orders from the federal government, as well as low backlogs in certain commercial sections may impede earnings growth over the near term. Emphasis on selecting niche markets with high growth and profitability, especially those which have barriers to entry, benefits margins. Continued emphasis on diversification and internal development, as well as carefully choosing acquisitions, and new-venture investments, bodes well over the long term.

STATISTICS:

YEAR	GROSS REVS. ($mill.)	OPER. PROFIT MARGIN %	RET. ON EQUITY %	NET INCOME ($mill.)	WORK CAP. ($mill.)	SENIOR CAPITAL ($mill.)	SHARES (000)	EARN. PER SH.$	DIV. PER SH.$	DIV. PAY %	PRICE RANGE	P/E RATIO	AVG. YIELD %
76	251.0	7.1	15.2	9.6	53.4	12.4	31,012	0.34	0.04	12	4⅞ - 3⅜	12.1	1.0
77	375.9	6.1	10.0	13.1	70.4	12.1	31,560	0.42	0.09	22	5⅛ - 3⅞	11.2	1.9
78	440.5	6.2	26.7	16.7	55.7	11.4	26,096	0.61	0.11	17	8¼ - 4⅛	10.1	1.7
79	522.2	6.3	25.2	20.6	71.0	11.0	26,404	0.79	0.15	19	12¼ - 6⅜	11.9	1.6
80	631.1	6.3	24.1	26.3	95.8	12.4	27,510	0.97	0.20	21	24¼ - 11¼	18.4	1.1
81	704.2	7.4	24.8	34.1	120.7	10.8	28,355	1.21	0.25	21	22 - 16⅛	5.8	1.3
82	800.8	6.7	22.9	40.2	139.8	12.2	29,595	1.38	0.32	23	30⅝ - 14½	16.3	5.3
83	904.2	6.5	21.7	46.6	153.6	11.3	30,256	1.56	0.36	23	38⅛ - 26	20.6	1.1
84	1,071.7	7.5	35.7	53.5	40.2	15.3	30,384	1.88	0.40	21	36⅛ - 26⅛	16.6	1.3
85	1,177.1	7.5	27.4	55.7	84.2	15.8	27,427	2.07	0.48	23	43 - 31	17.9	1.3

◆Long-Term Price Score — Short-Term Price Score; see page 4a. STATISTICS ARE AS ORIGINALLY REPORTED. Adjusted for 100% stock dividend 2/82 and 2/80. a-Incl. securities convertible into common.

INCORPORATED:
Nov. 13, 1947 – Mass.

PRINCIPAL OFFICE:
45 William Street
Wellesley, Mass. 02181
Tel: (617) 237-5100

ANNUAL MEETING:
Fourth Tuesday in April

NUMBER OF STOCKHOLDERS:
18,000

TRANSFER AGENT(S):
The First National Bank of Boston
Boston, Mass.

REGISTRAR(S):

INSTITUTIONAL HOLDINGS:
No. of Institutions: 173
Shares Held: 13,087,176

OFFICERS:
Chmn. & C.E.O.
  D.W. Freed
President
  J.M. Kucharski
Vice Pres. & Counsel
  L.M. Kelly
Treasurer
  P.A. Broadbent
Dir. Investor Relations
  P.F. Chapski

FIGURE 4–2 A sample page from Moody's *Handbook of Common Stocks*.
Source: Taken from Moody's *Handbook of Common Stocks,* Fall 1986 Edition. Reprinted by permission.

the United States. The *VL* covers over 1700 stocks (including NYSE, AMEX, and some OTC) organized into 90+ industries on a regular basis, reviewing each once every three months; specifically, each weekly issue covers several industry groupings, completing the cycle every quarter. In addition to this "Ratings and Reports," every week subscribers also receive a "Summary and Index" and a "Selection and Opinion" section containing an overall review of the market, a highlighted stock, a record of insider transactions, and numerous other data.

The *VL* is both a reference service and a recommendation service. Essential information is presented for each industry grouping as a whole as well as

CORPORATE BONDS **Duq-Eat 55**

Title-Industry Code & Co. Finances (In Italics)	*Ind*	*Chgs. 1983*		*Times Earn. 1984*	*1985 Yr. End*	*Cash &Eqv*	*Current Assets* (Million $)	*Liabs Date* (Million $)	*L. Term Debt (Mil $)*	*Debt % Prop*										
Individual Issue Statistics Exchange	Interest Dates	S&P Quality rating	Eligible	Bond Form	Legality M a N H N Y	Redemption Provisions Refund Earliest/Other	Call Price For S.F.	Call Price Regular	Out-st'd'g (Mil$)	Underwriter Firm	Underwriter Year	Price Range 1972-85 High	1972-85 Low	1986 High	1986 Low	1987 High	1987 Low	Mo. End Price Sale(s) or Bid	Curr Yield	Yield to Mat.
Duq Lt 1st 10¼s '92	jD	BBB	X	R	- - -	[1]100	[2]100	±108.20	75.0	S1	'85	102¾	100	107⅜	101⅞	105⅞	105¼	105⅝	9.70	8.98
• 1st 10¾s '95	Jd	BBB	X	R	- - -	[3]102.89	100	±108.68	50.0	F2	'85	99⅜	99⅜	108	100¼	108	108	107¾	9.98	9.38
1st 5⅛s '96	Fa	BBB	X	R	√ - √	....	±100.54	±101.74	22.8		'66	77	38½	74⅝	66¼	76	74½	76	6.74	9.08
1st 5¼s '97	Fa	BBB	X	R	√ - √	....	±100.55	±101.96	24.6	F2	'67	78	38	73½	65	74¾	73¼	74¾	7.02	9.15
1st 6⅜s '98	Fa	BBB	X	R	√ - √	....	±100.59	±102.55	34.7	F2	'68	90	43⅜	79½	71	80¾	79⅛	80¾	7.89	9.19
1st 7s '99	Jj	BBB	X	R	√ - √	....	±100.33	±102.85	30.0	W6	'69	97¼	46	83	74	84¼	82⅜	84¼	8.31	9.20
1st 7¾s '99	jJ	BBB	X	R	√ - √	....	±100.24	±103.32	28.9	B9	'69	103½	49⅝	88	78⅝	89¼	87½	89¼	8.68	9.22
• 1st 8¾s 2000	Ms	BBB	X	R	√ - √	....	100	103.52	30.0	F2	'70	112	53⅛	97⅜	82½	100	95⅞	96¼	9.09	9.25
1st 7⅞s 2001	Ms	BBB	X	R	√ - √	....	±100.38	103.76	35.0	B9	'70	104⅜	49⅛	87¾	78⅛	89⅛	87⅜	89⅛	8.84	9.27
1st 7½s 2001	jD	BBB	X	R	√ - √	....	100	±103.38	26.5	B9	'71	101¾	46¾	84⅜	75	86	84⅛	86	8.72	9.25
1st 7½s 2002	Jd	BBB	X	R	√ - √	....	100	±103.88	28.5	F2	'72	101⅛	46⅝	84	74½	85½	83⅜	85½	8.77	9.29
1st 7¼s 2003	Jj	BBB	X	R	√ - √	....	100	±103.32	32.7	W6	'72	99¼	45	81⅝	72¼	83⅛	81⅜	83⅛	8.72	9.30
1st 7¾s 2003	jJ	BBB	X	R	√ - √	....	100	±103.97	35.0	F2	'73	99½	47⅝	85⅜	75⅝	87	85	87	8.91	9.31
1st 8⅝s 2004	Ao	BBB	X	R	√ - √	....	100	±104.59	44.1	B9	'74	106⅛	52½	92¼	82⅛	93⅞	91⅞	93⅞	9.19	9.34
1st 9½s 2005	Ms	BBB	X	R	√ - √	....	±100.27	105¾	50.0	M4	'75	114¼	57⅜	99⅝	88¾	101¼	99⅛	101¼	9.38	9.35
• 1st 9s 2006	Jd	BBB	X	R	√ - √	....	100	±105.90	80.0	S1	'76	107	53	97	82¾	100	96⅛	96¾	9.30	9.36
• 1st 8⅜s 2007	Ao	BBB	X	R	√ - √	....	100¼	±105.97	97.4	F2	'77	102⅛	49⅝	91	77⅝	92¾	91	90¾	9.23	9.40
• 1st 10⅛s 2009	Fa	BBB	X	R	√ - √	....	100	±107.17	100	M7	'79	102⅞	59¼	104½	91	106	102¾	106¼	9.53	9.44
• 1st 12¼s 2010	Jj	BBB	X	R	√ - √	....	100	±108.73	60.0	S1	'80	104	70½	111	101¾	109¼	108	109⅜	11.20	11.11
• 1st 12⅛s 2013	Ao	BBB	X	R	√ - √	[4]109.54	100	±110.33	60.0	F2	'83	104	84¼	110	103⅛	108	108	107½	11.28	11.23
• 1st 13s 2013	jD	BBB	X	R	√ - √	[5]110.03	100	±110.86	50.0	M4	'83	105½	82	110	105¼	110½	110	110⅜	11.78	11.72
1st 11⅝s 2015	jD	BBB	X	R	- - -	[6]109.10	[2]100	±110.92	125	S1	'85	102¼	99¾	108¼	100⅛	107¼	105⅞	105⅞	10.98	10.95
1st 9½s 2016	jD	BBB	X	R	- - -	[7]107.13	[8]100	±109½	100	M4	'86	....	....	100	100	100½	99¾	99¾	9.52	9.52
• SF Deb 5s 2010	Ms	BBB-	X	CR	√ - √	....	±100.69	±102.85	9.17	F2	'60	72½	38	60	48	58⅝	56½	58⅛	8.60	9.51
Dyco Petroleum..........................	*49a*	*1.58*		*1.66*	*1.46 Dc*	*0.22*	*28.8*	*11.6 9-86*	*140*	*74.9*										
• Sr Sub Nts 13s '88	Mn	BB+	Y	R	- - -	....	....	NC	49.8	D7	'83	102⅞	93⅞	104⅛	102	No Sale		102⅞	12.64	10.48
[9]***Early Calif Indus***.......................	*27b*	*0.58*		*0.47*	*d0.99 Mr*	*5.65*	*68.6*	*38.6 9-86*	*47.5*	*117*										
Sub SF Deb 12½s '93	jD	CCC	Y	R	- - -	....	100	100	[10]18.3	W2	'78	104	66	92¾	79⅜	92	89⅛	90⅝	13.79	14.72
Eastern Air Lines[11].........................	*4*	*0.21*		*0.83*	*1.00 Dc*	*300*	*920*	*1226 9-86*	*2113*	*79.3*										
◆SecEqCtf'A' 17½s '98	Jj	CCC	Y	R	- - -	z100	*100	[12]100	39.0	M4	'81	115	87	114⅞	96⅛	113	111¾	s112	15.63	15.21
◆SecEqCtf'B' 17½s '97	jJ	CCC	Y	R	- - -	z100	*100	[12]100	41.9	M4	'81	115	87⅛	115	97¾	113½	112	s113	15.49	14.99
◆SecEqCtf'C' 16⅛s 2002	aO15	CCC	Y	R	- - -	z100	[13]100	[14]100	[10]188	M4	'82	110	87⅜	108⅞	98¼	106	103½	s104	15.50	15.44
Eastern[15]***Edison Co.***[16]................	*72a*	*2.00*		*2.17*	*2.04 Dc*	*0.44*	*49.1*	*80.4 9-86*	*227*	*41.4*										
1st & CT 16⅞s '92	Jd	A-	X	R	√ √ -	[17]107.24	100	±109.05	24.0	K1	'82	119	99⅜	119	109⅞	110⅞	110⅝	110⅝	15.25	13.98
[16]1st & CT 4½s '93	aO	A-	X	CR	√ √ -	....	±100.42	±101.14	5.00		'63	69½	38⅛	77⅛	68½	78¼	77	78¼	5.75	8.89
[18]1st & CT 6½s '97	Jd	A-	X	R	√ √ -	....	±101.18	±102.94	7.00	E1	'67	89⅜	43⅞	81½	72½	82¾	81¼	82¾	7.85	9.11
[16]1st & CT 8⅜s '99	Jd	A-	X	R	√ √ -	....	±101.39	±104.27	5.00	E1	'69	109	52⅜	92¾	83⅛	94¼	92½	94¼	8.89	9.16
[16]1st & CT 7⅞s 2002	jJ	A-	X	R	√ √ -	....	±101.60	±105.11	8.00		'72	103¼	48	87⅜	77¼	88⅞	87	88⅞	8.86	9.24
[16]1st & CT 8⅜s 2003	mS	A-	X	R	√ √ -	....	±101.59	±105.70	10.0	S1	'73	102	50½	91	80⅜	92½	90½	92½	9.05	9.26
1st & CT 12¼s 2013	Mn	A-	X	R	√ √ -	[19]109.48	100	±110.27	40.0	P5	'83	106⅛	79¼	115¼	103⅝	116¼	114¾	115	10.65	10.55
1st&CT 9⅝s 2016	jJ	A-	X	R	- √ -	[20]106.94	z100	±108.38	55.0	M8	'86	....	....	100¼	96¾	100¾	99¼	100¼	9.60	9.59
Eastman Kodak...........................	*40d*	*9.72*		*15.25*	*3.90 Dc*	*612*	*6023*	*3669 9-86*	*★1115*	*17.3*										
• Deb 8⅝s 2016	Jd15	AA	X	R	- √ -	[21]103.19	[22]100	±106.38	300	M8	'86	....	....	101	95	104¾	101½	s104	8.29	8.26
Eaton Corp....................................	*8*	*3.26*		*8.39*	*7.19 Dc*	*319*	*1809*	*650 9-86*	*★731*	*77.3*										
• SF Deb 7.60s '96	mS15	A	X	R	- √ -	....	100	±101.90	20.8	M4	'71	103¼	52½	96	80	98	98	94½	8.04	8.44
• SF Deb 8¾s 2001	jJ15	A	X	R	- √ -	....	[23]100	±104	37.4	M4	'76	106¼	55	98	79⅝	No Sale		98⅜	8.89	8.95
• SF Deb 7⅞s 2003	jD	A	X	R	- √ -	....	100	±103.78	49.0	M4	'73	100	48⅛	92¾	74¼	No Sale		91⅞	8.57	8.80
• SF Deb 9s 2016	Ms15	A	X	R	- √ -	[24]104¼	[25]100	±108½	100	M4	'86	....	....	99½	99½	No Sale		99¼	9.07	9.07
Deb[26] 8s '96	[27]fA15	A	X	R	- √ -	....	....	NC	100	M4	'86	....	....	103¼	98⅛	104¼	101¼	101¼	7.90	7.81

Uniform Footnote Explanations—See Page 1. Other: [1]Red rest'n(10 3/8%)to 12-1-90. [2]Fr 10-1-87. [3]Red rest'n(10.85%)to 6-1-90. [4]Red rest'n(12.2%)to 4-1-88. [5]Red rest'n(13.12%)to 12-1-88. [6]Red rest'n(11.76%)to 12-1-90. [7]Red rest'n(9.59%)to 12-1-91. [8]Fr 10-1-88. [9]Now ERLY Indus. [10]Incl disc. [11]Subsid of Texas Air. [12]Fr 7-1-91. [13]Fr 10-15-93. [14]Fr 10-15-87. [15]Subsid of Eastern Util Assoc. [16]Was Brocton Edison. [17]Red rest'n(17.29%)to 6-1-87. [18]Was Blackstone Valley Elec. [19]Red rest'n(12.43%)to 5-1-88. [20]Red rest'n(9.82%)to 7-1-91. [21]Red rest'n(8.84%)to 6-15-96. [22]Fr 6-15-97. [23]Fr 7-15-87. [24]Red rest'n(9.048%)to 3-15-96. [25]Fr 3-15-97. [26](HRO)On 8-15-96 at 100. [27]Due 8-15-2006.

FIGURE 4–3 A sample page from Standard & Poor's *Bond Guide*, January 1984.
Source: Standard & Poor's *Bond Guide,* New York, Standard & Poor's Corporation, September 1986. Reproduced by permission of Standard & Poor's Corporation.

for each individual company. For example, 23 series of financial and operating statistics are provided for each company for the previous 15 years and estimated for the next one or two years. These statistics can be seen in the middle of Figure 4–4, which shows a typical page of coverage for a company, in this case EG&G, a manufacturer of scientific products. This report, issued in late March 1987, contained historical data through 1986 and estimated data for 1987 (some data for 1986 was estimated).

As for recommendations, the *VL* ranks each company from 1 (top) to 5 (bottom) on the basis of its "probable safety in the future" and its timeliness ("probable price performance in the next 12 months") in relation to the other 1700+ stocks. The top 100 and bottom 100 stocks are in Group I and Group V; the next 300 top and 300 bottom, respectively, in Groups II and IV; and the middle 900 in Group III. Value Line recommends that investors choose stocks out of the top 400 (Groups I and II) that meet their standards for safety and current yield. If any of the selected stocks falls below the investor's standards, a switch is made into those that currently conform. This is convenient for investors because the weekly Summary & Index section shows the current performance and safety ratings for each of the 1700 stocks as well as their estimated yields and latest earnings.

Value Line's stock rankings are based on a computer model developed and modified over many years. The model includes price history over both a short and long period, earnings changes, and an earnings surprise factor to account for actual earnings significantly above or below those predicted by their analysts. The *VL* discloses the methodology for computing the ranks and regularly reports on how well the ranks have done in practice.

As Figure 4–4 shows, the *VL* coverage also provides such information as the beta (to be discussed in Chapter 5) and the P/E ratio (Chapter 9). Additional information includes the company's financial strength, the price stability of the stock, the price growth persistence, and the earnings predictability. Quarterly sales, earnings, and dividends are shown on both a historical and an estimated basis. Note (in the upper left corner) that both institutional and insider decisions are shown.

As part of its company coverage, Value Line issues an industry report for each of the 90+ industries it covers. This is typically a two-page report preceding the companies assigned to that industry by Value Line. This discussion analyzes the current and prospective situation for the industry and has a table of composite statistics, including both historical and estimated figures.

Value Line also publishes a separate Options and Convertibles service, which covers all listed options, convertibles, and warrants. Each of the options covered is assigned a performance rank. Value Line also publishes an OTC Special Situations Service and a New Issues Service.

Other advisory services and letters   There are many other investment advisory services. A few of the well-known ones include Zweig Forecast, Dow

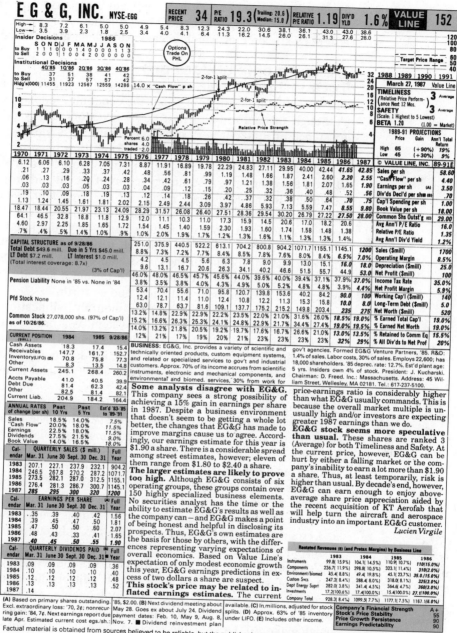

FIGURE 4–4 A page from a weekly issue of *Ratings and Reports, The Value Line Investment Survey.*

Source: *Ratings and Reports, The Value Line Investment Survey*, Edition 1, Part 3, March 27, 1987, p. 152. © 1987 Value Line, Inc. Reprinted by permission.

Theory Forecasts, The Holt Investment Advisory, The Professional Tape Reader, Babson Reports, and United Business Survey. A number of market letters exist, some of which occasionally generate national news.

Government Publications

The federal government, through a variety of agencies and departments, provides much information about the economy, industries, and companies. Although this information is free to investors, many do not know of its existence or utilize it very often. Generally, it is more specialized than the previous sources discussed and therefore it has been placed after them.

Government publications are a primary source for data concerning the state of the economy. A summary report of recent and prospective activity is contained in the *Economic Report of the President*, which is sent by the president to the Congress. The report includes over 200 pages covering such issues as monetary policy, inflation, tax policy, the international economy, and review and outlook. In addition, it contains over 100 pages of tables showing historical data for the Gross National Product (GNP), price indices, savings, employment, production and business activity, corporate profits, agriculture, international statistics, and so forth.

The Federal Reserve Bulletin, a monthly publication of the Board of Governors of the Federal Reserve System, is a prime source for monetary data, money and credit data, and figures on GNP, labor force, output, and the international economy. It also contains data pertinent to the Federal Reserve System, including member-bank reserves and reserve requirements, and open market transactions.

Most of the 12 Federal Reserve Banks also have their own publications, featuring data and analyses of economic activity. The Federal Reserve Bank of St. Louis produces several publications of special interest to economists and other economic observers. For example, *U.S. Financial Data* is a weekly analysis of money market conditions, and *National Economic Trends* is a monthly publication dealing with aggregate business.

Economic Indicators is a monthly publication of the Council of Economic Advisors. It contains data on income, spending, employment, prices, money and credit, and other factors on both a monthly and annual basis.

Business Conditions Digest (BCD), published monthly by the Department of Commerce, contains data on indicators of the economy from the National Bureau of Economic Research (which will be discussed in Chapter 10). Some 90 indicators, and over 300 components, are included. These indicators are important in attempting to discern the economy's movements, which make *BCD* a valuable information source for those interested in forecasting economic activity. *BCD* contains the basic data for many of the charts of economic activity often seen by investors.[7]

---

[7] The Federal Reserve also publishes a monthly *Chart Book* showing numerous financial and economic series.

A third monthly source of economic data is the Department of Commerce's *Survey of Current Business*. This source provides detailed information on the national income accounts, as well as data on such variables as industrial production, employment and wages, and interest rates. The *Survey* also reviews recent developments in the economy.

The government also produces data on industries, primarily through the Census Bureau. These data include employment figures, number of companies, and sales. Investors who choose to do their own detailed security analysis may find such information of real value. A good source of industry accounting data is *Quarterly Financial Report for Manufacturing Corporations*, published by the Federal Trade Commission and the Securities and Exchange Commission. This report contains aggregate balance sheet and income statement data for all manufacturing corporations. Data are broken down by industry and by size (assets).

Finally, the role of the government in providing investors with information on companies should be noted. Very extensive accounting and financial data are provided to investors in virtually all companies of interest through the requirements of the SEC. Annual reports must be filed within 90 days of the close of the fiscal year with the SEC in 10-K statements, which provide very detailed information. The 10-K statements contain information not available in a company's annual report. Interim reports (8-K) must also be filed if important transactions occur. These reports are available to investors from the SEC and can also be found in many libraries. In many respects, the 10-K report is the most detailed source of company information that can be obtained by an investor.

Academic and Professional Journals

Like government publications, the academic press is available to investors but is not often used. First, investors are often unaware of these journals. Second, in most cases they are too difficult to be read easily. And third, academic journals often contain many articles not of direct interest to the practicing investor.

The more difficult academic journals, of limited use to most investors, include *The Journal of Finance*, *The Journal of Financial and Quantitative Analysis*, *The Journal of Financial Economics*, *The Journal of Business*, *The Journal of Financial Research*, the *Financial Review*, and the *Journal of Business Research*.

Several journals of both an academic and professional nature are available. Of particular interest to some investors with a good basic understanding of investments is the *Journal of Portfolio Management*, a quarterly intended to make available academic research for the professional portfolio manager. The *Financial Analysts Journal* is a bimonthly with articles intended for financial analysts. This journal is published by the Financial Analysts Federation, a nonprofit corporation devoted to advancing security analysis and investment management. Although the average investor may not understand all of the articles in these two journals, much of this material is valuable to those with some knowledge of the field.

The Financial Analysts Federation is associated with the Institute of Chartered Financial Analysts, a professional organization composed of members called Chartered Financial Analysts (CFA). This professional designation is awarded to people meeting recognized standards of competency and conduct. To earn the CFA designation, a candidate must complete a series of three comprehensive examinations offered once a year in June. The subject areas studied include economics, financial accounting, quantitative techniques, ethical and professional standards, fixed-income securities analysis, equity securities analysis, and portfolio management. The candidate must also accumulate three years work experience in positions related to investments. The CFA designation, first awarded in 1963, is widely respected and continues to gain recognition in the investment community.

BOX 4–2 CHARTERED FACT ASSEMBLERS?

"You went down to Charlottesville to see the ICFA?" asks the young female portfolio manager, a recent survivor of the chartered financial analysts Level One examination. "Do they have beds of nails and those things you stretch people out on?"

Not torture racks exactly, but their intellectual equivalent. The Virginia-based Institute of Chartered Financial Analysts requires candidates for its CFA designation to endure three separate daylong examinations, spaced at least a year apart and each entailing up to an estimated 150 hours of study that must be added on top of demanding full-time jobs (every CFA must have at least three years' practical experience). Fewer than 30% will get through on the first attempt.

Still, at a time when financial careers are a hot item, the ICFA has no trouble attracting victims. A record 2366 attempted its Level One exam, the first hurdle, in 1986, confirming a dramatic upswing that began in the late 1970s. For comparison, a total of only 9,645 charters have been granted since the program began in 1963.

Partly, the CFA surge is a bull market symptom, and partly it reflects the CFA's increasing clout. "Peer group pressure" is the first explanation ICFA officials give for their popularity. Some peers are more equal than others: Mark Mallon, director of research at Pittsburgh's Federated Research, says getting a CFA isn't mandatory at his firm, but "de facto, it comes as close as it can to being an official company edict."

But nobody seems to be asking the important question: Does possession of a CFA make one a better analyst or investor? There's no evidence that anything in the CFA course (or anywhere else for that matter) helps analysts to make better stock picks. And there's considerable evidence that qualifications like the CFA too easily assist guilds of practitioners to cartelize their professions by raising barriers to entry—a process sociologists call "credentialism."

The subjects covered are undeniably worthy: economics, accounting, fixed income and equity securities analysis, portfolio management, quantitative techniques—and "ethical and professional standards'' (the ICFA's *Standards of Practice Handbook* now extends to 122 pages).

The CFA course emphasizes practical techniques used in the field, complementing, rather than directly challenging, the more abstract approach of the business schools. But one investment technique that is widely employed in practice rarely appears in the CFA exam, although it's included in the assigned readings. The frequent omission is technical analysis, the prediction of security price movements solely on the basis of their past activity. ICFA officials say this is because technical analysis has ''no theoretical justification.'' Translation: It throws business school academics into screaming fits.

Technical analysis directly contravenes the central tenet of even the mildest, or ''narrow,'' form of the Efficient Market Hypothesis, which specifically denies that information about price movements has predictive power. But most academics support a broader form of EMH that maintains that all public information about a stock is already reflected in its price. This would mean that further financial analysis, chartered or otherwise, can't successfully anticipate a stock's subsequent direction. In its most extreme form, the EMH would have to mean that the CFA is useless.

Alfred C. (Pete) Morley, 59, the tough, Trumanesque president of the ICFA, permits himself a slight smile when asked about the paradox of professional training that has no obvious relation to results. ''Securities analysis is not a science,'' he says carefully. ''In the final analysis, it's an art. The greatest characteristic of the successful analyst is imagination. But imagination can only be employed after all the facts have been gathered.''

More to the point, Morley offers another, pragmatic defense of the CFA (chartered fact assembler?): ''CFAs are compensated at a higher level than non-CFAs.''

Morley says he isn't seeking legislation to bar the business to all except CFAs—traditionally the ultimate objective of professional groups. And he did oppose a similar move by the New York Society of Security Analysts in the 1970s, when he was research director of institutional broker H. C. Wainwright.

But Morley also was recently appointed chief executive officer of the Financial Analysts Federation, the linked professional association that, unlike the ICFA, is legally able to lobby. He's strategically placed if he changes his mind.

Source: Peter Brimelow, ''Chartered Fact Assemblers,'' *Forbes,* October 20, 1986, p. 70. Reprinted by permission of *Forbes* magazine, October 20, 1986. © Forbes, Inc., 1986.

The C.F.A. Digest, a monthly publication of the Chartered Financial Analysts Institute, contains abstracts of published articles from academic, government, and professional sources that are felt to be of interest to security analysts and portfolio managers. Each issue may contain 25 to 30 abstracts.

A third professional journal is *Institutional Investor,* intended for money managers. Published monthly, its emphasis is on the current state of the money management industry.

Computerized Investments Information

Although the previous discussion demonstrates the tremendous amount of published financial information that exists, a large and growing amount of computer-based information is also available. In some cases the latter is similar to the published information, but it is much more convenient for those with access to both it and a computer. Individuals wishing to study securities and to analyze data can accomplish far more with the computer than they could ever hope to accomplish without it.

For several years investors have been able to obtain either data bases or computer-based services, or both, from specialized financial service firms. In the case of data bases, the buyer typically receives a tape (or tapes) containing substantial financial information on a large number of companies and processes this information on a mainframe computer. Computer-based services, on the other hand, provide the client with the means to access the data bases from the client's terminal (again, traditionally, some type of large computer). These data bases are almost always quite expensive, often thousands of dollars, as are the computers themselves.

Obviously, most investors do not have computers or computerized sources of information. However, the rise of the microcomputer has changed this situation dramatically and will continue to have a major impact in the future. Investors currently can access or process an incredible array of computerized information from their homes and the number doing so undoubtedly will grow.

For organizational purposes, we will first discuss the traditional sources of computerized information and services that remain important to many users, particularly researchers who wish to analyze and manipulate substantial amounts of data for hundreds, or even thousands, of companies. We will then review the microcomputer potential, which is of immediate use to individual investors with access to a microcomputer. It should be noted, however, that the division between these two components is not sharp and distinct. For example, Compustat now has available a floppy disk version of its data, and the Media General databank can be accessed by micros.

Traditional Computerized Data Bases and Services

Compustat Probably the best known source of financial information for studies of corporate securities and their issuers is Standard & Poor's Compustat Services, Inc. This financial data base consists of various tapes that can be regularly updated. For example, the Compustat® II/175-Item Annual and 100-Item Quarterly Format option available to universities consists of 12 data bases on over 6400 active companies (as of 1986).[8] The annual format

---

[8] One of the 12 data bases, the Research file, contains an additional 3600 inactive companies that have filed for bankruptcy, gone private, were acquired or liquidated, or no longer report.

presents 175 data items for 20 years, while the quarterly format presents 97 data items for 40 quarters.[9]

Compustat provides these tapes to many universities and colleges at greatly reduced rates, thereby making them available for scholarly research.[10] Many investments articles have used these data in their analysis.

CRSP The Center for Research in Security Prices at the University of Chicago produces a set of tapes containing both month-end and daily stock prices for every NYSE stock, starting in 1926.[11] These data are in both raw form (prices and dividends) and returns form. Market indices are also available on a daily and monthly basis.

The CRSP tapes allow researchers to document the price (return) performance of every NYSE stock, either by itself or in relation to a market index, for almost 60 years. Thus, the reaction of a stock, or group of stocks, to a particular event or series of events can be studied.

Media General The publishers of *The Media General Financial Weekly,* referred to earlier, also sell a databank containing major financial information for close to 3000 companies. The tapes include current and historical price and volume information as well as balance sheet and income statement data.

ISL Interactive Data Corporation (IDC) produces a quarterly tape containing daily price and volume information for all NYSE and AMEX securities, as well as some OTC stocks. Quarterly dividends and earnings are also contained on the tapes.

Investors can obtain computer-based information without having to purchase a data base such as those described here. For example, IDC is a time-sharing computer service company that specializes in providing financial information through the connection of a client's computer terminal to the IDC computer. The client can obtain data and services from the organizations' data bases by leasing time and space. IDC provides numerous data bases, including some of those mentioned earlier such as Compustat. It also has data bases covering price data, municipal securities data, foreign exchange data, international securities data, and other information. IDC offers the Value Line Data Base, which covers the 1700 companies in *The Value Line Investment Survey* described earlier.

Microcomputer Possibilities

The microcomputer is opening up numerous possibilities for investors, providing them with the opportunity to examine large amounts of data in an

---

[9] These data bases also contain business segment and aggregate industry data.

[10] For example in 1986 the Compustat II option described had a $10,000 annual fee for universities, while commercial rates totaled more than $60,000.

[11] Tapes for the American Stock Exchange are also available.

almost endless variety of ways. Until the rise of the microcomputer and its mushrooming related-support services, these opportunities were simply beyond the scope of all but a very few individual investors.

Several million personal computers have been sold, and projections call for a vastly expanding market. As more and more individual investors purchase a personal computer, the demand for investment services they can use will increase. The only additional hardware needed by an investor is a modem to connect the personal computer by telephone lines to another computer.

It is impossible to describe all of the services and packages now available to investors through the use of microcomputers. Existing products change rapidly, and in some cases disappear, as new ones appear daily. What we can do, however, is to organize this area into its principal products and services and describe a few of the better known offerings. Readers must keep in mind that this is a nonexhaustive list intended only as a general guide.[12]

Our organization is based on the following structure:

1. On-Line Financial Services
2. Floppy Disk Data Bases
3. Software packages
   a. for security analysis
      1. technical analysis
      2. fundamental analysis
   b. for portfolio management

On-line financial services Two general sources of information widely known and available to all micro users are *Compuserve* and *The Source*. *Compuserve* offers current and historical price data, financial statements, and earnings estimates. It also offers the ability to screen some 46,000 U.S. and Canadian securities according to your predefined criteria. As of 1986, *The Source* offered the retrieval of price quotes and research reports.

A major source of investment information for micros is the *Dow Jones News/Retrieval,* produced by the publishers of *The Wall Street Journal*. This service provides up-to-the-minute news and information from Dow Jones, which has a vast array of information stored in its computers. This information set includes news from *The Wall Street Journal, Barron's* and the Dow Jones News Service, Dow Jones Quotes, Media General Financial Services (covering 3200 companies and 170 industries), Disclosure II (detailed data on over 6000 publicly held companies, including data filed with the SEC), an update of weekly economic information, forecasts of corporate earnings for 2400 of the most widely followed companies, weekly forecasts of monetary and economic indicators, and other services. Users must pay a per-minute

---

[12]No endorsement of any of the products mentioned here is intended or implied.

fee to use the various parts of the service, with different parts having different rates.[13]

The *Dow Jones News/Retrieval* offers a total of 35 databases. It is considered by many investors to be the premier on-line financial service.

Several other on-line services are available. For example, Charles Schwab & Co., a discount brokerage firm, offers Schwab's Electronic Brokerage Service. Using its software package, *The Equalizer,* investors can access information from the *Dow Jones News/Retrieval* and from several other organizations such as Standard & Poor's. E. F. Hutton, a full-service brokerage firm, offers *Huttonline,* containing information on accounts, research reports and current prices, to its clients. *Newsnet* offers over 300 specialized newsletters, while *FCI-Invest/Net: The Insider Trading Monitor* offers information on insider trading activities for a large number of companies. Warner Computer Systems, Inc., *Nite-Line,* and *Merlin Dial/Data* offer primarily historical price data on large numbers of securities.

Typical of the new types of services available to investors through the use of micros is CitiQuote Investor from Citicorp Information Services. Using the software provided, investors have access to 67,000 securities updated daily with nine years of history. The information available includes price data, dividend and earnings data, and over 40 other items. The financial instruments covered include stocks, bonds, options, and government mortgage instruments.

Floppy disk databases Two packages available from well-known investment advisory services are Stock Pak II from Standard & Poor's, and Value/Screen Plus from Arnold Bernhard & Company (publisher of *The Value Line Investment Survey*). Stock Pak II consists of separate data disks covering NYSE, AMEX, and over-the-counter stocks. Users can design their own screening criteria to use with these data disks and screen the database for all companies meeting the criteria. Value/Screen Plus, on the other hand, is an investment management package that selects stocks and keeps portfolio records. It contains almost 40 data points on roughly 1700 companies with subscribers receiving an updated disk monthly or quarterly. Users can screen this database using Value Line's criteria such as timeliness and safety, and can load the data into spreadsheets.

Compustat data, described earlier, is now available in limited form for the personal computer. The initial package, first offered in 1985, covered the Standard & Poor 500 population for limited historical periods.

Economica and *Citibase* offer *Econ-DB,* a comprehensive PC database. Over 700 widely used economic time series, such as GNP, exports, consumption, and retail sales, are available on diskette in monthly, quarterly, or one-time only form.

---

[13]Non-prime-time rates are cheaper than prime-time rates.

Software packages Many software packages are now available for the micro, offering both security analysis and portfolio management. We will discuss each of these areas briefly.

In a special issue reviewing investment software in April 1986, *PC Magazine* reviewed 25 programs designed for technical analysis, which essentially means that they help you to prepare a chart of the price and/or volume movements for a particular company.[14] These programs typically come with the ability to access the on-line financial services in order that the necessary data can be downloaded. Personal computers are well suited to producing graphs of various types, which form the basis of technical analysis.

The same issue also reviewed seven fundamental analysis software packages, including Stock Pak II and Value/Screen Plus mentioned previously. It is clear that much less software has been produced in this area. The reason for this may become apparent after we study fundamental analysis.

Numerous software programs for the micro are available to manage the portfolio by valuing it, separating items by tax categories, tracking brokerage commissions, and so on. Essentially, these programs build a database (your portfolio information) and allow you to make calculations and generate reports from that database. These programs tend to be divided into two categories, those for professional portfolio managers and those for individual investors. The prices of such programs reflect this, with some ranging into the thousands of dollars.

Summary

Since the investment process is basically information-oriented, investors need to know about the various sources of investment information. Because of the large amount and variety available, a primary problem for investors is finding what is needed and likely to be useful from the vast quantity of information available.

Users of information can be broadly divided into two groups: individual investors and institutional investors. Individuals are usually part-time investors with neither the time nor the ability to digest a complex flow of information. This group must recognize its needs and limitations and act accordingly. Institutional investors, on the other hand, have the resources and the need to collect and process considerable information. They should be—and are—aware of various types of information.

Information sources can be separated into printed and computerized material. Published material is abundant and will continue to be so. Computerized information is already quite important to investors and is destined to become more so because of the tremendous expansion of microcomputers.

---

[14] See *PC Magazine*, Vol. 5, No. 7, April 15, 1986.

Published sources of information can be organized in rough order of general availability and use by investors. They include the financial press (newspapers and magazines), which is widely available as a source of such features as news stories, economy, industry and company analysis, price and volume information, and columnists. Corporate reports are sent automatically by companies to shareholders and other investors can easily obtain them. Brokerage firms provide a steady flow of information and recommendations. Because many investors deal with one or more brokers, they have access to considerable information.

Investment information services provide both information and recommendations. Standard & Poor's and Moody's are well known as sources of information of various types. Both services publish a variety of reports, manuals, and guides, and probably form the basis of investment information in this country while also recommending securities. On the other hand, numerous investment advisory services exist, which, though they provide information, are usually thought of as "recommendation" services. *The Value Line Investment Survey* is the largest and probably best known advisory service.

Other sources of information include government publications and the financial and professional journals. The federal govenment provides a wide variety of information on the economy, industries, and companies. Economy data are of particular importance and the government is the primary source of this type of information. Several professional journals offer articles on the current state of the art in investments.

Computerized investment information includes the traditional mainframe-oriented databases, a necessity in analyzing securities and researching investment questions and strategies, and computer-based services that allow subscribers to access information through time-sharing techniques. Perhaps more importantly to most investors, certainly individual investors, microcomputers now offer anyone a way to access information and services from their homes and offices. Included in this area are the on-line financial services, floppy disk databases, and various types of software for both security analysis and portfolio management. Growth in this market has been, and will continue to be, explosive.

Key Sources of Information

The Financial Press
  Newspapers
    The Wall Street Journal
    Barron's
    The M/G Financial Weekly
  Magazines
    Forbes

Business Week
Fortune
Annual Reports
Brokerage Firms
Investment Information Services
  Standard & Poor's Corporation
    Bond Guide

Bond Outlook
Corporate Records (Daily News)
Outlook
Stock Guide
Stock Reports
Moody's
 Bond Survey
 Handbook of Common Stocks
 Investors Fact Sheets
 Manuals (Industrial, OTC Industrial, Public Utility, Bank & Finance, Municipal & Government, Transportation, and International)
 Stock Survey
Investment Advisory Services
 The Value Line Investment Survey
 Others
Government Publications
 Economic Report of the President
 The Federal Reserve Bulletin
 Federal Reserve Bank of St. Louis
 U.S. Financial Data
 National Economic Trends
 Economic Indicators

Business Conditions Digest
Survey of Current Business
Quarterly Financial Report for Manufacturing Corporations
Academic and Professional Journals
 Academic Journals
 Professional Journals
  Financial Analysts Journal
  Journal of Portfolio Management
  Institutional Investor
  The C.F.A. Digest
Computerized Databases and Services
 Compustat
 CRSP
 ISL
 Media General
 Interactive Data Corporation
Microcomputers
 On-Line Financial Services
 Floppy Disk Databases
 Software Packages
  Security Analysis
   Technical Analysis
   Fundamental Analysis
 Portfolio Management

QUESTIONS AND PROBLEMS

1. How should individual investors approach the problem of obtaining investment information?
2. What sources of price and volume information for securities are investors most likely to use?

3. How does *The Wall Street Journal* and *Barron's* differ in price and volume quotations?

4. How can annual reports help investors in trying to analyze the "quality" of a corporation's earnings?

5. How do discount brokers and full-service brokers differ in providing investment information?

6. Describe how, using Standard & Poor's services, an investor can go from very detailed information about a common stock to a quite brief summary of pertinent information.

7. What does a Value Line rating of "4" for timeliness mean?

8. Would you expect each stock rated by Value Line to perform in accordance with its rank in every year? What about each of the five groups?

9. Outline government publications that would be of help in analyzing the economy.

10. What sources of information are available from the government on industries and on companies?

11. Which government publication is particularly useful in forecasting economic activity? Why?

12. Where could an investor find abstracts of recent articles of interest to security analysts and portfolio managers?

13. Explain what Compustat is and its value.

14. How could Compustat aid investors in testing possible investment strategies?

15. Of what additional value are the CRSP tapes in relation to Compustat?

16. What is meant by "time-sharing"?

17. What is the Dow Jones News/Retrieval?

18. Describe the types of software and services available for microcomputer users.

Selected References

The CFA Digest, The Institute of Chartered Financial Analysts, P. O. Box 3668, Charlottesville, Virginia 22903.

Dow Jones & Co. (*The Wall Street Journal* and *Barron's*). Subscriptions—200 Barnett Road, Chicopee, Massachusetts 01021.

Dow Jones News/Retrieval, P. O. Box 300, Princeton, New Jersey 08540.

Federal Reserve Bank of St. Louis, P. O. Box 442, St. Louis, Missouri 63166.

Federal Reserve Bulletin—Division of Administrative Services, Board of Governors of the Federal Reserve System, Washington, D.C. 20551.

Forbes, 60 Fifth Avenue, New York, New York 10014.

Interactive Data Corporation, 1114 Avenue of the Americas, New York, New York 10036.

Media General Financial Weekly, Media General Financial Services, Inc., P. O. Box C-32333, Richmond, Virginia 23293.

Moody's Investor's Services, Inc., 99 Church Street, New York, New York 10007.

Standard & Poor's Corporation, 345 Hudson Street, New York, New York 10014.

The Value Line Investment Survey and other Value Line services. Arnold Bernhard and Company, Inc., 5 East 44th Street, New York, New York 10017.

CHAPTER 5

RISK AND RETURN CONCEPTS

Investments has been traditionally dichotomized into security analysis and portfolio management. Starting in Chapter 6 and extending for several chapters, security analysis for fixed income and equity securities will be discussed. The heart of security analysis is the valuation of financial assets. Value, in turn, is a function of return and risk. These two concepts, therefore, are very important in the study of investments. In fact, in the final analysis the investment decision can be described as a return–risk trade-off.

Return and risk will be described, measured, and used throughout the text. Particular concepts of return and risk will be used when needed, but it is extremely valuable before beginning an analysis of the various securities to obtain a working knowledge of these concepts. This is the purpose of this chapter.

The Concept of Return

As noted in Chapter 1, the objective of investors is to maximize expected returns, although subject to constraints, primarily risk. Return is the motivating force in the investment process; that is, it is the reward for undertaking the investment.

Return is not as simple a concept as it first appears, for the following reasons.

1. In most cases, return is not guaranteed. It is expected, but it may not be realized.
2. There are various ways to measure return.

Regardless of difficulty, return is of crucial importance to investors. It is the only rational way (after allowing for risk) for investors to compare alternative investments that differ in what they offer. The measurement of actual (historical) returns is necessary for investors to assess how well they have done. And finally, the historical return plays a large part in the estimation of future, unknown returns, that is, expected returns.

Realized versus Expected Return

It is important at the outset to distinguish clearly between the two concepts of return described in Chapter 1: realized return and expected return. Both terms will be used extensively.

Realized return is what the term implies: it is ex post (after the fact) return, or return that was or could have been earned. This return has occurred. For example, a deposit of $100 in a bank on January 1, 1988, at a stated annual interest rate of 5¼% will be worth $105.25 one year later. The actual or realized return for 1988 is, therefore, $5.25/$100, or 5.25%. Similarly, the total annual return on the Standard & Poor 500 Composite Index for 1980 was about 31.5%. This was the actual (realized) return if an investor bought the entire index on January 1, 1980 and sold on December 31, 1980.

Expected return is the return from an asset that investors anticipate (expect) they will earn over some future period. It is a predicted return, subject to uncertainty, and may or may not occur. Investors are willing to purchase a particular asset if the expected return is adequate, but they understand that their expectation may not materialize. If not, the realized return will differ from the expected return. In fact, realized returns on securities show considerable variability. Although investors may receive their expected returns on risky securities on a long-run average basis, they generally do not do so on a short-run basis.

The Components of Return

Return on a typical investment consists of two components. The basic component that usually comes to mind is the periodic cash receipts (or income) on the investment, either interest or dividends. The second component is also important, particularly for common stocks but also for longer term bonds and other fixed-income securities. This is the appreciation (or depreciation) in the price of the asset, commonly called the capital gain or loss. It is the difference between the purchase price and the price at which the asset can be or is sold and can, therefore, be a gain or a loss.

Income

The income from an investment opportunity consists of one or more cash payments paid at specified intervals of time. Interest payments on most bonds, for example, are paid semiannually, whereas dividends on common stocks are paid quarterly. The distinguishing feature of these payments is that they are paid in cash by the issuer to the holder of the asset.

The term **yield** is often used in connection with this component of return. Yield refers to the return in relation to some price of a security. For example, the current yield on a 10% coupon bond purchased at a price of $900 is 11.11% ($100/$900). The current yield on a common stock paying $5 in dividends per year and selling today for $50 per share is 10%. And the current yield on a 5½% passbook savings account is 5½%. There are other yield measures, several of which will be discussed in the next chapter.

Price Appreciation (Depreciation)

The other component of return is the change in price on the asset (if any). Price appreciation is the amount by which the sale price of a security exceeds the purchase price (this is often referred to as a **capital gain**); a sale price lower than the purchase price results in price depreciation, often referred to as a **capital loss.**[1] Many investors invest primarily for capital gains or losses. This component is often expected by investors to be larger than the income component.

This concept involves only the difference between the proceeds from selling a security and its original cost. An investor can buy an asset and sell it one day, one hour, or one minute later for a capital gain or loss.

Total Return

Having examined the two components of a security's return, it remains to add them together (algebraically) to form total return, which for any security is defined as

$$\text{Total return} = \text{Income} \begin{cases} + \text{ Price appreciation} \\ - \text{ Price depreciation} \end{cases} \qquad (5\text{--}1)$$

Equation 5–1 is a conceptual statement for total return. To actually implement this concept, it should be stated differently, as is done in the following material. The important point is that a security's total return consists of the sum of two components, income and price change. Note that either component can be zero for a given security over any given time period. For example, a bond purchased at par and held to maturity provides a stream of income in the form of interest payments. A bond purchased for $800 and held to maturity provides both income and a price change. The purchase of a

---

[1] Capital gains and losses can be either paper gains (losses) or realized gains (losses). The security must be sold before a gain or loss is realized.

nondividend-paying stock that is sold six months later produces either a capital gain or loss, but no income.

Measuring Returns

Investors need to measure returns, whether realized or expected. A correct measurement must incorporate the two components of return, income and price change. Such a measurement is available and is called the holding period yield (HPY) or, alternatively, in slightly different form, the holding period return (HPR) and can be used for any security discussed in this text. Returns across time or from different securities can be measured and compared using the holding period yield or the holding period return.

Holding Period Yield

The **holding period yield (HPY)** is a percentage return concept relating all the cash flows received by an investor during any designated time period to the amount of money invested in the asset. HPY is defined as

$$HPY = \frac{\text{Any cash payments received} + \text{Price change over the period}}{\text{Price at which the asset is purchased (beginning price)}}$$

(5–2)

All the items in Equation 5–2 are measured in dollars. The cash payments received can be interest payments or dividends. The price change (in dollars) over the period, defined as the difference between the beginning price and the ending price, can be either positive (sales price exceeds purchase price) or negative (purchase price exceeds sales price). Netting the two items in the numerator together and dividing by the purchase price results in a percentage return figure. Note that in using the HPY, the two components of return, income and price change, have been measured.[2]

Consider the following examples, first for a bond, and then for a common stock, and finally for a warrant.

$$\text{Bond HPY} = \frac{I_t + (P_E - P_B)}{P_B} = \frac{I_t + PC}{P_B}$$

(5–3)

where I_t is the interest payment(s) received during the period, P_B and P_E are the prices at the beginning and end, respectively, of the measurement period t, and PC is the change in price during the period.

---

[2]This can be seen more easily by rewriting Equation 5–2 to specifically show its income and price change components.

$$HPY = \frac{\text{Cash payments received}}{\text{Purchase price}} + \frac{\text{Price change over the period}}{\text{Purchase price}}$$

The first term is a yield component whereas the second term measures the price change.

Example. Assume the purchase of a 10% coupon Treasury bond at a price of $960, held one year, and sold for $1020. Using Equation 5–3, the HPY for this bond for the one-year holding period would be

$$\text{Bond HPY} = \frac{100 + (1020 - 960)}{960} = \frac{100 + 60}{960} = 0.1667 \text{ or } 16.67\%$$

$$\text{Stock HPY} = \frac{D_t + (P_E - P_B)}{P_B} = \frac{D_t + PC}{P_B} \qquad (5\text{–}4)$$

where D_t = the dividend(s) paid during the period and all other terms are defined as before.

Example. Assume the purchase of 100 shares of XYZ corporation at $30 per share, the payment of a $2 dividend per share, and the sale of the 100 shares one year later at $26 per share. Although the HPY can be computed on a per share basis or total-dollar basis, the per-share basis is used in this text.[3] Based on Equation 5–2,

$$\text{Stock HPY} = \frac{2 + (26 - 30)}{30} = \frac{2 + (-4)}{30} = -0.0667 \text{ or } -6.67\%$$

$$\text{Warrant HPY} = \frac{C_t + (P_E - P_B)}{P_B} = \frac{C_t + PC}{P_B} = \frac{PC}{P_B} \qquad (5\text{–}5)$$

where C_t = any cash payment received by the warrant holder during the period. Because warrants pay no dividends, the only return to an investor from owning a warrant is the change in price during the period.

Example. Assume the purchase of warrants of XYZ corporation at $3 per share, a holding period of six months, and the sale at $3.75 per share. Using Equation 5–5,

$$\text{Warrant HPY} = \frac{0 + (3.75 - 3.00)}{3.00} = \frac{0.75}{3.00} = 0.25 \text{ or } 25\%$$

Notice that C_t is zero in this case (as it could be in the case of any other asset). Also notice that the length of the holding period in this case is six months. Although one year is often used for convenience, the HPY calculation can be applied to periods of any length.

In summary, the holding period yield is valuable as a measure of return because it is all-inclusive, measuring the total return per dollar of original investment. It facilitates the comparison of asset returns over a specified period, whether the comparison is of different assets, such as stocks versus bonds, or different securities within the same type, such as several common stocks. Remember that using the HPY concept does not mean that the securities are actually sold and the gains or losses realized.

---

[3] On a total dollar basis, the HPY would be [200 + (−400)]/3000 = −6.67%.

Holding Period Return

It is often necessary to measure returns on a slightly different basis. This is particularly true when calculating a compound rate of return, or geometric mean (explained later) because negative numbers cannot be used. The **holding period return (HPR)** solves this problem by adding 1.0 to the HPY. For example, an HPY of 0.10 is equal to an HPR of 1.10, and an HPY of -0.15 is equal to an HPR of 0.85. Although HPRs may be less than 1.0, they will always be greater than zero, thereby eliminating negative numbers.

Equation 5–2 can be modified to HPR form by using the price at the end of the holding period in the numerator, rather than the change in price, as in Equation 5–6.

$$HPR = \frac{\text{Cash payments received } + \text{ Price at the end of period}}{\text{Purchase price}} \quad (5\text{–}6)$$

Example. The HPR for the bond example shown above is

$$\text{Bond HPR} = \frac{100 + 1020}{960} = 1.1667$$

Example. The HPR for the stock example is

$$\text{Stock HPR} = \frac{2 + 26}{30} = 0.9333$$

Example. The HPR for the warrant example is

$$\text{Warrant HPR} = \frac{3.75}{3.00} = 1.25$$

To convert from an HPR to an HPY, subtract 1.0 from the HPR.

Using Returns Measures

As an illustration of the calculation and use of HPYs, consider Table 5–1, which shows the Standard & Poor (S&P) 500 Stock Composite Index for the years 1926 through 1986. Included in the table are end-of-year values for the index, from which capital gains and losses can be computed, and dividends on the index, which constitute the income component. The HPYs for every year from 1927 through 1986 can be calculated as shown at the bottom of the table, where, as a demonstration of these calculations, the HPY for 1981 is calculated. In 1981, the market, as measured by the S&P 500 Composite Index, had an HPY of -4.85%, or an HPR of .9515. In 1982, in contrast, the same market index showed an HPY of 20.37%, or an HPR of 1.2037.

The HPY (or HPR) is a useful measure of return for a specified period of time. Also needed in investment analysis are statistics to describe a series of returns. For example, investing in a particular stock for 10 years or in a different stock in each of 10 years could result in 10 HPYs, which must be described by one or more statistics.

TABLE 5-1 Standard & Poor's 500 Composite Index (1941 – 1943 = 10), Dividends in Index Form and Holding Period Yields (HPYs), 1926–1986.

Year	End-of-Year Index Value	Div.	HPY%	Year	End-of-Year Index Value	Div.	HPY%
1926	13.49	0.69	—	1956	46.67	1.74	6.44
1927	17.66	0.77	36.620	1957	39.99	1.79	− 10.478
1928	24.35	0.85	42.695	1958	55.21	1.75	42.436
1929	21.45	0.97	− 7.926	1959	59.89	1.83	11.791
1930	15.34	0.98	−23.916	1960	58.11	1.95	.284
1931	8.12	0.82	−41.721	1961	71.55	2.02	26.605
1932	6.89	0.50	− 8.990	1962	63.10	2.13	− 8.833
1933	10.10	0.44	52.975	1963	75.02	2.28	22.504
1934	9.50	0.45	− 1.485	1964	84.75	2.50	16.302
1935	13.43	0.47	46.316	1965	92.43	2.72	12.271
1936	17.18	0.72	33.284	1966	80.33	2.87	− 9.986
1937	10.55	0.80	−33.935	1967	96.47	2.92	23.727
1938	13.21	0.51	30.047	1968	103.86	3.07	10.843
1939	12.49	0.62	− .757	1969	92.06	3.16	− 8.319
1940	10.58	0.67	− 9.928	1970	92.15	3.14	3.509
1941	8.69	0.71	−11.153	1971	102.09	3.07	14.118
1942	9.77	0.59	19.217	1972	118.05	3.15	18.719
1943	11.67	0.61	25.691	1973	97.55	3.38	−14.502
1944	13.28	0.64	19.280	1974	68.56	3.60	−26.028
1945	17.36	0.66	35.693	1975	90.19	3.68	36.917
1946	15.30	0.71	− 7.776	1976	107.46	4.05	23.639
1947	15.30	0.84	5.490	1977	95.10	4.67	− 7.165
1948	15.20	0.93	5.425	1978	96.11	5.07	6.393
1949	16.76	1.14	17.763	1979	107.94	5.70	18.240
1950	20.41	1.47	30.549	1980	135.76	6.16	31.480
1951	23.77	1.41	23.371	1981	122.55	6.63	− 4.847
1952	26.77	1.41	17.711	1982	140.64	6.87	20.367
1953	24.81	1.45	− 1.167	1983	164.93	7.09	22.312
1954	35.98	1.54	51.229	1984	167.24	7.53	5.966
1955	45.48	1.64	30.962	1985	211.28	7.90	31.057
				1986	242.17	8.28	18.539

$$\text{HPY\%} = \frac{(P_t - P_{t-1}) + D_t}{P_{t-1}} (100)$$

for 1981

$$\text{HPY\%} = \frac{(122.55 - 135.76) + 6.63}{135.76} (100)$$

$$= -4.85\%$$

Source: Standard & Poor's Statistical Service, *Security Price Index Record*, 1986 ed., New York: Standard & Poor's pp. 134–137. Updated from monthly issues of Standard & Poor's *Current Statistics*. Reprinted by permission of Standard & Poor's Corporation.

TABLE 5–2   Calculation of the Arithmetic and Geometric Mean for the Years 1970–1979 for the S&P 500 Stock Composite Index

Year	S&P 500 Index HPYs (%)	S&P 500 Index HPRs
1970	3.51	1.0351
1971	14.12	1.1412
1972	18.72	1.1872
1973	− 14.50	0.8550
1974	− 26.03	0.7397
1975	36.92	1.3692
1976	23.64	1.2364
1977	− 7.17	0.9283
1978	6.39	1.0639
1979	18.24	1.1824

$$\text{Arithmetic mean} = \frac{3.51 + 14.12 + 18.72 + \ldots + 18.24}{10}$$

$$= 7.38\%$$

$$\text{Geometric mean} = [(1.0351)(1.1412)(1.1872) \ldots (1.1824)]^{1/n} - 1$$

$$= (1.7534)^{1/10} - 1$$

$$= 1.0578 - 1$$

$$= 0.0578 \text{ or } 5.78\%$$

Source: Based on data in Table 5–1.

Arithmetic mean   The most familiar statistic to any investor, or individual, is the arithmetic mean. Therefore, the word *mean* will refer to the arithmetic mean unless otherwise specified. The arithmetic mean, customarily designated by the symbol $\bar{X}$ (X bar), is

$$\bar{X} = \frac{\Sigma X}{n} \tag{5–7}$$

or the sum of each of the values being considered divided by the total number of values n.

Using data from Table 5–1 for the 10 years of the 1970s ending in 1979, the arithmetic mean is calculated in Table 5–2.

Geometric mean   The arithmetic mean return is appropriate as a measure of the central tendency of a distribution consisting of returns calculated for a particular time, such as a year. However, when percentage changes in value over time are involved, the arithmetic mean of these changes can be misleading. A different mean, the **geometric mean,** is needed to accurately describe the ''true'' average rate of return over multiple periods. The geometric mean return is the most descriptive reflection of compound, cumulative returns over time. It is often used in investments and finance, its most familiar guise being "compound interest."

The geometric mean is defined as the nth root of the product resulting from multiplying a series of returns together, as in Equation 5–8.

$$G = [(1 + r_1)(1 + r_2) \ldots (1 + r_n)]^{1/n} - 1 \qquad (5\text{–}8)$$

where r is a series of returns in HPY form. Note that adding 1.0 to each return, or r, produces an HPR. HPRs are used in calculating geometric mean returns, since HPYs, which can be negative, cannot be used.[4]

Continuing the example from Table 5–1, consisting of the 10 years of data ending in 1979 for the S&P 500, the geometric mean would be as shown in Table 5–2.

$$G = [(1.0351)(1.1412)(1.1872)(.855) \ldots (1.1824)]^{1/10} - 1$$

$$= 1.0578 - 1$$

$$= 0.0578 \text{ or } 5.78\%$$

The geometric mean reflects compound, cumulative returns over time. Thus, $1 invested in the S&P 500 Composite Index would have compounded at an annual rate of 5.78% over the period 1970–1979. Notice that this geometric average rate of return is considerably lower than the arithmetic average rate of return of 7.38%. The geometric mean will always be less than the arithmetic mean unless the values being considered are identical. The spread between the two depends on the dispersion of the distribution: the greater the dispersion, the greater the spread between the two means.

Arithmetic versus geometric mean   Which mean should be used to measure the performance of the market over multiple periods? The answer depends on the investor's objective. The arithmetic mean is a useful measure of average (typical) performance over single periods, whereas the geometric mean is a better measure of the change in wealth over more than a single period.

As an illustration of how the arithmetic mean can be misleading in investments, consider the following data that show the movements in price for two stocks over two successive holding periods. Both stocks have a beginning price of $10. Stock A rises to $20 in period 1 and then declines to $10 in period 2. Stock B falls to $8 in period 1 and then rises 50% to $12 in period 2. For stock A, the indicated average arithmetic rate of return per year is 25%. This is clearly not sensible because the price of stock A at the end of period 2 is $10, the same as the beginning price. The geometric mean calculation gives the correct average of 0% per year.

---

[4] An alternative method of calculating the geometric mean is to find the log of each X, sum them, divide by n, and take the antilog.

In the case of stock B, the arithmetic average of the annual percentage changes is 15%. However, if 15% were actually earned each period, the ending value in period 2 would be $10 \times 1.15 \times 1.15 = \$13.23$. We know that this is not correct because the price at the end of period 2 is $12. The annual geometric rate of return, 9.5%, produces the correct price at the end of period 2: $10 \times 1.095 \times 1.095 = \$12$.

As these simple examples demonstrate, over multiple periods the geometric mean provides the true average rate of growth; that is, the rate at which an invested dollar grows.

Stock	Period 1	Period 2	Annual Arithmetic Rate of Return	Annual Geometric Rate of Return
A	$20	$10	$[100\% + (-50\%)]/2 = 25\%$	$[2.0(.5)]^{1/2} - 1 = 0\%$
B	$ 8	$12	$[-20\% + (50\%)]/2 = 15\%$	$[.8(1.5)]^{1/2} - 1 = 9.5\%$

Compounding and discounting The use of compounding in the previous section points out the importance of this concept, and its complement, discounting. Both are important in investment analysis and are used often. Compounding involves **future values** resulting from compound interest—earning interest on interest. **Present value** (discounting) is the value today of a dollar to be received in the future. Such dollars are not comparable because of the time value of money; in order to be comparable, they must be discounted back to the present. Tables are readily available for both compounding and discounting, and calculators and computers make these calculations a simple matter. These tables are available at the end of this text.

Estimating Returns

A frequency distribution is used to describe a group of numbers representing past events, that is, actual occurrences. Frequency distributions of returns summarize some sample data. Analysts often refer to the realized returns for a security, or class of securities, over time.

Realized returns are important, particularly in that they help investors to form expectations about future returns. In the final analysis, however, investors must concern themselves with their best estimate of return over the next year, or six months, or whatever. What about the estimation of returns, which, realistically, is what investors must contend with in managing their portfolios?

Holding Period Yield Again
The HPY is applicable whether measuring realized returns or estimating future (expected) returns. It considers everything the investor can expect to receive over any specified future period; therefore, because it is inclusive, the HPY is useful in conceptualizing the estimated returns from securities.

To estimate the returns from various securities, investors must estimate the future streams of payments these securities are likely to provide. The basis for doing this for bonds and stocks will be covered in their respective chapters. For now, it is sufficient to remind ourselves of the uncertainty of estimates of the future, a problem emphasized at the outset of our discussion in Chapter 1.

Dealing with Uncertainty

The future is uncertain, which means that the returns expected from securities involves risk. The future return is not known but must be estimated; to repeat, it is an expected return and it may or may not actually be realized. An investor may expect the HPY on a particular security to be 0.10 for the coming year, but in truth this is only a "point estimate." Risk, or the chance of an unexpected return, is involved when investment decisions are made.

Probability distributions To deal with the uncertainty of returns, investors need to think explicitly about a security's distribution of probable HPYs. In other words, investors need to keep in mind that though they may expect a security to return 10%, for example, this is only a one-point estimate of the entire range of possibilities. Given that investors must deal with the uncertain future, a number of possible returns can, and will, occur.

In the case of a Treasury bond paying a fixed rate of interest, only one outcome is possible for the next interest payment. Barring total collapse of the economic system, the interest payment will be made with 100% certainty; that is, its probability of occurrence is 1.0, because no other outcome is possible. With the possibility of two or more outcomes, which is the norm for common stocks, each possible likely outcome must be considered and a probability of its occurrence assessed. The result of considering these outcomes and their probabilities together is a probability distribution; that is, the specification of the likely returns that may occur and the probabilities associated with these likely returns.

Probabilities represent the likelihood of various outcomes and are typically expressed as a decimal (sometimes fractions are used). The sum of the probabilities of all possible outcomes must be 1.0 because they must completely describe all of the (perceived) likely occurrences.

How are these probabilities and associated outcomes obtained? In the final analysis, they are subjective estimates. Past occurrences (frequencies) are usually relied on heavily in estimating the probabilities. However, the past must be modified for any changes expected in the future.

Probability distributions can be either discrete or continuous. With a discrete probability distribution, a probability is assigned to each possible outcome. In Figure 5–1a, five possible HPYs are assumed for a stock for next year. Each of these five possible outcomes has an associated probability, with the sum equal to 1.0.

With a continuous probability distribution, as shown in Figure 5–1b, an

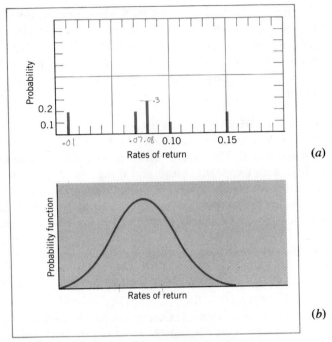

FIGURE 5–1 (*a*) **A discrete probability distribution.**
(*b*) **A continuous probability distribution.**

infinite number of possible outcomes exist. Because probability is now measured as the area under the curve in Figure 5–1*b*, the emphasis is on the probability that a particular outcome is within some range of values.

The most familiar continuous distribution is the normal distribution depicted in Figure 5-1*b*. This is the well-known "bell-shaped curve" often used in statistics. It is a two-parameter distribution in that the mean and the variance fully describe it.

To describe the single most likely outcome from a particular probability distribution, it is necessary to calculate its **expected value,** or expected return. The expected value is the average of all possible outcomes, where each outcome is weighted by its respective probability of occurrence. Expected value for any security or portfolio *i* is, therefore,

$$EV_i = \sum_{i=1}^{n} X_i \, P(X_i) \tag{5–9}$$

where

EV_i = the expected value of the distribution for security or portfolio *i*.
X_i = the value of the *i*th possible outcome.
$P(X_i)$ = the probability of the *i*th possible outcome.
n = the number of possible outcomes.

The expected value of the discrete probability distribution in Figure 5–1a is 0.08.[5]

The Concept of Risk

Risk and return go together in investments and finance. It is not sensible to talk about returns without talking about risk because investment decisions involve a risk–return trade-off. Investors must constantly be aware of the risk they are assuming, know what it can do to their investment decisions, and be prepared for the consequences.

Risk was defined in Chapter 1 as the chance that the actual outcome from an investment will differ from the expected outcome. Specifically, what is of concern to most investors is that the actual outcome will be less than the expected outcome. The more variable the possible outcomes that can occur—that is, the broader the range of possible outcomes—the greater the risk.

It is important to remember how expected return and risk go together. An investor cannot reasonably expect larger returns without being willing to assume larger risks. Consider the investor who wishes to avoid any risk (on a practical basis). Such an investor can deposit money in an insured savings account, thereby earning a guaranteed return of a known amount. However, this return will be fixed and the investor cannot earn more than this rate. Although risk is effectively eliminated, the chance of a larger return is also. To have the opportunity to earn a larger return, investors must be willing to assume larger risks.

Consider, from Table 5–1, an investor who purchased stocks at the beginning of 1972 and planned to "cash in" after three years. The HPYs for 1972, 1973, and 1974 were 18.72, −14.50, and −26.03, respectively. The average annual arithmetic return for these three years was −7.27%. Table 5–2 showed that for the years 1970 through 1979 the average annual arithmetic rate of return for the S&P 500 Index was +7.38%. Therefore, this hypothetical investor suffered an average annual arithmetic loss over those three years that was almost exactly equal to the average annual arithmetic gain for the decade of the 1970s. Such is the nature of risk!

Sources of Risk

What makes a financial asset risky? Traditionally, investors have talked about several sources of risk, such as interest rate risk and market risk. The

---

[5] $EV_i = \sum_{i=1}^{n} X_i P(X_i) = 0.01(0.2) + 0.07(0.2) + 0.08(0.3) + 0.10(0.1) + 0.15(0.2) = 0.08.$

sources of risk applicable to bonds and stocks will be discussed separately in Chapters 6 and 8, but only briefly now. Our purpose here is simply to point out that the total risk for a financial asset is a function of one or more of these sources.

Interest Rate Risk

This is the variability in a security's return resulting from changes in the level of interest rates. Such changes affect all securities inversely; that is, other things being equal, security prices move inversely to interest rates. The reason for this is tied up with the valuation of securities, a subject discussed later. Interest rate risk affects bonds more directly than common stocks, and is a major risk faced by all bondholders. As interest rates change, bond prices change in an inverse direction.[6]

Market Risk

Market risk is the variability in returns due to fluctuations in the overall market—that is, the aggregate stock market. All securities are exposed to market risk, although it affects primarily common stocks.

Market risk includes a wide range of factors exogenous to securities themselves, including recessions, wars, structural changes in the economy, and changes in consumer preferences.

Inflation Risk

A factor affecting all securities is purchasing power risk, or the chance that the purchasing power of invested dollars will decline. With uncertain inflation, the real (inflation-adjusted) return involves risk even if the nominal return is safe (e.g., a Treasury bond). This risk is related to interest rate risk since interest rates generally rise as inflation increases because lenders demand additional inflation premiums to compensate for the loss of purchasing power.

Business Risk

The risk of doing business in a particular industry or environment is called business risk. For example, USX faces unique problems as it competes in the steel business. Similarly, General Motors faces unique problems as a result of such developments as the global oil situation and Japanese imports.

Financial Risk

Financial risk is associated with the use of debt financing by companies. The larger the proportion of assets financed by debt (as opposed to equity), the larger the variability in the returns, other things being equal. Financial risk involves the concept of financial leverage.

---

[6]Interest rate risk is examined in detail in Chapter 6.

Liquidity Risk

This is the risk associated with the particular secondary market in which a security trades. An investment that can be bought or sold quickly and without significant price concession is considered liquid. The more uncertainty about the time element and the price concession, the greater the liquidity risk. A Treasury bill has little or no liquidity risk whereas a small OTC stock may have substantial liquidity risk.

Total Risk

Investors must do more than simply be aware of the sources of risk. They must be able to quantify risk; that is, risk must be measured. We will therefore discuss the measurement and estimation of the total risk to an investor from one or more financial assets and then do the same for a specific measure of risk that is a widely discussed and used cornerstone of modern portfolio theory.

Measuring Total Risk

Risk is often associated with the dispersion in the likely outcomes. Dispersion refers to **variability**. Risk is assumed to arise out of variability, which is consistent with our definition of risk as the chance that the actual outcome of an investment will differ from the expected outcome. If an asset's return has no variability, in effect it has no risk. Thus, a one-year Treasury bill purchased to yield 10% and held to maturity will, in fact, yield (a nominal) 10%. No other outcome is possible barring default by the U.S. government, a possibility not considered reasonable.

Consider an investor analyzing a series of returns (HPYs) on the major types of financial assets over some period of years. Knowing the mean of this series is not enough. The investor needs to know something about the variability in the returns. A **histogram** presents a frequency distribution pictorially, using a vertical bar for each class in a frequency distribution. The vertical axis of such a diagram shows the frequency (or relative frequency) and the horizontal axis represents the value of the class. Figure 5–2 shows the histograms (distributions) of returns for major financial assets for the period 1926–1986. Common stocks show the largest variability (dispersion) in returns, with "small" common stocks showing even greater variability.[7] Corporate bonds have a much smaller variability and therefore a more compact distribution. Long-term government bonds are less risky, and Treasury bills the least.[8] These distributions are therefore even more compact.

---

[7] In the Ibbotson–Sinquefield analysis, "size" refers to the capitalization (price times number of shares outstanding). The smallest quintile of NYSE stocks, based on capitalization, is chosen to represent the equities of smaller companies.

[8] The reason for the distribution of Treasury bonds, which have no practical risk of default,

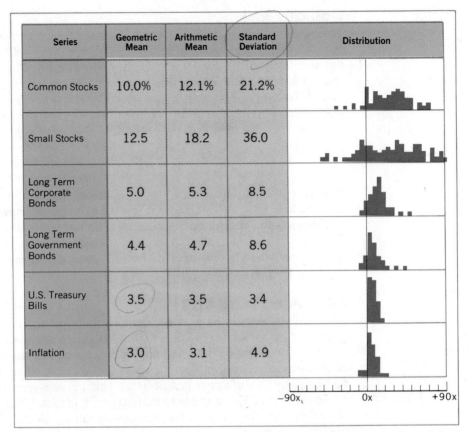

Series	Geometric Mean	Arithmetic Mean	Standard Deviation	Distribution
Common Stocks	10.0%	12.1%	21.2%	
Small Stocks	12.5	18.2	36.0	
Long Term Corporate Bonds	5.0	5.3	8.5	
Long Term Government Bonds	4.4	4.7	8.6	
U.S. Treasury Bills	3.5	3.5	3.4	
Inflation	3.0	3.1	4.9	

FIGURE 5–2 **Average annual geometric and arithmetic returns on major financial assets plus inflation, 1926–1986**
Source: Ibbotson, Roger G., and Rex A. Sinquefield, *Stocks, Bonds, Bills, and Inflation (SSBI),* 1982, updated in *SSBI 1987 Yearbook,* Ibbotson Associates, Chicago, 1987.

The risk of these distributions can be assessed with an absolute measure of dispersion, or variability. The most commonly used measure of dispersion over some period of years is the variance or its square root, the standard deviation. The variance (or standard deviation) measures the deviation of each observation from the mean of the observations and is a reliable measure of variability because all the information in a sample is used.

The variance (**standard deviation**) is a measure of the total risk of an asset or a portfolio. It captures the total variability in the asset's or portfolio's return, whatever the source(s) of that variability.

The variance and standard deviation can be calculated as

is that this is a distribution of annual returns, where negative numbers are possible. Thus, a Treasury bond purchased at $1000 on January 1 could decline to, say, $900 by December 31, resulting in a negative HPY.

$$s^2 = \frac{\Sigma(X - \bar{X})^2}{n - 1} \qquad\qquad (5\text{--}10)$$

$$s = \sqrt{s^2} \qquad\qquad (5\text{--}11)$$

where

s^2 = variance.

s = standard deviation.

X = each observation in the sample.

$\bar{X}$ = the mean of the observations.

n = the number of returns in the sample.

Knowing the returns from the sample, one can calculate the variance or standard deviation fairly easily. As an example, the standard deviation of the 10 HPYs (1970–1979) for the Standard & Poor's 500 Index, as shown in Table 5–2, can be calculated as follows:

Year	HPY (%), X	$X - \bar{X}$	$(X - \bar{X})^2$
1970	3.51	−3.87	14.98
1971	14.12	6.74	45.43
1972	18.72	11.34	128.6
1973	−14.50	−21.88	478.73
1974	−26.03	−33.41	1116.23
1975	36.92	29.54	872.61
1976	23.64	16.26	264.39
1977	−7.17	−14.55	211.70
1978	6.39	−.99	.98
1979	18.24	10.86	117.94

$$\Sigma(X - \bar{X})^2 = 3251.59$$

$$\frac{3251.59}{9} = 361.29$$

$$(361.29)^{1/2} = 19.01\%$$

The variance is the standard deviation squared. The variance and the standard deviation are similar and can be used for the same purposes; specifically, in investment analysis, both are used as measures of risk. The standard deviation, however, is used more often.

Referring back to Figure 5–2, notice the standard deviations for each of the listed assets. The standard deviation reflects the dispersion of the returns over the 61-year period covered in the data. The histograms clearly show the wide dispersion in the returns from common stocks compared with bonds and Treasury bills. Furthermore, smaller common stocks (i.e., the smallest quintile of stocks on the NYSE, based on market values) can logically be expected to be riskier than all common stocks taken together, and the histogram shows a wider dispersion. Notice how the standard deviations reflect this information. Common stocks had a standard deviation of returns of 21.2%, more than twice that of bonds and six times that of Treasury bills.

Common stocks are more risky, with more variable returns (greater dispersion), and this is reflected in their standard deviation. Again, the smallest quintile of NYSE stocks is even more risky; therefore, the standard deviation is considerably higher—36.0%—than the 21.2% for all stocks taken together.

In summary, the standard deviation of return measures the total risk of one security or the total risk of a portfolio of securities. The historical standard deviation can be calculated for individual securities or portfolios of securities using HPYs for some specified period of time. This ex post value is useful in evaluating the total risk that occurred for a particular historical period and in estimating the total risk that is expected to prevail over some future period, a subject to which we now turn.

Estimating Total Risk

To estimate the total risk expected over some future time period the standard deviation is used once again. In this discussion we are concerned with the total risk expected to prevail over some future time period, which may differ (sometimes significantly) from that which occurred in the past.

To measure the expected variability in outcomes, probability distributions can be used. The standard deviation is a measure of the spread or dispersion in the probability distribution. The larger this dispersion, the larger the standard deviation.

To calculate the standard deviation from the probability distribution, first calculate the expected value of the distribution using Equation 5–9. Essentially the same procedure used previously to measure risk is also used to estimate risk, but now the probabilities associated with the outcomes must be included, as in Equation 5–12.

$$s = \sqrt{\sum_{i=1}^{n} [(X_i - EV_i)^2 P(X_i)]} \tag{5-12}$$

where all terms are as defined previously.

The standard deviation of the hypothetical stock i's returns shown in Figure 5–2a is calculated as follows:

(1) Possible Return	(2) Probability	(3) (1) × (2)	(4) $X_i - EV_i$	(5) $(X_i - EV_i)^2$	(6) $(X_i - EV_i)^2 P(X_i)$
0.01	0.2	0.002	−0.07	0.0049	0.00098
0.07	0.2	0.030	−0.01	0.0001	0.00002
0.08	0.3	0.024	0	0.0000	0.00000
0.10	0.1	0.010	0.02	0.0004	0.00004
0.15	0.2	0.014	0.07	0.0049	0.00098
	1.0	0.080			0.00202

$$s = (0.00202)^{1/2} = 0.0449$$

The standard deviation, combined with the normal distribution referred to earlier, can provide some useful information about the dispersion. In a normal distribution, the probability that a particular outcome will be above (or below) a specified value can be determined. With 1 standard deviation on either side of the expected value of the distribution, 68.3% of the outcomes will be encompassed; that is, there is a 68.3% probability that the actual outcome will be within 1 (plus or minus) standard deviation of the expected value. The probabilities are 95% and 99% that the actual outcome will be within 2 or 3 standard deviations, respectively, of the expected value.

Calculating a standard deviation ex ante (before the fact) using probability distributions involves subjective estimates of the probabilities and the likely returns. However, this cannot be avoided because future returns are uncertain. The prices of securities are based on investors' expectations about the future. The relevant standard deviation in this situation is the ex ante standard deviation and not the ex post based on realized returns. Although standard deviations based on realized returns are often used as proxies for ex ante standard deviations, investors should be careful by remembering that the past cannot always be extrapolated into the future without modifications. Ex post standard deviations may be convenient, but they are subject to errors.

One important point about the estimation of standard deviation is the distinction between individual securities and portfolios. Standard deviations for well-diversified portfolios are reasonably steady across time, and therefore historical calculations may be fairly reliable in projecting the future. Moving from well diversified portfolios to individual securities, however, renders historical figures much less reliable.

Components of Total Risk

The standard deviation is a statistical measure of variability and, as such, is a proper measure of the variability in the returns from securities. However, standard deviation measures total risk, whereas only part of the total risk may be relevant in portfolios held by investors.

The traditional sources of risk identified previously as causing variability in returns seem to be of two general types: those that are pervasive in nature, such as market risk or interest rate risk, and those that are specific to a particular security issue, such as business or financial risk. Therefore, a logical way to divide total risk into its components is to make a distinction between a general (market) component and a specific (issuer) component. These two components are referred to in investment analysis as systematic risk and unsystematic risk. These two components are additive, so that

Total risk = Systematic risk + Unsystematic risk

The variability in a security's total returns that is not related to overall market variability is called the **unsystematic (nonmarket) risk.** This is the risk that is unique to a particular security.

Unsystematic risk is related to such factors as business and financial risk.

Although all securities tend to have some unsystematic risk, it is generally referred to in connection with common stocks.

As will be shown in Part Seven on portfolio management, an investor can construct a diversified portfolio and eliminate part of the total risk, the diversifiable or nonmarket part (unsystematic part). What is left is the nondiversifiable portion, or the market risk (systematic part). This part of the risk is inescapable because no matter how well an investor diversifies, the risk of the overall market cannot be avoided. If the stock market declines sharply, most stocks will be adversely affected; if it rises strongly, as in the last few months of 1982, most stocks will appreciate in value. These movements occur regardless of what any single investor does. Clearly, market risk is of critical importance to all investors.

Systematic (Market) Risk

Variability in a security's total returns that is directly associated with overall movements in the general market or economy is called **systematic** or **market risk.** Virtually all securities have some systematic risk, whether bonds or stocks, because systematic risk directly encompasses interest rate risk, market risk, and inflation risk. In the discussion, however, the emphasis will be on the systematic risk of common stocks. In this case, systematic risk is that part of the variability correlated with the variability of the stock market as a whole.

A measure is needed of this unavoidable systematic or nondiversifiable risk. Based on modern portfolio theory, the **beta** (β) has emerged as such a measure. Beta's usefulness as a measure of risk is briefly discussed here. The measurement of risk for common stocks will be discussed in Chapter 8.

Beta is a relative measure of risk—the risk of an individual stock relative to the market portfolio of all stocks.[9] If the security's returns move more (less) than the market's returns as the latter changes, the security is said to be more (less) volatile than the market. For example, a security whose returns rise or fall on average 15% when the market return rises or falls 10% is said to be an aggressive security.

Beta is the slope of the regression line relating a security's returns to those of the market. If the slope of this relationship for a particular security is a 45-degree angle, as shown for security B in Figure 5–3, beta is 1.0. This means that for every 1% change in the market's return, *on average* this security's returns change 1%. If the line is higher, beta is higher, meaning that the **volatility** (market risk) is greater. For example, security A's beta of 1.5 indicates that, on average, security returns are 1.5 times as volatile as market returns, both up and down. If the line is less steep than the 45-degree

---

[9]The market as a whole can be thought of in terms of a market index such as the Standard & Poor 500 Composite Index or the Dow Jones Industrial Index.

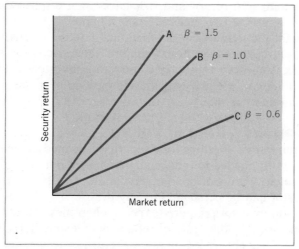

FIGURE 5–3 **Risk–return trade-offs representing betas of 1.5 (A), 1.0 (B), and 0.5 (C).**

line, beta is less than 1.0; this indicates that, on average, a stock's returns have less volatility than the market as a whole. For example, security C's beta of 0.6 indicates that stock returns move up or down generally only 60% as much as the market as a whole.

In summary, the aggregate market has a beta of 1.0. More volatile (risky) stocks have larger betas and less volatile (risky) stocks have betas smaller than 1.0. As a relative measure of risk, beta is very convenient. If an investor is considering a particular stock and is informed that its beta is 1.9, this investor can recognize immediately that the stock is very risky, in relation to the average stock, because the average beta for all stocks is 1.0. Many brokerage houses and investment advisory services report betas as part of the total information given for individual stocks. For example, *The Value Line Investment Survey* referred to in Chapter 4 reports the beta for each stock covered, as do brokerage firms such as Merrill Lynch.

The Risk–Return Relationship

In Chapter 1 and again in this chapter, the emphasis has been on how risk and return go together in investments. The foundation of investment decisions, the risk–return trade-off, was shown in Chapter 1 (Figure 1–1). That trade-off shows a positive linear relationship between expected return and risk, with expected return increasing as risk increases. Again, rational risk-averse investors will not willingly assume more risk unless they expect to receive additional (and adequate) return.

Now that both return and risk have been discussed in this chapter, it remains to put the two together, as in Chapter 1. However, this will now be done slightly differently in order to facilitate the discussion and analysis in subsequent chapters. Although the previous discussion about expected return–risk is entirely appropriate and valid, investors usually think in terms of a required rate of return; therefore, it is necessary to relate risk and required rate of return.

The Required Rate of Return

The **required rate of return** for a security is defined as the minimum expected rate of return needed to induce an investor to purchase it. That is, given its risk, a security must offer some minimum expected return before a particular investor can be persuaded to buy it.

What do investors require (expect) when they invest? First of all, investors can earn a riskless rate of return by investing in riskless assets such as Treasury bills. This risk-free rate of return is designated RF. Investors will expect this risk-free rate as a minimum; furthermore, they will expect a risk premium to compensate them for the additional risk assumed by investing in a risky asset. These two components constitute the required rate of return.

The risk-free rate of return   The risk-free rate of return, RF, such as the return on Treasury bills, is a nominal return. It consists of a real rate of return and an inflation premium. The real rate of return (i.e., the pure time value of money) is the basic exchange rate in the economy, or the price necessary to induce someone to forego consumption and save in order to consume more in the next period. This real rate of interest is defined within a context of no uncertainty and no inflation. What matters are the investment opportunities available to investors, which are dependent on the real growth rate of the economy.[10]

Because inflation, in fact, is present in the economy, the nominal RF rate must contain a premium for expected inflation. Investors strive to actually realize the rate of exchange between present and future consumption, which assumes no price changes. If they anticipate a rise in prices, an additional premium is required to maintain the real rate of interest. For example, if the real rate of interest is about 3% (a number often used for this purpose) and investors anticipate 5% inflation for the next year, the risk-free rate should *approximate* 8%. Such a premium should maintain the purchasing power of the real rate of interest to be earned over the next year, 3%. In summary, as an approximation[11]

---

[10] The economy's real growth rate is a function of the basic determinants of economic growth: (1) change in the size of the labor force and the number of hours worked and (2) the productivity of the labor force.

[11] The actual calculation involves adding 1.0 to both the real rate and the inflation premium, multiplying the two together, and subtracting the 1.0 from the product. In the example given, $[(1 + 0.03)(1 + 0.05)] - 1.0 = 0.0815$ or 8.15%.

$$\text{Risk-free rate of return} = \text{Real rate of return} + \text{Inflation premium} \quad (5\text{--}13)$$

The risk premium   In addition to the risk-free rate of return available from riskless assets, rational risk-averse investors purchasing a risky asset expect to be compensated for this additional risk. There would be no reason for risk-averse investors to purchase a risky asset that offered no return beyond that available from a riskless asset. Therefore, risky assets must offer **risk premiums** above and beyond the riskless rate of return. And the greater the risk of the asset, the greater the promised risk premium must be.

The risk premium must reflect all the uncertainty involved in the asset. Thinking of risk in terms of its traditional sources, such components as the business risk and the financial risk of a corporation would certainly contribute to the risk premium demanded by investors for purchasing the common stock of the corporation. After all, the risk to the investor is that the expected income (return) will not be realized because of unforeseen events. The particular business that a company is in clearly will affect significantly the risk to the investor. One has only to look at the automobile and steel industries in the last few years to see this. And the financial decisions that a firm makes (or fails to make) will also affect the riskiness of the stock.

Understanding the required rate of return   The required rate of return for any investment opportunity can be expressed as in Equation 5–14.

$$\text{Required rate of return} = \text{Risk-free rate} + \text{Risk premium} \quad (5\text{--}14)$$

It is important to note that there are many financial assets, and therefore many different required rates of return. The average required rate of return on bonds is different from the average required rate of return on preferred stocks, and both are different from that generally required from common stocks, warrants, or puts and calls. Furthermore, within a particular asset category such as common stocks, there are many required rates of return. Common stocks cover a relatively wide range of risk, from conservative utility stocks to small, risky, high-technology stocks.

It is also important to be aware that the level of required rates of return changes over time. For example, required rates of return change as inflationary expectations change because the inflation premium is a component of the risk-free rate of return, which in turn is a component of the required rate of return. Required rates of return were higher at year-end 1980 than at year-end 1982 because of the large difference in inflationary expectations between those two periods.

The overall level of required rates of return also changes as the risk premiums change. Investor pessimism will increase the risk premium and the required rate; investor optimism lowers both.

Risk and Required Rate of Return

Figure 5–4 integrates the required rate of return with risk. Although this figure closely resembles Figure 1–1, there are two important differences.

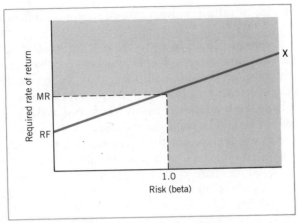

FIGURE 5–4 **The trade-off between the required rate of return and risk (beta)—the capital asset pricing model or security market line.**

1. Required rate of return is on the vertical axis, whereas expected return was used in Figure 1–1. Remember, however, that the required return is simply the minimum expected return that will induce investors to purchase a security.
2. Risk is still on the horizontal axis, but now it is measured specifically as beta, the measure of relative market risk.

Figure 5–4 shows that the intercept on the vertical axis remains RF. The relationship between the required rate of return and risk (beta) is linear, as represented by the line RFX. Securities with high (low) betas have high (low) risk, and therefore high (low) required rates of return.

The market as a whole (as proxied by an index such as the Standard & Poor 500 Composite Index) has a beta of 1.0. Its required rate of return is MR, as shown by the dotted line in Figure 5–4 extending from the linear trade-off where a beta of 1.0 is represented. This required rate of return on the market index, MR, equals the expected rate of return on the market index when the market is in equilibrium. That is, assuming that the forces of supply and demand in the market have stabilized, the expected return for the market is equal to the required return. Although both rates can and do change over time, in an efficient market it is reasonable to assume equilibrium unless there are indications to the contrary.

The linear trade-off depicted in Figure 5–4 is a very important concept in investments and finance. This relationship is expressed in equation form as

$$RR_i = RF + B_i(MR - RF) \qquad (5–15)$$

where

RR_i = the required (expected) rate of return for asset i.
RF = the risk-free rate of return.

B_i = the beta for security i.

MR = the required (expected) rate of return on the stock market as a whole.

Equation 5–15 is called the **capital asset pricing model (CAPM)**. It is also referred to (in Figure 5–4) as the **security market line (SML)**. Because of its importance, it will be discussed both here and in other parts of the text.

Capital Asset Pricing Model (CAPM)

The CAPM relates the required rate of return for any security i with the relevant risk measure for that security, its beta. Beta is the relevant measure of risk that cannot be diversified away in a portfolio of securities and, as such, is the measure that investors should consider in their portfolio management decision process.

The CAPM is a simple but elegant statement. It says that the required rate of return on an asset is a function of the two components of the required rate of return—the risk-free rate and the risk premium. Thus,

$$RR_i = \text{Risk-free rate} + \text{Risk premium}$$

$$= RF + B_i(MR - RF)$$

The CAPM provides an explicit measure of the risk premium. It is the product of the beta for a particular security i and the **market risk premium,** $MR - RF$.[12] Thus,

$$\text{Risk premium for security i} = B_i(\text{market risk premium})$$

$$= B_i(MR - RF) \qquad (5-16)$$

Equation 5–16 shows that securities with betas greater than the market beta of 1.0 should have larger risk premiums than that of the average stock and therefore, when added to RF, larger required rates of return.[13] This is exactly what investors should want since beta is a measure of risk, and greater risk should be accompanied by greater return. Conversely, securities with betas less than that of the market are less risky and should have required rates of return lower than that for the market as a whole. This will be the indicated result from the CAPM because the risk premium for the security will be less than the market risk premium and, when added to RF, will produce a lower required rate of return for the security.[14]

---

[12] The slope of the line RFX in Figure 5–4 is the market risk premium, $MR - RF$. This is the excess return for the market as a whole; that is, the return above the risk-free rate for assuming the risk of the market as a whole. The market risk premium reflects the additional return that investors usually expect for buying risky securities rather than the riskless asset.

[13] The assumption throughout this discussion is that MR is greater than RF. This is the only reasonable assumption to make because the CAPM is concerned with expected returns (i.e., ex ante returns). After the fact, this assumption may not hold for particular periods; that is, over historical periods such as a year RF has exceeded MR, which is sometimes negative.

[14] The risk premium on the security will be less than the market risk premium because we are multiplying by a beta less than 1.0.

Conclusions on Risk and Return

Return and risk go together. Investors expect larger returns to be associated with larger risks. They must anticipate a required rate of return before they can be induced to purchase a security. This required rate is related to risk both intuitively—clearly, risk and return go together—and formally through the CAPM.

Summary

The purpose of this chapter is to point out how return and risk go together in investments—indeed, these two parameters are the underlying basis of the subject. Everything an investor does, or is concerned with, is tied directly or indirectly to risk and return.

The term *return* can be used in different ways. It is important to distinguish between realized (ex post or historical) return and expected (ex ante or anticipated) return.

The two components of return are income and price change. These two components are captured in the holding period yield, a percentage return concept that can be used for any security. A variation of this concept is the holding period return, which adds 1.0 to the holding period yield. The latter is used when calculating the geometric mean of a series of returns, which measures the compound rate of return over time. The arithmetic mean, on the other hand, is simply the average return for a series and is used to measure the typical performance for a single period.

Historical returns can be described in terms of a frequency distribution and their variability measured by use of the standard deviation. When returns are estimated over the future, it is important to remember the uncertainty involved. Probability distributions can be used to express the possible outcomes.

Risk is the other side of the coin—risk and expected return should always be considered together. An investor cannot reasonably expect to earn large returns without assuming greater risks.

The components of risk have traditionally been categorized into interest rate risk, market risk, inflation risk, business risk, financial risk, and liquidity risk. The modern components of risk are systematic risk attributable to exogenous (market) forces, and the unsystematic risk attributable to unique (nonmarket) forces. Unsystematic risk can be diversified away.

Risk must be measured. The two often used measures of risk in investments are the standard deviation and the beta. After the expected value of a probability distribution is calculated as the weighted average of all possible outcomes, the standard deviation can be estimated using probabilities. It provides useful information about the distribution of returns and aids investors in assessing the possible outcomes of an investment.

A modern measure of risk is the beta coefficient, or the volatility in a security's returns. Beta is a relative measure of risk, relating the movements in the return of a given security to the movements in the market's returns. A high beta (compared to the market beta of 1.0) indicates larger volatility and larger risk. Like standard deviation, beta must be estimated over the future.

Return and risk must be considered together, and a risk–return trade-off diagram is a natural way of doing this. This diagram relates the required rate of return demanded by investors to the risk actually assumed in a portfolio—the systematic risk represented by beta. The required rate of return consists of the risk-free rate of return available to investors without assuming risk plus a risk premium. The risk-free rate of return is composed of a real rate of return plus an inflation premium. The risk premium is the beta for a security times the market's risk premium.

The formal statement relating the required rate of return for a security to its risk, as represented by beta, is called the capital asset pricing model (CAPM) or security market line (SML). The CAPM is a very sensible and logical concept, which states that the required rate of return is related to the relevant risk of an asset, given the risk-free rate of return available to all investors. Higher risk requires a higher expected return.

Key Words

Beta	Present value
Capital asset pricing model	Required rate of return
Capital gain	Risk premium
Capital loss	Security market line
Expected value	Standard deviation
Future value	Systematic (market) risk
Geometric mean	Unsystematic (nonmarket) risk
Histogram	Variability
Holding Period Return (HPR)	Volatility
Holding Period Yield (HPY)	Yield
Market risk premium	

QUESTIONS AND PROBLEMS

1. Distinguish between historical return and expected return.
2. How long must an asset be held in order to calculate an HPY?

3. Assume an investor in a 28% marginal tax bracket buys 100 shares of a stock for $40, holds it for five months, and sells it at $50. What tax, in dollars, will be paid on the gain?

4. Define the components of total return. Can any of these components be negative?

5. Calculate HPY for the following assets:
   a. A preferred stock bought for $70 per share, held one year during which $5 per share dividends are collected, and sold for $63.
   b. A warrant bought for $11 and sold three months later for $13.
   c. A 12% bond bought for $870, held two years during which interest is collected, and sold for $930.

6. Distinguish between HPY and HPR. Calculate HPRs for the three assets in Question 5.

7. When should the geometric mean return be used to measure returns? Why will it always be less than the arithmetic mean (unless the numbers are identical)?

8. Calculate the geometric mean rate of return per year for the Standard & Poor 500 Composite Index (Table 5–1) for the years 1980 through 1985.

9. Calculate the future value of $100 at the end of 5, 10, 20, and 30 years, given an interest rate of 12%. Calculate the present value of $1 to be received at the end of those same periods, given the same interest rate.

10. What is the difference between a frequency distribution and a probability distribution?

11. Refer to Figure 5–2. How can you explain the standard deviation for riskless government bonds compared to that of corporate bonds?

12. According to Figure 5–2, common stocks have generally returned more than bonds. How, then, can they be considered more risky?

13. Distinguish between market risk and business risk. How is interest rate risk related to inflation risk?

14. Classify the six traditional sources of risk as either systematic or unsystematic types of risk.

15. Define risk. How does the use of the standard deviation as a measure of risk relate to this definition of risk?

16. Calculate the standard deviation of HPYs (from Table 5–1) for the years 1980 through 1985.

17. Why is beta a relative measure of risk? Is standard deviation?

18. Given a stock with a beta of 0.85, what would investors expect its return to do if the market rose 15%? Would it surprise you if this stock failed to do as expected?

19. How can the standard deviation for a particular stock be estimated? How reliable is the estimate for a particular stock compared with a portfolio of stocks?

20. What is meant by the required rate of return for a security? How is it related to risk?

21. What are the components of the required rate of return? What role does the inflation premium play in this concept?

22. What could cause a change in the required rate of return? When the United States experienced an oil embargo in 1974, what effect, if any, do you think this had on investors' required rates of return?
23. What is the equation for required rate of return? Which variable in the equation would appear to be the most difficult to obtain?
24. In Figure 5–4, do you think the line RFX could slope downward?
25. What is the significance of the CAPM? What is the difference between the market's risk premium and an individual security's risk premium?

EXTENDED PROBLEMS, WITH EXAMPLES

I. **Example.** The following information is for XPO, a hypothetical company.

Year	(1) End-of-Year Price (P_t)	(2) Calendar-Year Dividends (D_t)	(3) Capital Gain $(P_t - P_{t-1})$	(4) Total Return $(2) + (3) = $ TR	(5) Holding Period Yield % $[100(4) \div P_{t-1}]$
19X1	$24.70	$1.105	—	—	1.20
19X2	27.20	1.26	$2.50	$ 3.76	15.22
19X3	36.30	1.42	9.10	10.52	38.68
19X4	35.75	1.58	−.55	1.03	2.84
19X5	38.25	1.62			

The three blanks for 19X5 are to be calculated.

A. Capital gain (capital loss) and income. The 19X5 income is the calendar-year dividend of $1.62. The 19X5 capital gain (loss) is the end-of-year price in 19X5 minus the end-of-year 19X4 price—$38.25 minus $35.75 = $2.50. The total return for calendar-year 19X5 is equal to Income + Capital gain = $1.62 + $2.50 = $4.12. Had you bought XPO on January 1, 19X5 for $35.75 per share and held for the calendar year, you would have had a total return of $4.12 per share.

B. What was this return (r) in percentage form (r%)?

$$\text{HPY} = \frac{\text{TR}}{P_{t-1}} = \frac{\$4.12}{\$35.75} = 0.1152 = r, \ r\% = 100r = 11.52\%$$

C. The same result is obtained as

$$r = \frac{D_{X5}}{P_{X4}} + \frac{PC}{P_{X4}} = \frac{\$1.62}{\$35.75} + \frac{\$2.50}{\$35.75} = 0.0453147 + 0.069930 \approx 0.1152$$

$$= r, r\% = 11.52$$

Problem 1. With the additional information that the price at the end of calendar-year 19X0 was $25.50, show that the values for 19X1 in the above example are (A) capital gain $= -\$0.80$, and total return is $0.305. The HPY% is equal to 1.20%.

Problem 2. For IBM, for the years 19X0 through 19X5, the values for columns 1 and 2 are provided. Calculate the capital gain (loss) and total return for the years 19X1–19X5 (columns 3 and 4 from above example), and confirm the 19X3 and 19X4 HPYs.

Year (t)	(1) End-of-Year Price (P_t)	(2) Calendar-Year Dividends (D_t)	HPY%
19X0	$ 74.60	$2.88	—
19X1	64.30	3.44	− 9.2%
19X2	67.70	3.44	10.6
19X3	56.70	3.44	−11.2
19X4	96.25	3.44	75.8
19X5	122.00	3.71	30.6

II. **Example.** The *arithmetic* mean of the holding period for IBM, 19X1–19X5.

$$\frac{\Sigma(HPY\%)}{n} = \frac{96.6}{5} = 19.32\%$$

Problem. For the five years from 19X1 to 19X5, calculate the mean HPY% of XPO.

III. **Example.** The *geometric* mean of the holding period for IBM, 19X1–19X5. The geometric mean is the fifth root of the product of the $(1 + r)$ version of the HPY%. Let us take it by steps. We formed the HPY% by multiplying the decimal by 100 to get r%. Now back up to the $(1 + r)$:

Year	HPY% = r%	r	$(1 + r)$
19X1	− 9.2%	−0.092	0.908
19X2	10.6	0.106	1.106
19X3	−11.2	−0.112	0.888
19X4	75.8	0.758	1.758
19X5	30.6	0.306	1.306

The geometric mean is: $GM = [(1 + r_1)(1 + r_2) \ldots (1 + r_n)]^{1/n} - 1$. So, we want the fifth root of the product $(0.908)(1.106)(0.888)(1.758)(1.306) = 2.047462654$, and

$$(2.047462654)^{1/5} = 1.1541 = (1 + r), r = 0.1541, r\% = 100r = 15.41\%$$

Problem. Show that the geometric mean holding period yield for XPO for the five years 19X1 to 19X5 is 13.15%.

IV. **Example.** The differences in meaning of the arithmetic and geometric mean, holding IBM stock over the period January 1, 19X1 through December 31, 19X5, for two different investment strategies:

> Strategy A—keep a fixed amount (say, $1000) invested, and *not* reinvest earnings.
> Strategy B—reinvest earnings and allow compounding.

First take IBM's HPYs and convert them to decimal form (r) for strategy A, and then to $(1 + r)$ form for strategy B.

Strategy A					Strategy B			
Jan. 1 Year	Amt. Inv. ×	r_t	=	Return	Jan. 1 Year	Amt. Inv. ×	$(1 + r_t)$ =	Terminal Amt.
19X1	$1000	−0.092		−$92.00	19X1	$1000.00	0.908	$908.00
19X2	1000	0.106		106.00	19X2	908.00	1.106	1004.25
19X3	1000	−0.112		−112.00	19X3	1004.25	0.888	891.77
19X4	1000	0.758		758.00	19X4	891.77	1.758	1567.74
19X5	1000	0.306		306.00	19X5	1567.74	1.306	2047.46
19X6	1000				19X6	2047.46		

Using strategy A, keeping $1000 invested at the beginning of the year, total earnings for the years 19X1 through 19X5 were $966, or $193.20 per year average ($966/5), which on a $1000 investment is $193.20/1000 = 0.1932, or 19.32% per annum—the same value as the arithmetic mean in Example II, above.

Using strategy B, compounding gains and losses total return was $1047.46 (the terminal amount $2047.46 minus the initial $1000). The average annual rate of return in this situation can be found by taking the nth root of the terminal/initial amount:

$$[2047.46/1000]^{1/5} = (2.04746)^{1/5} = 1.1541 = (1 + r), r\% = 15.41\%$$

which is exactly the set of values we ended up with in Problem III previously when calculating the geometric mean.

Problem. Replicate the example using XPO. You could also do the problem backward. Knowing the arithmetic mean, you could calculate the total return for strategy A, or with the geometric mean you could calculate the terminal amount from strategy B.

V. **Example.** The calculation of the standard deviation: Using the HPY values for IBM for the five years 19X1 to 19X5, the deviation of the values from the mean ($\bar{Y}$) can be illustrated graphically:

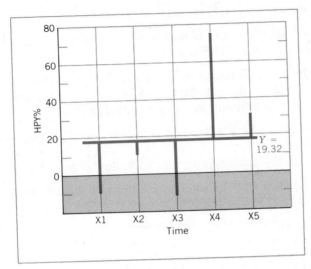

The numerator for the formula for the variance of these Y_t values is $\Sigma(Y_t - \bar{Y})^2$ which we will call SS_y, the sum of the squared deviations of the Y_t around Y. Algebraically, there is an alternative formula that is simpler:

$$SS_y = \Sigma(Y_t - \bar{Y})^2 = \Sigma Y_t^2 - \frac{(\Sigma Y_t)^2}{n}$$

Using IBM's annual holding period yields, the SS_y will be calculated both ways.

Year	$Y_t = HPY$	$(Y_t - \bar{Y})$	$(Y_t - \bar{Y})^2$	Y_t^2
19X1	− 9.2%	−28.52	813.3904	84.64
19X2	10.6	− 8.72	76.0384	112.36
19X3	−11.2	−30.52	931.4704	125.44
19X4	75.8	56.48	3189.9904	5745.64
19X5	30.6	11.28	127.2384	936.36
Sum	96.6	0	5138.1280	7004.44

$$\bar{Y} = 19.32\%$$

$$SS_y = \Sigma(Y_t - \bar{Y})^2 = 5138.128, \text{ and also}$$

$$SS_y = \Sigma Y_t^2 - \frac{(\Sigma Y_t)^2}{n} = 7044.44 - \frac{(96.6)^2}{5} = 5138.128$$

The variance is the "average" squared deviation from the mean:

$$s^2 = \frac{SS_y}{(n-1)} = \frac{5138.128}{4} = 1284.532 \text{ "squared percent"}$$

The standard deviation is the square root of the variance:

$$s = (s^2)^{1/2} = (1284.532)^{1/2} = 35.84\%$$

The standard deviation is the same units of measurement as the original observations, as is the arithmetic mean.

Problem. Show that the standard deviation for XPO's 5 annual HPYs is equal to 15.042%. Explain what the difference between the standard deviation of the HPYs of these two companies means about their relative "risk."

VI. **Example.** The calculation of annual holding period yields for bonds: we will look at bond prices on the basis of $100 par, as bond prices are quoted in *The Wall Street Journal*. The coupon rate on this long term bond was 10% at the time of purchase—January 1, 19X1. Market interest rates moved upward at that time and the price of the bond fell, recovered somewhat in 19X4, but fell off again in 19X5. The coupon rate of 10%, however, guaranteed a $10 per annum interest return (I_t). The data were:

	(1) P_B Beginning Year Price	(2) P_E End-of- Year Price	(3) I_t (0.10)($100)	(4) $P_E - P_B = PC$	(5) Return (3) + (4)	(6) HPY% [(5)/(1)]100
19X1	$100.00	$88.00	$10.00	−$12.00	−$ 2.00	−2.00%
19X2	88.00	74.50	10.00	− 13.50	− 3.50	−3.98
19X3	74.50	66.00	10.00	− 8.50	1.50	2.01
19X4	66.00	76.00	10.00	10.00	20.00	30.30
19X5	76.00	72.00	10.00			

First let's fill in the blanks for columns 4, 5, and 6. The change in price, PC, is

$$P_E - P_B = \$72 - \$76 = -\$4$$

and the return is $I_t = \$10$ minus the $4 capital loss, or $6.00. The HPY is

$$HPY = \frac{10 + (-4)}{76} = \frac{6}{76} = 0.078947, \text{ or } 100(0.0789) = 7.89\%$$

VII. **Example.** Risk-free rate, inflation premium, and required rate of return for IBM. An investor on January 1, 19X7, has the following expectations for the calendar year 19X7: Market return 15%; inflation rate 5%; real rate of return 3%; and B_i for IBM = 1.1.

$$RF = 3\% + 5\% = 8\%$$

the risk premium for IBM would be:

Risk premium (IBM) = $(1.1)(15 - 8) = (1.1)(7) = 7.7\%$

and the required rate of return for IBM would be

RR $= 8 + 7.7 = 15.7\%$

Problem. If you use the same expectations as the investor in the example, along with your expected $B_i = 0.9$ for PepsiCo, show that your required rate of return would be 14.3%. What would be the required rate of return if the expected inflation rate were 3%, the real rate of return 3%, and the expected market yield 12%?

Selected References

Ben-Horim, Moshe, and Levy, Haim. *Statistics: Decisions and Applications in Business and Economics*. New York: Random House Business Division, 1981.

Brigham, Eugene F. *Fundamentals of Financial Management*, 4th ed. Chicago: Dryden Press, 1986.

Clayton, Gary E., and Spivey, Christopher B. *The Time Value of Money*. Philadelphia: W. B. Saunders, 1978.

Curley, Anthony J., and Bear, Robert M. *Investment Analysis and Management*. New York: Harper & Row, 1979.

Fisher, Lawrence, and Lorie, James H. *A Half Century of Returns on Stocks and Bonds*. Chicago: The University of Chicago Graduate School of Business, 1977.

Harrington, Diana R. *Modern Portfolio Theory & The Capital Asset Pricing Model: A User's Guide*. Englewood Cliffs, N.J.: Prentice-Hall, 1983.

Ibbotson Associates, Inc. *Stocks, Bonds, Bills and Inflation: Yearbook*. Annual. Chicago, Illinois: Ibbotson Associates.

Jones, Charles P., Tuttle, Donald L., and Heaton, Cherrill P. *Essentials of Modern Investments*. New York: Ronald Press, 1977.

Latané, Henry A., Tuttle, Donald L., and Jones, Charles P. *Security Analysis and Portfolio Analysis*, 2nd ed. New York: Ronald Press, 1975.

Tinic, Seha M., and West, Richard R. *Investing in Securities: An Efficient Markets Approach*. Reading, Mass.: Addison-Wesley, 1979.

Valentine, Jerome L., and Mennis, Edmund A. *Quantitative Techniques For Financial Analysis*, rev. ed. Homewood, Ill.: Richard D. Irwin, 1980.

PART TWO

FIXED-INCOME SECURITIES: ANALYSIS AND VALUATION

CHAPTER 6

THE BASICS OF BONDS

Bonds are an important part of the investment alternatives available to investors. One of the basic types of securities, bonds offer investors the opportunity to earn stable nominal returns with low risk of loss of principal if held to maturity. Bonds also offer investors the chance to earn large returns by speculating on interest rate movements. Given the increase in interest rate volatility that has occurred in recent years these potential returns—and potential losses—have increased.

Bonds vary widely in individual features, giving investors an opportunity to choose those that closely match their risk preferences, maturity needs, or tax situations. For these reasons investors should understand the fundamentals of bonds, which will be covered in this chapter. In the following chapter, the discussion centers on how to analyze and manage bonds.

Understanding Bonds

General Characteristics
Bonds can be described simply as long-term debt instruments representing a contractual obligation (or IOU) on the part of the issuer. The buyer of a newly issued bond is lending money to the issuer who, in turn, agrees to pay interest on this loan and repay the principal at a stated maturity date.

149

Bonds are fixed-income securities because the interest payments and the principal repayment for a typical bond are specified at the time the bond is issued and fixed for the life of the bond. At the time of purchase, the bond buyer knows the future stream of payments to be received from buying and holding the bond to maturity. Barring default by the issuer, these payments will be received at specified intervals until maturity, at which time the principal will be repaid. However, if the buyer decides to sell the bond before maturity, the price received will depend on the level of interest rates at that time. In this case, the bond buyer is exposed to both default risk and interest rate risk, and the bond returns that will be realized for any particular holding period are by no means certain.

The **par value** (principal) of many bonds is $1000, and we will use this number as the amount to be repaid at maturity.[1] Most bonds are **coupon bonds,** where coupon refers to the periodic interest payments paid by the issuer to the holder of the bonds. Interest on bonds is typically paid every six months. A 10% coupon bond has a dollar coupon of $100 (10% of $1000), with interest of $50 paid every six months; therefore, knowing the coupon payment in dollars is the same as knowing the percentage coupon rate.[2] The terms *interest income* and *coupon income* are interchangeable.

The typical bond matures (expires) on a specified date and is technically known as a term bond. The phrase **term-to-maturity** is used to denote how much longer the bond will be in existence. In contrast, a serial bond has a series of maturity dates. Thus, one issue of serial bonds may mature in specified amounts year after year, and each specified amount could carry a different coupon.

It is important to note the legal ramifications of a bond. Failure to pay either interest or principal on a bond constitutes default for that obligation. Default, unless quickly remedied by payment or a voluntary agreement with the creditor, leads to bankruptcy. A filing of bankruptcy by a corporation initiates litigation and involvement by a court, which works with all parties concerned.[3]

---

[1] The par value almost never is less than $1000, although it easily can be more.

[2]
$$\text{Coupon rate} = \frac{\text{Stated (coupon) interest per year}}{\text{Par (face) value of the bond}}$$

The coupon rate is a fixed rate, given the bond's issuance. It can never vary.

[3] Several options are available in the case of bankruptcy. The firm could be liquidated if its liquidation value is likely to exceed its value if it continued to operate under a reorganization plan. If liquidated, proceeds must be divided among creditors and other claimants according to bankruptcy procedures. Alternatively, a court can seek a reorganization of a firm if its assets appear valuable enough in a going concern. Such a plan requires substantial concurrence by the affected creditors, who receive new claims on the reorganized firm. A third alternative for a firm is to voluntarily seek an "arrangement" under Chapter XI of the Federal Bankruptcy Act. The firm is protected by the court from its creditors while it attempts to work out a plan for paying its debt that creditors will accept.

Specific Characteristics

Every bond issue is a contractual obligation between the seller (issuer) and the buyers (investors). Legal conditions that must be met by the issuer are spelled out in an indenture or contract. A trustee is appointed to ensure that the issuer meets its obligations. Although the typical bond investor will not get involved with most of the provisions of the indenture, bond investors should be concerned with certain aspects of a particular bond they may be considering.

The most important aspect to many investors is the **call feature,** which gives the issuer the right to "call in" the bonds, thereby depriving investors of that particular fixed income security. Exercising the call right becomes attractive when market interest rates drop enough below the coupon rate on the outstanding bonds for the issuers to save money.[4] Although they will incur some costs to call the bonds, such as a "call premium" and administrative expenses, issuers expect to sell new bonds at a lower interest cost, in effect replacing existing higher interest cost bonds with new, lower interest cost bonds.[5]

The call feature is a disadvantage to investors who must give up the higher yielding bonds. The wise bond investor will note carefully the bond issue's provisions concerning the call, carefully determining the earliest date at which the bond can be called. Some investors have purchased bonds at prices above face value and suffered a loss when the bonds were unexpectedly called in and paid off at face value.[6] It is also important to determine what a bond's yield will be if it is called at the earliest date possible. Some bonds are not callable. *Most* Treasury bonds, for example, cannot be called before the maturity date.

A second characteristic of many bond issues is the requirement of a sinking fund, which provides for the orderly retirement of the bond issue during its life. The provisions of a sinking fund vary widely. It can be stated as a fixed or variable amount and as a percentage of the particular issue outstanding or the total debt of the issuer outstanding.[7]

Any part or all of the bond issue may be retired through the sinking fund by the time the issue matures. One procedure for carrying out the sinking fund requirement is simply to buy the required amount of bonds on the open

---

[4]There are different types of call features. Some bonds can be called anytime during their life, given a short notice of 30 or 60 days. Many callable bonds have a "deferred call" feature, meaning that a certain time period after issuance must expire before the bonds can be called. Popular time periods in this regard are 5 and 10 years.

[5]The call premium often equals one year's interest if the bond is called within a year; after the first year, it usually declines at a constant rate.

[6]A bond listed as "nonrefundable" for a specified period can still be called in and paid off with cash in hand. It cannot be refunded through the sale of a new issue carrying a lower coupon.

[7]Payments may be required beginning in the year after issue, or beginning several years later.

market each year.[8] A second alternative is to call the bonds randomly. Again, investors should be aware of such provisions for their protection.

A third characteristic of bonds that may be important to the bondholder is the security behind them. Bonds are senior securities; that is, they are senior to any preferred stock and to the common stock of a corporation in terms of priority of payment and in case of bankruptcy and liquidation. However, within the bond category itself there are various degrees of security. A *mortgage bond*, for example, represents a secured position whereby the issuing corporation pledges certain real assets as security. For example, first (second) mortgage bonds are secured by a first (second) mortgage on real estate.

A common type of unsecured bond is the **debenture,** that is, a bond backed only by the general viability of the issuer. Investors who purchase debentures are general creditors, protected by the overall assets of the issuer. Obviously, financially strong corporations are the more likely sellers of debentures, whereas the financially weak will likely have to resort to pledging some of their assets as collateral. Debentures can be subordinated, resulting in a claim on income that stands below (subordinate to) the claim of the other debentures.[9]

A fourth characteristic of some bond issues is convertibility, which means that the holder has the option, under specified terms, to exchange the convertible bonds for shares of common stock. By turning the bonds into the corporation, the convertible owner receives a stated number of shares of common stock, which presumably will be worth more than the bond itself; otherwise, the owner would not convert. An owner of convertibles enjoys the income stream of a fixed income security while holding an option on the underlying common stock. Investors do not receive this option free, however; the issuer sells such bonds at a lower interest rate than would otherwise be paid, resulting in a lower interest return to investors. Convertibles will be analyzed in Chapter 16.

New Bond Features

In Chapter 2 we discussed some new bond securities that have been created. In the corporate area, bond "fads" come and go.[10] The traditional corporate "vanilla" bond (i.e., the basic fixed-income security with no special features) is in style when inflation is under control and no other significant

---

[8] If the issue is being held by an institutional investor, the trustee (or issuer) can negotiate directly with the institution for the repurchase of the bonds.

[9] Other types of corporate bonds exist, including *collateral trust bonds* that are backed by other securities; for example, a parent firm may pledge the securities of one of its subsidiaries as collateral. *Equipment obligations* (or equipment trust certificates) are backed by specific real assets such as railroad engines, airplanes, and so forth. A trustee is typically used to hold the assets involved with both collateral trust bonds and equipment obligations.

[10] This discussion is based on Daniel Hertzberg, "Some Gimmicks Used to Sell Bonds Sour as Rates Fall, Inflation Slows," *The Wall Street Journal*, December 14, 1982, p. 33.

external forces distort the marketplace. For example, in July 1982, which approximates the beginning of the great bond market rise of 1982, only 46% of the corporate bond offerings were of the conventional variety; by November 1982, 81% of new corporate issues were vanilla bonds because the need for new features had subsided.[11]

Zero coupon bonds are the most radical innovation in the format of a traditional bond. An example of corporate zero coupon bonds is the Amax, Inc. issue of 1982. The bonds had an issue price of $225 per $1000 bond, with maturity in 1992. Bondholders must pay income taxes annually on the interest although no cash is received.

Variations of the zero coupon bond are also the big innovation in federal securities. These include the receipts, such as "tigers," that are sold at discount and backed by Treasury bonds.

Municipal bonds have several new features. The "put" bond can be resold by the investor to the municipality that issued it at a stated price (e.g., 95% of par value). This option, in effect, provides a floor for the bond's price and thereby protects investors from most of the loss possibility arising from interest rate risk.

A new wrinkle for municipal bond issuers is to offer a replacement issue for an outstanding issue of high coupon bonds and use the proceeds to buy enough Treasury bonds to cover the interest obligations on the old issue until they can be called. The federal backing raises the effective rating of the old bond to the highest category, causing a jump in its market value.[12] The owners are then able to trade these bonds for a larger number of the new issue, and thus can own more bonds at no additional cost.

Still another variation in this area is the municipal bond guarantee. This irrevocable guarantee, by a private party other than the issuer, is made for the bonds at time of issuance. In effect, the issuer insures the bonds because the guarantor is a source of collateral. Approximately 25% of the municipal bonds sold in 1985 carried bond insurance, with another 20% backed by letters of credit issued by banks.

Guaranteed bonds should help the issuer, who requests and pays for the insurance, by lowering costs. They may comfort the bondholder—in the industry, this practice is called "sleep insurance"—who ultimately pays the cost in the form of lower yields. It is estimated that the cost of insurance on long-term bonds to investors is about 25 basis points. It should be noted

---

[11] Several, but not all, of the new bond features were intended as inflation hedges and included: commodity-backed bonds with face values indexed to certain commodity prices that might be expected to outpace inflation; stock-indexed bonds linking the interest rate paid on the bond to some stock market factor; floating rate bonds with interest rates that periodically increase with market interest rates in general; and warrants sold with bonds allowing the owners to buy, within a stated period, more bonds at the same yield. Because these warrants are generally detachable from the bonds, they can be sold in the marketplace to speculators.

[12] Since the period to call is generally less than 10 years, the new quality and shorter maturity (less risk) raises the value of the bonds.

BOX 6–1   ZERO COUPON BOMBS

Come 2005, some holders of Baltimore City Housing Corp. zero coupon bonds for Baltimore School 100 are going to get a nasty surprise. Their investments will be worth only 15 cents for each dollar they expected to receive.

That's because the bonds were called last June, 19 years before the zeros were supposed to mature. Holders who heard about the call got $14.97 per $100 of face value, a nice gain from the $10.38 original cost. Holders who didn't hear about the call will come to the teller's window in 2005 and get only the $14.97, not the $100 they expected.

It's one of the lesser known hazards of zeros. After a call, the value of the bond freezes. There is no further "accretion" of interest.

It's not as big a problem with conventional bonds that pay semiannual interest. If the investor misses a call notice, the absence of the next coupon payment quickly sends a signal that something is wrong. But with a zero, the investor could lose a few decades of interest—almost the entire value of his investment.

You may have bought zeros because you were attracted to the idea of locking in an interest rate for 30 years. Unfortunately, you don't always get this feature. Plenty of tax-exempt zeros are callable. I've come across two dozen muni zeros that have been called over the past year. Interest rates have been falling, and the issuers don't want you to have the high rates you bargained for.

The Massachusetts Housing Finance Agency in 1982 sold zeros due in 2014 at $2 per $100 of face, for a yield of 12.7% to maturity. Two years later the agency called some of the bonds at $2.51 per $100. Other zero coupon issuers that have recently put out partial calls: Maryland Community Development Administration, Delaware State Housing Authority, Tarrant County (Tex.) Housing Finance and Smith County (Tex.) Housing Finance. Many housing finance agencies set up to provide money for home mortgages have issued partial calls after discovering that demand for mortgages was not up to expectations.

Why might a called bond go unredeemed? Those who have bearer bonds are hardly likely to hear of the call. Surprisingly, sometimes even owners who have registered their bonds—that is, given the paying agent their names and addresses—are also in the dark. An administrator at the Equitable Bank of Baltimore, the paying agent for the Baltimore school issue, says many of the bonds are still outstanding even though they are six months past the time when they have stopped drawing interest.

Equitable sends a notice by registered mail to all known holders 30 days before payment of the call. If the letter is returned, and some are, a second notification is sent. Could you miss a letter like that? Sure. Owners who move several times can get separated from mailed notices in the post office maze.

The bank does advertise its calls. But maybe you missed the ad—it ran in *The Bond Buyer,* a $1350-a-year daily trade paper with a circulation of about 2560.

If banks don't hire detectives to track down lost holders, you can hardly blame them. Banks get free use of unclaimed funds until the money has to be turned over to the state treasurer, the recipient of abandoned property in most states. The time period varies, but banks usually get the free lunch for three to five years.

How much is going unclaimed? Equitable Bank won't say what portion of the Baltimore issue is unclaimed. Of $13.8 million in zero and full-coupon Tarrant County bonds (accreted value) called last August, $514,000 sits in a no-interest account at paying agent Texas American Bank in Fort Worth. About 2% of a $7 million call by Maryland Community Development is unclaimed at Mercantile-Safe Deposit & Trust Co. in Baltimore.

Bondholders could sleep a little better if redemption money went into an interest-bearing account. It never does. "We can't invest the money because of the bond indenture," was the sanctimonious explanation from an administrator at Texas American. "If we paid interest, it would be hard to determine who was entitled to the interest, and we would have 1099 [IRS] forms to fill out," said a banker at Interfirst Bank in Fort Worth, which is sitting on $43,000 un-

claimed from one Texas muni that was called.

If paying agent banks don't particularly regret the lack of communication with investors, the issuers seem to care even less. They feel their fiduciary duty was fulfilled when they handed cash over to the paying agent.

The moral: If you own zeros—munis or corporates—pay attention to call notices or have a broker who does. Your registered representative can check on the status of a bond through the Kenny Information Service's "called bond data bank." And if you change your address, notify the paying agent. Bearer munis are no longer issued— a 1982 tax law did away with them—but if you have one of the old ones, you may want to ask the paying agent to notify you of any call.

Source: Ben Weberman, "Zero Coupon Bombs," *Forbes,* January 26, 1987, p. 103. Reprinted by permission of *Forbes* magazine, January 26, 1987. © Forbes Inc., 1987.

that the companies providing debt-service guarantees vary in their own creditworthiness.[13]

The 1986 tax act authorized the sale of "stripped" municipals, which separate the interest payments on the bonds from principal payments (in effect, each becomes a separate zero coupon security). The first of these bonds were sold in late 1986, immediately after the tax bill became law.

Information on Bonds

Bond Ratings

Bonds are rated as to the relative probability of default by several organizations, the best known of which probably are two financial services companies—Standard & Poor's (S&P) and Moody's. These organizations pro-

---

[13] See Ben Weberman, "Promises, Promises," *Forbes,* June 16, 1986, p. 179.

vide investors with **bond ratings,** that is, a current opinion on the quality of most large corporate and municipal bonds, as well as commercial paper. As independent organizations with no vested interest in the securities, Standard & Poor's and Moody's can render objective judgments on the securities' relative merits. This helps the investor to judge the quality of an issue. The rating firms, in effect, perform the *credit analysis* for the investor, carefully analyzing the issues in great detail.

Ratings, which are made by committees within the rating organizations, are assigned to specific issues of bonds and not the issuer itself; therefore, a corporation could have outstanding two bond issues carrying different ratings. The ratings reflect Standard & Poor's and Moody's judgments of the ability and determination of the issuer to fulfill its contractual obligations. It is not the collateral behind a bond that is important, but the earning power of the corporation (or the financial soundness of the government that issues the bonds); that is, the emphasis is on the likely prosperity of the issuer, not on the resources the investor can expect in the event of financial difficulties. The ratings are tied closely to the financial statements of the issuer. A particular bond issue's rating will change if the conditions of the issuer change enough to warrant it.

Standard & Poor's bond ratings consist of letters ranging from AAA, AA, A, BBB, and so on to D (Moody's corresponding letters are Aaa, Aa, A, Baa, etc., to D). Plus or minus signs can be used to provide more detailed standings within a given category.[14] Figure 6–1 shows Standard & Poor's rating definitions. Included is a brief explanation of the considerations on which the ratings are based, as well as a description of bond investment quality standards.

The first four categories, AAA through BBB, represent "investment grade" securities. AAA securities are judged to have very strong capacity to meet all obligations, whereas BBB securities are judged to have adequate capacity. Institutional investors typically must confine themselves to bonds in these four categories. Other things being equal, bond ratings and bond yields are inversely related.

Bonds rated BB, B, CCC, and CC are considered as speculative securities in terms of the issuer's ability to meet its contractual obligations. There are significant uncertainties with these securities although they are not without positive factors. Bonds rated C are currently not paying interest, and bonds rated D are in default.

Of the large number of corporate bonds outstanding, more than 80% have usually been rated A or better (based on the value of bonds outstanding). Utilities and finance companies have the fewest low-rated bonds, and transportation companies the most (because of problems with bankrupt railroads). Less is known about the ratings of state and local government bonds,

---

[14] Moody's uses numbers (i.e., 1, 2, and 3) to further designate quality grades. For example, bonds could be rated Aa1 or Aa2.

S&P'S DEBT RATING DEFINITIONS

A Standard & Poor's corporate or municipal debt rating is a current assessment of the creditworthiness of an obligor with respect to a specific obligation. This assessment may take into consideration obligors such as guarantors, insurers, or lessees.

The debt rating is not a recommendation to purchase, sell, or hold a security, inasmuch as it does not comment as to market price or suitability for a particular investor.

The ratings are based on current information furnished by the issuer or obtained by S&P from other sources it considers reliable. S&P does not perform an audit in connection with any rating and may, on occasion, rely on unaudited financial information. The ratings may be changed, suspended, or withdrawn as a result of changes in, or unavailability of, such information, or for other circumstances.

The ratings are based, in varying degrees, on the following considerations:

1. Likelihood of default—capacity and willingness of the obligor as to the timely payment of interest and repayment of principal in accordance with the terms of the obligation;
2. Nature of and provisions of the obligation;
3. Protection afforded by, and relative position of, the obligation in the event of bankruptcy, reorganization, or other arrangement under the laws of bankruptcy and other laws affecting creditors' rights.

AAA Debt rated 'AAA' has the highest rating assigned by Standard & Poor's. Capacity to pay interest and repay principal is extremely strong.

AA Debt rated 'AA' has a very strong capacity to pay interest and repay principal and differs from the highest rated issues only in small degree.

A Debt rated 'A' has a strong capacity to pay interest and repay principal although it is somewhat more susceptible to the adverse effects of changes in circumstances and economic conditions than debt in higher rated categories.

BBB Debt rated 'BBB' is regarded as having an adequate capacity to pay interest and repay principal. Whereas it normally exhibits adequate protection parameters, adverse economic conditions, or changing circumstances are more likely to lead to a weakened capacity to pay interest and repay principal for debt in this category than in higher rated categories.

Debt rated 'BB', 'B', 'CCC', 'CC', and 'C' is regarded as having predominantly speculative characteristics with respect to capacity to pay interest and repay principal. 'BB' indicates the least degree of speculation and 'C' the highest. While such debt will likely have some quality and protective characteristics, these are outweighed by large uncertainties or major exposures to adverse conditions.

BB Debt rated 'BB' has less near-term vulnerability to default than other speculative issues. However, it faces major ongoing uncertainties or exposure to adverse business, financial, or economic conditions which could lead to inadequate capacity to meet timely interest and principal payments. The 'BB' rating category is also used for debt subordinated to senior debt that is assigned an actual or implied 'BBB −' rating.

B Debt rated 'B' has a greater vulnerability to default but currently has the capacity to meet interest payments and principal repayments. Adverse business, financial, or economic conditions will likely impair capacity or willingness to pay interest and repay principal. The 'B' rating category is also used for debt subordinated to senior debt that is assigned an actual or implied 'BB' or 'BB −' rating.

CCC Debt rated 'CCC' has a currently identifiable vulnerability to default, and is dependent upon favorable business, financial, and economic conditions to meet timely payment of interest and repayment of principal. In the event of adverse business, financial, or economic conditions, it is not likely to have the capacity to pay interest and repay principal. The 'CCC' rating category is also used for debt subordinated to senior debt that is assigned an actual or implied 'B' or 'B −' rating.

CC The rating 'CC' is typically applied to debt subordinated to senior debt that is assigned an actual or implied 'CCC' rating.

C The rating 'C' is typically applied to debt subordinated to senior debt which is assigned an actual or implied 'CCC −' debt rating.

CI The rating 'CI' is reserved for income bonds on which no interest is being paid.

D Debt rated 'D' is in default. The 'D' rating category is also used when interest payments or principal repayments are expected to be in default at the payment date, and payment of interest and/or repayment of principal is in arrears.

Plus (+) or minus (−): The ratings from 'AA' to 'CCC' may be modified by the addition of a plus or minus sign to show relative standing within the major rating categories.

Provisional ratings: The letter 'p' indicates that the rating is provisional. A provisional rating as-

(FIGURE 6–1 continued)

sumes the successful completion of the project being financed by the debt being rated and indicates that payment of debt service requirements is largely or entirely dependent upon the successful and timely completion of the project. This rating, however, while addressing credit quality subsequent to completion of the project, makes no comment on the likelihood of, or the risk of default upon failure of, such completion. The investor should exercise his or her own judgment with respect to such likelihood and risk.

L The letter 'L' indicates that the rating pertains to the principal amount of those bonds where the underlying deposit collateral is fully insured by the Federal Savings & Loan Insurance Corp. or the Federal Deposit Insurance Corp.

* Continuance of the rating is contingent upon S&P's receipt of an executed copy of the escrow agreement or closing documentation confirming investments and cash flows.

N.R. Indicates no rating has been requested, that there is insufficient information on which to base a rating, or that S&P does not rate a particular type of obligation as a matter of policy.

Debt Obligations of Issuers outside the United States and its territories are rated on the same basis as domestic corporate and municipal issues. The ratings measure the creditworthiness of the obligor but do not take into account currency exchange and related uncertainties.

Bond Investment Quality Standards: Under present commercial bank regulations issued by the Comptroller of the Currency, bonds rated in the top four categories ('AAA', 'AA', 'A', 'BBB', commonly known as "investment grade" ratings) are generally regarded as eligible for bank investment. In addition, the laws of various states governing legal investments impose certain rating or other standards for obligations eligible for investment by savings banks, trust companies, insurance companies and fiduciaries generally.

FIGURE 6–1 Standard & Poor's debt rating definitions.
Source: Standard & Poor's Credit Week, January 19, 1987, p. 8. Reprinted by permission of Standard & Poor's Corporation.

but the majority apparently are rated in the top three categories based on value. Many individual issues, however, carry lower ratings.

Investors, both institutions and individuals, rely heavily on bond ratings in evaluating the relative quality of an issue because Standard & Poor's and Moody's have compiled excellent records in making their judgments. Since the Depression, very few defaults have occurred, and this is particularly true of the bonds in the top four investment grade categories. However, this excellent record does not solve all of the bond investor's problems. In roughly one-fourth of the cases the two agencies disagree on their evaluations. Furthermore, since most bonds are in the top four categories, it seems safe to argue that not all issues in a single category (such as A) can be equally risky. And it is standard practice to rate unsecured debentures one rating lower than the mortgage bonds of the same corporation, although both are directly tied to the prosperity of the same issuer. Finally, it is extremely important to remember that bond ratings are a reflection of the *relative* probability of default, which says little or nothing about the absolute probability of default.

Using Bond Information

Several sources of information, referred to in Chapter 4, are of particular value to the potential bond investor. These include government sources such as the *Federal Reserve Bulletin* and the *Treasury Bulletin* as well as the publications provided by Standard & Poor's and Moody's.[15] These sources will provide bond investors with all the technical information they are likely to require. If they wish to do fundamental analysis on a particular corporate issuer, Moody's and Standard & Poor's sources provide balance sheet and income statement data that permit investors to assess the availability of earnings for servicing debt obligations, the amount of fixed charges the corporation has obligated itself to pay, and so forth. These same sources also provide the bond ratings that were discussed earlier, and bond investors rely heavily on these ratings because they are so well known and have proven to be so reliable. Thus, investors can easily and quickly obtain an indication of the relative likelihood of default by the issuer. They must then decide for themselves if they are willing to assume the risk of, say, a BBB-rated bond. Although the return will exceed that of a higher rated bond, the quality is presumably lower.

Bond investors need information other than that pertaining to the details of the bond issue itself. They should pay particular attention to current and prospective economic conditions such as the trend of the economy. Specifically, investors should be concerned with the likely movement of interest rates, which directly affects bond prices. No one can consistently make accurate predictions of interest rate movements; therefore, the uncertainty is great when investors purchase bonds and subject themselves to interest rate risk.

Some sources of information about interest rate movements, both actual and prospective, are brokerage houses and investment advisory services. Merrill Lynch, for example, publishes the *Bond Market Comment,* which contains useful information on interest rate movements and analysis.

It is possible to find considerable information about bonds in the popular press. Well-known financial papers such as *The Wall Street Journal* and *Barron's* carry bond quotes and feature articles about interest rates, bond issues, current economic projections, strategies being followed by various investors, and other subjects.[16] *Forbes* and *Business Week* also carry features about bonds when appropriate.

---

[15] Reviewing from Chapter 4, these include the Standard & Poor's *Bond Guide,* published monthly, which contains various types of financial information on a large number of bonds, and Moody's *Bond Record,* which provides similar information. In addition, Moody's publishes various manuals, including the *Municipal and Government Manual,* the *Industrial Manual,* and the *OTC Industrial Manual,* which provide detailed information on the various bond issues. For a current weekly source of information, Moody's *Bond Survey* discusses conditions in the marketplace and lists both recent and forthcoming bond offerings.

[16] This source provides information for U.S. government bonds that are publicly traded and for many of the agency bonds that are of interest. It carries only listed issues of corporate bonds, however, just a small part of the total outstanding. If current market quotes are needed for bonds not carried in the *Journal* or *Barron's,* alternative sources are available, although not necessarily easily accessible. The *Bank and Quotation Record* summarizes price information on a monthly basis for many corporate issues, as well as U.S. governments, agencies, and municipals. In addition, *The Blue List* contains extensive price quotes for municipal issues and is widely used by institutions.

Reading Bond Information

Figure 6–2 is an excerpt from the bond page carried daily in *The Wall Street Journal* that reports on corporate and (a few) foreign bonds traded on the New York Stock Exchange. This page also shows AMEX bonds. The summary information at the top of the page shows the total volume for the preceding day, the number of issues traded (including advances, declines, and no changes), and some information on the Dow Jones Bond Averages. Note that the total volume on the day shown was only $47 million and that only 763 domestic and two foreign bonds traded on the exchange. As noted in Chapter 3, the bond market is primarily an over-the-counter market.

Consider the *second* bond listed, that of AMR Corporation. This is a 10¼% coupon bond, maturing in 2006—bond investors would refer to it as the "10¼s of '06." AMR will pay 10¼% of $1000 ($102.50) in interest per year per bond with the actual payments to be made semiannually ($51.25 every six months). On maturity in 2006, AMR will repay the holders of the bonds the $1000 principal, and this bond issue will terminate.

The first column after the name and coupon-year description is the "cur yld" (current yield), which is the rounded-off ratio of the coupon to the current market price (in this example, it is exactly 10%—$10.25/102½). As explained later in this chapter, this is only one measure of return for a bond and not the best. The next column is the volume figure, or the number traded on a given day.

The next three columns on the bond page are the high, low, and close, respectively, for that day's trading; the last column indicates the net change in closing price from the preceding day's closing (or from the last day the issue was traded). It is important to note that bond prices are quoted, by convention, without the last digit. For example, a price of 90 represents $900, whereas a price of 55 represents $550. Each "point," or a change of "1," represents 1% of $1000, or $10. The easiest way to convert quoted bond prices to actual prices is to remember that they are quoted in percentages, with the common assumption of a $1000 par value.[17] This bond gained $5 (+ ½) in price from the previous day's closing price.

It would appear from this example that an investor could purchase the AMR bond for $1025 on that day. Actually, bonds trade on an **accrued interest** basis. This means that the bond buyer must pay the bond seller the price of the bond plus the interest that has been earned (accrued) on the bond since the last semiannual interest payment; therefore, an investor can sell a bond anytime without losing the interest that has accrued. It is important that bond buyers remember this additional "cost" when buying a bond. For example, a 10% coupon bond purchased shortly before the next interest payment date would cost almost $50 more than the stated price of the bond.

---

[17] For example, the closing price for the AMR bond, 102½, represents 102.5% of $1000, or $1025.

NEW YORK EXCHANGE BONDS

Wednesday, January 14, 1987

Total Volume $47,050,000

	Domestic Wed.	Domestic Tue.	All Issues Wed.	All Issues Tue.
Issues traded	763	877	765	880
Advances	338	388	339	389
Declines	229	292	229	293
Unchanged	196	197	197	198
New highs	102	134	102	135
New lows	7	8	7	9

SALES SINCE JANUARY 1

1987	1986	1985
$392,756,000	$411,405,000	$284,444,000

Dow Jones Bond Averages

−1985− High	−1985− Low	−1986− High	−1986− Low	−1987− High	−1987− Low		−−−Wednesday−−− −1987−		−1986−		−1985−	
83.73	72.27	93.65	83.73	95.03	93.43	20 Bonds	95.03	+0.20	84.11	+0.38	72.88	+0.32
82.88	68.62	95.79	81.85	97.44	95.64	10 Utilities	97.44	+0.11	82.37	+0.52	69.37	+0.45
84.58	75.61	91.64	84.82	92.61	91.21	10 Industrial	92.61	+0.28	85.86	+0.24	76.42	+0.21

CORPORATION BONDS
Volume, $46,940,000

Bonds	Cur Yld	Vol	High	Low	Close	Net Chg.
AGS 7½11	cv	15	131	129	131	+ 2
AMR 10¼06	10.0	45	102½	102½	102½	+ ½
ANR 8⅝93	8.8	8	98⅜	98⅜	98⅜	− ¼
ARX 9⅜05	cv	39	111	109½	110¼	− ¾
AVX 13½00	12.9	10	105	105	105	...
Advst 9s08	cv	5	108½	108½	108½	− ½
AetnLf 8⅛07	8.3	5	97⅜	97⅜	97⅜	+ ⅞
AirbF 7½11	cv	50	118	118	118	...
AlaP 9s2000	8.9	5	101	101	101	− ¼
AlaP 8½s01	8.5	8	99¾	99¾	99¾	− ¾
AlaP 7¾s02	8.3	5	93⅛	93⅛	93⅛	− ⅜
AlaP 8⅞s03	8.8	12	100½	100⅜	100½	+ ⅛
AlaP 9¾s04	9.4	15	104¼	104⅛	104¼	− ⅜
AlaP 8¾07	8.8	11	100	100	100	...
AlaP 8⅝87	8.6	9	100⅝	100½	100½	− 1
AlaP 9½08	9.1	35	104¼	104	104	+ ⅛
AlaP 12⅝10	11.8	170	107¼	106½	107	− ⅝
AlskA 9s03	cv	91	130	126	128⅛	+ 4⅝
AlskH 16¼99	13.4	14	120⅞	120⅞	120⅞	− ⅛
AlskH 17¾91	14.4	9	123½	123½	123½	...
AlskH 10¾93	10.3	50	104	104	104	...
AlskH 11½93l	11.0	35	104⅛	104⅛	104⅛	...
Alco 8½10	cv	80	123	122	123	+ 2
Allgl 10.4s02	14.1	37	73⅞	72⅜	73⅞	+ 2
AlldC zr92	...	1	64⅛	64⅛	64⅛	− ⅜
AlldC zr96	...	30	47½	47½	47½	+ 1½
AlldC zr98	...	50	36¾	36	36¾	+ ½
AlldC zr2000	...	20	30½	30	30	− 2
AlldC zr87	...	5	96½	96½	96½	− ½
AlldC zr97	...	5	40¾	40¾	40¾	+ ⅝
AlldC zr09	...	50	13⅝	13⅝	13⅝	− ⅜
Alcoa 9s95	8.8	10	101¾	101¾	101¾	− ¼
AMAX 9⅜00	10.5	5	89	89	89	+ ⅛
AMAX 14½94	12.7	32	118	114½	114½	− 2¼
AForP 5s30	8.9	11	56	56	56	...
AAirl 5¼98	7.1	10	74	74	74	+ 2
AExC 7.8s92	7.7	25	101½	101½	101½	+ ½
AExC 11¼00	10.2	10	110¼	110¼	110¼	...
AExC 12⅞91	12.0	15	107⅜	107⅜	107⅜	+ ⅜
AmMed 9½01	cv	123	103½	103	103½	+ ½
AmMed 11¾99	11.3	10	103⅝	103⅝	103⅝	+ ⅛
ATT 3⅞s90	4.2	131	92⅛	92	92⅛	...
ATT 8¾00	8.5	301	103⅝	103	103⅛	+ ⅛
ATT 7s01	7.7	124	90¾	90½	90½	− ⅛
ATT 7⅛s03	7.9	62	90⅞	90⅜	90¾	+ ¼
ATT 8.80s05	8.6	432	102¾	102⅛	102½	...
ATT 8⅝s07	8.6	137	101⅛	100¾	100¾	...
Ames 10s95	9.9	20	101½	101½	101½	+ ½
Amfac 5¼94	cv	3	88	88	88	+ 1
Amoco 6s91	6.1	51	98½	98½	98½	...
Amoco 6s98	6.8	65	89	88½	88⅞	+ ⅜
Amoco 9.2s04	8.9	5	104	103¾	103¾	− ¼
Amoco 7⅞07	8.4	5	94¼	94¼	94¼	− ⅜
Amoco 14s91	12.6	40	111	109¾	111	+ 1¼
Ancp 13⅞02f	cv	30	100	100	100	...
Anxtr 8¼03	cv	20	101	101	101	...
Apch 8.5s06	7.5	5	113½	113½	113½	+ 1
ArmS 8.7s95	12.3	40	72	71	71	− 2
ArmS 9.2s00	14.3	970	64⅞	64	64½	+ ¼
Arms 8½01	13.8	51	61½	59	61½	...
ArRub 7¾11	cv	3	99½	99½	99½	+ ½
Asar 9¾2000	11.0	25	90	88½	88½	− 1½
AshO 8.2s02	8.5	92	97	94½	97	+ 2½
AshO 11.1s04	10.5	15	106	106	106	+ ½
ARich 5⅝97	6.0	25	93	93	93	+ 5
ARich 13⅝11	12.0	70	114	113	114	+ 1½
ARch dc7s91	7.1	20	98¾	98¾	98¾	...
ARch 12½12	11.2	5	112	112	112	+ 1⅞
ARch 10⅜95	9.0	10	115	115	115	...
AutDt 6½11	cv	130	124	122½	124	...
AvcoC 7½93	7.9	45	94⅞	94⅛	94⅞	+ ¾
Avnet 8s13	cv	26	102	100	102	+ 2¾
Bally 6s98	cv	53	93	92½	93	...
Bally 10s06	cv	29	103	102¾	102¾	− ¼
B O 4¼95	4.7	10	90½	90½	90½	...
BalGE 8⅜06	8.5	10	98¾	98¾	98¾	− ¾
BalGE 8¼07	8.4	5	98¾	98¾	98¾	+ ⅛
BalGE 9⅜08	9.0	5	103⅝	103⅝	103⅝	+ ⅛
BkBos 10.65s87	10.4	10	102 3/16	102 3/16	102 3/16	+ 1/32
BkNY 8¼10	cv	20	130½	130½	130½	+ ½
Banka 7⅞03	9.2	15	85¼	85¼	85¼	− ¾
Banka 8⅞05	9.6	44	93	92	92⅜	+ ⅞
Banka 8¾01	9.5	10	92	92	92	...
Bkam zr87A	...	7	95 3/16	95 3/16	95 3/16	+ 1/32
Bkam zr90s	...	6	72	71⅞	71⅞	− ⅛
Bkam zr92s	...	260	58⅞	58½	58⅞	+ ⅛
Bkam zr87D	...	20	92¼	92 5/32	92¼	...
Bkam zr91s	...	9	69⅞	68⅜	68⅝	− ⅝
Bkam zr93s	...	264	56	55	55¼	+ ⅜
BkAm 11½95	11.4	60	100½	100½	100½	+ ½
BkAm 11⅜96	11.2	12	102	101⅞	101⅞	− ⅛
BnkTr 8⅝02	8.8	5	98	98	98	− 1
BarcNA 11⅝03	9.9	10	117	117	117	− ¾
BASIX 8¾05	cv	51	92½	92¼	92½	+ ½
BaxL 4¾s01	cv	10	202	202	202	+ 6
v|Beker 15⅞03f	...	38	21	20⅝	21	...
BellPa 8⅝06	8.5	1	101	101	101	...
BellPa 7⅛12	8.0	5	89	89	89	+ 1¼
BellPa 9⅝14	9.1	40	105⅞	105½	105½	...
BellPa 8¾15	8.7	28	100¾	100⅝	100¾	...
BellPa 8⅛17	8.4	10	97	97	97	+ ⅜
Bendx 11.20s05	10.4	10	108	108	108	+ ⅛
BestPr 12⅝96	12.4	25	102⅛	102	102⅛	+ ⅝
BethSt 4½90	8.1	732	55¾	55	55¾	+ ¾
BethSt 5.4s92	9.0	25	60	60	60	...
BethSt 6⅞99	14.4	397	47⅝	46	47⅝	+ ⅝
BethSt 9s00	15.7	254	58	56	57¼	+ 1¾
BethSt 8.45s05	16.5	1330	51½	50¾	51⅛	+ 1⅜
CATS zr11-91	...	9	71½	70½	71½	+ 1
Champ 6½11	cv	68	127	125	127	+ 2
v|ChtCo 10⅝98f	...	10	65	65	65	− ½
v|ChtC dc14¾02f	...	25	62	61⅞	61⅞	...
ChsCp 6½96	cv	10	137	137	137	+ 1
ChsCp 6.35s99t	6.4	15	100	100	100	+ 1½
ChsCp 6½09t	6.7	10	97⅝	97⅝	97⅝	+ ⅞
Chelse 5¼93	cv	3	140	140	140	+ 2
Chmtrn 9s94	10.8	5	83	83	83	...
CPoM 7¼12	8.2	20	88⅝	88½	88½	− 2
Chvrn 7s96	7.3	10	96¼	96¼	96¼	− ¾
Chvrn 8¾05	8.7	2	100½	100½	100½	− ½
Chrysl 8⅞95	8.8	6	100⅞	100⅞	100⅞	+ ⅛
Chryslr 8s98	8.3	6	96⅝	96½	96⅝	+ ¼
Chryslr 12s15	10.6	50	113½	113½	113½	...
ChryF 8.35s91	8.3	55	100¾	100½	100¾	+ ¼
ChryF zr90	...	6	74⅞	74⅞	74⅞	− 1⅛
ChryF 9¾90D	9.0	10	108¼	108¼	108¼	...
CirclK 8¼05	cv	10	132	132	132	− 3
CirclK 7¼06	cv	138	106	104	106	...
Citicp 7.2s89t	7.2	35	99⅞	99⅞	99⅞	− ⅜
Citicp 8.45s07	8.7	45	97⅞	96⅞	96⅞	− 1
Citicp 8⅛07	8.5	10	95½	95½	95½	+ ½
Citicp 12¼93	11.3	6	108¼	107⅛	108¼	+ ¼
Citicp 12s90	11.7	20	103⅛	102¾	102¾	− 1
Citicp 12⅞89	12.3	60	105	104⅞	105	+ ⅛
CitSv 6⅛97	7.9	5	78	78	78	...
CitSv 13⅞11	12.4	10	112¼	112¼	112¼	− 1⅝
CitSvc zr87	...	1	94	94	94	...
CitSvc zr88	...	107	86¾	86¼	86¾	+ ⅜
CitSvc zr89	...	9	79⅝	79⅝	79⅝	+ ¼
ClkEq 7.85s91	8.0	5	98	98	98	− 1⅞
Claytn 7¾01	cv	6	111	110	111	+ 1
ClevEl 7⅛90	7.3	22	98	98	98	+ ⅞
ClevEl 9¼09	9.4	6	100	98¾	98¾	+ ⅝
ClevEl 9.85s10	9.7	10	102	101½	101½	− ⅝
Coastl 11¼96	11.1	282	102	101	101½	− ½
Coastl 11¾06	11.5	179	102¼	100¾	102¼	+ ¼
Coleco 14⅜02	14.7	136	98	98	98	− ½
Coleco 11s89	cv	8	101½	101½	101½	+ ⅜
Coleco 11⅛01	13.7	54	81½	80¼	81½	+ 1¼
Coltln 10⅛95	10.1	78	100	99½	100	+ 1
ColuG 9⅛95	8.9	10	102½	102	102½	+ 1¾
ColuG 8¼96	8.3	15	99½	99½	99½	− ¼
ColuG 9⅝89	9.4	1	102	102	102	− ⅛
ColuG 10⅛95	9.8	4	103½	103½	103½	+ ½
Cmdis 8s03	cv	51	100¼	100	100¼	...
Cmdis 9.65s02	10.4	61	92⅞	90	92⅞	+ 2⅞
Cmdis 10s94	9.8	100	102	102	102	+ 1½
CmwE 8s03	8.4	12	95	94½	95	+ ½
CmwE 8¾05	8.7	30	101	100	101	+ 1
CmwE 9⅜04	9.0	40	104	104	104	...
CmwE 8⅛07J	8.7	2	93½	93½	93½	− 1
CmwE 8¼07	8.6	21	96⅛	96	96⅛	− 1¼
CmwE 9⅛08	8.9	5	102½	102½	102½	...
CmwE 14⅞87	14.8	10	100 27/32	100 27/32	100 27/32	...
CmwE 15⅜00	12.8	6	120½	120½	120½	− ⅜
CmwE 14s91	13.1	100	108	107¼	107¼	− ⅞
CmwE 16s90	15.3	53	104¾	104¾	104¾	...
CmwE 14¼92	13.2	10	108	108	108	+ ¼
Cmpvsn 8s09	cv	87	86½	86	86½	− ½
ConEd 4¾91	5.3	5	89⅞	89⅞	89⅞	...
ConEd 4⅝91	5.2	5	89	89	89	− ½
ConEd 4⅝93	5.5	40	84⅛	84	84⅛	...
ConEd 9⅜00	9.0	30	104⅛	103⅞	103⅞	...
ConEd 7.9s01	8.1	10	98	97⅝	97⅝	− ¼
ConEd 7.9s02	8.2	10	96¾	96¾	96¾	− 1
ConEd 7¾03	8.1	15	95⅜	95⅜	95⅜	+ ¼
ConEd 8.4s03	8.5	34	100	99⅜	99⅜	...
ConEd 9⅛04	8.9	11	103	103	103	...
CnNG 8¼94	8.3	5	100	100	100	...
CnPw 5⅞96	7.3	7	81	81	81	− 1
CnPw 6⅞98	8.3	2	83¼	83¼	83¼	− 1½
CnPw 7⅝99	8.7	5	87¼	87¼	87¼	− ⅞
CnPw 7½02O	8.7	10	86⅜	86	86	− ¼
CnPw 8⅝03	9.4	20	92¼	92⅛	92⅛	− 1⅜
CnPw 11⅜94	10.7	6	105⅞	104	105⅞	+ 2½
CnPw 9s06	9.4	29	98⅛	96¼	96¼	− 1½
CtlInf 9s06	cv	125	117	115¼	117	+ 2
CtlDat 12¾91	11.9	130	107⅞	107½	107½	− ½
CtlDat 8½11	cv	110	118¾	118⅜	118⅜	− 1⅝
Coopvsn 8⅝05	cv	36	93	93	93	...
CrnPd 5¾92	6.3	5	91½	91½	91½	− 1½
CornG 7¾98	7.8	7	99	99	99	+ 4
CntryCr 7s11	cv	56	121	121	121	...
Crane 6½92	6.8	10	96	96	96	+ 2½
Crane 7s94	8.0	81	87¾	86¾	87¾	+ 1
Crane 8¾05	cv	77	138	136½	138	...
CrayRs 6⅛11	cv	36	132½	132	132½	+ ½
CritAc 12.35s14	12.0	40	103	103	103	− 4¼
CritAc 13.10s14	12.3	6	106¾	106¾	106¾	+ ¼
CritAc 11½15	11.2	7	103⅛	103	103	+ ⅛
CritAc 11¼15	10.8	1	104	104	104	+ 1¾
CritAc 11.85s15	11.4	5	104	104	104	+ ⅛
CrocN 8.6s02	8.8	5	97⅝	97⅝	97⅝	− 1⅛
Dana dc5⅞06	cv	130	90¾	90⅛	90½	+ ½
Datpnt 8⅞06	cv	45	69	68⅝	68⅝	...
Deere 5½01	cv	48	91	91	91	...
Deere 9s08	cv	191	100¼	99¾	100	...
DetEd 9s99	8.9	10	101	101	101	+ ¼
DetEd 9.15s00	9.1	60	101½	100½	101	+ 1
DetEd 7½03	8.5	15	88½	88½	88½	+ ⅛
DetEd 9⅞04	9.6	30	102¾	102¾	102¾	− ⅛
DetEd 11⅞00	10.9	8	108¾	106⅞	108¾	+ 1⅞
DetEd 10⅝06	10.2	7	105¼	103¾	103¾	− 1¾
DiaSh 9⅛00	9.5	15	96	96	96	+ 1⅛
DiaSh 8½08	9.8	115	87	86½	87	+ ½
DiaSh 7.7s01	9.3	50	82⅜	82⅜	82⅜	− ⅛
Dow 7.75s99	8.0	25	96½	96½	96½	+ 1
Dow 8½s05	8.6	10	98½	98½	98½	− 1½
Dow 8⅝08	8.8	13	98	98	98	− 2
FreptM 10[illegible]s01	10.9	1	100	100	100	− 2
Fruf 13½96	13.1	25	103	103	103	+ ½
FrufF 8s87	8.0	100	99½	99½	99½	...
Fuqua 9½98	9.6	54	99⅜	98⅛	99¼	+ ¾
Fuqua 9⅞97	9.9	22	100	100	100	+ ½
GAF 11⅜95	10.9	75	104½	104	104	− 1⅜
GATX 11½96	11.0	43	104⅜	104	104¼	...
Gelco 14⅝99	13.9	2	105¼	105¼	105¼	− ¼
Gelco 14s01	cv	7	106¼	106¼	106¼	+ ¼
Gelco 14¼87	13.8	5	103	103	103	+ 1¾
GCinem 10s08	cv	10	233	233	233	...
GCinem 10s09	cv	25	195	195	195	− 1
GdDyn 5¾11	...	5	116	116	116	...
GnEl 7½96	7.5	195	100	99⅞	99⅞	...
GElCr 7⅝88	7.5	17	101⅛	101⅛	101⅛	+ ⅜
GElCr 11¾05	10.2	2	115¾	115¾	115¾	+ ⅝
GElCr 14s90	13.8	91	101¼	101	101⅛	− ⅜
GFood 14⅜89	14.1	130	102	101½	102	...
GHost 7s94	8.2	10	85	85	85	...
GnInst 5s92	cv	2	104½	104½	104½	+ 2
GMills 8s99	8.0	15	100	100	100	...
GMills zr88s	...	35	93 11/32	93 11/32	93 11/32	+ 1/16
GMA 4⅞87	4.9	30	98¾	98¾	98¾	...
GMA 6¼88	6.3	105	99⅝	99½	99⅝	...
GMA 8s93m	7.9	17	102	101¾	101¾	− ¼
GMA 7⅛92	7.2	390	99⅝	99⅝	99⅝	− ¼
GMA 7.85s98	7.9	70	100	98⅝	99¾	+ 2¼
GMA 8⅞99	8.6	15	103	103	103	+ ⅝
GMA 8¾s00	8.6	10	101⅞	101⅞	101⅞	...
GMA 8.65s08	8.6	45	100⅝	100⅝	100⅝	...
GMA 14⅜91	13.1	20	109⅜	108¾	109⅜	...
GMA dc6s11	7.8	28	76⅝	76½	76⅝	− ⅛
GMA 14⅝89	14.1	38	103⅝	103	103⅝	+ ⅜
GMA 10½89	9.7	5	108	108	108	...
GMA 10s90	9.5	25	105⅜	105⅜	105⅜	...
GMA 8s96	8.0	71	100½	100¼	100½	...
GMA 8¼16	8.4	10	98½	98½	98½	+ ½
GMA 8s93J	7.9	95	102	101¾	101⅞	+ ⅛
GMA 7.80s93	7.8	100	100½	100¼	100½	+ ⅛
GTE 10⅛95	9.5	12	106⅛	106⅛	106⅛	...
GTE 9⅜99	9.0	15	103⅞	103⅞	103⅞	...
Gene 14¼94	14.0	2	102	102	102	+ ⅛
Genrad 7¼11	cv	10	92½	92½	92½	+ 6
GaPw 8⅞00	8.9	50	100¼	100	100⅛	− ⅝
GaPw 7⅜01	8.3	5	89¼	89¼	89¼	...
GaPw 7⅝01	8.3	5	91½	91½	91½	+ ⅜
GaPw 7½02D	8.3	10	90⅜	90⅜	90⅜	+ ⅞
GaPw 8⅝04	8.8	30	98⅞	97¾	98½	− ⅜
GaPw 11⅝00	10.9	10	106½	106½	106½	+ ⅜
GaPw 11¾05	10.9	6	107½	107½	107½	− ¼
GaPw 9⅞06	9.5	6	103½	103½	103½	+ ½
GaPw 9⅝08	9.5	6	102½	101	101	− ⅝
GaPw 9¾08	9.5	14	102¾	102¾	102¾	...
GaPw 10½09	10.0	24	104⅞	104⅛	104⅞	+ ¾
GaPw 11s09	10.5	10	105	104¾	104¾	− 2¼
GaPw 14½10	13.1	61	110½	109⅝	110½	...
GaPw 16s14	13.8	121	116	115½	116	+ ⅛
GaPw 10s16A	9.5	25	105⅜	104¾	105⅜	+ ⅞
GlbFn 9¼08	cv	95	107	106⅝	107	...
v|GloMr 12⅜98f	...	3	22	22	22	...
v|GloMr 16⅛02f	...	202	23¼	21⅛	21¾	+ ¼
v|GloM dc13s03f	cv	57	22	21½	22	+ 1
GNgF dc8⅜93	9.2	16	91	91	91	+ ½
Gdrch 8¼94	8.4	17	98	98	98	+ ½
Gdrch 7s97	8.3	6	84¼	84¼	84¼	− ⅛
Gdyr 8.6s95	8.6	27	101	100	100	− 1⅛
Grace 4¼90	cv	13	99¾	99¾	99¾	− ½
GranC 4⅝94	cv	3	66	66	66	+ ½
GWstFn 8½10	cv	26	144	143	143½	− ¼
GrnTr dc8¼95	9.6	10	86¼	86¼	86¼	...
Greyh 9⅜01	9.3	25	100⅞	100⅞	100⅞	...
GreyF 12½00	11.5	12	108¼	108	108¼	+ ¾
GreyF 16⅛92	14.1	3	115	114⅜	114⅜	− ⅝
GreyF zr94	...	175	48⅛	47¼	48⅛	+ ¾
Grolr 13⅝03	12.9	19	105¼	105⅛	105¼	− ¾
Grolr 9½05	cv	10	137	137	137	...
GrowGp 8½06	cv	10	111	111	111	...
Grumn 9¼09	cv	15	106½	106	106½	+ ½
GlfWn 7s03A	8.3	54	85	84	84	...
GlfWn 7s03B	8.3	17	83⅞	83⅞	83⅞	+ ¼
GlfRes 12½04	12.5	56	100	100	100	+ ¾
Harns dc12s04	11.9	12	100½	100½	100½	...
Hellm zr03	...	106	31	30½	31	+ ½
Hellr 9⅛91	9.0	10	101½	101½	101½	+ 1
ITTF 14¾91	13.8	13	107⅛	107⅛	107⅛	− 1⅞
IllBel 7⅝06	8.2	23	94	93⅜	93⅜	+ ⅜
IllPw 8⅝06	8.7	10	98⅞	98¾	98⅞	+ 1⅝
IllPw 8⅞08	8.8	10	100½	100½	100½	+ ¼
IllPw 14½90	13.9	30	104	103½	104	+ ⅜
Inco 12⅜10	11.8	5	105	105	105	+ 1
IndBel 8s14	8.2	15	97¾	97¾	97¾	...
Inexc 8½00	cv	185	83	81	83	+ 2
InldStl 8¾95	9.7	19	90½	90½	90½	...
InldStl 9½00	10.5	10	90¾	90¾	90¾	+ 1
InldStl 7.9s07	11.0	30	72	72	72	− ⅜
InldStl 11¼90	11.0	10	102	102	102	+ ⅜
Insilco 9s10	cv	3	122¾	122¾	122¾	− ½
ItgRs 10¾96	11.1	58	97⅞	97¼	97¼	− ¼
Intrfst 7¾05	cv	109	70½	70	70	...
IBM 9⅜04	9.0	67	105¼	104½	104½	− ⅞
IBM 7⅞04	cv	1683	111½	110½	111½	+ ½
InMin 9.35s00	9.4	9	100	100	100	...
IntRec 9s10	cv	77	79	76¾	79	+ 3
Intnr 10½08	cv	176	127	126	126¾	+ ¾
Intnr 11s95	10.4	5	106	106	106	...
Jamswy 8s05	cv	2	110	110	110	...
v|JnM 7.8504f	...	6	104¾	104¾	104¾	− 1½
v|JnM 9.7s85mf	...	9	112	111	112	+ 1
v|JonsLl 6¾94f	...	1	16¼	16¼	16¼	+ ⅛
v|JonsLl 6½88f	...	12	17	16½	16½	− 1
v|JoneL 9⅞95f	...	25	39⅜	39¼	39¼	...
v|JoneL 8s98f	...	5	39	39	39	...
v|JoneL 9¾96f	...	10	39	39	39	...
Kaisr 9s05	cv	35	103½	103½	103½	...
Kellwd 9s99	cv	4	265	265	265	+ 10½
KerrMc 8½06	8.9	1	95⅜	95⅜	95⅜	+ ⅛
Kystn 8½05	cv	10	113	113	113	+ 1
Kolmrg 8¾09	cv	37	90	90	90	...
Krogr 8.7s98	8.5	9	102¾	102¾	102¾	+ ¾
Krogr 14⅜91	13.6	10	106	106	106	− ⅞
v|LTV 5s88f	...	247	22	20⅝	22	+ 1½
v|LTV 9¼97f	...	44	30	28⅜	28½	− 1½
v|LTV 11s07f	...	231	21	20½	20½	− ⅛
v|LTV 13⅞02f	...	5	31	31	31	...
v|LTV 14s04f	...	62	29¼	28¾	29	+ ⅜
v|LTV 11½97f	...	5	22⅜	22⅜	22⅜	− 1⅝
v|LTV 7⅞98f	...	28	17⅝	17¼	17¼	− ⅜
v|LTV 8¾98f	...	8	18¼	18¼	18¼	− ¼
LaQuin 10s02	cv	8	104	104	104	− ½
LearS 10s04	10.2	2	97⅝	97⅝	97⅝	− 2¼
LearS 11¼98	11.3	82	101	99¾	99⅞	− ⅛
Leget 6½06	cv	14	100½	100¼	100½	...
LincFt 8½96	8.5	2	100½	100½	100½	+ ⅝
Litton 11½95	10.4	8	110½	110½	110½	+ 1½
Litton 12⅝05	10.5	32	120	120	120	+ ⅝
LomN zr01	...	238	30⅛	29½	29½	− 1
LomN 9s10	cv	26	132	132	132	...
LomN 7s11	cv	17	99½	99	99½	...
LglsLt 12⅝92	12.1	25	104½	103½	104½	− ½
LglsLt 13½13	12.4	5	109	108¾	109	+ ¼
LglsLt 13¼95	12.1	42	109¾	109	109½	+ ½
LglsLt 11¼96	11.3	90	101	100	100	− ¾
LglsLt 11⅞15	11.8	9	101	101	101	...
LglsLt 11.7s93	11.4	34	102½	102	102½	+ ½
LglsLt 11¾94	11.5	22	102½	102½	102½	...
LglsLt 11½14	11.7	37	99	97¾	98	+ ¼
Loral 7¼10	cv	160	116	115½	116	...
Lorilld 6⅞93	7.2	33	95	95	95	...
LouGs 9¼00	8.9	21	104	103⅛	104	...
v|Lykes 7½94f	...	80	16⅛	16	16	− 1½
MACOM 9¼06	cv	6	93	93	93	+ 1
MacMl 7½10	...	15	129½	129½	129½	+ ½
McyCr 13⅞91	13.1	140	105⅞	105½	105¾	+ ¼
MfrH 8⅛04	8.7	5	93½	93½	93½	− 1
MfrH 6s87t	6.1	10	99	99	99	...
MarO 8.5s06	9.6	45	89	87⅝	89	+ 1⅜
MarO 12½94	12.4	1144	100¾	100 19/32	100⅝	+ 1/32
Mattel 11⅝03	11.9	87	100	98	98	− ¾
McCro 7½94	10.5	1	71⅛	71⅛	71⅛	− ⅞
McDe 10s03	10.0	50	99⅝	99⅝	99⅝	− ⅜
McDnl zr94	...	35	58⅜	58	58	− ⅜
McKes 6s94	cv	6	229	229	229	+ 4
v|McLn 12s03f	...	65	13½	13	13	− 1
v|McLn 14¼94f	...	239	13¼	12½	13	+ ¼
MerLy zr06	...	628	25	24⅝	24⅝	+ ⅛
MesaCap 12s96	11.3	48	106⅝	106	106½	+ 2⅜

FIGURE 6–2 **Part of the "New York Exchange Bonds" page from *The Wall Street Journal* for January 15, 1987.** *Source: The Wall Street Journal,* January 15, 1987, p. 46. Reprinted by permission of *The Wall Street Journal,* © Dow Jones & Company, Inc., 1987. All Rights Reserved.

The reason for the price of the AMR bond is that interest rates declined slightly after this 10¼% coupon bond was issued. The higher coupon is more than competitive with the going market interest rate for bonds of this type, and the price rose to reflect this. Many of the bond prices to be seen in Figure 6–2 were selling at **premiums** (prices above par value), reflecting a decline in market rates after that particular bond was sold. Quite a few were selling at **discounts** (prices below par value of $1000) because the stated coupons are less than the prevailing interest rate on a comparable new issue.

Other items of interest in Figure 6–2 are the number of different bond issues a single corporation may have outstanding at a given time. Alabama Power (AlaP), for example, had nine different issues outstanding. Other utilities show the same pattern, as do some nonutilities—notice, for example, GMA (General Motors Acceptance Corporation) with 17 different issues outstanding.

Now consider the first bond listed on the page, "AGS." The small "cv" under the current yield column indicates that this is a convertible bond, which can be converted at the holder's option into common stock of the same corporation. These bonds require a different type of analysis and will be discussed in Chapter 16.

Finally, note the number of zero coupon bonds in the figure, as shown by the designation "zr." Of course, they have no current yield and they must always sell at a discount.

The Wall Street Journal also carries quotations on government securities, including Treasury bills, notes and bonds, and agency issues. Figure 6–3 shows quotations excerpted from "Treasury Bonds, Notes, and Bills" starting with 1990 maturities.

With Treasury notes and bonds, maturities are available for various periods up to the year 2017 (in Figure 6–3), with coupons ranging from 3.25% to about 15%. Note that U.S. government bond prices are quoted in 32nds; therefore, a bond price of 100.4 means 100 and 4/32. One other difference between government bonds and corporate bonds is that for the former the "yield" column is the yield to maturity, whereas for the latter it is current yield. These can be quite different, as will be explained later in the chapter.

Treasury bills pay no coupons; instead, they are sold at a discount from par value (the minimum denomination is $10,000). These are pure discount instruments, the total return being attributable to the difference between the price paid for the bill and its maturity value. The yields on Treasury bills are calculated and quoted on an *annualized yield basis* in both primary and secondary markets.[18]

---

[18] The yield, or discount rate, on a Treasury bill can be calculated as

$$\text{Discount rate} = \frac{\text{Face value} - \text{Issue price}}{\text{Face value}} \times \frac{360}{\text{Days to maturity}}$$

For example, consider a Treasury bill with a face value of $10,000 issued at a price of $9777,

TREASURY BONDS, NOTES & BILLS

Thursday, June 18, 1987

Representative mid-afternoon Over-the-Counter quotations supplied by the Federal Reserve Bank of New York City, based on transactions of $1 million or more.

Decimals in bid-and-asked and bid changes represent 32nds; 101.1 means 101 1/32. a-Plus 1/64. b-Yield to call date. d-Minus 1/64. k-Nonresident aliens exempt from withholding taxes. n-Treasury notes. p-Treasury note; nonresident aliens exempt from withholding taxes.

Treasury Bonds and Notes

Rate	Mat.	Date	Bid	Asked	Bid Chg.	Yld.
8½s,	1987	Jun p	100.2	100.6		0.00
10½s,	1987	Jun n	100.4	100.8		0.00
8⅞s,	1987	Jul p	100.10	100.14		4.63
8⅞s,	1987	Aug p	100.16	100.20		5.41
12⅜s,	1987	Aug p	100.29	101.1	– .1	5.18
13¾s,	1987	Aug n	101.4	101.8	– .1	5.06
9s,	1987	Sep p	100.23	100.27		5.75
11⅛s,	1987	Sep n	101.10	101.14		5.64
8⅞s,	1987	Oct p	100.26	100.30		6.11
7⅝s,	1987	Nov n	100.13	100.17	– .1	6.20
8½s,	1987	Nov p	100.29	101.1		6.06
11s,	1987	Nov p	101.24	101.28		6.09
12⅝s,	1987	Nov n	102.14	102.18		6.07
11¼s,	1987	Dec n	102.12	102.16	– .1	6.31
7⅞s,	1987	Dec p	100.21	100.25		6.33
8⅛s,	1988	Jan p	100.25	100.29	– .1	6.58
12⅜s,	1988	Jan n	103.9	103.13	+ .2	6.14
10⅛s,	1988	Feb n	102.2	102.6		6.64
10⅜s,	1988	Feb p	102.6	102.10		6.73
8s,	1988	Feb p	100.25	100.29		6.64
12s,	1988	Mar n	103.26	103.30	+ .1	6.70
7⅛s,	1988	Mar p	100.5	100.9		6.75
6⅝s,	1988	Apr p	99.21	99.25		6.89
13¼s,	1988	Apr n	105.5	105.9		6.50
8¼s,	1988	May n	101.1	101.5		6.90
7⅛s,	1988	May p	100.3	100.7		6.88
9⅞s,	1988	May n	102.13	102.17	– .1	6.92
10s,	1988	May p	102.16	102.20	– .1	6.93
7s,	1988	Jun p	99.31	100.3		6.90
13⅝s,	1988	Jun n	106.16	106.20		6.81
6⅝s,	1988	Jul p	99.15	99.19		7.01
14s,	1988	Jul n	107.1	107.8		6.91
6⅛s,	1988	Aug p	98.27	98.31		7.04
9½s,	1988	Aug p	102.19	102.22	+ .1	7.03
10½s,	1988	Aug n	103.21	103.25		7.02
6⅜s,	1988	Sep p	99.1	99.5		7.08
11⅜s,	1988	Sep p	105.1	105.5		7.10
15⅜s,	1988	Oct n	110.25	110.29	+ .2	6.59
6⅜s,	1988	Oct p	98.31	99.3	+ .1	7.09
6¼s,	1988	Nov p	98.22	98.26		7.13
8¾s,	1988	Nov n	102	102.4		7.13
8⅝s,	1988	Nov p	101.26	101.30		7.14
11¾s,	1988	Nov n	105.29	106.1		7.14
10⅝s,	1988	Dec p	104.24	104.28		7.19
6¼s,	1988	Dec p	98.22	98.26	+ .5	7.13
6⅛s,	1989	Jan n	98.8	98.12		7.21
14⅝s,	1989	Jan n	110.25	110.29	– .1	7.13
8s,	1989	Feb p	101	101.4		7.26
6¼s,	1989	Feb p	98.8	98.12	– .1	7.21
11⅜s,	1989	Feb n	106.7	106.11	+ .1	7.23
11¼s,	1989	Mar p	106.11	106.15		7.30
6⅜s,	1989	Mar p	98.12	98.16		7.29
7⅛s,	1989	Apr p	99.17	99.19	– .1	7.36
14⅜s,	1989	Apr n	111.26	111.30	– .1	7.24
6⅞s,	1989	May p	99.1	99.5	– .1	7.36
9¼s,	1989	May n	103.9	103.13	– .2	7.30
8s,	1989	May n	101.1	101.3	– .1	7.38
11¾s,	1989	May n	107.17	107.21		7.35
9⅝s,	1989	Jun p	104	104.4	– .1	7.39
14½s,	1989	Jul n	113.7	113.11	– .1	7.41
6⅝s,	1989	Aug p	98.8	98.12	– .2	7.46
13⅞s,	1989	Aug n	112.14	112.18	– .2	7.45
9⅜s,	1989	Sep p	103.26	103.30		7.46
11⅞s,	1989	Oct n	109.2	109.6	– .1	7.48
6⅜s,	1989	Nov p	97.15	97.19	– .2	7.49
10¾s,	1989	Nov n	106.30	107.2		7.48
12¾s,	1989	Nov p	111.8	111.11		7.49
8⅜s,	1989	Dec p	101.26	101.30		7.52
10½s,	1990	Jan n	106.20	106.24	– .1	7.56
3½s,	1990	Feb	91.30	92.30	– .4	6.44
6½s,	1990	Feb k	97.14	97.18	– .1	7.53
11s,	1990	Feb p	107.30	108.2	+ .1	7.59
7¼s,	1990	Mar p	99.1	99.5	– .1	7.59
10½s,	1990	Apr n	107	107.4		7.64
7⅞s,	1990	May k	100.18	100.20	– .3	7.63
8¼s,	1990	May	102.31	103.7		7.00
11⅜s,	1990	May p	109.12	109.16	– .1	7.66
7¼s,	1990	Jun p	98.25	98.29	– .2	7.66
10¾s,	1990	Jul n	108.2	108.6	– .1	7.70
9⅞s,	1990	Aug p	105.27	105.31	– .1	7.71
10¾s,	1990	Aug n	108.6	108.10	– .2	7.73
6¾s,	1990	Sep p	97.3	97.7	– .4	7.73
11½s,	1990	Oct n	110.19	110.23	– .3	7.77
9⅝s,	1990	Nov k	105.13	105.17	– .2	7.74
13s,	1990	Nov n	115.10	115.14	– .2	7.75
6⅝s,	1990	Dec p	96.16	96.20	– .2	7.74
11¾s,	1991	Jan n	111.31	112.3	– .2	7.80
9⅛s,	1991	Feb k	104.1	104.5	– .3	7.80
6¾s,	1991	Mar p	96.20	96.22	– .3	7.78
12⅜s,	1991	Apr n	114.19	114.23	– .3	7.84
8⅛s,	1991	May p	100.31	101.3	– .3	7.79
14½s,	1991	May n	122.2	122.6	– .4	7.79
13¾s,	1991	Jul n	120.1	120.5	– .4	7.86
7½s,	1991	Aug p	98.25	98.29	– .5	7.81
14⅞s,	1991	Aug n	124.10	124.14	– .6	7.86
12¼s,	1991	Oct p	115.17	115.21	– .5	7.90
6½s,	1991	Nov p	95.5	95.9	– .3	7.79
14¼s,	1991	Nov n	123.12	123.16	– .2	7.83
11⅝s,	1992	Jan p	113.25	114.1	– .4	7.70
6⅝s,	1992	Feb p	95.6	95.10	– .4	7.85
14⅝s,	1992	Feb n	125.17	125.21	– .7	7.92
11¾s,	1992	Apr	114.25	115.1	– .3	7.93
6⅝s,	1992	May k	94.28	95	– .5	7.87
13¾s,	1992	May n	122.30	123.2	– .3	7.97
10⅜s,	1992	Jul p	109.24	109.28	– .4	7.97
4¼s,	1987-92	Aug	91.25	91.27	– .3	5.90
7¼s,	1992	Aug	99.23	99.31	– .2	7.26
8¼s,	1992	Aug p	101.15	101.17	– .6	7.87
9¾s,	1992	Oct p	107.13	107.17	– .3	7.98
10½s,	1992	Nov n	110.21	110.25	– .5	8.00
8¾s,	1993	Jan p	103.6	103.10	– .5	8.00
4s,	1988-93	Feb	92.5	93.5	– .4	5.42
6¾s,	1993	Feb	95.2	95.10	– .6	7.79
7⅞s,	1993	Feb	99.20	99.28	– .4	7.90
10⅞s,	1993	Feb n	112.17	112.21	– .5	8.04
7⅜s,	1993	Apr p	96.26	96.30	– .6	8.04
10⅛s,	1993	May n	109.14	109.18	– .4	8.06
7¼s,	1993	Jul p	96.3	96.7	– .4	8.05
7½s,	1988-93	Aug	97	97.8	– .3	8.08
8⅝s,	1993	Aug	102.17	102.25	– .5	8.04
11⅞s,	1993	Aug n	117.26	117.30	– .9	8.11
7⅛s,	1993	Oct p	95.7	95.11	– .4	8.08
8⅝s,	1993	Nov	102.20	102.28	– .4	8.04
11¾s,	1993	Nov	117.21	117.25	– .4	8.13
7s,	1994	Jan	94.12	94.16	– .7	8.10
9s,	1994	Feb	104.7	104.15	– .6	8.12
7s,	1994	Apr p	94.7	94.11	– .6	8.10
4⅛s,	1989-94	May	91.30	92.30	– .5	5.36
13⅛s,	1994	May p	125.24	125.28	– .8	8.14
8¾s,	1994	Aug	103.6	103.14	– .7	8.11
12⅝s,	1994	Aug p	123.23	123.27	– .9	8.16
10⅛s,	1994	Nov	110.15	110.23	– .7	8.17
11⅝s,	1994	Nov	118.24	118.28	– .9	8.17
3s,	1995	Feb	92.3	93.3	– .3	4.06
10½s,	1995	Feb	112.17	112.25	– .5	8.22
11¼s,	1995	Feb p	116.24	117	– .6	8.21
10⅜s,	1995	May	111.30	112.6	– .9	8.24
11¼s,	1995	May p	117.1	117.9	– .7	8.23
12⅝s,	1995	May	124.30	125.6	– .10	8.23
10½s,	1995	Aug p	112.29	113.1	– .8	8.27
9½s,	1995	Nov p	107.5	107.9	– .7	8.28
11½s,	1995	Nov	119.2	119.10	– .9	8.27
8⅞s,	1996	Feb p	103.11	103.15	– .7	8.30
7⅜s,	1996	May p	94.5	94.13	– .7	8.28
7¼s,	1996	Nov p	93.6	93.10	– .8	8.29
8½s,	1997	May k	101.17	101.19	– .8	8.26
7s,	1993-98	May	90.10	90.18	– .13	8.33
3½s,	1998	Nov	92.1	93.1	– .3	4.28
8½s,	1994-99	May	100.13	100.29	– .12	8.32
7⅞s,	1995-00	Feb	95.15	95.23	– .8	8.43
8⅜s,	1995-00	Aug	99.4	99.12	– .13	8.45
11¾s,	2001	Feb	126.2	126.10	– .5	8.46
13⅛s,	2001	May	136.31	137.7	– .10	8.51
8s,	1996-01	Aug	96.22	96.30	– .8	8.37
13⅜s,	2001	Aug	139.8	139.16	– .18	8.52
15¾s,	2001	Nov	159.11	159.19		8.50
14¼s,	2002	Feb	146.30	147.6	– .13	8.54
11⅝s,	2002	Nov	125.25	126.1	– .12	8.55
10¾s,	2003	Feb	118.10	118.18	– .9	8.57
10¾s,	2003	May	118.21	118.29		8.55
11⅛s,	2003	Aug	121.22	121.30	– .9	8.59
11⅞s,	2003	Nov	128.6	128.14	– .14	8.61
12⅜s,	2004	May	132.29	133.5	– .15	8.61
13¾s,	2004	Aug	145.22	145.30	– .14	8.52
11⅝s,	2004	Nov k	126.22	126.30	– .6	8.61
8¼s,	2000-05	May	97.14	97.22	– .9	8.50
12s,	2005	May k	130.9	130.17	– .13	8.62
10¾s,	2005	Aug k	119.14	119.22	– .5	8.82
9⅜s,	2006	Feb k	107.16	107.24	– .13	8.54
7⅝s,	2002-07	Feb	91.16	91.24	– .16	8.50
7⅞s,	2002-07	Nov	93.22	93.30	– .25	8.51
8⅜s,	2003-08	Aug	97.21	97.29	– .22	8.59
8¾s,	2003-08	Nov	100.31	101.7	– .13	8.61
9⅛s,	2004-09	May	104.5	104.13	– .16	8.62
10⅜s,	2004-09	Nov	115.8	115.16	– .15	8:64
11¾s,	2005-10	Feb	127.11	127.19	– .16	8.67
10s,	2005-10	May	112.5	112.13	– .15	8.63
12¾s,	2005-10	Nov	136.25	137.1	– .22	8.68
13⅞s,	2006-11	May	147.20	147.28	– .22	8.68
14s,	2006-11	Nov	149.8	149.16	– .20	8.68
10⅜s,	2007-12	Nov	116.11	116.19	– .16	8.63
12s,	2008-13	Aug	131.25	131.29	– .17	8.68
13¼s,	2009-14	May	144.9	144.17	– .21	8.67
12½s,	2009-14	Aug k	137.10	137.14	– .21	8.67
11¾s,	2009-14	Nov k	130.21	130.25	– .16	8.62
11¼s,	2015	Feb k	128.16	128.20	– .17	8.54
10⅝s,	2015	Aug k	122.11	122.19	– .14	8.50
9⅞s,	2015	Nov	114.4	114.12	– .14	8.52
9¼s,	2016	Feb k	107.23	107.31	– .16	8.50
7¼s,	2016	May k	86.18	86.22	– .12	8.49
7½s,	2016	Nov k	89.10	89.14	– .13	8.48
8¾s,	2017	May k	103.7	103.9	– .12	8.45

U.S. Treas. Bills

Mat. date	Bid (Discount)	Asked (Discount)	Yield	Mat. date	Bid (Discount)	Asked (Discount)	Yield
-1987-				10-29	5.86	5.84	6.05
6-25	4.21	4.05	4.11	11- 5	5.83	5.79	6.00
7- 2	5.28	5.24	5.32	11-12	5.84	5.80	6.02
7- 9	5.54	5.50	5.59	11-19	5.82	5.78	6.00
7-16	5.28	5.24	5.33	11-27	5.90	5.86	6.10
7-23	5.25	5.21	5.31	12- 3	5.88	5.84	6.08
7-30	5.28	5.24	5.34	12-10	5.90	5.86	6.11
8- 6	5.50	5.48	5.59	12-17	5.90	5.88	6.14
8-13	5.50	5.48	5.60	12-24	5.94	5.90	6.17
8-20	5.49	5.45	5.58	-1988-			
8-27	5.51	5.47	5.60	1-21	5.90	5.88	6.15
9- 3	5.65	5.61	5.75	2-18	6.08	6.00	6.35
9-10	5.62	5.60	5.75	3-17	6.15	6.11	6.42
9-17	5.65	5.63	5.79	4-14	6.23	6.21	6.55
9-24	5.64	5.62	5.78	5-12	6.31	6.29	6.66
10- 1	5.76	5.74	5.91	6- 9	6.29	6.27	6.67
10- 8	5.70	5.66	5.84				
10-15	5.72	5.68	5.87				
10-22	5.78	5.74	5.94				

Source– Federal Reserve Bank.

FIGURE 6–3 **"Treasury Bonds, Notes & Bills" quotations from *The Wall Street Journal*, January 14, 1987.**

Source: Excerpted from *The Wall Street Journal*, January 14, 1987, p. 43. Reprinted by permission of *The Wall Street Journal*, © Dow Jones & Company, Inc., 1987. All Rights Reserved.

Reading the daily "Treasury Bills" section of *The Wall Street Journal* (the Treasury bill section is shown in the last part of Figure 6–3), an investor can see the bid quote, the ask quote, and the discount rate yield for Treasury bills trading in the secondary market (with Treasury bill quotes, the decimal assumes the normal meaning).

Do not be confused because the bid is larger than the ask. The bid and ask quotes are percentage discounts from face value. The bid quote is the discount rate derived from the price that dealers in these securities will pay to buy them from investors. The larger the discount, the smaller the price.[19] The ask quote is the discount rate derived from the prices at which dealers will sell to investors—the smaller the ask rate, the larger the price. Therefore, as you would expect in the over-the-counter market, dealers stand ready to sell Treasury bills to investors for a price exceeding what they would pay investors wishing to sell. The difference between the bid and ask quotes represents the dealers' spread, or profit.

Treasury bills trade on the basis of a 360-day year, whereas bonds typically trade on a 365-day-year basis. Treasury bills can be adjusted to a bond equivalent (or investment yield) basis, allowing investors to compare bill yields with the returns from securities with coupons.[20]

The Bond Market

Traditionally, the market for long-term bonds has differed from the stock market in that it is basically a primary market—a market for new issues. Institutional investors have been major purchasers of bonds because regulatory constraints favored such purchases, and on an overall basis they dominate the bond market. Institutional investors buy in large volume and often hold the bonds until maturity; therefore, the volume of trading for existing bonds (the secondary market) has historically been small. Although the sec-

---

maturing in 91 days. The discount rate is

$$\frac{\$10,000 - \$9777}{\$10,000} \times \frac{360}{91} = 8.82\%$$

[19] That is, the seller of a one year maturity Treasury bill would receive the bid price, or $(100\% - x.x\%)$ \$10,000, where $x.x\%$ is the stated "bid" yield.

[20] The bond equivalent basis is

$$\text{Bond equivalent basis} = \frac{\text{Total dollar discount}}{\text{Purchase price}} \times \frac{365}{\text{Days to maturity}}$$

For the Treasury bill illustrated above,

$$\text{Bond equivalent basis} = \frac{\$223}{\$9777} \times \frac{365}{91} = 9.15\%$$

Note that the bond equivalent yield is always greater than the yield in discount form.

ondary market for bonds is increasingly important, the historical nature of the bond market must be recognized.

New Trends in the Bond Market—Junk Bonds

No discussion of the bond market would be complete without considering one of the major events in bonds in the 1980s—the creation and use of "junk bonds." These bonds have a major impact on financial markets and corporate America, and have generated considerable media attention.

Junk bonds are high-risk, high-yield bonds; that is, they carry bond ratings of BB or lower, with correspondingly higher yields (as shown in Figure 6–1, bonds rated BB or below are regarded as "having predominantly speculative characteristics with respect to capacity to pay interest and repay principal"). An alternative—and more reassuring—name used to describe this area of the bond market is the *high-yield debt market*.[21]

Junk bonds are issued in connection with

1. Mergers.
2. Leveraged buyouts.
3. Companies with heavy debts to repay—such as bank loans.
4. Stock buybacks by corporations.

As with many other investment items, junk bonds illustrate how our dynamic capital markets adjust to new developments. Rising interest rates caused institutional investors to consider the relative attractiveness of lower-rated, and therefore higher-yielding, securities. At the same time, the upsurge in takeovers and mergers created a need for a new approach to financing these transactions. Such well known figures as T. Boone Pickens used junk bonds to help finance their takeover attempts while Drexel Burnham Lambert helped to develop this market by persuading institutions to buy such bonds. Drexel became both the biggest underwriter and the biggest dealer in the junk-bond market.

The junk-bond market has grown significantly with over 100 new issues in 1984 alone, totaling $14 billion. The total market exceeded $120 billion by 1986. Furthermore, institutional investors, such as insurance companies, pension funds, and bond mutual funds, have become significant holders of junk bonds. The high-yield mutual bond funds, representing in effect individual investors, own about one-fourth of all junk bonds.

The impact of junk bonds is immense. They have revolutionized takeover tactics and clearly contributed to the rash of hostile takeover bids in the 1980s. In effect, they have made possible the overthrow of many corporate managers. Since takeovers—both real and rumored—have a significant impact on the stock market as the prices of potential candidates are rapidly

---

[21] See Edward I. Altman and Scott A. Nammacher, *Investing in Junk Bonds: Inside the High Yield Debt Market* (New York: John Wiley, 1987) for a good discussion of this market.

BOX 6–2 THE IMPACT OF JUNK BONDS

It's quite a change, but 1987 will go down as the year the junk-bond market became, well, just another market. Drexel's eroding power signals more than the twilight of the takeover buccaneer using junk to finance audacious raids on established companies. Competition among other investment bankers for a chunk of Drexel's juicy junk business is shifting the focus from the Mike Milken mystique to the nuts and bolts of everyday corporate finance.

It's true that until recently financial manipulators and bust-up artists have adroitly abused these securities, pushing corporate leverage to new extremes. But junk bonds, so called because they rank as less-than-investment-grade securities, are rapidly establishing a place in the nation's capital markets: The more than $100 billion of junk outstanding is now nearly a quarter of all publicly traded corporate bonds.

The junk business will still have to be purged of remaining excesses before it can attain a fuller measure of respectability. And the most significant problem won't pass with the Boesky scandal. Instead, the extra risk that defines junk issues is coming home to roost in the form of rising defaults. Last year more than $3 billion worth of junk—some 3% of the issues on the market—defaulted. That's triple the average rate for the previous three years, and quite a few issues narrowly escaped default only through being exchanged for a new basket of securities.

NO REWARD. According to First Boston Corp., defaults cut last year's total return—from interest payments and price changes—by two-and-a-half percentage points, to 15.63%, based on an index composed of 159 junk issues. By contrast, safer investment-grade issues, as measured by a Salomon Brothers corporate index, showed a 17.03% return. Thus junk investors were not being rewarded for their extra risk. "The fact that there were over 3% defaults in a good growth year doesn't bode well for what defaults would be in a bad year," says New York University professor Edward I. Altman.

Already defaults are spreading from the steel and energy debacles of 1986 to a wider spectrum of issuers. Media companies, once junk-market darlings, are a prime example of how excessive leverage can hurt. Two junk-bond issuers tied to Drexel—WTTV in Indianapolis and Miami's Grant Broadcasting System Inc.—have filed for Chapter 11 bankruptcy protection from creditors. Moreover, as in many recent mergers and leveraged buyouts in other fields, some media companies have issued junk bonds on the basis of "leverage being redeemed not through earnings but through asset sales," explains newsletter publisher and junk critic James Grant. It's a risky strategy.

Grant points to the recent experience of SCI Holdings Inc., formerly Storer Communications Inc. When Lorimar-Telepictures pulled out of its $1.4 billion agreement to buy SCI's seven television stations, investors soon found that it's not always easy to sell assets to pay down debt. Lorimar had discovered, belatedly, that its bid was too high by 40%. Why? Advertising revenues had deteriorated since the deal was announced, reducing the value of those properties. SCI still has lots of time and room to maneuver, because it has other assets that it can sell to raise cash. Still, "I'm wary of media deals," says one longtime junk-bond buyer.

Problems could also multiply among

leveraged buyouts that leave little margin for error. Worries one junk expert: "The market has been accepting issues of companies that are highly leveraged and cyclical in earnings." Investor nervousness over Mary Kay Cosmetics Inc., for one, has sent the yield on its zero-coupon junk bonds to nearly 20%. Pacific Lumber Co. is struggling to boost cash flow to meet its debt obligations (BW—Feb. 2). And investors are getting leery of junk issuers in volatile industries such as construction, housing, and transportation.

QUALITY JUNK. Higher future default rates, however, do not mean the end of junk financings. "What the market needs is a true recession" which would clear away the weaker issues, says Atalanta/Sosnoff Capital Corp. Senior Vice-President Robert Kobel. "Yes, 5% to 6% of the market will default, but at least 90% of the market will fly right through." The junk market is big enough to have a broad spectrum of relatively high-quality issues.

Companies that voluntarily restructure their balance sheets, for example, will create a steady stream of issues that barely deserve the appellation "junk." Having learned from battles for corporate control, more managers are, in effect, "raiding" their own company before someone else does. By tapping the junk-bond market, managers accomplish several things at once. First, they keep their jobs. Second, they satisfy institutional investors seeking high income: "Junk is merely another form of equity with a high dividend" and no voting rights, says Dean LeBaron, head of Batterymarch Financial Management Corp. Finally, managers can gain more control over the equity with voting rights.

Colt Industries Inc. exemplifies this new breed of issuer. It recently quadrupled its debt—heavily in junk bonds—to $1.4 billion and increased its retirement fund's holdings of Colt common from 7% to 30%. Colt's stock surged from 66¾ to 93⅝ when the plan was announced last July.

The junk-bond market will return to its roots as other investment banks refine the skills that made Drexel its kingpin. Financing and developing long-term relationships with entrepreneurs, such as MCI Communication Corp.'s William G. McGowan, is one of the junk-bond market's greatest strengths. An entire generation of entrepreneurs and small companies that previously depended on banks and floating-rate, short-term money has been liberated from those uncertainties by the long-term, fixed-rate junk-bond market. The current climate of suspense—over the next default, the next indictment—will obscure that benefit for a while longer. But once the junk market weathers these storms, its wares will prove a durable financing tool for a significant part of Corporate America.

Source: Reprinted from February 16, 1987 issue of *Business Week* by special permission, © 1987 by McGraw-Hill, Inc.

driven up, and junk bonds are often used to finance the takeover (or stock buyback by the corporation), junk-bond activities can definitely affect the entire stock market.

Investors in the Bond Market

A variety of institutional investors, government agencies, foreign governments, and the Federal Reserve system channel funds into Treasury (government) and agency securities. Households (including personal trusts and nonprofit organizations) steadily increased their ownership over the period from 1978 to 1986, holding almost $590 billion of Treasuries and agencies by the end of 1986 (including $80 billion in savings bonds).

As for corporate bonds, households directly held only $71 billion in 1978, and only $64 billion by the end of 1986. This amounted to less than 10% of the corporate bonds outstanding. These figures are consistent with the traditional situation in the bond market—that life insurance companies and pension funds (including state and local funds) are major purchasers of corporate bonds. Private financial institutions held about $720 billion of corporate bonds by year-end 1986.

Finally, the municipal bond market has typically been an institutional market with commercial banks and property and casualty insurance companies buying substantial amounts of these bonds in any one year. However, individuals have become a strong force in the municipal bond market because inflation has pushed them into higher tax brackets, where the tax-exempt feature of municipals becomes attractive. Individuals were the major force in municipals by 1981, and in 1982 they became the market with over 95% of the net new supply of municipals being bought by individuals either directly or indirectly through investment company funds specializing in tax-exempts. Household ownership of municipals has increased every year from 1978 through 1986, at which time the total owned exceeded $250 billion.

The Tax Reform Act of 1986 may enhance the appeal of municipals to investors, particularly high-bracket investors, because it devastated tax shelters in general and eliminated or limited many other deductions. Municipal bonds emerged as one of the major investment opportunities available to investors. Investors need to remember that tax reform established three categories of municipals: (1) most municipals remain exempt from federal income taxes; (2) some municipals are exempt from federal income taxes but are subject to the alternative minimum tax; (3) some municipals are subject to both federal income taxes and the alternative minimum tax.[22]

Trading Bonds

Chapter 3 outlined trading conditions in the secondary bond markets. As noted, the secondary bond market is primarily an over-the-counter market, with dealers making a market in the various issues. These may be brokerage firms or commercial banks, which are well-known dealers in governments, agencies, and municipals. Although some corporate bonds are traded on the exchanges, primarily the NYSE, these few listed issues constitute only a small part of total bond trading. For example, in 1986 the trading volume for bonds traded on the NYSE averaged only $30 to $40 million a day. There-

---

[22] All municipal bonds issued on or before August 7, 1986 are exempt from federal income taxes and the alternative minimum tax.

fore, the *listed* market in bonds is small and thin. Most corporate bonds are traded over the counter, as are all governments, agencies, and municipals.

Some sectors of the bond market, such as U.S. government bonds, have been quite active and are becoming more so. The large amounts of government securities outstanding and the continuing large flows into these securities make this the dominant segment of the bond market for most investors. Henry Kaufman, a well known Wall Street commentator on interest rates, has called the U.S. government market the leader in establishing prices in the bond market.[23]

Unlike the homogeneous government bond market, the corporate bond market faces growing heterogeneity and declining credit quality. Although some issues may be actively traded, such as utility issues because of the interest in high-yielding securities, other issues may be quite inactive. Individual investors are well advised to consider the relative illiquidity of a small (less than $100,000) position in corporate bonds. Such a position can be liquidated, but it may take longer than a comparable trade in government bonds or common stocks and price concessions must often be made. On the New York Stock Exchange, the spread can range from one to two points (one point = $10) on active issues and up to five points or more on inactive issues. Including commissions, an investor could pay as much as $600 on a $10,000 order. Some experts recommend that the average investor not buy bonds in amounts less than $100,000 unless he or she plans to hold them 5 or 10 years.[24]

The municipal securities market is generally not active. Because of the large number of small bond issues in this market, substantial illiquidity exists and potential bond purchasers should be aware of this before transacting. Although more individual investor funds are flowing into this market, it remains an over-the-counter dealer market subject to difficulties in trading.

Bond Returns and Risks

Why Buy Bonds?

A wide range of investors participate in the fixed income securities marketplace, ranging from individuals who own a few government or corporate bonds to large institutional investors, who own billions of dollars of bonds. Most of these investors are presumably seeking the basic return–risk characteristics that bonds offer; however, quite different overall objectives can be accomplished by purchasing bonds. It is worthwhile to consider these points. As fixed-income securities, bonds are desirable to many investors

---

[23] See Henry Kaufman, "New Precepts of Interest Rates," Salomon Brothers, 1980.
[24] This information is based on Ben Weberman, "Comparison Shopping," *Forbes*, October 6, 1986, p. 203.

because they offer a steady stream of interest income over the life of the obligation and a return of principal at maturity. The promised yield on a bond held to maturity (assuming default does not occur) is known at the time of purchase. Investors who buy bonds and hold them to maturity can, in effect, lock in an expected return and plan accordingly. Barring default by the issuer, the buyers will have the bond principal returned to them at maturity, and by holding to maturity, they can escape the risk that interest rates will rise, thus driving down the price of the bonds.

Other investors are interested in bonds exactly because bond prices will change as interest rates change. If interest rates rise (fall), bond prices will fall (rise). These investors are not interested in holding the bonds to maturity but rather in the possible capital gains they can earn if they correctly anticipate movements in interest rates. Because bonds can be purchased on margin, large potential gains are possible from speculating on interest rates; of course, large losses are also possible.

Bond speculators encompass a wide range of participants, from financial institutions to individual investors. All are trying to take advantage of an expected movement in interest rates.

Much speculation has occurred recently in the bond markets. In the past, bonds were viewed as very stable instruments whose prices fluctuated very little in the short run. This situation has changed drastically, however, with the bond markets becoming quite volatile. Interest rates in the early 1980s reached record levels, causing large changes in bond prices.

Now that we know why investors purchase and sell bonds, we can analyze some basic information about the returns from, and risks of, investing in bonds. This will allow us to proceed directly with the valuation and analysis of bonds in the next chapter.

Bond Returns

As noted in Chapter 5, the return (HPY) on bonds can be separated into two parts, which helps to explain why bonds can appeal to both conservative investors seeking steady income and aggressive investors seeking capital gains. Conservative investors usually view bonds as "fixed income securities," meaning that they expect specified payments from the bonds at specified times. The payments are going to consist of either coupon income on a semiannual basis and the return of principal at maturity or, with zero discount bonds, the return of principal at maturity.

The second source of potential returns to bondholders arises from the behavior of bond prices. Capital gains and losses occur because bonds are purchased and sold before maturity. Bond prices are determined by several factors, including time to maturity, coupon, and the general level of interest rates (these factors are discussed in the next chapter). The most important variable that affects a bond at any time is the behavior of interest rates in the marketplace. Holding other factors constant, the determining factor in the behavior of bond prices is the behavior of interest rates. There is an inverse relationship between the two—as market interest rates rise (fall), bond prices decline (rise). Therefore, investors can earn capital gains (or suffer losses) from bonds just as they do with stocks. If they purchase bonds and market interest rates fall, the prices of the bonds will rise; conversely, if interest rates rise after the purchase, the prices of the bonds will decline.

The behavior of bond prices is more complex than the inverse relationship between bond prices and market interest rates. Different bonds react in different ways to a given change in market rates. Other factors that affect prices include the time to maturity, the coupon, the call feature, and the rating on the bond. The result is a complex system of bond price changes, but the end result is still that investors have the opportunity to earn large returns by speculating on the behavior of bond prices.

Measuring Returns

Several measures of the yield, or return, on a bond are available and sometimes used by investors. We will discuss three of these measures in this chapter. The first is included only for purposes of terminology since it is not a measure of the total return to an investor. The most commonly used measure of yield, or promised return, for a bond is the yield to maturity. This concept is introduced in this chapter and used in the next to discuss the valuation of bonds. Finally, the holding period yield is a measure of the total return on a security.

Current yield   A more accurate measure than coupon yield is the **current yield,** defined as

$$\text{Current yield} = \frac{\text{Stated (coupon) interest per year}}{\text{Current market price}} \qquad (6\text{--}1)$$

Assume, for example, that a 10-year, 10% coupon bond is currently selling for $1075 because interest rates declined after the bond was issued. The dollar coupon is $100 (10% of $1000), and the annual current yield is $100/$1075 = 9.3%.

The current yield is clearly superior to the coupon rate because it uses the current market price. However, it is not a true measure of the return to a bond purchaser because it does not account for the difference between the bond's purchase price and its eventual redemption at par value.

Yield to maturity   The rate of return on bonds most often quoted by investors is the **yield to maturity** (YTM), defined as the indicated (promised) semiannually compounded rate of return an investor will receive from a bond purchased at the current market price and held to maturity. The calculation of yield to maturity involves equating the current market price (MP) of a bond with its discounted future coupon payments and principal repayment; that is, the yield to maturity is the discount rate that equates the present value of all net cash flows to the cost (MP) of the bond, as shown by

Equation 6–2.[25] Note that the market price, the coupon, the number of years to maturity, and the face value of the bond are known, and the discount rate or yield to maturity is the variable to be determined.[26]

$$MP = \sum_{t=1}^{2n} \frac{C_t/2}{(1 + YTM/2)^t} + \frac{FV}{(1 + YTM/2)^{2n}} \qquad (6-2)$$

where

MP = the market price of the bond in question.
YTM = the yield to maturity.
  C = the coupon in dollars.
  n = the number of years to maturity.
FV = the face or par value.

Consider the following example designed to illustrate the concept of calculating a yield to maturity. A 10% coupon bond has 10 years remaining to maturity. Assume that the bond is selling at a discount with a current market price of $885.30. Because of interest rate risk, we know that yields have risen since the bond was originally issued because the price is less than $1000. Using Equation 6–2 to solve for yield to maturity, we would have

$$\$885.30 = \sum_{t=1}^{20} \frac{\$50}{(1 + YTM/2)^t} + \frac{\$1000}{(1 + YTM/2)^{20}} = 12\%$$

---

[25] This is identical to calculating the internal rate of return, which involves a trial-and-error (iteration) process.

[26] A traditional method for calculating YTM, used by bond traders and others, is the use of bond tables. These tables provide investors with a YTM, given the coupon rate, the price of the bond, and the time to maturity. They can also be used to determine the price of a bond when the yield (and the other factors) are known.

To find the YTM on a bond using these tables, the following steps are performed.

1. Choose the page in the bond table corresponding to the appropriate coupon rate. There is a page for each different coupon.
2. Select the column with the appropriate maturity date.
3. Find the price of the bond in the appropriate maturity column and read across this row to the left column that contains the resulting YTM.

An approximation formula exists for calculating YTM. It relates the net annual effective cash flow to the average amount of money invested in the bond during the ownership period. Effectively, the investor is assumed to have an average investment of this amount in the bond as the price gradually converges to $1000, as it must by the maturity date.

$$\text{Approximate yield to maturity} = \frac{\text{Coupon interest} \begin{cases} + \text{ Amortized discount} \\ \text{or} \\ - \text{ Amortized premium} \end{cases}}{(\text{Current market price} + \text{Par value})/2}$$

As an example of calculating the approximate YTM, consider a bond with a 10% coupon and a term to maturity of 10 years. If it is purchased by an investor as an assumed current market price of $1075, the approximate yield to maturity is [$100 − ($75/10)]/[$1000 + 1075)/2] = 8.92%.

Since the left side of Equation 6–2 and the numerator values (cash flows) on the right side are known, the equation can be solved for YTM. Because of the semiannual nature of interest payments, the coupon (which in this example was $100) is divided in half and the number of periods (ten in this example) is doubled. What remains is a trial-and-error process to find a discount rate (YTM) that will equate the inflows from the bond (coupons plus face value) with its current price (cost). Different YTMs would have to be tried until the left-hand and right-hand sides were equal. In this example, the solution is 12%.[27]

$885.30 = $50 (present value of an annuity, + $1000 (present value factor,
6% for 20 periods)   6% for 20 periods)

$885.30 = $50(11.4699) + $1000(0.3118)

$885.30 = $885.30

These problems are easily solved today by calculator or computer. The preceding analysis simply demonstrates what is happening with the YTM.

It is important to understand that YTM is a *promised* yield because investors will earn the indicated yield only if the bond is held to maturity. Obviously, no trading can be done if the YTM is to be earned. The investor simply buys and holds. What is not so obvious to many investors, however, is the reinvestment implications of the YTM measure.

The YTM calculation assumes that the investor reinvests all coupons received from a bond at a rate equal to the computed YTM, thereby earning interest on interest over the life of the bond. For a bond with a YTM of 10%, for example, this 10% will be earned *only* if each of the coupons are reinvested at a 10% rate. If the investor spends the coupons, or reinvests them at a rate different from the assumed reinvestment rate of 10%, the **realized yield** actually earned will differ from the promised YTM. Coupons could be reinvested at rates higher or lower than the computed YTM.

This interest-on-interest concept significantly affects the realized return. Its impact is a function of coupon and time to maturity, with reinvestment becoming more important as either coupon or time to maturity rises, or both. Consider what happens when investors purchase bonds at high YTMs, such as when interest rates were at very high levels in the summer of 1982. Unless they reinvested the coupons at the promised YTMs, investors did not actually realize these high promised yields. For the promised YTM to become a realized YTM, coupons had to be reinvested at the record rates existing at that time, an unlikely situation for a high-YTM bond with a long maturity. The subsequent decline in interest rates during the fall of 1982 illustrates the

---

[27] The present value of an annuity factor for 6% for 20 periods, 11.4699, is taken from Table A–4 at the end of the text; 0.3118, the present value of a $1 for 6% for 20 periods, is taken from Table A–2.

TABLE 6–1 Realized Yield, Using Different Reinvestment Rate Assumptions, for a 10% 20-Year Bond Purchased at Face Value

Coupon Income[1] ($)	Assumed Reinvestment Rate (%)	Amount Attributable to Reinvestment[2] ($)	Total Return[3] ($)	Realized Return[4] (%)
2000	0%	0	2000	5.57
2000	5%	1370	3370	7.51
2000	8%	2751	4751	8.94
2000	9%	3352	5352	9.46
2000	10%	4040	6040	10.00
2000	11%	4830	6830	10.56
2000	12%	5738	7738	11.14

[1] Coupon income = $50 coupon received *semiannually* for 20 years = $50 × 40 periods.

[2] Amount attributable to reinvestment = total return minus coupon income. This is also known as the interest on interest.

[3] Total return = sum of an annuity for 40 periods, $50 semiannual coupons (Example: at 10% reinvestment rate, $50 × [5%, 40 period factor of 120.80] = $6040).

[4] Realized return = [Future Value per Dollar Invested]$^{1/N}$ − 1 where future value per dollar invested = (total return + the cost of bond)/cost of the bond. The result of this calculation is the realized compound return on a semiannual basis. To put this on an annual basis, this figure must be doubled.

fallacy of believing that one has "locked up" record yields during a relatively brief period of very high interest rates.

To illustrate the importance of interest on interest in YTM figures, Table 6–1 shows the total realized return under different assumed reinvestment rates for a 10% noncallable 20-year bond purchased at face value. If the reinvestment rate is exactly equal to the YTM of 10%, the investor will realize a 10% compound yield when the bond is held to maturity, with $4040 of the total dollar return from the bond attributable to interest on interest. At a 12% reinvestment rate, the investor realizes an 11.14% compound return, with almost 75% of the total return coming from interest on interest ($5738/7738). With no reinvestment of coupons (spending them as received), the investor would achieve only a 5.57% realized return. Clearly, the reinvestment portion of the YTM concept is critical.

Bond investors today often make specific assumptions about future reinvestment rates in order to cope with the reinvestment rate problem. Given their assumption, they can calculate the realized yield to be earned if that assumption turns out to be accurate.

One of the advantages of a zero coupon bond is the elimination of reinvestment rate risk. Investors know at the time of purchase the YTM that will be realized when the bond is held to maturity.

Most corporate bonds, and some government bonds, are callable by the issuers, typically after some deferred call period. For bonds likely to be called, the yield to maturity calculation is unrealistic. A better calculation is the promised **yield to call.** The end of the deferred call period, when a bond first can be called, is often used for the yield to call calculation. This is particularly appropriate for bonds selling at a premium (i.e., high coupon bonds with market prices above par value).[28]

To calculate the yield to first call, the YTM formula (Equation 6–2) is used, but with the number of periods until the first call date substituted for the number of periods until maturity; in addition, the call price is substituted for face value. These changes are shown in Equation 6–3.

$$MP = \sum_{t=1}^{2c} \frac{C_t/2}{(1 + YTC/2)^t} + \frac{CP}{(1 + YTC/2)^{2c}} \qquad (6\text{--}3)$$

where

    CP = the call price to be paid if the bond is called.
  YTC = yield to first call.
     c = number of periods until the call date.

It is important to remember that bond prices are calculated on the basis of the lowest yield measure. Therefore, for premium bonds selling above a certain level, yield to call replaces yield to maturity because it produces the lowest measure of yield.[29]

Holding period yield As explained in Chapter 5, a measure of the total return for any security is available in the form of holding period yield (HPY). The formula for a bond's HPY is repeated as Equation 6–4.[30]

$$HPY = \frac{I_t + PC}{P_B} \qquad (6\text{--}4)$$

Using the current yield example, assume that the investor holds this bond for one year, collects $100 in interest, and sells the bond for $1050. The HPY for this one year period is

$$\text{One year HPY} = \frac{100 + (-25)}{1075}$$

$$= 6.98\%$$

---

[28] That is, bonds with high coupons (and high yields) are prime candidates to be called.

[29] The technical name for the point at which yield to call comes into play is the "crossover point," which is a price and is approximately the sum of par value and one year's interest. For a discussion of this point, see S. Homer and M. Leibowitz, *Inside the Yield Book* (Englewood Cliffs, N.J.: Prentice-Hall, 1972), Chapter 4.

[30] The subscript t stands for time and refers to a holding period. I is the bond's coupon interest payment in dollars during holding period t. P_B is the bond's price at the beginning of holding period t, and PC is the change in bond price over the period.

On the other hand, assume the investor had held this only six months, collected one $50 coupon (bond interest is paid semiannually), and sold the bond for $1110. The HPY in this case would be

$$\text{Six-month HPY} = \frac{50 + 35}{1075}$$

$$= 7.91\%$$

Bond Risk

Bonds have their own sources of risk, just as common stocks and other securities. Bondholders are promised a stream of interest payments and a repayment of the principal or par value, but they are subject to several sources of risk in actually realizing these returns, specifically, (1) interest rate, (2) inflation, (3) default, (4) maturity, (5) call, and (6) liquidity risks.

Interest rate risk A major risk facing all bondholders is changing interest rates, which thereby change the price of the bonds. Prices of outstanding bonds must change inversely with changes in current market interest rates. When the market interest rate declines (rises), prices of bonds outstanding rise (fall).

Interest rate risk is the change in the price of a security as a result of changes in market interest rates. This variability in prices is caused by changes in interest rate levels, which are very powerful forces that affect all securities markets. Although investors normally discuss interest rate risk in connection with bond analysis, it is important to remember that this risk has significant implications for common stocks. It will be discussed again when we consider the sources of risk to an owner of common stocks.

To illustrate how interest rate risk applies to fixed-income securities, consider a new issue of corporate bonds by IBM. If IBM bonds are rated AAA and if existing AAA corporate bonds with comparable features are yielding 10%, the new IBM bonds will yield approximately 10%. Let us assume that IBM can in fact sell new bonds today by contracting to pay the purchasers 10% (of $1000) annually in interest and by guaranteeing to redeem the bonds in, say, 20 years. An investor buying these bonds today for $1000 each will receive $100 in interest income each year for 20 years and will have $1000 returned for each bond at the end of the 20 years unless IBM defaults—a most unlikely event. Barring default, and recognizing the erosion of all financial assets by inflation, the investor takes no further risk by holding the bonds to maturity. However, if the bonds must be sold before maturity in order to raise money, the investor is exposed to interest rate risk.

To continue the example, assume that the investor needs to sell the bonds five years after purchasing them and that the interest rate on comparable bonds has risen to 12%. Potential investors in this bond will not pay the original purchaser $1000 for the five-year-old IBM bonds. Why should they, when they can buy new bonds with comparable features yielding 12%? As a result of the upward shift in interest rates, the price of these bonds must decline below $1000, allowing the purchaser to receive approximately 12% on them.

The same forces apply in the opposite direction. If interest rates decline, bond prices rise. Obviously, investors would prefer the higher interest rates on the old bonds, other things being equal. By purchasing old, higher yielding bonds, they will drive the price up and the yield down until yields again reach an equilibrium.

(2) **Inflation risk**   Fixed-income securities, by definition, promise specified payments at specified periods. Since the payment in dollars is fixed, the value of the payment in real terms declines as the price level rises. This risk of the real return being less than the nominal (dollar) return is referred to as inflation risk.

Inflation risk will be accounted for in the next chapter when the level of interest rates is discussed. However, it can be noted that inflation risk is really the risk of unanticipated inflation. If anticipated, inflation is reflected in nominal riskless interest rates that investors use in valuing bonds. Thus, investors are compensated for that part of inflation that is anticipated but may not be compensated for unanticipated inflation.

(3) **Default risk**   Corporate bonds and municipals, as discussed earlier, are subject to default—the failure to pay the specified interest payments or repay the principal at the time specified in the indenture. Bonds carry strict obligations and the failure to make a specified payment as called for is a serious event.

Default risk does not exist for U.S. Treasury securities, at least on a practical basis. Although some U.S. agency securities are not directly guaranteed by the federal government, the belief is that the Treasury would not permit one of these agencies to default. Corporates and municipals are always subject to some risk, however small, of default by the issuer. The two major rating agencies, Standard & Poor's and Moody's, are good sources of information on default risk.

(4) **Maturity risk**   Maturity risk refers to the fact that the further into the future an investor goes in purchasing a long-term security, the more risk there is in the investment (other things being equal). The environment 30 years from now, when some long-term bonds mature, can scarcely be envisioned today. Thus, investing for the long term involves substantial risk, and bond investors wish to be compensated for this risk with an additional premium for lending long term rather than short term.

(5) **Call risk**   As explained earlier in the chapter, many corporate bonds are callable. Issuers have the option of redeeming a bond before the maturity date, typically after the first five years a bond is outstanding. Bonds will not

be called unless it is to the issuer's advantage—it is not likely to be to the bondholder's advantage. When interest rates decline, bonds carrying higher coupons are likely to be called. The call risk to a bondholder, therefore, is that higher coupon bonds will have to be given up.

(6) **Liquidity risk** Liquidity risk is concerned with the secondary market where a security is traded. A security is liquid if it can be sold easily and quickly with (at most) small price concessions. While Treasury securities are very liquid, the corporate bond market is less so. This is particularly true for "small" positions (less than $100,000).

Measuring Risk

As noted, there are several sources of risk for bonds. In measuring risk, however, there is no measure comparable to the beta for equity securities (at least in the sense of being widely recognized and used). Nevertheless, it is always appropriate to talk about the dispersion in expected returns.

Recall from Chapter 5 that the risk of an investment involves the idea that the actual outcome on any security or portfolio will be different from the expected outcome. Risk is typically assessed by measuring the dispersion in actual outcomes—the greater the dispersion, the greater the risk. Standard deviation, or variance, is a measure of dispersion or total risk; this is the most widely used measure of dispersion.

Whether they realize it or not, investors are dealing with a probability distribution of possible HPYs when they consider investing in a bond. Assuming this distribution is normal, a comparison of the returns from bond A with those from bond B will indicate which is riskier. If the standard deviation of A is 5% and that of B is 3%, A can be said to be riskier.

Useful information can be derived from historical data using the standard deviation (and the assumption that the distribution of returns is normal, or approximately so). One standard deviation on either side of the mean or expected value encompasses about 68% of the HPYs in the distribution; ±2 encompasses about 95% of the HPYs, and ±3 encompasses about 99%. Thus, knowing that all AAA corporate bonds had an average HPY of 12% per year for the last 10 years with a standard deviation of 2%, and that the distribution was normal, you know that 68% of the HPYs were within the range of 10% to 14%, or 2% on either side of the mean. In this scenario, investors experienced little risk roughly two-thirds of the time, and even 95% of the time the HPYs did not go below 8%. Based on this information, investors can decide if they are willing to take the risk of these outcomes.

As another example, consider the situation where someone says that the expected HPY on a bond rated "B" for the next year is 18%, but that the estimated standard deviation is 10%. The significance of this statement can be understood quickly. Two standard deviations around this expected value encompass *negative* HPYs.

The Historical Returns and Risk on Bonds

Investments is a forward looking subject, with participants interested in what will happen over some future holding period. Throughout this text we are discussing the valuation and analysis of securities in order to help us make intelligent estimates of the future returns from, and risks of, securities. Nevertheless, it is important to know what has happened in the past. Otherwise, investors have no reasonable basis for judging their future estimates. For example, if during the last 50 years, which encompasses severe depressions as well as periods of very high inflation, bonds in any one year never returned 30% or experienced a 20% loss, it would be unlikely for them to do so in the foreseeable future. It would not be impossible, however; the past therefore cannot simply be extrapolated into the future with no adjustments and no considerations. But knowing what the returns and risk on the major types of securities have been in the past is useful information.

One of the best known series of returns for the major types of securities, used in Chapter 5, was compiled by Ibbotson and Sinquefield. The original study, covering the period 1926–1976, has been updated periodically.[31] The relevant portion of the Ibbotson–Sinquefield data used in Chapter 5 (Figure 5–2) to discuss the distribution of returns and their standard deviations is reproduced as Table 6–2.

The Ibbotson–Sinquefield report is a statistical examination of the total rates of return (HPYs) on a monthly and annual basis for common stocks, long-term corporate bonds, long-term U.S. government bonds, and inflation. In addition, for stocks and U.S. government bonds, the total returns are broken down into returns attributable only to income and only to capital appreciation.

Table 6–2 shows the returns and risk, as measured by the standard deviation, on bonds for the period 1926–1986. Notice that both arithmetic mean and geometric mean returns are shown. As discussed in Chapter 5, the

TABLE 6–2 **Rates of Return on Long-Term Bonds and Treasury Bills, 1926–1986**

Series	Geometric Mean (%)	Arithmetic Mean (%)	Standard Deviation (%)
Long-term corporate bonds	5.0	5.3	8.5
Long-term government bonds	4.4	4.7	8.6
U.S. Treasury bills	3.5	3.5	3.4
Inflation	3.0	3.1	4.9

Source: Ibbotson, Roger G., and Rex A. Sinquefield, *Stocks, Bonds, Bills and Inflation* (SSBI), 1982, updated in *SSBI 1987 Yearbook,* Ibbotson Associates, Chicago, 1987.

---

[31] This data is available on a regular basis. Both an annual volume and quarterly volumes are sold, and monthly updates are available.

geometric mean for each of the series represents the compound annual rate of return, and is less than the arithmetic mean. Geometric means measure the change in wealth over time, whereas the arithmetic mean is a better measure of the "typical" performance over individual periods.

Table 6–2 shows that, over this 61 year period, long-term corporates and governments had annual geometric mean HPYs of 5.0% and 4.4% respectively, and similar arithmetic mean annual returns. The standard deviations were 8.5% and 8.6%, respectively. Although in the late 1970s and early 1980s investors became accustomed to high interest rates and the idea that bond returns should be considerably higher than these numbers indicate, for many years bond returns were low because inflation was very low or nonexistent. Also, it is important to recognize that the measurement process used to produce these numbers produces, on an annual basis, some losses on corporates and governments in certain years; that is, since the returns are measured annually based on year-end prices, bond price declines during the year can produce negative HPYs *for that year*.

The fact that the measurement of returns on an annual basis can result in some negative HPYs on bonds can be clearly demonstrated in connection with an additional point about bond returns and risk. An investor in fixed income securities always has as one important option choosing between long-term bonds and short-term instruments. Assume the investor has an investment horizon of one year and decides what to invest in (i.e., short-term instruments or long-term bonds) at the beginning of each year. How would such an investor have fared over a period encompassing the recent major inflationary experience of the United States as well as the great up markets of the mid-1980s?

Consider the annual returns on a long-term government bond index and short-term Treasury bills for the 20 year period 1967–1986.[32] Inflation started its upward trend in the late 1960s as a result of President Johnson's financing policies, and interest rates and inflation declined dramatically in the last half of 1982. Therefore, this is an excellent period in which to demonstrate the potential returns on bonds, as well as their riskiness.

The annual total returns on long-term bonds were negative in 8 of the 20 years between 1967 and 1986, with 4 negative years in a row (1977–1980). Because of their short-term nature, Treasury bills always produce a positive total annual return. Furthermore, shorts outperformed longs in three additional years when bond returns were positive (1974, 1981, and 1983). Thus, investing in long-term bonds on an annual basis is not a riskless strategy. In 11 out of 20 recent years short-term money market instruments outperformed long-term bonds. On an average annual compound rate of return

---

[32] These figures are based on *Stocks, Bonds, Bills and Inflation: 1987 Yearbook,* Ibbotson Associates; Chicago, 1987.

basis, Treasury bills outperformed long-term government bonds for the period 1967–1986.

Of course, in particular years long-term bond returns can be extraordinary. Bond investors earned larger total returns during 1982 as a result of the sharp drop in interest rates. Bond prices soared, raising total returns to unprecedented heights. In 1982, assuming more risk by purchasing longs instead of shorts paid off handsomely. The same was true for 1985, when returns on bonds averaged 30% or more.

On the very first page of this text the following question was posed: is it possible to have earned 40% or more in one year by investing in default-free Treasury securities? The answer is yes! Two agency issues, one from the Federal Home Loan Mortgage Corporation and one from the Federal Housing Administration, produced incredible annual returns of roughly 49% each in 1982. A 30-year Treasury bond, the safest long-term instrument known to humankind, produced an annual return of 41%. High-grade corporate bonds did even better![33]

Summary

Because bonds are a major financial asset, investors need to understand them and be aware of what they offer. They are creditor instruments and, by definition, fixed income securities; that is, a typical (i.e., coupon) bond offers a stream of fixed interest payments and the return of a specified par value (typically, $1000), all at designated dates. Bonds involve specific contractual obligations on the part of the issuer; failure to meet such obligations results in default and possibly bankruptcy.

Important characteristics of a bond include the call feature, giving the issuer the right to call in a bond issue by paying it off; the sinking fund, representing periodic payments by the issuer to pay off the bond; the security behind the bond, which may range from none (for a debenture) to the pledge of real property (for a mortgage bond); and the convertibility feature, allowing the bondholder to turn in the bond to the issuer for a specified number of shares of common stock.

Bonds change over time. Zero coupon bonds are a radical departure from the traditional bond format. New corporate bond features were offered in the early 1980s primarily because of inflationary conditions. New municipal bond features include federal backing, guarantees, "stripped" format, and put bonds.

Bonds are rated, primarily by Standard & Poor's Corporation and by

---

[33] See Martin L. Leibowitz, "Future Directions of Bond Portfolio Management," reprinted in *The Revolution in Techniques for Managing Bond Portfolios,* The Institute of Chartered Financial Analysts, 1983.

Moody's, as to their relative probability of default. These ratings have been very successful and they relieve the investor of having to make this judgment; however, the investor still must gauge the absolute risk and the attractiveness of bonds in general. Ratings range from AAA (the highest) to D (those bonds in default) with the first four grades (AAA through BBB) considered investment grade. Municipal bonds and commercial paper are also rated.

Several information sources are available for bonds. These are divided into two broad types: specific information on the issuer and information on the economy and interest rates, the major factor affecting bond price changes. Bond price information is available daily in the financial press.

The bond market is basically a primary market, that is, a market for new issues. Institutional investors have traditionally dominated this market, although individuals became the major force in municipals in 1981 and 1982. Some corporate bonds are traded on exchanges (primarily, the NYSE); however, most bond trading is done over the counter. Although the U.S. government and agency markets are very active, the corporate and municipal markets are not active markets for the average investor. Junk bonds have become an important component of the bond market, having significantly impacted both corporate managements and bond investors.

Bonds offer steady returns as well as a chance for capital gains; therefore, bonds attract both income seekers and speculators. As measures of return, the current yield is inadequate. The yield to maturity is a mainstay in bond analysis. Yield to maturity is the promised (expected) fully compounded rate of return an investor receives by purchasing a bond and holding it to maturity. Although promised, a yield to maturity may not be realized because the calculation assumes reinvestment of all coupons at the computed YTM rate. The interest-on-interest concept is an important part of the YTM calculation. HPY is always a useful measure of total return, for both bonds or any other asset.

The major source of bond risk is interest rate risk, whereby a change in interest rates causes an inverse change in bond prices; inflation risk, default risk, maturity risk, call risk, and liquidity risk are other sources. Risk can be measured with the standard deviation.

According to the Ibbotson–Sinquefield data for 1926–1986, the compound annual return on bonds has been 5.0% for corporates and 4.4% for governments. Bonds have been much safer than common stocks—as shown by standard deviations that are only 40% those for stocks. However, even within fixed-income securities, short-term instruments may outperform long-term bonds in certain years; for example, between 1967 and 1986 shorts outperformed longs in 11 of 20 years. Finally, the returns on fixed-income instruments can be dramatic from time to time. In 1982, Treasury bonds returned over 41% and were outperformed by several other fixed-income securities; furthermore, in 1985 the annual return on Treasury bonds was 31%.

Key Words

Accrued interest	Debenture	Premium
Bond	Discount	Realized yield
Bond ratings	Interest on interest	Term-to-maturity
Call feature	Interest rate risk	Yield to call
Coupon bond	Junk bond	Yield to maturity
Current yield	Par value	

QUESTIONS AND PROBLEMS

1. Are all bonds fixed-income securities?
2. Distinguish between a term-to-maturity bond and a serial bond.
3. Is the call feature an advantage or disadvantage to an investor? In what interest rate environment would you expect issuers to call in bonds, other things being equal?
4. Distinguish between a vanilla bond, a zero coupon bond, and a floating rate bond. How can a bond be guaranteed?
5. What is the probability of default for an "A" rated bond? Why might an investor purchase a "B" rated bond, which is below investment grade?
6. What "macro" information should be of primary concern to bond investors? What are some sources of such information?
7. Turning to the "New York Exchange Bonds" page in *The Wall Street Journal,* consider the second bond listed. What is the annual coupon in dollars for this bond, and when does it mature? Of what significance is the current yield? What other yield measure should investors consider?
8. Referring again to Question 7, find the first convertible bond on the page and decide whether it is selling as a "bond" or because it is valuable currently to convert it into common stock. Find the first premium bond and explain why this bond is selling at a premium.
9. Referring again to Question 7, translate the closing price of the second bond listed into its "true" price (based on $1000 par).
10. In the case of Treasury bills whose yields are quoted in *The Wall Street Journal,* why is the bid price larger than the asked price?
11. What is the relative size of the government securities market versus the corporate and municipal sectors? List, in order of descending importance, the role of individual investors in these three markets.

12. How are bonds traded? Where? What limitations, if any, do individual investors face in trading the various types of bonds?
13. How can bonds appeal to the most conservative investor as well as the speculator?
14. Calculate the HPY for a 9% bond purchased at 86, held one year, and sold for 92. Given this information, what statements can be made about interest rates?
15. Given the following information, calculate the current yield, the yield to maturity, and the HPY for each bond:
    a. A bond priced at $940, maturing in three years, with an 8% coupon.
    b. A bond priced at $1150, maturing in 10 years, with a 15% coupon.
    c. A bond bought at par, with a coupon of 12%, which matures in one year.
16. Calculate the two components of total return for a 13% coupon bond bought at $73, and sold three years later for $83.
17. Name the sources of risk for a bond. Which sources are most applicable to corporate bonds? to Treasury bonds?
18. How can bond risk be measured?
19. Assume a normal distribution for the corporate bond information in Table 6–2. Roughly two-thirds of the time, what range would be expected for annual returns? 95% of the time?
20. How have money market instruments performed, in relation to high-grade corporates, on an annual basis over the period 1967–1986? What are the implications to bond investors?
21. What directly accounts for the dramatic bond returns in 1982 and 1985? What are the implications to bond investors?
22. What is the relationship between the level of, and changes in, interest rates, and bond speculation?
23. Why is the current yield not a true measure of a bond's return?
24. What are the disadvantages to an investor of purchasing 10 or 15 corporate bonds?

Selected References

Altman, Edward I., and Nammacher, Scott A. *Investing in Junk Bonds: Inside the High Yield Debt Market.* New York: John Wiley, 1987.

Anthony, Robert N. "How to Measure Fixed-Income Performance Correctly." *The Journal of Portfolio Management,* Winter 1985, pp. 61–65.

Darst, David M. *The Complete Bond Book.* New York: McGraw-Hill, 1975.

Fabozzi, Frank J., and Pollack, Irving M., editors. *The Handbook of Fixed Income Securities,* 2nd ed. Homewood, Ill.: Dow Jones-Irwin, 1986.

Gup, Benton E. *The Basics of Investing,* 3rd ed. New York: John Wiley, 1987.

Hertzberg, Daniel. "Some Gimmicks Used to Sell Bonds Sour as Rates Fall, Inflation Slows." *The Wall Street Journal,* December 14, 1982, p. 33.

Homer, Sidney. "Historical Evolution of Today's Bond Market." *Journal of Portfolio Management,* Spring, 1975, pp. 6–11.

Ibbotson Associates. *Stocks, Bonds, Bills, and Inflation: 1987 Yearbook.* Chicago: Ibbotson Associates, 1987.

Kidwell, David S., and Peterson, Richard L. *Financial Institutions, Markets, and Money,* 3rd ed. Chicago: Dryden Press, 1987.

Maginn, John L., and Tuttle, Donald L., editors. *Managing Investment Portfolios.* Boston: Warren, Gorham & Lamont, 1983.

Nelson, Wayne F. *How to Buy Money.* New York: McGraw-Hill, 1981.

Tuttle, Donald L. editor. *The Revolution in Techniques for Managing Bond Portfolios.* Charlottesville, Va.: The Institute of Chartered Financial Analysts, 1983.

Weberman, Ben. "Make Mine Vanilla." *Forbes,* August 30, 1982, p. 169.

Yawitz, Jess B., and Marshall, William J. "Risk and Return in the Government Bond Market." *Journal of Portfolio Management,* Summer 1977, pp. 48–52.

CHAPTER 7

BOND VALUATION AND ANALYSIS

What determines the price of a security? The answer is value! A security's estimated value determines the price that investors place on it in the open market.

A security's **intrinsic value,** or economic value, is the present value of the expected cash flows (or returns) from that asset. Any security purchased is expected to provide one or more cash flows some time in the future. These cash flows could be periodic, as interest or dividends, a terminal price or redemption value, or a combination of these. Since these cash flows occur in the future, they must be discounted at an appropriate rate to determine their present value. The sum of these discounted cash flows is the economic (intrinsic) value of the asset. Calculating intrinsic value, therefore, requires the use of present value techniques. Equation 7–1 expresses the concept

$$\text{Value}_{t=0} = \sum_{t=1}^{n} \frac{\text{Cash flows}}{(1 + r)^t} \qquad (7\text{--}1)$$

where

$\text{Value}_{t=0}$ = the value of the asset now (time period 0).

Cash flows = the future receipts and repayment (or sales price of the asset).

r = the appropriate discount rate.

n = number of periods over which the cash flows are
expected.

To solve Equation 7–1 and derive the intrinsic value of a security, it is
necessary to determine the following:

1. The expected *cash flows* from the security. This includes the size and
   type of cash flows, such as dividends, interest, face value to be received at maturity, or expected price of the security at some point in
   the future.
2. The *timing* of the expected cash flows. Since the returns to be generated from a security occur at various times in the future, they must be
   properly documented for discounting back to time period zero (today).
   Money has a time value, and the timing of future cash flows significantly affects the value of the asset today.
3. The *discount rate*, or required rate of return demanded by investors.
   The discount rate used will reflect the time value of the money and the
   risk of the security. It is an opportunity cost, representing the rate
   foregone by an investor in the next best alternative with comparable
   risk.

Bond Valuation

Given the intrinsic value model for valuing any security, the value of a bond
is equal to the present value of its expected cash flows.[1] The coupons and the
principal repayment are known and the present value is determined by discounting these future payments from the issuer at an appropriate discount
rate, or market yield, for the issue.

The formula for calculating the present value of a coupon bond can be
stated as follows:

$$PV = \sum_{t=1}^{n} \frac{C_t}{(1 + r)^t} + \frac{FV}{(1 + r)^n} \qquad (7–2)$$

where

  PV = the present value of the bond today (time period 0).
   C = the coupons or interest payments.
  FV = the face value (or par value) of the bond.
   n = the maturity of the bond.
   r = the appropriate discount rate or market yield for the bond.

---

[1] As discussed in Chapter 6, an investor purchasing a bond must also pay to the seller the
accrued interest on that bond.

The present value process for a typical coupon-bearing bond involves three steps, given the dollar coupon on the bond, the face value, and the current market yield applicable to a particular bond.

1. Using the present value of an annuity table (Table A–4 in the Appendix), determine the present value of the coupons (interest payments).
2. Using the present value table (Table A–2 in the Appendix), determine the present value of the face value of the bond; for our purposes, the face value will always be $1000.
3. Add the present values determined in steps 1 and 2 together.

Consider newly issued bond A with a three-year maturity, sold at par to yield 10%. Assuming *annual* interest payments of $100 per year for each of the next three years, the value of bond A, based on Equation 7–2, is

$$PV(A) = \frac{\$100}{(1 + 0.10)} + \frac{\$100}{(1 + 0.10)^2} + \frac{\$100 + \$1000}{(1 + 0.10)^3}$$

$$= \$1000$$

which, of course, agrees with our immediate recognition that the bond's value would have to be $1000 since it has just been sold at par.

Now consider bond B, with characteristics identical to A's, issued five years ago when the interest rate demanded for such a bond was 7%. The coupon per year is $70. Assume that the current discount rate (or market yield) on bonds of this type is 10%, and that the bond has three years left to maturity. Investors will certainly not pay $1000 for bond B and receive $70 per year when they can purchase bond A and receive $100 per year. They will, however, pay a price determined by the use of Equation 7–2.

$$PV(B) = \frac{\$70}{(1 + 0.10)} + \frac{\$70}{(1 + 0.10)^2} + \frac{\$70 + \$1000}{(1 + 0.10)^3}$$

$$= \$925.38$$

Thus, bond B is valued, as is any other asset, on the basis of its future stream of benefits (cash flows), using a discount rate that properly reflects the risk involved. Since the numerator is always specified for coupon-bearing bonds at time of issuance, the only problem in valuing a typical bond is to determine the denominator—the discount rate. This can be done by observation in the marketplace. The discount rate is the current market interest rate being earned by investors on comparable investments such as new bonds with the same features (in other words, it is an opportunity cost). Thus, the effect of interest rates is incorporated into the discount rate used to solve the present value model; that is, the discount rate reflects the current market yield for the issue.

In order to conform with existing payment practices on bonds of paying interest semiannually rather than annually, Equation 7–2 must be modified. This is accomplished by dividing the discount rate being used (r), and the coupon (C_t), by 2 and doubling the number of periods. The three steps previously given are still applicable, and Equation 7–2 will now look as follows:

$$PV = \sum_{t=1}^{2n} \frac{C_t/2}{(1 + r/2)^t} + \frac{FV}{(1 + r/2)^{2n}} \qquad (7\text{–}3)$$

Equation 7–3 is the procedure used for published bond quotes and standard bond practices. Solving the previous examples using semiannual calculations rather than annual,

$$PV(A) = \sum_{t=1}^{6} \frac{\$50}{(1 + 0.05)^t} + \frac{\$1000}{(1 + 0.05)^6} = \$50(5.0757) + \$1000(0.7462)$$

$$= \$999.99$$

$$PV(B) = \sum_{t=1}^{6} \frac{\$35}{(1 + 0.05)^t} + \frac{\$1000}{(1 + 0.05)^6} = \$35(5.0757) + \$1000(0.7462)$$

$$= \$923.85$$

Explaining Bond Prices and Yields

Borrowers supply securities to the financial markets, while lenders seek securities as an investment. Equilibrium security prices and interest rates (yields) are determined simultaneously as part of the same process; that is, the price of a security and its rate of return or yield are determined at the same time as different aspects of the borrowing and lending of loanable funds.

An important part of the interest rate–security price determination process is the effect of an increase or decrease in the demand for loanable funds. An increase in the demand for loanable funds leads to an increase in the supply of securities, a new lower equilibrium price for securities, and a higher equilibrium interest rate on loanable funds. An increase in the supply of loanable funds leads to an increase in the demand for securities, a new higher equilibrium price for securities, and a lower equilibrium interest rate on loanable funds.

This analysis summarizes a fundamental fact about the relationship between bond prices and bond yields: bond prices move inversely to interest rates. When the level of interest rates demanded by investors on new issues changes, the yields that they require on all bonds already outstanding will change also. In order for these yields to change, the prices of these bonds must change. Therefore, the market yields and prices of all bonds—both new and outstanding—are directly related to interest rate behavior. It is obvious, therefore, that current market interest rates, and any expected change in market interest rates, are the key variables to analyze and monitor in understanding the behavior of bond prices and yields.

In the following discussion, we will consider the basic components of market interest rates because of their critical importance in the bond decision process. In analyzing the components of nominal interest rates, we will pay particular attention to two important dimensions of interest rate *behavior*.

1. The differences in yields for a given category of bonds, which is known as the term structure of interest rates.
2. The differences in yields that exist between different sectors or types of bonds, typically referred to as yield spreads.

The Level of Market Interest Rates: A Simple Explanation

Explaining interest rates is a complex task that involves substantial economics reasoning and study. This is not feasible in this text.[2] What is feasible is to assess the basic determinants of actual interest rates with an eye toward recognizing the factors that affect market interest rates and cause them to fluctuate. The bond investor who understands the foundations of market rates can then rely on expert help for more details, and be in a better position to interpret and evaluate such help.

The basic foundation of market interest rates is the marginal physical productivity of capital—that is, the rate at which capital physically reproduces itself. It is the opportunity cost of foregoing consumption, representing the rate that must be offered to individuals to persuade them to save rather than consume. This rate is sometimes referred to as the **real rate of interest,** because it is not affected by price changes or risk factors.[3] It is assumed by some economists to be about 2–3% a year.[4] It is designated RR in this discussion.

Nominal interest rates on top quality securities are composed of the RR plus an adjustment for inflation. A lender who lends $100 for a year at 10% will be repaid $110. But if inflation is 12% a year, the $110 that the lender receives upon repayment of the loan is worth only (1/1.12 of $110), or $98.21.

---

[2] Most money and banking texts contain a good, concise discussion of interest rates. A detailed analysis can be found in James C. Van Horne, *Financial Market Rates and Flows,* 2nd ed. Englewood Cliffs, N.J.: Prentice-Hall, 1984.

[3] The real rate of interest cannot be measured directly. It is often estimated by dividing (1.0 + MIR) by (1.0 + EI), where MIR is the market interest rate and EI is expected inflation. This result can be approximated by subtracting estimates of inflation from nominal (market) interest rates (on either a realized or expected basis). Some economists believe estimates of the real rate are subject to large errors. See G. Santoni and C. Stone, "The Fed and the Real Rate of Interest," *Review, FRB of St. Louis,* Vol. 69, No. 10 (December 1982), pp. 8–18.

[4] There is a common perception that real interest rates have been high in the 1980s. See Stephen G. Cecchetti, "High Real Interest Rates: Can They Be Explained?" *Economic Review: Federal Reserve Bank of Kansas City,* September/October 1986, pp. 31–41.

Lenders therefore expect to be compensated for the expected rate of price change in order to leave the real purchasing power of wealth unchanged. This inflation adjustment can, *as an approximation,* be added to the real rate of interest. Unlike RR, which is often assumed to be reasonably stable with time, adjustments for expected inflation vary widely with time. For example, the annual change in the implicit price deflator for the Gross National Product (GNP) ranged from 1.6% in 1960 to about 10% in 1980.

Thus, for short-term risk-free securities, such as three-month Treasury bills, the nominal interest rate is a function of the real rate of interest and inflationary premiums. This is expressed as Equation 7–4, in which EI = the expected inflation and MIR_{RF} = market interest rates for short-term, risk-free securities.

$$MIR_{RF} = RR + EI \qquad (7\text{–}4)$$

The short-term risk-free rate of interest changes as these two variables change. They could move in the same direction or opposite directions. The change in inflationary expectations is the key variable affecting the change in the risk-free rate of interest. The wide fluctuations in the Treasury bill rate that occur over time are primarily attributable to changes in inflation.

All market interest rates, whether for risk-free (Treasury) securities or for risky securities, are affected by a time factor. That is, while long-term Treasury bonds are free from default risk in the same manner as Treasury bills, Treasury bonds typically yield more than bills. The maturity factor generally increases the bond investor's risk. Normally, the longer the term of maturity, the higher the yield on a bond, everything else held constant. This is true for all types of bonds, whether Treasuries, corporates, or municipals. We will discuss the term structure of interest rates, which accounts for the relationship between time and yield for a given type of bond, below.

Most market interest rates are also affected by a third factor, a risk premium, which lenders require as compensation for the risk involved. This risk premium is associated with the issuer's own particular situation or with a particular market factor; in contrast, both RR and EI are economic factors that originate from forces external to the bond issuer or market factor. These *issue characteristics* unique to a given issuer that constitute the risk premium (RP) include whether the bonds are callable or not, whether they are secured or unsecured, the degree of marketability, and the tax treatment accorded certain securities. Another important characteristic discussed in Chapter 6 is the risk of default. Both corporate and municipal bonds carry some risk of default for which investors expect to be compensated. Market interest rates for corporate bonds exceed those for U.S. Treasury securities, with everything else held constant, because there is some risk of default on the corporates.

The risk premium is often referred to as the yield spread or yield differential. We will consider it following the discussion on the term structure of interest rates.

Term Structure of Interest Rates

The **term structure of interest rates** refers to the relationship between time to maturity and yields for a particular category of bonds. This relationship holds for a given time; ideally, other factors are held constant, particularly the risk of default. The easiest way to do this is to examine U.S. Treasury securities, which have no risk of default, no sinking fund, and are taxable. By eliminating those that are callable, and those that have some special features, a quite homogeneous sample of bonds can be obtained for analysis.

Yield curves The term structure is usually plotted in the form of **yield curves,** which are a graphical depiction of the relationship between yields and time for bonds that are identical except for maturity. The horizontal axis represents time to maturity, while the vertical axis represents yield to maturity. Figure 7–1 shows some typical (possible) yield curves, each of which indicate that interest rates vary with the time to maturity.

Curve 1 in Figure 7–1 is an upward sloping yield curve, which is considered typical; that is, interest rates that rise with maturity are considered the "normal" pattern. Since the early 1930s, upward-sloping yield curves have predominated. Yield curves sometimes slope downward, often when interest rates have reached their peak. Curve 2 in Figure 7–1 is a downward-sloping curve. Curve 3 is a "humped" yield curve—a curve with a peak in the short-to-intermediate-range maturities. Finally, curve 4 is a flat yield curve.

Figure 7–1b shows the yield curves for U.S. Treasuries at the start of the big interest rate movement in the summer of 1982 and roughly six months later. The curve at 7/7/82 was downward sloping, as would be expected when interest rates are at a peak. Six months later, the yield curve had returned to "normal"—upward sloping. The curves in Figure 7–1b indicate basically a parallel downward shift in the term structure of interest rates.

Term structure theories A theory of the term structure of interest rates is needed to explain the shape and slope of the yield curve and why it shifts over time. There are three competing theories today: the expectations theory, the liquidity premium theory, and the market segmentation theory.

1. The **expectations theory** of the term structure of interest rates states that the long-term rate of interest is equal to an average of the short-term rates that are expected to prevail over the long-term period. In effect, the term structure consists of a set of forward rates and a current known rate. Forward rates are rates that are expected to prevail in the future; that is, they are unobservable but anticipated future rates.

Under the expectations theory, long rates must be an average of the present and future short-term rates. For example, a three-year bond would carry an interest rate that is an average of the current rate for one year and the expected *forward rates* for the next two years. Technically, the average involved is a geometric rather than an arithmetic average. The same princi-

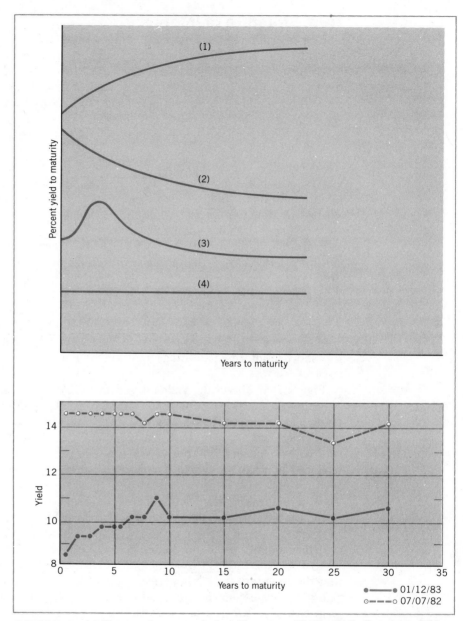

FIGURE 7–1 (*a*) **Shapes of some typical yield curves.** (*b*) **The U.S. Treasury yield curves for 7/7/82 and 1/12/83.**

Source: (*b*) Merrill Lynch, Pierce, Fenner & Smith, Inc., *Fixed Income Selector*, First quarter 1983, p. 9. This graph is reprinted by permission of Merrill Lynch, Pierce, Fenner & Smith Incorporated. © 1983 Merrill Lynch, Pierce, Fenner & Smith Incorporated.

ple holds for any number of periods; therefore, the market rate for any period to maturity can be expressed as an average of the current rate and the applicable forward rates.

For expositional purposes:[5]

$_tR_n$ = the current known yield (i.e., at time t), on a security with n periods to maturity

$_{t+1}r_n$ = the yield expected to prevail one year from today (at time $t + 1$) for n periods—these are forward rates

The rate for the three-year bond referred to above must be a geometric average of the current one-year rate ($_tR_1$) and the expected forward rates for the subsequent two years.

Therefore, in equation form

$$(1 + {_tR_3}) = [(1 + {_tR_1})(1 + {_{t+1}r_1})(1 + {_{t+2}r_1})]^{1/3} - 1.0 \qquad (7\text{--}5)$$

where

$(1 + {_tR_3})$ = the rate on a three-year bond.
$(1 + {_tR_1})$ = the current known rate on a one-year bond.
$(1 + {_{t+1}r_1})$ = the expected rate on a bond with one year to maturity beginning one year from now.
$(1 + {_{t+2}r_1})$ = the expected rate on a bond with one year to maturity beginning two years from now.

Example. Assume the current one-year bond rate ($_tR_1$) is 0.07, the two forward rates are 0.075 ($_{t+1}r_1$) and 0.082 ($_{t+2}r_1$). The rate for a three-year bond, $(1 + {_tR_3})$, would be

$$(1 + {_tR_3}) = [(1.07)(1.075)(1.082)]^{1/3} - 1.0$$

$$= 1.07566 - 1.0$$

$$= 0.07566 \text{ or } 7.566\%$$

The same principle applies for any number of periods. Any long-term rate is a geometric average of consecutive one-period rates.

Forward rates cannot be easily measured, but they can be inferred for any one-year future period. The expectations theory, however, does not say that these future expected rates will be correct; it simply says that there is a relationship between rates today and rates *expected* in the future.

Under this hypothesis, investors can expect the same return regardless of the choice of investment. Any combination of securities for a specified pe-

---

[5]This discussion is based on J. C. Poindexter and C. P. Jones, *Money, Financial Markets and the Economy*. St. Paul, Minn.: West Publishing, 1980. Chapter 9.

riod will have the same expected return. For example, a five-year bond will have the same expected return as a two-year bond held to maturity plus a three-year bond bought at the beginning of the third year. The assumption under this hypothesis is that expected future rates are equal to computed forward rates. Profit-seeking individuals will exploit any differences between forward rates and expected rates, ensuring that they equilibrate.

2. The **liquidity preference theory** states that interest rates reflect the sum of current and expected short rates, as in the expectations theory, plus liquidity (risk) premiums. Because uncertainty increases with time, investors prefer to lend for the short run. Borrowers, however, prefer to borrow for the long run in order to be assured of funds. Investors receive a liquidity premium to induce them to lend long term, while paying a price premium (in the form of lower yields) for investing short term.

The difference between the liquidity preference theory and the expectations theory is the recognition that interest-rate expectations are uncertain. Risk-averse investors seek to be compensated for this uncertainty. Forward rates and estimated future rates are not the same. They differ by the amount of the liquidity premiums.

3. The third hypothesis for explaining the term structure of interest rates is the **market segmentation theory.** Under this hypothesis, rates on securities with different maturities are effectively determined by the conditions that prevail in the different maturity segments of the market. Thus, securities with different maturities are imperfect substitutes for one another. Changes in the interest rates of various maturities affect the rates on other maturities little or not at all.

In the segmented markets approach, market participants may operate only within certain maturity ranges, or at least concentrate their activities in such ranges. Banks, for example, emphasize short-term assets because of their emphasis on liquidity. Life insurance companies, on the other hand, have traditionally taken a long-run view. They can predict their future liabilities quite well because of the accuracy of mortality estimates, and can afford to invest in longer term securities. Under this hypothesis, the shape of the yield curve is significantly influenced by the various market participants and the relative quantity of funds they have for investment.

All three of these theories have implications for the slope of the yield curve. As noted, under the market segmentation theory, the yield curve will change as the demand for or supply of securities in various parts of the maturity range changes. Such changes may have little or no effect on other parts of the yield curve. Under the liquidity preference theory, upward sloping curves should predominate because of the uncertainty premiums on longer term securities. The yield curve will shift as expectations about future rates change. Finally, under the expectations theory, the shape of the yield curve at any point in time has implication about the expectations of market participants:

1. If the yield curve is rising, the implication is that future short rates are expected to rise.
2. If the yield curve is downward sloping, the implication is that future short rates are expected to fall.
3. If the yield curve is horizontal (flat), the implication is that future short rates are expected to equal the current short rate. Such a curve reflects a state of transition.

Which of these theories is correct? The issue of the term structure has not been resolved; although many empirical studies have been done, the results are at least partially conflicting. Therefore, definitive statements cannot be made. In actual bond practice, market observers and participants tend not to be strict adherents to a particular theory. Rather, they accept the reasonable implications of all three and try to use any information in assessing the shape of the yield curve. Thus, many will focus on expectations, but allow for liquidity premiums.

Since the 1930s upward-sloping yield curves have been the norm, as would be predicted by the liquidity preference theory. And this theory is more compatible than the other two with the study of investments, which emphasizes the risk–return trade-off that exists. The liquidity preference theory stresses the idea that because of larger risks, longer maturity securities require larger returns or compensation.[6]

Regardless of which of the three theories of the term structure of interest rate is correct, it seems reasonable to assert that investors demand a premium from long-term bonds because of their additional risk. After all, uncertainty increases with time and long-term bonds are more sensitive to interest rate fluctuations than are short-term bonds. Given that this is a logical argument, what does the historical evidence indicate?

Ibbotson and Sinquefield, referred to earlier in connection with the returns on financial assets, have calculated bond maturity premiums for the years 1926 through 1986.[7] A bond maturity premium is defined as the return on long-term Treasury bonds minus the return on Treasury bills. The data indicate that the annual arithmetic mean maturity premium for that period was 1.2 (the geometric mean was 0.9). According to Ibbotson–Sinquefield, long-term bondholders undoubtedly demand a positive maturity premium before investing; however, they may not receive one over certain periods because unanticipated and rising inflation may result in large unanticipated capital losses. Thus, investors may not anticipate part of the inflation that occurs (for example, each of the five years from 1977 to 1981 showed a negative maturity premium).

---

[6] The expectations theory categorizes investors as return maximizers, whereas the market segmentation theory categorizes investors as risk minimizers.
[7] See R. Ibbotson and R. Sinquefield, *Stocks, Bonds, Bills and Inflation: 1987 Yearbook*, p. 46.

Risk Premiums—Yield Spreads

Assume that market interest rates on risk-free securities are determined as just explained, if the expected rate of inflation rises, the level of all rates rises also. Similarly, if the real rate of interest were to decline, market interest rates would decline—that is, the level of rates would decrease. Furthermore, as seen in the term structure analysis, yields vary over time for issues that are otherwise homogeneous in nature. The question that remains is, why do rates differ between different bond issues or segments of the bond market?

The answer to this question lies in what is referred to in bond analysis as yield spreads (or yield differentials or risk differentials). **Yield spreads** refer to the relationships between bond yields and the particular issuer and issue characteristics and constitute the risk premiums referred to earlier. Yield spreads are often calculated among different bonds holding maturity constant. They are a result of the following factors:

1. Differences in quality, or risk of default. Clearly other things being equal, a bond rated BAA will offer a higher yield than a similar bond rated AAA because of the difference in default risk.
2. Differences in call features. Bonds that are callable have higher YTMs than otherwise identical noncallable bonds. If the bond is called, bondholders must give it up, and they can replace it only with a bond carrying a lower YTM. Therefore, investors expect to be compensated for this risk.
3. Differences in coupons. High coupon bonds are more likely to be called if interest rates drop sharply.
4. Differences in marketability. Some bonds are more marketable than others, meaning that their liquidity is better. They can be sold either quicker or with less of a price concession, or both. The less marketable a bond, the higher the YTM.
5. Differences in tax treatments.

Clearly, yield spreads are a function of the variables connected with a particular issue or issuer. Investors expect to be compensated for the risk of a particular issue, and this compensation is reflected in the risk premium. However, investors are not the only determining factor in yield spreads. The actions of borrowers also affect them. Heavy Treasury financing, for example, may cause a narrowing of the yield spreads between governments and corporates as the large increase in the supply of Treasury securities pushes up the yields on Treasuries.

Yield spreads among alternative bonds may be positive or negative at any time. Furthermore, the size of the yield spread changes over time. Whenever the differences in yield become smaller, the yield spread is said to "narrow"; as the differences increase, it "widens." It seems reasonable to assume that yield spreads widen during recessions because of increasing risk-averseness on the part of investors. Since the probability of default is

TABLE 7–1 Yield Spreads—Municipal Bonds vs. Corporates and Treasuries

Month	Corporate Aaa Bonds	Long-term Treasury Securities
January 1986	197	151
February 1986	223	168
March 1986	192	108
April 1986	159	43
May 1986	155	53
June 1986	126	41
July 1986	137	38
August 1986	151	54
September 1986	178	100
October 1986	178	98
November 1986	183	98

Source: U.S. Financial Data, The Federal Reserve Bank of St. Louis, December 18, 1986.

greater during a recession, investors demand more of a premium. On the other hand, yield spreads narrow during boom periods. There is some historical support that this occurs.[8]

As one example of yield spreads, consider Table 7–1 which shows selected spreads between municipal bonds on the one hand and corporate Aaa bonds and Treasuries on the other. As noted, one of the factors causing risk premiums or yield spreads is different tax treatments. During 1986, investors contemplated the significant tax law changes that were ultimately signed by President Reagan in late 1986. Through the first eight months of 1986, expectations of tax liabilities caused the spreads between municipal bonds and other long-term securities to fluctuate substantially. The reason was the great uncertainty about the prospects of tax reform and what would happen to both the overall tax rate and the treatment of municipal bonds (which, of course, were always exempt from federal taxes).

As Table 7–1 shows, the spreads between municipals and both corporates and Treasuries fluctuated substantially from January through August, 1986. The basis-point spread (100 basis points = 1%) between municipals and corporates ranged from 126 to 223, and for Treasuries the range during this period was from 38 to 168. However, once the general shape of the tax package became relatively clear in September, the spreads between munic-

---

[8] See Calvin M. Boardman and Richard W. McEnally, "Factors Affecting Seasoned Corporate Bond Prices," *Journal of Financial and Quantitative Analysis,* 1981, pp. 207–226.

ipals and these other two securities stabilized.[9] Notice the very small differences for September, October, and November.

Although the structure of yield spreads and their changes over time are complex, some general relationships account for most of the yield spreads that do exist.

1. Different types of bonds, for example, U.S. Treasuries versus corporates and municipals.
2. Different qualities within the same type of bond, for example, AAA corporates versus A corporates.
3. Different coupons within the same type or quality, for example, a high coupon Treasury bond versus a low coupon Treasury bond.

Relationships between Bond Yields and Prices

The previous section examined the nature of market interest rates and the periodic changes in them. It was shown that investors need to be concerned with three types of changes in interest rates: changes in the level of rates, the term structure, and the yield spread. When the level of rates for new securities changes, investors also change their required returns on outstanding bonds. To obtain this change in required return or yield, the bond price must change.

What is the exact relationship between changes in yields (interest rates) and price? The response of a bond's price to a change in yield is a function of several variables, which will be described in the next section as a set of bond theorems. Furthermore, understanding the concept of duration provides important insights about the sensitivity of bond price changes to changes in interest rates. Therefore, duration will be explained following the discussion of bond theorems and will subsequently be useful in understanding one of the bond strategies used today.

Malkiel's Bond Price Theorems

Burton Malkiel has derived five theorems about the relationship between bond prices and yields.[10] Using the bond valuation model, Malkiel has shown that the changes in the price of a bond (i.e., its volatility), given a change in yields, are a function of the following:

- Time to maturity
- Coupon
- Prevailing interest rate

---

[9]The changes in the tax treatment of certain types of municipals was made retroactive to August 15, 1986.

[10]Burton G. Malkiel, "Expectations, Bond Prices, and the Term Structure of Interest Rates," *Quarterly Journal of Economics*, May 1962, pp. 197–218.

Malkiel's five bond price theorems are

1. Bond prices move inversely to bond yields (given a fixed coupon). This principle needs no elaboration beyond the present value analysis. The nature of interest rate risk is that if bond yields increase (decrease), bond prices will decrease (increase). The bond valuation model, as described in Equation 7–2, clearly indicates that, by the nature of present value analysis, discounting the cash flows by a higher discount rate (yield) must lead to a lower present value (price).

2. For a given change in market yield, the change in bond price that occurs will be greater the longer the term to maturity is; that is, bond price volatility and time to maturity are directly related. As an example, for a given drop in interest rates, the price of a 10% coupon bond with 15 years to maturity (bond A) would rise less than a 10% coupon bond with 25 years to maturity (bond B).

Assume market rates drop from 10% to 8%, and that both bonds were selling for par before the drop.

Bond A: $50 (present value annuity factor, 5%; 30 periods) = $ 768.60
           $1000 (present value factor, 5%; 30 periods)   =   231.40
                                                  $1000.00

Bond B: $50 (present value annuity factor, 5%; 50 periods) = $ 912.80
           $1000 (present value factor, 5%; 50 periods)   =   87.20
                                                  $1000.00

At the new market rate of 8%, the prices of the bonds are as follows:

Bond A: $50 (present value annuity factor, 4%; 30 periods) = $ 864.60
           $1000 (present value factor, 4%; 30 periods)   =   308.30
                                                  $1172.90

Bond B: $50 (present value annuity factor, 4%; 50 periods) = $1074.10
           $1000 (present value factor, 4%; 50 periods)   =   140.70
                                                  $1214.80

As we can see, the price of bond B, with the longer maturity, has risen more than the price of bond A. If market rates had increased, the price of bond B would have declined more than that of bond A.

3. The percentage price change described in Theorem 2 increases at a diminishing rate as the term to maturity increases. For example, the price of the 15-year 10% coupon bond in Theorem 2 increased $172.90, or 17.29% when market rates declined by 2%. Although the price of the same bond with a maturity of 25 years increased more in total dollars than the 15-year bond, the percentage increase was only 21.48%. Thus, the marginal precentage change in price decreases as maturity increases.

4. Holding maturity constant, a decrease in yields raises bond prices more than a corresponding increase in yields lowers prices. This means that for a given change in yields (e.g., 1%), the capital gains that result from a decrease always exceed the capital losses that result from an increase (in absolute terms), whatever the maturity. The practical implication of this is that investors can expect to make more on a long bond position for a given rate decrease than on a short bond position for a comparable rate increase.

As an example of this theorem, consider the 15-year 10% coupon bond illustrated earlier. Contrast the price of this bond if market rates were to decline from 10% to 8% with the price if they rose from 10% to 12%. At 10%, of course, the price of this bond is $1000. At each of the other two rates, the prices would be: 8% ($1172.90, as calculated above) and 12% ($862.25).

Thus, the decrease in yield from 10% to 8% increased the price of the bond $172.90, whereas an increase in yields from 10% to 12% lowered the price $137.75. In absolute terms, the capital gains resulting from a decline in market yields will exceed the capital losses resulting from a comparable increase in market yields.

5. The higher the coupon on a bond, the smaller the *percentage* price change for any given change in yields. This means that bond price fluctuations (volatility) and bond coupons are inversely related. If a bond carries a high coupon (high in relation to the average bond coupon), its percentage price change for a given change in bond yield will be less than if the coupon had been low.

To illustrate this theorem, we can contrast the 15-year 10% coupon bond with a 15-year 15% coupon bond as market yields decline from 10% to 8%. As we have seen, the price of the 10% coupon bond will rise to $1172.90, an increase of 17.3%. The price of the 15% coupon bond will rise from $1383.98 to $1604.90, an increase of only 16% (note, however, that the change in *absolute dollars* is larger).

The practical implication of Malkiel's derivations for bond investors is the conclusion that the two bond variables of major importance in assessing the change in the price of a bond, given a change in interest rates, are its coupon and its maturity. It can be summarized as

> **THE PRACTICAL IMPLICATION OF THE BOND PRICE THEOREMS:**
> A decline (rise) in interest rates will cause a rise (decline) in bond prices, with the most volatility in bond prices occurring in longer maturity bonds and bonds with low coupons.

Therefore (1) a bond buyer, in order to receive the maximum price impact of an expected change in interest rates, should purchase low coupon, long-maturity bonds, and (2) if an increase in interest rates is expected (or feared), an investor holding bonds or contemplating their purchase should concentrate on those with large coupons or short maturities, or both.

These five relationships provide useful information for bond investors by demonstrating how the price of a bond changes as interest rates change. However, it is cumbersome to calculate various possible price changes on the basis of these theorems. What is needed is a measure that relates the price sensitivity of a bond to all of these factors. Such a measure, called duration, is available.

Duration

Although maturity is the traditional measure of a bond's lifetime, it is inadequate because of its focus on only the return of principal at the maturity date. Two 20-year bonds, one with an 8% coupon and the other with a 15% coupon, do not have identical *economic* lifetimes. The investor will recover the original purchase price much sooner with the 15% coupon bond. Therefore, a measure is needed that accounts for the entire pattern (both size and timing) of the cash flows over the life of the bond. The concept for such a measure, called **duration,** was conceived some 50 years ago by Frederick Macaulay.[11]

Duration = Number of years needed to fully recover purchase price of a bond, given present values of its cash flows

= Weighted average time to recovery of all interest payments plus principal

$$= \sum_{t=1}^{n} t \left[\frac{\dfrac{C_t}{(1 + YTM)^t}}{\displaystyle\sum_{t=1}^{n} \dfrac{C_t}{(1 + YTM)^t}} \right] \tag{7-6}$$

where

C_t = the cash receipt in period t (interest or principal).
YTM = the yield to maturity on the bond.
t = time period when any cash receipt occurs.

The denominator of Equation 7–6 is simply the price or present value of a bond, as given previously in Equation 7–2. The numerator of Equation 7–6 is the present value of any year's cash receipt. Therefore, the cash receipt in each year is weighted in relation to the price (total present value) of the bond. By multiplying each year's weighted cash receipt by the number of years when each is to be received, and summing, duration is obtained. Note that duration is measured in years.

Table 7–2 provides an example of calculating the duration for a bond. The hypothetical bond is a 10% coupon bond with six years remaining to maturity. For simplicity, coupons are assumed to be paid annually (in actual practice they are paid semiannually) and the bond is priced at par (resulting in a YTM of 10%).

---

[11] Frederick R. Macaulay, *Some Theoretical Problems Suggested by the Movements of Interest Rates, Bond Yields, and Stock Prices in the United States since 1856.* New York: National Bureau of Economic Research, 1938.

TABLE 7-2 **An Example of Calculating the Duration of a Bond Using a 10% Coupon, Six-Year Maturity Bond Priced at $1000.**

(1) Year	(2) Cash Flow	(3) Present Value Factor	(4) Present Value of (2)	(5) Present Value ÷ Price	(6) (1) × (5)
1	100	0.9091	$ 90.91	0.09091	0.09091
2	100	0.8264	82.64	0.08264	0.16528
3	100	0.7513	75.13	0.07513	0.22539
4	100	0.6830	68.30	0.06830	0.27320
5	100	0.6209	62.09	0.06209	0.31045
6	1100	0.5645	620.95	0.62095	3.72570
Total			$1000	1.00000	4.79093 = 4.79

The cash flows consist of the six $100 coupons plus the return of principal at the end of the sixth year. Notice that the sixth year cash flow of $1100 ($100 coupon plus $1000 return of principal) accounts for 62% of the value of the bond and contributes 3.73 years to the duration of 4.79 years. In this example, the other five cash flows combined contributed roughly one year to the duration. The duration of 4.79 years is almost 1.2 years less than the term to maturity of 6 years. As explained following, duration will always be less than time to maturity for bonds that pay coupons.

What does duration tell us? It tells us the difference in the effective lives of alternative bonds. For example, with an 8% yield to maturity and an 8% coupon, a 10-year bond has an effective life (duration) of 7.25 years, whereas a 20-year bond has an effective life of 10.60 years—quite a different perspective, given that the second has a term to maturity of twice the first. Furthermore, under these conditions, a 50-year bond has an effective life of only 13.21 years.[12] The reason for the sharp differences between the term to maturity and the duration is that cash receipts received in the distant future have very small present values and therefore add little to a bond's value.

How is duration related to the key bond variables previously analyzed?

1. The coupon is inversely related to duration. This is logical because higher coupons result in quicker recovery of the bond's value, resulting in a shorter duration.
2. As illustrated earlier, duration expands with time to maturity but at a decreasing rate, particularly beyond 15 years time to maturity. Even between 5 and 10 years time to maturity, duration is expanding at a significantly lower rate than in the case of a time to maturity of up to 5 years, where it expands rapidly.

---

[12] These numbers, and the basis for this discussion, are taken from Richard W. McEnally, "Duration as a Practical Tool for Bond Management," *The Journal of Portfolio Management*, Summer 1977, pp. 53–56.

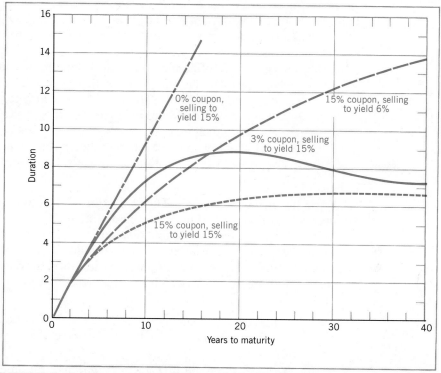

FIGURE 7–2   An illustration of duration versus time to maturity for some hypothetical bonds.

Source: William L. Nemerever, "Managing Bond Portfolios Through Immunization Strategies," Reprinted in *The Revolution in Techniques for Managing Bond Portfolios,* The Institute of Chartered Financial Analysts, Charlottesville, Va., 1983, p. 104. Reproduced from *The Revolution in Techniques for Managing Bond Portfolios,* The Institute of Chartered Financial Analysts, 1983. By permission.

3. Duration and yield to maturity are inversely related. Higher yields produce lower present values of cash receipts received far out in time, thereby diminishing their relative value.

Figure 7–2 illustrates some relationships between time to maturity and duration.[13] Primarily, it shows how much duration varies across instruments and environment.

The following observations can be made from Figure 7–2:

1. In general, duration increases with maturity.
2. For all bonds paying coupons, duration is always less than maturity.

---

[13] This discussion is based on William L. Nemerever, "Managing Bond Portfolios Through Immunization Strategies," reprinted in *The Revolution in Techniques for Managing Bond Portfolios.* Charlottesville, Va.: The Institute of Chartered Financial Analysts, 1983.

3. For a zero coupon bond, duration is equal to time to maturity.
4. For a deep discount bond (the 3% coupon bond selling to yield 15%), a point is reached at which duration actually decreases as maturity increases.
5. During periods of high interest rates, long-term bonds resemble intermediate term bonds much more than when interest rates are low, based on duration. The 15% coupon bond selling to yield 15% in Figure 7–2, illustrating a period of high interest rates, has a duration that does not increase much as time to maturity increases.
6. In a period of low interest rates, as illustrated by the 15% coupon bond selling to yield 6%, duration increases rapidly with time to maturity.

Using the duration concept   The real value of the duration measure to bond investors is that it combines coupon and maturity, the two key variables to be manipulated in response to expected changes in interest rates. As noted earlier, duration is positively related to maturity and negatively related to coupon. However, bond price changes are directly related to duration, as shown by Equation 7–7 (which is an approximation).

$$\text{Percentage change in bond price} = \frac{-D}{(1 + \text{YTM})} \times \text{Percentage point change in the YTM} \qquad (7\text{–}7)$$

For example, the bond in Table 7–2 with a duration of 4.79 years would decline in price approximately 8.70% if the YTM changed by 2 percentage points, from 10% to 12%. (The adjusted duration would be $-4.79/1.10 = 4.35$; multiplying by the 2-percentage-point rise in YTM produces an expected change in price for the bond of about 8.70%, or a new price of about $913.)

What does this mean to bond investors? It means that to obtain the maximum (minimum) price volatility from a bond, investors should choose bonds with the longest (shortest) duration. If an investor already owns a portfolio of bonds, he or she can act to increase the duration of the portfolio if a decline in interest rates is expected and the investor is attempting to achieve the largest price appreciation possible. Fortunately, duration is additive, which means that a bond portfolio's duration is a weighted average of each individual bond's duration.

It should be noted that although duration is one measure of bond risk, and an important one, it is not necessarily always the appropriate one. Duration measures volatility, which is important but is only one aspect of the risk in bonds. If an investor considers volatility an acceptable proxy for risk, duration is the measure of risk to use. Duration may not be a complete measure of bond risk, but it does reflect some of the impact of changes in interest rates.

Bond Strategies and Management

It is appropriate to end this chapter with a discussion of the approaches that bond investors can use in managing their bond portfolios, or the bond portion of their overall portfolio. This requires more than understanding the basic factors affecting the valuation and analysis of bonds, which were discussed earlier in this chapter.

Bond investing has become increasingly popular, no doubt as a result of record interest rates in recent years. Unfortunately, the theoretical framework for bond portfolio management has not been developed to the extent of that for common stocks. In some ways common stocks have been more "glamorous," and more attention has been devoted to them. Furthermore, more data exist for common stocks, undoubtedly because the most prominent stocks trade on the New York Stock Exchange where daily prices can be collected and analyzed. The same is not true for bonds. Even today an investor cannot call most brokers and obtain instantaneous, current quotes on many bonds.

Despite the lack of a complete theory of bond portfolio management, investors must manage their bond portfolios and make investment decisions. Different bond investors have derived different strategies to follow, depending on their risk preferences, knowledge of the bond market, and investment objectives.

For organizational purposes, and because this scheme corresponds to the two broad strategies an investor can follow, we will first discuss passive management of bond portfolios and then active management.

Passive Management Strategies

A number of investors accept the idea that securities are fairly priced in the sense that the expected return is commensurate with the risk taken. This belief can justify a **passive management strategy,** meaning that the investor does not actively seek out trading possibilities in an attempt to outperform the market. Such a position is supported by evidence of the type presented in Figure 7–3, which shows the performance of bond managers during the years 1981–1985. The results in Figure 7–3 shows that during this period more managers fell below the bond index than exceeded it.

A passive investment strategy does not mean that investors do nothing. They still must monitor the status of their portfolios in order to match their holdings with their risk preferences and objectives. Conditions in the financial markets change quickly, and investors must do likewise when necessary. Passive management does not mean that investors accept changes in market conditions, securities, and so on if these changes cause undesirable changes in the securities they hold.

In following a passive management approach, bond investors must first assess the factors that were discussed earlier to determine if the bonds to be

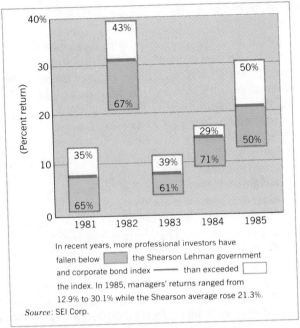

In recent years, more professional investors have fallen below ▨ the Shearson Lehman government and corporate bond index ▬ than exceeded ☐ the index. In 1985, managers' returns ranged from 12.9% to 30.1% while the Shearson average rose 21.3%.

Source: SEI Corp.

FIGURE 7–3 **Bond managers vs. bond averages.**
Source: George Anders, "Returns Seesaw for Managers Seeking to Top Index on Bond," *The Wall Street Journal,* April 21, 1986, p. 37. Reprinted by permission of *The Wall Street Journal,* © Dow Jones & Company, Inc. 1986. All Rights Reserved.

held are suitable investment opportunities. Thus, investors must assess default risk and diversify their holdings to protect themselves against changes in the probability of default. Likewise, call risk must be examined at the outset. Ideally, investors may be able to find bonds that are not callable over the period that they will be held. The higher the coupon on a bond, the more likely it is to be called. A third factor affecting investors is the marketability of a bond. Some bonds cannot be readily sold without a price concession, a lag in the time required to sell the bond, or both.

Other factors for the passive bond investor to consider at the outset of the program and to monitor during the life of the investment include a current income requirement and taxes. Some bond investors need large current yields. This suggests large coupons, other things being equal. Taxes are also a factor, because what matters is the after-tax return one achieves. Municipal securities may be a good choice for investors in high marginal tax brackets because of their exemption from federal taxes; U.S. Treasury securities, on the other hand, are exempt from state (and most city) taxes.

Strategies for investors following a passive bond management approach include the following.

1. *Buy and hold*. This is an obvious strategy for any investor interested in nonactive trading policies. Having considered the factors just mentioned, this investor chooses a portfolio of bonds and does not attempt to trade them in a search for higher returns. An important part of this strategy is to separate from that set the most promising bonds that meet the investor's requirements. This requires some knowledge of bonds and markets. Simply because an investor is following a basic buy-and-hold strategy does not mean that selection is unimportant. It is important to know such facts as the yield advantage of agency securities over U.S. Treasuries, the yield advantage of utilities over industrials, and other factors.

A buy-and-hold strategy can accommodate various degrees of investor passivity. At one extreme, investors could try to duplicate the overall bond market by purchasing a broad cross-section of bonds. This strategy has now become easy to accomplish as the result of bond index funds, a relatively new creation which is gaining in popularity. An example is the Vanguard bond market fund, a highly diversified fund which seeks to match the performance of the Salomon Brothers Broad Investment-Grade Bond Index. There are no investment advisory fees to pay with this fund, and total annual operating expenses are expected to be 25 cents per $100 of fund assets. Given the performance of bond managers shown in Figure 7–3, bond index funds may become a popular alternative with investors.

Other buy-and-hold investors may search out alternatives that are better than current holdings and trade accordingly. Finally, some investors may use timing considerations, switching from short maturities to long and back again as conditions warrant.

2. *Immunization*. **Immunization** is the strategy of immunizing (protecting) a portfolio against interest rate risk (i.e., changes in the general level of interest rates). To see how such a strategy works, think of interest rate risk as being composed of two parts:

a. The **price risk,** resulting from the inverse relationship between bond prices and required rates of return.
b. The **reinvestment rate risk,** resulting from the uncertainty about the rate at which future coupon income can be reinvested. The YTM calculation assumes that future coupons from a given bond investment will be reinvested at the calculated yield to maturity. If interest rates change such that this assumption is no longer operable, the bond's realized YTM will differ from the calculated (expected) YTM.

Notice that these two components of interest rate risk move in opposite directions. If interest rates rise, reinvestment rates (and therefore income) rise, whereas the price of the bond declines; of course, the converse of this statement also holds. In effect, the favorable results on one side can be used to offset the unfavorable results on the other. This is what immunization is all about—protecting the portfolio against interest rate risk by canceling out its two components.

The duration concept discussed earlier is the basis for immunization theory. Specifically, a portfolio is said to be immunized (the effects of interest rate risk neutralized) if the duration of the portfolio is made equal to a preselected investment horizon for the portfolio. Note carefully what this statement says. An investor with, say, a 10-year horizon does not choose bonds with 10 years to maturity but bonds with a duration of 10 years—quite a different statement. This will usually require holding bonds with maturities in excess of the investment horizon.[14]

Active Management Strategies

Although bonds can be and often are purchased to be held to maturity, they often are not. Henry Kaufman, a well-known forecaster of interest rates, has formulated some new precepts of interest rates, one of which is that "bonds are bought for their price appreciation potential and not for income protection."[15] Many bond investors feel this way and use **active management strategies**. Three levels of active strategy will be discussed briefly.

Forecasting interest rates   Changes in interest rates are the key factor affecting bond prices because of the inverse relationship between changes in bond prices and changes in interest rates. When interest rate declines are projected by the investor, action should be taken to invest in bonds, and the right bonds, for price appreciation opportunities. When interest rates are expected to rise, the objective is to minimize losses by not holding bonds or holding bonds with short maturities.

Assuming that an investor has a forecast of interest rates, what strategy can be taken? The basic strategy is to change the maturity of the portfolio; specifically, an investor should lengthen (shorten) the maturity of a bond portfolio when interest rates are expected to decline (rise).

It is important to be aware of the trade-offs in strategies involving maturity.

1. Short maturities sacrifice price appreciation opportunities and usually offer lower coupons (income), but serve to protect the investor when rates are expected to rise.
2. Longer maturities have greater price fluctuations: therefore, the chance for bigger gains (and bigger losses) is magnified. However, longer maturities may be less liquid than Treasury bills.

---

[14] For additional information on reinvestment rate risk, see R. W. McEnally, "How to Neutralize Reinvestment Rate Risk," *The Journal of Portfolio Management*, Spring 1980. Also, see Nemerever, "Managing Bond Portfolios."

[15] Henry Kaufman, "New Precepts of Interest Rates" (Salomon Brothers Inc.) reprinted in *1982 C.F.A. Study Guide III*. Charlottesville, Va.: The Institute of Chartered Financial Analysts, 1981.

2 **Bond swaps** Managers of bond portfolios attempt to adjust to the constantly changing environment for bonds (and all securities) by engaging in what are called **bond swaps**. The term usually refers to the purchase and sale of bonds in an attempt to improve the rate of return on the bond portfolio. Although there are several different types of bond swaps, only the best known are discussed briefly here.[16]

1. The substitution swap involves bonds that are perfect (or very close) substitutes for each other with regard to characteristics such as maturity, quality rating, call provisions, marketability, and coupon payments. The only difference is that, at a particular time, the two bonds sell at slightly different prices (and, therefore, a different yield to maturity). The swap would be made into the higher yielding bond which, if its yield declines to that of the other bond, will provide capital gains as well as a higher current yield.

2. A pure yield pickup swap involves no expectations about market changes, as does the substitution swap (where the buyer expects the yield on the higher yielding bond to drop). This swap simply involves selling a lower yielding bond and purchasing a higher yielding bond of the same quality and maturity. The motivation is strictly to obtain higher yield.

3. The rate anticipation swap is based on a forecast of interest rates. When rates are expected to rise (fall), swaps are made into short (long) maturity bonds (or cash). Because of greater interest rate fluctuations in recent years, interest rate anticipation swaps will probably become increasingly popular relative to other types of swaps.

4. The intermarket spread (sector) swap is designed to take advantage of expected changes in the yield spread relationships between various sectors of the bond market. For example, a bond investor may perceive a misalignment between Treasury bonds and utility bonds. If the yield spread between the two sectors is too wide and is expected to narrow, a switch may be made into the higher yielding security.

3 **Use of newer techniques** The bond markets have changed rapidly in recent years because of numerous structural changes and the record level of interest rates that have occurred. Along with these changes have come new techniques for the active management of fixed-income portfolios.

The distinction between the bond market and the mortgage market is now blurred, with mortgage instruments competing in the capital markets in the same manner as bonds. The mortgage has been transformed into a security, and the mortgage market has become more uniform and standardized. These securities are alternatives to bonds, especially corporate bonds, and can be used in the portfolio as substitutes.

---

[16]For a complete discussion of these swaps, see Homer and Leibowitz, *Inside the Yield Book*.

Financial futures are now a well-known part of the investor's alternatives. The use of futures has grown tremendously. They are used to hedge positions and to speculate on the future course of interest rates. Futures will be discussed in more detail in Chapter 17.

Building a Bond Portfolio

Having reviewed some active and passive strategies for managing a bond portfolio, it is appropriate to consider how to go about building a bond portfolio. The first consideration, which is true throughout the range of investment decisions, is to decide on the risk–return trade-off that all investors face. If an investor seeks higher expected returns, he or she must be prepared to accept a greater risk. Figure 1–1 is applicable to bonds alone. To see this, think of the two broad objectives that investors can have with a bond portfolio, as discussed in Chapter 6.

1. Conservative investors view bonds as fixed income securities that will pay them a steady stream of income. In most cases, the risk is small and with federal government issues there is no practical risk of default. These investors tend to use a buy-and-hold approach.

Investors following this strategy seek to maximize their current income subject to the risk (quality of issue) they are willing to assume—corporates should return more than Treasury issues, BAA should return more than A or AA or AAA, longer maturities should return more than short maturities, and so on.

Even conservative investors in bonds must consider a number of factors. Assume that an investor wishes to purchase only Treasury issues, thereby avoiding the possible risk of default. Careful consideration should be given to the maturity of the issue, since the range is from Treasury bills of a few months maturity to bonds maturing in the twenty-first century. Obviously, this will depend to a large extent on interest rate forecasts. Even conservative buy-and-hold investors probably should avoid long-term issues if interest rates are expected to rise over an extended period of time. Finally, these investors may wish to consider the differences in coupons between issues. Previous discussion has shown that the lower the coupon on a bond, the higher the price volatility. Although many investors in this group may plan to hold to maturity, conditions can change.

2. Aggressive investors are interested in capital gains arising from a change in interest rates. There can be a substantial range of aggressiveness, from the really short-term speculator to a somewhat less aggressive investor willing to realize capital gains over a longer period while possibly earning high income yields.

The short-term speculator studies interest rates carefully and moves into and out of securities on the basis of interest rate expectations. If rates are expected to fall, this investor can buy long-term, low-coupon issues and achieve maximum capital gains if the interest rate forecast is correct. Treasury bonds can be bought on margin to further magnify gains (or losses).

Treasury securities, for example, can be purchased on 10% margin. Note also that the speculator often uses Treasury issues (the highest quality bond available) or high-grade corporates in doing this kind of bond trading. It is not necessary to resort to low quality bonds.

Another form of aggressive behavior is seeking the highest total return, whether from interest income or capital gains. These investors will plan on a long horizon in terms of holding a portfolio of bonds but will engage in active trading during certain periods when such actions seem particularly appropriate. One such period was 1982, when bonds were offering record yields to maturity and interest rates were widely expected to decline. Even mildly aggressive investors could purchase Treasury bonds yielding high-coupon income and have a reasonable expectation of capital gains. The downside risk in this strategy at this time was small. These investors still needed to consider maturity and coupon questions, however, because no interest rate decline can be assumed with certainty.

Summary

This chapter has discussed bond valuation, analysis, and management. The emphasis is on understanding the determinants of a bond's value and how to use this intelligently as a bond investor.

Any security's intrinsic value is the sum of its discounted cash flows. To find this value, it is necessary to identify the amount and timing of the cash flows and the appropriate discount rate to be used in the present value process.

Bond valuation is relatively straightforward because the expected cash flows are known precisely when the bond is issued. Using an appropriate market yield for the discount rate, the present value (price) of a bond can easily be found using present value tables or a calculator. If the price of the bond is known, the yield to maturity (discount rate) can be determined.

The key to bond yields and prices is interest rates. Three aspects of importance are the level of rates over time, the term structure of interest rates, and yield spreads. The level of market interest rates for short-term, risk-free securities is a function of the real rate of interest and inflationary expectations. Inflationary expectations is the key variable in understanding changes in market rates for short-term, default-free securities.

The term structure of interest rates denotes the relationship between market yields and time to maturity. A yield curve graphically depicts this relationship with upward sloping curves being the norm. None of the three prevalent theories to explain term structure—the expectations theory, the liquidity preference theory, and the market segmentation theory—is dominant.

A risk premium is an important component of risky securities. Yield spreads are the relationship between bond yields and particular bond features such as quality and callability. Differences in type, quality, and coupon account for most of the yield spreads.

Malkiel's bond theorems show that bond price volatility is a function of the time to maturity, coupon, the par value of the bond, and the prevailing interest rate. The two variables of major importance are coupon and maturity. Maximum price volatility is achieved with low coupon, long maturity bonds.

Duration is the weighted average time (years) to recovery of all interest payments plus maturity, and it shows the effective life of a bond. Bond price changes are directly related to duration, which combines coupon and maturity, the two key variables affecting a bond's price. Duration is one measure of bond risk.

Bond strategies may be active or passive. Passive strategies include buy and hold and immunization. Active management strategies include forecasting interest rates, bond swaps, and other new techniques such as the use of futures. Whichever strategy is followed, bond portfolios must be built and managed. Different investors will follow different approaches, depending on their return–risk preferences.

Key Words

Active management strategy
Bond swaps
Duration
Expectations theory
Immunization
Intrinsic value
Liquidity preference theory
Market segmentation theory

Passive management strategy
Price risk
Real rate of interest
Reinvestment rate risk
Term structure of interest rates
Yield curve
Yield spread

QUESTIONS AND PROBLEMS

1. How is the intrinsic value of any asset determined? How are intrinsic value and present value related?
2. How is the price of a bond determined? Why is this process relatively straightforward for a bond?

3. What effect does the use of semiannual discounting have on the value of a bond in relation to annual discounting? Calculate the price of a 10% coupon bond with eight years to maturity, given an appropriate discount rate of 12%, using both annual and semiannual discounting.

4. Define YTM. Describe three methods of determining YTM for a bond.

5. Why is YTM important?

6. Distinguish between promised yield and realized yield. How does interest on interest affect realized return?

7. How can bond investors eliminate the reinvestment rate risk inherent in bonds?

8. Describe three aspects of market interest rates, carefully distinguishing between the three.

9. How can one describe, verbally and graphically, the relationship between time to maturity and yields for a particular category of bonds?

10. Briefly discuss the three existing theories of the term structure of interest rates.

11. What factors explain yield spreads?

12. What are the implications of Malkiel's bond price theorems to bond investors? Which two bond variables are shown to be of major importance in assessing bond price changes?

13. How does duration differ from time to maturity? What does duration tell you?

14. How is duration related to time to maturity? To coupon? Do the same relationships hold for a zero coupon bond?

15. Calculate the duration of a 12% coupon bond with 10 years remaining to maturity and selling at par.

16. Given the duration calculated in Question 15, calculate the percentage change in bond price if the yield to maturity for this bond changes to 14%.

17. Assume that a bond investor wishes to maximize the potential price volatility from a portfolio of bonds about to be constructed. What should this investor seek in the way of coupon, maturity, and duration?

18. Is duration a complete measure of bond risk? Is it the best measure?

19. Identify and explain two passive bond management strategies.

20. Explain the concept of immunization. What role, if any, does duration play in this concept?

21. Identify and explain two specific active bond management strategies. Are the two related?

22. What does an upward-sloping yield curve imply about the expectations of investors? A downward-sloping curve?

23. It is August 1, 1982, and you have correctly forecast that interest rates will soon decline sharply. Assuming that you will invest only in fixed-income securities and that your time horizon is one year, how would you construct a portfolio?

24. When would investors find bonds with long maturities, selling at large discounts, particularly unattractive as investment opportunities?

25. Calculate the price for a 12% coupon bond with 10 years to maturity, if the going rate for this bond is 14%.
26. What is the YTM for a bond selling at $900 with an 11% coupon and 10 years remaining to maturity?
27. Which bond is more affected by interest-on-interest considerations?

   Bond A—12% coupon, 20 years to maturity
   Bond B—6% coupon, 25 years to maturity

28. Compare the difference between annual and semiannual discounting for a 10-year bond with a 12% coupon, if the current going rate for such a bond is 8%.
29. Describe the four bond swaps. Indicate the assumption(s) being made by an investor in undertaking these swaps.
30. The YTM on a 10%, 15-year bond is 12%. What is its price?

EXTENDED PROBLEMS, WITH EXAMPLES

I. **Example.** Calculating the price of a bond, illustrating Formula 7–2 and Formula 7–3. Consider a bond with the following characteristics:

   C = an $80 coupon = (0.08)($1000).
   PAR = $1000 face value.
   r = 0.10, the discount rate—the going market interest rate on similar securities.
   n = exactly three years—the time to maturity.

under two different conditions:

   a. Annual coupon payments, $80 is received at the end of each year.
   b. Semiannual coupon payments, $40 is received every six months.

Under either condition the price of the bond is the present value of the discounted future returns. The returns, and their discounted values, are as follows:

Future Date	Assumption A			Assumption B		
6 months				$40 ÷ (1.05)	=	38.095
1 year	$80 ÷ (1.10)	=	72.726	$40 ÷ (1.05)²	=	36.281
1.5 years				$40 ÷ (1.05)³	=	34.554
2 years	$80 ÷ (1.10)²	=	66.116	$40 ÷ (1.05)⁴	=	32.908
2.5 years				$40 ÷ (1.05)⁵	=	31.341
3 years	$80 ÷ (1.10)³	=	60.105	$40 ÷ (1.05)⁶	=	29.849
3 years	$1000 ÷ (1.10)³	=	751.315	$1000 ÷ (1.05)⁶	=	746.215
Price			$950.26			$949.243

Since the discount rate (10%) exceeds the coupon rate (8%), the bond is selling at a discount, but the prices differ because of the timing of the coupon payments.

Problems
1. If the coupon rate of the $1000 bond was 10% (the coupon = $100), and the discount rate was 8%, with the same three years to maturity, show that the price of the bond is: $1051.54, with annual compounding; $1052.24, with semiannual compounding.
2. What would be the price of this bond if both the coupon rate and the discount rate were 10%?

II. **Example.** Equivalent formula, used in bond tables, that appears more complex, but is easier to calculate. For the bond described in Example I, the value of the sum of the coupon payments can be calculated together with the discounted value of par. For the annual coupons (condition A above):

$$P = \frac{C}{r}\left[1 - \frac{1}{(1 + r)^t}\right] + \frac{Par}{(1 + r)^t} = \frac{80}{0.10}\left[1 - \frac{1}{(1.10)^3}\right] + \frac{1000}{(1.10)^3}$$

$$= 198.948 + 751.315 = \$950.26$$

with semiannual compounding:

$$P = \frac{C/2}{r/2}\left[1 - \frac{1}{(1 + r/2)^{2t}}\right] + \frac{Par}{(1 + r/2)^{2t}}$$

$$= \frac{40}{0.05}\left[1 - \frac{1}{(1.05)^6}\right] + \frac{1000}{(1.05)^6}$$

$$= 203.028 + 746.215 = \$949.24$$

Problems
1. Repeat the problems in Example I using these formulas.
2. What would be the price of the bond used in these examples if the coupon were paid quarterly?

3. What effect does the use of semiannual discounting have on the value of a bond in relation to annual discounting? Refer to the problems and examples above. Illustrate further by calculating the price of a 10% coupon bond with eight years to maturity, given an appropriate discount rate of 12%, using both annual and semiannual discounting.

4. Put the known values, for each semiannual period, into Equation 7–3 for a bond selling at a price of $1052 with a 10% coupon, paid semiannually, with three years to maturity. What are the arithmetic problems in calculating YTM?

5. Calculate the yield to first call for a bond selling at $885, callable at $1100, bearing a 12% coupon paid semiannually, with two years to go to first call and four to maturity.

III. **Problems.** Using the present value tables:
1. Calculate the YTM for Problem II–4.
2. Calculate the YTM for Problem II–5.

IV. **Example.** Calculating duration. Using Example I, with semiannual coupon payments for the bond, and referring to Equation 7–6 and Table 7–2, show that the values in the last column of Assumption B correspond to column 4 of Table 7–2, and the sum of that column is the price of the bond.

Future Date	(4)	(5) = (4) ÷ 949.243	(1)	(6) = (5) × (1)
6 months	38.095	0.04132	0.5	0.02066
1 year	36.281	0.03822	1.0	0.03822
1.5 years	34.554	0.03640	1.5	0.05460
2 years	32.908	0.03467	2.0	0.06934
2.5 years	31.341	0.03302	2.5	0.08255
3 years	29.849	0.03145	3.0	0.09435
3 years	746.215	0.78612	3.0	2.35836
Sum	949.243	1.00120		2.71808

Notice that Equation 7–6 will have to be revised to use (YTM/2) and $2t$ as the power.

Problems
1. For the bond in Problem I with semiannual coupons, 10% coupon rate, $1000 par, discount rate of 8%, and our calculated price of $1052.24, calculate the duration, and explain what it means.
2. Do you think, generally, that the duration is longer (or shorter) for a security selling at a premium (or discount)?

Selected References

Cecchetti, Stephen G. "High Real Interest Rates: Can They Be Explained?" *Economic Review: Federal Reserve Bank of Kansas City,* September–October 1986, pp. 31–41.

Diller, Stanley. "Analyzing the Yield Curve: A New Approach." *Financial Analysts Journal,* March–April 1981, pp. 23–41.

Dyl, Edward A., and Martin, Stanley A. "Another Look at Barbells Versus Ladders." *The Journal of Portfolio Management,* Spring 1986, pp. 54–59.

Fabozzi, Frank J., and Pollack, Irving M., eds. *The Handbook of Fixed Income Securities,* 2nd ed. Homewood, Ill.: Dow Jones-Irwin, 1986.

Fong, H. Gifford. *Bond Portfolio Analysis.* Monograph No. 11. Charlottesville, Va.: The Financial Analysts Research Foundation, 1980.

Fong, H. Gifford, and Fabozzi, Frank J. "How to Enhance Bond Returns with Naive Strategies." *The Journal of Portfolio Management,* Summer 1985, pp. 57–60.

Gatti, James F. "Risk and Return on Corporate Bonds: A Synthesis." *Quarterly Review of Economics and Business,* Summer 1983, pp. 53–70.

Homer, S., and Leibowitz, Martin L. *Inside the Yield Book.* Englewood Cliffs, N.J.: Prentice-Hall, 1972.

Ibbotson Associates, Inc. *Stocks, Bonds, Bills and Inflation: 1987 Yearbook.* Chicago, Ill.: Ibbotson Associates, 1987.

Macaulay, Frederick. *Some Theoretical Problems Suggested by the Movements of Interest Rates, Bond Yields, and Stock Prices in the United States since 1856.* New York: National Bureau of Economic Research, 1938.

Malkiel, Burton G. "Expectations, Bond Prices, and the Term Structure of Interest Rates." *Quarterly Journal of Economics,* May 1962, pp. 197–218.

Maloney, Kevin J., and Yawitz, Jess B. "Interest Rate Risk, Immunization, and Duration." *The Journal of Portfolio Management,* Spring 1986, pp. 41–48.

McEnally, Richard W. "How to Neutralize Reinvestment Rate Risk." *The Journal of Portfolio Management,* Spring 1980, pp. 59–63.

McEnally, Richard W. "Duration as a Practical Tool for Bond Management." *The Journal of Portfolio Management,* Summer 1977, pp. 53–57.

Santoni, S., and Stone, C. "The Fed and the Real Rate of Interest." *Review, FRB of St. Louis,* December 1982, pp. 8–18.

Speakes, Jeffrey K. "Fixed-Income Risk Measurement and Risk Management." *The Journal of Portfolio Management,* Winter 1984, pp. 66–70.

Tuttle, Donald L., ed. *The Revolution in Techniques for Managing Bond Portfolios.* Charlottesville, Va.: The Institute of Chartered Financial Analysts, 1983.

APPENDIX 7–A

A TRANSITION FROM BONDS TO COMMON STOCKS: THE ANALYSIS AND VALUATION OF PREFERRED STOCK

In Chapter 2 preferred stock was classified for investment analysis purposes as a fixed-income security, although technically it is an equity security. It is best described as a hybrid security, having some characteristics similar to fixed-income securities (i.e., bonds) and some similar to common stocks. It seems appropriate, therefore, to discuss the analysis and valuation of preferred stock between the valuation of bonds (this chapter) and the valuation of common stocks (Chapter 9). Preferred stock serves as a transition between these two basic types of securities.

Analysis

Preferred stock can be described as a perpetuity, or perpetual security, since it has no maturity date and will pay the indicated dividend forever. Although perpetual, many preferred stock issues carry a sinking fund, which provides for the retirement of the issue, usually over a period of many years. Furthermore, many preferred stocks are callable by the issuer, which also potentially limits the life of preferreds. Finally, roughly half of all preferred stocks issued in recent years is convertible into common stock. Therefore, although preferred stock is perpetual by definition, in reality many of the issues will not remain in existence in perpetuity.

Preferred stock dividends, unlike common stock dividends, are fixed when the stock is issued and do not change. These dividends are specified as an annual dollar amount (although paid quarterly) or as a percentage of par value, which is often either $25 or $100. The issuer can forego paying the preferred dividend if earnings are insufficient. Although this dividend is specified, failure to pay it does not result in default of the obligation, as is the case with bonds. Most preferred issues have a cumulative feature, which requires that all unpaid preferred dividends must be paid before common stock dividends can be paid.

Investors regard preferred stock as less risky than common stock because the dividend is specified and must be paid before a common stock dividend can be paid. They regard preferreds as more risky than bonds, however, because bondholders have priority in being paid and in case of liquidation. Investors should, therefore, require higher rates of return on preferred stock than on bonds of the same issuer, but a smaller required return than on common stocks. A complicating factor in this scenario, however, is that 80% of dividends received by one corporation from another are excludable from corporate income taxes, making preferred stock attractive as an investment for corporations. As a result of this tax feature, preferred stocks often carry slightly lower yields than bonds of comparable quality.

Valuation

The value of any perpetuity can be calculated as follows:

$$V_p = \frac{C}{(1 + k_p)} + \frac{C}{(1 + k_p)^2} + \ldots$$

$$= \frac{C}{k_p} \qquad \qquad (7A-1)$$

where

V_p = the value of a perpetuity today
C = the constant annual payment to be received
k_p = the required rate of return appropriate for this perpetuity

Because preferred stock is a perpetuity, Equation 7A–1 is applicable in its valuation. We simply substitute the preferred dividend (D) for C and the appropriate required return (k_{ps}) for k_p, resulting in Equation 7A–2.

$$V_{ps} = \frac{D}{k_{ps}} \qquad \qquad (7A-2)$$

A preferred stock, or any perpetuity, is easy to value because the numerator of Equation 7A–2 is known, and fixed, forever. No present value calculations are needed for a perpetuity, which simplifies the valuation process considerably. If any two of the values in 7A–2 are known, the third can easily be found.

As an example of the valuation analysis, consider the $2.675 cumulative preferred stock of Carolina Power and Light Company (CP&L), with a par value of $25. This $2.675 annual dividend is fixed. To value this preferred, investors need to estimate the required rate of return appropriate for a preferred stock with the degree of riskiness of CP&L. Suppose the k, or required rate of return, is 10%. The value of this preferred would be

$$V_{CP\&L} = \frac{\$2.675}{0.10}$$

$$= \$26.75$$

On the other hand, a required rate of return of 11% would result in a value of $24.32.

If the current price for this preferred, as observed in the marketplace, is used in Equation 7A–2, the yield can be solved by using Equation 7A–3.

$$k_{ps} = \frac{D}{P_{ps}} \qquad (7A–3)$$

In the case of CP&L, a recent price was about $30, indicating a yield, or required rate of return, of about 8.92%.

Notice from Equation 7A–2 that as the required rate of return rises, the price of the preferred stock declines; obviously, the converse is also true. Because the numerator is fixed, the value (price) of a preferred stock changes as the required rate of return changes. At the time of the price observation for CP&L, the range for the preceding 52 weeks was $26⅝ to $30⅞. The $30⅞ price indicates that interest rates (and required returns) declined during this 52-week period to such a level as to make the value of the preferred rise to this price.

The 1971–1986 price for the CP&L preferred ranged from $17⅞ to $31. A price of $31 implies a required return of 8.63% at some point during this time span, and the price of $17⅞ implies a required rate of return of 14.97%. Clearly, investors' required rates of return fluctuate across time as interest rates and other factors change. As rates fluctuate, so do preferred stock prices.

PART THREE

COMMON STOCKS: ANALYSIS AND VALUATION

CHAPTER 8

COMMON STOCKS

After discussing fixed income securities in the preceding two chapters, the next logical step is to consider common stocks (equity securities). In many respects common stocks are easier to describe because they do not have the many technical features of fixed income securities, such as sinking funds, call features, and maturity risks. On the other hand, they are much more difficult to analyze and value. Several chapters are needed to consider the basic approaches to valuing and selecting common stocks.

Understanding Common Stocks

General Characteristics

The general characteristics of common stocks can be explained much more briefly than fixed-income securities. Quite simply, common stocks denote an equity (ownership) interest in a corporation. The stockholders are the owners of the corporation, entitled to all remaining income after the fixed-income claimants (including preferred stockholders) have been paid; also, in case of liquidation of the corporation, they are entitled to the remaining assets after all other claims (including preferred stock) are satisfied. Because they are entitled to any income and assets remaining after payments to all other claimants, common stockholders are referred to as the residual claimants of a corporation.

Common stockholders, as the owners, have control of a corporation—at least in principle. They also have limited liability, meaning that the stockholders cannot lose more than their investment in the corporation. In the event of financial difficulties, creditors have recourse only to the assets of the corporation; the stockholders are protected. This is perhaps the greatest advantage of the corporation and the reason it has been so successful.

Specific Characteristics

There are certain terms and features of common stocks that should be understood by investors. These features are each outlined here and described briefly.

1. The *charter* is the document issued by a state to permit the formation of a corporation. Because each state has its own laws of incorporation, some states (such as Delaware) with relatively favorable laws issue more charters than others. Charters are generally uniform on many details, including the collective rights of the stockholders and their specific rights as individual owners.[1] In effect, stockholder rights are governed by the laws of the state granting the charter. Charters can be amended with approval of a specified percentage of the voting stock and with approval from the appropriate officials of the chartering state.

2. The *voting rights* of the stockholders give them legal control of the corporation. In theory, the board of directors controls the management of the corporation, but in many cases the effective result is the opposite. Stockholders can regain control if they are sufficiently dissatisfied.

Stockholders are entitled to attend the annual meeting and vote on major corporate issues such as electing directors and issuing new shares of stocks. Most vote by *proxy,* meaning that the stockholder authorizes someone else (typically management) to vote his or her shares. Sometimes proxy battles occur, whereby one or more groups unhappy with corporate policies seek to bring about changes.

3. The *preemptive right* in a corporation's charter grants existing stockholders the first right to purchase any new common stock sold by the corporation. The "right" is a piece of paper giving each stockholder the option to buy a specified number of new shares, usually at a discount, during a specified short period of time. Because of this, rights are valuable and can be sold in the market.[2]

4. *Par value* for a common stock, unlike a bond or preferred stock, is not a significant economic variable. Corporations can make the par value any

---

[1] Collective rights include amending the charter, electing directors, issuing securities, and entering into mergers. Specific rights include the right to vote, the right to sell shares, and the right to share in the residual assets of the corporation if it is dissolved.

[2] Rights are one of the corporate-created options discussed in Chapter 2.

number they choose; $1 is often used today. Some corporations issue no-par stock. New stock is usually sold for more than par value, with the difference recorded on the balance sheet as "capital in excess of par value."

5. The **book value** of a corporation is the value of the equity as shown on the books (i.e., balance sheet). It is the sum of common stock outstanding, capital in excess of par value, and retained earnings. Dividing this sum (total book value) by the number of common shares outstanding produces the book value per share. In effect, book value is the accounting value of the equity. Although book value per share may not be irrelevant in making investment decisions, market value per share remains the critical item of interest to investors.

6. The **market value** (i.e., price) of the equity is what we are concerned with in our analysis. The aggregate market value for a corporation, calculated by multiplying the market price per share of the stock by the number of shares outstanding, represents the total value of the firm as determined in the marketplace. The market value of one share of stock, of course, is simply the observed current market price.

7. Dividends are the only cash payments regularly made by corporations to their stockholders. They are decided on and declared by the board of directors and can range from zero to virtually any amount the corporation can afford to pay (typically, up to 100% of earnings). Stockholders have no guarantees about dividends. At best, they can reasonably "expect" the dividend to be a certain amount in the future or to grow by a certain amount. The ratio of dividends to earnings is known as the payout ratio.

Dividends are declared and paid quarterly. To receive a declared dividend, an investor must be a *holder of record* on the specified date that a company closes its stock transfer books and compiles the list of stockholders to be paid. However, to avoid problems the brokerage industry has established a procedure of declaring that the right to the dividend remains with the stock until four *business* days before the holder-of-record date. On this fourth day, the right to the dividend leaves the stock; for that reason this date is called the *ex-dividend* date.

As an example, assume that the board of directors meets on June 10 and declares a quarterly dividend, payable on July 15. June 10 is called the *declaration date*. The board will declare a *holder-of-record* date—say July 5. The books close on this date, but the stock goes *ex-dividend* on July 1. In order to receive this dividend, an investor must purchase the stock by June 30. The dividend will be mailed to the stockholders of record on the *payment date*, July 15.

8. Stock dividends and stock splits attract considerable investor attention. A **stock dividend** is a payment by the corporation in shares of stock instead of cash. For example, a 5% stock dividend would entitle an owner of 100 shares of a particular stock to an additional five shares. A **stock split** involves the issuance of a larger number of shares in proportion to the existing shares outstanding (e.g., a 2 for 1 or 3 for 1 split). With a stock split, the book value and par value are changed; for example, each would be cut in half with a 2 for 1 split. On a practical basis, there is little difference between a stock dividend and a stock split.[3]

The important question to investors is the value of the distribution, whether a dividend or a split. It is clear that the recipient has more shares (i.e., more pieces of paper), but has anything of real value been received? The answer is that, other things being equal, these additional shares do not represent additional value. Remember that if you own 100 shares of a corporation that has 1000 shares of stock outstanding, your proportional ownership is 10%; if a 2 for 1 stock split occurs, your proportional ownership is still 10% because you now own 200 shares out of a total of 2000 shares outstanding. If you were to sell your newly distributed shares, however, your proportional ownership would drop to 5 percent.

Of course, if a stock dividend is accompanied by a higher cash dividend resulting from higher earnings, the price of the stock could, and probably should, be bid up. But the increase in value is due to the fundamental determinants of stock prices—in this case, earnings and dividends—and not to the stock dividend itself.

Stock dividends and stock splits may increase stock ownership by reducing the price at which shares can be purchased. In fact, it is widely believed by corporations and investors that an optimal price range exists for a particular stock. Therefore, if the stock price should rise above this range, the corporation may attempt to bring the price back into the perceived optimal range by declaring a stock split.

Stock Information

Using Stock Information

As discussed in Chapter 4, a common stock investor has numerous sources of information. These sources can be "free" (brokerage or financial press recommendations) or costly (subscription fee to an investment advisory or information service). The information can be in the form of recommended stocks (and portfolios) or basic (raw) data and/or data calculated for specific purposes (e.g., financial ratios or time series trends of changes in the money supply). Finally, information is available in both published and computerized formats.

In order to understand the valuation process for stocks, common stock investors should organize and think about information as it is used in secu-

---

[3] In fact, the New York Stock Exchange considers any distribution amounting to less than 25% of the outstanding shares to be a stock dividend.

rity analysis. At the end of the next chapter, as a lead-in to Chapters 10 through 12 on fundamental security analysis, a suggested framework for common stock analysis will be presented. This framework calls for first analyzing the economy and overall state of the stock market, next analyzing industries, and finally, analyzing individual companies. Each of these chapters will review information pertaining to their respective stages of analysis.

Reading Common Stock Information

Figure 8–1 is an excerpt from the New York Stock Exchange (NYSE) page carried daily in *The Wall Street Journal.* A similar page appears in virtually every daily newspaper.

We will use as an example the first company listed on the page, AAR corporation. The first two figures reported are the high and low prices during the preceding 52 weeks. This information aids investors in assessing the range over which the stock has traded during the previous year. Following the abbreviation for the name of the company, the current annual dividend per share is shown. AAR paid an annual dividend equal to $0.50 per share. Since dividends are paid quarterly, the actual payment would be $0.125 per share per quarter. Also shown is the dividend yield in percentage form, 1.8 for AAR. This is found by dividing the annual dividend by the current market price (and rounding off). × 100

The next figure, 20, is the P/E ratio, or multiplier, for AAR. This is the ratio of the current price to the latest 12-month earnings. It is an indication of how much the market (all investors) is willing to pay for AAR per dollar of earnings generated. Obviously, it is an identity as reported since it is calculated simply by dividing the current price by the latest 12-month earnings. However, it is often used in the valuation of common stocks, as explained in the next chapter. In fact, the P/E ratio, in its various forms, is a well-known variable to most investors.

Following the P/E ratio is yesterday's sales in hundreds of shares. For the day being reported, 67,400 shares of AAR stock were traded.

The last three entries are the high, low, and close, respectively, for AAR during its trading on the previous day. This stock reached a high of $28 per share on one of the markets listed at the top of the exhibit and it also declined to a low of $27 per share on one of these markets. It actually closed, or last traded, at $27.25 per share. The net change in the last column, $-\frac{3}{4}$, refers to the difference between yesterday's closing price and the previous day's closing price. In the case of AAR, the stock closed down 75 cents per share from the preceding day's closing price.

The letters "wt" following any name abbreviation refer to a warrant for that particular corporation. Information identical to stocks is reported for warrants, except that warrants pay no dividends. However, an investor desiring additional information about this or any other warrant—such as the terms of conversion into common stock—must consult some source of infor-

NEW YORK STOCK EXCHANGE COMPOSITE TRANSACTIONS

Tuesday, January 20, 1987

Quotations include trades on the Midwest, Pacific, Philadelphia, Boston and Cincinnati stock exchanges and reported by the National Association of Securities Dealers and Instinet

FIGURE 8–1 An excerpt from the New York Stock Exchange composite transactions page from *The Wall Street Journal* for January 21, 1987.

Source: The Wall Street Journal, January 21, 1987, p. 48. Reprinted by permission of *The Wall Street Journal*, © Dow Jones & Company, Inc., 1987. All Rights Reserved.

mation such as an investment advisory service that carries information on warrants.[4]

Consider next the twentieth entry listed, "Adob pf". This represents a preferred stock issue for that corporation (actually, this company had two different preferred issues listed). Again, all information is identical to that of a common stock except the P/E ratio is not reported because it has no relevance in the case of preferred stock. The preferred pays a fixed dividend; therefore, other things being equal, increased earnings will not result in a higher valuation for the preferred. These securities generally move like bonds, responding to interest rates. Notice that a corporation may have several issues of preferred stock outstanding. (See "AlaP" as an example.)

One last point to note is the letters that appear beside certain stocks, such as an "s" or an "n." These letters refer to footnotes, carried on a nearby page, that provide additional information, particularly dividend information.

Information about the American Stock Exchange (AMEX) is identical to that for the New York Exchange, though there are fewer companies, and the companies are typically smaller. Warrants and some preferreds are carried on the American, just as on the New York.

Investors should also know how to read information about stocks in the over-the-counter market. As explained in Chapter 3, an increasing number of OTC stocks are being traded in the NASDAQ National Market System. The information for these issues will resemble that of the organized exchanges, as the following hypothetical example for Coors Beer shows

365-day High Low			Yld.	P/E	Sales (hds)	High	Low	Last	Net Chg.
39⅓	12¼	Coors Co B .50	1.9	15	1150	21	20¾	21	−⅜

The only differences between this information and that shown on the NYSE is that the first two prices are listed as "365-day High Low" (rather than as "52 Weeks High Low"), and there is no column explicitly labeled "Div." although the dollar dividend amount is shown, as in the case of the $0.50 for Coors.

In the case of the "traditional" over-the-counter stocks, for NASDAQ-traded stocks only a bid price and an asked price are reported, as opposed to high, low, and close prices on the exchanges. Consider the following hypothetical example for Adobe Systems:

	Sales 100s	Bid	Ask	Net Chg.
Adobe Systems	122	30¼	31¼	−1⅛

---

[4]For example, the *Value Line Options and Convertibles Service* or the *R.H.M. Survey of Warrants, Options, and Low-Priced Stock.*

The bid price is what a dealer is willing to pay for the stock, and therefore what an investor should be able to sell shares for; the asked price is what the dealer will sell the shares for, and therefore what an investor will have to pay (of course, brokerage commissions will also be due in most cases). In the case of Adobe, there is a 1 point ($1) spread between the bid and asked price. The net change figure shown for over-the-counter stocks is the difference between *bid* prices on successive days.

The other information carried for these stocks includes the dividend, although many of these companies pay no dividend, and the sales in hundreds of shares for the previous day. Adobe paid no dividend, and 12,200 shares were traded on this hypothetical day.[5]

The Stock Market

In contrast to the bond market, the stock market is basically a secondary market. The aggregate amount of new common stock issued by corporations every year is small compared to the trading on the organized exchanges— the New York Stock Exchange, the American Stock Exchange, the regional exchanges—and the over-the-counter market. During the years 1983 through 1986 new common stock offerings averaged roughly $37 billion per year. However, when we compare this to activity in the secondary markets for common stocks, the relative importance is clear. For example, in 1986, the reported dollar volume on the New York Stock Exchange alone was about $1.4 trillion dollars. Clearly, it is the secondary market for common stocks that is of major importance.

Investors in the Stock Market

Households, a proxy for individual investors, have traditionally been the major owner of common stocks. Therefore, individual investors play an important role in the stock market, at least in terms of ownership.

In 1980 institutional investors owned about 35% of the market value of all NYSE-listed stocks, suggesting the importance of these investors in the stock market, at least for the larger stocks. Ownership figures, however, do not tell the complete story. It is also important to look at the trading activity of these investors. Institutional investors are the dominant single force in the market. By 1980 they were accounting for 50% of the value and almost 50% of the shares traded. By 1986 about 50% of the reported volume on the NYSE was large block transactions.

It is important to note that, although institutional investors dominate the NYSE, individuals may dominate the other markets. They account for a

---

[5] Additional OTC quotes are carried in papers such as *The Wall Street Journal*. Only bid and ask quotes are shown for these stocks.

substantial portion of public activity and public share volume in other markets. This suggests that individual investors recognize the opportunities in these other markets and pursue them. Also, in some cases institutional investors are restricted from these markets because the stocks are often too small to meet their criteria or legal requirements. As will be seen in Chapter 10, the other markets—the AMEX and the over-the-counter market—have outperformed the NYSE in recent years. Individual investors may know exactly what they are doing by not being the major force on the NYSE!

Trading Stocks

Some parallels exist between the stock market and the bond market in terms of trading. As noted in Chapter 6, although the market for U.S. government and agency bonds are active, liquid markets, the corporate and municipal sectors are much less so, at least for the average investor. In the case of stocks, the New York Stock Exchange is a very active, liquid market, with trades occurring smoothly within a carefully monitored framework. Prices may fluctuate sharply as a result of changes in investor expectations, but such changes are orderly, and investors can buy or sell with reasonable confidence that the prices are "fair" (i.e., represent orderly transactions within a monitored environment).

The American Stock Exchange is designed to imitate the NYSE, and thus has similar trading procedures.[6] The role of the specialist is essentially the same as on the NYSE, although capital requirements are smaller. Active stocks are usually assigned to specialist firms that may have several partners at the post to handle orders. Certain trading policies are different because of the relatively "thin" supply of shares for many AMEX stocks.[7]

In the over-the-counter market, the corporations being traded may range from very large (e.g., Food Lion Supermarkets and Coors Beer) to very small firms unknown to most investors; therefore, the market for particular shares may be very active or very inactive. Bid–ask spreads may range from ⅛ point to 2 points or more. The small investor can trade in the OTC market more easily than in the corporate or municipal bond markets, investing only a few hundred dollars or less. The OTC market is of increasing importance and continues to enhance its position relative to the organized exchanges (see Box 8–1).

The extent of active stock market trading by individual investors should depend on several factors. One is their knowledge. Do they understand how stocks are valued, traded, and managed? A second factor is their belief about the relationship between a security's value and its price. Are the two usually identical, and if not, can a typical investor expect to spot the difference? A

---

[6]This discussion is indebted to R. Teweles and E. Bradley, *The Stock Market*, 4th ed. New York: John Wiley & Sons, 1982, pp. 198–199.

[7]For example, specialists cannot accept stop orders for round lots.

BOX 8–1 AND THEN THERE WERE THREE

Who's got the hot-selling stuff? In the old days there wasn't much contest so far as equities were concerned: The class goods went on the New York Stock Exchange, the Amex was the bargain basement, and the counter markets were for pushcart peddlers.

New companies would go public, mature to where they could meet Amex sales and earnings requirements, and if all went well, the day would come when the champagne corks would pop to announce the Big Board listing.

No longer. The counter market—better known as the Nasdaq list, after its sponsoring body, the National Association of Securities Dealers—has done quite a lot of maturing itself. It is no longer a place from which companies are in a hurry to graduate. The counter market has "gotten its act together," concedes Big Board Chairman John J. Phelan Jr., to the point where it is holding on to many more of its stocks for a longer period.

It has got much harder to sell first-tier stocks, such as Apple Computer or MCI Communications, on the prestige values of a Big Board or (to a lesser degree) an Amex listing. The sell is particularly hard with the high-tech stocks Phelan needs to add excitement to a list that is heavily Smokestack America.

Some of those relative newcomers give every sign of staying put over-the-counter. To the institutional investors that own 46% of Intel Corp., says investor relations liaison officer Jim Jarrett, "it makes no difference" whether the big memory chip producer trades on the Big Board or over-the-counter. "Today," he adds, "there is less rationale to list on the NYSE."

The pinch is even worse across Trinity churchyard at the Amex. Its list is heavily weighted to energy stocks, many of them Canadian, that are at the moment not in brisk demand. "We really need 100 companies a year just to show a net gain in listings," says Amex President Kenneth Leibler, "and 100 companies is not easy in an auction market."

It's not easy for the Big Board, either. Its listings have slipped from a recent peak of 1581 in 1978 to the current total of 1540; the Amex, from 1200 in 1976 to 940.

NASD-traded issues, on the other hand, have been climbing almost without interruption—from 2495 in 1976 to 4136. Both listed exchanges have been bedeviled by merger mania. In the last two years alone the Big Board has lost 157 listings to buyouts of one kind or another. The more vulnerable Amex has lost 97 over the same time period. The NASD has taken its lumps, too: about 264 wipeouts on what is, of course, a much broader listing base. But in an era when new companies are being created at a record pace, NASD has no trouble replacing the losses.

It has real momentum going for it in the flood of new issues washing over its doorstep. The high mark of initial public offerings rises and recedes with speculative fever—there were a record 863 such issues in 1983, for example; 526 in 1984; and only 494 last year.

Since many new issues do not meet the listing minimums for either exchange, the counter market has a quasi-monopoly on newer companies—quasi because both exchanges have begun to make heavy promotional moves, with some success, on new issues that do measure up for immediate listing. The semi-lock on new issues explains in part why the counter market's share of trading volume has risen so dramatically.

Why the need for protection against a market that little more than a decade ago was notorious for slipshod marketmaking, well-after-the-fact price reporting, and speculative forays that left many an untutored player for dead? "There was a lack of visibility and credibility," recalls National Association of Securities Dealers President Gordon Macklin.

Forget about the nuts and bolts of a real-time electronic trading system, though it has played an important part in the rise of the counter market. The big impetus came from the realization of Big Board member firms—"the usual household names," says Securities & Exchange Commission official Richard Chase—that the counter market could be turned into a major profit center.

Big firms like Merrill Lynch, Shearson Lehman and Goldman, Sachs found they could underwrite a company, make a market in it, stir up retail interest with research reports and turn a profit almost every step of the way. As John Phelan notes, investors will never again think of the counter market as "1½ brokers operating out of Rome, N.Y."

The pain of relative slippage has been somewhat eased for the two exchanges by the general boom in stock trading. But the worry is there. "Though volume is at a high level and so are our resources," says Amex Chairman Arthur Levitt, "I'm not lulled into a sense of security. We've got to compete aggressively to protect our franchise."

Suppose the NASD market slice continues to expand at the same rate as in the last five years. Could the Big Board, feeding on only bite-size rations of dynamic new listings, be boxed into the limited role of a predominantly institutional market trading only old-line, big-capitalization stocks? Could the Amex lose still more of its equity base and fade into a predominantly options market?

Arthur Levitt, like John Phelan, argues that dealer markets like the NASD tend to dwindle when stocks go down and are unable to supply the liquidity needed to cushion a decline—who can forget 1974–75, when small company stocks were almost unsalable? But that was a decade ago, and the counter market's growth rate has persisted through too many turns now for it to be dismissed as merely cyclical.

Both Phelan and Levitt have been around The Street too long to take their own argument too literally. They are selling hard, making listing more attractive by throwing in ancillary services (like lobbying and recruiting directors) and diversifying into futures and options contracts that generate more volume in stocks already on the list.

The Big Board still has a huge lead in terms of dollar value of trading ($970.5 billion, vs. $235.5 billion for the NASD list and $26.7 billion for the Amex) and thinks it has a prestige edge in the battle for a potentially big trading market that is still several years down the road—the market in "global" stocks. However, the Amex and the NASD are beginning to plug into that one, too. Nobody's got the business locked up these days.

Source: Richard Phalon, "And Then There Were Three," *Forbes*, April 21, 1986, pp. 31–32. Reprinted by permission of *Forbes* magazine, April 21, 1986. © Forbes Inc., 1986.

third factor is the trade-offs to be made between direct investing and indirect investing through the purchase of investment company shares.

Each of these issues will be addressed in subsequent chapters. Readers can then decide for themselves the extent to which active stock market trading is desirable.

Common Stock Returns and Risks

As we did with bonds, we need to analyze basic information about the returns from, and risks of, investing in common stocks. This information will form a basis for the discussion of the valuation and analysis of stocks in the next chapter.

Common Stock Returns

The returns on common stocks can be separated into two parts: dividends and capital gains or losses. The total return from common stocks is

$$TR = \text{Dividend yield} + CG(L) \tag{8-1}$$

where TR is the total return on a stock during any specified period, dividend yield is the ratio of dividend to market price, and CG(L) is the capital gain or loss resulting from the purchase of a stock at one price and its subsequent sale at a different price.[8]

Dividends can be a substantial part of the total return from a common stock; in fact, some common stocks (in particular, utilities) are bought primarily for their dividend yield. Historically (1926–1976), dividends have constituted almost half of the total return from common stocks.[9] Nevertheless, most investors think of common stocks as vehicles for large (hopefully!) capital gains, although quite a few end up with capital losses. It is this part of the total return that really excites most investors in common stocks.

Measuring Returns

The income component of common stock returns is measured by the **dividend yield,** defined as the ratio of dividends to stock price. For example, the current yield on a stock is the current annual dividend divided by the current market price. The estimated yield on a stock is the estimated dividend to be paid for some period, such as for the next twelve months, divided by the current market price. As noted, dividend yield measures only part of the total return from a common stock.

As a conceptual measure, the HPY is a proper measure of the total return

---

[8] Note that in the case of a short sale, the capital gain or loss would be the difference between the sale price and the subsequent purchase price.

[9] See L. Fisher and J. Lorie, *A Half Century of Returns on Stocks and Bonds.* Chicago: University of Chicago Graduate School of Business, 1977.

on a common stock. It captures both components of the possible return from a stock, and therefore accounts for everything that an investor receives (or will receive).

Reviewing once again (from Chapter 5), the formula for HPY on a common (or preferred) stock is

$$\left[\quad \text{HPY}_{cs} = \frac{D_t + PC}{P_B} \quad \right] \qquad (8-2)$$

where D_t represents the dividend received during a given period t, such as a year, a month, or a quarter, PC measures the change in price during the period, and P_B represents the beginning or purchase price.

Holding period yield is a useful measure of return. It is easy to use as a measure of the return that has occurred, say over the past year, for one stock, a portfolio, or the market as a whole. It is also useful in trying to estimate the future returns from securities. To do so, however, an investor must estimate the future price in order to calculate the PC term, and estimating price at any point in the future is difficult, at best. Such an estimation process requires the use of probability distributions and expected values, as explained in Chapter 5.

Common Stock Risks

Sources of risk Common stocks have their own sources of risk, just as bonds. We discussed the sources of risk applying to all securities in Chapter 5 and those applying to bonds in particular in Chapter 6. We will do the same here for common stocks before considering the modern components of risk widely used today in investment analysis.

1. *Market Risk*. The chance of losses due to fluctuations in the stock market as a whole is referred to as market risk. For example, the Dow Jones Average dropped almost 25 points in less than one-half hour when news of President Kennedy's assassination reached the floor of the New York Stock Exchange (it was closed early as a result). And there are other examples of prices on stocks varying dramatically from what could be reasonably expected on the basis of informed estimates at the time.

One can argue that many sharp movements in the market (either up or down) are unjustified from an economic standpoint. Nevertheless, the possibility of such movements always exists, and they do occur.

2. *Interest Rate Risk*. Interest rate risk, a major risk facing all bondholders, was explained in Chapter 6. Market interest rates tend to move up or down together over longer periods. Not only bonds but all securities are affected by such movements, and the effect is usually the same—namely, other things being equal, the prices of securities move inversely to interest rates.

Interest rate risk affects common stocks in part because the market interest rate is a discount rate. In Chapter 7 it was shown that as the interest payments on bonds are discounted at higher interest (discount) rates, the present values (price) of the bonds decline. The same principle applies to common stocks, with everything else held constant. If interest rates rise, discount rates will be higher and stock prices (present values) will be lower. Furthermore, higher interest rates on debt securities decrease the attractiveness of equities to investors, other things being equal. In 1982 investors could purchase some bonds with coupons of 15, 16, and even 18%. With an opportunity for capital gains if interest rates were to subsequently decline, such purchases appeared very attractive. Finally, interest rates can affect margin purchases inversely, with higher rates leading to less demand for equities purchased on margin.

3. *Inflation Risk.* Inflation affects the values of all assets, because it decreases the dollar value of the returns received from the investment. Inflation risk involves uncertainty about the future purchasing power of funds that have been invested. As noted in Chapter 6, inflation risk is technically the risk of unanticipated inflation, since investors should adjust for anticipated inflation.

Historically, common stocks have been promoted as inflation hedges. However, several studies of this possibility indicate that stocks have been inadequate hedges against inflation on a monthly or even yearly basis.[10] To be a complete inflation hedge, common stocks should provide a nominal return equal to the noninflationary return required on the investment plus an amount to compensate for actual inflation exceeding expected inflation.

4. *Other Risks.* Various writers on the subject sometimes refer to other risks in connection with common stocks, including business risk, financial risk, industry risk, political risk, and management risk. The last two are self-explanatory, and somewhat abstract. **Business risk** involves the probability of a company suffering losses or profits less than expected for a given period because of adverse circumstances in that company's particular line of activity. This risk could occur because of external forces such as trade restrictions, a worldwide recession, or hostilities with a foreign country that constitutes much of the market for a company's products. Internally, business risk comes about because of such factors as efficiency considerations, poor planning, or illegal activities by employees.

Financial risk involves the use of debt in financing the assets of a firm. The use of fixed-cost financing affects the earnings per share available to the stockholders, magnifying both gains and losses. This process is called **leverage**. Because of the risk of default, and therefore possible bankruptcy, arising from the use of debt, variability in a company's returns should increase with the use of financial leverage. The same is true of operating leverage, defined as the change in operating profit resulting from a change in sales volume. The higher the operating leverage, other things being equal, the higher the variability in returns accruing to the common stockholders.

---

[10] See, for example, Charles R. Nelson, "Inflation and Rates of Return on Common Stock," *Journal of Finance*, May 1976, pp. 471–483; and Zvi Bodie, "Common Stocks as a Hedge Against Inflation," *Journal of Finance*, May 1976, pp. 459–470.

Industry risk refers to the possibility of virtually all firms in a given industry being adversely affected by some common factor that does not affect, or affects to a much lesser degree, firms outside that industry. The troubled auto industry of the early 1980s is one example.

Systematic and unsystematic risk   The previous discussion indicates that the risk applicable to common stocks can be divided into two types: (1) A general component, representing that portion in the variability of a stock's total returns that is directly associated with overall movements in general economic (or stock market) activity; (2) A specific (issuer) component, representing that portion in the variability of a stock's total return that is not related to the variability in general economic (market) activity. In Chapter 5 we labeled these two components systematic and unsystematic risk, and the following summarizes our earlier discussion:

   1. Systematic risk is that part of the total variability directly associated with the variability in the overall market. That is, the variability in the returns of all stocks together explains a significant part of the variability in the returns of any one individual stock. Thus, systematic risk is related to and is often referred to as market risk.

   2. Unsystematic risk is that part of the total risk not related to the overall market variability—the portion of total variability remaining after the systematic part has been removed. Because it is unrelated to overall market risk, it is sometimes called nonmarket risk. It is attributable to the unique factors affecting a particular company.

   Partitioning of common stock total risk into these two components has become commonplace in investment analysis. The usefulness of this separation will be more evident when we discuss portfolio management.

Measuring Risk

As discussed in Chapter 5, risk is often associated with dispersion in the likely outcomes, and dispersion refers to variability. The standard deviation captures the dispersion or variability and is used as a measure of the total risk for a common stock. The standard deviation can easily be squared to form the variance, which is an alternative measure of dispersion or risk. Sometimes it is convenient to use standard deviation, and at other times it is convenient to use variance.

   The statistical measure of total risk for a common stock, standard deviation or variance, can be quantitatively separated into its two components, systematic risk and unsystematic risk (which was also discussed in Chapter 5). When this is done, the significance of systematic risk can be seen.

$$\text{Total Risk for Stock i} = \text{Systematic Risk} + \text{Unsystematic Risk} \qquad (8\text{-}3)$$
$$= \text{Market Risk} + \text{Nonmarket Risk}$$
$$= \text{Nondiversifiable Risk} + \text{Diversifiable Risk}$$

The unsystematic risk measures that part of the total risk of a common stock that is not related to the aggregate market for all stocks. As shown in the chapters on portfolio management later in the text, when an investor builds a portfolio of stocks the unsystematic risk is diversified away, or nearly so. This means that the unsystematic risk term in Equation 8–3 will disappear or be reduced to a very small amount. What remains is the first term, which measures systematic risk.

Systematic risk refers to that part of the total risk that is attributable to the aggregate market for all stocks. A key component of the systematic risk is a stock's beta, which was previously explained in Chapter 5. Beta is a relative measure of risk—the risk of an individual stock in relation to the overall market, as measured by the volatility of its returns. To summarize, the average beta for all stocks is 1.0; that is, the beta for the overall market is 1.0. Thus, a stock with a beta of 1.5 would be considered an aggressive (risky) security, whereas a stock with a beta of 0.5 would be considered defensive (conservative). *On average,* if the beta of a stock was 2, its returns would be twice as volatile as the overall market, moving up or down twice as much. For example, if the overall market declined 5%, this stock's returns should decline, on the average, 10%; if the market rose 10%, its returns should rise 20%. On the other hand, with a beta of 0.8, if the market declined 5%, this stock's returns should decline only 0.8 as much, or 4%; likewise, a market rise of 10% should bring about a smaller increase in returns for this stock, 8%. Betas can also be negative, which would indicate expected changes in return in the opposite direction to the market.

It is important to remember that beta is an index measure of the systematic risk for a common stock. It is measured on a ratio scale; that is, a beta of 2.0 is twice as large as a beta of 1.0, and a beta of 0.5 is half as large. Beta is useful for comparing the relative systematic risk of different stocks and, in practice, is used by investors to judge a stock's riskiness. Stocks can be ranked by their betas—because the variance of the market is a constant across all securities for a particular period, ranking stocks by beta is the same as ranking them by their absolute systematic risk.[11] Stocks with high (low) betas are said to be high (low) risk securities.

Betas are estimated from historical data, regressing HPYs for the individual security against the HPYs for some market index. As a result, the usefulness of beta will depend on, among other things, the validity of the regression equation. Regardless of how good the fit is, however, beta is an estimate subject to errors.

It is important to note that most calculated betas are ex post betas. What is actually needed in investment decisions is an ex ante beta measuring expected volatility. The common practice of many investors is simply to calculate the beta for a security and assume it will remain constant in the

---

[11] The absolute systematic risk for a stock is the product of the stock's beta and the variance of the return for the overall market.

future, a risky assumption in the case of individual securities. Similar to standard deviations, portfolio betas are quite often stable across time whereas individual security betas are often notoriously unstable. However, this is not an unfavorable outcome for investors because the basic premise of portfolio theory is the necessity of holding a portfolio of securities rather than only one or a few securities.

One method of estimating beta is to employ the historical regression estimate but subjectively modify it for expected or known changes. In fact, it is logical to begin the estimation of beta using the best estimate of the historical beta.

Substantial evidence has been presented that betas tend to move toward 1.0 over time.[12] Betas substantially larger (smaller) than 1.0 should tend to be followed by betas that are lower (higher), and closer to 1.0. Thus, forecasted betas should be closer to 1.0 than the estimates based solely on historical data would suggest. Several models have been advocated for adjusting betas for this tendency to "regress toward the mean."[13] As a result, it is not unusual to find "adjusted" betas rather than historical betas. Merrill Lynch, for example, adjusts betas for this tendency. Investors who obtain beta information from such sources are actually using estimated betas.

The Historical Returns and Risks on Common Stocks

As with the discussion of bonds, this chapter concludes with an analysis of the historical returns on common stocks. Knowledge of the past 60 years of returns on risky assets, both on an absolute basis and in relation to other financial assets, is useful. Perhaps more important, this information should be useful in helping investors to estimate the future returns from stocks. In the absence of extraordinary inflation or major structural changes in our economy, it is simply unrealistic to expect future annual returns on common stocks over many years, to average, say, 30%; on the other hand, investors need not be overly worried that they will return as little as, say, 5% a year.

The Ibbotson–Sinquefield (IS) data, discussed in Chapter 5 (Figure 5–2), provide detailed figures for the returns and risk of common stocks. In that study IS report monthly and annual returns for Standard & Poor's 500 Composite Index for the years 1926 through 1986. These returns include both dividends and capital gains or losses (i.e., they are monthly or yearly HPYs).

---

[12] See M. Blume, "Betas and Their Regression Tendencies," *Journal of Finance*, Vol. X, No. 3 (June 1975), pp. 785–795; and R. Levy, "On the Short-Term Stationarity of Beta Coefficients," *Financial Analysts Journal*, Vol. 27, No. 5 (December 1977), pp. 55–62.

[13] See M. Blume, "On the Assessment of Risk," *Journal of Finance*, Vol. V, No. 1 (March 1971), pp. 1–10; and O. Vasichek, "A Note on Using Cross-Sectional Information in Bayesian Estimation of Security Betas," *Journal of Finance*, Vol. 8, No. 5 (December 1973), pp. 1233–1239.

TABLE 8–1 **Annual Rates of Return and the Equity Risk Premium for Common Stocks, 1926–1986**

	Geometric Mean (%)	Arithmetic Mean (%)	Standard Deviation (%)
Common stocks	10.0	12.1	21.2
Small stocks	12.5	18.2	36.0
Common stock risk premium (stocks − Treasury bills)	6.3	8.6	21.7

Source: Ibbotson, Roger G., and Rex A. Sinquefield, *Stocks, Bonds, Bills, and Inflation* (SSBI), 1982, updated in *SSBI 1987 Yearbook,* Ibbotson Associates, Chicago, 1987, pp. 21 and 46. Reprinted by permission.

Table 8–1 repeats (from Figure 5–2) the arithmetic mean, geometric mean, and standard deviation of annual returns for common stocks for the years 1926 through 1986. The geometric annual rate of return has averaged 10.0% for this 61-year period, an impressive figure in comparison with alternatives such as bonds. This return, or the 12.1% average annual arithmetic mean, was not achieved without significant risk, however, as shown by the standard deviation of 21.2%. This standard deviation is two to three times that of government and corporate bonds, and roughly six times that of Treasury bills (refer to Figure 5–2).

Table 8–1 also shows the returns and risk of "small" common stocks. Small in this case refers to the bottom quintile of New York Stock Exchange stocks ranked by market value. It is reasonable to expect these smaller stocks to be more risky than the largest stocks on the NYSE such as IBM or AT&T; therefore, the returns should generally be larger. The average annual compound return for this long period was 2.5 percentage points higher, and the annual arithmetic return was over 6 percentage points higher. The trade-off, however, was the large jump in risk from 21.2% to 36.0%, as measured by the standard deviation. This is another good demonstration of the risk–return trade-off.

Finally, Table 8–1 shows the so-called **equity risk premium** for common stocks, defined as the difference between the return on common stocks and the return on riskless assets (Treasury bills). In other words, this is the additional annual average compensation that investors received for assuming the additional risk of common stock ownership. Each investor has to decide if this average risk premium is adequate compensation for the additional risk; furthermore, if it can be expected to continue, will it be adequate in the future.

The message from Table 8–1, in conjunction with Figure 5–2, is very clear. Common stocks have provided twice the annualized return of government bonds over a 61-year period, but at a cost of two to three times the risk; for "small" stocks, the comparable figures are two to three times as much return, but at over four times the risk. Most investors in common stocks

TABLE 8–2 Compound Annual Rates of Return on Standard & Poor's 500 Index, 1967–1986

To the End of	From the Beginning of																			
	1967	1968	1969	1970	1971	1972	1973	1974	1975	1976	1977	1978	1979	1980	1981	1982	1983	1984	1985	1986
1967	24.0																			
1968	17.3	11.1																		
1969	8.0	0.8	−8.5																	
1970	7.0	1.9	−2.4	4.0																
1971	8.4	4.8	2.8	9.0	14.3															
1972	10.1	7.5	6.7	12.3	16.6	19.0														
1973	6.2	3.5	2.0	4.8	5.1	0.8	−14.7													
1974	1.4	−1.5	−3.4	−2.4	−3.9	−9.3	−20.8	−26.5												
1975	4.9	2.7	1.6	3.3	3.2	0.6	−4.9	0.4	37.2											
1976	6.6	4.9	4.1	6.0	6.4	4.9	1.6	7.7	30.4	23.8										
1977	5.3	3.6	2.8	4.3	4.3	2.8	−0.2	3.8	16.4	7.2	−7.2									
1978	5.4	3.9	3.2	4.5	4.6	3.3	0.9	4.3	13.9	7.0	−0.5	6.6								
1979	6.3	5.0	4.5	5.9	6.1	5.1	3.2	6.6	14.8	9.7	5.4	12.3	18.4							
1980	8.0	6.9	6.5	8.0	8.4	7.8	6.5	9.9	17.5	13.9	11.6	18.7	25.2	32.4						
1981	7.1	6.0	5.6	6.9	7.2	6.5	5.2	7.9	14.0	10.6	8.1	12.3	14.3	12.2	−4.9					
1982	8.0	7.0	6.7	7.9	8.3	7.7	6.7	9.4	14.9	12.1	10.2	14.0	16.0	15.2	7.4	21.4				
1983	8.8	7.9	7.7	8.9	9.3	8.9	8.0	10.6	15.7	13.3	11.9	15.4	17.3	17.0	12.3	22.0	22.5			
1984	8.6	7.8	7.6	8.7	9.1	8.7	7.9	10.2	14.8	12.5	11.2	14.1	15.4	14.8	10.7	26.5	14.1	6.3		
1985	9.7	9.0	8.9	10.1	10.5	10.2	9.6	11.9	16.2	14.3	13.3	16.2	17.6	17.5	14.7	20.2	19.8	18.5	32.2	
1986	10.2	9.5	9.4	10.6	11.0	10.8	10.2	12.4	16.4	14.7	13.8	16.4	17.7	17.6	15.3	19.9	19.5	18.5	25.1	18.5

Source: Ibbotson, Roger G., and Rex A. Sinquefield, *Stocks, Bonds, Bills and Inflation* (SSBI), 1982, updated in *SSBI 1987 Yearbook,* Ibbotson Associates, Chicago, 1987, p. 103. Reprinted by permission.

should continue to enjoy higher returns than investors in fixed-income securities, but they will have to assume higher risk to do so. In any one year or over a period of years, their returns may be less than those available in alternative assets.

We can better appreciate the risk, as well as the return potential, of common stocks by considering a shorter segment of time such as periods of years. Table 8–2 shows the annual returns on the same index considered before, the Standard & Poor's 500 Composite Index, for the years 1967 through 1986. These data clearly demonstrate both the potential returns and the riskiness of common stocks. The average return over a longer period can be high in comparison with other securities such as bonds, but over shorter periods the variability, both up and down, can be great.

The returns in Table 8–2 are total returns, calculated as "percent per annum compounded annually." For example, the compound annual rate of return on this stock index for the years 1980 and 1981 was 12.2%, consisting of a gain of 32.4% in 1980 and a loss of 4.9% in 1981, calculated as

$$1.324(0.951) = 1.259$$

$$(1.2591)^{1/2} = 1.122$$

$$1.122 - 1.0 = 0.122 \text{ or } 12.2\%$$

Over the entire period 1967–1986, the annual compound return was 10.2%, whereas for the last 10 years (1977–1986) it was 13.8%, for the last five years (1982–1986) it was 19.9%, and for the last three years it was 18.5%. Thus, the compound annual rate of return on common stocks for periods of a few years depends significantly on the exact years measured.

As the number of years increases, the compound average return is likely to approach the long-run compound average return on common stocks of about 9–10%. However, investors run the risk of investing at the beginning of 1973, for example, and finding that at the end of 1977 their compound annual total rate of return is only −0.2%. They are motivated, though, with the hope of being one of those who invested at the beginning of 1982, for instance, and found that at the end of 1986 their compound annual total rate of return was 19.9%.

Note (by reading down the diagonal in Table 8–2) that over the 10-year period 1977–1986, only two years out of 10 showed losses. Historically (for the period 1926–1986), 30% of the time the returns have been negative.

Summary

Common stocks (equity securities) represent an ownership position in corporations. The stockholders are the owners, exercise control, and have limited liability.

Specific characteristics of common stocks include the charter issued by the state to establish the corporation and the voting rights of the stockholders, which may be protected by the preemptive right of the stockholders to purchase any new shares sold. The par value of a common stock is relatively insignificant. The book value is the accounting value of the equity; market value, however, is the variable of interest to stockholders because on a per share basis it is the price of the stock, and stock prices are the key variable for investors.

Stockholders may or may not receive quarterly dividends, the only cash payments made by a corporation, depending on the board of directors. If they do, the payment procedure involves several specific steps. Stock dividends and stock splits represent a repackaging of the pieces of paper (stock shares) evidencing ownership. Other things being equal, they do not represent direct economic value.

Much information is available on stocks and should be organized along market–industry–company lines. Daily price and volume information is readily available in major newspapers.

The stock market is primarily a secondary market in which existing shares are traded among investors. Institutional investors have dominated the NYSE for many years, accounting for a substantial portion of its total activity. Individual investors dominate the other exchanges.

Trading on the New York Stock Exchange is very smooth and orderly. Overall, AMEX trading is similar, but supplies of many of these stocks are thin. Over-the-counter trading ranges from very active to very inactive, depending on the particular issue.

Returns on common stocks consist of the dividend yield plus the capital gain (or loss). Dividend yield measures the income component of the total return, while the HPY is applicable as a measure of total return.

Common stock risk sources include market risk, interest rate risk, inflation risk, and others. These sources of risk can be separated into systematic and unsystematic components. The total risk for a common stock is measured by the standard deviation or variance. A relative measure of systematic risk is the beta coefficient, which measures the volatility of a stock's returns. Unsystematic risk can be diversified away in a portfolio, leaving the systematic risk which cannot be diversified away.

Historically (1926–1986), common stocks have averaged 10.0% compound annual return, but with a standard deviation two and a half times that of government and corporate bonds. "Small" common stocks have had even larger average returns and risk. Common stocks may average high returns over longer periods of time, but significant risks may be incurred over shorter periods of time. An investor who has to sell could suffer significant losses. On the other hand, gains can be quite large over short periods of time.

Key Words

Book value	Leverage
Business risk	Market value
Dividends	Stock dividend
Dividend yield	Stock split
Equity risk premium	Systematic risk
Financial risk	Unsystematic risk

QUESTIONS AND PROBLEMS

1. What are the advantages and disadvantages of being a common stockholder of IBM as opposed to being a bondholder?
2. Distinguish between par value, book value, and market value for a corporation.

3. Assume that a company in whose stock you are interested will pay their regular quarterly dividend soon. Looking in *The Wall Street Journal*, you see a dividend figure of $3.20 listed for this stock. The board of directors has declared the dividend payable on September 1, with a holder-of-record date of August 15. When must you buy the stock to receive this dividend, and how much will you receive if you buy 150 shares?

4. Of what value to investors are stock dividends and splits?

5. How does the reporting in *The Wall Street Journal* for a "standard" over-the-counter stock differ from those over-the-counter stocks traded on the NASDAQ National Market?

6. Why is the stock market considered a "secondary" market?

7. How important are institutional investors in NYSE total trading?

8. How does trading in the over-the-counter market compare to trading in the corporate and municipal bond markets from the standpoint of the average individual investor?

9. What is the relative importance, historically, of the two components of common stocks returns?

10. How can you measure the income component of stocks?

11. What are the sources of risk for common stocks?

12. Distinguish between systematic and unsystematic risk.

13. What is meant by the risk premium for common stocks? Looking at the historical record, would you expect to find much variation in annual risk premiums?

14. How is the systematic risk, in relative terms, calculated for a stock?

15. What are some factors that have affected the unsystematic return for Chrysler Corporation during the 1980s?

16. Why is beta a relative measure of risk?

17. How can the total risk of a common stock be measured? How is beta related to this measure?

Selected References

Bodie, Zvi. "Common Stocks as a Hedge Against Inflation." *Journal of Finance*, May 1976, pp. 459–470.

Brealey, Richard A. *An Introduction to Risk and Return from Common Stocks*, 2nd ed. Cambridge, Mass.: MIT Press, 1983.

Brigham, Eugene F. *Fundamentals of Financial Management*. 4th ed. Chicago: Dryden Press, 1986.

Elton, Edwin J., and Gruber, Martin J. *Modern Portfolio Theory and Investment Analysis*, 3rd ed. New York: John Wiley, 1987.

Farrell, James L., Jr. *Guide to Portfolio Management*. New York: McGraw-Hill, 1983.

Gup, Benton E. *The Basics of Investing*, 3rd ed. New York: John Wiley, 1987.

Ibbotson Associates, Inc. *Stocks, Bonds, Bills, and Inflation: Yearbook.* Annual. Chicago, Ill.: Ibbotson Associates, 1986.

Kidwell, David S., and Peterson, Richard L. *Financial Institutions, Markets, and Money,* 3rd ed. Chicago: Dryden Press, 1987.

Malkiel, Burton G. *A Random Walk Down Wall Street.* New York: W. W. Norton, 1975.

New York Stock Exchange Fact Book. Annual. New York: New York Stock Exchange, Inc.

Sharpe, William F., and Cooper, G. M. "Risk–Return Classes of New York Stock Exchange Stocks, 1931–1967." *Financial Analysts Journal,* March–April 1972, pp. 46–54.

Teweles, Richard J., and Bradley, Edward S. *The Stock Market,* 4th ed. New York: John Wiley, 1982.

Tinic, Seha M., and West, Richard R. *Investing in Securities: An Efficient Markets Approach.* Reading, Mass.: Addison-Wesley, 1979.

CHAPTER 9

COMMON STOCK VALUATION AND ANALYSIS

Why do investors buy common stocks? What determines the value of a common stock? What approaches are commonly used by investors interested in stocks? These questions will be answered in the next six chapters. Because of the complexity of common stocks and the related questions that are raised in their analysis, several chapters are needed to adequately describe the most frequently used analysis and selection processes.

There are three well-known approaches for analyzing and selecting common stocks: fundamental analysis, technical analysis, and efficient market considerations. The discussion of common stocks will therefore be built around these three approaches.

Traditionally, fundamental analysis has occupied the majority of resources devoted to the analysis of common stocks. All investors should understand the logic of, and rationale for, fundamental analysis. It deserves, and will receive, careful consideration. The other two approaches, technical analysis and the efficient markets concept, are analyzed in detail in Chapters 13 and 14, respectively.

Each of these three approaches will be described briefly, starting in reverse order with efficient market concepts. This will allow us to develop the fundamental approach in some detail in the remainder of this chapter and set the stage for the next three chapters, which analyze the fundamental approach in a specific, recommended order.

Efficient Market Concepts

One of the most significant developments in the last 10 to 15 years is the proposition that securities markets are efficient. This idea has generated considerable controversy concerning the analysis and valuation of securities because of its significant implications for investors. Regardless of how much (or how little) an investor learns about investments, and regardless of whether an investor ends up being convinced by the efficient markets literature, it is prudent to learn something about this idea early in one's study of investments. Much evidence exists to support the basic concepts from this hypothesis, and it cannot be ignored simply because one is uncomfortable with the idea or because it sounds too improbable. Therefore, it is appropriate to consider this concept at the outset of any discussion about the valuation of common stocks.

The efficient market (EM) hypothesis is concerned with the assessment of information by investors. Security prices are determined by expectations about the future. Investors use the information available to them in forming their expectations. If security prices fully reflect all the relevant information that is available and usable, a securities market is said to be efficient.

If the stock market is efficient, prices reflect their fair economic value as estimated by investors. Even if this is not strictly true, prices may reflect their approximate fair value after transactions costs are taken into account, a condition known as "economic efficiency." In such a market, where prices of stocks depart only slightly from their fair economic value, investors should not employ trading strategies designed to "beat the market" by identifying undervalued stocks.

The implications of an efficient market are extremely important for investors. They include one's beliefs about how to value securities in terms of the other two approaches—the fundamental and the technical approach. This, in turn, encompasses questions about the time and effort to be devoted to these two approaches. Other implications include the management of a portfolio of securities—should management be active or passive? Efficient market proponents often argue that less time should be devoted to the analysis of securities for possible inclusion in a portfolio and more to such considerations as reducing taxes and transaction costs and maintaining the chosen risk level of a portfolio over time.

The rise, and increasing acceptance, of the efficient markets concept has had an impact on traditional investing practices. Hardest hit has been technical analysis, to be discussed in the next section. If prices fluctuate in accordance with the efficient markets model, there is little chance that pure technical analysis can have any validity.

The EM concept also has implications for fundamental analysis. If the market is efficient, prices will react quickly to new information. With many active investors buying and selling, prices should be close to their fair economic values. However, fundamental analysis is still needed in an efficient market; if it was not being done, the market would be less efficient. In fact, one can argue that it is the very fact that investors do fundamental analysis, in the belief that the market is not efficient, that makes the market efficient.

Technical Strategies

One of the two traditional strategies available to investors before the formulation of the efficient markets concept is technical analysis. In fact, technical analysis is the oldest strategy, being traceable back to at least the late nineteenth century.

The rationale behind technical analysis is that the value of a stock is primarily a function of supply and demand conditions. These conditions, in turn, are determined by a range of factors, from scientific to opinions and guesses. The market uses all of these factors in determining the changes in prices. These prices will move in trends that may persist, with changes in trends resulting from changes in supply and demand conditions. The idea that these changes can be detected by analyzing the action of the market itself characterizes technical analysis.

The term technical analysis refers to the methodology of forecasting fluctuations in securities prices. This methodology can be applied either to individual securities or to the market as a whole (i.e., forecasting a market index such as the Dow Jones Industrial Average).

In its purest sense, technical analysis is not concerned with the underlying economic variables that affect a company or the market. The causes of demand and supply shifts are, therefore, not important. The basic question to be asked can be stated as follows: does excess demand exist for a stock, and can it be detected by studying either the patterns of past price fluctuations or the movements of certain technical indicators or rules? Technicians study the market using graphical charting of price changes and volume of trading over time. Also, a number of technical indicators are used.

Technical analysis will be considered more fully in Chapter 13 and efficient markets in Chapter 14. The efficient markets concept presents a direct challenge to technical analysis; if prices fluctuate as predicted by this hypothesis, past price changes are of no value in predicting future price changes.

Fundamental Analysis

Fundamental analysis is based on the premise that any security (and the market as a whole) has an intrinsic value at any given time. This value is a function of underlying economic values—specifically, expected returns and risk. By assessing these fundamental determinants of the value of a security, it is possible to determine an estimate of its intrinsic value. This estimated intrinsic value can then be compared to the current market price of the security. Similar to the decision rules used for bonds in Chapter 7, there are decision rules for common stocks when fundamental analysis is used to calculate intrinsic value. These rules will be stated later in the chapter.

A basic assumption of fundamental analysis is that market price and intrinsic value can differ from time to time, but eventually investors will recognize the discrepancy and act to bring the two values together. Those investors who can perform good fundamental analysis and spot discrepancies should be able to profit by acting before this occurs.

Two basic fundamental approaches to the valuation of common stocks are typically used in the securities world: the present value approach and the P/E ratio (multiple of earnings) approach. The present value analysis is similar to the process considered for bonds in Chapter 7. The future stream of benefits to be received from a common stock is discounted back to the present at the investor's required rate of return. The P/E ratio approach is probably more widely used by practicing security analysts. A stock is said to be worth some multiple of its future earnings; therefore, investors determine the value or price of a stock by deciding how many dollars (the multiple) they are willing to pay for every dollar of expected earnings.

We will now consider each of these fundamental approaches to the valuation of common stock in turn, starting with the present value approach.

The Present Value Approach

The traditional method of calculating intrinsic value involves the use of present value analysis. As explained in Chapter 7, the price of any security is determined by its value, and this value is usually determined by a present value process involving the capitalization (discounting) of income. That is, the current value of a security is equal to the discounted (present) value of the future stream of economic benefits that the investor expects to receive from the asset. To use such a model, the investor must estimate a discount rate, or appropriate required rate of return (which is the sum of the risk-free rate and risk premium as explained in Chapter 5), and the amount and timing of the future stream of economic benefits. These two components are used in a present value model to estimate the intrinsic value, which is then compared to the current market price of the security.

Figure 9–1 summarizes the present value process used in fundamental analysis. It emphasizes the factors that go into valuing common stocks. The exact nature of the present value process used by investors in the marketplace will depend on assumptions made about the growth in the expected stream of benefits, as explained later.

The required rate of return for a common stock   The general concept of a required rate of return was discussed in Chapter 5 and was used in Chapter 7 to value bonds. It is appropriate to review this concept for the case of common stocks.

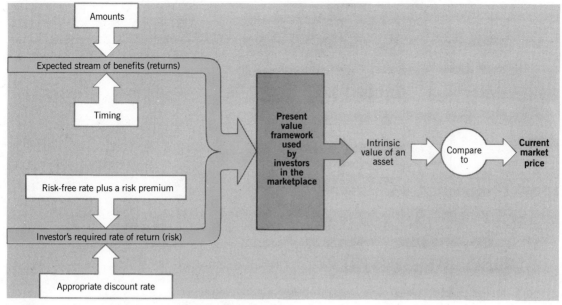

FIGURE 9–1   **The present value approach to valuation.**

An investor who is considering the purchase of a common stock must consider its risk and, given its risk, the minimum expected rate of return that will be required to induce the investor to make the purchase. This minimum expected return, or required rate of return, is an opportunity cost.

What is the relationship between the required rate of return and risk for a common stock? Chapter 1 described the underlying premise of investments—a trade-off between risk and return in which the larger the risk assumed, the larger the return should be to compensate for the risk. Remember, however, that the return referred to is *expected* return. Expectations may not materialize because of unforeseen events, or simply because expected return is a probability distribution with less than 100% probability of a particular return occurring.

The trade-off between the required rate of return and risk is considered to be linear, as shown in Figure 9–2, which reviews and enhances the discussion in Chapter 5. Required rate of return (usually represented in finance by the letter k) is on the vertical axis, risk is on the horizontal axis, and the vertical intercept is the risk-free rate of return that can be earned on a riskless asset. It is important to remember that the horizontal axis in Figure 9–2 uses beta to measure risk. As explained in the previous chapter, beta is a measure of nondiversifiable or systematic risk for a stock. It is the relevant measure of risk when investors hold portfolios of common stocks.

Figure 9–2 indicates that the required rate of return increases as the risk, measured by beta, increases. The stock market taken as a whole has a beta

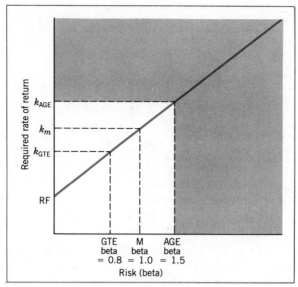

FIGURE 9–2 **The trade-off between required rate of return and risk for common stocks.**

of 1.0, indicated by point M in the diagram. The required rate of return for all stocks is therefore k_M. Now consider a stock with a beta lower than 1.0; for example, assume that General Telephone and Electronics has a beta of 0.8. Its required rate of return, k_{GTE}, will be below k_M because its risk (beta) is less than that of the market. On the other hand, if a stock such as A. G. Edwards, a large publicly traded brokerage firm, has a beta of 1.50, this would indicate substantially greater risk than the market as a whole; therefore, investors would require a higher rate of return, k_{AGE}.

Recall from Chapter 5 that the required rate of return—the risk trade-off shown in Figure 9–2—can be expressed in equation form. The required rate of return for any common stock (e.g., stock i):[1]

$$k_i = RF + B_i(MR - RF)$$

where

k_i = the required rate of return for stock i (the RR_i in Chapter 5).
RF = the risk-free rate.
MR = the required rate of return on the market.
B_i = the risk (beta) of stock i.

This equation is known as the capital asset pricing model, or CAPM. It is one of the key developments in finance and, rightly or wrongly, underlies

---

[1]This equation was explained in detail in Chapter 5.

much of modern investment analysis. The CAPM provides us with a statement for the required rate of return for a common stock.

The expected stream of benefits for a common stock   The other component that goes into the present value framework is the expected stream of benefits. Just as the value of a bond is the present value of any interest payments plus the present value of the bond's face value that will be received at maturity, the value of a common stock is the present value of all the cash flows to be received from the issuer (corporation). The questions are, what are the cash flows for a stock, how much can be expected, and when will they be received?

To find which cash flows are appropriate in the valuation of a common stock, ask yourself a question. If I buy a particular common stock and place it in a special trust fund for the perpetual benefit of myself and my heirs, what cash flows will be received? The answer is dividends, because this is the only cash distribution that a corporation actually makes to its stockholders. Although a firm's earnings per share in any year belong to the stockholders, corporations generally do not pay out all of their earnings to their stockholders.

Stockholders may plan to sell their shares sometime in the future, resulting in a cash flow from the sales price. As shown later, however, even if investors think of the cash flows from common stocks as a combination of dividends and a future price at which the stock can be sold, this is equivalent to the stream of all dividends to be received on the stock.

What about earnings? Are they important? Can they be used as the expected stream of benefits? The answer is yes to both questions. Dividends are paid out of earnings, so earnings are clearly important. And the second approach to fundamental analysis, to be considered later, uses the earnings and a P/E ratio to determine intrinsic value. Therefore, earnings are an important part of fundamental analysis; in fact, earnings receive more attention from investors than any other single variable.

If all earnings are paid out as dividends, they will be accounted for as dividends. If earnings are retained by the corporation, they will presumably be reinvested, thereby enhancing future earnings and, ultimately, dividends. The present value analysis should not count the earnings reinvested currently and also paid later as dividends. If properly defined and separated, these two variables would produce the same results; therefore, more than one present value model is possible.[2] It is always correct, however, to use dividends in the present value analysis.

Because dividends are the cash flow stream to be directly received by investors, it seems appropriate to have a valuation model based on dividends. The dividend valuation model is such a model.

---

[2] Besides dividends and earnings, cash flow (earnings after tax plus depreciation) has been suggested for these models.

The dividend valuation model One widely used approach for valuing common stocks involves the application of Equation 7–1, repeated here and now labeled (9–1).[3]

$$\text{Value} = \sum_{t=1}^{n} \frac{\text{Cash flows}}{(1 + k)^t} \qquad (9\text{--}1)$$

where

k = the required rate of return

In adapting this general equation specifically to value common stocks, the cash flows are dividends expected to be paid in each future period. Since dividends are the only cash payment a stockholder receives directly from a firm, they are the foundation of valuation for common stocks. An investor or analyst using this approach would carefully study the future prospects for a company and estimate the likely dividends to be paid. Also, the analyst would estimate an appropriate required rate of return or discount rate based on the risk foreseen in the dividends, and given the alternatives available. Finally, he or she would discount to the present and add together the estimated future dividends, properly identified as to amount and timing.

The present value approach to calculating the value (price) of a common stock is conceptually no different from the approach used in Chapter 7 to value bonds, or in Appendix 7–A to value preferred stock. Specifically, Equation 9–1 adopted for common stocks, where dividends are the cash flow, results in Equation 9–2. This equation, known as the **dividend valuation model,** states that the value of a stock today is the discounted value of all future dividends:

$$\text{PV}_{cs} = \frac{D_1}{(1 + k_{cs})} + \frac{D_2}{(1 + k_{cs})^2} + \frac{D_3}{(1 + k_{cs})^3} + \ldots + \frac{D_\infty}{(1 + k_{cs})^\infty}$$

$$= \text{The Dividend Valuation Model} \qquad (9\text{--}2)$$

where D_1, D_2, and so on are the dividends expected to be received in each future period, and k_{cs} is the discount rate applicable for an investment with this degree of riskiness (again, the opportunity cost of a comparable risk alternative).

Two immediate problems with Equation 9–2 can be observed:

1. The last term in (9–2) indicates that investors are dealing with infinity; that is, they must value a stream of dividends that may be paid forever since common stock has no maturity date.
2. The dividend stream is uncertain; there are no specified number of dividends, if in fact any are paid at all. Dividends must be declared

---

[3] For a good discussion of common stock valuation, see Eugene F. Brigham, *Fundamentals of Financial Management,* 4th ed. Chicago: Dryden Press, 1986.

periodically by the firm's board of directors (technically, they are declared quarterly). Furthermore, the dividends for most firms are expected to grow over time; therefore, investors usually cannot simplify Equation 9–2 as in the case of a preferred stock.[4] Only if dividends are not expected to grow could such a simplification be made. Although such a possibility exists, it is unusual.

How are these problems resolved? The first problem, that Equation 9–2 involves an infinite number of periods and dividends, will actually be resolved when we deal with the second problem, specifying the expected stream of dividends. However, from a practical standpoint this problem is not as troublesome as it first appears. At reasonably high discount rates such as 12, 14, or 16%, dividends received 40 or 50 years in the future are worth very little today, so that investors need not worry about them.

The conventional solution to the second problem is to make some assumptions about the growth of dividends over time. The investor or analyst is trying to estimate the future stream of dividends or a price that is expected to exist at some point in the future, or both. To do this, the investor should classify each stock into one of three cases, depending on the expected growth rate of the dividends. In summary, *the dividend valuation model is operationalized by estimating the expected future dividends to be paid by a company. This is accomplished by modeling the expected growth rate(s) in the dividend stream.*

A time line will be used to represent the three alternative growth rate versions of the dividend valuation model. All stocks that pay a dividend, or that are expected to pay dividends sometime in the future, can be modeled as one of these three cases. It is important to keep in mind during this discussion that the dividend currently being paid on a stock (or the most recent dividend paid) is designated as D_0 and is, of course, known. Investors must estimate the future dividends to be paid, starting with D_1, the dividend expected to be paid in the next period. The three growth rate cases for dividends are:

1. A constant dividend equal to the current dividend being paid, D_0, to be paid every year from now to infinity. This is typically referred to as the no-growth case:

D_0	D_0	D_0	D_0	. . .	D_0	
0	1	2	3	. . .	∞	Time Period

2. A dividend that is growing at a constant rate g, starting with D_0. This is typically referred to as the constant or normal growth version of the

---

[4] Refer to Appendix 7–A for the valuation of preferred stock.

dividend valuation model:

D_0	$D_0(1+g)^1$	$D_0(1+g)^2$	$D_0(1+g)^3$	$\ldots$	$D_0(1+g)^\infty$	
0	1	2	3	$\ldots$	∞	Time Period

3. A dividend that is growing at variable rates, for example, g_1 for the first four years and g_2 thereafter. This is typically referred to as the supernormal growth version of the dividend valuation model:

D_0	$D_1=D_0(1+g_1)$	$D_2=D_1(1+g_1)$	$D_3=D_2(1+g_1)$	$D_4=D_3(1+g_1)$
0	1	2	3	4

$D_5=D_4(1+g_2)$	$\ldots$	$D_\infty=D_{\infty-1}(1+g_2)$	
5	$\ldots$	∞	Time Period

The constant dollar dividend case (case 1) reduces to a perpetuity; that is, assuming a constant dividend (i.e., no growth), Equation 9–2 would simplify to the no-growth case shown as Equation 9–3.

$$\boxed{PV_{cs} = \frac{D_0}{k_{cs}} = \begin{array}{l}\text{Constant dollar version} \\ \text{of the dividend valuation model}\end{array}} \qquad (9\text{--}3)$$

where D_0 is a constant dividend expected for all future time periods and k_{cs} is the opportunity cost or required rate of return.

The no-growth case is equivalent to the valuation process for a preferred stock because, exactly like a preferred stock, the dividend (numerator of Equation 9–3) is fixed forever. Therefore, a no-growth common stock is a perpetuity and is easily valued when k_{cs} is determined.

Cases 2 and 3 indicate that to establish the benefits stream, which is to be subsequently discounted, it is first necessary to compound some beginning dividend into the future. Obviously, the higher the interest rate used, the greater the future amount; furthermore, the longer the time period, the greater the future amount.

Case 3 involves variable growth rates, or what some analysts refer to as supernormal growth. In this case, firms may grow at a rapid rate for some years and then slow down to an "average" growth rate. At least two different growth rates are involved. Case 3 is explained in Appendix 9–A.

A more likely scenario is Case 2 in which dividends are expected to grow at a constant rate over time. This **constant growth model** is shown as Equation 9–4.[5]

$$PV_{cs} = \frac{D_0(1+g)}{(1+k_{cs})} + \frac{D_0(1+g)^2}{(1+k_{cs})^2} + \frac{D_0(1+g)^3}{(1+k_{cs})^3} + \ldots + \frac{D_0(1+g)^\infty}{(1+k_{cs})^\infty}$$

$$(9\text{--}4)$$

---

[5] The constant growth model is often referred to as the Gordon model (named after Myron J. Gordon, who played a large part in its development and use).

where D_0 is the current dividend being paid, which will grow at the constant rate g, and k_{cs} is the appropriate discount rate.

Equation 9–4 can be simplified to the following equation.[6]

$$PV_{cs} = \frac{D_1}{k - g} = \begin{array}{l}\text{Constant growth version of} \\ \text{the dividend valuation model}\end{array} \qquad (9\text{–}5)$$

where D_1 is the dividend expected to be received at the end of year 1.

Equation 9–5 is used whenever it is reasonable to assume a constant growth rate for dividends. In actual practice it is used quite often because of its simplicity and because it is the best description of the actual behavior of a large number of companies and, in many instances, the market as a whole.

As an example, assume ABC corporation is currently paying $1.00 per share in dividends and investors expect dividends to grow at the rate of 5% a year for the foreseeable future. For investments at this risk level, investors require a return of 15% a year. The estimated value (or price) will be

$$P = V = \frac{D_1}{k - g}$$

$$P_{ABC} = V_{ABC} = \frac{\$1(1.05)}{0.15 - 0.05} = \$10.50$$

Note that the current dividend of $1.00 ($D_0$) must be compounded one period because Equation 9–5 specifies the dividend expected to be received one period from now (D_1). In valuation terminology, D_0 represents the dividend currently being paid, and D_1 represents the dividend expected to be paid in the next period. If D_0 is known, D_1 can always be determined.

$$D_0 = \text{Current dividend}$$

$$D_1 = D_0(1 + g)$$

where g is the expected growth rate of dividends.

An examination of Equation 9–5 can quickly demonstrate the factors affecting the price of a common stock, assuming the constant growth version of the dividend valuation model to be the applicable valuation approach. If the market lowers the required rate of return for a stock, price will rise (other things being equal). If investors decide that the expected growth in dividends will be higher as the result of some favorable development for the firm, price will also rise (other things being equal). Of course, the converse for these two situations also holds—a rise in the discount rate or a reduction in the expected growth rate of dividends will lower price.

Notice how sensitive the present value is to the estimates used in Equation 9–5. In the ABC example, assume the following:

---

[6] Note that k must be greater than g or nonsensical results are produced. Equation 9–4 collapses to Equation 9–5 as the number of periods involved approaches infinity.

1. The discount rate used (k) is 16% instead of 15%, with other variables held constant

$$P_{ABC} = \frac{\$1(1.05)}{0.16 - 0.05} = \$9.55$$

   In this example, a 1-percentage-point rise in k results in a 9% decrease in price, from \$10.50 to \$9.55.

2. The growth rate (g) is 6% instead of 5%, with other variables held constant

$$P_{ABC} = \frac{\$1(1.06)}{0.15 - 0.06} = \$11.77$$

   In this example, a 1-percentage-point rise in g results in a 12% increase in price, from \$10.50 to \$11.77.

3. The discount rate rises to 16% while the growth rate declines to 4%

$$P_{ABC} = \frac{\$1(1.04)}{0.16 - 0.04} = \$8.67$$

   In this case, the price declines from \$10.50 to \$8.67, a 17% change.

   These differences suggest why stock prices constantly fluctuate as investors make their buy and sell decisions. Even if all investors use the constant growth version of the dividend valuation model to value a particular common stock, many different estimates of value (price) will be obtained because of the following:

1. Each investor has his or her own required rate of return, resulting in a relatively wide range of values of k.
2. Each investor has his or her own estimate of the expected growth rate in dividends. Although this range may be reasonably narrow in most valuation situations, small differences in g can produce significant differences in price, when everything else is held constant.

   Thus, at any point for any given stock, some investors are willing to buy whereas others wish to sell, depending on their evaluation of the stock's prospects. This helps to make markets active and liquid. In practice, the dividend valuation model is used in various forms (see Box 9–1).

Dividends, Dividends—What about capital gains?   In their initial study of valuation concepts, investors are often bothered by the fact that the dividend valuation model contains only dividends, and an infinite stream of dividends at that. Although this is true, most investors are sure that (1) they will not be here forever and (2) they really want capital gains. Dividends may be nice, but buying low and selling high is wonderful! Since so many investors are interested in capital gains, which by definition involves the difference between the price paid for a security and the price at which this security is later sold, a valuation model should seemingly contain a stock price

BOX 9–1 USING THE DIVIDEND VALUATION MODEL IN PRACTICE

Is it possible to assign a "true" value to stocks? Fans of so-called dividend discount investing think they have just such a philosopher's stone. This is their reasoning: people buy a stock to get the dividends. Indeed, so goes the theory, dividends are ultimately the *only* reason to buy a stock. Even growth stocks like Apple or Genentech, with no payouts, are valuable only because of the expectation that their businesses will someday mature and throw off cash to the owners.

Because a dollar of dividends in the future is worth less than a dollar today, the dividend stream must be discounted. For example, the prospect of getting a $1 payout in 1997 is worth only 39 cents now, if the discount rate is 10% a year. Take each projected dividend, discount it to get a present value, and sum the numbers. The total is supposedly what the stock is worth today. This theory assumes stocks are not all that much different from bonds, except that the dividend stream is less predictable than the stream of interest payments.

The dividend discount theory has had some success in the real world. "Historically, dividend discount valuation has been the most successful model at figuring which stocks will give an investor the highest rate of return," boasts George Reid, a former mathematics and philosophy professor at St. Louis University, who helped create just such a model for money manager Sanford C. Bernstein & Co. in New York City.

Since 1981 Bernstein claims to have beaten the market an average of 5% a year using Reid's discount model as its principal tool in picking stocks. An independent evaluation by CDA Investment Technologies puts Bernstein 16th among 129 managers for performance over the past five years. Bernstein & Co. has been raking in a lot of dough with its dividend discounting since its assets under management have grown from $800 million in 1981 to over $6 billion today.

Wells Fargo Bank has had impressive results attracting pension money with a dividend discount model. Here Wells Fargo is not picking individual stocks but simply using the formula to divine when stocks are cheap relative to bonds.

What does Bernstein's model currently recommend? Reid won't say, so we turned to Ford Investor Services for an illustration of how this system works. Ford, a small database and newsletter firm in San Diego, publishes stock picks based on a dividend discount model.

David Morse, author of the Ford model, is not a purist. Rather than attempting to project dividends into the distant future, as Reid does, Morse takes the forecasting out only 10 years. In lieu of summing dividends for years 11 through eternity, he takes a termination stock value for 1997 and discounts that into 1987 dollars.

To project dividends, Morse first estimates future earnings on the strength of current earnings growth and published forecasts from Wall Street analysts. Then he assumes that a constant proportion of earnings will be paid out as dividends. Morse uses discount rates most often in the 8%-to-10% range, with higher rates for riskier, debt-heavy companies.

Getting a termination value for a company is straightforward, if somewhat chancy. Since the model has already come up with a 1997 earnings figure, based on an assumption about earnings growth, all that is needed is a price/earnings ratio. The Ford formula assumes a 1997 P/E equal to the inverse of the discount rate. If the discount rate is 8%, for example, the 1997 P/E multiple will be the inverse of 8%, or 12.5.

The shortcomings of this system are obvious. In estimates of earnings growth rates such factors as competition, technological breakthroughs and lawsuits can't be fully anticipated, so future earnings are guesses at best. Cautions Barton M. Biggs, chairman of Morgan Stanley Asset Management, which uses the Ford service only to suggest which market sectors are overpriced: "An analyst can make a stock's value come out any way he wants to simply by changing the growth rates."

The system, however, isn't sold as a precise forecaster of 1996 earnings per share, but as a way of knowing which stocks are relatively cheap. Significantly, the model tends to favor stocks with either high yields or rapidly rising dividends (that's how such high-P/E stocks as Limited Inc. get on the list). The discipline of discounting distant returns forces the analyst to put a low value on profits that won't turn into hard cash for the shareholder until the next century. Genentech and Apple are rated as grossly overpriced, tobacco stocks as bargains.

The table of stocks that the dividend model rates among the best buys shows the key components that go into calculating an intrinsic value. The exercise makes a mathematical case for buying American Brands. But no computer can discount for the possibility that the courts will rule against the tobacco industry in one of those product liability suits.

Source: Michael Ozanian, "Bird-in-hand-theory," *Forbes*, February 23, 1987, pp. 104, 108. Reprinted by permission of *Forbes* magazine, February 23, 1987. © Forbes Inc., 1987.

somewhere. Thus, in computing present value for a stock, investors are interested in the present value of the expected price two years from now, or six months from now, or whatever the expected, and finite, holding period is. How can price be incorporated into the valuation—or should it be?

In truth, the only cash flows that an investor needs to be concerned with are dividends. Expected price in the future is built into the dividend valuation model given by Equation 9–2—it is simply not visible. To see this, ask yourself at what price you can expect to sell a common stock that you have bought. Assume, for example, that you purchase today and plan to hold for three years. The price you receive three years from now will reflect the buyer's expectations of dividends from that point forward (at the end of years 4, 5, etc.). That is, the price today of the stock will equal

$$P_0 = \frac{D_1}{(1 + k_{cs})} + \frac{D_2}{(1 + k_{cs})^2} + \frac{D_3}{(1 + k_{cs})^3} + \frac{P_3}{(1 + k_{cs})^3} \quad (9\text{–}6)$$

But P_3 (the price of the stock at the end of year 3), is, in turn, equal to the discounted value of all future dividends from year 4 to infinity. That is,

$$P_3 = \frac{D_4}{(1 + k_{cs})^4} + \frac{D_5}{(1 + k_{cs})^5} + \ldots + \frac{D_\infty}{(1 + k_{cs})^\infty} \quad (9\text{–}7)$$

Substituting Equation 9–7 into 9–6 produces Equation 9–2, the basic dividend valuation model. Thus, the result is the same whether investors discount only a stream of dividends or a combination of dividends and price. Since price at any point in the future is a function of the dividends to be received after that time, the price today for a common stock is best thought of as the discounted value of all future dividends.

Intrinsic value   After making careful estimates of the expected stream of benefits and the required rate of return for a common stock, the intrinsic value of the stock is obtained through the present value analysis—that is, the dividend valuation model. This is the objective of fundamental analysis.

What does intrinsic value imply? The traditional rule in investments specifies a relationship between the intrinsic value of an asset and its current market price. Specifically,

> If intrinsic value exceeds current market price, the asset is undervalued and should be purchased or held if already owned.
>
> If intrinsic value is less than current market price, the asset is overvalued and should be avoided, sold if held, or possibly sold short.
>
> If the two values are equal, this implies an equilibrium in that the asset is correctly valued.

An important question to ask at this point is, what do you really have when you have valued an asset and you have determined its intrinsic value? The intrinsic value of an asset is that value which exists when the asset is correctly valued. Intrinsic value and present value are closely related; specifically, calculation of intrinsic value is simply the present value concept used in a financial context.

A problem with intrinsic value is that it is derived from a present value process involving estimates of uncertain (future) benefits and use of (varying) discount rates by different investors. Therefore, the same asset may have many intrinsic values—it depends on who, and how many, are doing the valuing. This is why, for a particular asset on a particular day, some investors are willing to buy and some to sell. Because future benefits are uncertain and investors have differing required rates of return, the use of fundamental valuation models will result in varying estimates of the intrinsic value of an asset. The market price of an asset at any point in time is, in this sense, the consensus intrinsic value of that asset for the market.

Does the problem of varying estimates of value render valuation models useless? No, because individual investors cannot make intelligent investment decisions without having an intelligent estimate of the value of an asset. Is General Motors worth, say, $60 a share to you? It may or may not be, depending on your own required rate of return (discount rate), your estimate of the future benefit stream to be derived from owning GM, and certain other factors.[7]

---

[7] As shown in Part Seven, securities should be chosen on the basis of a portfolio concept— that is, how they fit together to form a unified whole.

Let us assume that you require 18% to invest in GM; that is, your opportunity cost for alternative investment opportunities of similar risk is 18%. Also, assume that the current dividend is $6.25 and is expected to grow at the rate of 6% a year for the indefinite future. Based on these figures and using the dividend valuation model, the intrinsic value (justified price) of GM to you might be estimated to be $55 per share. Based on the intrinsic value principle, GM is undervalued and should be purchased if the current market price of GM is less than $55 per share. What is of direct importance is that the valuation process tells you that if you pay $55 per share for GM, you will earn your required rate of return of 18%, *if* the assumed dividend growth rate is correct. You can, therefore, pay $40 per share, or $45, or $48, and earn more than the required rate of return.

Other investors with different opinions about k and g may be on the margin valuing this security, only slightly higher or slightly lower than $55. They are potential traders if the price moves slightly, or if news causes even slight variations in their k or their g. The valuation process can establish justified prices for assets or indicate whether or not you can *expect* to earn your required rate of return on a prospective asset. Remember, however, that you are not assured of earning your required rate of return. Investments is always a forward-looking process. Estimates are made under uncertainty, based on the best information available. But even the best estimates may not be realized. As discussed in Chapter 1, uncertainty will always be the dominant feature of the environment in which investment decisions are made.

The Multiplier or P/E Ratio Approach

An alternative method of valuation often used by practicing security analysts is the **P/E ratio** or **earnings multiplier** approach. In fact, this method is used more often than present value techniques in actual practice. It is consistent with the present value analysis because it concerns the value of a stock or the aggregate market, just as before. Using the P/E ratio approach,

$$\text{Price} = \text{Earnings per share} \times \text{P/E ratio} \qquad (9\text{--}8)$$

The multiplier approach is concerned with the price–earnings multiple, or P/E ratio. It is based on the following identity:

$$\text{P/E ratio} = \frac{\text{Current price}}{\text{Actual earnings this year}} \qquad (9\text{--}9)$$

Obviously, Equation 9–8 is nothing more than an identity. It simply states that current price is some multiple of earnings (which is why this is referred to as the multiplier approach). It is convenient to refer to stocks as selling at, say, 10 times earnings, or 15 times earnings. Such a classification has traditionally been used by investors to categorize stocks. Growth stocks, for example, have typically sold at high multiples (compared to the average stock) because of their expected high earnings growth. In the 1960s, such stocks as McDonald's, Avon, and Disney sold at 40 to 60 times earnings (i.e., the P/E ratio was 40 to 60). The average stock during that time might have been selling for 10 to 18 times earnings, reflecting their average growth in earnings prospects—and average risk. Conservative blue chip stocks usually sell at relatively low P/E ratios.

In practice, various P/E ratios are used.[8] *The Wall Street Journal*, for example, uses the most recent 12-month earnings to calculate the daily P/E ratios reported. Such a ratio may be useful information for assessing the relative risk of a stock (e.g., it could be compared to the multiplier for the Dow Jones Industrial Average, which is reported once a week in the *Journal*).[9] It cannot, however, be indiscriminately used to predict the future price of a stock. Again, next period's price is a function of next period's earnings and next period's multiplier, and both of these variables must be carefully estimated in order to obtain an accurate assessment of future price.

How can the multiplier concept be used in valuation? After all, although current P/E multiplied by current earnings equals current price, the current market price of a stock can be found by looking in today's *Wall Street Journal*! The operational version of Equation 9–9 divides current price by estimated earnings for the next period (typically, the next 12 months), as in Equation 9–10:

$$\text{P/E Ratio} = \frac{\text{Current price}}{\text{Estimated Earnings for next period}} \qquad (9\text{–}10)$$

As an example, a stock with expected earnings of $3 per share will sell for $45 if investors are willing to pay 15 times next period's expected earnings. The stock price should change as estimates of expected earnings change.

What determines a P/E ratio? To answer this question, the P/E ratio can be derived from the dividend valuation model which, again, is the foundation of valuation for common stocks. Start with Equation 9–5, the value of a stock using the constant growth version of the model—this is the version most often used in practice.

$$P_0 = \frac{D_1}{k - g} \qquad (9\text{–}5)$$

Divide both sides of Equation 9–5 by expected earnings, E_1, to obtain

$$P_0/E_1 = \frac{D_1/E_1}{k - g} \qquad (9\text{–}11)$$

---

[8] In calculating P/E ratios, on the basis of either the latest reported earnings or the expected earnings, problems can arise when comparing P/E ratios among companies if some of them are experiencing, or are expected to experience, abnormally high or low earnings. To avoid this problem, some market participants calculate a *normalized* earnings estimate. Normalized earnings are intended to reflect the "normal" level of a company's earnings; that is, transitory effects are presumably excluded, thus providing the user with a more accurate estimate of "true" earnings.

[9] Since this is the arithmetic mean of only 30 P/E ratios, one should exercise caution. In 1983, one company with near-zero earnings had a P/E ratio that was extremely large as a result of unusual circumstances. This caused this average to be *over 100*.

D_1/E_1, the ratio of dividends to earnings, is referred to as the **payout ratio.** Equation 9–11 uses the expected payout ratio, not the current payout ratio.

Equation 9–11 indicates those factors that affect the P/E ratio, which are the factors on the right side of (9–11): (1) the expected dividend payout ratio, D_1/E_1, (2) the required rate of return, and (3) the expected growth rate of dividends.

Variables 2 and 3 are typically the most important factors because a small change in either can have a large effect on the P/E ratio. To see this, assume that the payout ratio is 60%. By varying k and g, and therefore changing the difference between the two (the denominator in Equation 9–11), investors can assess the effect on the P/E ratio as follows:

Assume $k = 0.15$ and $g = 0.07$ $\qquad$ $P/E = \dfrac{D_1/E_1}{k - g}$

$$P/E = \frac{0.60}{0.15 - 0.07}$$

$$= \frac{0.60}{0.08} = 7.5$$

Now assume $k = 0.16$ and $g = 0.06$ $\quad \downarrow P/E = \dfrac{0.60}{0.10} = 6$

or that $k = 0.14$ and $g = 0.08$ $\qquad \uparrow P/E = \dfrac{0.60}{0.06} = 10$

Think about each of these P/E ratios being used as a multiplier with an expected earnings for stock i for next year of $3.00. The possible prices for stock i would be $22.50, $18, and $30 respectively, which is quite a range given the small changes in k and g that were made.

P/E ratios and interest rates   The P/E ratio reflects investor optimism and pessimism. It is related to the required rate of return. As the required rate of return increases, other things being equal, the P/E ratio decreases, as can be seen from Equation 9–11.

The required rate of return, in turn, is related to interest rates, which are the required returns on bonds. As interest rates increase, required rates of return on all securities, including stocks, also generally increase. As interest rates increase, bonds become more attractive compared to stocks on a current return basis.

Based on these relationships, an inverse relationship between P/E ratios and interest rates is to be expected. As interest rates rise (decline), other things being equal, P/E ratios should decline (rise). Table 9–1 shows interest rates (yields) on corporate, federal, and municipal bonds, yields on preferred stocks, and P/E ratios for the Standard & Poor's 500 Composite Index for the years 1976 through 1986. Although the interest rate data are based on averages of monthly data during the year while the P/E ratio data are based

TABLE 9-1 The Relationship between Yields and P/E Ratios, 1976–1986

| Year | Yields | | | | |
	AAA Industrial	Long-Term U.S. Bonds	Municipal State & Local	Preferred Stock	S&P P/E Ratio
1986	9.02	8.14	6.95	8.76	16.52
1985	11.37	10.75	8.60	10.49	14.15
1984	12.71	11.99	9.61	11.59	9.95
1983	12.04	10.84	8.80	11.02	11.67
1982	13.79	12.23	10.86	12.53	11.13
1981	14.17	12.87	10.43	12.36	7.98
1980	11.94	10.81	7.85	10.57	9.16
1979	9.63	8.74	5.92	9.07	7.31
1978	8.73	7.89	5.52	8.25	7.79
1977	8.02	7.06	5.20	7.60	8.73
1976	8.43	6.78	5.66	7.97	10.84

Source: Federal Reserve *Bulletins,* Page A24, Dec. 1979, 1982, 1985, June 1987. The P/E ratios for the Standard & Poor 500 Stock Index are based on calendar year earnings and end of year prices from Standard & Poor's Statistical Service, *Security Price Index Record,* 1987 edition. Reprinted by permission.

on year-end figures, the inverse relationship between the two can be seen clearly. As interest rates rose from 1976 through 1981, the P/E ratio on the S&P 500 Composite Index declined. Conversely, as interest rates declined from 1982 through 1986, the P/E ratio on the stock composite rose.

Notice in Table 9–1 how the yields on preferred stocks track the yields on bonds. Preferred stock, although technically an equity security, behaves like a fixed-income security because of the fixed dividend payment. Preferred stocks are substitutes for bonds in the eyes of many investors interested in obtaining a fixed, steady stream of payments.

Which Approach to Use?

We have described the two most often used approaches in fundamental analysis—the dividend valuation model and the P/E ratio (multiplier) model. Which should be used?

In theory, the dividend valuation model is a correct, logical, and sound position. The best estimate of the current value of a corporation is probably the present value of the (estimated) dividends to be paid by that corporation to its stockholders. However, some analysts and investors feel that this model is unrealistic. After all, they argue, no one can forecast dividends into the distant future with perfect accuracy. Technically, the model calls for an estimate of all dividends from now to infinity, which is an impossible task. Finally, many investors want capital gains and not dividends, so for some investors it is not desirable to be focusing only on dividends.

The previous discussion dealt with these objections that some raise about the dividend valuation model. Can you respond to these objections based on this discussion?

Possibly because of the objections to the dividend valuation model cited here, or possibly because it is easier to use, the earnings multiplier or P/E model remains a popular approach to valuation. It is a less sophisticated and more intuitive model. In fact, understanding the P/E model can help investors to understand the dividend valuation model. Because dividends are paid out of earnings, investors must estimate the growth in earnings before they can estimate the growth in dividends or dividends themselves.

Rather than view these approaches as alternatives, it is better to view them as complements. Each is useful, and together they provide analysts with a better chance of valuing common stocks. There are several reasons for viewing them as complementary.

1. The P/E model can be derived from the constant growth version of the dividend valuation model. They are, in fact, alternative methods of looking at value. In the dividend valuation model, the future stream of benefits is discounted. In the P/E model, an estimate of expected earnings is multiplied by a P/E ratio or multiplier.

2. Dividends are paid out of earnings. To use the dividend valuation model, it is necessary to estimate the future growth of earnings. The dividends used in the dividend valuation model are a function of the earnings for the firm, an estimate of which is used in the earnings multiplier model.

3. Finally, investors must always keep in mind that valuation is no less an art than a science and estimates of the future earnings and dividends are subject to error. In some cases it may be desirable to use one or the other method, and in other cases both methods can be used as a check on each other. The more procedures investors have to value common stocks, the more likely they are to obtain reasonable results.

In the three chapters that follow, we will utilize extensively the overall logic of the fundamental valuation approach—namely, that the intrinsic value of a common stock, or the aggregate market, is a function of its expected returns and accompanying risk, as proxied by the required rate of return. The dividend valuation model and the P/E ratio model will be used interchangeably to illustrate the fundamental valuation process. It is necessary now to outline the fundamental analysis process.

A Framework for Fundamental Analysis

It is obvious that under either of these fundamental approaches an investor will have to work with individual company data. Does this mean that the investor should plunge into a study of company data first and then consider other factors such as the industry within which a particular company operates or the state of the economy? The answer is NO!!! The proper order in which to proceed in fundamental analysis is, first, to analyze the overall economy and securities markets. Second, analyze the industry within which a particular company operates. Finally, analysis of the company, which involves the factors affecting the valuation models described earlier, should be considered.

Thus, the preferred order for fundamental security analysis is (1) the economy and market, (2) the industry, and (3) the company. This approach will be used for the next three chapters. Following is the justification for this approach.

Economy/Market

It is very important to assess the state of the economy and the outlook for primary variables such as corporate profits and interest rates. Investors are heavily influenced by these variables in making their everyday investment decisions. If a recession is likely, or underway, stock prices will be heavily affected at certain times during the contraction. Conversely, if a strong economic expansion is underway, stock prices will be heavily affected, again at particular times during the expansion. Thus, the status of economic activity has a major impact on overall stock prices. It is, therefore, very important for investors to assess the state of the economy and its implications for the stock market.

In turn, the stock market impacts on each individual investor. Investors cannot very well go against market trends. If the market goes up (or down) strongly, the majority of stocks are carried along. Company analysis is likely to be of limited benefit in a year such as 1974 when the stock market was down 26%. Conversely, many investors did well in the years 1975 and 1976 regardless of their specific company analysis because the market was up 37% and 24% respectively.

In a well-known study several years ago, Benjamin King analyzed the relationship between market returns and individual stock returns.[10] (He also assessed industry effects, which we will consider later.) King found that for an earlier period of time (1927–1960), roughly half of the variance for an average stock was explained by the overall market. Although the impact of the overall market on a stock's returns seems to have declined in the years following those studied, it remains very substantial.

Another indication of the overall market impact is that on earnings for a particular company. Available evidence suggests that from one-fourth to one-half of the variability in a company's annual earnings is attributable to the overall economy (plus some industry effect).[11]

---

[10] See B. King, "Market and Industry Factors in Stock Price Movements," *Journal of Business,* vol. 39 (1966), pp. 139–190.

[11] See Edwin J. Elton and Martin J. Gruber, *Modern Portfolio Theory and Investment Analysis,* 3rd ed. New York: John Wiley, 1987.

The economy also significantly affects what happens to various industries. One has only to think of the effects of import quotas, record high interest rates, and so forth to see why this is so. Therefore, economy analysis must precede industry analysis.

Industry Analysis

After completing an analysis of the economy and the overall market, an investor can decide if it is a favorable time to invest in common stocks. If so, the next step should be industry analysis. King identified an industry factor as the second component (after overall market movements) affecting the variability in stock returns.

Individual companies and industries tend to respond to general market movements, but the degree of response can vary significantly. Industries undergo significant movements over both relatively short and relatively long periods. Industries will be affected to various degrees by recessions and expansions. For example, the heavy goods industries will be severely affected in a recession (think of the auto and steel industries in the 1981–1982 recession). Consumer goods will probably be much less affected during such a contractionary period. During a severe inflationary period such as the late 1970s and very early 1980s, regulated industries such as utilities were severely hurt by their inability to pass along all price increases. Finally, new "hot" industries emerge from time to time and enjoy spectacular (if short-lived) growth. Examples include synthetic fuels and genetic engineering.

Company Analysis

Although the first two steps are important and should be done in the indicated order, great attention and emphasis should be placed on company analysis. Security analysts are typically organized along industry lines, but the reports that they issue usually deal with one (or more) specific companies.

The bottom line for companies, as far as most investors are concerned, is earnings per share. There is a very close relationship between earnings and stock prices, and for this reason most attention is paid to earnings. Dividends, after all, are paid out of earnings. The dividends paid by companies are closely tied to earnings, but not necessarily the current quarterly (or even annual) earnings.

A number of factors are important in analyzing a company; but, because investors tend to focus on earnings and dividends, we need to understand the relationship between these two variables, and between them and other variables. We also need to consider the possibilities of forecasting earnings and dividends.

Because dividends are paid out of earnings, we will concentrate on earnings in our discussion of company analysis in Chapter 12. Earnings are the real key to the fundamental analysis of a common stock. A good understanding of earnings is vital if an investor is to understand, and carry out, fundamental analysis.

The Framework in Perspective

It is useful to summarize the framework for fundamental analysis we are using because the following three chapters will be based on this framework.

Figure 9–3 depicts the fundamental valuation process. We will examine the economy and market first, then industries, and finally individual companies. Fundamental valuation is usually done within the context of a present value model, primarily the dividend valuation model, or a multiplier (P/E ratio) model. In either case, the two components of the value of any security being examined are (1) the expected stream of benefits, either earnings or dividends, and (2) the required rate of return or discount rate—alternatively, the multiplier or P/E ratio.

It is these two factors on which we need to concentrate as we systematically proceed through the three levels of analysis: economy/market, industry, and company.

Summary

Three approaches for analyzing and selecting common stocks are fundamental analysis, technical analysis, and efficient market considerations. Technical analysis is dependent on stock price changes being predictable, whereas the efficient market hypothesis states that prices reflect known information.

Fundamental analysis concerns the intrinsic value of a stock, which is a function of its expected returns and risk. Two fundamental approaches to determining value are the present value approach and the earnings multiplier (P/E ratio) approach. Both are correct, acceptable methods that should be viewed as complementary.

The present value approach for common stocks is similar to that used with bonds. A required (minimum) expected rate of return must be determined, based on the risk-free rate and a risk premium. There is a direct relationship between beta and required return, represented by the CAPM, which provides an equation for the estimation of required return. As for expected returns, either dividends or earnings can be used. Since dividends are the only cash flows directly paid by a corporation, they are the logical choice for a present value model.

According to the dividend valuation model, the value of a stock today is the discounted value of all future dividends. In order to account for an infinite stream of dividends, stocks to be valued are classified by their expected growth rate in dividends. If no growth is expected, the model reduces to a perpetuity. If two or more growth rates are expected, a supernormal growth must be used in which the future stream of dividends is identified before being discounted.

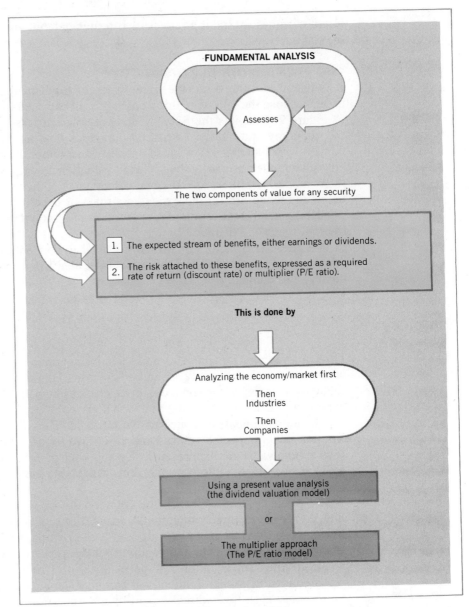

FIGURE 9–3 **A framework for fundamental analysis.**

The constant-growth version of the dividend valuation model is most often used; it reduces to the ratio of the dividend expected next period to the difference between the required rate of return and the expected growth rate in dividends. This model is sensitive to the estimates of the variables used in it; therefore, investors calculate different prices for the same stock while using an identical model. This model implicitly accounts for the terminal price of a stock.

The multiplier or P/E ratio approach is based on the identity that a stock's price is the product of earnings per share and the P/E ratio. The P/E ratio can be calculated by dividing the current price by the estimate of next period's earnings. The P/E ratio itself is a function of the dividend payout ratio, the required rate of return, and the expected growth rate of dividends. Also, P/E ratios are inversely related to interest rates because interest rates are directly related to required rates of return.

In order to perform fundamental analysis correctly, investors need a framework. The proper order for fundamental analysis is to analyze the market and economy first, then industries, and then companies. The aggregate market is the most pervasive influence on any single stock, carrying most stocks with it as it moves up or down; therefore, assessing the overall situation should be the first step in analyzing stocks. Because stocks grouped as industries tend to move together, industries should be analyzed second. Finally, individual companies must be analyzed. The basic techniques of fundamental analysis, the present value approach and the P/E ratio approach, can be used at each of the three levels—market, industry, and company.

Key Words

Constant growth model	Fundamental analysis
Dividend valuation model	Payout ratio
Earnings multiplier	P/E ratio

QUESTIONS AND PROBLEMS

1. What is meant by "intrinsic value"? How is it determined?
2. How can the required rate of return for a stock be estimated? What difficulties are likely to be encountered?

3. Why can earnings not be used as readily as dividends in the present value approach?

4. What is the dividend valuation model? Write this model in equation form.

5. What problems are encountered in using the dividend valuation model?

6. Describe the three possibilities for dividend growth. Which is the most likely to apply to the typical company?

7. Since dividends are paid to infinity, how is this problem handled in the present value analysis?

8. Demonstrate how the dividend valuation model is the same as a method that includes a specified number of dividends and a terminal price.

9. Assume that two investors are valuing General Foods Company and have agreed to use the constant growth version of the dividend valuation model. Both use $3.00 a share as the expected dividend for the coming year. Are these two investors likely to derive different prices? Why or why not?

10. Once an investor calculates intrinsic value for a particular stock, how does he or she decide whether or not to buy it?

11. How valuable are the P/E ratios shown daily in *The Wall Street Journal*?

12. What factors affect the P/E ratio? How sensitive is it to these factors?

13. What is the recommended order for doing fundamental analysis? Why is this sequence deemed proper?

14. Some investors prefer the P/E ratio model to the present value analysis on the grounds that the latter is more difficult to use. State these alleged difficulties and respond to them.

15. Diversified Conglomerates (DC) is currently selling for $40 a share with an expected dividend in the coming year of $3.00 per share. If the growth rate in dividends expected by investors is 9%, what is the required rate of return for DC?

16. Assume that Amalgamated Clothiers is expected by investors to have a dividend growth rate over the foreseeable future of 7% a year and that the required rate of return for this stock is 14%. The current dividend being paid (D_0) is $2.40. What is the price of the stock?

17. Wolfman Hair Products is currently selling for $50 per share and pays $2.00 in dividends ($D_0$). Investors require 15% return on this stock. What is the expected growth rate of dividends?

18. Frank's Ghoulish Productions pays $1.00 a year in dividends, which is expected to remain unchanged. Investors require 10% on this stock. What is its price?

19. (a) Given a preferred stock with an annual dividend of $3.00 per share and a price of $40, what is the required rate of return? (b) Assume now that interest rates rise, leading investors to demand a required rate of return of 9%. What will the new price of this preferred stock be?

20. An investor purchases the common stock of a well-known house builder, Drac's Shacks, for $25 per share. The expected dividend for the next year is $3.00 per share and the investor is confident that the stock can be sold one year from now for $30. What is the implied required rate of return?

21. (a) The current risk-free rate (RF) is 10% and the expected return on the market for the coming year is 15%. Calculate the required rate of return for: (1) stock A, with a beta of 1.0, (2) stock B, with a beta of 1.7, and (3) stock C, with a beta of 0.8. (b) How would your answers change if RF in part (a) were to increase to 12%, with the other variables unchanged? (c) How would your answers change if the expected return on the market changes to 17%, with the other variables unchanged.

22. Classy Copper, Inc. is currently selling for $60 and paying a $2.00 ($D_0$) dividend. (a) If investors expect dividends to double in 12 years, what is the required rate of return for Classy? (b) If investors had expected dividends to approximately triple in six years, what would the required rate of return be?

23. Bright Brass, Inc. is currently selling for $36, paying $1.80 in dividends, and investors expect dividends to grow at a constant rate of 8% a year. (a) If an investor requires a rate of return of 14% for a stock with the riskiness of Bright Brass, is it a good buy for this investor? (b) What is the maximum an investor with a 14% required return should pay for Bright Brass? If the required return is 15%?

24. Foxy Productions sells at $32 per share, and the latest 12-month earnings are $4 per share with a dividend payout of 50%. (a) What is Foxy's current P/E ratio? (b) If an investor expects earnings to grow by 10% a year, what is the projected price for next year if the P/E ratio remains unchanged? (c) Assuming that the payout ratio will remain the same, the expected growth rate of dividends is 10%, and an investor has a required rate of return of 16%, would this stock be a good buy? Why or why not? (d) If interest rates are expected to decline, what is the likely effect on Foxy's P/E ratio?

25. Indicate the likely direction of change in a stock's P/E ratio if (a) the dividend payout decreases, (b) the required rate of return rises, (c) the expected growth rate of dividends rises, (d) the riskless rate of return decreases.

EXTENDED PROBLEMS, WITH EXAMPLES

I. **Example.** Many of the valuation techniques used in Chapter 9 will be illustrated using hypothetical data. Assume the common of XRO trades on the NYSE. For the period 1978–1987 the following values are for the end-of-year price (P), calendar-year earnings (E), and dividends (D). The values in columns 4 through 7 are calculated using the data in the first three columns. *Calculate* the 1987 values that are left blank.

Year	(1) P	(2) E	(3) D	(4) P/E	(5) (D/P) (%)	(6) (D/E) (%)	(7) HPY (%)
1978	$7.40	$1.05	$0.52	7.0	7.03	49.5	—
1979	9.60	1.10	0.52	8.7	5.42	47.3	36.8
1980	12.10	1.20	0.52	10.1	4.30	43.3	31.5
1981	11.30	1.42	0.52	8.0	4.60	36.6	−2.3
1982	12.00	2.02	0.58	5.9	4.83	28.7	11.3
1983	13.50	2.46	0.62	5.5	4.59	25.2	17.7
1984	13.40	2.61	0.76	5.1	5.67	29.1	0.5
1985	14.70	2.88	0.82	5.1	5.58	28.5	15.8
1986	18.60	3.22	0.91	5.8	4.89	28.3	32.7
1987	27.40	3.42	1.12	___	___	___	___

1. For Formula 5–15, the beta for XRO is 1.14. If the expected risk-free rate is 5% and the market return (say the expected HPY for the S&P 500) is 15%, then the required rate of return for XRO is

   $$k = 5 + 1.14(15 - 5) = 5 + 11.4 = 16.4\%$$

2. The dividend valuation model, assuming a constant dividend flow for XRO, may be shown to be a limit of the formula used in Example II of Chapter 7. The formula was for the price of a bond, with a constant coupon flow of C.

   $$P = \frac{C}{r}\left[1 - \frac{1}{(1 + r)^t}\right] + \frac{Par}{(1 + r)^t}$$

   Because common stock is not redeemable, there is no Par and the second term of the formula falls away. Because $t = \infty$, $(1 + r)$ to the infinite power is infinitely large, and the reciprocal is zero; therefore, the bracketed term is equal to 1.0, and

   $$P = \frac{C}{r}, \text{ or for common stock, } P = \frac{D}{k} \text{ (which is Equation 9–3).}$$

   If it were assumed that XRO would pay a constant dividend of $1.12 per annum over all future time periods, then the warranted price would be dividend divided by the required rate of return (using $k = 16.4\%$ from No. 1):

   $$P = \frac{1.12}{0.164} = \$6.83$$

which is considerably less than the 1987 closing price of $27.40. The reason for the wide disparity can be found by looking at the dividends in column 3, which seem to be steadily increasing over time.

3. Equations 9–4 and 9–5 incorporate the per-annum growth rate of dividends (g) into the valuation formula. Let us calculate some past growth rates of dividends using the formula

$$[\text{Ending value/Beginning value}]^{1/n} = (1 + g)$$

From 1978 to 1987

$$(1 + g) = [1.12/0.52]^{1/9} = 1.089; g\% = 8.9\%$$

From 1986 to 1987 (one year only)

$$(1 + g) = [1.12/0.91] = 1.231; g\% = 23.1\%$$

From 1982 to 1987

$$(1 + g) = [1.12/0.58]^{1/5} = 1.141; g\% = 14.1\%$$

Many additional past dates could be used to calculate ex post values of g. The important thing, however, is what g is expected to be ex ante. Assume a particular investor expects, for XRO, a $g\%$ of 11%. Using Equation 9–5, we could calculate a warranted price, using $k = 0.164$ from No. 1 above.

$$\text{Expected dividends for 1988} = (1 + g)D_{87} = (1.11)(1.12) = 1.2432$$

and

$$P = \frac{1.2432}{(0.164 - 0.11)} = \$23.02$$

Problem. Calculate the price for

$g = 0.12$ ($28.51)
$g = 0.13$ ($37.22)
$g = 0.14$ ($53.20)
$g = 0.15$ ($92.00)

Notice that as g approaches the value of k, $(k - g)$ becomes smaller and the calculated P becomes quite large.

4. The end-of-year P/E ratios for XRO are shown in column 4, and are ex post values from Equation 9–9. Equation 9–10 requires an ex ante earnings value for 1988. If the earnings expected for 1988 were $3.70, the P/E ratio would be 7.4 based on the last price of $27.40.

Problem. If you expect XRO to earn $4.00 next year, and expect a P/E ratio of 8, calculate the estimated price. If the current price is $27.80, is the security over- or undervalued?

5. Equation 9–11 can be illustrated using some of the ex post values in column 6 above. Assume that the (D/E) is 0.30 (30% in column 6). In No. 1 above we used $k = 0.164$, and in No. 3, we used $g = 0.11$. So Equation 9–11 could be evaluated as

$$P/E = \frac{(0.30)}{(0.164 - 0.11)} = 5.6$$

Problem. Now assume $k = 0.15$, and calculate the new P/E. How does the P/E ratio change? If the k remains at 0.164 and g at 0.11 but the payout rises to 0.40, what will happen to the P/E ratio?

Selected References

Beaver, William, and Morse, Dale. "What Determines Price–Earnings Ratios?" *Financial Analysts Journal,* July–August 1978, pp. 65–76.

Bing, Ralph. "Survey of Practitioners' Stock Evaluation Methods." *Financial Analysts Journal,* May–June 1971, pp. 55–69.

Black, Fischer, "The Dividend Puzzle." *Journal of Portfolio Management,* Winter 1976, pp. 5–8.

Brealey, Richard A. *An Introduction to Risk and Return from Common Stocks,* 2nd ed. Cambridge, Mass.: MIT Press, 1983.

Brigham, Eugene F. *Fundamentals of Financial Management,* 4th ed. Chicago: Dryden Press, 1986.

Capstaff, John. "Interpreting Price Earnings Ratios: How Much Does the Market Judge Future Earnings Growth?" *The Investment Analyst,* October 1985, pp. 18–28.

Elton, Edwin J., and Gruber, Martin J. *Modern Portfolio Theory and Investment Analysis,* 3rd ed. New York: John Wiley, 1987.

Farrell, James L. "The Dividend Discount Model: A Primer." *Financial Analysts Journal,* November–December 1985, pp. 16–25.

Gordon, Myron J. *The Investment, Financing and Valuation of the Corporation.* Homewood, Ill.: Richard D. Irwin, 1962.

Graham, Benjamin. "The Future of Common Stocks." *Financial Analysts Journal,* September–October 1974, pp. 20–30.

Hawkins, D. "Toward an Old Theory of Equity Valuation." *Financial Analysts Journal,* November–December 1977, pp. 48–53.

Hunt, Lacy. "Determinants of the Dividend Yield." *Journal of Portfolio Management,* Spring 1977, pp. 43–48.

Latané, Henry, Joy, Maurice, and Jones, Charles. "Quarterly Data, Sort–Rank Routines, and Security Evaluation," *Journal of Business,* July 1970, pp. 427–438.

Lorie, James H., and Hamilton, Mary T. *The Stock Market: Theories and Evidence.* Homewood, Ill.: Richard D. Irwin, 1973.

Malkiel, Burton G. *A Random Walk Down Wall Street*, College Edition Revised. New York: W. W. Norton, 1975.

Malkiel, Burton G., and Cragg, John. "Expectations and the Structure of Share Prices," *American Economic Review*, September 1970, pp. 601–617.

Nagorniak, John J. "Thoughts on Using Dividend Discount Models." *Financial Analysts Journal*, November–December 1985, pp. 13–15.

Rie, Daniel. "How Trustworthy Is Your Valuation Model?" *Financial Analysts Journal*, November–December 1985, pp. 42–48.

APPENDIX 9—A

SUPERNORMAL GROWTH

As explained in this chapter, common stocks are valued, using the dividend valuation model, by classifying the expected growth rate in dividends into one of three categories: no (zero) growth, constant (normal) growth, and supernormal growth. In this appendix we will examine supernormal growth.

Supernormal growth is defined as a situation in which the expected future growth in dividends must be described using two or more growth rates; although any number of growth rates is possible, most stocks can be described using two or possibly three. A number of companies have experienced growth of this type—that is, during part of their lives their growth exceeded that of the average company in the economy, but later the growth rate slowed. Examples from the past include McDonald's, Disney, Polaroid, and Xerox.

To capture the expected growth in dividends under this scenario, it is necessary to define the dividend stream over the periods of different growth. It is reasonable to assume that at some point the company's growth will slow down to that of the economy as a whole; that is, at some time, the company's growth can be described by the constant growth model (Equation 9–5). What remains, therefore, is to model the dividend stream up to the point at which dividends slow to a normal growth rate, and find the present value of all the components. This can be described in equation form as

$$P_0 = V_0 = \sum_{t=1}^{n} \frac{D_0(1 + g_1)^t}{(1 + k)^t} + \frac{1}{(1 + k)^n} P_n \qquad (9A-1)$$

280

where

$P_0 = V_0 =$ the price or value of the stock today.

$D_0 =$ the current dividend.

$g_1 =$ the supernormal growth rate.

$k =$ required rate of return.

$n =$ the number of periods of supernormal growth.

$P_n =$ the price of the stock at the end of the supernormal growth period, based on growth at a rate g_2 from $n + 1$ to ∞.[1]

Notice in Equation 9A–1 that the first term on the right side defines a dividend stream covering n periods, growing at a growth rate of g_1, and discounted at the required rate of return k. This term covers the period of supernormal growth, at which time the stock is expected to slow down and grow at a constant rate forever. In Equation 9A–1, the valuation process conceptually is

$P =$ Discounted value of all dividends through the supergrowth period n
+ discounted value of the price of the stock at the end of period n

Now consider what P_n is in Equation 9A–1. It is the price of the stock derived from the constant growth model as of the end of period n; that is, the constant growth version of the dividend valuation model is used to solve for price at the end of period n, which is the beginning of period $n + 1$. Therefore,

$$P_n = \frac{D_{n+1}}{k - g_2}$$

Because P_n is the price of the stock at the end of period n, it must be discounted back to the present using the present value table (Table A–2, Appendix). When added to the value of the discounted dividends from the first term, the price of the stock today (P_0) is produced.

Figure 9A–1 illustrates the concept of valuing a supernormal growth company. In this example, the current dividend is $1.00 and it is expected to grow at a supernormal rate (g_1) of 12% a year for five years, at the end of which time the new growth rate (g_2) is expected to be a constant 6% a year forever. The required rate of return is 10%.

The first step in the valuation process is to determine the dollar dividends in each year of supernormal growth. This is done by compounding the beginning dividend, $1.00, at 12% for each of five years, producing the following:[2]

---

[1] The end of period n is the same as the beginning of period $n + 1$.

[2] The beginning dividend can be multiplied by each year's factor, found from Table A–1. Alternatively, each successive dividend can be multiplied by $(1 + g)$.

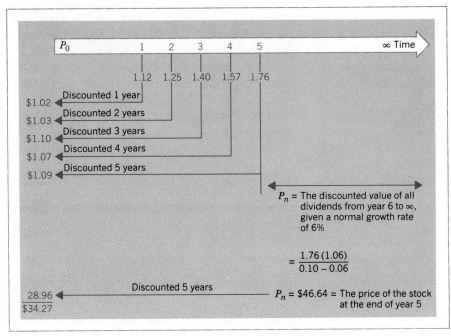

FIGURE 9A-1   Illustration of a hypothetical supernormal growth company.

$$
\begin{aligned}
D_0 &= \$1.00 \\
D_1 &= \$1.00(1.12) &= \$1.12 \\
D_2 &= \$1.00(1.12)^2 &= \$1.25 \\
D_3 &= \$1.00(1.12)^3 &= \$1.46 \\
D_4 &= \$1.00(1.12)^4 &= \$1.57 \\
D_5 &= \$1.00(1.12)^5 &= \$1.76
\end{aligned}
$$

Once the stream of dividends over the supergrowth period has been determined, they must be discounted to the present using the required rate of return of 10%. Thus,

$$
\begin{aligned}
\$1.12(0.909) &= \$1.02 \\
\$1.25(0.826) &= \$1.03 \\
\$1.46(0.751) &= \$1.10 \\
\$1.57(0.683) &= \$1.07 \\
\$1.76(0.621) &= \underline{\$1.09} \\
&\quad\ \ \$5.31
\end{aligned}
$$

Summing the five discounted dividends produces the value of the stock for its first five years *only,* which is \$5.31. To evaluate years 6 on, when constant growth is expected, the constant growth model will be used.

$$P_n = \frac{D_{n+1}}{k - g_2}$$

$$= \frac{D_6}{k - g_2}$$

$$= \frac{D_5(1.06)}{k - g_2}$$

$$= \frac{1.76(1.06)}{0.10 - 0.06}$$

$$= \$46.64$$

Thus, $46.64 is the price of the stock at the beginning of year 6 (end of year 5). It must be discounted back to the present, using the present value factor for five years and 10%, 0.621. Therefore,

$$P_n \text{ discounted to today} = P_n \ (PV \text{ factor, 5 years, 10\%})$$
$$= \$46.64(0.621)$$
$$= \$28.96$$

The last step is to add the two present values together:

$ 5.31 = Present value of the first five years of dividends.

28.96 = Present value of the price at the end of year 5, representing the discounted value of dividends from year 6 to ∞.

──────

$34.27 = P_0 the price or value of this supernormal growth stock today.

PART FOUR

COMMON STOCKS: THE FUNDAMENTAL APPROACH

CHAPTER 10

MARKET ANALYSIS

As discussed in the last chapter, the recommended procedure in fundamental security analysis is to first analyze the aggregate stock market, then the industries, and finally individual companies. This chapter considers the first step—market analysis.

We will examine several aspects of market analysis. First, what is meant by the "market"? Although it is a popular expression among investors, what does it really mean? Second, the importance of market analysis needs to be considered. Why is market analysis the first step in fundamental analysis?

Ultimately, investors must make intelligent judgments about the current state of the market and possible changes in the future. Is it at unusually high or low levels, and what is it likely to do in the next three months or year or five years? A logical starting point in assessing the market is to understand the economic factors that determine stock prices. Understanding the current and future state of the economy is the first step in understanding what is happening and what is likely to happen to the market.

Based on a knowledge of the economy–market relationship, a valuation of the market can be made using the procedures discussed in Chapter 9; that is, valuation concepts can be applied to the market as well as to individual securities. The final issue we consider in this chapter is the process involved in forecasting the market. Although investors cannot reasonably expect to be consistently correct in doing this, they can expect to make some intelligent inferences. Because of the market's impact on investor success, investors should at least attempt some basic forecast of the market's likely direction over some future period.

What Is the "Market"?

How often have you heard someone ask "How did the market do today?" or, "How did the market react to that announcement?" These popular questions are probably asked daily by investors. Virtually all investors in stocks want a general idea of how the overall market for equity securities is performing, both to guide their actions and as a benchmark against which to judge the performance of their securities. Furthermore, several specific uses of market indicators can be identified, as discussed in the next section.

Uses of Market Indicators

Market indicators are needed to tell investors how all stocks in general are doing at any time; that is, to give them a "feel" for the market. Many investors are encouraged to invest if stocks are moving upward, whereas downward trends may encourage some to liquidate their holdings and invest in money market assets or funds.

Historical records of market averages are useful for gauging where the market is in a particular cycle and possibly shedding light on what will happen. Assume, for example, that the market has never fallen more than $X\%$, as measured by some index, in a six-month period. Although this is no guarantee that such a decline will not occur, this type of knowledge aids investors in evaluating their potential downside risk over some period of time.

Market averages and indices are useful to investors in quickly judging their overall portfolio performance. Because stocks tend to move up or down together, the rising or falling of the market will indicate to the investor in a general way how he or she is likely to do. Of course, to determine the exact performance of each investor, portfolios must be measured, a topic to be discussed in Chapter 21.

Technical analysts need to know the historical record of the market in seeking out patterns from the past that may repeat in the future. Detection of such patterns is the basis for forecasting the future direction of the market using technical analysis, considered in Chapter 13.

Market averages and indices are also used to calculate betas, an important measure of risk discussed in Chapters 5 and 8. An individual security's returns are regressed on the market's returns in order to estimate the security's beta, or relative measure of systematic risk.

Because the "market" is simply the aggregate of all security prices, it is most conveniently measured by some index or average of stock prices. Investors, therefore, need to know about the various market indicators.

Stock Market Indicators

The major indicators or measures of the market will be discussed in this section. First, however, we need to consider the issues involved in constructing a market index. Furthermore, a basic distinction between an index and an average must be made.

Constructing a Stock Market Indicator

Several issues must be dealt with in the construction of a stock market index or indicator. The most important involve the composition of the index, the weighting procedure used, and the method of calculation.

What is the composition of the index? Is a subsample of one exchange to be used, or a subsample from the major exchanges; furthermore, should a subsample from the over-the-counter (OTC) market be included? Alternatively, should every stock on an exchange, or exchanges, be used, and if so, how should OTC stocks be handled (e.g., every active OTC stock, or every OTC stock for which daily quotes are available)?

If investors need a broad measure of stock performance, several markets (NYSE, AMEX, and OTC) need to be included. If investors want to know the performance of the "largest" stocks, a measure of NYSE performance may be sufficient. Some market indicators use subsamples of one or more markets, whereas others use every stock on one or more markets. It is important to be aware of compositional differences among the various market indicators.

A second issue involves the weighting procedure used in constructing the index. Does each stock receive equal weight, or is each weighted by its market value (i.e., market price multiplied by shares outstanding). Alternatively, the indicator could be price weighted, resulting in higher priced stocks carrying more weight than lower priced stocks.

The third issue is the calculation procedures used. The primary question here is whether an index or an average is being used.

Averages and Indices

A **market average** is an arithmetic average of the prices for the sample of securities being used. It shows the arithmetic mean behavior of the prices at a given time. A **market index,** on the other hand, measures the current price behavior of the sample in relation to a base period established for a previous time. Indices, therefore, are expressed in relative numbers, whereas averages are simply arithmetic means (weighted or unweighted). The use of an index allows for more meaningful comparisons over long periods of time because current values can be related to established base period values.

The first market measures discussed, the Dow Jones Averages, are arithmetic averages. All the other measures discussed are indices.

The Dow Jones Averages

The best-known average in the United States is the Dow Jones Industrial Average (DJIA), probably because it is carried by *The Wall Street Journal*.[1] It is the oldest market indicator, originating in 1896 and modified over the years.[2] The DJIA is computed from 30 leading industrial stocks whose composition changes slowly over time to reflect changes in the economy. This average is said to be composed of **blue chip stocks**, meaning large, well-established, and well-known companies.

The level of the Dow Jones Industrial Average is an indication of what the average price of the 30 stocks would be *if no splits or dividends had occurred;* for example, a figure of 1000 points (it is quoted in points) for the DJIA would indicate an average of $1000 per share. Over time, however, the divisor has changed because of stock splits and stock dividends; for example, in 1986 it was less than 1.0. As a result, a one-point change in the DJIA does not represent a change of one dollar in the value of an average share but rather of a few cents.

It is important to note that the DJIA is a price-weighted series. Although it gives equal weight to equal *dollar* changes, high-priced stocks carry more weight than low-priced stocks. A 5% change in the price of stock A at $50 will have a larger effect on the DJIA than a 5% change in stock B at $20. This also means that as high-price stocks split, and their prices decline, they lose relative importance in the calculation of the average; on the other hand, nonsplit stocks increase in relative importance. This bias against growth stocks, which are the most likely stocks to split, can result in a downward bias in the DJIA.

The DJIA has been criticized because of its use of only 30 stocks, because it is price weighted (rather than value weighted), and because the divisor is not adjusted for stock dividends of less than 10%. Nevertheless, it is the oldest continuous indicator of the stock market, and it remains *the* prominent index for many investors. It does fulfill its role as a "blue chip" indicator. Proposals have been made to make it more representative in the 1980s.[3]

Judgments by investors about the overall market, based on movements in the Dow Jones Industrial Average, should be put into perspective. For example, is the market "too high" at 2200 at a particular point in time? Or

---

[1] There are three additional Dow Jones averages: the transportation, the public utility, and the composite. The first two encompass 20 and 15 stocks, respectively, and the composite consists of these two groups plus the DJIA (i.e., 65 stocks). Each average is calculated similarly to the DJIA, with changes made in the divisor to adjust for splits and other factors. Daily information on these averages can be found in *The Wall Street Journal* and other newspapers.

[2] The first average of U.S. stocks appeared in 1884 and consisted of 11 stocks, mostly railroads. See H. L. Butler and R. F. DeMong, "The Changing Dow Jones Industrial Average," *Financial Analysts Journal*, July–August 1986, pp. 59–62.

[3] For an article on improving the Dow Jones Industrial Average, see Butler and DeMong, op. cit.

2500? You cannot really answer this question because the construction of the DJIA is arbitrary. See Box 10–1 for an insightful view of what it means for the Dow index to reach particular levels.

Standard & Poor's Stock Price Indices

Standard & Poor's Corporation, which publishes financial data for investors, also publishes five market indices, including a 400-stock Industrial Average, a 40-stock Utility Average, a 20-stock Transportation Average, a 40-stock Financial Average, and finally, all of these combined into a 500-stock Composite Index.[4] The latter is carried in the popular press and is often referred to by investors as a "good" indicator of what the market is doing.

Unlike the Dow Jones Industrial Average, the S&P 500 Composite Index (hereafter, S&P 500) is a market value index, meaning that it is expressed in relative numbers with a base period set to 10 (1941–43). To calculate the index, the market value of all firms is calculated (current market price times number of shares) and this total value is divided by the market value of the 500 securities for the base period; this relative value is multiplied by 10, representing the base period.[5] As an example, a current value of 200 for the S&P 500 would indicate that the average price of the 500 stocks in the index has increased by a factor of 20 in relation to the base period.

The S&P 500 is obviously a much broader measure than the Dow, and should be more representative of the general market. However, it does consist primarily of NYSE stocks and is clearly dominated by the largest corporations.[6] All stock splits and dividends are automatically accounted for in calculating the value of the index because the number of shares currently outstanding (i.e., after the split or dividend) and the new price are used in the calculation. Unlike the Dow Jones averages, each stock's importance is based on relative total market value instead of relative per-share price.

New York Stock Exchange Indices

The NYSE Composite Index is broader still, covering all stocks listed on the NYSE. It is similar to the S&P Indices in that it is a total-market–value-weighted index. The base index value is 50 (as of year-end 1965).[7]

The NYSE Composite Index, although comparable to the S&P Indices, is a true reflection of what is happening on the NYSE because it covers all stocks listed.[8] Thus, an investor who purchases a variety of NYSE stocks

---

[4] Standard & Poor's also publishes indices for various groupings of stocks, covering specific industries, low-priced stocks, high-grade stocks, and so on.

[5] Before multiplying by 10, the S&P 500 at any point in time can be thought of as the price, in relation to the beginning price of $1, of all stocks in the index weighted by their proportionate total market values.

[6] The S&P 500 contains some bank and insurance company stocks traded in the OTC market.

[7] Subindexes are available and include Industrial, Utility, Transportation, and Financial.

[8] This is the only available index limited only to the NYSE but covering all the stocks on it.

BOX 10–1 MEANINGLESS SIGNALS?

Are you frightened to see the Dow Jones industrials pushing to new highs? Or maybe you are elated. In either case, forget it; a new high on the Dow signifies very little. Let me tell you why.

Far from being an accurate proxy for the stock market as a whole, the Dow index—and many of the other indexes—are just lists of stocks selected by a committee.

Take the Dow Jones industrial average. It is made up of 30 stocks using a relatively complex equation. Trouble is that the stocks in the average have been changed over the years, based on the decisions of a small group working within the Dow Jones organization. Little is known about how these people pick stocks for the average, yet their choices can significantly change the level of this index.

On Mar. 14, 1939 one particular stock was dropped from the index. Why? It was "just another dull office equipment supplier." The name of the stock was IBM. AT&T was substituted. You know the rest: With stock dividends, splits and rights offerings, IBM moved up 635.2 times over the next four decades before the keepers of the gate saw fit to restore it to their index in June of 1979. Its replacement, AT&T, moved up 6 times in the same period. Had IBM been kept throughout, the Dow would be around 2100 today. (Nearer 3500 if the appreciation were not adjusted downward after each stock split, to equally weight the average.)

You see, in a sense, the Dow keepers are just stock pickers—and just as fallible. When the time came to restore IBM, something had to be dropped. It was Chrysler, then barely breathing. Kicked out of the index, Chrysler staged a sensational come-

back. Since then, Chrysler has appreciated 450% to IBM's 74%, or 6 times as much. Chalk up a bunch more points had IBM not been added back.

I could go on. The committee was certainly active that June day in 1979. Its final decision was to drop Esmark from the Dow, replacing it with Merck. Again, you can guess the outcome. Merck has risen a respectable 75%, but Esmark has increased 566%. This change cost the Dow about 100 points.

Had the Dow guardians left their index untouched in 1979, it would be over 2200 today, or more than 60% higher. Never underestimate the ability of a committee to arrive at the wrong decision.

So: Is the market too high? Or too low? My point is, you can't tell by looking at the Dow averages.

Okay, how about the S&P's 500? Similar pattern. In the late Sixties, for example, the REITs (Real Estate Investment Trusts) were added very near their alltime highs, only to be dropped in 1974 at a fraction of those prices near their lows.

The makeup of many indexes, then, simply reflects the conventional stock picker wisdom of a given time. Investors believe stock market indexes mirror markets completely insulated from popular fashions. Not true. Because stock selection or deletion is important if not critical, the index is not a mirror but more like a painting that differs, and sometimes dramatically, from the reality it attempts to portray. This subjective element in stock indexes is something most people, including experts, are unaware of.

Hundreds of institutional investors, controlling tens of billions of dollars, have been convinced by the professors to put their money into funds mirroring various market indexes. The academics claim that this is the only objective way to buy stocks, completely unaware of the underlying subjective manner in which index stocks are selected. In the end, the academics and index investors get exactly what they attempted to avoid—human error.

Since there are many indexes, some are performing much better than others at any time. Small stock indexes were popular well after the small cap markets turned south in mid-1983. The Value Line index, which is a long-standing record of 1700 equally weighted stocks, did sensationally in the past 10 years, but only because it recovered from the sharp drop in the prior 10. On a 20-year basis, it has moved up only marginally, while the Dow and the S&P's are significantly higher.

To get back to the original point: should we be elated or alarmed by the Dow's new high? The answer: neither. It doesn't matter all that much. Its significance is vastly exaggerated.

Source: Adapted from David Dreman, "Meaningless Signals," *Forbes,* December 16, 1985, p. 230. Reprinted by permission of *Forbes* magazine, December 16, 1985. © Forbes Inc., 1985.

---

may find this index to be a better reflection of average performance against which to measure the performance of his or her securities.

American Stock Exchange Index

The American Exchange introduced a new index in 1973, replacing the previous index based on price changes. The base period, August 31, 1973, was assigned an index number of 100. It is similar to the S&P and NYSE indices in that it is based on market values. All common stocks, warrants, and American Depository Receipts (ADRs) listed on the AMEX are covered in this Index. ADRs are tradable receipts for the shares of foreign corporations, with the actual shares remaining in the country of origin.

NASDAQ Indices

The National Association of Security Dealers produces seven NASDAQ indices that cover industrials, banks, insurance, other finance, transportation, utilities, and a Composite Index, which includes all companies.[9] These indices are similar to the S&P and NYSE indices. The base period January 1971 is assigned a value of 100 for the Composite Index and the Industrial Index.

In addition to these, the NASDAQ/NMS Industrial Index and the NASDAQ/NMS Composite Index were begun on July 10, 1984. The initial value of each was 100.

---

[9]In addition, the following indices are available: the NASDAQ-100™ and the NASDAQ-Financial, both of which began on February 1, 1985 at a value of 250. Each consists of the 100 largest market-capitalized firms in their respective categories.

Value Line Index

The Value Line Investment Survey, discussed in Chapter 4, publishes several indices including a Composite Index.[10] The VL Index is different, however, in that it is an equally weighted geometric average of stock prices. Also, it is based on the roughly 1700 companies in the 90+ industries that Value Line chooses to cover in its reports.[11] June 1961 is assigned the base index of 100.

Since Value Line is a well known investment advisory service, its indices receive attention. Investors, however, should be aware of how these unique indices differ from the others. All stocks are equally weighted; that is, since a daily net percentage change in price is computed for the stocks, each stock in the index has the same percentage weight.[12] Therefore, a 20% movement in a stock's price has the same impact on the index whether 10 million or 100 million shares are outstanding. The small, low-priced stocks covered by Value Line will have the same impact as the larger stocks. In effect, the Value Line Composite is an unweighted index covering a broad cross-section of stocks. Some market observers feel that because it is unweighted, it is more reflective of general market trends.

The Media General Composite Market Value Index

The Media General Financial Weekly publishes the Media General (M/G) Composite Index, which covers all NYSE and AMEX stocks as well as over 800 OTC stocks. It is a market-value based index, which uses January 2, 1970 as its base. This index is very broad, second only to the Wilshire 5000 discussed next, and is available weekly in *The Media General Financial Weekly,* which provides detailed information on market measures and market activity.[13]

The Wilshire 5000

The broadest of all indicators is the *Wilshire 5000,* representing the dollar market value of all NYSE and AMEX stocks plus all actively traded OTC stocks; in effect, it is the total price of all stocks for which daily quotations can be obtained. It is quoted in billions of dollars.

---

[10] Specifically, Value Line publishes an Industrial, Rail, Utility, and Composite Index.

[11] The vast majority (more than 80%) of these stocks are listed on the NYSE.

[12] To compute the VL Index, the closing price of each stock for a given day is divided by the preceding day's close (which is set at an index of 100). The geometric average of these indexes of change is calculated by finding the nth root of the product of the n changes (where n is approximately 1700). Finally, the geometric average of change for the day is multiplied by the preceding value of the average to obtain the new value.

[13] *The Media General Financial Weekly* also carries the DJIA (monthly high and low) on an inflation-adjusted basis.

Relationship between Market Averages

Figure 10–1 shows most of the market indicators just discussed. In part *a*, the similarity between the market value-weighted indices—Standard & Poor's, NYSE Composite, and the AMEX—can be seen, as well as how they performed in comparison with the arithmetic average of the Dow Jones Industrials. In part *b*, the Wilshire 5000 is compared with the Dow Jones Industrials; the broadest market measure, covering all the stocks for which daily quotations are available, is shown together with the market measure using the fewest stocks (30).[14] Based on Figure 10–1, the following observations can be made:

1. As would be expected, the S&P 500 and the NYSE Composite Index are virtually identical in their patterns. The S&P 500 stocks are contained within the NYSE Composite Index and account for most of its total market value.[15]

2. Although the DJIA contains only 30 stocks, and has often been criticized because of this and the manner in which the average is computed, it parallels the movements of the broader market value-weighted indices *involving NYSE stocks*. The correlation between the price changes for the three indices (S&P, NYSE, and DJIA) has been quite high; however, this does not mean that the DJIA will show similar percent changes over all intervals of time.

3. The greatest divergence in market indices occurs when comparisons are made between those indices that involve only NYSE stocks and those that cover other exchanges or NYSE stocks plus stocks from other exchanges. Figure 10–1 shows that (a) the AMEX Index and the NASDAQ Composite have been very strong performers in recent years, far outperforming the NYSE-related indices; (b) the Wilshire 5000 and the DJIA roughly parallel each other. The broader index reflects the changes made by smaller stocks, which is not captured by the DJIA, and tends to be more volatile.

In addition to the long-term movements in market measures indicated in Figure 10–1, investors may wish to consider short-term movements. In this case, dramatic differences can, and do, occur between the various market measures. Table 10–1 shows the percent change for five of the market measures previously discussed for 4- and 52-week periods as of August 16, 1982, and August 15, 1983—one year apart.

Table 10–1 indicates that for the four weeks preceding August 16, 1982, all five market measures were up, with the DJIA doubling the broader market measures. On the other hand, for the preceding four weeks one year

---

[14] Keep in mind that the Wilshire 5000 is the total market value of the securities whereas the Dow Jones Industrials is an arithmetic average.

[15] The importance of this can be realized by noting that the 50 biggest companies in the S&P 500 Index account for more than 50% of its weighting.

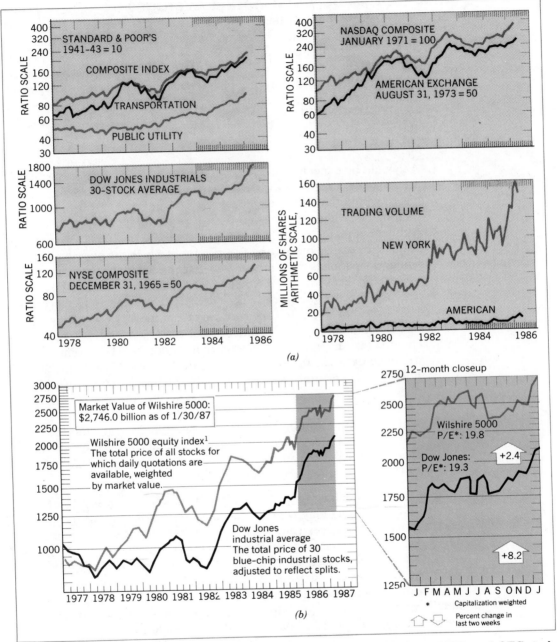

FIGURE 10-1 (*a*) **Graphs of market measures for NYSE, AMEX, and OTC-stocks, 1978-1986.** (*b*) **A comparison of the Wilshire 5000 Index with the Dow Jones Industrial Average, 1977-early 1987.**
Source: (a) *Federal Reserve Chart Book*, Board of Governors of the Federal Re-

TABLE 10–1 **Four and Fifty-Two Week Percentage Changes in Five Measures of the Stock Market as of Mid-August 1982 and 1983**

	Wilshire 5000	DJIA	NYSE Composite	AMEX	NASDAQ Composite
August 16, 1982					
Last 4 weeks	1.6	3.4	1.7	1.7	1.0
Last 52 weeks	−16.3	−11.3	−14.5	−30.0	−17.3
August 15, 1983					
Last 4 weeks	−1.2	−0.8	−1.1	0.5	−2.5
Last 52 weeks	57.9	48.2	53.2	92.8	86.3

Source: Forbes, August 16, 1982, p. 83, and August 15, 1983, p. 107. Reprinted by permission.

later, four market indicators were down and the AMEX was up; furthermore, the DJIA declined less than the other three.

Table 10–1 also indicates the substantial differences that can occur in market indicators over a period of one year. For the year preceding August, 1982, the AMEX was down twice as much as the other market measures with the DJIA showing the smallest (but still substantial) decline. For the year preceding August, 1983, all market indicators reflect the great bull market for that period, but the AMEX gain was almost twice that of the DJIA. Notice how well AMEX and NASDAQ stocks performed, with the Wilshire 5000 performance in between that of the NYSE-based measures and the measures covering non-NYSE stocks.

Why Is Market Analysis Important?

Now that we know what the "market" is, we can consider again the importance of market analysis. As noted in Chapter 9, 30 to 50% of the variability in an individual stock's return is attributable to aggregate market effects. The aggregate market remains the largest single factor explaining fluctuations in individual stock prices.

Of even greater importance is the market's effect on a diversified portfolio. As shown in Chapter 18, the basic tenet of portfolio theory is to diversify into a number of securities (properly chosen). For adequately diversified portfolios, market effects account for 90% and more of the variability in the portfolio's return. In other words, for a well-diversified portfolio, which each investor should hold, the market is the dominant factor affecting the variability of its return.

serve System, September 1986, p. 70; (b) The Forbes/Wilshire 5000 Review, *Forbes* magazine, February 23, 1987. Excerpted by permission of *Forbes* magazine, February 23, 1987. © Forbes Inc., 1987.

In the final analysis, most investors are heavily influenced and affected by the market. If it goes up strongly, as it did in the latter part of 1982 and again in 1985 and 1986, most investors make money. If it goes down sharply, as in 1974, most investors lose money. It is quite difficult to successfully go against the market.

Table 10–1 dramatically shows the importance of market analysis for one-year periods, which can be generalized to other time periods. Over the period from mid-August 1981 through mid-August 1982, most investors lost money, because all of the markets were down substantially. On the other hand, the corresponding period one year later was one of the record high periods in modern stock history. Virtually all investors gained during this period, whether they held NYSE stocks or other stocks, whether they were conservative or aggressive, and whether they knew anything at all about valuing stocks or were simply astute enough to invest in August 1982 because they correctly discerned the future trend of the market.

Understanding the Stock Market

Now that we know what "the market" is and why market analysis is important, what remains is to understand, value, and forecast the market. This section is concerned with understanding the market.

What determines stock prices? We have established, in Chapter 9, the two determinants of stock prices—the expected benefits stream (earnings or dividends) and the required rate of return (or its counterpart, the P/E ratio). Although these are the ultimate determinants of stock prices, a more complete model is desirable when attempting to understand the stock market. Such a model is shown in Figure 10–2, which is a flow diagram of stock price determination described by Keran several years ago; that is, it shows the variables that interact together to ultimately determine stock prices.[16]

In Figure 10–2, there are four exogenous (independent) variables that ultimately affect stock prices: the potential output of the economy (Y^*), which is a nonpolicy variable, and three policy variables (i.e., variables subject to government policy decisions)—the corporate tax rate (t_x), changes in government spending or fiscal policy (ΔG), and changes in nominal money (ΔM). All variables to the right of the dotted line are determined within the economy (and are called endogenous variables).

The two primary exogenous policy variables, ΔG and ΔM, affect stock prices through two channels.

---

[16] See Michael W. Keran, "Expectations, Money, and the Stock Market," *Review*, Federal Reserve Bank of St. Louis, Vol. 53, No. 1 (January 1971), pp. 16–31.

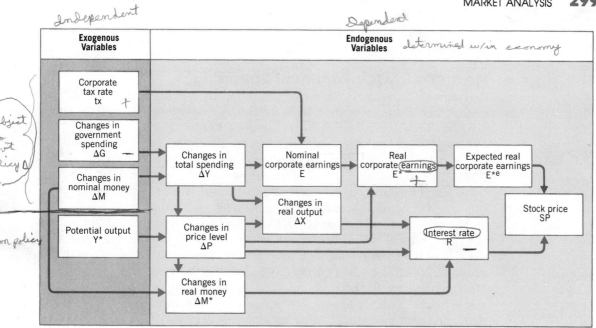

FIGURE 10–2 A flow diagram of stock price determination.
Source: Michael W. Keran, "Expectations, Money, and the Stock Market," *Review,* Federal Reserve Bank of St. Louis, January 1971, p. 27.

1. They affect total spending (ΔY), which, together with the tax rate (t_x), affects corporate earnings.[17] Expected changes in (real) corporate earnings (E^*) are *positively* related to changes in stock prices (SP).

2. They affect total spending, which together with the economy's potential output (Y^*) and past changes in prices, determine current changes in prices (ΔP). ΔY and ΔP determine current changes in real output (ΔX). Changes in ΔX and ΔP generate expectations about inflation and real growth, which in turn influence the current interest rate (R). Interest rates have a *negative* influence on stock prices (SP).

Although alternative flow diagrams of the type shown in Figure 10–2 could be constructed, this model is entirely reasonable and logical as a description of stock price determination. It indicates the following major factors that determine stock prices. Three active policy variables—fiscal policy (government spending), monetary policy (money supply), and the corporate tax rate—plus potential output affect three changes. These changes—total spending, price level, and real money—ultimately affect corporate earnings and interest rates which, in turn, determine stock prices.

---

[17]Technically, both the current level and lagged changes in Y affect corporate earnings.

This discussion will use Table 10–2, which contains a variety of macro data for 1960–1986, as a reference.

Fiscal Policy (Government Spending)

Government activity, in the form of fiscal policy and tax policy, is clearly a major force in the economy and its evolution across time. Federal spending accounted for about 24% of Gross National Product (GNP) by 1986.

Government spending may augment or substitute for private spending. Fiscal policy can be expansive, encouraging spending and growth, or contractionary, dampening spending and growth. Tax policies can be designed to be accommodating or not, depending on corporate and personal marginal rates, depreciation schedules, and investment tax credits.

The president and Congress together determine government spending and tax rates, which, when carried out in the prevailing conditions, determine the size of the federal budget deficit. Deficits tend to vary inversely with the economy, with the trend of deficits indicating the government's posture. How deficits are financed is important to the economy, and ultimately to stock prices. Deficits financed by money creation can have significant inflationary consequences.[18] More government debt may also raise the price level (through its impact on desired money balances), which, as Figure 10–2 shows, has an impact on the interest rate.

Large deficits can place a strain on the capital markets as the government seeks to raise the necessary funds. An increase in government demand can drive up real interest rates. A concern about large deficits is "crowding out," whereby government borrowing crowds out potential private borrowers because the government can pay the going rate on its securities, which are of the highest credit quality. Private borrowers may find less funds available, or more expensive funds, and lower their investment spending. The occurrences of "crowding out" have been difficult to document, resulting in some controversy as to whether this scenario is actually a significant problem.

Table 10–2 shows the government's budget surplus or deficit from the GNP accounts (column 8). Clearly, the deficits have been large and growing in recent years, and have become an item of great concern to many observers. By 1985, the large deficits had become a major political controversy.[19]

Monetary Policy (Money Supply)

Although most observers will agree that money influences economic activity, the amount (and sometimes the direction) of the influence remains controversial. Monetarism has been widely discussed in recent years and, to

---

[18] Deficits are inflationary if the debt is monetized or if additional debt continually grows as a percentage of GNP.

[19] A good discussion of issues such as this, as well as current fiscal and monetary policy, can be found in the annual *Economic Report of the President*, available each February.

TABLE 10–2 Selected Economic Variables, 1960–1986[a]

Year	(1) %Δ CPI	(2) %Δ Real GNP	(3) %Δ M1	(4) %Δ M2	(5) LTB Rate	(6) TB Rate	(7) S or D (billions of $)
1960	1.5	2.2	0.6	4.9	4.1	2.9	3.0
1961	0.7	2.6	3.3	7.4	3.9	2.4	−3.9
1962	1.2	5.3	1.8	8.1	4.0	2.8	−4.2
1963	1.6	4.1	3.7	8.4	4.0	3.2	0.3
1964	1.2	5.3	4.7	8.0	4.2	3.5	−3.3
1965	1.9	5.8	4.7	8.1	4.3	4.0	0.5
1966	3.4	5.8	2.5	4.5	4.9	4.9	−1.8
1967	3.0	2.9	6.6	9.2	5.1	4.3	−13.2
1968	4.7	4.1	7.7	8.0	5.6	5.3	−6.0
1969	6.1	2.4	3.2	4.1	6.7	6.7	8.4
1970	5.5	−0.3	5.2	6.6	7.4	6.5	−12.4
1971	3.4	2.8	6.6	13.5	6.2	4.3	−22.0
1972	3.4	5.0	9.2	13.0	6.2	4.1	−16.8
1973	8.8	5.2	5.5	6.9	6.8	7.0	−5.6
1974	12.2	−0.5	4.4	5.5	7.6	7.9	−11.6
1975	7.0	−1.3	4.9	12.6	8.0	5.8	−69.4
1976	4.8	4.9	6.6	13.7	7.6	5.0	−53.5
1977	6.8	4.7	8.1	10.6	7.4	5.3	−46.0
1978	9.0	5.3	8.3	8.0	8.4	7.2	−29.3
1979	13.3	2.5	7.2	7.8	9.4	10.0	−16.1
1980	12.4	−0.2	6.6	8.9	11.5	11.5	−61.3
1981	8.9	1.9	6.5	10.0	13.9	14.0	−63.8
1982	3.9	−2.5	8.8	8.9	13.0	10.7	−145.9
1983	3.8	3.6	9.8	12.0	11.1	8.6	−176.0
1984	4.0	6.4	6.0	8.6	12.4	9.6	−170.0
1985	3.8	2.7	12.2	8.1	10.6	7.5	−198.0
1986	1.1	2.5	16.6p	9.3p	7.7	6.0	−204.0p

[a]Key to abbreviations: (p = preliminary)

%ΔCPI = percentage change in the Consumer Price Index (December to December).
%Δ real GNP = percentage change in real GNP.
%ΔM1 = percentage change in the money supply (M1 definition).
%ΔM2 = percentage change in the money supply (M2 definition).
LBT rate = interest rate on 10-year U.S. government bonds.
TB rate = three-month Treasury bill rate.
S or D = federal government budget surplus or deficit (−) from GNP accounts (in billions of dollars)—calendar yr. basis.

Source: Economic Report of the President, 1987.

some extent, increasingly accepted. But widespread disagreement over its role remains. Some economists feel that monetary factors are the primary force in the economy, whereas others view it as only one part of a complex set of factors. The available evidence on its impact remains in dispute.

Monetarists believe that control of the money supply is critical in controlling output, unemployment, and inflation, and that changes in the growth of money are highly correlated with changes in the rate of total spending.[20] Accelerations in money growth result in accelerations in nominal GNP, whereas sharp decelerations over a period of months can lead to recessions. Another monetarist position is that the growth of money is closely related to growth in the monetary base, which to a large extent is under the control of the Federal Reserve.[21]

Many economists agree that, in the long run, a causal link exists between money growth and inflation. Money is important to inflation, which cannot continue unless the money supply increases. The rise in inflation from the mid-1960s through 1980 was associated with an upward drift in the trend rate of money growth. Significant slowdowns in money growth are usually reflected in subsequent movements in the inflation rate (with a lag of one or two years).

Measures of money supply have been important variables in interpreting the economy for many years. Because of changes in the U.S. economy, new definitions of these variables have been introduced to assist observers in keeping up with the money supply. M1 is the basic measure of money supply, sometimes called the narrow monetary aggregate. It is the sum of currency plus demand deposits plus other checkable deposits.[22] M2 starts with M1 and adds savings and small time deposits at all depository institutions plus Money Market Deposit Accounts and shares in money market funds. M3 is an even broader measure, adding to M2 large time deposits at all depository institutions and other small items.[23] Disagreement continues as to which of these three measures is the most appropriate measure of the money stock.

It is important to note how monetary policy affects the economy. Figure 10–2 indicates that changes in nominal money affect changes in total spending (ΔY). The transmission mechanism of monetary policy runs from the Federal Reserve System to ΔY (i.e., nominal GNP growth) in the following manner.

---

[20] This discussion is based on Lawrence K. Roos, "An Insider's View of Innovations and Monetary Policymaking: Implications for the Economy," reprinted in *The C.F.A. Study Guide I*, 1984 (Charlottesville, Va.: The Institute of Chartered Financial Analysts, 1983), pp. 114–119.

[21] The monetary base is defined as the sum of currency in circulation and financial institution deposits at the Federal Reserve.

[22] Other checkable deposits include NOW accounts, automatic transfer accounts (ATS), and credit union shares.

[23] M3 includes large repurchase agreements and money market funds restricted to institutional investors (which is not counted in M2).

Tools of monetary control → Monetary aggregate growth
→ Nominal GNP growth

The tools of monetary control are (1) open market operations, which are the most important, (2) changes in reserve requirements, and (3) changes in the discount rate (the rate at which banks can borrow from the Federal Reserve). Traditionally, the Federal Reserve has focused on M1, which is intended to measure transactions balances held by the public, as the monetary aggregate to control. Some observers believe that the regulatory changes in the early 1980s—allowing institutions to pay unregulated rates of return on checkable deposits—cause significant problems for the Federal Reserve's conduct of monetary policy, which is based on the monetary aggregates. By 1984 the Fed was paying less attention to a strict interpretation of M1.

As indicators of the Federal Reserve's policy positions, Federal Reserve open market operations, and the related changes in money supply (and interest rates), are widely watched by market observers in order to predict what the economy, and therefore the market, will do. If the Fed increases the money supply (and interest rates fall), the assumption is that the Fed wishes to encourage economic growth. If the money supply decreases (or the rate of increase slows), and interest rates rise, the assumption is that the Fed is attempting to restrict economic growth.

Columns 3 and 4 of Table 10–2 show the percentage change from year to year in M1 and M2. Notice how large percentage changes in the CPI (column 1) usually follow large percentage changes in the money supply, but with roughly a two-year lag. For example, the largest change in the CPI in the 1960s occurred in 1969 (6.1%), two years after a large percentage change in the money supply; large changes in the CPI occurred in 1973 and 1974, following large percentage changes in the money supply in 1971 and 1972.

The explicit policy of the Fed in the early 1980s was to attempt to control the monetary aggregates rather than interest rates. Money supply figures, released weekly on Thursday afternoons (starting in 1984), are keenly followed by many market observers.

The Corporate Tax Rate

As Figure 10–2 indicates, the corporate tax rate, together with the level and changes in total spending (ΔY), determine nominal corporate earnings. Under the Tax Reform Act of 1986, the corporate *marginal tax rate* (the tax on the last dollar of income) became 34%.[24] Marginal tax rates exceed (or equal) average tax rates, defined as the total tax liability divided by the total taxable income.

The marginal corporate tax rate declined to 46% in the early 1980s. Before this time, the marginal rate was 48%. Thus, the change in corporate tax rates

---

[24] This rate became effective on July 1, 1987.

in 1986 was an historic change. Other factors being equal, a decline in the marginal tax rate will raise corporate earnings. However, the 1986 act decreased or eliminated several corporate deductions, easing the tax code's traditional tilt toward heavy industry. The loss of the investment tax credit and scaled-back new depreciation allowances negatively impacted companies investing heavily in plant and equipment. Projections made in 1986 estimated that corporate taxes would increase about $120 billion over five years. Roughly speaking, this would return the corporate tax to its levels in the 1970s.

Output

The level of economic activity is important in understanding the aggregate securities markets in general and the stock market in particular. In the Keran model, changes in total spending (ΔY) represent nominal GNP whereas changes in real output represent real GNP.

The most basic and widespread measure of the economy's activities is **Gross National Product (GNP)**, the market value of all goods and services produced during some time period (typically, one year).[25] GNP is measured either by adding together all incomes generated in the economy (wages, rents, interest, etc.) or by adding together all expenditures made in the economy (by consumers, business, governments, etc.).

The Department of Commerce supplies GNP data every quarter and publishes the details regularly.[26] These data are revised as a result of new information, and new estimates appear frequently. Because of its widespread use as a measure of economic activity, GNP figures and forecasts are available from numerous sources, both government and private.

Nominal GNP has increased year after year. Real GNP, on the other hand, has not. Table 10–2 (column 2) shows that the percentage changes in real GNP in 1970, 1974, 1975, and 1980 were negative, whereas the years 1976 to 1978 showed percentage gains of over 5%. The year 1984 was also a year of strong growth in real GNP.

The Price Level

Figure 10–2 indicates that changes in the price level (ΔP) are affected by changes in total spending, which is affected by monetary policy and fiscal policy.[27] As the figure shows, changes in the price level affect interest rates indirectly by affecting real output and real money, which affect interest rates. In addition, changes in the price level directly affect the interest rate.

---

[25] A second measure of the economy's activities is industrial production, an index of the output of the pricing sectors of the economy. GNP and industrial production should move together as the business cycle unfolds across time.

[26] GNP data are available in the *Survey of Current Business.*

[27] Changes in the price level are also affected by the relationship between actual and potential output.

Furthermore, changes in the price level help to determine real corporate earnings.

Table 10–2 (column 1) shows percentage changes in the Consumer Price Index on a year-to-year basis. Note that high rates of change in prices were usually associated with low or negative percentage changes in real GNP. Interest rates (columns 5 and 6) tend to be higher when price level changes are high. Also notice that corporate profits (column 7) are usually negatively affected by high rates of price level changes.

Price levels are important because of investor expectations. If inflation is expected, interest rates will be high, which negatively affects stock prices. If inflation is expected to decrease, a drop in interest rates will be anticipated and stock prices will rise (other things being equal).

Corporate Earnings, Interest Rates, and Stock Prices

It is logical to expect a close relationship between corporate profits and stock prices. The discussion of fundamental analysis in Chapter 9 showed that price, or value, for one stock or the market as a whole should be a function of the expected stream of benefits to be received (cash flows) and the required rate of return demanded by investors. Therefore, if the economy is prospering, investors would expect corporate earnings to rise and, other things being equal, stock prices to rise.

Figure 10–3 shows the relationship between corporate profits after taxes and the S&P 500 Index. There is an approximate parallel between earnings dips and price declines, with declines occurring in stock price before earnings. A relationship between upward trends in corporate earnings and stock prices can also be seen. In analyzing data such as Figure 10–3, however, remember that two factors determine the price or value of the market (or a single stock)—earnings (or dividends) and a risk factor (discount rate). Thus, other things often are not equal—earnings may rise, but the discount rate may also rise, and if strong enough can cause a decline in stock prices. Or, as in late 1982, stock prices may rise sharply while corporate profits rise very little or even decline.

Interest rates, the other component of determining stock prices in Figure 10–2, are a basic component of discount rates, with the two usually moving together. It is necessary, therefore, to consider the relationship between interest rates and stock prices.

Figure 10–3 also shows the relationship between interest rates and stock prices. There is clearly a relationship, just as in GNP and corporate profits, but in this case the relationship is inverse—as interest rates rise (fall), stock prices fall (rise), other things being equal.

To understand the relationship between stock prices and interest rates, consider the following in Figure 10–3. Interest rates rose in 1974 and stock prices declined, whereas the opposite occurred in 1980. Notice the sharp decline in 1980 in both the Treasury bill rate and the corporate bond rate, and the sharp rise in stock prices. Also notice the dramatic decline in interest

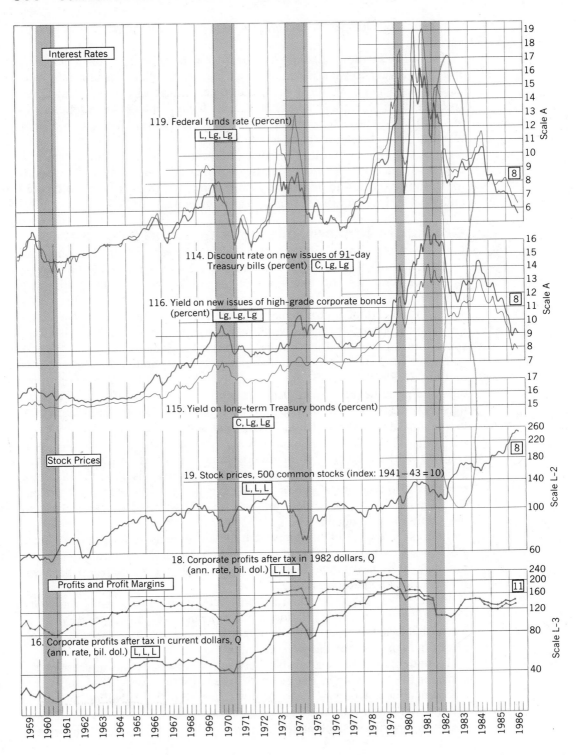

Interest Rates

119. Federal funds rate (percent)
L, Lg, Lg

114. Discount rate on new issues of 91-day
Treasury bills (percent) C, Lg, Lg

116. Yield on new issues of high-grade corporate bonds
(percent) Lg, Lg, Lg

115. Yield on long-term Treasury bonds (percent)
C, Lg, Lg

Stock Prices

19. Stock prices, 500 common stocks (index: 1941−43 =10)
L, L, L

18. Corporate profits after tax in 1982 dollars, Q
(ann. rate, bil. dol.) L, L, L

Profits and Profit Margins

16. Corporate profits after tax in current dollars, Q
(ann. rate, bil. dol.) L, L, L

Scale A
Scale A
Scale L-2
Scale L-3

rates in the latter half of 1982 and the very strong rise in stock prices. Finally, note the decline in interest rates in 1985 and 1986 and the strong rise in stock prices. Again, precise relationships do not occur in all years because two factors determine stock prices—earnings and a discount (interest) rate.

Why is there an inverse relationship? Recall from Chapter 9 that the basic fundamental valuation model is given by the following equation (assuming the constant growth version of the dividend valuation model):

$$P_0 = \frac{D_1}{k - g} \qquad (10\text{--}1)$$

The k in equation 10–1 is the required rate of return (discount rate) to be used by investors in discounting future cash flows. It is the required rate of return that investors expect to earn by investing in common stocks. This rate can be thought of as the sum of a riskless rate of return plus a risk premium determined by the riskiness of the stock being valued. Most observers use the rate on Treasury securities as a proxy for the riskless rate of return because Treasuries have no practical risk of default. Therefore, the discount rate k is intimately tied to interest rates, and that is why the Keran model (or any other model) can use interest rates in discussing stock price determination. In summary, if interest rates in the economy rise, the riskless rate rises because it is tied to interest rates and normally the required rate of return (discount rate) rises because the riskless rate is one of its two components.

Valuing the Market

To value the market using the fundamental analysis approach explained in Chapter 9, determinants of the market, as previously explained, are used—specifically, the expected stream of benefits and the rate of return required by investors (or, alternatively, a multiplier or P/E ratio). The following estimates are needed: (1) the stream of benefits—earnings or dividends—and (2) the required rate of return or the earnings multiplier.

These estimates are used in Equations 10–1 and 10–3, which were explained in Chapter 9:

$$P = \frac{D_1}{k - g} \qquad (10\text{--}1)$$

$$P/E = \frac{D_1/E_1}{k - g} \qquad (10\text{--}2)$$

$$P = P/E(E) \qquad (10\text{--}3)$$

FIGURE 10–3 **Stock prices, corporate profits after taxes, and long and short-term interest rates, 1959 to mid-1986.**

Source: Business Conditions Digest, August 1986, pp. 28 and 34 combined.

where

D_1 = dividends expected to be paid in the next period.
E_1 = earnings expected in the next period.
k = discount rate or required rate of return.
g = expected growth rate in dividends or earnings.

These equations apply equally to the aggregate market or an individual stock; however, this analysis is concerned with an aggregate market index such as the S&P 500 Composite Index. Conceptually, the value of this index is the discounted value of all future cash flows to be paid (i.e., the index value of dividends); alternatively, it is the expected earnings on the S&P 500 Index multiplied by the estimated P/E ratio, or multiplier. In summary,

$$\text{Value of S\&P 500 today} = \frac{\text{Dividends to be paid on Index next year}}{\begin{array}{cc} \text{Required rate} & \text{Expected growth} \\ \text{of return} & \text{in dividends} \end{array}}$$

or

Value of S&P 500 = Expected earnings on the index $\times$ (estimated multiplier)

For reasons explained in Chapter 9, this discussion focuses on the multiplier approach.

The Earnings Stream

Estimating expected earnings for a market index for a future period is not easy. Several steps are involved.

The item of interest is the earnings per share for a market index or, in general, corporate profits after taxes. The latter variable is related to GNP, the broadest measure of economic activity. Corporate earnings after taxes is derived from corporate sales, which in turn is related to GNP.

A detailed, complete fundamental analysis would involve estimating each of these variables, starting with GNP, then corporate sales, working down to corporate earnings before tax, and finally to corporate earnings after taxes. Each of these steps can involve various levels of difficulty, as the following points suggest.

1. To move from GNP to corporate sales, it may be possible to use a regression equation with percentage change in GNP as the independent variable and percentage change in corporate sales as the dependent variable. Based on this regression equation, a prediction could be made of sales given a forecast of change in GNP.
2. To obtain corporate earnings after tax, it is necessary to estimate a net profit margin, which is a volatile series. An alternative is to estimate a gross profit margin by considering those factors that affect the gross margin, including unit labor costs, the utilization rate of plant and equipment, and the inflation rate. After obtaining an estimate of the

gross profit margin, multiplying by the sales (per share) estimate would provide an estimate of earnings before depreciation and taxes. Both of these factors would have to be estimated and deducted to obtain an estimate of expected earnings (per share) for an index for the coming year.

Figure 10–4*a* shows corporate before-tax and after-tax profits, as well as the tax liability and undistributed profits (earnings after tax minus dividends). This figure clearly shows the volatility in earnings. It also demonstrates the impact of the tax liability, which somewhat smooths out the sharp movements in profits before taxes.

The Multiplier

The multiplier to be applied to the earnings estimate is equally as important as the earnings estimate. Investors sometimes mistakenly ignore the multiplier and concentrate only on the earnings estimate. The multiplier is more volatile than the earnings component and, therefore, more difficult to predict. In order to understand why, consider Figure 10–4*b*, which shows the Standard & Poor's 500 Composite Stock Price Index and the P/E ratio annual range for the period 1969 through mid-1986.

The P/E ratio for the market was low in the postwar period, perhaps because investors were expecting record inflation resulting from stifled demand. As the economy progressed and the dire predictions did not materialize, the P/E ratio began to rise in the early 1950s, reaching 19 by 1958 and remaining around that level through 1972 (as shown by the four rectangles for the years 1969–1972). In Figure 10–4*b*, the years 1969 through 1972 might be considered "normal" in terms of the annual range for the Standard & Poor's 500's P/E ratio. The figure shows that as inflation heated up in 1973, the multiplier started to decline, and by 1974 it was about half its previous level—a drastic cut for such a short period of time. Therefore, what was considered normal (about 17) in the 1960s and early 1970s was not the norm in the late 1970s and early 1980s. The lesson from this analysis is obvious: investors cannot simply extrapolate P/E ratios because dramatic changes occur over time. Perhaps the most that can be said is that in the postwar period, P/E ratios of broadly based indices have ranged from an average of about 7 to an average of about 17.

Putting the Two Together

It should be obvious by now that valuing the aggregate market is no easy job. Nor will it ever be, because it involves estimates of the uncertain future. And if valuing the aggregate market were relatively easy to do, many investors would become wealthy by knowing when to buy and sell stocks.

As noted, it is difficult to analyze all of the complicated details required to do fundamental market analysis. It involves studying utilization rates, tax rates, depreciation, GNP, and other factors, plus applying some sophis-

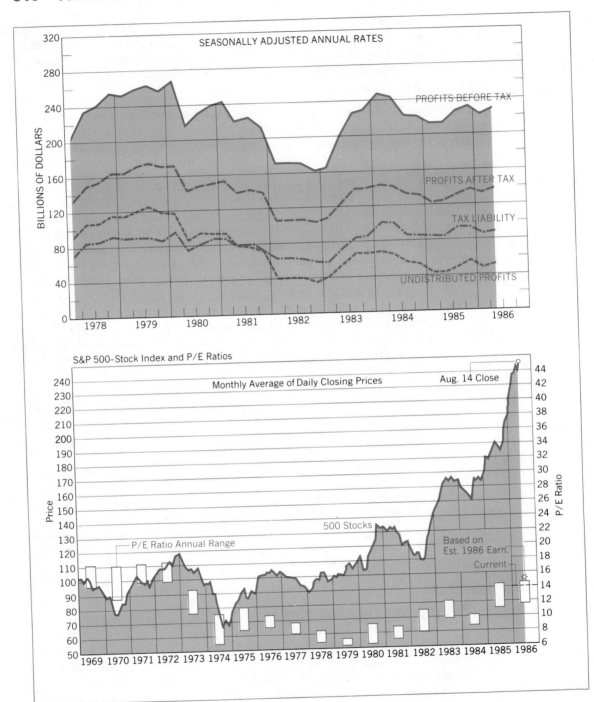

SEASONALLY ADJUSTED ANNUAL RATES

BILLIONS OF DOLLARS

PROFITS BEFORE TAX

PROFITS AFTER TAX

TAX LIABILITY

UNDISTRIBUTED PROFITS

S&P 500-Stock Index and P/E Ratios

Monthly Average of Daily Closing Prices

Aug. 14 Close

Price

P/E Ratio

P/E Ratio Annual Range

500 Stocks

Based on
Est. 1986 Earn.

Current

ticated statistical techniques. It is instructive, however, to analyze some general results of our basic valuation techniques. Regardless of the difficulty in doing market analysis, and the extent to which an analyst or investor goes, the methodology just outlined is the basis on which to proceed.

As an example of *conceptually* valuing the market, consider the information in Table 10–3, keeping in mind that these are end-of-year values for the Standard & Poor's 500 Composite Index. Be very careful to understand what will be done here. We will "value" the market in *hindsight*, based on ex post (and year end) values; that is, we will interpret what actually happened. In order to value the market, an investor must forecast the two components of value, earnings and P/E ratios; however, the reasoning process we will use is applicable whenever and however one values the market.

Consider what happened to the market in 1974. Earnings on the S&P 500 Composite Index increased from year-end 1973 to 1974 ($8.16 to $8.89), but investors became pessimistic because of the energy crisis. The required rate of return demanded by investors rose, which is the same as saying the multiplier (P/E ratio) declined. Stock prices declined sharply, from 97.55 to 68.56, because the steep decline in the multiplier more than offset the increase in earnings for the year. The important point of this analysis is that an investor trying to value the market for the year ahead, at the beginning of 1974, had to estimate what was likely to happen to the earnings stream for the market and to the P/E ratio (or discount rate). Estimating the earnings is only half the story, and the less important half in many cases.

Stock prices rose sharply in 1975, although earnings declined, indicating that the multiplier recovered some of the ground lost in the previous year as investor confidence started to increase. In 1976, earnings rose significantly (from $7.96 to $9.91) and stock prices moved up strongly; based on year-end values, the P/E ratio declined slightly.

In 1977 the market moved down sharply despite a strong showing in earnings. Why? The multiplier must have declined again. In 1978, a good increase in earnings was not reflected in prices, which remained essentially unchanged; therefore, investors must have raised their required returns (Figure 10–3 shows a rise in market interest rates for 1978). In 1979 earnings increased strongly and stock prices rose; on a year-end basis, the P/E ratio declined slightly. In 1980, a strong rise in stock prices occurred while earnings remained essentially unchanged, meaning that investors lowered their required rate of return. (Figure 10–3 shows a decline in interest rates in

---

FIGURE 10–4 (a) Corporate profits before and after tax, undistributed profits, and tax liability, 1978 to mid-1986; (b) S&P 500 Composite Index and the annual range of the P/E ratio, 1969 to mid-1986.

Source: (a) *Economic Indicators,* prepared for the Joint Economic Council by the Council of Economic Advisers, June 1986, p. 8; (b) *The Outlook,* Standard & Poor's Corporation, Vol. 58, No. 31 (August 20, 1986), p. 614. Reprinted by permission.

TABLE 10–3 Prices, Earnings, Dividends, and Several Calculated Variables for the Standard & Poor's 500 Index, 1960–1986[a]

	End-of-Year Prices	Earnings	Dividends	HPY(%)[b]	P/E[c]	Based on Year-End Prices Dividend Yield (D/P)100(%)	Dividend Payout (D/E)100(%)
1960	58.11	3.27	1.95	0.28	17.77	3.36	59.63
1961	71.55	3.19	2.02	26.60	22.43	2.82	63.32
1962	63.10	3.67	2.13	−8.83	17.19	3.38	58.04
1963	75.02	4.02	2.28	22.50	18.66	3.04	56.72
1964	84.75	4.55	2.50	16.30	18.63	2.95	54.95
1965	92.43	5.19	2.72	12.27	17.81	2.94	52.41
1966	80.33	5.55	2.87	−9.99	14.47	3.57	51.71
1967	96.47	5.33	2.92	23.73	18.10	3.03	54.78
1968	103.86	5.76	3.07	10.84	18.03	2.96	53.30
1969	92.06	5.78	3.16	−8.32	15.93	3.43	54.67
1970	92.15	5.13	3.14	3.51	17.96	3.41	61.21
1971	102.09	5.70	3.07	14.12	17.91	3.01	53.86
1972	118.05	6.42	3.15	18.72	18.39	2.67	49.07
1973	97.55	8.16	3.38	−14.50	11.95	3.46	41.42
1974	68.56	8.89	3.60	−26.03	7.71	5.25	40.49
1975	90.19	7.96	3.68	36.92	11.33	4.08	46.23
1976	107.46	9.91	4.05	23.64	10.84	3.77	40.87
1977	95.10	10.89	4.67	−7.16	8.73	4.91	42.88
1978	96.11	12.33	5.07	6.39	7.79	5.28	41.12
1979	107.94	14.76	5.70	18.24	7.31	5.28	38.62
1980	135.76	14.82	6.16	31.48	9.16	4.54	41.57
1981	122.55	15.36	6.63	−4.85	7.98	5.48	43.75
1982	140.64	12.64	6.87	20.37	11.13	4.88	54.35
1983	164.93	14.03	7.09	22.31	11.67	4.30	50.53
1984	167.24	16.72	7.53	5.97	9.99	4.50	45.04
1985	211.28	14.93	7.90	31.06	14.15	3.74	52.91
1986	242.17	14.66	8.28	18.54	16.52	3.42	56.48

[a]Values for recent years are subject to revision.

[b]HPY $= 100[(P_t - P_{t-1} + D_t)/P_{t-1}]$.

[c]P/E is earnings during the calendar year divided by the end-of-year price; the dividend yield is calculated similarly. The dividend yield is defined differently from that reported in Standard & Poor's sources.

Source: From Standard & Poor's Statistical Service; Security Price Index Record, 1980 ed. pp. 134–137: Plus update issues of Current Statistics through May 1987. Reprinted by permission.

1980.) The years 1981 and 1982 offer a good contrast. Stock prices declined in 1981 and rose in 1982, whereas earnings rose in 1981 and declined in 1982. The multipliers must have been moving in the opposite direction (interest rates moved in opposite directions in these years—see Figure 10–3).

The year 1982 offers a good example for market valuation. A very strong bull market began in August of 1982, which was widely attributed to a decline in interest rates and to investor belief that this decline would continue. Interest rates are closely related to discount rates (required rates of return). With a decline in the discount rate or, equivalently, an increase in the multiplier, stock prices rose, although earnings on the S&P declined for the year.

Good returns continued in 1983 as earnings rose strongly. Although earnings also increased sharply in 1984, prices (and returns) were up only slightly as the P/E ratio declined. In contrast, earnings declined in 1985 but stock prices moved ahead dramatically, with an HPY for the year of 31%. Clearly, investors were willing to pay more per dollar of earnings in 1985. Interest rates declined sharply in 1985, and again in 1986.

The conclusion of this analysis is that to value the market, an investor must analyze both factors that determine value: earnings (or dividends) and multipliers (or required rates of return). More important, the investor must forecast these variables in order to forecast the market.

Forecasting Likely Changes in the Market

Investors must consider how to forecast likely trends and changes in the market. They must be aware not only of what the market is doing currently, and why, but also where it is most likely to go in the future.

It is important to note that we are not going to discuss exact future market levels or even precise changes in the market. This is impossible for anyone to do consistently. As will be shown in Chapter 14, there is strong evidence that the market is efficient, one implication of which is that changes in the market cannot be predicted on the basis of information about previous changes. What we are seeking are general clues as to the market's direction and the duration of a likely change. To say, for example, that we are confident the market will go to 3000, or 1000, (as measured by the Dow Jones Industrial Average) one year from now is foolish.

This discussion is organized around two approaches. First, some of the techniques related to the economic variables that affect the business cycle and stock prices will be used. The second approach involves the fundamental valuation model used in the discussion of market valuation.

Using Economic Variables to Forecast the Market

The business cycle The **business cycle** reflects movements in economic activity as a whole, which is comprised of many diverse parts. The diversity of the parts ensures that business cycles are virtually unique, with no two parts identical. However, cycles do have a common framework, with a beginning (a trough), a peak, and an ending (a trough). Thus, economic activity starts in depressed conditions, builds up in the expansionary phase, and ends in a downturn, only to start again (perhaps because of government stimulus).

The typical business cycle in the United States seems to consist of an expansion averaging about three and a half years and a contraction averaging about one year. Obviously, however, these are only averages and cannot be relied on exclusively to interpret current or future situations. The longest expansion on record, for example, covered 106 months from February 1961 through December 1969, and the March 1975 to January 1980 expansion lasted 58 months. Business cycles cannot be neatly categorized as to length and turning points at the time they are occurring. Only in hindsight can such nice distinctions be made.

To make use of business cycle data, an investor needs to monitor indicators of the economy. A good source of help in this regard is the National Bureau of Economic Research (NBER), a private nonprofit organization.

The NBER dates the business cycle when possible. The duration of the contraction and expansion is measured in addition to other pertinent data. In its examination process, the NBER attempts to identify those components of economic activity that move at different times from each other. Such variables can serve as indicators of the economy in general.

Current practice is to identify leading, coincident, and lagging **composite indices of general economic activity.** This information can be found in *Business Conditions Digest,* including the median lead or lag for each series in relation to the business cycle and several characteristics of each series.

The NBER has focused on 12 leading indicators as representing the best combination of desirable characteristics, including stock prices and money supply. The 12 indicators taken as a composite have, generally, turned up three to four months before a recovery, and down eight to nine months before a recession begins.

The coincident and lagging indicators serve to confirm (or not) the indications of the leading series. If the leading index signal is not confirmed first by the coincident index and then by the lagging index, investors should reconsider the signal.[28]

Figure 10–5 shows these three composite indices for the years 1950 through mid-1986. The index of leading indicators moves roughly in line with stock prices, as can be seen by comparing the index in Figure 10–5 to the plot of stock prices in Figure 10–3. The similarity in the two is striking (look, for example, at the years 1970 and 1974).

---

[28] The Bureau of Economic Analysis now publishes a "composite index of four roughly coincident indicators" to condense the information from the most important monthly indicators into a summary measure. See Keith M. Carlson, "Monthly Economic Indicators: A Closer Look at the Coincident Index," *Review,* Federal Reserve Bank of St. Louis, November 1985, pp. 20–30.

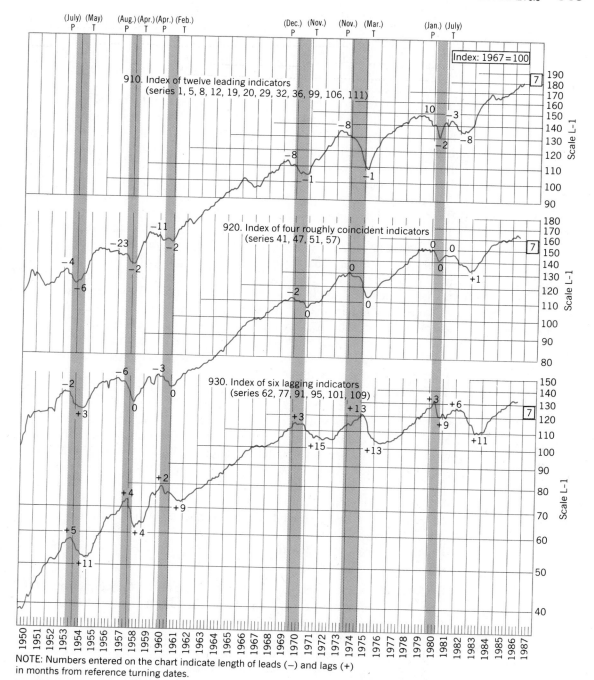

NOTE: Numbers entered on the chart indicate length of leads (−) and lags (+) in months from reference turning dates.

FIGURE 10–5 **Composite indices of leading, coincident, and lagging indicators, 1950 to mid-1986.**

Source: Business Conditions Digest, U.S. Department of Commerce, August 6, 1986, p. 10.

We have now established that certain composite indices can be helpful in forecasting or ascertaining the position of the business cycle. However, stock prices are one of the leading indicators; that is, they tend to lead the economy's turning points, both peaks and troughs. What is the investor who is trying to forecast the market to do?

This leading relationship between stock prices and the economy must be taken into account in forecasting likely changes in stock prices. Stock prices generally decline in recessions, and the steeper the recession, the steeper the decline. However, investors need to think about the business cycle's turning points months before they occur in order to have a handle on the turning points in the stock market. If a business cycle downturn appears likely in the future, it is also likely that the market will turn down some months ahead of the economic downturn.

It is possible to be somewhat more precise about the leading role of stock prices. Because of this tendency to lead the economy, the holding period yield on stocks (on an annual basis) could be negative (positive) in years in which the business cycle peaks (bottoms). Stock prices have almost always risen as the business cycle is *approaching* a trough. These increases have been large, so that investors do well during these periods. Furthermore, stock prices often drop suddenly as the business cycle enters into the initial phase of recovery. After the previous sharp rise as the bottom is approached, a period of steady prices or even a decline typically occurs. The economy, of course, is still moving ahead.

This business cycle–stock price relationship was again confirmed in the 1982–1983 expansion and stock market boom.[29] The recession worsened in late 1982, but the stock market soared; in early 1983, when the economy showed signs of recovery, stock prices wavered for a time. This action was consistent with the previous 10 major business slumps since 1929. Measuring the Dow Jones Industrial Average from the low point in a slump to the point when the economy started to recover, the index rose an average of 27.8%. In the following 12 months, it rose an average of only 17%. In only three cases of the 10 did the index rise faster after business turned up than before.

Thus, the investor forecasting the market using business cycle factors should note the following.

1. If the investor can recognize the bottoming out of the economy before it occurs, the market rise can be predicted, at least based on past experience, before the bottom is hit.
2. As the economy recovers, stock prices may level off or even decline. Therefore, a second significant movement in the market may be predictable, again based on past experience.

---

[29] This discussion is based on Alfred L. Malabre, Jr., "Perverse Stocks," *The Wall Street Journal*, February 2, 1983, p. 1.

Why is the market a forecaster of the economy? Basically, investors are discounting future earnings because, as the valuation analysis in Chapter 9 showed, stocks are worth today the discounted value of all future cash flows; that is, current stock prices reflect investor expectations of the future. Stock prices adjust quickly if investor expectations of corporate profits change. Of course, the market can misjudge corporate profits, resulting in a false signal about future movements in the economy.

An alternative explanation for stock prices leading the economy involves an investor change in the required rate of return, which again would result in an immediate change in stock prices. Note that the valuation model allows for a change in confidence (psychological elements) because a change in investor confidence changes the required rate of return (in the opposite direction). Thus, our valuation model encompasses psychological elements, which are sometimes used in explaining market movements.

Monetary variables Because of its importance in the economy, monetary policy is assumed to have an important effect on stock prices. Thus, to understand stock prices, investors must understand monetary variables; and to forecast the market, investors must take into account likely changes in the money supply.

The supposed relationship between changes in the money supply and changes in stock prices is direct, with the former leading the latter.[30] Several studies have examined this relationship; most of the earlier studies found that a relationship does exist and that money leads stock prices.[31] There is good evidence, however, that the market anticipates the changes in monetary growth, so that investors cannot use past changes in money supply as a means of outperforming the market. Rozeff, for example, found that stock market movements were related to money supply movements, both current and future; that is, the market has the lead role.[32] This is another indication of market efficiency, an issue considered in Chapter 14. A recent study found that excess money growth causes a negative reaction in stock prices at the time of announcement only. This effect was the result of the "unexpected" portion of the money growth rate. Causality tests supported "causality" only from stock returns to money growth.[33]

---

[30] This relationship was first hypothesized by Beryl Sprinkel, *Money and Stock Prices*. Homewood, Ill.: Irwin Publishing, 1964.

[31] See, for example, Kenneth Homa and Dwight Jaffe, "The Supply of Money and Common Stock Prices," *The Journal of Finance*, December 1971; and Michael Hamburger and Lewis Kochin, "Money and Stock Prices: The Channels of Influence," *The Journal of Finance*, May 1972.

[32] See Michael Rozeff, "The Money Supply and the Stock Market—The Demise of a Leading Indicator," *Financial Analysts Journal*, September–October 1975.

[33] John Sims, "Money Supply and Stock Returns—Does a Relationship Exist?" Unpublished manuscript, University of North Carolina, 1982.

Interest rates   Stock prices are clearly related to changes in interest rates, as established earlier. The implications of this relationship are clear. If interest rates are expected to decline, stock prices will be expected to rise. An excellent example of this can be found in 1982, when interest rates were at record highs and finally began to decline in the late summer (see Figure 10–3). Stock prices rose sharply over the next 12 months. A second example of this relationship is the period mid-1984 to mid-1986.

Using Valuation Models to Forecast the Market

Given the valuation models developed earlier, it is necessary to use one of two approaches.

1. Forecast D_1, k and g, and use Equation 10–1, $D_1/(k - g)$.
2. Forecast E and P/E, and use the equation $P = P/E(E)$ (Equation 10–3), where $P/E = (D_1/E_1)/(k - g)$ (Equation 10–2).

As an example of trying to make some forecast of the market, consider Figure 10–6, which shows Value Line's "Industrial Composite" (IC) of over 900 industrial, retail, and transportation companies, accounting for about 80% of all income earned by nonfinancial corporations in the United States. Per-share figures are based on the total number of shares outstanding for all the companies in the composite; that is, the IC is weighted by company size.[34] The data shown in Figure 10–6 include actual and forecasted earnings per share (*EPS*), dividends per share (*DPS*), growth rates for these variables as well as others, and several other variables and ratios.

Note that the performance of the IC during the recession periods conforms with our previous discussion. Also notice that in mid-1986, when this figure was published, the IC was at its highest point, reflecting this superstrong market rise since mid-1982.

First, we can analyze two of the figures given at the top of Figure 10–6: a recent price of 39 and a P/E ratio of 14.2. Value Line's estimate of the *EPS* for 1986 at this time (mid-1986) was $2.75, as shown on the third row of the data. Since

$$P = P/E(E)$$

$$P = 14.2 \times \$2.75$$

$$= \$39$$

Thus, the recent price of the IC is a combination of a P/E of 14.2 and expected earnings for 1986 of $2.75.

---

[34] The price action of the Industrial Composite is influenced by company size, with larger corporations having a greater influence than smaller corporations. In contrast, the Value Line averages are unweighted; that is, they are influenced equally by the price movements of each stock.

July 25, 1986   VALUE LINE *Selection & Opinion*   page 953

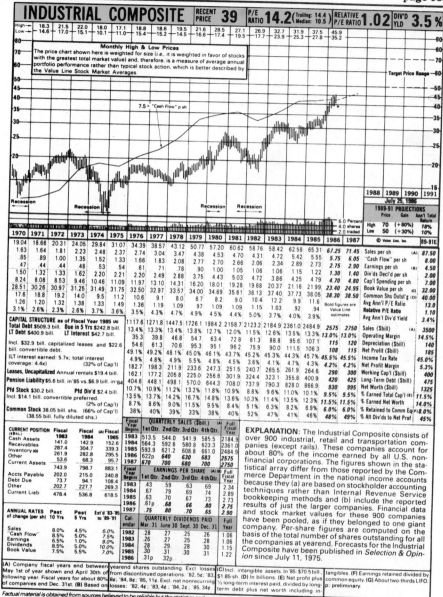

INDUSTRIAL COMPOSITE   RECENT PRICE **39**   P/E RATIO **14.2** (Trailing: 14.4 / Median: 10.5)   RELATIVE P/E RATIO **1.02**   DIV'D YLD **3.5%**

EXPLANATION: The Industrial Composite consists of over 900 industrial, retail and transportation companies (except rails). These companies account for about 80% of the income earned by all U.S. nonfinancial corporations. The figures shown in the statistical array differ from those reported by the Commerce Department in the national income accounts because they (a) are based on stockholder accounting techniques rather than Internal Revenue Service bookkeeping methods and (b) include the reported results of just the larger companies. Financial data and stock market values for these 900 companies have been pooled, as if they belonged to one giant company. Per-share figures are computed on the basis of the total number of shares outstanding for all the companies at yearend. Forecasts for the Industrial Composite have been published in *Selection & Opinion* since July 11, 1975.

FIGURE 10–6   **Value Line's Industrial Composite of over 900 industrial, retail, and transportation companies, 1970 to mid-1986.**

Source: The Value Line Investment Survey, Selection and Opinion, July 25, 1986, p. 953. © 1986 Value Line, Inc. Reprinted by permission.

Assuming a constant growth model, the estimated required rate of return for 1986 is[35]

$$k = D_1/P + g$$
$$= 1.35/39 + 0.10$$
$$= 0.134$$

Solving Equation 10–2

$$P/E = \frac{D_1/E_1}{k - g}$$
$$= \frac{1.35/2.82}{0.134 - 0.10}$$
$$= 14.1$$

Thus, the models and variables previously discussed seem to be internally consistent with these data.

Now, what about forecasts, or at least likely possibilities? First, assume that in 1987 the spread between k and g, 0.034, will hold. Using Value Line's 1987 estimates of D and E

$$\text{Estimated 1987 P/E} = \frac{1.40/2.90}{0.034}$$
$$= \frac{0.482}{0.034}$$
$$= 14.2$$

In this scenario the P/E would remain approximately constant. Earnings in 1987, however, are estimated to be higher than the 1986 estimate. Therefore,

$$\text{Estimated } P_{1987} = \text{estimated 1987 P/E}(E_{1987})$$
$$= 14.2(2.90)$$
$$= \$41.18$$

The estimated 1987 price for the IC, $41.18, is 5.6% higher than the price at the time of estimate (mid-1986), $39. What if the spread narrows to 0.024, as a result of k declining from 0.134 to 0.124?

Previous $k - g = 0.134 - 0.10 = 0.034$

New $k - g = 0.124 - 0.10 = 0.024$

---

[35] The $1.35 estimate is taken from the fourth row as the average of the estimated 1986 and 1987 dividends (thereby extending the figure one year ahead to mid-1987 from mid-1986) in Figure 10–6. The g value of 0.10 is taken from the estimates of growth through 1989–1991 in the bottom left panel. E_1 is also calculated as an average of the 1986 and 1987 estimates.

$$\text{New estimated 1987 P/E} = \frac{0.48}{0.024}$$

$$= 20$$

$$\text{New estimated } P_{1987} = \text{estimated 1987 P/E}(E_{1987})$$

$$= 20 \times 2.90$$

$$= \$58$$

A one percentage point decline in k, leading to a one percentage point drop in the spread between k and g, therefore, results in a substantial gain on the IC for 1987, from $39 in mid-1986 to $58 at the end of 1987, a 49% change.

On the other hand, assume that k rises one percentage point because of an increase in either the riskless rate of return or the risk premium demanded by investors. In this scenario,

$$\text{New estimated 1987 P/E} = \frac{0.48}{0.144 - 0.10}$$

$$= 10.9$$

and

$$\text{New estimated } P_{1987} = \text{estimated 1987 P/E}(E_{1987})$$

$$= 10.9(\$2.90)$$

$$= \$31.64$$

Assuming no change in the estimated 1987 earnings, these calculations suggest a market (i.e., the IC) decline from $39 in mid-1986 to $31.64 at the end of 1987.

The foregoing examples illustrate the fundamental analysis approach to forecasting the market. Such forecasts are not easy, at best, and are clearly subject to errors, some often substantial. The unexpected will occur. Nevertheless, it is possible for the average investor to make some intelligent and useful forecasts of the market at certain times, at least as to direction. In 1974, for example, it was not too difficult to believe that the market could rise in the future, given the low point it had reached. If the economy could be expected to improve after the shock of the energy crunch, earnings could be expected to hold steady or improve. More importantly, if investor pessimism could be expected to decrease to any extent, the P/E ratio had to increase, and therefore stock prices had to increase. And this is exactly what happened!

Another example is 1981–1982, when interest rates had reached record levels in the United States and the economy was in a recession. Investors had only to convince themselves that some recovery would occur, thereby increasing earnings, or more important, that interest rates would decline, thereby lowering the required rate of return (i.e., raising the P/E ratio). This is exactly what happened, of course, launching the great bull market of mid-1982 to mid-1983.

There is an interesting piece of information about P/E ratios and recessions.[36] Based on the last 10 economic slumps, the P/E ratio is higher at the end of the slump than at its low point in the slump; in other words, the market P/E usually rises just before the end of the slump. It then remains roughly unchanged over the next year.

Investors should attempt to apply the foregoing type of analysis to the current situation—that is, estimating for the future. Although it is not a perfect process by any means, useful forecasts of likely market trends can be made.

Summary

This chapter had two broad objectives: first, to consider the commonly used measures of market performance (i.e., the market indicators), and second, to demonstrate how investors can logically understand the stock market, which will help them in the difficult tasks of valuing the market and forecasting likely trends. Although the details of market analysis are complex, the basic concepts for understanding the market are straightforward.

The "market" is the aggregate of all security prices and is conveniently measured by some average or, most commonly, by some index of stock prices. These measures range from the narrowest New York Stock Exchange measure, the Dow Jones arithmetic mean averages, to the broadest, the Wilshire 5000. In between are two broader measures of the NYSE, the Standard & Poor's Indices and the New York Stock Exchange Indices. The American Stock Exchange has an index, as does the OTC market—the NASDAQ and NASDAQ/NMS Indices. *The Value Line Investment Survey* publishes indices based on the 1700 stocks it covers, as does a weekly newspaper, *The Media General Financial Weekly,* which covers all NYSE and AMEX stocks plus some 800 OTC stocks. Finally, the Wilshire 5000 index is composed of all stocks for which daily price quotations are available.

The three indices based on NYSE stocks (Dow Jones, S&P, and NYSE Composite Index) show high correlations between daily percentages of price changes. There are major divergences between these three indices and those covering other exchanges, such as the AMEX and the OTC market. Over short-run periods, significant differences do occur among the various market measures.

---

[36] See Malabre, "Perverse Stocks."

Total

Aggregate market analysis is important because a substantial part of the average stock's return is attributable to the market. Movements in the overall market are the dominant factor affecting the return of a diversified portfolio.

To understand the market (i.e., what determines stock prices) it is necessary to think in terms of a valuation model. The two determinants of stock prices are the expected benefits stream (earnings or dividends) and the required rate of return (alternatively, the P/E ratio). Keran's model is useful for visualizing the economic factors that combine to determine stock prices. In trying to understand the market in conceptual terms, it is appropriate to think of corporate earnings and interest rates as the determinants of stock prices. Corporate earnings are directly related to stock prices, whereas interest rates are inversely related.

To value the market, it is necessary to estimate expected corporate earnings and the P/E ratio (alternatively, the dividend valuation model could be used). Corporate earnings will be a function of sales, which in turn is related to GNP, tax rates, depreciation, and interest expense. It is a volatile series, as is the P/E ratio or multiplier. Although valuing the market can never be easy, it is possible to make some intelligent estimates by considering what is likely to happen to corporate profits and P/E ratios (or interest rates) over some future period, such as a year. It is possible to determine likely changes in either or both of these parameters, particularly at major turning points. Although investors may not time their actions exactly, they will nevertheless benefit from determining important rises and declines in either series.

In forecasting likely changes, investors can examine economic variables such as money supply, output, price levels, and government spending that affect the business cycle and stock prices. Leading, lagging, and coincident indicators may be helpful in predicting changes in the market. It is important to remember that stock prices typically lead the economy.

An alternative approach to forecasting likely changes in the market is to apply the valuation model based on dividends or earnings. Using information such as that available for Value Line's Industrial Composite, estimates of the market can be made on the basis of the multiplier model (i.e., estimated price = estimated earnings × estimated P/E ratio).

Key Words

Blue chip stocks	M1
Business cycle	M2
Composite indices of general economic activity	M3
	Market average
Gross National Product (GNP)	Market index

Market Indices and Averages

Averages
  The Dow Jones Industrial Average
  (also, Transportation, Public Utility, and Composite averages)
Indices (arranged from smallest number of companies in index to largest)
  New York Stock Exchange
    Standard & Poor's 400 Industrial Index
    Standard & Poor's 500 Composite Index
    New York Stock Exchange Index
  American Stock Exchange
    American Stock Exchange Index
  Over-the-Counter
    NASDAQ Indexes
  Composite Indices
    The Value Line Industrial Average
    The Value Line Composite Average
    The Media General Composite Index
    The Wilshire 5000

QUESTIONS AND PROBLEMS

1. Name at least four distinct uses for market indicators.
2. What are the advantages and disadvantages of using the Dow Jones Industrial Average?
3. Express, in equation form, the method for calculating the S&P 500 Composite Index.
4. What is the difference between the S&P 500 Composite Index and the NYSE Composite Index? How closely can they be expected to parallel each other?
5. Why is the Value Line index unique among market indicators?
6. Why is market analysis so important?
7. What are the two determinants of stock prices? How are these two determinants related to a valuation model?
8. How can the Keran model use interest rates as one of the two determinants of stock prices when the interest rate does not appear in either the dividend valuation model or the earnings multiplier model?

9. In terms of the Keran model, how can the Federal Reserve affect stock prices?
10. What is the historical relationship between stock prices, corporate profits, and interest rates?
11. How can investors go about valuing the market?
12. What was the primary cause of the rise in stock prices in 1982?
13. What is the "typical" business cycle–stock price relationship?
14. If an investor can determine when the bottoming out of the economy will occur, when should stocks be purchased—before, during, or after such a bottom? Would stock prices be expected to continue to rise as the economy recovers (based on historical experience)?
15. Can money supply changes forecast stock price changes?
16. What is the historical relationship between the market's P/E ratio and recessions?
17. Based on Figure 10–4, what is the likely explanation for the stock market's lackluster performance in the last half of the 1970s?
18. Suppose that you know *with certainty* that corporate earnings next year will rise 15% above this year's level of corporate earnings. Based on this information, should you buy stocks?
19. In the text the Value Line Industrial Composite is used in an example of market valuation. For this problem, the Standard & Poor's 400 Industrial Index and Equations 10–1, 10–2, and 10–3 are used. The annual data for the years 19X1 through 19X6 are provided:

Year	End-of-Year Price (P)	Earnings (E)	Dividends (D)	P/E	(D/E)100 (%)	(D/P)100 (%)
19X1	107.21	13.12	5.35	8.17	40.78	4.99
19X2	121.02	16.08	6.04	7.53	37.56	4.99
19X3	154.45	16.13	6.55	9.58	40.61	4.24
19X4	137.12	16.70	7.00	8.21	41.92	5.11
19X5	157.62	13.21	7.18	11.93	54.35	4.56
19X6	186.24	15.24	6.97			

a. Calculate the 19X6 values for those columns left blank.
b. Why would you expect this index to differ from the Value Line Index?
c. On the assumption that $g = 0.095$, calculate k for 19X6 using the formula $k = (D/P) + g$.
d. Using the 19X6 values in Equation 10–2, show that P/E $= 12.22$.
e. Assuming a Value Line projection that 19X7 earnings will be 25% greater than the 19X6 value, show that projected earnings for the S&P 400 is expected to be 19.05 in 19X7.

f.   Assuming further that the dividend–payout ratio will be 0.40, show that projected dividends for 19X7 will be 7.62.

g.   Using the projected earnings and dividends for 19X7, and the same k and g used in Problem c, show that Equation 10–2 yields an expected P/E for 19X7 of 10.69.

h.   Using these expected values for 19X7, evaluate Equation 10–3, and show that the expected price is 203.61.

i.   Recalculate the values for 19X7 P/E and P, using the same $g = 0.095$, but with (1) $k = 0.14$; (2) $k = 0.13$; (3) $k = 0.12$.

Selected References

Barth, James R., and Monell, Stephen O. "A Primer on Budget Deficits." *Economic Review*. Federal Reserve Bank of Atlanta, August 1982, pp. 6–17.

Bernstein, Peter L., and Silbert, Theodore H. "Are Economic Forecasters Worth Listening To?" *Harvard Business Review*, September–October 1984, pp. 32–40.

Butler, Hartman L., Jr., and DeMong, Richard E. "The Changing Dow Jones Industrial Average." *Financial Analysts Journal*, July–August 1986, pp. 59–62.

Carlson, Keith M. "Monthly Economic Indicators: A Closer Look at the Coincident Index." *Review*. Federal Reserve Bank of St. Louis, November 1985, pp. 20–30.

Federal Reserve Bank of St. Louis. *National Economic Trends* weekly.

Forbes, "The Forbes/Wilshire 5000 Review," bimonthly.

Friedman, Benjamin M. "Money, Credit and Interest Rates in the Business Cycle." *National Bureau of Economic Research*, Working Paper No. 1482, October 1984.

Hoehn, James G. "Monetary Aggregates as Indicators of General Economic Activity." *Economic Review*. Federal Reserve Bank of Dallas, November 1982, pp. 1–11.

Keran, Michael W. "Expectations, Money and the Stock Market." *Review*. Federal Reserve Bank of St. Louis, January 1971, pp. 16–31.

King, Benjamin. "Market and Industry Factors in Stock Price Behavior." *Journal of Business*, January 1966, pp. 139–190.

Kopcke, Richard W. "How Erratic Is Money Growth?" *New England Economic Review*. Federal Reserve Bank of Boston, May–June 1986, pp. 3–20.

Malabre, Alfred L., Jr. "Just as the Economy May Be Recovering, Share Prices Wobble." *The Wall Street Journal*, February 2, 1983, pp. 1, 22.

McNees, Stephen K. "Which Forecast Should You Use?" *New England Economic Review*. Federal Reserve Bank of Boston, July–August 1985, pp. 36–42.

Pearce, Douglas K. "Stock Prices and the Economy." *Economic Review*. Federal Reserve Bank of Kansas City, November 1983, pp. 7–22.

Renshaw, Edward F. "The Anatomy of Stock Market Cycles." *The Journal of Portfolio Management*, Fall 1983, pp. 53–57.

Roley, V. Vance. "Which Forecast Should You Use?" *New England Economic Review*. Federal Reserve Bank of Boston, July–August 1985, pp. 36–42.

Schiller, Robert J. "Theories of Aggregate Stock Price Movements." *The Journal of Portfolio Management,* Winter 1984, pp. 28–37.

Schiller, Robert J. "Do Stock Prices Move Too Much to Be Justified by Subsequent Changes in Dividends?" *American Economic Review,* June 1981, pp. 421–436.

Sheehan, Richard G. "Weekly Money Announcements: New Information and Its Effects." *Review.* Federal Reserve Bank of St. Louis, August–September 1985, pp. 25–34.

The Value Line Investment Survey, "Selection and Opinion," weekly.

Umstead, David. "Forecasting Stock Market Prices." *Journal of Finance,* May 1977, pp. 427–441.

United States Government Printing Office, *Economic Report of the President,* yearly.

Walsh, Carl E. "New Views of the Business Cycle: Has the Past Emphasis on Money Been Misplaced?" *Business Review.* Federal Reserve Bank of Philadelphia, January–February 1986, pp. 3–12.

CHAPTER 11

INDUSTRY ANALYSIS

The second step in the fundamental analysis of common stocks is industry analysis. Convinced that the economy and the market are attractive from the standpoint of investing in common stocks, the investor should proceed to consider those industries that promise the most opportunities in the coming years. From the perspective of the 1980s, for example, investors cannot view basic U.S. industries such as auto and steel industries with the same enthusiasm they would have 15 or 20 years earlier. On the other hand, it was obvious that the telecommunications and computer-related industries were going to change the way in which most Americans live by introducing home microcomputers that could communicate with information banks throughout the country—or the world!

In this chapter we will analyze industries in terms of their expected returns and multipliers (or discount rates), concentrating on the conceptual issues involved in industry analysis. The basic concepts of industry analysis can be easily understood, given our previous analysis. Although the actual analysis may be tedious, these concepts can be applied by investors in several ways, depending on the degree of rigor sought, the amount of information available, and the specific models used.

The significance of industry analysis can be established by considering the performance of various industries over multiple-year periods. This analysis will indicate the value to investors of selecting certain industries while avoiding others. We will also establish the need for investors to continue analyzing industries by showing the inconsistency of industry performance over consecutive yearly periods. Such a demonstration justifies an analysis of industries, which will be done following this discussion.

The Value of Industry Analysis

Before embarking on fundamental industry analysis, it is worthwhile to consider its value. If resources are to be devoted to it, industry analysis should be valuable. We will, therefore, assess the value of industry analysis at the outset of our discussion.

In order to assess the value of industry analysis, the performance of industry groups over long periods of time can be examined.[1] Standard & Poor's calculates weekly stock price indices for a variety of industries, with data available for a 40-year period. Since the data are reported in index numbers, price data from different industries are comparable and long-term comparisons of price performance can be made.

Table 11–1 shows the price performance of selected industries for the years 1973 and 1950 (using 1941–43 as the base), for 1960 (using 1950 as a base), for 1973 (using 1960 as a base), and for 1982 and 1986 (using 1941–43 as the base). The S&P 400 Industrial Index in 1973 was 12 times (121/10) its 1941–43 level, a continuously compounded average in excess of 8% annually over this 31-year period. However, this average growth rate consisted of widely varying performance over the industries covered by Standard & Poor's.

Over the 31-year period 1943–1973, office and business equipment did extremely well (145 times what it was in 1941–43), thanks primarily to IBM; without IBM, this industry was still 43 times larger than its base. The electronics industry also did well, rising to almost 69 times its beginning level (685/10). At the other extreme, the lead and zinc industry was less than two times its beginning level, and the sugar and textile apparel industries were only three times their beginning levels. Notice how the capital goods industry paralleled the Industrial Average.

Even over shorter periods of time, as the last two columns at the top of Table 11–1 show, industries perform quite differently. During the 1950s, for example, the price index for the electronics industry increased almost tenfold (i.e., the index was 96), while that for the textile apparel industry increased only twofold, with the sugar and lead–zinc industries doing much worse.

Standard & Poor's has changed industry classifications over time because of changes in the economy. The lower half of Table 11–1, therefore, shows

---

[1]This discussion is taken from H. A. Latané, D. L. Tuttle, and C. P. Jones, *Security Analysis and Portfolio Management*. New York: Ronald Press, 1975, pp. 427–431.

TABLE 11–1 Standard & Poor's Weekly Stock Price Indices for Selected Industries Using 1973 Data and Three Different Base Periods, and Selected Price Indices Using 1982 and 1986 Data and a Base of 1941–43 = 10

	1941–1943 = 10		1950 = 10	1960 = 10
	1973	1950	1960	1973
Computer and business equipment	1450 /₁₀ =145 20		113	46
(without IBM)	433 /₁₀ = 43 17		59	42
Electronics (major companies)	685	23	96	31
Drugs	245	14	43	41
Oil (composite)	145	22	30	23
Capital goods	119	18	33	20
S&P 400 Industrial Average	121	18	32	20
Gold mining	64	10	16	39
Aerospace	46	12	38	10
Sugar	30	16	13	15
Textile apparel	31	13	21	11
Lead and zinc	17	12	8	18

	1941–1943 = 10	
	1982	1986
Oil well equipment and service	1312	999
Computer and business equipment	1412	2032
Drugs	248	540
S&P 400 Industrial Average	156	270
Textile apparel	63	174
Aerospace	179	322
Chemicals (diversified)	57	32
Copper	55	52
Broadcast media	889	2255
Steel	32	28
Shoes	108	149

Sources: H. A. Latané, D. L. Tuttle, and C. P. Jones, *Security Analysis and Portfolio Management.* New York: Ronald Press, 1975, pp. 427–429; Standard & Poor's *Statistical Service: Security Price Index Record,* April 1987 ed. Price data are as of December 1982 and 1986 (monthly averages of weekly indices). Reprinted by permission of John Wiley & Sons, Inc. and Standard & Poor's.

selected Standard & Poor's Industry Stock Price indices for the end of 1982 and the end of 1986, based on 1941–43. This provides both a 40-year-plus picture of industry performance, which approximates the maximum investing lifetime of many individuals, and a look at how much change can occur in a four-year period. Again, tremendous differences exist for industries, ranging from the 131-fold increase for oil well equipment and service to slightly in excess of a tripling for steel by the end of 1986. Broadcast media did very well over the period ending in 1986, and more than doubled from the

1982 level. Copper, on the other hand, has been a poor long-term performer, and its performance has also worsened in the short run.

Consistency of Industry Performance

The previous section established the value of industry analysis from a long-term perspective. Those investors who select the growth industries and maintain their positions will generally receive far better returns than those who have the misfortune to concentrate in industries that perform poorly over long periods of time.

Can relative industry performance be predicted reliably on the basis of past success, as measured by the previous price performance? To answer this question, consider Table 11–1 again. Assume that an investor calculated the top part of the table sometime in 1974, when the 1973 data were available. Should this investor count on past performance to carry him or her through the next several years—for example, through 1982? The answer is NO!

The computer business and equipment industry, a spectacular performer through 1973, was lower by 1982—in other words, the great growth was over. Although this was still a phenomenal industry over the 40 years 1943–1982 with a 141-fold increase, it was an even better 31-year performer (through 1973), with a 145-fold increase. The drug industry, a strong performer over the 1943–1973 period, was virtually unchanged in 1982. On the other hand, textile apparel showed an index of 63 by 1982, compared to 31 in 1973, and aerospace showed 179 versus 46. Furthermore, both of these industries showed dramatic increases over the four-year period 1982–1986.

What about industry performance over shorter periods of time? Should investors screen industries to find those that are currently performing well and are, therefore, likely to be the source of the most promising opportunities, from which company analysis will be done? To answer this question, consider Table 11–2, which shows price performance by industries for 52-week periods ending in mid-November of the years 1980, 1981, and 1982.[2]

In 1980, the rare metals industry ranked first (out of 60 covered) for the 52-week period ending in mid-November of that year. This industry as a whole had experienced a 121% increase in price over the previous year. However, an investor choosing this industry on the basis of this performance would have been disappointed over the subsequent two years, as the rank and performance dropped to 60 (last) in 1981 with a one-year decline of 39%, and was in fifty-fourth place in 1982 with a one-year decline of 11%. Similarly, the oil and natural gas services industry went from third place in 1980 with a previous year gain of 104%, to fifty-third place in 1981 (−26%) and sixtieth place (last) in 1982 with a decline of 41%.

---

[2] The author wishes to thank *The Media General Financial Weekly* for providing these data.

TABLE 11–2 Media General Industry Ranks and Percentage Price Performance over 52-Week Periods Ending in Mid-November 1980, 1981, and 1982 and in Late September 1984, 1985, and 1986 for Selected Industries

| | Previous 52-Week Price Performance as of Mid-November | | | | | |
| | 1980 | | 1981 | | 1982 | |
	Rank	Percent Change	Rank	Percent Change	Rank	Percent Change
Oil, natural gas services	(3)	104	(53)	−26	(60)	−41
Metals, rare	(1)	121	(60)	−39	(54)	−11
Savings and loans	(52)	9	(56)	−30	(5)	55
Shoes	(19)	39	(9)	16	(7)	50
Automotive	(60)	−8	(44)	−16	(10)	44
Retail-department stores	(57)	−1	(14)	9	(1)	80
Electronics	(6)	70	(29)	−1	(42)	15

| | Previous 52-Week Price Performance as of Late September | | | | | |
| | 1984 | | 1985 | | 1986 | |
	Rank	Percent Change	Rank	Percent Change	Rank	Percent Change
Aerospace	(8)	7	(24)	15	(53)	10.5
Textile manufacturing	(53)	−19	(10)	22	(8)	56
Shoes-leather	(58)	−28	(18)	19	(12)	43
Savings and loans	(60)	−30	(4)	35	(5)	52
Airlines	(24)	−7	(3)	40	(52)	12
Drug manufacturers	(36)	−11	(8)	27	(7)	48
Food-meats-dairy	(20)	10	(7)	28	(3)	57

Source: The Media General Financial Weekly, issues of November 17, 1980, November 16, 1981, and November 15, 1982, September 24, 1984, September 23, 1985, and September 22, 1986, p. 1. Courtesy of *The Media General Financial Weekly.*

On the other hand, consider the retail department store industry, which was in fifty-seventh place in 1980 (−1%). By 1981, it was in the fourteenth position (9%), and by 1982 in the first position with a previous yearly gain of 80%. The automotive industry also showed a dramatic turnaround, rising from last place in 1980 to tenth place in 1982.

Finally, note the leather shoes industry. It was a steady performer during this three-year period, rising from the top third of the 60 industries in 1980 to almost the top decile in 1982.

The bottom part of Table 11–2 tells the same basic story for the years 1984–1986. Aerospace went from eighth place to fifty-third, while savings and loans went from sixtieth to fifth. Textiles and leather shoes improved dramatically from 1984 to 1986.

Table 11–2 is compiled from *The Media General Financial Weekly,* which provides a front-page ranking of 60 industries, including industry performance (rank and percentage change) for the current week, as well as the last 4, 13, and 52 weeks. This analysis also shows the company in each industry with the highest and lowest performance for each of the four periods. These weekly data are unique and provide a valuable source of information to investors. However, when using short-term information an investor must remember an important point about fundamental analysis of industries. Although industry analysis is clearly valuable over time, with some industries far outperforming others, industry rankings on some periodic basis (e.g., yearly or quarterly) are not consistent. Investors cannot simply choose those industries that have performed well recently and expect them to continue to do so for the next several periods. Perhaps just as important, investors should not ignore industries simply because their recent performance has been poor. Their subsequent performance over relatively short periods of time may be, and often is, at the opposite extreme! It is necessary, therefore, to learn the basic concepts of industry analysis. First, however, let us consider exactly what an industry is.

What Is an Industry?

At first glance, the term *industry* may seem self-explanatory. After all, everyone is familiar with the auto industry, the drug industry, and the electric utility industry. But are these classifications as clear-cut as they seem? For example, a consumer can drink beer out of glass containers or aluminum cans or steel cans. Does this involve one industry—containers—or three—the glass, steel, and aluminum industries (or perhaps two: glass and metals)?

The problem becomes even more messy when companies in diversified lines of business are considered. In 1986, for example, Harvey Group, an American Stock Exchange company, showed the following breakdown by sales: retailing of professional and home audio and video equipment, 56%; food brokerage, 44%; however, by percentage of total profits the breakdowns are 32% and 68%, respectively. In what industry is Harvey Group? It is not easy to classify such a company, particularly in relation to Cascade Natural Gas, for example, a New York Stock Exchange company whose only activity is the distribution of natural gas in 84 communities in Washington and Oregon.

There are complications in classifying even a seemingly "clear" example such as General Motors, the world's largest automobile manufacturer. In 1984 GM acquired EDS, a computer services firm, and in 1985 it acquired Hughes Aircraft.

The message is clear. Industries cannot casually be identified and classified—at least in many cases. It seems safe to assert that industries have been, and will continue to become, more mixed in their activities and less identifiable with one product or service.

Classifying Industries

Regardless of the problems, analysts and investors need methods with which to classify industries. One well-known and widely used system is the **Standard Industrial Classification (SIC) system** based on Census data and developed to classify firms on the basis of what they produce.[3] SIC codes have 11 divisions, designated A through K. For example, agriculture-forestry-fishing is Industry Division A, mining is B, retail trade is G, and K, the last group, is nonclassifiable establishments. Within each of these divisions are several major industry groups, designated by a two-digit code. The primary metal industries, for example, are a part of Division D, manufacturing, and are assigned the two-digit code 33.

The major industry groups within each division are further subdivided into three-, four-, and five-digit SIC codes to provide more detailed classifications. A specific industry is assigned a three-digit code, as are entire companies.[4] Plants carrying out specific functions (such as producing steel) are assigned four-digit SIC codes. A five-digit code indicates a specific product. Thus, the larger the number of digits in the SIC system, the more specific the breakdown.

SIC codes have aided significantly in bringing order to the industry classification problem by providing a consistent basis for describing industries and companies. Analysts using SIC codes can focus on economic activity in as broad, or as specific, a manner as desired.

Other Industry Classifications

The SIC system of industry classification is probably the most consistent system available, and possibly the easiest to use. However, it is not the only industry designation in actual use. Standard & Poor's Corporation, at the end of 1982, provided weekly stock indices on some 101 industry groupings (or parts of industries).[5] Many of these series go back 30 or 40 years.

The Value Line Investment Survey covers roughly 1700 companies, divided into 90+ industries, with a discussion of industry prospects preceding the company analysis. As discussed later, these industry classifications could be important because *Value Line* ranks their expected performance (relatively) for the year ahead.

Still another very useful industry classification system is that of *The Media General Financial Weekly,* discussed earlier, which divides stocks into 60 industries. Since Media General is one of the few consistent (weekly) sources of past price performance by industries, these classification systems can also be quite useful to investors.

---

[3] See *Census of Manufacturers*. Washington, D.C.: U.S. Government Printing Office.

[4] Companies involved in several lines of activity are assigned multiple SIC codes.

[5] The 101 number excludes investment companies but includes industries both with and without the dominant company (e.g., AT&T and IBM). See Standard & Poor's Statistical Service *Current Statistics,* December 1982.

Other sources of information use different numbers of industries in presenting data. The important point to remember is that no one industry classification system is widely used in the standard investment publications.

Analyzing Industries

Industries, as well as the market and companies, are analyzed through the study of a wide range of data, including sales, earnings, dividends, capital structure, product lines, regulations, innovations, and so on. Such analysis requires considerable expertise and is usually performed by industry analysts employed by brokerage firms and other institutional investors.

A useful first step is to analyze industries in terms of their stage in the life cycle. The idea is to assess the general health and current position of the industry. A second step is to assess the position of the industry in relation to the business cycle and macroeconomic conditions. A third step involves a qualitative analysis of industry characteristics designed to assist investors in assessing the future prospects for an industry. Each of these steps will be examined in turn.

The Industry Life Cycle

Many observers believe that industries evolve through at least three stages: the pioneering stage, the expansion stage, and the stabilization stage. There is an obvious parallel in this idea to human development. The concept of an **industry life cycle** could apply to industries or product lines within industries. The industry life cycle concept is depicted in Figure 11–1, and each stage is discussed in the following section.

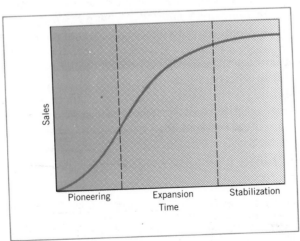

FIGURE 11–1 The industry life cycle.

Pioneering stage In this stage, rapid growth in demand occurs. Although a number of companies within a growing industry will fail at this stage because they will not survive the competitive pressures, most experience rapid growth in sales and earnings, possibly at an increasing rate. The opportunities available may attract a number of companies, as well as venture capital. Considerable jockeying for position occurs as the companies battle each other for survival, with the weaker firms failing and dropping out. Investor risk in an unproven company is high, but so are expected returns if the company succeeds. At the pioneering stage of an industry it can be difficult for security analysts to identify the likely survivors, just when the ability to identify the future strong performers is most valuable. By the time it becomes apparent who the real winners are, their prices may have been bid up considerably beyond what they were in the earlier stages of development.

In the early 1980s, the microcomputer business—both hardware and software—offered a good example of companies in the pioneering stage. Given the explosion in expected demand for these products, many new firms entered the business hoping to capture some share of the total market. By 1983, there were an estimated 150 manufacturers of home computers, a clearly unsustainable number over the longer run.

Expansion stage In this second stage of an industry's life cycle the survivors from the pioneering stage are identifiable. They continue to grow and to prosper, but the rate of growth is more moderate than before.

At the expansion stage of the cycle, industries are improving their products and perhaps lowering their prices. They are more stable and solid, and at this stage they often attract considerable investment funds. Investors are more willing to invest in these industries now that their potential has been demonstrated and the risk of failure has decreased.

Financial policies become firmly established at this stage. The capital base is widened and strengthened. Dividends often become payable, further enhancing the attractiveness of these companies to a number of investors.

Stabilization stage Finally, industries evolve into the stabilization stage (sometimes referred to as the maturity stage), at which the growth begins to moderate. Sales may still be increasing, but at a much slower rate than before. Products become more standardized and less innovative, the marketplace is full of competitors, and costs are stable rather than decreasing through efficiency moves and so on. Industries at this stage continue to move along, but without significant growth. Stagnation may occur for considerable periods of time, or intermittently.

Assessing the industry life cycle This three-part classification of industry evolvement is helpful to investors in assessing the growth potential of different companies in an industry. Based on the stage of the industry, they can better assess the potential of companies within that industry. However, there are limitations to this type of analysis. First, it is only a generalization, and investors must be careful not to attempt to categorize every industry, or all companies within a particular industry, into neat categories that may not apply. Second, even the general framework may not apply to some industries that are not categorized by many small companies struggling for survival. Finally, the bottom line in security analysis is stock prices, a function of the expected stream of benefits and the risk involved. The industrial life cycle tends to focus on sales and share of the market and investment in the industry. Although all of these factors are important to investors, they are not the final items of interest. Given these qualifications to industry life-cycle analysis, what are the implications to investors?

The pioneering stage may offer the highest potential returns, but it also offers the greatest risk. Several companies in a particular industry will fail, or do poorly. Such risk may be appropriate for some investors, but many will wish to avoid the risk inherent in this stage.

The maturity stage is to be avoided by investors interested primarily in capital gains. Companies at this stage may have relatively high dividend payouts because their growth prospects are fewer. These companies often offer stability in earnings and dividend growth.

Perhaps a fourth stage could be added to the analysis of the industrial life cycle—decline, on either a relative or absolute basis. Clearly, investors should seek to spot industries in this stage and avoid them. In the 1980s, as the United States enters the era of information processing, certain industrial sectors will decline (in some cases, this decline has already started).

It is the second stage, expansion, that is probably of most interest to investors. Industries that have survived the pioneering stage often offer good opportunities as the demand for their products and services is growing more rapidly than the economy as a whole. Growth is rapid, but orderly, an appealing characteristic to investors.

Business-Cycle Analysis

A second way to analyze industries is by their operating ability in relation to the economy as a whole. That is, some industries perform poorly during a recession whereas others are able to weather it reasonably well. Some industries move closely with the business cycle, outperforming the average industry in good times and underperforming it in bad times. Investors, in analyzing industries, should be aware of these relationships.

Most investors have heard of, and are usually seeking, growth companies. In **growth industries,** earnings are expected to be significantly above the average of all industries, and such growth may occur regardless of setbacks in the economy. Drugs have been a growth industry in the past, as have color television, office equipment, and computers. Recent growth industries include genetic engineering, microcomputers, and new medical devices. Current and future growth industries might include robotics and cellular radios. Clearly, one of the primary goals of fundamental security analysis is to identify the growth industries of the near and far future.

At the opposite end of the scale are the **defensive industries,** which are least affected by recessions and economic adversity. Food has long been considered such an industry. People must eat and they continue to drink beer, and so on, regardless of the economy. Public utilities might also be considered a defensive industry.

Cyclical industries are most volatile—they do unusually well when the economy prospers and are likely to be hurt more when the economy falters. Durable goods are a good example of the products involved in cyclical industries. Autos, refrigerators, and stereos, for example, may be avidly sought when times are good, but such purchases may be postponed during a recession because consumers can often make do with the old units. Counter-cyclical industries also exist, actually moving opposite to the prevailing economic trend. The gold mining industry is known to follow this pattern.

These three classifications of industries according to economic conditions do not constitute an exhaustive set. Additional classifications are possible and logical. For example, some industries are **interest-sensitive,** that is, particularly sensitive to expectations about changes in interest rates. The financial services industry, the banking industry, and the real estate industry are obvious examples of interest-sensitive industries. Another is the building industry.

What are the implications of these classifications to investors? To predict performance of an industry over shorter periods of time, investors should carefully analyze the stage of the business cycle and the likely movements in interest rates. If the economy is heading into a recession, cyclical industries are likely to be affected more than other industries, whereas defensive industries are the least likely to be affected. With such guidelines, investors may make better buy or sell decisions. Similarly, an expected rise in interest rates will have negative implications for the savings and loan industry and the home-building industry, whereas an expected drop in interest rates will have opposite effects.

These statements reinforce the importance of market analysis. Not only do investors need to know the state of the economy and market before deciding to invest, but such knowledge is valuable in selecting, or avoiding, particular industries.

As an example of applying business cycle considerations to industry analysis, consider the situation in 1982–1983. The great bull market of 1982–1983 officially began on August 13, 1982. One year later, the market, as measured by the Dow Jones Industrial Average, was up approximately 50%. Every industry appreciated during this span, ranging from more than 250% for the brokerage industry to less than 1% for the entertainment industry.

Investors who understood the economy–industry relationship realized that the cyclical industries were likely to do well as the economy improved. And, in fact, some of the largest gains were made by cyclical industries: metals, up 135%; autos, up 98%, airlines, up 80%; and aluminum, up 76%. Some of these industries were still showing depressed earnings well into the bull market, but as several popular press articles noted in 1983, investors recognized that cyclical movements should occur in certain industries and acted accordingly.[6]

The interest-sensitive industries soared before and during this period, as investors anticipated a drop in interest rates. By mid-1982, many investors were, or already had been, looking for an improvement in the business cycle, with a corresponding drop in interest rates. Realizing that this situation would be favorable for industries substantially affected by interest rates, investors bought accordingly. And finally, lower interest rates, other things being equal, mean higher stock prices. Higher stock prices, in turn, suggest the possibility of increasing trading by investors, resulting in more brokerage commissions for the brokerage industry, which, as noted, was the number one performer over this one-year period.

In 1980–1981, on the other hand, the economy experienced recession and sharply rising interest rates. Cyclical industries did poorly—autos were in last place in 1980 and forty-fourth in 1981; the November 1981 performance record for the previous 12 months showed metals in last place, with heavy building fifty-ninth, aerospace fifty-fourth, heavy machinery forty-eighth, chemicals forty-seventh, and so on.

Clearly, business-cycle analysis for industries is a logical and worthwhile part of fundamental security analysis. Industries are sensitive to the business conditions and interest rate expectations existing at any given time, and the smart investor will think carefully about these factors.

③ Qualitative Aspects of Industry Analysis

In analyzing industries, the analyst or investor should consider several important qualitative factors that can characterize an industry. Knowing about these factors will help investors to understand a particular industry and will aid in assessing its future prospects.

- **The historical performance**   As we have learned, some industries perform well and others poorly over long periods of time. Although performance is not always consistent and predictable on the basis of the past, an industry's track record should not be ignored. In Table 11–1, we saw that the lead and zinc industry performed poorly both in 1950 and 1960 (in relation to the base of 1941–43). It continued to do badly in 1973. The office and business equipment industry and the electronics industry, on the other hand, showed strength at the 1950 and 1960 checkpoints, and continued to do well in 1973.

  Investors should consider the historical record of sales and earnings growth and price performance. Although the past cannot simply be extrapolated into the future, it does provide some useful information.

- **Competition**   The nature of the competitive conditions existing in an industry can provide useful information in assessing its future. Is the industry

---

[6] See Gary Putka, "Some See Activity of Certain Groups as Sign of Possible Leadership Shift," *The Wall Street Journal,* June 13, 1983, p. 47.

protected from the entrance of new competitors as a result of control of raw materials, prohibitive cost of building plants, the level of production needed to operate profitably, and so forth? The domestic automobile industry, for example, is in effect protected from new domestic competitors because of the vast costs and scope of operations involved in manufacturing autos. Obviously, they are not completely protected from foreign competition, although they have enjoyed some protection, such as voluntary import restrictions.

According to one analysis, the intensity of competition in an industry determines that industry's ability to sustain above-average returns.[7] This intensity is not a matter of luck, but a reflection of underlying factors that determine the strength of five basic competitive factors.

1. Threat of new entrants.
2. Bargaining power of buyers.
3. Rivalry between existing competitors.
4. Threat of substitute products.
5. Bargaining power of suppliers.

These factors are seen as ranging from intense in some industries (e.g., tires and paper) where spectacular profits do not occur, to mild in other industries (e.g., cosmetics/toiletries) where high returns are not unusual.

Investors need to consider carefully the future ability of particular industries to compete against both domestic and foreign competitors. Assessing these five factors is a good way to start.

Government effects   Government regulations and actions can have significant effects on industries. The investor must attempt to assess the results of these effects or, at the very least, be well aware that they exist and may continue.

Consider the breakup of AT&T as of January 1, 1984. This one action has changed the telecommunications industry permanently, and perhaps others as well. As a second example, the deregulating of the financial services industries resulted in banks and savings and loans competing more directly with each other, offering consumers many of the same services. Such an action has to affect the relative performance of these two industries as well as some of their other competitors, such as the brokerage industry (which can now also offer similar services in many respects).

Structural changes   A fourth factor to consider is the structural changes that occur in the economy. As the United States continues to move from an industrial society to an information–communications society, major industries will be affected. New industries with tremendous potential are, and will

---

[7] See Michael E. Porter, "Industry Structure and Competitive Strategy: Keys to Profitability," *Financial Analysts Journal*, July–August 1980, pp. 30–41.

be, emerging, whereas some traditional industries, such as steel, may never recover to their former positions.

Structural shifts can occur even within relatively new industries. For example, in the early 1980s the microcomputer industry was a young, dynamic industry with numerous competitors, some of whom enjoyed phenomenal success in a short period of time. The introduction of microcomputers by IBM in 1982, however, forever changed that industry. Other hardware manufacturers sought to be compatible with IBM's personal computer and suppliers rushed to supply items such as software, printers, and additional memory boards. Virtually every part of the industry was significantly affected by IBM's decision to enter this market.

Valuing Industries

The fundamental valuation of industries is based on the principles discussed in Chapters 9 and 10. An estimate is needed of both the expected returns for an industry and the risk involved. It is easiest to think in terms of expected earnings and P/E ratios.

Expected Earnings

The objective in fundamental security analysis at the industry level is to produce an estimate of the expected earnings per share for the industry. This requires substantial analysis on the part of the estimator, including an estimate of sales per share for the industry and an estimate of the net profit margin for the industry. Multiply these together to obtain an estimate of expected earnings.

The mechanics for calculating expected earnings are complex and require some skill in security analysis. A number of assumptions must usually be made. However, the following points can be noted:

1. Sales can be estimated over a long-run or a short-run period. If the former is sought, techniques such as input–output analysis could be used.[8] If a short-run forecast is desired, the most convenient method would be regression analysis. For example, industry sales might be regressed on GNP or personal income.
2. The net profit margin is often a volatile series. Estimating a volatile series often involves substantial errors. It is probably preferable to estimate the gross profit margin and subtract estimates of depreciation and tax rates to obtain the net profit margin.

---

[8] Input–output analysis is a technique that shows the workings of the economy through the interdependence of the different sectors in the economy. It shows how each sector (industry) receives its inputs from other sectors and where its output goes. Although an interesting and promising technique, it is still in the development stage in terms of information supplied. Input–output analysis and data does not appear on a regular, timely basis.

3. Steps 1 and 2 require the use of good data, careful statistical techniques, and sound application.

One approach to forecasting industry sales and profits has been outlined by Wenglowski as follows:[9]

1. Translate a GNP forecast (and its major components) into a first set of sales estimates for industries.
2. Use industry financial analysts to help construct models for forecasting the sales of specific industry. An example of such a model for the office equipment industry is as follows:

> Sales of the S&P Office Equipment Group = a + b (Business investment in producers durable equipment) + c (IBM direct sales − IBM total revenues) + d (a dummy variable for major new computer model introduction dates) where: a, b, c, and d are coefficients estimated by multiple regression techniques.

3. Have the economists subjectively adjust these model forecasts for factors that may not have been picked up by statistical analysis of past trends.
4. Ensure that the sum of the industry sales forecast is consistent with the GNP forecast.
5. Reconcile the model's forecasts with adjustments by the economists and industry analysts, obtaining the best estimate of sales.
6. Use the derived forecast to predict industry profits, using a profit forecasting equation for each industry. The basic form of this equation, according to Wenglowski, is as follows:

> Industry before-tax profits = a + b (Industry sales) − c (Average hourly earnings of production workers in the industry) + d (Productivity proxy for the industry) where: a, b, c, and d are coefficients estimated by multiple regression techniques.

According to Wenglowski, these equations pick up an average of 90% of the movement in pretax profits.

The P/E Ratio

To assess the P/E ratio or multiplier for an industry, an investor can first examine the historical record. What has the multiplier been in relation to the market's multiplier? Is it likely to change, and why? Although the past cannot be used naively to extrapolate the future, it does offer a reasonable guide. It must be modified, however, for expected changes.

To assess why the multiplier may change, one must analyze the three

---

[9]See Gary Wenglowski, "Industry Profit Analysis—A Progress Report and Some Predictions," reprinted in *The C.F.A. Study Guide II, 1983*, Charlottesville, Va.: The Institute of Chartered Financial Analysts, 1982, pp. 102–106.

factors affecting the multiplier, which were discussed in Chapter 9. Based on Equation 9–11

$$P/E = \frac{D_1/E_1}{k - g} \qquad (11-1)$$

These factors are (1) the payout ratio, D/E, (2) the required rate of return, k, and (3) the expected growth in dividends, g.

Although the payout ratio does change over time, it would be expected to be reasonably stable at any given time. The likely sources of change are the required rate of return and the expected growth in dividends.

As previously established, the required rate of return consists of the risk-free rate plus a risk premium. The risk-free rate affects all investments across the board and should be adjusted for accordingly. Thus, other things being equal, rising interest rates will increase the risk-free rate and the required rate of return.

The risk premium is more important for individual industries. If the components of risk for an industry are increasing, so too is its risk premium, which can be viewed in two ways.

1. Traditional risk factors such as business risk, financial risk, political risk, and so on increase.
2. Systematic risk (beta) of the industry increases. Beta was discussed in Chapter 8 and the systematic risk in a portfolio context will be discussed in Chapter 19. By computing the beta for the industry and determining its change, an assessment of any increase or decrease in systematic risk can be made.

As for expected growth in earnings and dividends, the major factors affecting this are (1) the retention rate and (2) the return on equity (ROE).

Each of these variables would have to be examined for a particular industry to determine if expected growth was changing. Because the retention rate is defined simply as

$$\text{Retention rate} = 1 - \text{Payout rate} \qquad (11-2)$$

this component can be easily examined.

Return on equity is, itself, a function of two variables.[10]

1. The equity turnover, defined as net sales/equity.
2. The net profit margin, defined as net income/net sales.

An industry's return on equity could increase as a result of either (1) more efficient use of the equity (turning it over more often) or (2) an increase in the industry's net profit margin.

---

[10] These ratios will be discussed in Chapter 12.

Evaluating Future Industry Prospects

Ultimately, investors are interested in expected performance in the future. They realize that such estimates are difficult and are likely to be somewhat in error, but they know that equity prices are a function of expected parameters, not past, known values. How, then, is an investor to proceed?

Ideally, investors would like to value industries along the lines discussed in the previous section; that is, they would like to be able to estimate the expected earnings for an industry and the expected multiplier, producing an estimate of expected price. As we have seen, however, this is not easy to do. It requires an understanding of several relationships and estimates of several variables. Fortunately, considerable information is readily available to help investors in their analysis of industries. Investors should be aware of the primary sources of information about industries and the nature of the information available. These issues are discussed later.

The next best alternative to detailed industry analysis is to apply the concepts discussed here in a general way. To determine industry performance for shorter periods of time (e.g., one year), investors should ask themselves the following questions:

1. Given the current and prospective economic situation, which industries are likely to show improving earnings?
2. Which industries are likely to show improving P/E ratios; or, what is the likely direction of interest rates and which industries would be most affected by a significant change in interest rates? A change in interest rates, other things being equal, leads to a change in the discount rate (and a change in the multiplier).
3. Which industries are likely to be most affected by possible future political events, such as a new administration, renewed inflation, new technology, an increase in defense spending, and so on?

To forecast industry performance in the long run, investors should ask the following questions:

1. Which industries are obvious candidates for growth and prosperity over, say, the next decade? In the early 1980s, industries such as microcomputers, the software industry, telecommunications, and robotics could be identified.
2. Which industries appear likely to have difficulties as the United States changes from an industrial to an information-collecting and processing economy? Possible candidates are automobiles and steel.

Sources of Industry Information

General information   Several sources provide basic data on industries, including the following:

1. Standard & Poor's: (a) *The Annual Analysis Handbook* with monthly supplements provides per-share statistics for the industries covered. The data include sales, profit margin, income taxes, depreciation, earnings, dividends, capital expenditures, and so on. (b) The *Industry Survey* covers major industries with basic analysis revised annually and current analysis revised quarterly. (c) Standard & Poor's *Register* provides Standard Industrial Classification codes for all companies.[11]

2. *Robert Morris Associates Annual Studies* and *Dun & Bradstreet Key Business Ratios* provide ratios for a number of industries.

3. The *Quarterly Financial Report for Manufacturing, Mining and Trade Corporations*, published jointly by the Federal Trade Commission and the Securities and Exchange Commission, provides timely information on individual industries. Included are data on sales, net profit, and so forth. Individual industries can be compared to groups of industries (e.g., all mining corporations) and to all manufacturing corporations.

4. *Forbes* magazine has an annual rating of industry performance in their early January issue. Five-year figures on profitability and growth of sales and earnings are shown for a large number of industries and for individual companies within those industries.[12] An excerpt from the 1987 issue is shown in Figure 11–2.[13] Thus, this source provides investors with calculated information they can use to assess industries (and companies within those industries).

5. *The Value Line Investment Survey* covers both individual companies and the industries that the covered companies comprise. Companies are organized by industry with each weekly issue giving information on several industries at a time. A write-up of industry developments, financial data, and trends introduces each group of companies (industry) covered by *Value Line*. Investors can obtain data on such variables as industry sales, operating margin, profit margin, tax rate, and capital structure.

   Value Line estimates industry statistics both for the current year and the coming year. It also *ranks* all industries in terms of timeliness (probable performance over the next 12 months); therefore, investors have a unique and readily available short-term forecast. Figure 11–3 shows a weekly ranking of all industries covered by *Value Line*.

6. As discussed earlier in the chapter, *The Media General Financial Weekly* publishes up-to-date weekly information on 60 industries, showing price performance over four recent periods. This is a convenient source of recent industry performance.

---

[11] Using the four-digit code starting with industry 0111 and going through industry 9661, companies are listed under each code in alphabetical order.

[12] Additional information includes the debt/equity ratio, return on total capital, and the net profit margin.

[13] Figure 11–2 is excerpted from the "Computers and Electronics" grouping used by *Forbes*.

Yardsticks of management performance

Company	% in -segment- sales/profits	Profitability — Return on equity					Growth — Sales			Growth — Earnings per share			earnings stability
		rank	5-year average	latest 12 months	debt as % of equity	net profit margin	rank	5-year average	latest 12 months	rank	5-year average	latest 12 months	
Honeywell	29/34	15	12.0%	8.7%	28.0%	3.2%	21	5.6%	9.1%	14	-1.7%	20.4%	very low
Computervision	•/DD	16	11.2	def	81.6	def	10	17.9	-2.5		NM	D-D	NM
Unisys	•/•	17	8.5	10.1	117.8	4.0	15	12.1	33.7	5	22.2	10.4	high
Data General	•/•	18	8.2	0.8	34.9	0.5	14	14.0	2.4	17	-10.2	-77.2	very low
Amdahl	•/•	19	7.5	4.6	32.7	2.4	9	19.2	6.6	10	11.0	-35.3	very low
General Instrument	29/PD	20	7.1	def	6.0	def	24	-0.4	-10.7		NM	D-D	NM
Zenith Electronics	30/NA	21	5.8	def	64.8	def	17	7.5	9.6		NM	P-D	NM
Datapoint	•/DD	22	2.0	def	42.1	def	18	6.5	-14.5		NM	D-D	NM
Gould	35/PD	23	2.0	def	65.9	def	25	-8.9	-21.5		NM	D-D	NM
Control Data	•/•	24	0.0	def	47.9	def	19	6.1	-7.8		NM	D-D	NM
Storage Technology	•/DD	25	def	NE	NE	2.3	23	-0.1	3.6		NM	D-P	NM
Compaq Computer	•/•		NA	25.4	44.7	6.2		NA	29.2		NM	52.3	NA
Medians			13.1	9.5	24.2	3.5		14.6	7.6		1.9	-1.0	
Electronic equipment													
EG&G	•/•	1	29.7%	24.5%	3.3%	4.3%	3	13.9%	1.8%	2	16.1%	-7.1%	very high
AMP	•/•	2	20.2	14.0	3.9	7.6	8	9.2	12.0	5	1.5	10.3	very low
Pitney Bowes	87/88	3	18.2	20.2	17.5	8.4	11	7.6	8.3	3	14.4	11.9	high
Bairnco	28/25	4	15.1	12.1	55.5	3.6	1	33.0	10.3	1	25.7	-12.2	very high
Perkin-Elmer	46/41	5	14.1	10.3	12.0	5.3	14	4.3	-0.4	8	-0.9	-13.6	very low
Tyler	35/ 5	6	14.0	6.3	111.8	1.3	9	9.2	3.1	9	-1.7	-38.9	very low
Tektronix	•/•	7	13.4	6.0	1.3	3.7	10	7.8	-5.5	7	0.8	-32.3	very low
M/A-Com	•/•	8	13.0	2.7	48.8	2.2	2	19.1	-31.6	6	0.9	-68.5	very low
North Amer Philips	27/31	9	12.2	4.5	48.1	1.1	6	11.4	4.3	4	2.0	-50.9	very low
General Signal	48/49	10	12.1	3.8	13.6	2.1	16	8	-7.1	13	-12.7	-67.0	very low average

● 90% or more. **DD:** Segment deficit, total deficit. **DP:** Segment deficit, total profit. **PD:** Segment profit, total deficit. D–D: Deficit to deficit. D–P Deficit to profit. P–D: Profit to deficit. def. Deficit. NA: Not available. NE: Negative equity. NM: Not meaningful. ‡‡Three-year growth. For further explanation, see page 61.

FIGURE 11–2 *Forbes* annual industry analysis for the computers and electronics industry, 1987 (other companies were included in this grouping).
Source: Forbes. Yardsticks of Management Performance, January 12, 1987, Forbes, Inc., 1987.

Specific information   A large number of publications that contain specific industry information are available. Industry magazines are a good example, including such publications as *Chemical Week* and *Automotive News*. Another source of specific industry information is trade associations, which compile statistics for their particular industries; examples are the American Banker's Association and the Iron and Steel Institute.

Obviously, brokerage firms prepare many reports on both companies and industries. Because their research analysts are typically organized along industry lines, reports are often issued on specific industries.

Summary

Industry analysis is the second of three steps in fundamental security analysis, following aggregate market analysis but preceding individual company analysis. The objective in this analysis is to identify those industries that will perform best in the future in terms of returns to stockholders.

INDUSTRIES, IN ORDER OF TIMELINESS*

Arrow (▲▼) before name indicates that a **significant change in Rank** has occurred since the preceding week.

1	Computer Software & Svcs.	24	Apparel	47	Electric Utility (East)	70	Multiform
2	Metals & Mining (General)	25	Coal/Alternate Energy	48	Packaging & Container	71	Steel (General)
3	Home Appliance	26	Metal Fabricating	49▲	Machinery (Const. & Mining)	72	Toys & School Supplies
4	Newspaper	27	Chemical (Basic)	50	Shoe	73	Silver
5	Gold (No. American)	28	Financial Services	51	Telecommunications	74	Retail (Special Lines)
6	Trucking/Transp. Leasing	29	Bank	52	Furn./Home Furnishings	75	Natural Gas (Diversified)
7	Paper & Forest Products	30	Brewing/Soft Drink	53	Aerospace/Defense	76▲	Manu. Housing/Rec. Veh.
8	Drug	31	European Diversified	54	Auto & Truck	77	Metals & Mining (Industrial)
9	Food Processing	32	Retail Store	55	Food Wholesalers	78	Recreation
10	Toiletries/Cosmetics	33	Insurance (Diversified)	56	Precision Instrument	79	Building Supplies
11	Industrial Services	34▼	Japanese Diversified	57	Maritime	80	Electronics
12	Chemical (Specialty)	35	Insurance (Prop./Casualty)	58	Real Estate	81	Restaurant
13	Publishing	36	Investment Company	59	Electric Utility (West)	82	Auto Parts (OEM)
14	Copper	37	Bank (Midwest)	60▼	Household Products	83	Petroleum (Producing)
15	Distilling/Tobbaco	38	Grocery	61	Machine Tool	84	Drugstore
16	Medical Supplies	39	Electric Utility (Central)	62	Natural Gas (Utility)	85	Broadcasting/Cable TV
17	Air Transport	40	Aluminum	63▼	Medical Services	86	Advertising
18	Chemical/Diversified	41	Cement	64	Canadian Energy	87	Railroad
19	Securities Brokerage	42	R.E.I.T.	65	Auto Parts (Replacement)	88	Oilfield Services/Equipment
20	Tire & Rubber	43	Textile	66	Machinery	89	Bank (Texas)
21	Savings & Loan	44	Computer & Peripherals	67	Office Equipment & Supplies	90	Semiconductor
22	Steel (Specialty)	45	Petroleum (Integrated)	68	Insurance (Life)	91	Steel (Integrated)
23	Building	46	Electrical Equipment	69	Hotel/Gaming		

*Based on the Timeliness ranks of the stocks in the industry

FIGURE 11–3 **Weekly Industrial Ranking in order of timeliness by The Value Line Investment Survey.**
Source: The Value Line Investment Survey. Summary of Advices and Index, January 23, 1987, p. 24. © 1987 Value Line, Inc. Reprinted by permission.

Is industry analysis valuable? Yes, because over the long term, 30 and 40 years, for example, some industries perform much better than others. Industry performance, however, is not consistent; past price performance does not always predict future price performance. Particularly over shorter periods such as one or two years, industry performance rankings may completely reverse themselves. Therefore, investors relying on past price performance may be disappointed in both their selections and their lost opportunities.

Although the term "industry" at first seems self-explanatory, industry definitions and classifications are not straightforward, and the trend toward diversification of activities over the years has blurred the lines even more. The Standard Industrial Classification system, a comprehensive scheme for classifying major industry groups, specific industries, specific functions, and specific products, brings some order to the problem. SIC codes are not the only system of industry classification, however; a number of investment information services—such as Standard & Poor's, Value Line, and Media General—use their own industry classifications.

To analyze industries, a useful first step is to examine their stage in the life cycle, which in its simplest form consists of the pioneering, expansion, and maturity stages. Most investors will usually be interested in the expansion stage, in which growth is rapid and risk is tolerable. A second industry analysis approach is business-cycle analysis. Industries perform differently at various stages in the business cycle. Investors should be aware of these relationships. A third phase involves a qualitative analysis of important factors affecting industries.

To value industries, investors should think in terms of the expected earnings and P/E ratios. Both of these variables are difficult to estimate. Both factors, however, are affected by the same variables that are important in aggregate market analysis and in individual company analysis.

Investors interested in evaluating future industry prospects have a wide range of data available for their use. These data can be used for a detailed, in-depth analysis of industries using standard security analysis techniques, for examining recent ratings of industry performance (e.g., the *Forbes* data in Figure 11–2), or as a readily available ranking of likely industry performance (for example, the *Value Line* industry rankings in Figure 11–3).

Key Words

Cyclical industries
Defensive industries
Growth industries
Industry life cycle

Interest-sensitive industries
Standard Industrial Classification
  (SIC) system

QUESTIONS AND PROBLEMS

1. Why is it difficult to classify industries?
2. Why is industry analysis valuable?
3. Name some industries that you would expect to perform well in the next 5 years, and in the next 10 to 15 years.
4. How consistent is year-to-year industry performance?
5. What are the stages in the life cycle for an industry? Can you think of other stages to add?
6. Name an industry that is currently in each of the three life-cycle stages.
7. In which stage of the life cycle do investors face the highest risk of losing a substantial part of the investment?
8. Which industries are the most sensitive to the business cycle? The least sensitive?

9. Explain how aggregate market analysis can be important in analyzing industries in relation to the business cycle.
10. Explain the concept used in valuing industries.
11. What sources of information would be useful to an investor doing a detailed industry analysis?
12. Explain how Figure 11–2 might be useful to an investor doing industry analysis.
13. Compare the Value Line industry ranking shown in Figure 11–3 to those provided by Value Line one year later. How closely do they correspond?
14. Pepsico, over the period 1976–1978, pursued a strong policy of acquisition. Until that time, the company was essentially in the soft drink business. Their acquisitions included the following companies in different industries:

	Percentage of Total Revenues	Percentage of Total Profits
Beverages	39	31
Food products	31	47
Food service	17	17
Transportation	9	2
Sporting goods	4	3
	100	100

In addition, foreign operations accounted for 19% of 1982 revenues, and 3% of operating profits.

a. Based on these figures, in what industry would you expect to find Pepsico? Use *The Value Line Investment Survey* to determine the industry classification for Pepsico.
b. Regardless of its classification, do you see any problems in evaluating the industry containing Pepsico if it, and other members of that industry, have revenue and profit breakdowns like Pepsico's?
c. Do you see any commonality to the acquisitions in relation to soft drinks?
d. Would you expect to find a reasonably close association between the soft drink industry and the food processing industry in terms of relative performance? Examine Figure 11–3 to determine how they ranked in early 1987 and then examine the latest rankings in *The Value Line Investment Survey*.

Selected References

Aber, John. "Industry Effects and Multivariate Stock Price Behavior." *Journal of Financial and Quantitative Analysis,* November 1976, pp. 617–624.

Browne, Lynn E. "High Technology Industry in the World Marketplace." *New England Economic Review,* May–June 1986, pp. 21–25.

Farrell, James, "Analyzing Covariation of Returns to Determine Homogeneous Stock Groupings," *Journal of Business,* April 1974, pp. 186–207.

King, Benjamin. "Market and Industry Factors in Stock Price Behavior." *Journal of Business,* January 1966, pp. 139–190.

Latané, Henry A., Tuttle, Donald L., and Jones, Charles P. *Security Analysis and Portfolio Management.* New York: Ronald Press, 1975.

Livingstone, Miles. "Industry Movements of Common Stocks." *Journal of Finance,* June 1977, pp. 861–874.

Meyers, Stephen. "A Re-examination of Market and Industry Factors in Stock Price Behavior." *Journal of Finance,* June 1973, pp. 695–705.

Porter, Michael E. "Industry Structure and Competitive Strategy: Keys to Profitability." *Financial Analysts Journal,* July–August 1980, pp. 30–41.

Porter, Michael E. *Competitive Advantage: Creating and Sustaining Superior Performance.* New York: Free Press, 1985.

Reilly, Frank and Drzycimski, Eugene. "Alternative Industry Performance and Risk." *Journal of Financial and Quantitative Analysis,* June 1974, pp. 423–446.

Rosenberg, Barr. "Extra-Market Components of Covariance in Security Returns." *Journal of Financial and Quantitative Analysis,* March 1974, pp. 263–274.

Wenglowski, Gary. "Industry Profit Analysis—A Progress Report and Some Predictions." Reprinted in *The C.F.A. Study Guide II,* 1983. Charlottesville, Va.: The Institute of Chartered Financial Analysts, 1982.

CHAPTER 12

COMPANY ANALYSIS

Given that market analysis indicates a favorable time to invest in common stocks and that an investor has analyzed industries to find those with the most promising future, it remains to choose promising companies within those industries. The last step in fundamental analysis, therefore, is to analyze individual companies. An investor should think in terms of—and analyze to the extent practical—the two components of fundamental value: earnings or dividend streams, and a required rate of return or P/E ratio.

Fundamental Analysis

Fundamental analysis at the company level involves analyzing the basic financial variables of the company in order to estimate the intrinsic value (per share) of the company. These variables include sales, profit margins, depreciation, the tax rate, sources of financing, asset utilization, and other factors. Additional analysis could involve the firm's competitive position in its industry, labor relations, technological changes, management, foreign competition, and so on. The end result of fundamental analysis is an estimate of the two factors that determine a security's (or industry's or the market's) value: a payments stream and a required rate of return.

As discussed in Chapter 9, the dividend valuation model is one of two basic frameworks used for explaining common stock valuation. Assuming that the dividend growth rate for a particular company can be expected to be constant over the future, the dividend valuation model reduces to the normal constant growth version shown as Equation 12–1 (Equation 9–5 from Chapter 9):

$$\text{Intrinsic value} = PV_{cs} = \frac{D_1}{k - g} \qquad (12\text{--}1)$$

where

PV_{cs} = the present value of the common stock today.
D_1 = the expected dollar dividend to be paid next period.
k = the required rate of return.
g = the expected future growth rate of dividends.

In fundamental analysis, the **intrinsic value** of a stock is its justified price; that is, the price justified by a company's fundamental financial variables.

Alternatively, for a short-run estimate of intrinsic value the earnings multiplier model could be used. To use this approach, we need an estimate of next year's earnings per share and the P/E ratio expected to prevail.[1] Intrinsic value is the product of the estimated earnings for a company and the estimated multiplier or P/E ratio, as shown in Equation 12–2.

$$\text{Intrinsic value} = EPS \times P/E \text{ Ratio} \qquad (12\text{--}2)$$

Using either Equations 12–1 or 12–2, a stock's calculated intrinsic value is compared to its current market price. If the intrinsic value is larger than the current market price, the stock would be considered undervalued—a buy. If intrinsic value is less than the market price, the stock would be considered overvalued and should be avoided or possibly sold if owned; further, an overvalued security could also be sold short.

As explained in Chapter 9, the intrinsic value approach used in fundamental analysis is predicated on a present value analysis. The value of a share is equal to the present value of all cash flows to be received from it. These cash flows could be earnings, dividends, or perhaps the sum of earnings and noncash expenses (i.e., depreciation, etc.). If defined correctly, these variables give equivalent results in a valuation model. Recall from Equation 9–11 that the P/E ratio is a function of D_1/E_1, k, and g, as shown in Equation 12–3, thereby linking Equations 12–1 and 12–2.

$$\frac{P_0}{E_1} = \frac{D_1/E_1}{k - g} \qquad (12\text{--}3)$$

---

[1] Technically, to calculate the intrinsic value of a stock using the multiplier method, analysts often determine what is called the normalized EPS, defined as the normal earnings for a company under typical operating conditions. Thus, unusual impacts on earnings are adjusted for, such as nonrecurring earnings or extraordinary earnings.

Therefore, we can state that the intrinsic value of a share of stock is a function of (using the dividend valuation model)

$$\text{Intrinsic value} = f(D_1, k, \text{ and } g)$$

or, using the multiplier model

$$\text{Intrinsic value} = f(E_1, P/E)$$

Combining the two approaches, we find that the intrinsic value for a common stock is a function of earnings or dividends, the ratio of dividends to earnings (the **dividend payout ratio**), the required rate of return, and the expected growth rate in dividends (or earnings).[2]

Investors can use either the dividend valuation approach (Equation 12–1) or the earnings multiple approach (Equation 12–2) in company analysis. For purposes of discussion, however, we will concentrate on earnings and P/E ratios for several reasons.

1. Dividends are paid from earnings; therefore, the D value in Equation 12–1 is a function of next period's earnings.
2. The multiplier model is more often used in actual practice and requires an earnings figure.
3. The required rate of return is a key component of the P/E ratio. If the required rate of return can be understood and estimated, so can the P/E ratio.

Understanding Earnings

To understand **earnings per share (EPS)** for a company, we must understand how EPS is derived and what it represents. For investors, an EPS figure is the bottom line—the item of major interest—in a company's financial statements.

The Financial Statements

Investors rely heavily on the **financial statements** of a corporation. They provide the major financial data used in investment decisions. In order to illustrate certain points in this general discussion, we will examine the 1985 financial statements for EG&G, Inc., a producer of technical and scientific products and services for customers worldwide.

The balance sheet The balance sheet shows the stock of assets for a corporation, as well as its liabilities and owner's equity, at one point in time. The amounts at which items are carried on the balance sheet are dictated by

---

[2] Under the constant growth version of the dividend valuation model, the expected growth rate in dividends is equal to the expected growth rate in earnings and stock price.

accounting conventions. Cash is the actual dollar amount, whereas marketable securities could be at cost or market value (EG&G's is at cost). Stockholders' equity and the fixed assets reflect book value.

The balance sheet for EG&G, shown in Table 12–1, is for the year 1985 with 1984 included as well.[3] The asset side is divided into current assets and long-term assets (labeled as property, plant, and equipment) plus some "other assets." In the case of EG&G, the net property, plant, and equipment is small compared to the current assets, whereas in the case of General Motors, for example, the fixed assets exceed the current assets.

The liabilities on a balance sheet are divided between current liabilities (payable within one year) and permanent liabilities (which include the stockholders' equity). For 1985, EG&G had $184 million in current liabilities, $16 million in long-term debt, and $203 million in "stockholders' equity," plus miscellaneous items. Note that the stockholders' investment includes 27,431,000 shares of stock issued with a par value of one dollar, some capital in excess of par value, and a substantial amount of retained earnings ($173 million). It is important to recognize that the retained earnings from previous years do not represent "spendable" funds for a company; rather, they designate that part of previous earnings not paid out as dividends. Although 1 million shares of preferred stock have been authorized by the board of directors, no shares were outstanding at the end of 1985.[4]

A number of financial ratios can be calculated from balance sheet data that indicate the company's financial strength (e.g., the current ratio, a measure of liquidity, or the debt to total assets ratio, a measure of leverage). Some of these ratios will be demonstrated later in the analysis.

The income statement This statement is used more frequently by investors, not only to assess current management performance but also as a basis for estimating the future profitability of the company. The income statement represents flows for a particular period, usually one year. Table 12–2 shows the income statement for EG&G, covering the years 1985, 1984, and 1983 (many income statements show only the current and previous years).

The key item for investors on the income statement is the after-tax net income, which, divided by the number of common shares outstanding, produces earnings per share. Earnings from continuing operations are used to judge the success of the company and are almost always what is reported by the financial press. Nonrecurring earnings, such as net extraordinary items that arise from unusual and infrequently occurring transactions, are separated from income from continuing operations.

Table 12–2 clearly illustrates the "flow" in an income statement. Starting

---

[3] Standard practice in financial statements is to show at least two years of results, allowing comparisons to be made.

[4] As explained in Chapter 2, preferred stock, though often treated by investors as a fixed income security, is in fact an equity security and is shown as part of the stockholders' equity.

TABLE 12-1 Consolidated Balance Sheet, EG&G, Inc. 1985

As of December 29, 1985 and December 30, 1984 (Dollars in thousands)	1985	1984
Current Assets:		
Cash and short-term investments	$ 17,374	$ 18,326
Accounts receivable (including unbilled receivables of $40,500 in 1985 and $38,000 in 1984) less reserves of $5,100 in 1985 and $3,500 in 1984	161,755	147,656
Inventories	75,757	70,829
Other (including prepaid income taxes of $8,000 in 1985 and $4,500 in 1984)	13,505	8,249
Total Current Assets	268,391	245,060
Property, Plant and Equipment, at cost:		
Land	2,746	2,364
Buildings and leasehold improvements	27,656	26,389
Machinery and equipment	88,401	71,987
	118,803	100,740
Less—Accumulated depreciation and amortization	78,744	67,971
Net Property, Plant and Equipment	40,059	32,769
Other Assets:		
Marketable investments	72,921	70,705
Other investments	14,333	12,667
Intangible assets	26,571	16,704
Other	7,536	9,418
Total Other Assets	121,361	109,494
Total Assets	$429,811	$387,323
Current Liabilities:		
Short-term debt and current maturities of long-term debt	$ 62,265	$ 81,368
Accounts payable	40,534	41,028
Accrued expenses		
Payroll	6,856	6,064
Employee benefits	29,539	30,952
Federal, foreign and state income taxes	20,713	20,840
Other	24,330	24,640
Total Current Liabilities:	184,237	204,892
Long-Term Debt	15,767	15,256
Deferred Income Taxes	17,976	12,649
Other Long-Term Liabilities	8,430	4,680

(handwritten margin notes: "— LT Assets" next to Property, Plant and Equipment)

(*continued*)

TABLE 12–1 (*Continued*)

As of December 29, 1985 and December 30, 1984	1985	1984
Stockholders' Equity:		
Preferred stock—$1 par value, authorized 1,000,000 shares; none outstanding	—	—
Common stock—$1 par value, authorized 100,000,000 shares; issued 27,431,000 shares in 1985 and 30,494,000 shares in 1984	27,431	30,494
Capital in excess of par value	13,352	16,743
Retained earnings	173,378	219,070
Cumulative translation adjustments	(3,963)	(6,049)
	210,198	260,258
Less—Cost of shares held in treasury	6,797	110,412
Total Stockholders' Equity	203,401	149,846
Total Liabilities and Stockholders' Equity	$429,811	$387,323

Source: Annual Report to Stockholders, 1985, EG&G. Courtesy of EG&G, Inc., pp. 34–35.

TABLE 12–2 **Consolidated Statement of Income, EG&G, Inc. 1985**

For the Three Years Ended December 29, 1985	1985	1984	1983
(Dollars in thousands except per share data)			
Revenues	$1,155,104	$1,079,813	$910,137
Net sales, contract revenues and fees	22,013	19,658	18,203
Other income	1,177,117	1,099,471	928,340
Costs and Expenses			
Costs of sales	943,025	878,269	739,823
Selling, general and administrative expenses	130,137	120,825	105,753
Other expenses	15,390	15,395	5,054
	1,088,552	1,014,489	850,630
Income Before Income Taxes	88,565	84,982	77,710
Provision for federal and foreign income taxes	32,857	31,443	31,065
Net Income	$ 55,708	$ 53,539	$ 46,645
Earnings Per Share	$2.07	$1.88	$1.56

Source: Annual Report to Stockholders, 1985, EG&G. Courtesy of EG&G, Inc., p. 36.

with revenues (net sales plus other income), costs and expenses are deducted, the largest of which are cost of sales. The difference (adjusted for certain items as necessary) is income before income taxes, which for EG&G in 1985 was $89 million.[5] Subtracting out a provision for taxes leaves a net income (total dollars) of $56 million, which divided by the weighted number of shares outstanding produces EPS of $2.07.[6]

Certifying the Statements

The earnings on an income statement are derived on the basis of **generally accepted accounting principles (GAAPs)**. The company adheres to a standard set of rules developed by the accounting profession on the basis of historical costs, which can be measured objectively. An auditor from an independent accounting firm certifies that the earnings have been derived according to accounting standards in a statement labeled the "auditor's report." Note that the auditor's report does not guarantee the accuracy or the quality of the earnings in an absolute sense, but only that the statements present fairly the financial position of the company for a particular period. The auditors are certifying, in effect, that generally accepted accounting principles were applied on a consistent basis. The Financial Accounting Standards Board (FASB), which succeeded the Accounting Principles Board of the American Institute of Certified Public Accountants in 1972, currently formulates accounting standards.

The Problem with Earnings

Although earnings in particular, and financial statements in general, are derived on the basis of GAAPs and certified in an auditor's report, a problem exists with earnings. The problem, simply stated, is that reported EPS for a company (i.e., accounting EPS) is not a precise figure that is readily comparable over time, and the EPS for different companies may not be comparable to each other.

The problem with earnings is that alternative accounting principles can be used to prepare the financial statements. Many of the items in the balance sheet and income statement can be accounted for in at least two ways, resulting in what one might call the "conservative" treatment and the "liberal" treatment of EPS. Given the number of items that constitute the financial statements, the possible number of acceptable (i.e., that conform to GAAPs) combinations that could be used is enormous. Holding everything else constant—such as sales, products, and operating ability—a company could produce several legal and permissible EPS figures depending solely on the accounting principles used. *Forbes* magazine once illustrated how a

---

[5] Interest expense of $11 million is included in "other expenses."

[6] In 1985, the weighted average shares for EG&G, which is used to calculate EPS, was 26,955,000.

single company, using only two sets of principles (liberal and conservative), could produce in one year an EPS of $1.99 per share or an EPS of $3.14, a number more than 50% higher.[7] Although this may be an extreme example, the question is, which EPS best represents the "true" position of a company? A good example of how reported income can be made to vary is shown in Box 12–1.

Reported EPS is a function of the many alternative GAAPs in use. In truth, it is extremely difficult, if not impossible, for the "true" performance of a company to be reflected consistently in one figure. And each company is different. So is it reasonable to expect one accounting system to capture the true performance of all companies? The business world is complex, and one can make a case for the necessity of alternative treatments of the same item or process, such as inventories or depreciation.

It is also worthwhile to remember that accountants are caught in the middle between investors, who want a clean, clear-cut EPS figure, and company management, which wishes to present the financial statements in the most favorable light. After all, management hires the accounting firm, and, subject to certain guidelines, management can change accounting firms. As long as the company follows GAAPs it may be difficult for the accountant to resist management pressures to use particular principles. At some point, an accounting firm may resign as a company's auditor as a result of the problems and pressures that can arise—see Box 12–1 for a good illustration.

It is also true that the FASB faces conflicting demands when it formulates or changes accounting principles. Various interest groups want items accounted for in specific ways. The end result is that the "standards" issued by the FASB are often compromises that do not fully resolve the particular issue, and in some cases, they may create additional complications. Since its formation, the FASB has issued numerous standards and exposure drafts and has tackled some very difficult issues such as inflation accounting and foreign currency translations. Much remains to be done, however, and this will probably remain true for a long time.

Should the FASB falter in its job, or investors actively demand more action in the way of "tighter" accounting rules, the government could intervene and issue its own rulings. The Securities and Exchange Commission has the authority to do this because corporations must file detailed financial data with it. In fact, the SEC has issued some definitions of acceptable accounting practices over the years, thereby acting as a prod to the accounting groups to continue their progress.

In conclusion, it is important for all investors to remember that reported EPS is not the precise figure that it first appears to be. Unless adjustments

---

[7] See "What Are Earnings? The Growing Credibility Gap," *Forbes*, May 15, 1967, pp. 28–29.

You can get rather significant acctg Δ's from yr to yr.
Cautious investor understand + look at footnotes

BOX 12–1   NOW YOU SEE IT, NOW YOU DON'T

Without warning, Coopers & Lybrand resigned on April 24 as auditor for Baltimore's USF&G Corp. What's the deal? Big Eight accounting firms don't often up and quit an audit engagement after 14 years, especially one that brings in fees of probably $1 million a year from an $8 billion property/casualty insurance company. Something big? Big indeed. Two weeks before the resignation, USF&G, prodded by Coopers & Lybrand, had restated its financial statements for 1983, 1984 and the first nine months of 1985. The results were not pretty. The restatement cut 1983's operating income by 19%, to $140 million, and slashed 1984's operating income from plus $93 million to minus $41 million.

What happened? Battered by huge underwriting losses since 1981, USF&G needed help. It discovered it could use its investment portfolio to exploit some of the new financial abstractions Wall Street has dreamed up in recent years. Until Coopers & Lybrand finally blew the whistle, financial wheeling and dealing enabled USF&G to boost investment income and take it into operating income.

Explains David O'Leary, an insurance stock analyst at Hartford, Conn.'s Fox-Pitt, Kelton, Inc., "USF&G was basically transferring money from capital to income. While its [reported investment] income was going up, capital was getting killed."

How do you transfer money from the investment portfolio to operating income? One clever USF&G strategy involved selling covered call options—that is, selling investors the right to buy stock in USF&G's portfolio at a predetermined price.

Suppose, hypothetically, that USF&G owned IBM at a cost of $100 a share. IBM rises to $150, so USF&G has earned a capital gain of $50. But the insurer might sell a $140 call (the right to buy the stock for $140) against its IBM for a premium of $20.

The accounting question is, Where do you record that $20 premium? As part of "realized gains or losses on investments"? Or as part of operating income, along with gains or losses on underwriting? Operating income, remember, is what analysts and investors tend to look at when judging an insurer's performance.

Until the restatement, USF&G was recording the entire premium as operating income. It was doing so despite the fact that part of the premium ($10 in our example) reflected a capital gain already in the stock when the call was sold. Then, when the call was exercised, USF&G would show a $10 capital loss—the stock, carried at $150 on the books, was being "sold" for $140. By sticking $10 of what had been a capital gain into income, USF&G effectively depleted the capital account to augment the operating income account. Coopers & Lybrand, then, required USF&G to put some of these capital gains back into "realized gains on investments."

Another of USF&G's devices to boost reported income involved buying dividends. USF&G would buy stocks before the dividend date of record, entitling it to receive the dividend and record investment income. Then, still before the record date, USF&G would agree to sell the stock ex-dividend at a capital loss—that is, at the market price, minus the dividend payment the new owner would not receive. Again—taking money out of the capital account and putting it into operating income. According to the restatement, these dividend machinations overstated operating income by $81 million ($1.49 a share) in 1984 and $120 million ($2.02 a share) in 1985.

There was more. In order to take unrealized gains on some of its debt securities into net income, USF&G would sell and then immediately repurchase the securities. Similar "wash sales" are common to realize losses near the end of the year for tax purposes. But neither the IRS nor the accountants have any standards dealing with wash sales to realize gains. Only after Coopers & Lybrand argued that the economic substance of the wash sale transaction was not really a sale did USF&G restate the questionable gains—which had, it now appears, overstated net income by $52 million in 1984 alone.

USF&G executives seek to shift the blame to fuzzy accounting rules. "There are so many new ways to invest your money and trade your securities," contends Paul Schlough, USF&G's vice president for investor relations, "that the accounting treatment never really was very clear." Schlough might have a point—except for the rules of common sense, and the fact that other firms have been more conservative. Several mutual fund companies and at least two other insurers (Combined International and American General), for example, also write covered call options but mostly credit all proceeds to capital gains, not investment income.

Are USF&G's shenanigans unique? Probably not. The Securities & Exchange Commission was worried enough that it

asked the Financial Accounting Standards Board to put a major project concerning "financial instruments"—such as options—on the FASB's already crowded agenda. The board has its work cut out. "The area of financial instruments is one of the final frontiers," says John Deming, KMG Main Hurdman's director of accounting. "There is no real authoritative accounting literature, and anyway, Wall Street seems to come out with a new scheme every day."

What of Coopers & Lybrand's partners, without whose prodding USF&G might still be magically turning capital gains into income? The firm refuses to comment on the USF&G affair. That may be because Coopers rendered clean opinions for USF&G's 1983 and 1984 reports; those opinions may have helped USF&G in raising $268 million in much-needed capital through two stock offerings last year. A shareholder class action suit was filed against Coopers and USF&G soon after the restatement, alleging negligent misrepresentation and fraud.

Perhaps a little late, the accountants nonetheless did the courageous thing in forcing its client to stop playing accounting games. What a pity Coopers ends up paying for its courage by being sued as well as by losing a valuable account.

Source: John Heins, "Now You See It, Now You Don't," *Forbes*, June 30, 1986, pp. 110–111. Reprinted by permission of *Forbes* magazine, June 30, 1986. © Forbes Inc., 1986.

are made, EPS may not be comparable on either a time series or a cross-sectional basis. Such adjustments, however, are typically difficult to make and require considerable expertise in accounting and financial analysis. The best advice for the investor is to go ahead and use the reported EPS because it is all that is normally available, and the majority of investors will also have to rely on this figure. Investors should, however, be aware of the potential problems involved in EPS and constantly keep in mind its nature and derivation.

Some EPS figures are better than others in the sense that they have been derived using more reasonable (i.e., conservative) principles. In other words, they are of a higher quality. The quality of EPS is a concept that should be considered by thoughtful investors, and is examined in the next section.

The Concept of Earnings Quality

In a recent article on the "quality" of earnings, Bernstein and Seigel stated:[8]

> . . . a company's reported earnings figure is often taken by the unsophisticated user of financial statements as the quantitative measure of the firm's well-being. Of course, any professional knows that earnings numbers are in *large part* the product of conscious and often subjective choices between various accounting treatments and business options, as well as of various external economic factors. . . . If he wants to assess the true earning power of each company, the financial statement user must make some determination of the "quality" of its earnings" (emphasis added).

Although there are no absolute elements of earnings quality, the authors do present some guidelines for determining quality. These include the following:

1. *Liberal versus conservative accounting policy*. In general, conservatively determined earnings are of a higher quality because they are less likely to be overstated.
2. *Integrity of the reporting period*. To what degree do earnings benefit from past earnings or borrow from future earnings? Quality exists when the accounting policies used reflect "economic reality."
3. *Business choices—discretionary costs*. Earnings quality is related to proper provision for the maintenance of assets and earning power. Control over discretionary costs can be used to manipulate reported income.
4. *External factors—variability*. Earnings that are less variable are usually considered to be of higher quality.
5. *Balance sheet analysis*. The riskiness of the assets and liabilities can be analyzed as a complement to other checks on quality.

Overall, the authors argue that earnings figures should have integrity (be free of manipulations to increase reported income) and reliability (provide a good indication of earning power). However, although all investors would agree that earnings quality is important, the concept itself is elusive and in

---

[8] See Leopold Bernstein and Joel Seigel, "The Concept of Earnings Quality," *Financial Analysts Journal*, July–August 1979.

the final analysis, subjectively determined. Given this problem, is the concept used in practice?

Seigel surveyed accountants, security analysts, and financial managers to see how they view earnings quality.[9] The responses indicated that these groups are familiar with this concept and find it "meaningful and useful," although they also recognized the elusive nature of the quality of earnings. Regardless of its elusiveness, investors should pay some attention to the quality of EPS.

The Determinants of Earnings

On a company level, EPS is the culmination of several factors working in succession. We will examine these determining factors in steps by analyzing, through financial ratios, the variables that interact to determine the company's EPS. This financial ratio analysis can be useful to a company in assessing its strengths and weaknesses, and to investors in understanding earnings, both currently and prospectively. The ratios involved in each step are shown on the left side, and their application to EG&G's data for 1985 on the right side.

STEP 1   What Determines EPS?

$$\text{EPS} = \text{ROE} \times \text{Book value per share} \qquad (12\text{--}4)$$

$$2.07 = .274 \times 7.55$$

where ROE = return on equity and book value per share is the stockholders' equity.

		For EG&G	$	Return
EPS =	$\dfrac{\text{Net income after taxes}}{\text{Shares outstanding}}$	$\dfrac{\$55,708,000}{26,955,000}$	= \$2.07	—
ROE =	$\dfrac{\text{Net income after taxes}}{\text{Stockholders' equity}}$	$\dfrac{\$55,708,000}{203,401,000}$	= —	0.274
Book value =	$\dfrac{\text{Stockholders' equity}}{\text{Shares outstanding}}$	$\dfrac{\$203,401,000}{26,955,000}$	= \$7.55	—

Note that both factors, ROE and book value, determine the EPS. The ROE is the rate at which stockholders earn on their portion of the capital financing the company. Book value measures the accounting value of the stockholders' equity. In EG&G's case in 1985, the ROE was 27.4% and the book value was $7.55 per share.[10] Therefore, EPS equaled

$$\$7.55 \times 0.274 = \$2.07$$

---

[9] See Joel Seigel, "The 'Quality of Earnings' Concept—A Survey," *Financial Analysts Journal*, March–April 1982, pp. 60–64.

[10] This book value calculation uses weighted shares outstanding in 1985.

STEP 2   What Determines ROE?

The **return on equity (ROE)** is a result of the company's profitability on its assets and the manner in which it has financed those assets, as expressed in Equation (12–5).

$$ROE = ROA \times Leverage \qquad (12\text{–}5)$$

where ROA = return on assets and leverage reflects how the assets are financed (i.e., owners' money or creditors' money).

			Return	Leverage factor
ROE =	$\dfrac{\text{Net income}}{\text{Equity}}$	$\dfrac{\$55,708,000}{\$203,401,000}$ =	0.274	—
ROA =	$\dfrac{\text{Net income}}{\text{Total assets}}$	$\dfrac{\$55,708,000}{\$429,811,000}$ =	0.130	—
Leverage =	$\dfrac{\text{Total assets}}{\text{Equity}}$	$\dfrac{\$429,811,000}{\$203,401,000}$ =	—	2.11

Return on assets (ROA) is a fundamental measure of firm profitability, reflecting how effectively and efficiently the firm's assets are used. Obviously, the higher the net income for a given amount of assets, the better the return. For EG&G, the return on assets is 0.13. The ROA can be improved by increasing the net income more than the assets (in percentage terms), or by using the existing assets even more efficiently.

The **leverage** ratio measures how the firm finances its assets.[11] Basically, it can finance with either debt or equity. Debt is a cheaper source of financing, but a more risky method because of the fixed interest payments that must be systematically repaid on time to avoid bankruptcy. Leverage can magnify the returns to the stockholders (favorable leverage) or diminish them (unfavorable leverage). Thus, any given ROA can be magnified into a higher ROE by the judicious use of debt financing. The converse, however, applies—injudicious use of debt can lower the ROE below the ROA.

In 1985, EG&G's ratio of total debt to total assets was about 48% (not counting deferred federal income taxes). Thus, the creditors are financing about one-half of the assets, and the stockholders the other half. Dividing total assets by equity produces an *equity multiplier* of 2.11, which can be used as the measure of leverage.

Combining these two factors, ROA and leverage, for EG&G to obtain ROE results in

$$ROE = 2.11 \times 0.13 = 0.274$$

---

[11] Leverage can be measured in several ways, such as the ratio of total debt to total assets or the ratio of debt to equity.

In sum, both the investment decision (the ROA) and the financing decision (leverage) affect the returns to the stockholders. A firm can use its assets effectively, resulting in a high ROA, and decrease this ratio by poor financing decisions. Conversely, it can experience mediocre returns from its assets, but boost the ROA figure by clever financing. Finally, a firm could do a very good or very bad job on both determinants of ROE. To fully understand the EPS for a given company, investors should examine both how the assets are used and how they are financed.

As an example of the financing impact on EPS, assume the ROA for EG&G remains at 0.13, but that any asset increase is financed by additional debt. Let us assume that the leverage ratio goes to 2.20, which is the same as assuming that the debt ratio goes to 0.55 of total assets; that is, [1 − (1/2.20)] = 0.55.

$$ROE = 0.13 \times 2.20$$

$$= 0.286$$

In this example, the ROE is boosted a full percentage point which, in turn, would increase the EPS. In fact, as long as the marginal debt cost is less than the marginal return on assets, the additional debt financing will increase the ROE and therefore the EPS (although this is not evident in the analysis). What does not show here, however, is the impact of leverage on the risk of the firm. Remember that in this analysis we are examining only the determinants of EPS but that two factors, EPS and a multiplier, are required to determine value. An increase in leverage may raise the riskiness of the company more than enough to offset the increased EPS, thereby lowering the value of the company.

STEP 3   What Determines Return on Assets?

ROA is an important measure of a firm's profitability. It is determined by two factors, as shown in (12–6).

$$ROA = \text{Net income margin} \times \text{Turnover} \qquad (12\text{–}6)$$

where

$$ROA = \frac{\text{Net income}}{\text{Total assets}} \quad \frac{\$55,708,000}{\$429,811,000} = 0.13$$

$$\text{Net income margin} = \frac{\text{Net income}}{\text{Sales}} \quad \frac{\$55,708,000}{\$1,177,117,000} = 0.047$$

$$\text{Turnover} = \frac{\text{Sales}}{\text{Total assets}} \quad \frac{\$1,177,117,000}{\$429,811,000} = 2.739$$

The first item affecting ROA, the net income margin, measures the firm's earning power on its sales (revenue). How much net return is realized from sales, given all costs? Obviously, the more the firm earns per dollar of sales, the better. EG&G's net income margin is 4.7%.

Turnover is a measure of efficiency. Given some amount of total assets, how much in sales can be generated? The more sales per dollar of assets, where each dollar of assets has to be financed with a source of funds bearing a cost, the better it is for a firm. The firm may have some assets that are unproductive, thereby adversely affecting its efficiency. EG&G's turnover rate is almost three; combining the two ratios,[12]

$$\text{ROA} = 0.047 \times 2.739 = 0.129 \text{ or } 0.13$$

Again, one of the determinants of ROA may be able to offset poor performance in the other. The net income margin may be low, but the firm may generate more sales per dollar of assets than comparable firms. Conversely, poor turnover may be partially offset by high net profitability.

STEP 4 What Determines the Net Income Margin?

The net income margin is a function of two ratios.

$$\text{Net income margin} = \frac{\text{Net income}}{\text{EBIT}} \times \frac{\text{EBIT}}{\text{Sales}} \qquad (12\text{--}7)$$

where

$$\text{EBIT} = \text{earnings before interest and taxes}$$

$$\text{Net income margin} = \frac{\text{Net income}}{\text{Sales}} \quad \frac{\$55,708,000}{\$1,177,117,000} = 0.047$$

$$\text{Income ratio} = \frac{\text{Net income}}{\text{EBIT}} \quad \frac{\$55,708,000}{\$100,061,000} = 0.557$$

$$\text{Operating efficiency} = \frac{\text{EBIT}^{13}}{\text{Sales}} \quad \frac{\$100,061,000}{\$1,177,117,000} = 0.085$$

The income ratio relates the net income after tax to the EBIT. It reflects the impact of interest and taxes on net income. If these variables decline, the income ratio would rise, as would the net income margin (if other things are equal). Firms can lower taxes through the use of credits, such as the investment tax credit and a credit for net operating losses suffered in earlier years. Interest expense, for a given amount of debt, will decline as market interest rates decline. Of course, the firm could also change the amount of debt it uses to finance its assets.

The EBIT/sales ratio is a measure of the firm's ability to operate efficiently; that is, EBIT reflects the earnings before the financing decision is accounted for by subtracting the interest expense, and before the provision for income taxes. The larger the EBIT per dollar of sales, the better. In effect, the EBIT reflects the gross margin on sales.

---

[12] Rounding errors account for the difference between 0.13 above and 0.129 here.

[13] EBIT is computed as income before income taxes (from Table 12–2) plus 1985 interest expense of $11,496,000 (obtained from the footnotes accompanying the statements).

For EG&G, the net income margin is

$$0.557 \times 0.085 = 0.047 \text{ or } 4.7\%$$

The advantage of analyzing these earnings determinants is to be able to determine the strengths and weaknesses of a particular company. Various factors interrelate to determine EPS. Some of these factors—for example, the financing decision—are under the control of the company's management, but others are not—for example, the marginal tax rate paid by corporations and the level of market interest rates.

On a conceptual basis, it is easy to see how these factors affect EPS. Consider the manufacturers of home computers in the early 1980s. Early entrants in the business were able to expand volume as the total sales grew, thereby gaining operating efficiency. This increasing efficiency had an impact on EBIT/sales, and led to an increase in EPS (during this time, profit margins held). With increasing competition, however, the net income margin declined as prices were cut to meet the competition. The ROA was negatively affected and this led to a decline for most companies in ROE and EPS—in some cases by disastrous dimensions.

Importance of Analysis of Earnings

Investors devote considerable attention to earnings (EPS) because this is one of the two components of value. The reported earnings of corporations, both annual and quarterly, are studied intensively as clues to the profitability of the firm, both current and future. No one should underestimate the importance of EPS. Investors may not understand fully the many accounting principles on which earnings are based, but nearly all investors have access to reported EPS and pay attention to their announcement in *The Wall Street Journal* or other source.

Why all this attention to EPS? A graphic case for the emphasis on earnings can be made by examining Figure 12–1, which shows the 50 best and worst stocks for a five-year period. The top 50 stocks from the sample of 650 companies studied showed a five-year price appreciation of 182%, with a change in EPS of 199%; for the bottom 50 performers, with a price depreciation of −62%, the change in EPS was −61%. This figure dramatically demonstrates the importance of *reported* EPS in common stock analysis. Although all comparisons of earnings and stock prices are not as striking as Figure 12–1, EPS changes and price changes are usually closely related for the best performing and worst performing stock.

Figure 12–1 shows the importance of reported earnings. A logical question to ask next is, should stocks that experience the largest growth in EPS have the largest risk-adjusted returns? A study by Elton, Gruber, and Gultekin examined the risk-adjusted excess returns available from buying stocks

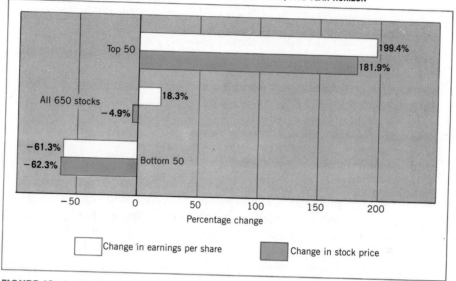

MEDIAN CHANGES IN EARNINGS AND STOCK PRICE, FIVE-YEAR HORIZON

Top 50 — 199.4% / 181.9%
All 650 stocks — 18.3% / −4.9%
Bottom 50 — −61.3% / −62.3%

Percentage change: −50, 0, 50, 100, 150, 200

☐ Change in earnings per share   ▨ Change in stock price

FIGURE 12–1 Median changes in earnings and stock price: five-year horizon, 1966–1970.

Source: V. Niederhoffer and P. J. Regan, "Earnings Changes, Analysts' Forecasts and Stock Prices," *Financial Analysts Journal,* Vol. 28 (May–June 1972), p. 71. Reprinted by permission.

on the basis of next year's growth in earnings.[14] They found that those stocks with the highest future growth in EPS showed the highest risk-adjusted returns. For the 30% of the companies with the highest growth in EPS, the risk-adjusted excess return was 7.48%; for the 30% with the lowest growth, the risk-adjusted excess return was −4.93%. Clearly, therefore, growth in reported earnings affects stock prices in a highly significant manner.

Note that the EPS that matters and is used to value stocks is the future (expected) EPS. Current stock price is a function of the future stream of earnings and the P/E ratio, not the past earnings. If investors knew what the EPS for a particular company would be next year, they could achieve good results in the market.

One method of assessing the future EPS for a company is to determine its EPS growth rate. Knowing the current EPS and the growth rate in EPS, future EPS can be calculated easily. That is

$$E_1 = E_0(1 + g)$$

---

[14] E. Elton, M. Gruber, and M. Gultekin, "The Usefulness of Analyst Estimates of Earnings," unpublished manuscript, 1978. This article is discussed in E. Elton and M. Gruber, *Modern Portfolio Theory and Investment Analysis,* 3rd ed. (New York: John Wiley, 1987), pp. 435–436.

where

E_1 = next period's EPS

E_0 = current EPS

g = the expected growth rate in EPS

$$E_2 = E_0(1 + g)^2$$

and so on.

The logical questions to answer, therefore, are what determines earnings growth and how well can such growth be predicted?

Determining the Earnings Growth

Investors are, and should be, concerned with future growth in the EPS for a company because, as shown in Figure 12–1, such changes will be closely associated with price changes. What determines the earnings growth rate?

The growth rate of earnings or dividends, g, is a function of the ROE (r) and the **retention rate** (b), as in Equation 12–8:[15]

$$g = rb \qquad (12\text{–}8)$$

where the retention rate = 1 − dividend payout ratio.

In order to estimate g, therefore, it is necessary to estimate r and b. Payout ratios for most companies vary over time, but reasonable estimates can often be obtained for a particular company. We have previously examined ROE and found that it is influenced by several variables.

ROE can be shown to be a function of three forces: asset efficiency, net income margin, and leverage. Using the ratios developed from the previous section,

$$\text{ROE} = \frac{\text{Sales}}{\text{Assets}} \times \frac{\text{Net Income}}{\text{Sales}} \times \frac{\text{Assets}}{\text{Equity}} \qquad (12\text{–}9)$$

EG&G's 1985 ROE, as discussed, was 0.274. Using Equation 12–9,

$$\text{ROE} = \frac{\$1,177,117,000}{\$429,811,000} \times \frac{\$55,708,000}{\$1,177,117,000} \times \frac{\$429,811,000}{\$203,401,000}$$

$$= 2.739 \times 0.047 \times 2.11$$

$$\text{ROE} = 0.272$$

---

[15] Technically, g is defined as the expected growth rate in dividends. However, the dividend growth rate is clearly influenced by the earnings growth rate. Although dividend and earnings growth rates can diverge in the short run, such differences would not be expected to continue for long periods of time. The standard assumption in security analysis is that g represents the growth rate for both dividends and earnings.

To estimate the future growth rate for EG&G, it is necessary to estimate those factors that will affect the ROE and the retention rate.

In the case of EG&G, the payout ratio for the years 1982 through 1985 averaged about 22%, although the ratio increased somewhat in 1985 to 23%. The retention rate is, therefore, about 78%. The ROE for these same five years averaged about 25%. For EG&G, investors might assume that the average of the previous five years is the best estimate of the future and, therefore, g is

$$g = 0.78(0.25) = 0.195$$
$$= 19.5\%$$

Although the payout ratio variable has been quite stable for EG&G, it is usually difficult to estimate the three factors that determine ROE—efficiency, net income margin, and leverage. EG&G financial ratios are reasonably stable, but they do change from year to year.

Equation 12–8 is one of the principal calculations in fundamental security analysis and is often used by analysts. An alternative to estimating the components of the growth rate is to use the past g values to predict future growth. Again, the important variable in company analysis is the change in earnings over some future period. How well does the past growth rate of earnings for a particular company predict the future growth rate?

Predicting Earnings Growth

As we have seen, the intrinsic value and actual market price of a common stock are directly (positively) related to the level and growth of its EPS. Therefore, one of the most important parts of company analysis, and of fundamental security analysis in general, is the projection of earnings growth. Other things being equal, those companies with strong earnings growth in the future are the most probable candidates for further strong price appreciation. Earnings changes (i.e., growth) are the key to fundamental stock analysis.

Given the importance of earnings growth, the logical question becomes, is past growth an indicator of future growth? An investor might naturally assume that stocks with previous high growth rates of EPS would have high growth rates in the future. Unfortunately, empirical studies do not support this assumption; according to available evidence, both British and American companies indicate the lack of persistence in earnings trends.[16] Two simple

---

[16] See, for example, I. M. D. Little, "Higgledy Piggledy Growth," *Bulletin of the Oxford University Institute of Economics and Statistics,* Vol. 24 (November 1962), pp. 389–412; R. Trent, "Corporate Growth Rates: An Analysis of Their Intertemporal Association," *Southern Journal of Business,* Vol. 4 (October 1969), pp. 196–210; and J. Lintner and R. Glauber, "Higgledy-Piggledy Growth in America," unpublished manuscript, 1969 (this article is discussed in Elton and Gruber, *Modern Portfolio Theory,* pp. 431–432).

examples suffice to establish this finding. Ford Motor Company showed an annual rate of change in EPS for the 10 years and five years ending in 1986 of 17% and 42%, respectively.[17] Was it reasonable to assume that such growth rates would persist in an industry as competitive as automobiles? In the case of EG&G, a relatively stable company that has demonstrated steady growth in EPS since 1969 (i.e., EPS increased in each successive year), the EPS growth rates for each of the three years ending in 1985 were 14%, 16%, and 13%, respectively. Which of these growth rates, if any, is most likely to continue in the future?

Because of the lack of consistency in earnings trends, investors, who need estimates of future EPS, cannot simply assume that trends will continue. They can estimate the expected growth in dividends or earnings, using Equation 12–8, or they can use EPS forecasts, provided either mechanically (i.e., by equation) or by security analysts. Since earnings forecasts are widely available from brokerage houses and other organizations, or can be computed by calculator or computer, investors need to consider the use, and value, of earnings forecasts.

Working with Earnings Forecasts

The preceding discussion has established two important points in the fundamental security analysis process for individual companies.

1. EPS is the key to future price changes in a common stock. Stocks with large earnings changes are the most likely candidate to show large price changes, either positive or negative.
2. The earnings growth rate, or persistence in the earnings trend, is not easily predicted. Investors cannot simply use the past rate of growth in EPS to predict the future rate of growth.

The investors' problem, therefore, is to determine (1) how to obtain an earnings forecast, (2) which forecast provides the more useful information (mechanical estimates or analysts' estimates), and (3) how expectations of future earnings can best be used in selecting stocks. We will consider each of these topics in turn.

Obtaining a Forecast of EPS

Security analysts and earnings forecasts   Among the most obvious sources of earnings forecasts are security analysts, who make such forecasts as a part of their job. Because of the widespread availability of this type of earnings information, it is worthwhile to examine how valuable the earnings projections of security analysts are.[18]

---

[17] *The Value Line Investment Survey*, December 26, 1986, p. 105.
[18] *The Value Line Investment Survey*, for example, forecasts quarterly earnings for several quarters ahead for each company covered.

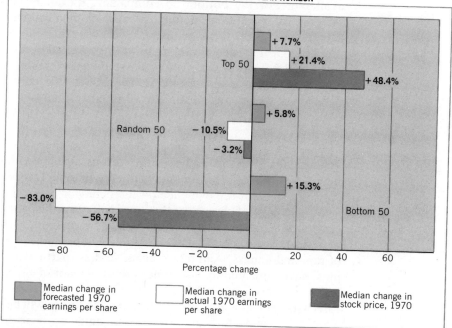

FIGURE 12–2 **Median changes in forecasted earnings, actual earnings, and stock price: one-year horizon.**
Source: V. Niederhoffer and P. J. Regan, ''Earnings Changes, Analysts' Forecasts and Stock Prices,'' *Financial Analysts Journal,* Vol. 28 (May–June 1972), p. 71. Reprinted by permission.

Malkiel and Cragg, in a well-known study of the earnings forecasts of security analysts, found that these estimates were not very accurate.[19] The correlations between the rate forecast and the realized growth rate were low. The analysts apparently relied heavily on past growth rates, which, as noted previously, is not a reliable method of forecasting earnings growth. The average correlation coefficient between actual earnings growth and forecast growth for the five institutional investors studied was only 0.35.

Niederhoffer and Regan, in the study that showed the association between earnings and stock prices (Figure 12–1), also examined analysts' ability to forecast earnings for a one-year horizon (1970). Figure 12–2 shows the top and bottom 50 companies (and a random 50 companies) from the sample in terms of actual price changes for one year, the actual earnings change, and the forecasted earnings change. For the top 50 companies, analysts underes-

---

[19]B. Malkiel and J. Cragg, ''Expectations and the Structure of Share Prices,'' *American Economic Review,* Vol. 60 (September 1970), pp. 601–617.

timated the earnings changes in 89% of the cases for which estimates were available. For the bottom 50 companies, the analysts overestimated the earnings for every single company for which data were available; that is, the actual earnings for these companies were less than the forecasted earnings.

Elton, Gruber, and Gultekin, in the study cited earlier, found that investors could not earn excess returns by buying and selling stocks on the basis of the consensus estimate of earnings growth (the consensus estimate was defined as the average estimate of security analysts at major brokerage houses).

Mechanical estimates of earnings forecasts   An alternative method of obtaining earnings forecasts is the use of various mechanical procedures such as time series models. In deciding what type of model to use, it is necessary to consider some of the evidence on the behavior of earnings over time.

Studies of the behavior of the time path of earnings have produced mixed results. Most of the early studies indicated randomness in the growth rates of annual earnings, as discussed earlier. Other studies found some evidence of nonrandomness. And more recent studies, particularly of quarterly earnings, have indicated that the time series behavior of earnings is not random.

Time series analysis involves the use of historical data to make earnings forecasts. The model used assumes that the future will be similar to the past. The series being forecast, EPS, is assumed to have trend elements—an average value, seasonal factors, and error. The moving average technique is a simple example of the time series model for forecasting EPS. Exponential smoothing, which assigns differing weights to past values, is an example of a more sophisticated technique. A regression equation would represent another sophisticated technique for making forecasts; the regression equation could handle several variables, such as trend and seasonal factors.

(2) Which Forecasts Are Best?

Evidence is mixed whether mechanical forecasts or estimates by security analysts are more reliable. Earlier studies found that analysts' forecasts were not more accurate than sophisticated time series forecasts.[20] A later study of Brown and Rozeff (BR) that received considerable attention found the opposite—the results "overwhelmingly" favored the analysts.[21] BR found that earnings forecasts made by *The Value Line Investment Survey* were consistently significantly better than those produced by well-known time series models, including the sophisticated Box–Jenkins method. Such a

---

[20] See J. Cragg and B. Malkiel, "The Consensus and Accuracy of Some Predictions of the Growth of Corporate Earnings," *Journal of Finance*, March 1968, pp. 67–84 and E. Elton and M. Gruber, "Earnings Estimates and the Accuracy of Expectational Data," *Management Science*, April 1972, pp. 409–424.

[21] L. Brown and M. Rozeff, "The Superiority of Analyst Forecasts as Measures of Expectations: Evidence from Earnings." *The Journal of Finance*, Vol. 33 (March 1978), pp. 1–16.

finding is reassuring from an economic theory standpoint because analysts' forecasts cost more than time series forecasts.

Even if investors accept the results of this study as to the *relative* superiority of analysts' forecasts, the message in Figure 12–2 remains true today. Analysts often over- or underestimate the earnings that are actually realized. For recent evidence of this see Box 12–2, which indicates that analysts, in estimating the earnings for the stocks in the Dow Jones Industrial Average for 1985 and 1986, made average errors in the range of 21% to 30%.

BOX 12–2 THE INACCURACY OF EARNINGS FORECASTS

The good news was that the Dow went way up. The bad news, for people who take Wall Street analysis seriously, is that the move was completely independent of earnings forecasts.

A year ago market watchers were talking about a 1900 Dow within 18 months. The scientific basis for this wild forecast, at a time when the Dow was a mere 1327, was earnings estimates. For those we turned to compilations by the Institutional Brokers Estimate System (IBES), which tracks the work of over 2,500 Wall Street analysts. The consensus was for the 30 Dow stocks to earn $133 in 1985 and $162 in 1986, a gain of 22%.

The price forecast came true in July, earlier than predicted. But the circumstances don't lend much credit to the forecasters. The consensus earnings forecasts were wildly wide of the mark. Instead of the $162 predicted for 1986, current expectation is $127.

Errors in the total Dow earnings, moreover, don't display the full fallibility of the forecasters, since high guesses for some companies offset low guesses for others. Consider them one at a time and it turns out that the average error was 21% for 1985. Assuming the current estimates for 1986 stand up—a generous assumption—the year-ahead estimates for 1986 were off by an average 30%.

Bethlehem Steel was supposed to earn $2.20 in 1986 but has already lost $2.16. Inco was going to earn $1.35 but now may only break even. The pros had no idea that 1986 would be terrible for IBM. Unexpected writeoffs can't explain away the mistakes.

Yet the stocks moved. The better earnings didn't come through, but higher price/earnings ratios did. Threatened takeovers of Goodyear and Union Carbide helped. More important is that the stock market has a distant horizon. Wall Street has, for example, rewarded Eastman Kodak for its staff cuts (stock up 45% since last October), though the restructuring could trim more than 80 cents from 1986's bottom line.

For next year, the Dow is supposed to earn $156. What if the earnings go up, but this time the P/Es go down? Stock analysts may make the stock market more interesting, but they don't do much to make it more predictable.

Source: Adapted from Michael Ozanian, "Right for the Wrong Reasons," *Forbes,* December 1, 1986, pp. 244–247. Adapted by permission of *Forbes* magazine, December 1, 1986. © Forbes Inc., 1986.

(3) Actual EPS versus Expectations about EPS

We have established that earnings changes and stock price changes are highly correlated. We have also discussed the necessity of forecasting EPS and how these forecasts can be obtained. What remains is to examine the role of expectations about earnings in selecting common stocks.

The association between earnings and stock prices is more complicated than simply demonstrating a correlation (association) between earnings changes and stock prices changes. Investor expectations are also important in an environment dominated by uncertainty. Investors must form expectations about EPS, and these expectations should be incorporated into stock prices if markets are efficient. Although these expectations will often be inaccurate, they play a key role in affecting stock prices. Malkiel and Cragg, in the study cited earlier, concluded that in making accurate one-year predictions, "It is far more important to know what the market will think the growth rate of earnings will be next year rather than to know the (actual) realized long-term growth rate."[22]

Similarly, Niederhoffer and Regan found in their study that the actual change in earnings of most of the best-performing companies was higher than that predicted by the analysts. For the worst performing companies, the actual change in earnings was less than predicted. Therefore, the difference, or *earnings surprise factor,* is associated with significant adjustments in the price of the stock.

As Latané and Jones have pointed out, new information about a stock is unexpected information.[23] What is important about EPS in terms of stock prices is the difference between what the market (i.e., investors in general) was expecting the EPS to be and what was actually reported by the company. Unexpected information about earnings calls for a revision in investor probability beliefs about the future and, therefore, an adjustment in the price of the stock.

To assess the impact of the surprise factor in EPS, Latané and Jones developed a model to express and use the earnings surprise factor in the quarterly EPS of companies. The resulting criterion represents the difference between the actual EPS for a company and the EPS "expected" by the market. The latter variable is obtained for one of the mechanical models referred to earlier—a simple time series regression involving the quarterly EPS of a particular company. By subtracting the expected EPS from the actual EPS, the "unexpected" earnings component is obtained. This is then standardized for size differences among companies, and the result is called **standardized unexpected earnings (SUE)**. SUE is calculated as[24]

---

[22] Malkiel and Cragg, "Expectations and the Structure of Share Prices," p. 616.

[23] H. Latané and C. Jones, "Standardized Unexpected Earnings—A Progress Report," *The Journal of Finance,* Vol. 32 (December 1977), pp. 1457–1465.

[24] This is explained in ibid., p. 1457. The standardization variable is the standard error of estimate for the estimating regression equation.

$$\text{SUE} = \frac{\text{Actual quarterly EPS} - \text{Forecasted quarterly EPS}}{\text{Standardization variable}} \quad (12\text{--}10)$$

The SUE concept is designed to capture the surprise element in the earnings just referred to; in other words, the difference between what the "market" expects the company to earn and what it actually does earn. A favorable earnings surprise, where the actual earnings exceed the market's expectation, should bring about an adjustment to the price of the stock as investors revise their probability beliefs about the earnings of the company; conversely, an unfavorable earnings surprise should lead to a downward adjustment in price—in effect, the market has been disappointed in its expectations.

Latané and Jones have shown that the absolute size of the SUE calculated for a large sample of stocks is nicely distributed around 0.0, with fewer observations in the tails of the distribution and more observations toward the center (i.e., SUEs around 0.0).[25] In doing this, stocks can be categorized by SUEs that are divided into increments of 1.0. Thus, SUE classifications can range from all stocks with a SUE ≤ 4.0 (category 1), all between -4.0 and -3.0 (category 2), and so on up to the most positive category, all stocks with SUEs >4.0 (category 10). The larger the SUE (either positive or negative), the greater the unexpected earnings and therefore, other things being equal, the larger the adjustment in the stock's return should be. Stocks with small SUEs (between $+1.0$ and -1.0) have little or no unexpected earnings and, therefore, should show little or no subsequent adjustment in stock return.

Jones, Rendleman, and Latané have documented the relationship between SUEs and stock returns for a very large sample of stocks (over 1400) for a nine-year period (third quarter 1971 through second quarter 1980).[26] This analysis used daily stock returns to measure the adjustment of stocks before, on, and after quarterly earnings announcements. The results indicate that SUE has been an effective discriminator of *average* stock performance; that is, stocks classified into SUE categories, as just described, performed as hypothesized. Category 10 did the best, category 1 did the worst, and the other eight categories had returns in between and in the correct order (from less negative for categories 2 through 5 to more positive for categories 6 through 9).[27] Analyzing the results from 20 days before the announcement to 90 days after suggested that roughly half the adjustment in returns occurs after earnings are announced (the other half occurs prior to and on the announcement date).

---

[25] H. Latané and C. Jones, "Standardized Unexpected Earnings—1971–77," *The Journal of Finance*, Vol. 34 (June 1979), pp. 717–724.

[26] See Charles P. Jones, Richard J. Rendleman, Jr., and Henry A. Latané, "Stock Returns and SUEs During the 1970s," *Journal of Portfolio Management*, Winter 1984, pp. 18–22.

[27] The average portfolio betas for each of the 10 SUE categories were virtually identical, and eight were not significantly different from 1.0 (the two that were, were in the middle categories—and had average beta values of 1.01 and 1.02, respectively).

In conclusion, stock prices are affected not only by the level of and growth in earnings but also by the market's expectations of earnings. Investors should be concerned with both the forecast for earnings and the difference between the actual earnings and the forecast. Therefore, fundamental analysis of earnings should involve more than a forecast, which is difficult enough—it should involve the role of the market's expectations about earnings.

The P/E Ratio

The other half of the valuation framework in fundamental analysis is the **price/earnings (P/E) ratio,** or multiplier. As a definition, the P/E ratio is simply the current market price of a stock divided by earnings, as shown in Equation 12–11. The most recent four quarters of earnings are often used as the denominator, although other earnings may be used.

$$\text{P/E ratio} = \frac{\text{Current stock price}}{\text{Earnings per share}} \qquad (12\text{–}11)$$

The P/E ratio indicates how much per dollar of earnings investors are willing to pay for a stock, that is the price for each dollar of earnings. In a sense, it represents the market's summary evaluation of a company's prospects. Investors are ultimately interested in the P/E ratio expected to prevail, not the current P/E ratio, because they buy a stock for its expected earnings. Investors are willing to pay a price today that reflects their expectations of growth. Thus, the P/E ratio can be restated as

$$\text{P/E ratio} = \text{Earnings multiplier} = \frac{\text{Current stock price}}{\substack{\text{Earnings expected} \\ \text{over the next year}}} \qquad (12\text{–}12)$$

Based on Equation 12–12, investors can derive a theoretical P/E ratio that reflects how much should be paid per dollar of future earnings. Together with an estimate of earnings for the next year, the current intrinsic value of a stock can be estimated in the following way:

$$\begin{aligned} \text{Current estimate of intrinsic value} &= \text{Expected earnings next year} \\ &\quad \times \text{Estimated P/E ratio} \\ &= E_1 \times \frac{P_0}{E_1} \qquad (12\text{–}13) \end{aligned}$$

In December 1986, Value Line estimated EG&G's 1986 and 1987 earnings at, respectively, $1.65 and $1.90.[28] EG&G was selling for about $30 per share at the time. Estimating for the year ahead (to December 1987) by averaging

---

[28] *The Value Line Investment Survey,* December 1986, p. 152, is the source of all data for EG&G used here.

these two earnings figures and obtaining $1.78, we find an estimated intrinsic value of

$$P_0 = 1.78 \times \frac{30}{1.78}$$

$$= 1.78 \times 16.9$$

$$= \$30$$

In December 1986, EG&G was selling for about 15 times 1985 earnings of $2.07, and 18 times Value Line's estimate for 1986 earnings of $1.65. The average annual P/E ratio for EG&G for the years 1981 to 1985 was 15.9, 14.5, 20.6, 17.0, and 18.2, respectively.

In effect, the P/E ratio is a measure of the relative price of a stock. In December 1986, for example, investors were willing to pay about 10 times the earnings for General Motors (GM), but 18 times the earnings for EG&G.[29] What are the reasons for such a large difference? To answer this question, it is necessary to consider the determinants of the P/E ratio.

Determinants of the P/E Ratio

Reviewing earlier discussion, the expected P/E ratio is conceptually a function of the three factors from Equation 12–3:[30]

$$\frac{P_0}{E_1} = \frac{D_1/E_1}{k - g}$$

where

D_1/E_1 = the expected dividend payout ratio.
k = the required rate of return for the stock.
g = expected growth rate in dividends.

Investors attempting to determine the P/E ratio that will prevail for a particular stock should think in terms of these three factors, and their likely changes. Each of these will be considered in turn.

The dividend payout ratio Dividends are clearly a function of earnings (although accounting earnings and cash, out of which dividends are paid, are not necessarily closely related). The relationship between these two variables, however, is more complex than simply current dividends being a function of current earnings. Dividends paid by corporations reflect established practices (i.e., previous earnings level) as well as prospects for the future (i.e., expected future earnings).

Most corporations in the United States act as if dividends matter significantly to investors. The majority of corporations listed on the NYSE

---

[29] These P/E ratios were based on the most recent four quarters of earnings.
[30] Equation 12–3 is based on the constant growth version of the dividend valuation model.

and AMEX pay dividends, and many of the actively traded over-the-counter stocks do also. Consequently dividends, once established at a certain level, are maintained at that level if at all possible. Dividends are not reduced until and unless there is no alternative. Also, dividends are not increased until it is clear that the new, higher level of dividends can be supported. The result of these policies is that dividends adjust with a lag to earnings.[31]

The P/E ratio can be expected to change as the expected dividend payout ratio changes. The higher the expected payout ratio, other things being equal, the higher the P/E ratio. However, "other things" are seldom equal. If the payout rises, the expected growth rate in earnings and dividends, g, will probably decline, thereby adversely affecting the P/E ratio. This decline occurs because less funds will be available for reinvestment in the business, thereby leading to a decline in the expected growth rate, g.

The required rate of return   As explained in Chapter 5 (Equation 5–19), the required rate of return, k, is a function of the riskless rate of return and a risk premium. Thus, k is equal to

$$k = RF + RP \qquad (12\text{--}14)$$

The riskless rate of return can be proxied by the Treasury bill rate. The risk premium is the additional compensation demanded by risk-averse investors before purchasing a risky asset such as a common stock.

Discounted cash flow models, discussed in Chapter 9, can be used to estimate the required rate of return for a company. Rearranging Equation 9–5 indicates that k is equal to the current dividend yield plus the expected growth rate in earnings. A recent study by Harris suggests that a consensus forecast of earnings growth by analysts can be used successfully as a proxy for the dividend growth rate in solving for k.[32] Since analysts' growth forecasts are readily available on a large number of stocks, this approach may offer a straightforward method of estimating required rates of return.

At the company level, the risk premium for a stock can be thought of as a composite of business risk, financial risk, and other risks, which were explained in Chapter 5. Business risk reflects the risk of being in a particular line of business. Financial risk is associated with the use of debt financing by a company. Debt financing is more risky to a company than equity financing, thereby increasing the variability in returns. Other risks could include the liquidity, or marketability, of a particular stock. As a general rule, large NYSE companies are more liquid than are small OTC stocks.

Based on Equation 12–14, the following statements can be made about a company's required rate of return:

---

[31] For a good discussion of corporate dividend policy, see O. M. Joy, *Introduction to Financial Management* (Homewood, Ill.: Richard D. Irwin, 1983), pp. 272–278.

[32] See Robert S. Harris, "Using Analysts' Growth Forecasts to Estimate Shareholder Required Rates of Return," *Financial Management*, Spring 1986, pp. 58–67.

1. Other things being equal, if the risk-free rate, *RF*, rises, *k* will rise. Thus, in periods of high interest rates such as 1980–1981, *k* typically will be higher than in periods such as 1982–1983, when interest rates had declined from the high levels of 1980–1981.
2. Other things being equal, if the risk premium rises (falls), as a result of an increase (decrease) in business risk, financial risk, or other risks, *k* will rise (fall).

The relationship between *k* and the P/E ratio is inverse: as *k* rises, the P/E ratio declines; as *k* declines, the P/E ratio rises. The required rate of return is a discount rate, and discount rates and P/E ratios move inversely to each other. To understand this, think of capitalizing earnings, rather than using an earnings multiplier. To do this, analysts use the **E/P ratio,** which is the reciprocal of the P/E ratio (i.e., E/P = [1/(P/E)]).

$$\text{Intrinsic value} = \frac{E_1}{E_1/P_0} \qquad (12\text{–}15)$$

Rather than use a multiplier of, say, 10, an E/P ratio or capitalization rate of 0.10 can be used. Because the intrinsic value is being estimated, earnings (E_1) must be estimated as well as the capitalization rate (E_1/P_0).

By combining Equation 12–15 with Equation 12–1 (the constant growth version of the dividend valuation model), the relevant variables can be expressed as a function of the E/P ratio.

$$\text{Intrinsic value} = \frac{D_1}{k - g} \qquad (12\text{–}1)$$

$$\text{Intrinsic value} = \frac{E_1}{E_1/P_0} \qquad (12\text{–}15)$$

$$\frac{D_1}{k - g} = \frac{E_1}{E_1/P_0} \qquad (12\text{–}16)$$

$$E_1/P_0 = \frac{k - g}{D_1/E_1} \qquad (12\text{–}17)$$

Equation 12–17 shows that the E/P ratio is positively (directly) related to *k*. Since the E/P is the inverse of the P/E ratio, *k* and P/E are inversely related.

The expected growth rate The third variable affecting the P/E ratio is the expected growth rate of dividends, *g*.[33] We know that *g* = *br*, making the expected growth rate a function of the return on equity (*r*) and the retention

---

[33] Remember that in the constant growth version of the dividend valuation model, the growth rate in dividends is equivalent to the growth rate in earnings and to the growth rate in the price of the stock for all future time periods.

rate (*b*). The higher either of these variables are, the higher *g* will be. What about the relationship between *g* and P/E? P/E and *g* are directly related—the higher the *g*, other things being equal, the higher the P/E ratio.

Investors should be willing to pay more for a company with expected rapid growth in earnings in relation to a company with expected slower growth in earnings. A basic problem in fundamental analysis, however, is determining how *much* more investors should be willing to pay for growth; in other words, how high should the P/E ratio be? There is no precise answer to this question. It will depend upon such factors as the following:

1. The confidence that investors have in the expected growth. In the case of EG&G, for example, investors may be well justified in expecting a rapid rate of growth for the next few years because of previous performance, management's ability, and the high estimates of growth described in investment advisory services. This may not be the case for another company where, because of competitive inroads and other factors, the high growth prospects are at great risk—consider Apple Computer, for example, which must face the IBM challenge in home computers.

2. The reasons for the earnings growth can be important. Is it a result of great demand in the marketplace, or a result of astute financing policies that could backfire if interest rates rise sharply or the economy enters a severe recession? Is growth the result of sales expansion or cost cutting (which will be exhausted at some point)?

EG&G's P/E Ratio

In analyzing the P/E ratio for EG&G, we first ask what model describes the expected growth for EG&G. Given this company's recent rapid growth and Value Line's estimate of its expected future growth, we probably would not choose the constant growth version of the dividend valuation model. Instead, we should evaluate EG&G by using a supernormal (abnormal) growth model as described in Appendix 9–A. EG&G is expected to enjoy rapid growth for at least a few more years. At some point, however, this growth can be expected to slow down to a more normal growth rate.

Given the growth prospects for EG&G, Equation 12–3 is not strictly applicable for estimating a P/E ratio because it assumes constant growth in dividends and earnings over all future time periods. However, the same variables will affect the P/E ratio. Furthermore, at some time in the future, the expected rate will slow down to a more normal rate of growth, and at that point the P/E ratio for the *next* year will be

$$\frac{P}{E_{n+1}} = \frac{D_{n+1}/E_{n+1}}{k - g}$$

where *n* is the year that the abnormal growth ends.

TABLE 12–3 The Stocks in The Value Line Investment Survey with the Highest and Lowest P/E Ratios as of January 30, 1987

LOWEST P/Es
Stocks whose estimated current P/E ratios are lowest

Page No.	Stock Name	Recent Price	Current P/E Ratio	Timeliness	Safety Rank	Industry Group	Industry Rank
1426	Wheeling-Pitts. Steel	8	1.3	–	5	Steel (Integrated)	90
1168	TransCapital Financial	13	3.2	3	4	Savings & Loan	17
1263	Robins (A.H.) Co.	9¼	3.3	–	5	Drug	7
1161	Gibraltar Fin'l	11	3.5	2	5	Savings & Loan	17
194	Long Island Lighting	11	3.7	4	5	Electric Utility(East)	53
1160	Fin'l Corp. Santa Barb.	12	3.7	2	5	Savings & Loan	17
674	Horizon Corp.	5	3.9	3	5	Real Estate	56
204	Public Serv. (N.H.)	8⅜	4.1	4	5	Electric Utility(East)	53
1157	Far West Fin'l	13	4.1	4	3	Savings & Loan	17
878	Owens-Corning	18	4.2	–	3	Building	21
1166	Imperial Corp. of Amer.	17	4.3	1	5	Savings & Loan	17
1159	Fin'l Corp. of America	9⅜	4.4	3	5	Savings & Loan	17
714	Gulf States Util.	8	4.5	4	5	Electric Util.(Central)	39
1162	GLENFED Inc.	25	5.3	2	3	Savings & Loan	17
2029	Manufacturers Hanover	47	5.3	3	3	Bank	24
1423	LTV Corp.	2⅛	5.3	–	5	Steel (Integrated)	90
210	United Illuminating	32	5.4	3	4	Electric Utility(East)	53
1107	Mohawk Data Sciences	2⅞	5.4	3	5	Computer & Peripherals	41
1165	Home Federal S&L (S.D.)	27	5.4	3	3	Savings & Loan	17
1155	CalFed Inc.	34	5.5	3	3	Savings & Loan	17
1404	Nortek Inc.	15	5.6	3	4	Multiform	71
2068	Southmark Corp.	9⅞	5.7	4	4	Financial Services	29
2010	Chase Manhattan	40	6.0	4	3	Bank	24
104	Chrysler	45	6.1	3	3	Auto & Truck	40
189	Duquesne Light	13	6.2	4	4	Electric Utility(East)	53
1163	Golden West Fin'l	37	6.3	3	4	Savings & Loan	17
2011	Chemical New York	48	6.4	3	3	Bank	24
729	Middle South Utilities	15	6.4	3	5	Electric Util.(Central)	39
105	Ford Motor	72	6.4	2	3	Auto & Truck	40
1164	G't Western Fin'l	47	6.5	3	3	Savings & Loan	17
1153	Ahmanson (H.F.)	22	6.5	3	3	Savings & Loan	17
197	Niagara Mohawk	18	6.8	5	4	Electric Utility(East)	53
652	First Chicago	33	6.8	2	3	Bank (Midwest)	28
2030	Marine Midland Banks	51	7.0	3	3	Bank	24
801	Tonka Corp.	22	7.1	3	4	Toys & School Supplies	72
2021	First Interstate Bancorp	57	7.2	3	3	Bank	24
2027	Irving Bank Corp.	51	7.2	3	2	Bank	24
260	KLM Royal Dutch Air	18	7.2	3	3	Air Transport	15
1507	Borman's Inc.	20	7.5	3	5	Grocery	43
1784	Resorts Int'l 'A'	45	7.5	5	3	Hotel/Gaming	83
873	M.D.C. Holdings	15	7.5	3	5	Building	21
708	Commonwealth Edison	36	7.6	2	3	Electric Util.(Central)	39
193	Gen'l Public Utilities	24	7.6	1	3	Electric Utility(East)	53
2050	Valley National	40	7.6	4	2	Bank	24
742	Texas Utilities	35	7.6	3	2	Electric Util.(Central)	39
711	Detroit Edison	18	7.6	2	3	Electric Util.(Central)	39
350	Banner Ind.	21	7.6	1	5	Industrial Services	9
2012	Citicorp	57	7.6	3	3	Bank	24
944	Pope & Talbot	33	7.6	1	3	Paper & Forest Products	6
712	El Paso Elec. Co.	20	7.7	3	4	Electric Util.(Central)	39
871	Kaufman & Broad	19	7.7	2	4	Building	21
2121	Intelogic Trace	5¾	7.7	–	4	Computer Software/Svcs	1
182	Cen. Hudson G. & E.	30	7.8	4	3	Electric Utility(East)	53
2064	Leucadia National	19	7.8	2	4	Financial Services	29
702	Centerior Energy	24	7.8	4	4	Electric Util.(Central)	39
2028	KeyCorp	25	7.8	3	2	Bank	24
2077	CIGNA Corp.	60	7.8	3	2	Insurance (Diversified)	32
566	Lockheed Corp.	51	7.8	2	3	Aerospace/Defense	44
2007	Bankers Trust NY	48	7.8	3	3	Bank	24
257	Delta Air Lines	55	7.9	1	3	Air Transport	15
2039	Security Pacific	40	7.9	2	3	Bank	24
717	Illinois Power	30	7.9	3	3	Electric Util.(Central)	39
111	Subaru of America	17	7.9	3	3	Auto & Truck	40
205	Rochester Gas & Elec.	24	8.0	4	3	Electric Utility(East)	53
561	Gen'l Dynamics	75	8.0	3	3	Aerospace/Defense	44
866	Elcor Corp.	16	8.0	2	4	Building	21
1680	Suave Shoe	8¾	8.1	2	3	Shoe	49
629	Chubb Corp.	60	8.2	3	3	Insurance(Prop/Casualty)	36
2033	Midlantic Banks	44	8.2	3	1	Bank	24
2003	Bank of Boston	30	8.3	1	2	Bank	24
660	Society Corp	62	8.3	3	1	Bank (Midwest)	28
2004	Bank of New England	33	8.3	3	3	Bank	24
651	First Bank System	30	8.4	2	2	Bank (Midwest)	28
707	Cincinnati Gas & Elec.	29	8.4	3	5	Electric Util.(Central)	39
1626	Fieldcrest Cannon	35	8.4	3	3	Textile	50
1586	Ultrasystems	9¾	8.4	3	4	Unassigned	—
208	Southern Co.	28	8.5	3	3	Electric Utility(East)	53
657	National City Corp.	29	8.5	2	1	Bank (Midwest)	28
656	NBD Bancorp	32	8.5	2	1	Bank (Midwest)	28
737	Public Serv. (Indiana)	16	8.6	3	5	Electric Util.(Central)	39
2031	Maryland Nat'l	45	8.6	2	2	Bank	24
196	N.Y. State Elec. & Gas	33	8.6	3	3	Electric Utility(East)	53
609	Gen'l Refractories	18	8.6	1	5	Steel (General)	80
2112	AST Research	15	8.6	–	4	Computer Software/Svcs	1
2041	Southeast Banking	41	8.6	3	3	Bank	24
648	Comerica Inc.	53	8.6	3	2	Bank (Midwest)	28
1631	United Merchants	13	8.7	5	4	Textile	50
184	Commonwealth Energy	40	8.7	3	2	Electric Utility(East)	53
715	Houston Inds.	37	8.7	3	3	Electric Util.(Central)	39
1678	Reebok Int'l	27	8.7	–	3	Shoe	49
2017	Dominion Bankshs.	19	8.8	3	2	Bank	24
608	Florida Steel	25	8.8	3	3	Steel (General)	80
2109	Cyclops Corp.	71	8.8	2	3	Steel (Specialty)	22
811	Superior Inds. Int'l	13	8.8	4	3	Auto Parts(Oem)	81
1485	Monfort of Colorado	49	8.9	2	3	Food Processing	11
644	AmeriTrust Corp.	38	8.9	4	1	Bank (Midwest)	28
2020	First Fidelity Bancorp	38	8.9	3	1	Bank	24
2072	Aetna Life & Casualty	61	8.9	3	1	Insurance (Diversified)	32
767	Dynascan	14	9.0	2	4	Telecommunications	46
2005	Bank of New York	42	9.0	2	2	Bank	24

HIGHEST P/Es
Stocks whose estimated current P/E ratios are biggest

Page No.	Stock Name	Recent Price	Current P/E Ratio	Timeliness	Safety Rank	Industry Group	Industry Rank
1232	Inspiration Resources	5⅛	85.0	3	4	Copper	12
1894	Grace (W. R.)	54	83.1	3	2	Chemical/Diversified	19
1801	Int'l Banknote	4⅞	81.7	3	4	Publishing	18
1698	Greenman Brothers	8⅞	80.9	5	3	Retail (Special Lines)	61
385	United Cable TV	28	80.0	4	4	Broadcasting/Cable TV	86
1090	Centronics Data Comp.	4¾	80.0	–	5	Computer & Peripherals	41
1092	Computer & Comm.	5¼	75.7	4	4	Computer & Peripherals	41
381	Malrite Communic.	9¾	75.4	5	4	Broadcasting/Cable TV	86
114	Champion Spark Plug	12	75.0	3	3	Auto Parts(Rep)	63
414	Murphy Oil Corp.	30	75.0	3	3	Petroleum (Integrated)	45
1582	Revlon Group	12	70.6	4	5	Unassigned	—
1077	National Semiconductor	14	70.0	3	4	Semiconductor	88
1344	Acme-Cleveland	11	68.8	3	3	Machine Tool	66
800	Mattel, Inc.	11	64.7	5	5	Toys & Scnool Supplies	72
386	Viacom Int'l	41	64.1	–	3	Broadcasting/Cable TV	86
454	Mitchell Energy & Dev.	13	61.9	3	4	Natural Gas(Diversified)	74
1040	CTS Corp.	33	61.1	–	3	Electronics	75
774	Mobile Communic. 'B'	22	59.5	3	4	Telecommunications	46
1357	Becor Western	13	59.1	3	3	Machinery(Const&Mining)	54
1456	Amfac, Inc.	24	58.5	4	3	Food Processing	11
1902	VLSI Technology	14	58.3	3	4	Unassigned	—
373	Adams-Russell Co.	21	58.3	–	4	Broadcasting/Cable TV	86
1811	Zondervan Corp.	28	58.3	–	5	Publishing	18
1235	Noranda Inc.	23	57.5	2	4	Metals & Mining(General)	2
1273	Zenith Labs.	8½	56.7	5	4	Drug	7
1808	Playboy Enterprises	8½	56.7	3	4	Publishing	18
676	Koger Properties	33	55.9	3	3	Real Estate	56
627	Northgate Expl'n Ltd.	4⅞	54.4	2	5	Metals & Mining (Ind'l)	78
1060	Varian Associates	25	54.3	4	3	Electronics	75
1358	Caterpillar Inc.	44	54.3	4	3	Machinery(Const&Mining)	54
679	Rouse Co.	33	54.1	2	3	Real Estate	56
966	Kerr Glass Mfg.	14	53.8	3	3	Packaging & Container	38
262	PS Group Inc.	36	53.7	–	4	Air Transport	15
1701	Lionel Corp.	5¾	52.7	3	5	Retail (Special Lines)	61
1567	Pioneer Elec. ADR	31	52.5	2	3	Japanese Diversified	33
1483	MEI Diversified	9⅜	52.2	–	3	Food Processing	11
625	Inco Limited	13	52.0	3	4	Metals & Mining (Ind'l)	78
1046	Gen'l Instrument	20	51.3	3	3	Electronics	75
461	Tenneco, Inc.	42	51.2	3	3	Natural Gas(Diversified)	74
1349	Monarch Mach. Tool	16	50.0	3	3	Machine Tool	66
123	Stewart-Warner	30	48.4	3	2	Auto Parts(Rep)	63
1237	Phelps Dodge	24	48.0	3	4	Copper	12
765	Murray Ohio Mfg.	20	47.6	4	3	Recreation	76
84	Apollo Computer	19	47.5	2	4	Computer & Peripherals	41
439	Mesa Ltd. Partners	17	47.2	–	4	Petroleum (Producing)	84
864	Dallas Corp.	15	46.9	4	3	Building	21
1682	Wolverine World Wide	9¾	46.7	4	4	Shoe	49
418	Phillips Petroleum	13	46.4	3	4	Petroleum (Integrated)	45
2126	Telecredit Inc.	64	46.0	1	4	Computer Software/Svcs	1
1231	Homestake Mining	27	45.0	3	3	Gold (No.American)	5
1073	Int'l Rectifier	8¾	44.0	4	5	Semiconductor	88
1259	Marion Labs.	46	43.8	2	3	Drug	7
771	M/A-COM, Inc.	14	43.8	4	3	Telecommunications	46
1561	Canon Inc. (ADR)	32	43.2	4	3	Japanese Diversified	33
415	Occidental Petroleum	31	43.1	3	3	Petroleum (Integrated)	45
1696	Gen'l Nutrition	5⅝	43.1	3	4	Retail (Special Lines)	61
417	Pennzoil Company	68	42.5	3	3	Petroleum (Integrated)	45
1838	Louisiana Land Expl.	31	42.5	3	3	Petroleum (Producing)	84
1397	Kuhlman Corp.	14	42.4	5	3	Multiform	71
435	Gulf Canada Corp.	13	41.9	–	3	Canadian Energy	60
427	Tosco Corp.	2½	41.7	4	5	Petroleum (Integrated)	45
135	Goodrich (B. F.)	51	41.5	3	3	Tire & Rubber	20
1367	Joy Mfg.	35	41.2	–	2	Machinery(Const&Mining)	54
1870	Trico Inds.	7¾	41.1	–	4	Oilfield Serv/Equip.	89
1513	Food Lion 'B'	16	41.0	2	3	Grocery	43
1227	Dome Mines	8⅝	41.0	2	5	Gold (No.American)	5
1635	Alexander's, Inc.	41	41.0	3	4	Retail Store	26
1833	Apache Corp.	11	40.7	3	4	Petroleum (Producing)	84
1226	Campbell Red Lake	22	40.7	2	3	Gold (No.American)	5
439	NOVA, AN ALBERTA	6⅞	40.6	3	3	Canadian Energy	60
148	Coherent, Inc.	13	40.6	4	4	Precision Instrument	55
1850	Camco Inc.	15	40.5	4	3	Oilfield Serv/Equip.	89
1577	Gen'l DataComm	9¼	40.4	4	4	Unassigned	—
1065	Zenith Electronics	25	40.3	3	3	Electronics	75
1228	Echo Bay Mines	26	40.0	2	3	Gold (No.American)	5
819	Neutrogena Corp.	41	39.8	2	3	Toiletries/Cosmetics	8
412	Kerr-McGee Corp.	31	39.7	3	3	Petroleum (Integrated)	45
1029	AVX Corp.	15	39.5	3	4	Electronics	75
1558	Zimmer Corp.	3⅞	39.0	4	5	Manu Housing/Rec Veh	67
536	Applied Biosystems	35	38.9	3	3	Unassigned	—
572	Northrop Corp.	41	38.7	5	3	Aerospace/Defense	44
380	LIN Broadcasting	58	38.7	1	3	Broadcasting/Cable TV	86
1225	Callahan Mining	18	38.3	3	3	Silver	73
604	Trinity Inds.	19	38.0	3	3	Metal Fabricating	25
1334	Reece Corp.	11	37.9	3	4	Machinery	69
2018	Equimark Corp.	4⅞	37.7	3	5	Bank	24
1568	Sony Corp. (ADR)	21	36.2	3	3	Japanese Diversified	33
1883	Pittston	13	36.1	3	3	Coal/Alternate Energy	34
1021	Mark Controls	13	36.1	3	3	Electrical Equipment	48
217	Bergen Brunswig 'A'	23	35.9	5	3	Medical Supplies	16
307	Kansas City South'n Ind.	49	35.8	4	3	Railroad	87
1329	Portec, Inc.	15	35.7	4	3	Machinery	69
680	Texas Pacific Land Trust	26	35.6	3	2	Real Estate	56
377	Chris-Craft	21	35.6	3	3	Broadcasting/Cable TV	86
1055	Safeguard Scientifics	16	35.6	1	5	Electronics	75
460	Southern Union Co.	12	35.3	4	3	Natural Gas(Diversified)	74
1813	Affiliated Publications	40	34.8	1	3	Newspaper	4
450	ENSERCH Corp.	19	34.5	3	3	Natural Gas(Diversified)	74
362	Rollins Environmental	29	34.5	1	4	Industrial Services	9
1406	Quixote Corp.	12	34.3	4	3	Multiform	71

Factual material is obtained from sources believed to be reliable, but the publisher is not responsible for any errors or omissions contained herein.

Source: The Value Line Investment Survey, Summary of Advice and Index, January 30, 1987, p. 35. © 1987 Value Line Inc. Reprinted by permission.

Why P/E Ratios Vary among Companies

Stock prices reflect market expectations about earnings. Companies that the market believes will achieve higher earnings growth rates will tend to be priced higher than companies that are expected to show low earnings growth rates. Thus, a primary factor in explaining P/E ratio differences among companies is investor expectations about the future growth of earnings. Variations in the rate of earnings growth will also influence the P/E.

Table 12–3 shows *The Value Line Investment Survey*'s ranking of the lowest and highest P/E stocks, on a current basis as of January 30, 1987, out of the more than 1700 companies covered. The lowest estimated current P/E ratios ranged from 1.3 to 9.0, whereas the highest ranged from 85.0 to 34.3.

The low P/E ratio stocks in Table 12–3 are dominated by the utility industry (historically, a low growth, low P/E industry), specifically, electric utilities whose rates are regulated. Banks were also heavily represented at this time, as were savings and loans. The high P/E ratio stocks include a wide variety of businesses, many of which appear to be good growth prospects in the latter part of the 1980s (e.g., ''computer and peripherals'' and ''electronics''), and some that appear to be highly speculative (e.g., ''gold'' and ''petroleum''). Other activities represented in the high P/E set include real estate, broadcasting/cable TV, drugs, publishing, and food processing. Each of these areas represented expected growth opportunities in the late 1980s, as assessed by investors in early 1987.

Additional Company Analysis

In modern investment analysis, the risk for a stock is based on its beta coefficient, as explained in Chapters 5 and 8. Beta reflects the relative systematic risk for a stock, or the risk that cannot be diversified away. The higher the beta coefficient, the higher the risk for an individual stock, and the higher the required rate of return.

Beta measures the volatility of a stock's returns—its fluctuations in relation to the market. According to *The Value Line Investment Survey*, the beta for EG&G was 1.20 at the end of 1986. Therefore, we know that EG&G has larger relative systematic risk than the market as a whole; that is, its return fluctuates more than the market's returns. If the overall market is expected to rise 20%, for example, over the next year investors could expect, generally, for EG&G to rise 24% based on its beta of 1.20. Investors who are seeking to outperform the market, and who believe that the market will rise, could be interested in EG&G in this hypothetical situation. However, remember that if, and when, the market declines, EG&G would be expected to decline more than the market. If the market declines 20%, for example, EG&G would be expected, on average, to decline in price by 26%.

It is extremely important in analyses such as these to remember that beta is a measure of volatility, indicating what can be expected to happen, *on average,* to a stock when the overall market rises or falls. In fact EG&G, or any other stock, will not perform in the predicted way every time. If it did, the risk would disappear. Investors can always find examples of stocks that, over some specific period of time, did not move as their beta indicated they would. This is not an indictment of the usefulness of beta as a measure of volatility; rather, it suggests that the beta relationship can only be expected to hold *on the average*.

In trying to understand and predict a company's return and risk, we need to keep in mind that the return will be a function of two components. The systematic component will be related to the return on the overall market and is the product of the beta coefficient and the return on the market, as explained. The other component is the unique part attributable to the company itself and not to the overall market. It is a function of the specific positive or negative factors that affect a company independent of the market.

Summary

This chapter focuses on the analysis of individual companies, the last of three steps in fundamental security analysis. On a broad level, this analysis would encompass all of the basic financial variables of the company, such as sales, management, competition, and so on. On a specific level, it involves applying the valuation procedures explained in earlier chapters.

Intrinsic value (a company's justified price) can be estimated using either a dividend valuation model or an earnings multiplier model. It is then compared to the current market price in order to determine if the stock is undervalued or overvalued. This analysis concentrates on the earnings multiplier model.

An important first step in fundamental analysis is to understand the earnings per share (EPS) of companies. To do this, the financial statements are used. The balance sheet shows the assets and liabilities at a specific date, whereas the income statement shows the flows during a period for the items that determine net income. Although these statements are certified by the accounting profession, alternative accounting principles result in EPS figures that are not precise, readily comparable figures. Investors should be aware of the process under which reported EPS are determined, and its limitations. The concept of earnings "quality" may help investors to do this.

EPS is the result of several variables interacting. The following statement indicates the more important components:

$$EPS \rightarrow ROE \rightarrow ROA \text{ and Leverage} \rightarrow \text{Net Income Margin and Turnover}$$

All of these factors affect EPS, and investors may wish to analyze some of these factors in detail.

Changes in earnings are directly related to changes in stock prices. To assess expected earnings, investors can consider the earnings growth rates, which is the product of ROE and the earnings retention rate. The lack of persistence in these growth rates may lead investors to consider EPS forecasts, available mechanically or from analysts. Both are subject to error and the evidence is mixed on which method is better, although a recent study favors analysts' forecasts.

The difference between actual and forecasted EPS is important because of the role of the market's expectations about earnings. "Surprises" are associated with price changes, both favorable and unfavorable. Standardized unexpected earnings (SUE) attempts to evaluate the unexpected portion of quarterly earnings.

The price/earnings (P/E) ratio is the other half of the earnings multiplier model, indicating the amount per dollar of earnings investors are willing to pay for a stock. It represents the relative price of a stock, with some companies carrying high P/E ratios while others have low ones. The P/E ratio is influenced directly by investors' expectations of the future growth of earnings and the payout ratio, and inversely by the required rate of return. Since the latter variable is a function of the riskless rate of return and a risk premium, the effect of changes in interest rates on P/E ratios can be assessed.

P/E ratios vary among companies primarily because of investors' expectations about the future growth of earnings. If investors lower their expectations, the price of the stock may drop while earnings remain constant or even rise.

Additional company analysis involves the beta coefficient, the measure of volatility for a stock. The beta indicates the *average* responsiveness of the stock's price to the overall market, with high (low) beta stocks exhibiting larger (smaller) changes than the overall market.

Key Words

Dividend payout ratio	Leverage
E/P ratio	Price/Earnings (P/E) ratio
Earnings per share (EPS)	Retention rate
Financial statements	Return on assets (ROA)
Generally accepted accounting principles (GAAPs)	Return on equity (ROE)
Intrinsic value	Standardized unexpected earnings (SUE)

QUESTIONS AND PROBLEMS

1. What is the intrinsic value of a stock?
2. How can a stock's intrinsic value be determined?
3. What are the limitations of using Equation 12–1 to determine intrinsic value?
4. What is meant by "GAAP"?
5. What are the problems with estimating accounting earnings?
6. What does the auditor's report signify about the financial statements?
7. Using *The Wall Street Journal, Barron's, Forbes,* and other business publications, find an example of a company whose recent accounting practices affected EPS in a way that illustrates the problem with earnings.
8. What is the concept of earnings quality?
9. Outline, in words, the determination process for EPS.
10. Explain the role that financing plays in a company's EPS.
11. Assuming that a firm's return on assets exceeds its interest costs, why would it not boost ROE to the maximum through the use of debt financing since higher ROE leads to higher EPS?
12. How can the earnings growth rate be determined?
13. How well do earnings growth rates for individual companies persist across time?
14. How can investors obtain EPS forecasts? Which source is better?
15. What role does earnings expectations play in selecting stocks?
16. How can the unexpected component of EPS be used to select stocks?
17. Explain the relationship between SUE and fundamental security analysis.
18. Describe at least two variations in calculating a P/E ratio.
19. Using the *Value Line Investment Survey,* list the average annual P/E ratio for the following companies for the years 1982 through 1986: Apple Computer, EG&G, General Electric, and Philadelphia Electric. What conclusions can you draw from this information?
20. What are the variables that affect the P/E ratio? Is the effect direct or inverse for each component?
21. Holding everything else constant, what effect would the following have on the P/E ratio of a company?
    a. An increase in the expected growth rate of earnings.
    b. A decrease in the expected dividend payout.
    c. An increase in the risk-free rate of return.
    d. An increase in the risk premium.
    e. A decrease in the required rate of return.
22. Why would an investor want to know the beta coefficient for a particular company? How could this information be used?

23. Is beta the only determinant of a company's return?

24. Using Table 12–3, update from *Value Line* the P/E ratios for the first 10 companies in both the lowest and highest set. What does this tell you about the stability of the P/E ratio over time?

25. The following data are for PepsiCo, for the years 1977 through 1981.

Year	Price	Earn-ings	Divi-dends	Book Value	P/E	(D/E)100	HPY%	ROE (Earn/ Book)
1977	$28.00	$2.15	$.83	$9.57	13.0	38.4%	—	22.5%
1978	25.50	2.43*	.98	10.85*	10.5*	40.1*	−5.4	22.4*
1979	24.70	2.85*	1.11	12.05*	8.7*	38.8*	1.2	23.7*
1980	27.20	3.20*	1.26	13.93*	8.5*	39.3*	15.2	23.0*
1981	36.30	3.61*	1.42	16.21*	10.1*	39.3*	38.7	22.3*

The 1977 and 1978 values are affected by acquisitions during those two years. Also, in late 1982 it was discovered that several managers and vice presidents had allegedly engaged in some "creative" accounting practices in valuing inventories and calculating profits of the foreign operation. This resulted in operating profits and book value being overstated for each of the years 1978–1981. The accounting errors had not been detected by PepsiCo, nor by the auditors. Taxes were paid and dividends were declared on the basis of the earnings shown previously. Every starred item is incorrect, as well as the historical profit and loss statements and the balance sheets. PepsiCo had to calculate a downward restatement of earnings of $92 million over the four years and write down $79 million in assets of the foreign bottling operations. Twelve officials of PepsiCo were dismissed, and suit was brought against PepsiCo for filing false and misleading financial information. The news of this event, as it developed, can be followed in *The Wall Street Journal,* Nov. 15, 1982, p. 55; Dec. 14, 1982, p. 5; Dec. 20, 1982, p. 8; and July 29, 1983, p. 1.

a. Relative to the section on The Problem with Earnings, discuss the problem of PepsiCo.

b. Instead of the earnings indicated, assume that the revised earnings are reported as: 1978, $2.40; 1979, $2.70; 1980, $2.86; and 1981, $3.22. The end-of-year prices, dividends paid, and the HPY% are correct with the data shown. Using the revised earnings data, calculate the P/Es, (D/E)100, and ROEs and compare them with the unrevised values.

c. On the basis of your comparison, discuss the problem of valuation of PepsiCo during the 1978–1981 period, as well as the problem of valuation even now.

d. The end-of-year price (P), annual earnings per share (E), dividends per share (D), and book value for 1982 and 1983 were as follows:

Year	P	E	D	Book
1982	$35.75	$2.40	$1.58	$15.14
1983	38.25	3.01	1.62	16.66

Calculate the standard ratios and the HPY% for 1982 and 1983, and compare them with the S&P 500 values.

e. How do you account for the decrease in book value from 1981 to 1982? What effect does this have on the estimated ROE, and the change in ROE, in 1982 relative to 1981?

26. Valuation of General Fudge (GF)

GF is a large producer of food products. In 19X5, the percentage breakdown of revenues and profits was as follows:

	Revenues(%)	Profits(%)
Packaged foods	41	62
Coffee	28	19
Processed meat	19	13
Food service–other	12	6
	100	100

International operations account for about 22% of sales and 17% of operating profit.

For the 19X1–19X5 fiscal years, ending March 31, the number of shares outstanding (in millions) and income selected statement data were (in millions of dollars) as follows:

Shares Outst.	Year	Reve- nues	Oper. Inc.	Cap. Exp.	Deprec.	Int. Exp.	Net Income Bef. Tax	Net Income After Tax
49.93	19X1	$5472	$524	$121	$77	$31	$452	$232
49.97	19X2	5960	534	262	78	39	470	256
49.43	19X3	6601	565	187	89	50	473	255
49.45	19X4	8351	694	283	131	152	418	221
51.92	19X5	8256	721	266	133	139	535	289

a. For each year calculate operating income as a percentage of revenues.
b. Net profits after tax as a percentage of revenues.
c. After-tax profits per share outstanding (EPS).

The balance sheet data for the same fiscal years (in millions of dollars) was as follows:

Year	Cash	Current Assets	Current Liab.	Total Assets	Long-Term Debt	Common Equity	Total Capital
19X1	$291	$1736	$845	$2565	$251	$1321	$1681
19X2	178	1951	1047	2978	255	1480	1845
19X3	309	2019	929	3103	391	1610	2121
19X4	163	2254	1215	3861	731	1626	2499
19X5	285	2315	1342	4310	736	1872	2804

d. Calculate the ratio of current assets to current liabilities for each year.

e. Calculate the long-term debt as a percentage of total capital.

f. For each year calculate the book value per share as the common equity divided by the number of shares outstanding.

g. Calculate ROE.

h. Calculate ROA.

i. Calculate leverage.

j. Calculate the net income margin.

k. Calculate turnover.

l. Calculate the EBIT.

m. Calculate the income ratio.

n. Calculate operating efficiency.

o. On the basis of Problems a–m, evaluate the current status of the health of GF, and the changes over the period.

27. Additional Valuation of General Fudge

Combining information from the S&P reports and some estimated data for 19X7, the following calendar-year data, on a per-share basis, are provided:

Year	Price Range Low	Price Range High	Earn-ings	Divi-dends	Book Value	(D/E) 100(%)	Annual Avg. P/E	ROE E/Book
19X1	$26.5	$35.3	$4.56	$1.72	$25.98	37.7	7.0	17.6%
19X2	28.3	37.0	5.02	1.95	29.15	38.8	6.2	17.3
19X3	23.5	34.3	5.14	2.20	32.11	42.8	5.8	16.0
19X4	27.8	35.0	4.47	2.20	30.86		7.7	
19X5	29.0	47.8	5.73	2.30	30.30		6.8	
19X6	36.6	53.5	6.75	2.40	39.85			
19X7			6.75	2.60	44.00			

a. Calculate the D/E, ROE, and HPY for 19X4, 19X5, and 19X6 (use the average of the low and high prices to calculate HPYs).

b. Show that from 19X2 through 19X6 the per annum growth rate in dividends was 6.9% and for earnings was 8.2%.

c. Using the current price of $47, with hypothesized projected earnings for

19X7 of $6.75, show that Equation 12–12 would be evaluated as P/E = 6.96.

d. On the basis of the annual average P/E ratios shown here and your estimate in Problem c, assume an expected P/E of 7. If an investor expected the earnings of GF for 19X7 to be $7.50, evaluate Equation 12–13, and show that the intrinsic value would be $52.50.

e. What factors are important in explaining the difference in the P/E ratios of EG&G and GF?

f. From your calculation of the growth rate of dividends in Problem b, assume that the annual rate is 7%. If the required rate of return for the stock were 12% and the expected dividend payout ratio is 0.4, evaluate Equation 12–3 and show that P/E = 8.

g. If the dividend payout ratio is 0.4, and the return on equity is 15%, evaluate Equation 12–8 and show that $g = 0.09$.

h. Using $k = 0.14$ and $g = 0.09$, with hypothesized expected 19X7 dividends, evaluate Equation 12–1 and show that the intrinsic value is $52.

i. Value Line's estimate of the "beta" for GF is 0.8, relative to EG&G's beta of 1.3. Is this information of any help in explaining the different P/E ratios of these two companies?

Selected References

Beaver, William, and Morse, Dale. "What Determines Price–Earnings Ratios?" *Financial Analysts Journal,* July–August 1978, pp. 65–76.

Benesh, Gary A., Keown, Arthur J., and Pinkerton, John M. "An Examination of Market Reaction to Substantial Shifts in Dividend Policy." *The Journal of Financial Research,* Summer 1984, pp. 131–142.

Bernstein, Leopold A., and Seigel, Joel. "The Concept of Earnings Quality." *Financial Analysts Journal,* July–August 1979, pp. 72–75.

Black, Fischer. "The Dividend Puzzle." *Journal of Portfolio Management,* Winter 1976, pp. 5–8.

Brealey, Richard A. *An Introduction to Risk and Return from Common Stocks.* 2nd ed. Cambridge, Mass.: The MIT Press, 1983.

Brown, Lawrence, and Rozeff, Michael. "The Superiority of Analyst Forecasts as Measures of Expectations: Evidence from Earnings." *Journal of Finance,* March 1978, pp. 1–16.

Capstaff, John. "Interpreting Price Earnings Ratios: How Much Does the Market Judge Future Earnings Growth?" *The Investment Analyst,* October 1985, pp. 18–28.

Chugh, Lal C., and Meador, Joseph W. "The Stock Valuation Process: The Analysts' View." *Financial Analysts Journal,* November/December 1984, pp. 41–48.

Elton, Edwin J., and Gruber, Martin J. *Modern Portfolio Theory and Investment Analysis.* 3rd ed. New York: John Wiley, 1987.

Jennings, Robert, and Starks, Laura. "Information Content and the Speed of Stock Price Adjustment." *Journal of Accounting Research,* Spring 1985, pp. 336–350.

Jones, Charles P., Rendleman, Richard J., and Latané, Henry A. "Stock Returns and SUEs During the 1970s." *The Journal of Portfolio Management,* Winter 1984, pp. 18–22.

Jones, Charles P., Tuttle, Donald L., and Heaton, Cherrill P. *Essentials of Modern Investments.* New York: Ronald Press, 1977.

Joy, O. Maurice. *Introduction to Financial Management.* Homewood, Ill.: Richard D. Irwin, 1983.

Latané, Henry A., and Jones, Charles P. "Standardized Unexpected Earnings— 1971–77." *The Journal of Finance,* June 1979, pp. 717–724.

Lintner, John, and Glauber, Robert. "Higgledy, Piggledy Growth in America." In J. H. Lorie and R. A. Brealey, eds., *Modern Developments in Investment Management,* 2nd ed. Hinsdale, Ill.: Dryden Press, 1978.

Malkiel, Burton, and Cragg, John. "Expectations and the Structure of Share Prices." *American Economic Review,* September 1970, pp. 601–617.

Nagorniak, John J. "Thoughts on Using Dividend Discount Models." *Financial Analysts Journal,* November–December 1985, pp. 13–15.

Niederhoffer, Victor, and Regan, Patrick J. "Earnings Changes, Analysts' Forecasts and Stock Prices." *Financial Analysts Journal,* May–June 1972, pp. 65–71.

Richards, Malcolm. "Analysts' Performance and the Accuracy of Corporate Earnings Forecasts." *The Journal of Business,* July 1976, pp. 350–357.

Rie, Daniel. "How Trustworthy Is Your Valuation Model?" *Financial Analysts Journal,* November–December 1985, pp. 42–48.

Seigel, Joel. "The 'Quality of Earnings' Concept—A Survey." *Financial Analysts Journal,* March–April 1982, pp. 60–64.

PART FIVE

CHAPTER 13

TECHNICAL ANALYSIS

As discussed in Chapter 9, technical analysis is the second approach for selecting stocks. This approach is entirely different from the fundamental approach discussed in the last four chapters and the efficient markets approach to be discussed in Chapter 14.

Although the oldest of the three approaches, dating back to the late 1800s, the technical approach to common stock selection is extremely controversial. The techniques discussed in this chapter appear at first glance to have merit because they seem intuitive and plausible; however, they have been severely challenged in the last two decades.

It is important for the reader to place this subject in proper perspective. On the one hand, someone learning about investments should be exposed to technical analysis because many investors, investment advisory firms, and the popular press talk about it and use it. As noted, it has been available for a long time and is widely known; furthermore, it may produce some insights into the psychological dimension of the market. Even if it is incorrect, many investors act as if it is correct. On the other hand, today's investors should be aware of and accept the best prevailing evidence about an approach or concept. As we shall see in Chapter 14, extensive evidence challenges the validity, and likelihood of success, of technical analysis. Therefore, the prudent course of action is to be exposed to the subject, but to be aware of its potential problems and limitations.

The discussion in this chapter seeks to strike a reasonable balance. Although it is desirable to know about technical analysis, the persuasive documentation questioning its usefulness argues for a streamlined approach to its study. Accordingly, we will not discuss the techniques in great detail. A number of technical strategies could be considered, and their interpretation is often a matter of judgment. In particular, we will not discuss pure technical analysis (charting) in detail because its validity is questionable and it is very subjective in interpretation. A reader interested in the fine points of charting should consult one of the references devoted to that subject.[1]

Although technical analysis can be applied to securities other than common stocks, conventional technical analysis emphasizes either the aggregate stock market or individual common stocks. Therefore, we will restrict our discussion in this chapter to common stocks.

What Is Technical Analysis?

Technical analysis can be defined as the use of published market data for the analysis of both the aggregate stock market and individual stocks. It is sometimes called market or internal analysis.

Technical analysis is based on published market data as opposed to fundamental data such as earnings, sales, growth rates, or government regulations. **Market data** include the price of a stock or the level of a market index, volume (number of shares traded), and technical indicators (explained later) such as the short interest ratio. Many technical analysts feel that only market data, as opposed to fundamental data, are relevant.

The objective of technical analysis is timing—predicting short-term price movements in either individual stocks or a market indicator. This is accomplished by studying the action of the market or stock through an analysis of price and volume data, or certain technical indicators. Note that technicians are interested not in price levels but in price changes. They attempt to forecast trends in price changes.

Recall that in fundamental analysis the present value model produces an estimate of a stock's intrinsic value, which is then compared to the market price. Fundamentalists believe that their data, properly evaluated, indicate the worth or intrinsic value of a stock. Technicians, on the other hand, believe that it is extremely difficult to estimate intrinsic value or to derive much benefit from such a number if it is estimated. Technicians believe that it is virtually impossible to consistently obtain and analyze *good* information; in particular, technicians are dubious about the value to be derived from an analysis of published financial statements. Instead, they focus on

---

[1]See, for example, R. Edwards and J. Magee, *Technical Analysis of Stock Trends,* 5th ed. (Springfield, Mass.: John Magee, 1966).

price changes as an indication of the forces of supply and demand for a stock or the market.

The following points summarize technical analysis:

1. Technical analysis is based on published market data.
2. The focus of technical analysis is timing. The emphasis is on likely price changes.
3. Technical analysis focuses on internal factors by analyzing movements in the market and/or a stock. Fundamental analysis, in contrast, focuses on economic and political factors—forces external to the market itself.
4. Technicians tend to concentrate more on the short run; the techniques of technical analysis are designed to detect likely price movements over a relatively short time. Fundamentalists, on the other hand, have a substantial interest in the intermediate and longer run.

The Rationale of Technical Analysis

Technical analysis is based on the proposition that prices are determined by the interaction of demand and supply and reflect the net optimism (pessimism) of market participants. Since all investors are not in agreement on price, the determining factor at any point in time is the net demand (or lack thereof) for a stock based on how many investors are optimistic or pessimistic. Furthermore, once the balance of investors becomes optimistic (pessimistic), this mood is likely to continue for the near-term and can be detected by various technical indicators.

Clearly, prices are set by the forces of supply and demand. Many market participants would agree that investors have differing amounts of information on which to base their decisions. A key question in assessing technical analysis concerns the information that investors use to make their decisions. Technicians believe that investors use a wide variety of factors, including those not related to the fundamental value of a company (e.g., rumors and irrelevant information). If this is the case, one cannot rely solely on a sound fundamental model to determine the intrinsic value of a stock; however, market data can be used to assess trends in market psychology.

A second key question concerns trends in prices and the detection of these trends. A major assumption in technical analysis is that trends in stock prices occur and continue for considerable periods of time. The rationale for this is that investors do not receive and interpret information equally—some receive it earlier or assess it better than other investors. For example, market professionals who follow the market daily may learn of important developments before the average investor. The same is true of the large institutional investors who constantly seek out new information about stocks.

The effect of the process by which prices adjust to new information, as far as technicians are concerned, is one of a *gradual adjustment* toward a new (equilibrium) price. As the stock adjusts from its old equilibrium level to its new level, the price tends to move in a trend. Stock prices require time to adjust to the change in supply and demand.

Technicians assume that the process of change from the old equilibrium to the new can be detected by the action of the stock (or the market) itself. What is important is to be able to recognize quickly a change in the supply–demand relationship and take the appropriate action. The reason the change is taking place is not important; only the fact that it is taking place is important.

The rationale of technical analysis can be summarized as follows:

1. Prices are determined by the forces of demand and supply.
2. Many factors affect demand and supply, including fundamental factors as well as "market psychology" factors.
3. Stock prices tend to move in trends as the stock price adjusts to a new equilibrium level.
4. Trends can be analyzed, and changes in trends detected, by studying the action of price movements and trading volume across time.

The Framework of Technical Analysis

Technical analysis is primarily a timing technique. What matters is the change (as opposed to the level) in prices. Technicians are attempting to discern trends in demand and supply in order to forecast short-term movements in price.

Technical analysis can be applied to both the aggregate market and individual stocks. Either can be analyzed by graphs (charts) and, in some cases, by technical indicators that are applicable to both.

Price and volume are the primary tools of the technical analyst. Technicians believe that the forces of supply and demand show up in patterns of price and volume. Volume data are used to gauge the general condition in the market and to help assess its trend. The evidence seems to suggest that rising (falling) stock prices are usually associated with rising (falling) volume. If stock prices rise but volume activity does not keep pace, technicians would be skeptical about the upward trend. An upward surge on contracting volume would be particularly suspect. A downside movement from some pattern or holding point, accompanied by heavy volume, would be taken as a bearish sign.

Figure 13–1 depicts the technical analysis approach to selecting common stocks. We will discuss aggregate market analysis first, then individual stock analysis. Although there is overlap, technical indicators are primarily concerned with the aggregate market, whereas charts are primarily associated with individual stocks.[2]

---

[2] A good source of current information on technical indicators is *Barron's,* a weekly newspaper.

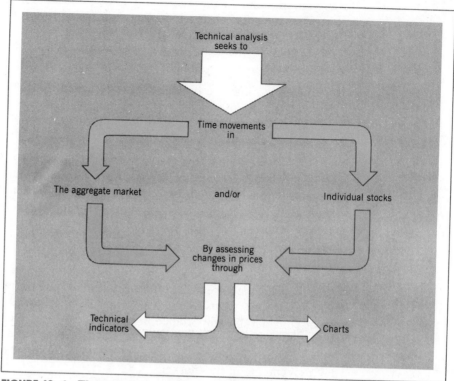

FIGURE 13–1 The technical analysis approach to common stock selection.

Aggregate Market Analysis

Technical analysis is often applied to the aggregate market, as represented by an index such as the Dow Jones Industrial Average or the Standard & Poor's 500 Composite Index. The purpose is to predict changes in the overall market.

The Dow Theory

The oldest and best known theory of technical analysis is the **Dow theory,** originally developed in the late 1800s by the editor of *The Wall Street Journal.*[3] Although Charles H. Dow developed it to describe past price movements, William Hamilton followed up by using it to predict movements in the market (it is not concerned with individual securities). The Dow theory

---

[3]For a good discussion of the Dow theory, see R. Teweles and E. Bradley, *The Stock Market,* 4th ed. (New York: John Wiley, 1982), pp. 307–322.

was very popular in the 1920s and 1930s, and is still discussed today as evidenced by a recent article in *The Journal of Portfolio Management* entitled "Dow Theory Is Alive and Well!"[4]

The basis of the Dow theory is the existence of three types of price movements.

1. Primary moves, a broad market movement that lasts several years.
2. Secondary (intermediate) moves, occurring within the primary moves, which represent interruptions lasting several weeks or months.
3. Day-to-day moves, occurring randomly around the primary and secondary moves.

The term **bull market** refers to an upward primary move, whereas a **bear market** is a downward primary move. A major upward move is said to occur when successive rallies penetrate previously obtained highs, whereas the declines remain above previously obtained lows. A major downward move is expected when successive rallies fail to penetrate previously obtained highs, while declines penetrate previously obtained lows.

The secondary or intermediate moves give rise to the so-called technical corrections, which are often referred to in the popular press. These corrections supposedly adjust for excesses that have occurred. These movements are of considerable importance in applying the Dow theory.

Finally, the day-to-day "ripples" occur often and are of minor importance. Even ardent technical analysts usually do not try to predict day-to-day movements in the market.

Figure 13–2 illustrates the basic concept of the Dow theory (numerous variations exist). The primary trend, represented by the dotted line, is up through time period 1. Although several downward (secondary) reactions occur, these "corrections" do not reach the previous low. Each of these reactions is followed by an upward movement that exceeds the previously obtained high. Trading volume continues to build over this period. Prices again decline after time period 1 as another correction occurs; however, the price recovery fails to surpass the last peak reached (this is referred to as an abortive recovery). When the next downward reaction occurs, it penetrates the previous low. This could suggest that a primary downturn (a new bear market) has begun (subject to confirmation, as mentioned later).

The Dow theory is intended to forecast the start of a primary movement; however, it will not forecast how long the movement will last. It is important to note that, as originally conceived, the Dow Jones Industrial and Rail Average (which was later replaced by the Transportation Average) must *confirm* each other for the movement to be validated. (It is also important to note that confirmation is up to each user of the Dow theory.) The trend will continue as long as the averages confirm each other. Only these averages

---

[4]See D. Glickstein and R. Wublels, "Dow Theory Is Alive and Well!" *The Journal of Portfolio Management*, Vol. 9 (Spring 1983), pp. 28–32.

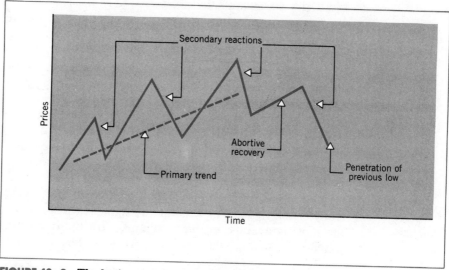

FIGURE 13–2 **The basic concept of the Dow theory.**

matter—extensive records are not required, chart patterns are not studied, and so on.

The Dow theory is subject to a number of criticisms.[5] Studies of its success rate have been disappointing (e.g., over periods of as much as 25 years, investors would have been more successful with a buy-and-hold policy in the same stocks). It is obvious that today's economy is vastly different from that existing when the theory was developed. Confirmations are slow to arrive, and often unclear when they do. The amount of price movement needed for a confirmation is unclear.

One problem with the Dow theory is the many versions available. The theory is interpreted in various ways by its users and may therefore be predicting different (and conflicting) movements at the same time.

Regardless of the problems with the Dow theory, its influence can be seen in research reports and other informational services. Consider the following excerpt from a weekly research comment issued by Merrill Lynch.

The DJIA made a new all time high last week without the accompaniment of most other market indexes including the cumulative advance decline index and the DJ Transports. There now exists what market students often refer to as unfavorable divergences. The theory is that strong markets are broad and confirmed down the line by the majority of issues. Narrow blue chip strength unconfirmed by the rank and file tends to occur late in uptrends prior to reversals of trend.[6]

---

[5]This discussion is based on Teweles and Bradley, *The Stock Market*, pp. 320–321.
[6]This quote was taken from Robert Farrell, *Merrill Lynch Investment News*, Research Comment: 2382, September 26, 1983. Quoted by permission.

Moving Averages

A popular technical technique for analyzing the market (and individual stocks) is that of moving averages of prices, which are used to detect both the direction and the rate of change. Some number of days of closing prices is chosen for the calculation of a moving average. A well-known average for identifying major trends is the 200-day moving average (alternatively, a 30-week moving average); for identifying intermediate trends, a 10-week moving average is often used. After initially calculating the average price, the new value for the moving average is calculated by dropping the earliest observation and adding the latest one. This process is repeated daily (or weekly). The resulting moving average line supposedly represents the basic trend of stock prices.

A comparison of the current market price to the moving average produces a buy or sell signal. The general buy signal is when actual prices rise through the moving average on high volume, with the opposite applying to a sell signal. As usual in technical analysis, variations of this general rule exist.

The Advance–Decline Line (Breadth of the Market)

The advance–decline line measures, on a cumulative basis, the net difference between the number of stocks advancing in price and the number of stocks declining in price. Subtracting the number of declines from the number of advances produces the net advance for a given day (which, of course, can be negative). The advance–decline line (often referred to as the breadth of the market) results from accumulating these numbers across time.

The advance–decline line is compared to a stock average—in particular the Dow Jones Industrial Average—in order to determine if movements in this market indicator have also occurred in the market as a whole. The two normally move together. If both are rising (declining), the overall market is said to be "technically strong (weak)." If the advance–decline line is rising while the average is declining, the decline in the latter should reverse itself. Particular attention is paid to a divergence between the two during a bull market. If the average rises while the line weakens or declines, this indicates a weakening in the market and the average would be expected to reverse itself and start declining.

The Confidence Index

The Confidence Index, published weekly by *Barron's*, attempts to measure investor optimism and pessimism by examining investor actions in the bond market. It is calculated as

$$\text{Confidence Index} = \frac{\text{Yield on 10 high-grade corporate bonds}}{\text{Average yield on 40 Dow Jones bonds}} \quad (13\text{--}1)$$

Since high-grade bonds should always yield less than lower quality bonds, the Confidence Index should always be less than 1.0. As investors become more optimistic about the future, the difference between the two yields in the index decreases (i.e., the default risk premium narrows and the ratio increases). As investors become more pessimistic about the future, the difference between the two yields increases (i.e., the default risk premium rises) and the ratio decreases. Because the bond market tends to be dominated by institutional investors, the Confidence Index is viewed by some as a barometer of sophisticated investors' expectations (and behavior).

Overall, the Confidence Index should move in the same direction as the stock market because increased confidence in the bond market should lead to increased confidence in the stock market. Therefore, an increase (decrease) in the index is a buy (sell) signal. If the Confidence Index leads the market, it can be useful as an indicator.[7] Because it is available weekly in *Barron's,* it is a convenient and accessible indicator.

Although the bond and stock markets generally move together, there is no theoretical reason why confidence in the bond market should precede confidence in the stock market. The latter is considered by most observers to be the preeminent discounter of future events. In fact, the Confidence Index does not always lead the market and has given a number of false signals. Thus, its record as a predictor is mixed.

Contrary Opinion, Old and New

Several indicators are based on the theory of **contrary opinion.** The idea is to trade opposite (contrary) to those investors who, supposedly, almost always lose—in other words, to go against the crowd. This is an old idea on Wall Street, and over the years technicians have developed several measures designed to capitalize on this concept. We will consider some of the best known traditional contrary opinion indicators and then examine a new approach to contrary analysis.

Odd-lot theory According to the **odd-lot theory,** small investors who often buy or sell odd-lots (less than 100 shares of stock) are usually wrong in their actions at market peaks and troughs. Supposedly, such investors typically buy (sell) when the market is at or close to a peak (bottom).

To take advantage of the (wrong) actions of these investors, an indicator must be calculated. Several are available, but a commonly used one is the odd-lot index, defined as

$$\text{Odd-lot index} = \frac{\text{Odd-lot sales}}{\text{Odd-lot purchases}} \qquad (13\text{--}2)$$

A decline in this index would indicate more purchases in relation to sales by small investors, suggesting they are optimistic. According to contrary opinion, it is time to sell—to go against the "man in the street." Conversely,

---

[7] Lead time is believed by advocates to be between two months and one year.

a rise in this index would indicate more sales relative to purchases, a sign of pessimism by small investors but an opportune time for a contrarian to buy.

The odd-lot short sales theory   A variation of the odd-lot index is the odd-lot short sales ratio, defined as[8]

$$\text{Odd-lot short sales ratio} = \frac{\text{Odd-lot short sales}}{\text{Total odd-lot sales}} \qquad (13\text{--}3)$$

As short sales by odd-lotters increase (decrease), these investors are becoming more pessimistic (optimistic). For a contrarian, it is time to buy (sell). The rationale for this ratio is the same as before. Odd-lotters are expected to sell short at precisely the wrong time; that is, prior to a rise in prices.

Regardless of which odd-lot indicator is used, odd-lot theories have not been particularly successful. Small investors have often been correct in their judgments, particularly since the 1970s. This analysis seems to have proven incorrect at least as often as it has proven accurate. Many market professionals today do not believe in odd-lot theories.

The opinions of investment advisory services   *Investors Intelligence,* an investment advisory service that summarizes other advisory services for its readers, calculates an index of investment service opinions.[9] It has found that, on average, these services are most bearish at the market bottom and least bearish at the market top. A "bearish sentiment index" can be calculated as the ratio of advisory services that are bearish to the total number with an opinion. When this index approaches 60%, the Dow Jones Industrial Average tends to go from bearish to bullish; as it approaches 10%, the opposite occurs. Thus, a contrarian should react in the opposite direction of the sentiment these services are exhibiting.

The reason for this seeming contradiction to logic—that investment advisory services are wrong at the extremes—is attributed to the fact that these services tend to follow trends rather than forecast them. Thus, they are reporting and reacting to what has happened rather than concentrating on anticipating what is likely to happen. (See Box 13–1 for the recent performance of this indicator.)

The new contrary opinion   The indicators of contrary opinion discussed previously are not new, and as indicated many market professionals no longer pay much attention to odd-lot theories. A new wave of contrary action has appeared in recent years, however, and has received considerable attention. Although it is not really technical analysis, we will discuss it here because of its natural relationship with the idea of contrary opinion.

---

[8]This ratio is often used by technicians to confirm the general odd-lot indicator.

[9]This discussion is based on J. Cohen, E. Zinbarg, and A. Zeikel, *Investment Analysis and Portfolio Management* (Homewood, Ill.: Richard D. Irwin, 1982), p. 317.

BOX 13–1 MARKET SIGNS: CALL THEM UNRELIABLE

Three Indicators That Have Gone Haywire

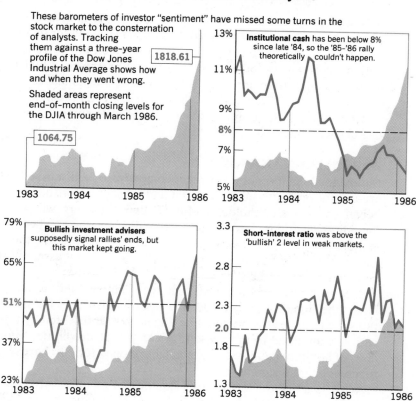

These barometers of investor "sentiment" have missed some turns in the stock market to the consternation of analysts. Tracking them against a three-year profile of the Dow Jones Industrial Average shows how and when they went wrong.

1818.61

Shaded areas represent end-of-month closing levels for the DJIA through March 1986.

1064.75

1983   1984   1985   1986

Institutional cash has been below 8% since late '84, so the '85-'86 rally theoretically couldn't happen.

13%
11%
9%
8%
7%
5%
1983   1984   1985   1986

79%
Bullish investment advisers supposedly signal rallies' ends, but this market kept going.
65%
51%
37%
23%
1983   1984   1985   1986

3.3
Short-interest ratio was above the 'bullish' 2 level in weak markets.
2.8
2.3
2.0
1.8
1.3
1983   1984   1985   1986

Source: Beatrice E. Garcia, "Market Signs: Call Them Unreliable," *The Wall Street Journal*, April 21, 1986, p. 37. Reprinted by permission of *The Wall Street Journal*, © Dow Jones & Company, Inc. (1986). All rights reserved.

The new contrarians are perhaps best illustrated by David Dreman, author of a book entitled *The New Contrarian Investment Strategy,* and a column in *Forbes* magazine entitled "The Contrarian." Dreman believes that the majority of investors, including institutional investors, are often wrong and that a good strategy is often to do what they are not doing. Consider the following excerpt from one of his *Forbes* columns.

Forget the timers who publish market letters telling you how to catch stock swings. A table in my Jan. 4 column showed that between 1971 and 1981 there was an almost perfect correlation between the investment advice they gave you and the future course of the market—unfortunately, almost perfectly wrong.

The advisers were always most bullish near market peaks and recommended the heaviest selling near bottoms, just prior to sharp rallies.[10]

Or consider this Dreman quote on "first-rate professional advice" from another column. "Wisdom? All the evidence I have seen suggests that the best way to treat such wisdom is to hear it out and then go 180 degrees against it."[11] Dreman has argued that a good strategy for investors to follow is that of buying low P/E stocks which, in effect, are currently out of favor with most investors (otherwise, they would be selling at higher P/E ratios). Thus, this contrarian approach is to buy good stocks that are not popular at the time with the "crowd" (i.e., they have low P/E ratios), and wait. We will consider the P/E ratio approach and some of Dreman's findings about the use of this strategy in Chapter 14.

Mutual Fund Liquidity

Mutual funds (a form of investment company, to be discussed in Chapter 18) are institutional investors who own and manage a portfolio of securities on behalf of their shareholders. Mutual fund managers will vary their cash (liquidity) positions across time, depending on their expectations for the market. Because of the availability of data on these funds, the ratio of cash and cash equivalents (e.g., Treasury bills) to the total assets of the fund can be obtained on a timely basis.

One technical position with regard to mutual fund liquidity is that the larger the liquidity percentage, the more bullish it is for the market. The rationale involves the potential buying power represented by this liquidity—as it is committed to the market, prices will be driven up. Similarly, a low level of liquidity indicates little available money for purchases by the mutual funds, a bearish sign.

What is a high or low level of liquidity? Probably 5–10% cash and cash equivalents is considered normal. A level of liquidity below 5–6% was considered bearish up until the mid-1970s, while 7–8% is the current range often used. A level above 10% is typically considered bullish, with recent emphasis on the 11–12% range.[12] Using these benchmarks, the 1985–1986 rally occurred despite institutional cash below 8%—see Box 13–1.

It is interesting to note that mutual fund liquidity can be used as a contrary opinion technique (and, therefore, could have been included in the previous section). Under this scenario, mutual funds are viewed in a manner similar to odd-lotters—they are presumed to act incorrectly before a market turning point. Therefore, when mutual fund liquidity is low because the funds are

---

[10] See David Dreman, "A Bernard Baruch Kind of Market," *Forbes,* August 30, 1982, p. 178.

[11] See David Dreman, "Consulting the Oracles," *Forbes,* November 7, 1983, p. 306.

[12] The liquidity level can be found in *Barron's* "Monthly Mutual Fund Indicators." It is listed as "Liquid Asset Ratio (Equity and Balanced)."

fully invested, contrarians believe that the market is at, or near, a peak. The funds should be building up cash (liquidity), but instead they are extremely bullish and are fully invested. Conversely, when funds hold large liquid reserves, it suggests that they are bearish; contrarians would consider this a good time to buy because the market may be at, or near, its low point.

This contrarian view is consistent with the first interpretation presented in terms of its predictions for future market movements. In either case, a high level of liquidity is a bullish sign and low liquidity is a bearish sign. For one piece of factual evidence, consider the liquidity position of common stock mutual funds in August 1982, the start of a very strong bull market. At that time, 12% of their assets were in cash.

Short Interest Ratio

The **short interest ratio** is defined as

$$\text{Short interest ratio} = \frac{\text{Total shares sold short}}{\text{Average daily trading volume}} \qquad (13\text{--}4)$$

The short interest (number of shares sold short) is calculated on the twentieth of the month and appears subsequently in *The Wall Street Journal*, listed by stock name for both the New York and American Exchanges. Although available for each stock, this information is typically used in aggregate market analysis.

The rationale for this ratio is somewhat unusual. Investors sell short when they expect prices to decline; therefore, the higher the short interest, the more investors are expecting a decline. However, this ratio is usually interpreted in the opposite manner. A *high* short interest ratio is taken as a bullish sign because the large number of shares sold short represent a large number of shares that must be repurchased in order to close out the short sales (if the ratio is low, the required purchases are not present). In effect, the short seller must repurchase, whether his or her expectations were correct or not. The larger the short sale ratio, the larger the potential demand that is indicated; therefore, an increase in the ratio indicates more "pent up" demand for the shares that have been shorted.

The short interest ratio for a given month can be interpreted only in relation to historical boundaries, which are approximately 1.0 to 2.0 for the NYSE. A short interest ratio above 2.0 is considered extremely bullish, while a ratio below 1.0 indicates weakness; therefore, if the ratio rises above normal, a buy signal is generated, and if it falls below 1.0, a sell signal is generated. However, increased trading in stock options and futures (discussed in Chapters 15 and 17 respectively), which provide investors with new ways to hedge and speculate, has distorted the historical boundaries. The short interest ratio has recently been above 2.0 on a regular basis, and it was above 2.0 when the market was weak—see Box 13–1.

Individual Stock Analysis

We turn our attention now from an analysis of the aggregate market to an analysis of individual common stocks. Technicians are interested in both.

Technical Indicators

Some of the technical indicators discussed previously can be applied to individual stocks as well as the aggregate market. Moving averages, for example, are used for individual stocks as well as the market. Moving average series are available from financial advisory services such as *Daily Graphs,* which offers weekly charts on over 2600 companies. Each chart includes both a 200-day and a 10-week moving average.

The short interest ratio can also be calculated for individual stocks, and the short interest on many NYSE and AMEX stocks is reported monthly in *The Wall Street Journal* along with the short interest position for the market. Overall, however, technical indicators are usually applied to the market.

To assess individual stock price movements, technicians generally rely on charts or graphs of price movements. A second popular technique is that of relative strength analysis.

Charts of Price Patterns

The **charting** of price patterns is one of the classic technical analysis techniques. Technicians believe that stock prices move in trends, with price changes forming patterns that can be recognized and categorized. By visually assessing the forces of supply and demand, technicians hope to be able to predict the likely direction of future movements.

Technical analysts rely primarily on bar charts and point-and-figure charts. We will discuss each of these in turn. During this discussion, keep in mind two terms often used by technicians—support level and resistance level. A **support level** is the level of price (or, more correctly, a price range) at which a technician expects a significant increase in the demand for a stock; a **resistance level,** on the other hand, is the level of price (range) at which a technician expects a significant increase in the supply of a stock. Support levels tend to develop when profit taking causes a reversal in a stock's price following an increase. Investors who did not purchase earlier are now willing to buy at this price, which becomes a support level. Resistance levels tend to develop after a stock declines from a higher level. Investors are waiting to sell the stocks at a certain recovery point. At certain price levels, therefore, a significant increase in supply occurs and the price will encounter resistance moving beyond this level.

Box 13–2 shows a technical opinion from a brokerage firm report. Several of the terms just discussed, such as resistance and support levels, are mentioned; furthermore, trends covering different periods of time are assessed.

BOX 13–2 A TECHNICAL OPINION FROM A BROKERAGE FIRM

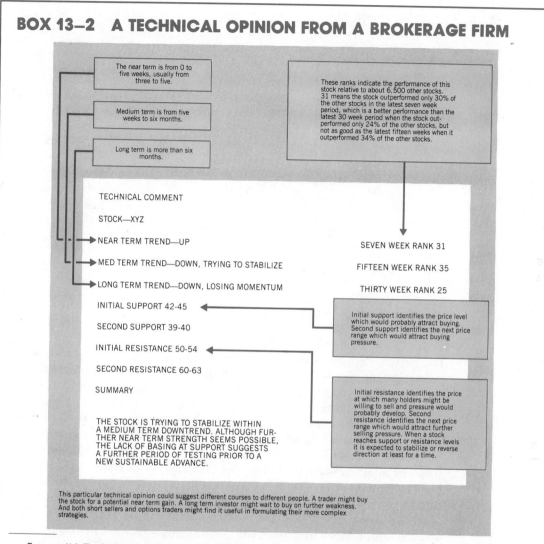

The near term is from 0 to five weeks, usually from three to five.

Medium term is from five weeks to six months.

Long term is more than six months.

These ranks indicate the performance of this stock relative to about 6,500 other stocks. 31 means the stock outperformed only 30% of the other stocks in the latest seven week period, which is a better performance than the latest 30 week period when the stock outperformed only 24% of the other stocks, but not as good as the latest fifteen weeks when it outperformed 34% of the other stocks.

TECHNICAL COMMENT

STOCK—XYZ

NEAR TERM TREND—UP

MED TERM TREND—DOWN, TRYING TO STABILIZE

LONG TERM TREND—DOWN, LOSING MOMENTUM

INITIAL SUPPORT 42-45

SECOND SUPPORT 39-40

INITIAL RESISTANCE 50-54

SECOND RESISTANCE 60-63

SUMMARY

THE STOCK IS TRYING TO STABILIZE WITHIN A MEDIUM TERM DOWNTREND. ALTHOUGH FURTHER NEAR TERM STRENGTH SEEMS POSSIBLE, THE LACK OF BASING AT SUPPORT SUGGESTS A FURTHER PERIOD OF TESTING PRIOR TO A NEW SUSTAINABLE ADVANCE.

SEVEN WEEK RANK 31

FIFTEEN WEEK RANK 35

THIRTY WEEK RANK 25

Initial support identifies the price level which would probably attract buying. Second support identifies the next price range which would attract buying pressure.

Initial resistance identifies the price at which many holders might be willing to sell and pressure would probably develop. Second resistance identifies the next price range which would attract further selling pressure. When a stock reaches support or resistance levels it is expected to stabilize or reverse direction at least for a time.

This particular technical opinion could suggest different courses to different people. A trader might buy the stock for a potential near term gain. A long term investor might wait to buy on further weakness. And both short sellers and options traders might find it useful in formulating their more complex strategies.

Bar charts Probably the most popular chart in technical analysis, and clearly the simplest, bar charts are plotted with price on the vertical axis and time on the horizontal axis. Each day's price movement is represented by a vertical bar whose top (bottom) represents the high (low) price for the day. (A small horizontal tic may be used to designate closing price for the day.)

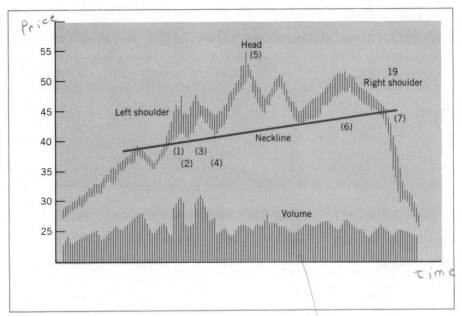

FIGURE 13–3 A bar chart for Unfloppy Disks, Inc.

The bottom of a bar chart usually shows the trading volume for each day, permitting the simultaneous observation of both price and volume activity. Note that the time intervals do not have to be days, but could be weeks, months, or anything else a particular preparer may choose. Figure 13–3 shows a daily bar chart for a hypothetical company, Unfloppy Disks, Inc.

The technician using charts will search for patterns in the chart that can be used to predict future price moves. Note in Figure 13–3 the strong uptrend occurring over a period of months. This trend ended with a rally on high volume (at point 1 in the figure) that forms part of the left shoulder of a famous chart pattern called a "head-and-shoulders" pattern. In the left shoulder there is initial strong demand followed by a reaction on lower volume (2), and then a second rally, with strong volume, carrying prices still higher (3). Profit taking again causes prices to fall to the so-called neckline (4), thus completing the left shoulder (the neckline is formed by connecting previous low points). A rally occurs, but this time on low volume, and again prices sink back to the neckline. This is the head (5). The last step is the formation of the right shoulder, which in this case occurs with light volume (6). Growing weakness can be identified as the price approaches the neckline. As can be seen in Figure 13–3, a downside breakout occurs on heavy volume, which is considered by technicians to be a sell signal.

What about other patterns? The number of such patterns considered by technicians is very large. Some of the possible patterns include flags, pennants, gaps (of more than one type), triangles of various types (e.g., symmetrical, ascending, descending, and inverted), the inverted saucer or dome, the triple top, compound fulcrum, the rising (and falling) wedge, the broadening bottom, the duplex horizontal, rectangles, and the inverted V.

It is obvious that numerous patterns are possible and can usually be found on a chart of stock prices. It is also obvious that most, if·not all, of these patterns are much easier to identify in hindsight than at the time they are actually occurring.

Point-and-figure charts   A **point-and-figure chart** is somewhat more complex in that it shows only significant price changes, and volume is not shown at all. It also attempts to predict the amount of the future price movements. Although the horizontal axis still depicts time, specific calendar time is not particularly important (some chartists do show the month in which changes occur).

An X is typically used to show upward movements, and O to show downward movements. Each X or O on a particular chart may represent $1 movements, $2 movements, $5 movements, and so on, depending upon how much movement is considered significant for that stock. An X or O is recorded only when the price moves by the specified amount.

Figure 13–4 shows a point-and-figure chart for several days for a hypothetical company called Gigantic Computers. Note the lack of a time dimension in this chart. Instead, only significant price changes, in this case $1, are recorded. An X is recorded for each $1 uptick and an O for each $1 downtick. A new column is started each time the direction of price change is reversed.

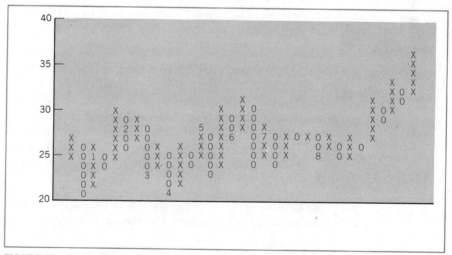

FIGURE 13–4   A point-and-figure chart for Gigantic Computers. X = $1 upward price change, 0 = $1 downward price change (numbers indicate months).

A point-and-figure chart is designed to compress many price changes into a small space. By doing this, areas of "congestion" can be identified. A congestion area is a compacted area of price fluctuations (i.e., a closely compacted horizontal band of Xs and Os). The technician studies a congestion area in search of a "breakout," which will indicate an expected upward or downward movement in stock price. In Figure 13–4, the congestion at month 8 leads to an upward breakout.

Some evidence on price charts   There are many chart patterns, some of which were mentioned earlier, and numerous technicians analyzing and interpreting these patterns. It is, therefore, impossible to "demonstrate" conclusively the lack of predictive significance in charting. Very few *scientific* studies of the ability of chart patterns to predict the future direction of price movements have been conducted. One such study is relevant in considering the likelihood of success of this activity.

Robert Levy studied the predictive significance of "five-point" chart patterns. A five-point chart pattern is one with two highs and three lows, or two lows and three highs. As Figure 13–5 shows, there are 32 possible forms that this chart can assume. As Levy noted:[13]

> The avid chartist will recognize, among the thirty-two patterns, several variations of channels, wedges, diamonds, symmetrical triangles, head and shoulders, reverse head and shoulders, triple tops, and triple bottoms. Each of these formations allegedly reflects underlying supply/demand and support/resistance conditions which have implications as to future price behavior. A common belief among chartists is that the appearance of certain patterns followed by a "breakout" gives a profitable buy or sell signal. (Reprinted from Robert A. Levy, "The Predictive Significance of Five-Point Chart Patterns," *The Journal of Business*, The University of Chicago Press, July 1971, p. 316. By permission of the University of Chicago Press. © 1971 by the University of Chicago.)

Using daily prices for 548 NYSE stocks over a five-year period (1964–1969), Levy found 19,077 five-point patterns. Of these, 9383 were followed by a breakout and were therefore studied. The results indicated that although some patterns did produce better results than others, none performed very differently from the market. Deducting brokerage commissions, *none* of the 32 patterns was found to have any "profitable forecasting ability in either (bullish or bearish) direction." The really surprising conclusion of this study, however, concerned the charts themselves. Again, to quote Levy:

> Even more important, an evaluation of the six distinct best and worst patterns for the four holding periods uncovers an extraordinary contradiction between

---

[13] See R. Levy, "The Predictive Significance of Five-Point Chart Patterns," *The Journal of Business*, Vol. 44 (July 1971), pp. 316–323. © 1971 by the University of Chicago. All rights reserved.

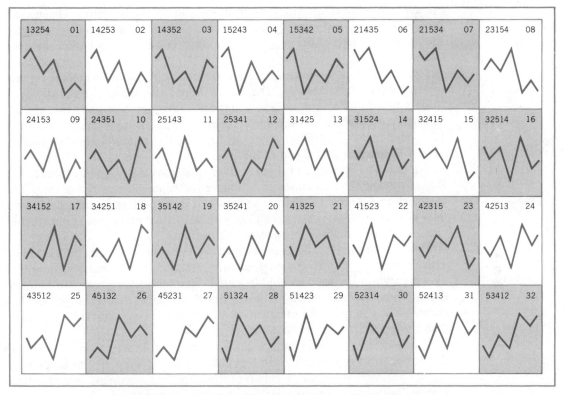

FIGURE 13–5   Possible forms of a five-point chart pattern.
Source: Robert A. Levy, ''The Predictive Significance of Five-Point Chart Patterns,'' *The Journal of Business,* The University of Chicago Press, July 1971, p. 317. By permission of the University of Chicago Press. © 1971 by the University of Chicago.

the lessons of the chartist's textbook and the empirical evidence generated by these tests. For example, the best performing patterns would probably be characterized as bearish by most technicians, and conversely, the worst performing patterns would, in two of the three cases, be characterized as bullish. (Reprinted from Robert A. Levy, ''The Predictive Significance of Five-Point Chart Patterns,'' *The Journal of Business*, The University of Chicago Press, July 1971, p. 322. By permission of the University of Chicago Press. © 1971 by the University of Chicago.)

Opinions about charting vary widely. The evidence is not conclusive—at least to everyone's satisfaction. The controversy will continue.

Relative Strength

A well-known technique used to forecast individual stocks (or industries) is relative strength analysis. The **relative strength** for a given stock is calculated as the ratio of the stock's price to a market index, or an industry index, or to the average price of the stock itself over some previous period. These ratios can be plotted to form a graph of relative price across time; that is, the graph shows the strength of the stock relative to its industry, the market, or whatever.

Numerous investment information services provide information on relative strength. For example, *The Value Line Investment Survey* divides a stock's price by the Value Line Composite Average and plots this relative strength ratio for each company it covers. In the example page from *Value Line* (shown in Chapter 4) covering EG&G, the relative price strength is shown in the plot at the top of the page.

The relative strength of a stock over time may be of use in forecasting. Because trends are assumed to continue for some time, a rising ratio indicates relative strength—that is, a stock that is outperforming the market and may continue to do so. As they do with most technical indicators, technicians interpret some of these signals in different ways.

Relative strength analysis lends itself well to computerized stock analysis. This probably accounts for its popularity among institutional investors who own highly automated and sophisticated data analysis systems. In fact, the extent to which a number of institutional investors use relative strength techniques, and have the means to observe changes at about the same time, could affect the volatility of a stock.

The relative strength concept gained considerable attention in 1967 with the publication of an article by Levy that claimed very strong investment results through the use of relative strength.[14] Subsequent investigations pointed out several deficiencies with Levy's study.[15] Nevertheless, the concept remains an important part of technical analysis today.

New work appears periodically supporting relative strength. For example, a 1981 paper by James Bohan indicated support for relative strength analysis over the years 1969–1980.[16] Bohan studied Standard & Poor's industry groups on an annual basis for those years. He found that for the top quintile, which consisted of the top 20% of industry groups from the preceding year, there was a 29% probability of a group remaining in the first quintile in the following year. The lowest quintile showed a 32% probability of remaining in the bottom. When the average annual returns for each quintile were calculated, the top quintile showed the largest average returns, whereas the bottom quintile showed the smallest returns (13.4% versus 2.8%

---

[14]R. Levy, "Random Walks: Reality or Myth," *Financial Analysts Journal,* Vol. 23 (November–December 1967), pp. 69–77.

[15]M. Jensen, "Random Walks: Reality or Myth," *Financial Analysts Journal,* Vol. 23 (November–December 1967), pp. 77–85; and M. Jensen and G. Bennington, "Random Walks and Technical Theories: Some Additional Evidence," *Journal of Finance,* Vol. 25 (May 1970), pp. 469–482.

[16]J. Bohan, "Relative Strength: Further Positive Evidence," *The Journal of Portfolio Management,* Vol. 8 (Fall 1981), pp. 36–39.

respectively, with the S&P 500 showing 5.3%). Furthermore, the first three quintiles were found to have betas not significantly different from the market, and the bottom two quintiles showed betas significantly higher than the market.

Some Conclusions about Technical Analysis

Technical analysis often appeals to those beginning a study of investments because it is easy to believe that stock prices form repeatable patterns over time or that certain indicators should be related to future market (or individual stock) price movements. Most people who look at a chart of a particular stock will immediately see what they believe to be patterns in the price changes and clear evidence of trends that should have been obvious to anyone studying it.

On the other hand, academicians (and numerous practitioners) are highly skeptical of technical analysis, to say the least. Virtually every academic article used at the college level will dismiss, or seriously disparage, this concept. The reasons are at least two-fold.

1. Tests of technical analysis techniques have failed to confirm their value, given all costs and considering an alternative, such as a buy-and-hold strategy.
2. Most empirical tests of the efficient market hypothesis (EMH), to be discussed in the next chapter, support this concept. As we shall see, a belief in the EMH is tantamount to a denial of the usefulness of technical analysis.

In addition to these reasons, other troubling features of technical analysis remain. First of all, several interpretations of each technical tool and chart pattern are not only possible, but usual. One or more of the interpreters will be correct (more or less), but it is virtually impossible to know ex ante (beforehand) who these will be. Ex post (after the fact), we will know which indicator or chart, or whose interpretation, was correct, but only those investors who used that particular information will benefit. Tools such as the Dow theory are well known for their multiple interpretations by various observers who disagree over how the theory is to be interpreted.

On the other hand, consider a technical trading rule (or chart pattern) that is, in fact, successful; that is, when it gives its signal on the basis of reaching some specified value (or forms a clear picture on a chart), it correctly predicts movements in the market or some particular stock. Such a rule or patterns, if observed by several market participants, will be self-destructive as more and more investors use it. Price will reach its equilibrium value quickly, taking away profit opportunities from all but the quickest. Furthermore, some observers will start trying to act before the rest on the basis of what they expect to happen (e.g., they may act before a complete head-and-shoulders forms). Price will then reach an equilibrium even quicker, so that only those who act earliest will benefit. Eventually, the value of any such rule will be negated entirely.

Finally, no inherent reason exists for stock price movements to repeat themselves. For example, flipping a fair coin 100 times should, on average, result in about 50 heads and 50 tails. There is some probability that the first 10 tosses could produce 10 heads. However, the chance of such a pattern repeating itself would be very small. As we shall see in the next chapter, there is strong evidence suggesting that stock price *changes* over time follow a "random walk"—in effect, any patterns formed are accidental, but not surprising. See Box 13–3 for a good discussion of random occurrences.

BOX 13–3 GAMBLER'S PARADOX

Many economists and those who use fundamental economic data in their work argue that commodity and stock prices are randomly generated, and, therefore, no matter what historically based method one might employ, it is impossible to predict tomorrow's or next month's prices. Technicians who employ such things as moving averages, chart and price patterns, computer programs and the like, of course, don't agree with such a position.

One reason that it is difficult to find common ground between the two schools of thought is that there is no general agreement about how commodity and stock prices are produced. If the underlying process is random and/or independent, it is probably impossible to predict future price movements. But if prices are either nonrandom and/or dependent, then there is some pattern to prices, and, with the appropriate tools, one should be able to detect that pattern.

The mathematical definitions of randomness and independence are not obvious, but the concepts can be made clear by an example. Suppose you have a small jar filled with 50 white and 50 black balls. Take out 1 ball at a time, note its color and replace it in the jar, then withdraw another ball. If you do this repeatedly, you will generate a random and independent sequence of colors. It is random because each and every ball had an equal chance of being selected. It is independent because the choice of the first ball had no effect on the selection of the second and succeeding balls.

If the process is truly independent and you have a "run" of six white balls, will that affect the probability of getting a white ball on the seventh selection? Of course not. But so many people believe the opposite that the phenomenon has been given a name—"the gambler's paradox" or "maturity of chance." Unfortunately, for gamblers and everyone else, if the process is truly independent—that is, if you have not inadvertently biased it in some way—then the probability of drawing a white ball is still 0.5. The previous six selections have no effect on the outcome of the seventh.

If you like challenges, try to convince someone who is holding a pair of so-called hot dice and has just rolled six consecutive sevens at a crap table that the seventh roll is completely independent of the previous six. According to John Scarne, a well-known writer on gambling, the longest color win recorded at roulette in an American casino occurred in Saratoga, N.Y. in

1943, when the color red came up 32 times. The odds against this happening are in the billions. Some might call this a miracle, but it is well to keep in mind that the odds are exactly the same against a series of alternate occurrences of red and black, odd, even or any other arbitrary series of 32 events.

The only thing that makes this run remarkable is that one color turned up in the string. Scarne reports in his book *Complete Guide to Gambling* that he witnessed a woman make 39 consecutive passes at the crap table. The odds against such an event make the roulette example seem like an everyday occurrence. Such events would normally break any gambling house, but table limits prevent the winnings from becoming astronomical. (I would still want to check the dice in the latter example.)

But back to commodity price behavior. If you believe that you can predict the behavior of commodity prices, then it is necessary to assume, at least implicitly, that prices are nonrandom, dependent or both. Otherwise, you are involved in a gambler's paradox, and, in the long run, whatever system you use will not work.

Source: Adapted from Stanley W. Angrist's column, by permission of *Forbes* magazine, December 2, 1985. © Forbes Inc., 1985.

What can we conclude about technical analysis? First, it is impossible to test all the techniques of technical analysis and their variations and interpretations; in fact, technical analysis has not been tested thoroughly. The techniques of technical analysis are simply too numerous; therefore, absolutely definitive statements cannot be made about the sum total of this subject. A good example of the omissions in this area is the use of volume in technical strategies. Although volume is a recognized part of technical analysis, few tests have been conducted on its use in conjunction with the rest of technical analysis.

Second, in fairness, many technical analysts recognize that technical analysis is not the key to riches and that it will not solve the investment problem of what stocks to buy, and when. These analysts view technical analysis as a supplement or complement to a broader analysis. They do not ignore fundamental analysis, but perhaps use technical analysis to screen for companies that will then be analyzed by fundamental analysis.

Third, on the basis of all available evidence, it is difficult to justify technical analysis. The studies that have been done in support of this concept have produced, at best, weak support. Studies done in support of the EMH, on the other hand, are much stronger and are nearly unanimous in their conclusions that technical analysis does not work. It is time, therefore, to turn to a consideration of the efficient market hypothesis.

Summary

This chapter discusses the second of three approaches to selecting securities—technical analysis. This is the oldest approach available to investors and in many respects the most controversial.

Technical analysis relies on published market data, primarily price and volume data, to predict the short-term direction of individual stocks or the market as a whole. The emphasis is on internal factors that help to detect demand–supply conditions in the market. The rationale is that the net demand (or lack thereof) for stocks can be detected by various technical indicators, and that trends in stock prices occur and continue for considerable periods of time. Stock prices require time to adjust to the change in supply and demand.

Price and volume are primary tools of the technical analyst, as are various technical indicators. Technical analysis can be applied to both the aggregate market and to individual stocks.

Aggregate market analysis originated with the Dow theory, the best-known technical theory. It is designed to detect the start of major movements, based on two market indicators confirming each other. Several versions of the Dow theory are in use, and several criticisms of this indicator can be made.

Other technical indicators of the aggregate market include, but are not limited to, the following:

1. Moving averages, used to detect both the direction and the rate of change in prices.
2. The advance–decline line (breadth of market), used to assess the condition of the overall market.
3. The Confidence Index, which attempts to measure investor optimism and pessimism.
4. Contrary opinion, which is designed to go against the crowd. Included here are the odd-lot theory, the odd-lot short sales theory, and the opinions of investment advisory services.
5. Mutual fund liquidity, which uses the potential buying power (liquidity) of mutual funds as a bullish or bearish indicator.
6. Short interest ratio, which assesses potential demand from investors who have sold short.

When applied to individual stocks, technical analysis can involve some of the same indicators just described. More importantly, it will involve the use of charts of price patterns to detect the trends that are believed to persist over time. The most often used charts are bar charts, which show each day's price movement as well as volume, and point-and-figure charts, which show only significant price changes as they occur.

Numerous chart "patterns" are recognizable to a technician; therefore, this type of technical analysis requires its own specialization. However, there is some scientific evidence available suggesting that patterns based on "five-point chart patterns" have no validity. Furthermore, all patterns are subject to multiple interpretations, as various technicians will read the same chart differently.

A second well-known technique used for individual stocks is that of relative strength, which shows the strength of a particular stock in relation to its average price, its industry, or the market. Although original claims for its effectiveness have been refuted, this concept remains active today with support for it appearing periodically.

Key Words

Bar chart	Odd-lot theory
Bear market	Point-and-figure chart
Bull market	Relative strength
Charting	Resistance level
Contrary opinion	Short interest ratio
Dow theory	Support level
Market data	Technical analysis

QUESTIONS AND PROBLEMS

1. Describe the rationale for technical analysis.
2. Differentiate between fundamental analysis and technical analysis.
3. What do technicians assume about the adjustment of stock prices from one equilibrium position to another?
4. What role does volume play in technical analysis?
5. What is the purpose of the Dow theory? What is the significance of the "confirmation" signal in this theory?
6. How does the Dow theory forecast how long a market movement will last?
7. Using a moving average, how is a sell signal generated?
8. Why is the advance–decline line referred to as an indicator of breadth-of-market?
9. Why would an increase in the Confidence Index be a buy signal?
10. What is the rationale for the theory of contrary opinion?
11. How is the odd-lot index calculated? How is it used as a buy or sell signal?
12. Why is a rising short interest ratio considered to be a bullish indicator?
13. Distinguish between a bar chart and a point-and-figure chart.
14. What is relative strength analysis?
15. On a rational economic basis, why is the study of chart patterns likely to be an unrewarding activity?
16. Is it possible to categorically prove or disprove technical analysis?
17. Assume that you know a technical analyst who claims success on the basis

of his or her chart patterns. How might you go about scientifically testing this claim?

18. How do the new contrarians differ from the more traditional contrarians?

19. Why do stock price movements repeat themselves?

20. Look at the bar chart of the Dow Jones Averages on the next to last page of *The Wall Street Journal*. Does this chart cover a sufficient time period to apply the Dow theory?

21. With reference to question 20, why would this chart, or possibly several of these charts covering a number of months, be useful in trying to apply the Dow theory?

22. What new financial instruments have caused the short interest ratio to be less reliable? Why?

23. Describe a bullish sign when using a moving average. A bearish sign. Do the same for the advance–decline line.

24. Consider the plot of stock X in the following diagram. The plot shows weekly prices for one year, based on a beginning price of $30.

    a. Using Figure 13–5, do you see any five-point chart patterns in this figure?

    b. Do you see any other patterns in this chart that might help you to predict the future price of this stock?

    c. What is your forecast of this stock's price over the next three months?

    d. If this price series were to be generated using random numbers, do you think it could resemble this plot?

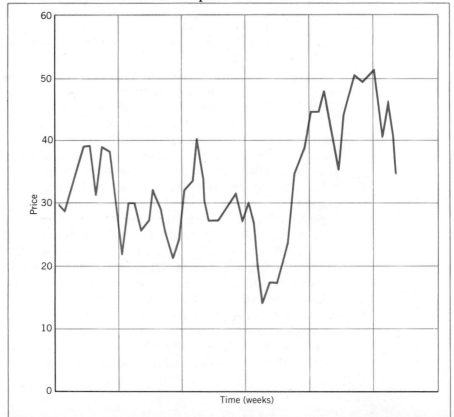

Time (weeks)

Selected References

Bohan, J. "Relative Strength: Further Positive Evidence." *The Journal of Portfolio Management,* Fall 1981, pp. 36–39.

Cootner, P. H., ed. *The Random Character of Stock Market Prices.* Cambridge, Massachusetts: MIT Press, 1964.

Edwards, R., and Magee, J. *Technical Analysis of Stock Trends.* 5th ed. Springfield, Mass.: John Magee, 1966.

Fama, Eugene F. "The Behavior of Stock Market Prices." *Journal of Business,* January 1965, pp. 34–105.

Fama, Eugene F., and Blume, Marshall E. "Filter Rules and Stock Market Trading." *Journal of Business,* January 1966, pp. 226–241.

Glickstein, D., and Wublels, R. "Dow Theory Is Alive and Well!" *The Journal of Portfolio Management,* Spring 1983, pp. 28–32.

Greene, M., and Fielitz, B. "Long-Term Dependence in Common Stocks Returns." *Journal of Financial Economics,* May 1977, pp. 339–349.

James, F. E., Jr. "Monthly Moving Averages—An Effective Investment Tool?" *Journal of Financial and Quantitative Analysis,* September 1968, pp. 315–326.

Jensen, Michael C. "Random Walks: Reality or Myth." *Financial Analysts Journal,* November–December 1967, pp. 77–85.

Jensen, Michael C., and Bennington, George A. "Random Walks and Technical Theories: Some Additional Evidence." *Journal of Finance,* May 1970, pp. 469–482.

Joy, O. M., and Jones, Charles P. "Should We Believe the Tests of Market Efficiency?" *Journal of Portfolio Management,* Summer 1986, pp. 49–54.

Kaish, Stanley. "Odd-Lot Profit and Loss Performance." *Financial Analysts Journal,* September–October 1969, pp. 83–90.

Levy, R. A. "Random Walks: Reality or Myth." *Financial Analysts Journal,* November–December 1967, pp. 69–77.

Levy, R. A. "The Predictive Significance of Five-Point Chart Patterns." *The Journal of Business,* July 1971, pp. 316–323.

Levy, R. A. "Conceptual Foundations of Technical Analysis." *Financial Analysts Journal,* July–August 1966, pp. 83–89.

Levy, R. A. "Relative Strength as a Criterion for Investment Selection." *The Journal of Finance,* December 1967, pp. 595–610.

Loeb, T. "Trading Cost: The Critical Link between Investment Information and Results." *Financial Analysts Journal,* May–June 1983, pp. 39–44.

Malkiel, Burton G. *A Random Walk Down Wall Street.* 2nd college ed. New York: W. W. Norton, 1981.

Roberts, Harry. "Stock Market 'Patterns' and Financial Analysis: Methodological Suggestions." *Journal of Finance,* March 1959, pp. 1–10.

Teweles, Richard J., and Bradley, Edward S. *The Stock Market,* 4th ed. New York: John Wiley, 1982.

Umstead, David. "Forecasting Stock Market Prices." *Journal of Finance,* May 1977, pp. 427–441.

Ying, C. "Stock Market Prices and Volume of Sales." *Econometrica,* July 1966, pp. 676–685.

Zweig, Martin E. *Understanding Technical Forecasting*. Princeton, N.J.: Dow Jones, 1978.

CHAPTER 14

EFFICIENT MARKETS

We have now considered fundamental and technical approaches for selecting stocks. An alternative approach is based on the concept that securities markets, in particular the market for common stocks, are efficient. As explained later, "efficient" refers to quick and accurate reflection of information in prices.

In an efficient market, many traditional investing activities, such as technical analysis and even "typical" fundamental analysis, are suspect at best and useless at worst. Needless to say, such a proposition has generated tremendous controversy, which continues today. The idea of an efficient market remains controversial, and a number of participants refuse to accept it. This is not surprising in view of the enormous implications that an efficient market has for everyone concerned with securities. Some market participants' jobs and reputations are at stake, and they are not going to accept this concept readily.

Because of its significant impact and implications, the idea that markets are efficient deserves careful thought and study. Beginners should approach it with an open mind. The fact that some well-known market observers and participants reject this idea does not reduce its validity. Nor is it going to disappear, because too much evidence exists to support it. The intelligent approach for investors, therefore, is to learn about it and from it.

First, we will consider what an efficient market is and what it means.

Although the concept of market efficiency applies to all financial markets, we will concentrate on the equities market. The evidence that has accumulated in support of the concept will be sampled, as well as some evidence of possible market anomalies (i.e., inefficiencies). Finally, the implications of efficient markets to investors will be considered.

What Is an Efficient Market?

As we know from our study of valuation models in previous chapters, stock prices are determined by investors on the basis of the expected cash flows to be received from a stock and the risk involved. Investors use all the information they have available or can reasonably obtain. This information set consists of both known information and beliefs about the future—that is, information that can reasonably be inferred. Regardless of its form, information is the key to the determination of stock prices; therefore, it is the central issue of the efficient markets concept.

 An **efficient market** (EM) is defined as one in which the prices of securities fully reflect all known information quickly and accurately. Let us consider the meaning of this definition.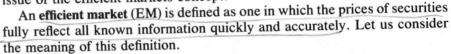

- *Prices*. Although we could talk in terms of the returns on securities, the EM concept usually refers to the prices of stocks.[1] If prices are determined in an efficient market, returns are also, because prices are the principal component of the return (HPY) calculation for many stocks.
- *Fully reflect*. The EM concept postulates that investors will assimilate all information into prices in making their buy and sell decisions. Therefore, the current price of a stock incorporates all information.
- *All known information*. The EM concept assumes that all known information is reflected in the price, including not only past information (e.g., last year's or last quarter's earnings), but also current information as well as events that have been announced but have not yet transpired (such as a forthcoming stock split). Furthermore, information that can reasonably be inferred is also assumed to be reflected in price. For example, if many investors believe that interest rates will soon decline, prices will reflect this belief before the actual decline occurs.
- *Quickly and accurately*. This part of the definition often causes beginners some problems. The EM concept does not require that the adjustment be literally instantaneous, only that it occur very quickly as information becomes known. Given the extremely rapid dissemination of information in the United States through electronic communications equipment, which virtually all brokerage houses and institutional inves-

---

[1] The term "price efficient" is sometimes used. It means that security markets are efficient in processing information.

tors have, information is spread very quickly, almost instantaneously, to market participants with access to these sources. For individual investors without this access, important information can be received, at the latest, the following day in such sources as *The Wall Street Journal*.

As for accurately, again the EM concept does not claim, or require, a perfect adjustment. Rather, it says that the adjustment in prices resulting from information is "unbiased." This means that the expected value of the adjustment error is zero—sometimes too large and at other times too small, but on average evening out and correct. The new price does not have to be the new equilibrium price, but only an unbiased estimate of the final equilibrium price that will be established after investors have fully assessed the input of the information.

Why the Market Can Be Expected to Be Efficient

If all this seems too much to expect, consider the situation from the following standpoint. It can be shown that an efficient market can exist if the following events occur:

[handwritten note: ? → not always there, can't be explained by formula]

[handwritten note in left margin: Assumptions behind EMH]

1. A large number of rational, profit maximizing investors exist who actively participate in the market by analyzing, valuing, and trading stocks. These investors are price takers; that is, one participant alone cannot affect the price of a security.
2. Information is costless and widely available to market participants at approximately the same time.
3. Information is generated in a random fashion such that announcements are basically independent of one another.
4. Investors react quickly and accurately to the new information, causing stock prices to adjust accordingly. *[handwritten note: → not always]*

These conditions may seem strict, and in some sense they are; however, consider how closely they parallel the actual investments environment. There is no question that there are a large number of investors who are constantly "playing the game." Both individuals and institutions follow the market closely on a daily basis, standing ready to buy or sell when they think appropriate. The total amount of money at their disposal at any one time is significant.

Although the production of information is not costless, it is true that for institutions in the investments business, generating various types of information is a necessary cost of business, and many participants receive it "free."[2] It is widely available to many participants at approximately the same time as information is announced on radio, television, and teletype around the country.

Information is, for the most part, generated in a random fashion in the

---

[2]Obviously, investors pay for such items in their brokerage costs and other fees.

sense that most investors cannot predict when companies will announce significant new developments, when wars will break out, when strikes will occur, when currencies will be devalued, when important leaders will suddenly suffer a heart attack, and so forth. Although there is some dependence in information events over time, by and large announcements are independent and occur more or less randomly.

Finally, ask yourself why investors should not react quickly to information as it is announced. Many monitor the market daily, have funds with which to act, and are seeking to make money. They are going to act, and act quickly. You have only to observe some stocks with the largest changes in price on the NYSE on a given day and then check the news stories for that day to see that this is true.

If, as we have shown, the above conditions for an EM are generally met in practice, the result is a market in which investors adjust security prices rapidly and accurately to reflect random information coming into the market. Prices reflect fully all available information. Furthermore, price changes are independent of one another and move in a random fashion. The price change occurring today is independent of the one yesterday because it is based on investors' reactions to new, independent information coming into the market today.

The implications of an efficient market are enormous. In assessing the impact of such a market, see Box 14–1.

BOX 14–1   THE MARKET IS BEATING THE INVESTMENT MANAGERS

In the 23 years he has spent scouting the higher reaches of Wall Street, business strategy consultant Charles Ellis figures he has logged "maybe 5000 days" assessing the capabilities of many of the nation's top money managers. What has he concluded about the profession from all these labors?

That by and large money managers are "tough, clever, tenacious," but he is underwhelmed by their performance. Ellis reckons that nearly two out of every three professionally managed funds, measured cumulatively over the last 15 years, have failed to do as well in equities as Standard & Poor's 500 stock average. "The fact is," says Ellis, "the investment managers are not beating the market. The market is beating them."

How to explain that mediocrity on the part of people who are "tough, clever, tenacious"? Ellis, who brings a nice blend of the theoretical and workaday experience to the topic, thinks the great mass of money managers have failed to recognize a dramatic change in the market.

Ellis is not in the business of managing money, but of advising a long list of blue-chip institutional clients on business strategy. Managing partner of the Connecticut-based Greenwich Associates, Ellis, now 48, first came to The Street in the early Sixties. In those days, he says, beating the game was no great shakes. Institutional investors accounted for only 30% of the market. Now, however, borne on a flood of rising cash flow, institutional investors account for what Ellis says is 80% of the market. The institutions have virtually become the stock market.

So? The market has been institutional for a long time. What's new? What's new, Ellis says, is that the thousands of analysts and money managers prowling the market sweep up most of the bargains before they become real bargains. The market, in short, has become highly efficient.

Since money managers spend a lot of time taking in one another's analytical wash, only a truly perceptive minority can consistently get the edge of superior knowledge over the rest of the mob. Look at *Forbes'* mutual fund ratings. Only a handful of managers—Lindner Fund, Sequoia Fund and Mutual Shares—keep popping up in the winner's circle.

Further, given the drag of management fees and other costs, it takes about 1.6% of assets for the average institutional investor to keep the joint running. Since investors demand an equity premium—a premium over the risk-free rate of return for choosing to invest in stocks—a money manager has to wring an extra 25% above the historical 6% equity premium to enable his client to keep up with the market. Ellis thinks that the majority of money men find grinding out even that bare minimum "surprisingly difficult."

That comes as no great epiphany to devotees of the efficient market theory, who argue that the anthill army of analysts at work have made the market so efficient that it is unbeatable over the long haul. You can beat the market only by joining it; in effect, by replicating it with a portfolio of "index" stocks.

Ellis brings something different to the party. He thinks there are rewards to be had in taking carefully measured above-market risks, and his consulting work has given him an unusual insight into where the money men have gone wrong.

Ellis thinks many money men would do better if clients understood long-term investing. Corporate pension funds, for example, are often administered by in-house bureaucrats whose long-range career paths lead to other jobs. The fund is just one more rung up the ladder. The result, says Ellis in his book (*Investment Policy, How to Win the Loser's Game*, Dow Jones-Irwin), is that the people who hire and fire the money managers prefer noncontroversial investment policies to the less stereotyped kind of investing that alone yields superior results. In Ellis' words, they seek "the most acceptable near-term balance between desires for superior returns and avoidance of unusual or unorthodox positions. . . . They above all . . . avoid distressing risk to their own careers."

And what's happening on the money managers' side of the portfolio? "The very same thing," says Ellis. "They are understandably cautious, compromising with a defensive tilt, seeking 'not to lose' over a three-to-five-year time horizon." Says Ellis of the corporate types who choose investment managers: "Most of these people are good corporate managers, but they act as any ordinary person with a minimum of investment experience would."

In short, they are we—fated to buy high and sell low because of a constitutional inability to make a long-range plan and stick to it. The psychological and tactical hazards of the game are such, Ellis argues, that the number of investors able to outdo the market over long periods is very small indeed.

Yes, there are people who can beat the market fairly consistently. Ellis bows in the direction of such standouts as T. Rowe Price; Warren Buffett, chairman of Berkshire Hathaway; and the Vanguard Group's John Neff. Ellis even has some of his own cash running with Buffett and Neff, whom he puts in the star-quality Pantheon of "maybe 20" individuals. Twenty, mind you, out of thousands.

Ellis advocates what he calls a "coffee-can portfolio," a term he borrowed from Bob Kirby of the Capital Group in Los Angeles to describe a cross section of the U.S.' best-managed companies held for the long pull. You can increase the reward potential by adding as much risk in the shape of more volatile stocks as you feel comfortable with. He also puts in a good word for a mix of well-managed mutual funds for individuals.

"It's not exciting," chuckles Ellis. "It takes the fun out of watching the averages and quarterly reports, talking to friends and worrying about the market." Maybe you prefer the fun of doing your own trading. That's okay, Ellis says, "but it's a loser's game. Don't try to win, try not to lose."

Source: Richard Phalon, "Winning a Loser's Game," *Forbes*, March 10, 1986, pp. 136–137 and 139. Reprinted by permission of *Forbes* magazine, March 10, 1986. © Forbes Inc., 1986.

How Efficient Is the Market?

If, as discussed, the conditions for market efficiency are actually met, exactly how efficient is the market, and what does this imply for investors? We will first consider the question of efficiency, including the major evidence in support of this concept. We will then consider the implications to investors of an efficient market.

We have defined an efficient market as one in which all information is reflected in stock prices quickly and, on balance, accurately. Thus, the key to assessing market efficiency is information, in all of its various forms. When we speak of information, we mean not only the type of information, but its quality and the speed with which it is disseminated among investors.

Standard practice since 1970 is to discuss the EM concept in the form of the **efficient market hypothesis (EMH),** which is simply the formal statement of market efficiency previously discussed.[3] The EMH is concerned with the extent to which security prices fully reflect all available information and, for expositional purposes, is divided into the following *cumulative* levels.

1. **Weak form**   One of the most traditional types of information used in assessing security values is the market data discussed in Chapter 13. If security prices are determined in an efficient market, historical price and volume (i.e., market) data should already be reflected in current prices and should be of no value in predicting future price changes. Since price and volume data are the basis of technical analysis, technical analysis that relies on the past history of price and volume information is of little or no value.

Tests of the usefulness of price and volume data are called **weak-form** tests of the EMH. If the weak form of the EMH is true, past price changes

---

[3] See E. Fama, "Efficient Capital Markets: A Review of Theory and Empirical Work," *Journal of Finance*, Vol. 25, No. 2 (May 1970), pp. 383–417.

should be unrelated to future price changes; that is, stock changes over time should be independent.

Note that the correct implication of a weak-form efficient market is that the past history of price and volume information is of no value in assessing future changes in price. It is not correct to state, as is sometimes done, that the best estimate of price at time $t + 1$ is the current (time t) price because this implies an expected return of zero. The efficient market in no way implies that the expected return on any security is zero.

2. Semistrong form A more comprehensive level of market efficiency involves not only known and publicly available price and volume data, but all *publicly* known and available data such as earnings, dividends, stock split announcements, new product developments, financing difficulties, and accounting changes. A market that quickly incorporates all such information into prices is said to be **semistrong** efficient. Note that a semistrong efficient market encompasses the weak form of the hypothesis because price and volume data are part of the larger set of all publicly available information.

Tests of the semistrong EMH are tests of the *lag* in the adjustment of stock prices to announcements of information. A semistrong efficient market implies that investors cannot act on new public information after its announcement and expect to earn above-average risk-adjusted returns. If lags exist in the adjustment of stock prices to certain announcements, the market is not fully efficient in the semistrong sense.

3. Strong form The most stringent form of market efficiency is the **strong form,** which asserts that stock prices fully reflect *all* information, public and nonpublic. If the market is strong-form efficient, no group of investors should be able to earn, over a reasonable period of time, excess rates of return by using publicly available information in a superior manner. Professionally managed portfolios are most often tested in this regard.

An extreme version of the strong form holds that all nonpublic information, including information that may be restricted to certain groups such as corporate insiders and specialists on the exchanges, is immediately reflected in prices. In effect, this version refers to monopolistic access to information by certain market participants.

Strong-form efficiency encompasses the weak and semistrong forms and represents the highest level of market efficiency. Figure 14–1 depicts graphically these three levels of market efficiency.

Evidence on Market Efficiency

Because of the significance of the concept of efficient markets to all investors, and because of the controversy that surrounds the EMH, we will examine the empirical evidence on market efficiency. Many studies have been done over the years, and continue to be done. Obviously, we cannot begin to discuss them all, nor is it necessarily desirable to discuss several in detail. Our purpose here is to obtain an idea of how these tests are done, the scope of what has been done, and their results. The empirical evidence will

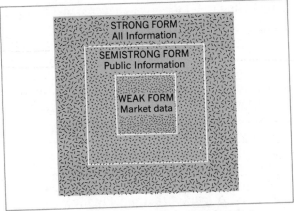

FIGURE 14–1 Cumulative levels of market efficiency and the information associated with each level.

be separated into tests of the three forms of market efficiency previously discussed.

It is important to note that the key to testing the validity of any of the three forms of market efficiency is the *consistency* with which investors can earn returns in excess of those commensurate with the risk involved. Short-lived inefficiencies appearing on a random basis do not constitute evidence of market inefficiencies, at least in an economic (as opposed to a statistical) sense.

Weak Form Evidence

As noted, weak-form efficiency means that price and volume data are incorporated into current stock prices. If prices follow nonrandom trends, stock price changes are dependent; otherwise, they are independent. Therefore, weak form tests involve the question of whether all information contained in the sequence of past prices is fully reflected in the current price.

The weak-form EMH is related to, but not identical with, an idea from the 1960s called the *random walk hypothesis*. If prices follow a random walk, price changes over time are random (independent).[4] The price change for today is unrelated to the price change yesterday, or the day before, or any other day. This is a result of the scenario described at the outset of the chapter. If new information arrives randomly in the market, and investors react immediately to it, changes in prices will also be random.

One way to test for weak-form efficiency is to statistically test the independence of stock price changes. If the statistical tests suggest that price

---

[4]Technically, the random walk hypothesis is more restrictive than the weak form EMH. Stock prices can conform to weak-form efficiency without meeting the conditions of a random walk.

changes are independent, the implication is that knowing, and using, the past sequence of price information is of no value to an investor; in other words, trends in price changes do not exist. It should be carefully noted that we are talking about price changes and not the level of price itself. Obviously, a $60 stock has a price on any given day that will be related closely to its price tomorrow, since it is unlikely in one day to go much above $62 or much below $58. Also, we are not concerned with whether the change in today's price, say $+ \frac{1}{2}$, is related to the change in tomorrow's price, say $- \frac{1}{4}$. Dollar price changes such as these are also related. The issue centers on percentage price changes over time—are they related or not?

A second way to test for weak-form efficiency, after testing the pure statistical nature of price changes, is to test specific trading rules that attempt to use the past price and volume data. If such tests legitimately produce risk-adjusted returns beyond that available from simply buying a portfolio of stocks and holding until a common liquidation date, after deducting all costs, it would suggest that the market is not weak-form efficient.

Statistical tests of price changes   Stock price changes in an efficient market should be independent. Two simple statistical tests of independence are the serial correlation test and the signs test. The first involves measuring the correlation between price changes for various lags, such as one day, two days, and so on. The second involves classifying each price change as to its sign; that is, whether it was $+$, 0, or $-$ (regardless of amount). Then the "runs" in the series of signs can be counted and compared to known information about a random series. If there are persistent price changes, the length of the runs will indicate this.

A test of randomness in stock prices can be traced back to the turn of this century, but modern tests began in the 1950s. A well-known test was conducted by Eugene Fama, who studied the daily returns on the 30 Dow Jones industrial stocks.[5] Using serial correlation analysis to test for statistically significant correlation coefficients, Fama tested lags ranging from one to 10 days. Of the 30 stocks and 10 possible lags, a few correlation coefficients were found to differ statistically from zero, but the level was small. Only a very small percentage of any successive price change could be explained by a prior change. Serial correlation tests by other researchers invariably reached the same conclusion.

The signs test also supports independence. Although some "runs" do occur, they fall within the limits of randomness, since a truly random series exhibits some runs (several $+$ or $-$ observations in succession). Fama found, using the same data, a very small tendency for 1-day runs to persist. Longer runs of 4, 9, and 16 days did not persist. Overall, the results would be expected from a random series.

---

[5] E. Fama, "The Behavior of Stock Market Prices," *The Journal of Finance*, Vol. 38, No. 1 (January 1965), pp. 34–105.

Technical trading rules The statistical tests described here demonstrate that trends, other than those consistent with a random series, do not exist in stock prices. However, those who believe that not only do such trends exist but that they can be used successfully argue that the statistical tests do not detect some sophisticated or realistic strategies that they can use. In general, we are talking about technicians who, as noted in the previous chapter, believe that stock prices exhibit trends that can be detected through technical analysis. Therefore, although statistical tests are important and support the idea that such technical trading will prove useless, it remains to investigate such rules, using actual trading strategies.

An almost unlimited number of possible technical trading rules could be tested. Obviously, all of them cannot be examined; however, if a sufficient number are examined and found to be ineffective, the burden of proof shifts to those who argue that such techniques have value. And this is exactly the situation that prevails. No one has yet satisfactorily demonstrated that a technical trading rule based solely on past price and volume data can, after all proper adjustments have been made, outperform a simple buy-and-hold strategy.

It is important to consider what constitutes a fair test of a technical trading rule. The adjustments that must be made include the following:

1. *Risk*. If the risk involved in two strategies is not comparable, a fair comparison cannot be made. As we know, other things being equal, a more risky strategy would be *expected* to outperform a less risky strategy.

2. *Transaction and other costs (e.g., taxes)*. Several technical trading rules appeared to produce excess returns before transaction costs were deducted. After such costs were deducted, however, the rules were inferior to a buy-and-hold strategy, which generates little costs.

3. *Consistency*. Can the rule outperform the alternative over a reasonable period of time, such as five or 10 years? Any rule may outperform an alternative for a short period, but it will not be too useful unless it holds up over some future periods.

4. *Out-of-sample validity*. Has the rule been tried on data other than that used to produce the rule? It is always possible to find a rule that works on a particular sample if only enough rules are tried; that is, it is possible to torture the data until it confesses.

A well-known technical trading rule is the so-called **filter rule.** A filter rule specifies a breakpoint for an individual stock or a market average, and trades are made when the stock price change is greater than this filter. As an example, consider the following rule: buy a stock if the price moves up 10% from some established base, such as a previous low, hold it until it declines 10% from its new high, and then sell it and possibly go short.

Several studies of filters have been conducted. Fama and Blume tested 24 filters (ranging from 0.5 to 50%) on each of the 30 Dow Jones stocks.[6] Before commissions, several of the filters were profitable, in particular the smallest (0.5%). After commissions, however, average returns were typically negative or very small. Brokerage commissions more than offset any gains that could be exploited. The low correlations found in the statistical tests were insufficient to provide profitable filter trading rules.

This is perhaps a good place in the discussion to note the difference between *statistical dependence* and *economic dependence* in stock price changes. The statistical tests discussed earlier detected some small amount of dependence in price changes.[7] All of the series could not be said to be completely statistically independent. However, they were economically independent in that one could not exploit the small statistical dependence that existed. After brokerage costs, excess returns disappear, and, after all, this is the bottom line for investors—can excess returns be earned with a technical trading rule after all costs are deducted?

A popular technical trading rule that often appears in investment advisory publications is relative strength, which was discussed in Chapter 13 as one of the principal techniques for the technical analysis of individual stocks. It is defined as the ratio of a stock's current price to that of an industry or market index (or the stock's average price over some previous period). Levy developed and claimed success for a relative strength technique based on the previous 26 weeks of price data for the stock and the market.[8] Stocks with the highest relative strength were selected and replaced as necessary when a new ranking showed a decline in one of the top group. Levy presented results for some cut-off points that were superior to a buy-and-hold strategy, after brokerage costs.

Subsequent work by others indicated several problems with Levy's work, including a failure to adjust for risk and taxes.[9] Specifically, Levy's portfolios were more risky than a buy-and-hold strategy and involved short-term gains, which were taxed at rates higher than for long-term gains. Perhaps most important, Levy fitted his model to the same data base for which he subsequently presented his results. He tried 68 variations of the basic idea. Independent analysis of his work, involving other time periods and risk adjustments, produced results that were inferior to a buy-and-hold strategy.

Obviously, many different variations of the relative strength technique can be tested by varying the time period over which the average price is calculated and the percentage of the top stocks selected. If we conduct enough tests, we can find a rule that produces favorable results on a particu-

---

[6]E. Fama and M. Blume, "Filter Rules and Stock-Market Trading," *The Journal of Business: A Supplement,* Vol. 39 (January 1969), pp. 2–21.

[7]Stock returns tend to exhibit a slight positive correlation.

[8]See Chapter 13, footnote 15.

[9]See Chapter 13, footnote 15.

lar sample. Therefore, before we conclude that a trading rule of this type is successful, we should conduct a "fair" test as outlined earlier. Risks must be comparable, appropriate costs must be deducted, and finally the rule should be tried on a different sample of stocks.

Semistrong Form Evidence

Weak-form tests of both the statistical and the trading rule types are numerous and unanimous in their findings (after necessary corrections and adjustments have been made). Semistrong tests, on the other hand, are less numerous and somewhat more diverse in their findings, although they clearly support the proposition that the market adjusts to new public information rapidly.

Semistrong form tests are tests of the speed of price adjustments to public information. The question is whether investors can use publicly available information to earn excess returns, after proper adjustments. As a benchmark, we can use a buy-and-hold strategy with equivalent risk, or perhaps the market as a whole.

We will consider a sampling of often-cited studies of semistrong efficiency without developing them in detail. What is important is to obtain a feel for the wide variety of information tested and the logic behind these tests. The methodology and a detailed discussion of the results are not essential for our purposes. We will consider five issues as examples of semistrong efficiency tests; of course, other examples exist and could have been chosen.

Following the discussion of strong-form efficiency evidence, we will consider some contraevidence to semistrong efficiency; that is, evidence that lags do occur in the adjustment of stock prices to certain information. Although these examples are not an exhaustive list either, fewer documented examples of lags in the adjustment of stock prices to information have been presented.

1. *Stock splits*. An often-cited study of the long-run effects of stock splits on returns was done by Fama, Fisher, Jensen, and Roll (FFJR).[10] This paper was the first to use the *cumulative abnormal returns (CAR)* methodology based on the capital asset pricing model discussed in Chapter 5. CARs are (cumulative) average company-unique returns based on the residual error terms from the CAPM; that is, the CAR technique adjusts for what a security should earn, given its systematic risk, leaving for examination that part of a security's return attributable to unique company events, from which the impact of the information being studied can be assessed. In other words, after adjusting for what the company's return should have been, given its systematic risk, any remaining return (the residual part) can be examined.

In and of itself, a stock split adds nothing of value to a company; therefore, it should have no effect on the company's total market value. If you

---

[10] E. Fama, L. Fisher, M. Jensen, and R. Roll, "The Adjustment of Stock Prices to New Information," *International Economics Review*, Vol. 10, No. 1 (February 1969), pp. 2–21.

own 100 shares of stock worth $50 per share, after a 2-for-1 stock split, you will own 200 shares of stock worth $25 per share. Although per share price is affected, total value is not, because only the pieces of paper representing the stock ownership change. Clearly, a security's return should be unaffected after a stock split if the market is efficient because this information should have been reflected in the stock's price at or before the announcement of the split.

FFJR found that although the stocks they studied exhibited sharp increases in price prior to the split, abnormal (i.e., risk-adjusted) returns after the split were very stable. Thus, the split itself did not affect prices. The results indicate that any price adjustments occurred prior to a split, not afterward, which supports the semistrong form of market efficiency. Furthermore, investors could not gain by purchasing stocks after the *announcement* of the split, but before the split itself. In other words, for a typical individual stock, by the time a stock split is announced the market has discounted any favorable effects implied, so that investors cannot gain by acquiring stocks after the announcement.

2. *Money supply changes.* As noted in Chapter 10, a relationship exists between money supply and economic activity, and between money supply and stock prices. Several studies, in assessing the relationship between money supply growth and stock prices, find that changes in the money supply growth rates that are anticipated are reflected in stock prices before the changes occur.[11] If the changes are unexpected, they are reflected in prices almost immediately on the disclosure of the information necessary to assess the situation. Therefore, the market appears to be semistrong efficient with respect to changes in the money supply.

3. *Accounting changes.* A large number of studies have examined the effects on stock prices of announcements of accounting changes. The accounting changes include depreciation, the investment tax credit, inventory reporting (LIFO versus FIFO), and other items.

The issue of accounting announcements requires some explanation. Essentially, two different types of changes are involved.

1. The change may affect only the manner in which earnings are reported to stockholders, and therefore should not affect stock prices. The reason for this is that such changes do not affect the firm's cash flows, and thus its real economic value.
2. The change may affect the economic value of the firm by affecting its cash flows. This is a true change and should therefore generate a change in market prices. In an efficient market, stock prices should adjust quickly to the announcement of this type of change.

Although a large number of studies of this type have been done, a definitive statement about announcements of accounting changes cannot be

---

[11] See Chapter 10.

made. In general, the studies indicate that the market is able to distinguish the superficial changes described in type 1 from the real changes described in type 2. For example, switching depreciation methods from accelerated to straight-line for *shareholder reporting purposes* will affect shareholder earnings but not cash flows, and the evidence indicates no long-lasting effect on stock prices.[12] This is the result that would be expected in an efficient market. On the other hand, a change from FIFO to LIFO decreases taxes for the firm making the switch, thereby affecting the real value of the firm positively by increasing the cash flows. In an efficient market, price changes associated with such a change should be positive. What is interesting is that studies have found an increase in stock prices for some period preceding the switch from FIFO to LIFO.[13]

4. *Dividend announcements*. Does the market anticipate changes in dividends? To answer this question, it is necessary to build a model of dividend policy in order to be able to make predictions of dividends. This allows a surprise in a dividend change to be separated from what is anticipated by the market. By concentrating only on the unanticipated dividend changes, some assessment of market efficiency can be made. At least two separate studies of this question have been done.[14] Both find that, in general, the market seems to adjust to the new information quickly; in fact, much of the adjustment is in anticipation of the announcement itself.

5. *Reactions to other announcements*. Investors are constantly given a wide range of information concerning both large-scale events and items about particular companies. Each of these types of announcements has been examined as to the effects on stock prices.

One study examined the impact of major world events on stock prices.[15] In an efficient market, the adjustment of stock prices to such announcements should be rapid, preventing investors from earning excess returns as the information becomes publicly available. Stock prices were examined prior to the announcement and at the market opening following the announcement as well as on the following two days. Although there were some variations in the results, investors would have been unable to profit by purchasing stocks when the market opened following the announcement. In general, a semi-strong efficient market was indicated.

Another example of this type of announcement or story concerns the

---

[12] R. Kaplan and R. Roll, "Investor Evaluation of Accounting Information: Some Empirical Evidence," *The Journal of Business*, Vol. 45, No. 2 (April 1972), pp. 225–257.

[13] R. Abdel-Khalik and J. McKeown, "Understanding Accounting Changes in an Efficient Market: Evidence of Differential Reaction," *Accounting Review* (October 1978), pp. 851–868.

[14] R. Pettit, "Dividend Announcements, Security Performance, and Capital Market Efficiency," *Journal of Finance*, Vol. 27, No. 5 (December 1972), pp. 993–1007; and R. Watts, "The Informational Content of Dividends," *The Journal of Business*, Vol. 45, No. 2 (April 1973), pp. 191–211.

[15] F. Reilly and E. Drzycimski, "Tests of Stock Market Efficiency Following Major World Events," *The Journal of Business Research*, Vol. 1 (Summer 1973), pp. 57–72.

usefulness of the "Heard in the Street" column in *The Wall Street Journal*. This daily feature highlights particular companies and analysts' opinions on stocks. This is often the first disclosure of such information to the general public; however, it is reasonable to assume that analysts' estimates have already been made available to their respective firms' customers.

A study of the impact of the publication of this information on stock returns showed a positive effect on the order of 1 to 2%.[16] Unless transaction costs are smaller than this, however, market efficiency would seem to prevail. This is an example of economic efficiency—the abnormal returns indicated are not large enough to justify exploiting the small discrepancies that appear to exist.

Strong Form Evidence

The strong form of the EMH states that stock prices immediately adjust to and reflect all information, public or otherwise. In general, this means that no group of investors can earn excess returns through a superior ability to analyze publicly available information; in other words, investors who transform public information into private information do not gain by doing so. At the extreme, the strong form holds that even those investors with monopolistic access to information cannot gain by using this information.

One way to test for strong-form efficiency is to examine the performance of groups presumed to have access to "true" nonpublic information. If such groups can consistently earn above average risk-adjusted returns, the extreme version of the strong form would not be supported. We will consider corporate insiders, a group who presumably fall into the category of having monopolistic access to information.

We will also consider the performance of professionally managed portfolios as a test of whether any group of investors can earn excess returns. The availability of data makes this group a logical one to analyze in assessing the strong-form assertion that all information is fully reflected in prices and that no type of investor can earn excess returns through superior ability.

Corporate insiders A corporate insider is an officer, director, or major stockholder of a corporation. Such individuals might be expected to have valuable inside information. Insiders are required by the Securities and Exchange Commission (SEC) to report their purchase or sale transactions each month. This information is made public several weeks later.

Most studies of corporate insiders find that they consistently earn above average profits.[17] Insiders have access to privileged information and are able to act on it and profit before the information is made public. This is logical

---

[16] P. Davies and M. Canes, "Stock Prices and the Publication of Second-Hand Information," *The Journal of Business*, Vol. 51 (January 1978), pp. 43–56.

[17] See, for example, J. Jaffe, "Special Information and Insider Trading," *The Journal of Business*, Vol. 47 (July 1974), pp. 410–428.

and not really surprising. It is a violation of strong-form efficiency, however, which requires a market in which no investor can consistently earn abnormal profits.

Investors without access to this private information can observe what the insiders are doing by studying the publicly available reports they must make to the SEC. Several investment information services compile this information and sell it to the public in the form of regularly issued reports. Furthermore, such services as *The Value Line Investment Survey* report insider transactions for each company they cover. Studies of the performance of stocks after publication of these SEC reports indicate that above average returns could have been earned on the basis of this publicly available information.[18] Which form of market efficiency do these findings point to, and why?

Portfolio managers An interesting test of market efficiency is the performance of professional portfolio managers, particularly mutual fund managers for whom much data are available. This can be considered a test of strong-form efficiency if it is assumed that these managers are free to use any type of information and stock selection techniques they choose. These managers operate the portfolios on a continual basis with staffs of experts to assist them. Presumably, if valuable information is available to be discovered, these investors should be among the first to discover and use it.

Most of the evidence available on the historical performance of mutual funds suggests that the managers of these portfolios have been unable to achieve consistently superior performance. A well-known study by Jensen analyzed 115 mutual funds during the period 1945–1964.[19] On a net basis (i.e., less fund expenses), the average fund earned 1.1% *less* per year than an unmanaged portfolio of similar risk. Jensen was unable to detect a management contribution sufficient to offset fund expenses, results which support strong-form efficiency.

In an article appearing several years after Jensen's, Norman Mains corrected what he felt to be biases in Jensen's article against the managed funds.[20] His results suggest a neutral performance, on average, on a net basis; however, on a gross basis the majority of funds performed positively. Thus, managers would seem to be able to earn enough to pay fund expenses (unlike Jensen's findings), but not enough to benefit the fund's shareholders.

An early study of mutual funds by William Sharpe supports the Jensen

---

[18] S. Pratt and C. DeVere, "Relationship Between Insider Trading and Rates of Return for NYSE Common Stocks, 1960–1966," included in J. Lorie and R. Brealey, eds., *Modern Developments in Investment Management* (New York: Praeger Publishers, 1972), pp. 268–279.

[19] M. Jensen, "The Performance of Mutual Funds in the Period 1945–1964," *The Journal of Finance*, Vol. 23 (May 1968), pp. 389–416.

[20] N. Mains, "Risk, the Pricing of Capital Assets, and the Evaluation of Investment Portfolios: Comment," *The Journal of Business*, Vol. 50 (July 1977), pp. 317–384.

findings.[21] Sharpe found that of 34 funds examined, only 11 performed equal to or better than the Dow Jones Industrial Average (on a net basis). A later study by John McDonald also supports Jensen, finding no benefit to shareholders from active management.[22] And, as noted, the majority of other studies has found similar results. On the other hand, Irwin Friend et al. found good performance for mutual funds compared to certain random selection techniques.[23]

If the Efficient Market Hypothesis Is True?

The nonexhaustive evidence on market efficiency presented here is impressive in its support of market efficiency. What are the implications to investors? How should investors analyze and select securities and manage their portfolios if the market is efficient?

As mentioned earlier, technical analysis and the EMH directly conflict with each other. Technicians believe stock prices exhibit trends that persist across time, whereas the weak-form EMH states that price (and volume) data are already reflected in stock prices. EMH proponents believe that information is disseminated rapidly and that prices adjust rapidly to this new information. If prices fully reflect the available information, technical trading systems that rely on a knowledge and use of past trading data cannot be of value.

Although technical analysis cannot be categorically refuted because of its many variations and interpretations, the evidence accumulated to date overwhelmingly favors the weak-form EMH and casts doubt on technical analysis. The evidence is such that the burden of proof has shifted to the proponents of technical analysis to demonstrate, in a correctly conducted test (e.g., adjusting for transaction costs and risk), that technical analysis outperforms a buy-and-hold strategy.

The EMH also has implications for fundamental analysis, which seeks to estimate the intrinsic value of a security and provide buy or sell decisions depending on whether the current market price is less than or greater than the intrinsic value. The sum total of all the evidence that has been accumulated to date suggests that discrepancies do, in fact, exist from time to time and from security to security. There is no theoretical reason why an investor cannot do a superior job of analysis and profit thereby. However, the EMH suggests that those investors who use the same data and make the same interpretations as other investors will experience only average results.

[21]W. Sharpe, "Mutual Fund Performance," *The Journal of Business,* Vol. 39 (January 1966), pp. 119–138.
[22]J. McDonald, "Objectives and Performance of Mutual Funds, 1960–1969," *Journal of Finance and Quantitative Analysis,* Vol. 9 (June 1974), pp. 311–333.
[23]I. Friend, M. Blume, and J. Crockett, *Mutual Funds and Other Institutional Investors* (New York: McGraw-Hill Book Company, 1970).

What is necessary in fundamental analysis, given the evidence on market efficiency, is to perform clearly *superior* fundamental analysis. For example, an investor must estimate future variables such as earnings better than other investors, or at least more consistently. This investor must derive more and better insights from information that is publicly available to all investors. The evidence on the EMH suggests that it is quite difficult, although by no means impossible, for investors to do this.

What about money management activities? Assume for a moment that the market is efficient. What would this mean to the money management process, that is, to professional money managers? The most important effect would be a reduction in the resources that would be devoted to assessing individual securities. For the manager to act in this respect, he or she would have to believe that an analyst had come up with some superior insights. Passive strategies would become the norm; nevertheless, the portfolio manager would still have tasks to perform in this efficient market. These tasks would consist of at least the following:[24]

1. *The degree of diversification.* As will be seen in Chapter 19, the basic tenet of good portfolio management is to diversify the portfolio. The manager would have to be certain that the correct amount of diversification had been achieved.
2. *The riskiness of the portfolio.* Depending on the type of portfolio being managed and its objectives, the manager must achieve a level of risk appropriate for that portfolio. This would involve assessing the risk and establishing the appropriate position.
3. *The maintenance of the desired risk level.* It may be necessary to make changes in the portfolio that will keep the risk level at the intended level.
4. *The tax status of the investor.* Investors are interested in the amount of return they are allowed to keep after taxes. Accordingly, their tax situation should be kept in mind as investment alternatives are considered. Tax-exempt portfolios have their own needs and interests.
5. *Transaction costs.* Trading costs can have a significant impact on the final performance of the portfolio. Managers should seek to reduce these costs to the extent possible and practical.

Before deciding that these tasks may be all that is left to do in the portfolio management process in the face of an efficient market, we should examine some evidence that suggests possibilities for investors interested in selecting stocks. This evidence is in contrast with that discussed thus far and constitutes a good conclusion for this chapter by indicating that regardless of how persuasive the case for market efficiency is, the final answer is not in and may never be.

---

[24] See J. Lorie and M. Hamilton, *The Stock Market: Theories and Evidence* (Homewood, Ill.: Richard D. Irwin, 1973), pp. 106–108.

Evidence of Market Anomalies

Having considered the type of evidence supporting market efficiency, we can appropriately consider some other work that raises questions. We will refer to these examples as possible market anomalies, meaning that the results are in contrast to what would be expected in a totally efficient market; furthermore, they cannot easily be "explained away." We will examine several anomalies that have generated much attention and have yet to be satisfactorily explained. In considering these anomalies, however, investors must be cautious in viewing any, or all, of them as a stock selection device guaranteed to outperform the market. There is no such guarantee because empirical tests of these anomalies may not approximate actual trading strategies that would be followed by investors. Furthermore, if anomalies exist and can be identified, investors should still hold a portfolio of stocks rather than concentrating on a few stocks identified by one of these methods. As we shall see in Chapter 19, diversification is crucial for all investors.

Earnings Announcements

The adjustment of stock prices to earnings announcements has been studied in several papers, opening up some interesting questions and possibilities. It is obvious that earnings announcements, because of the importance of earnings in the valuation process, are important to investors. Such announcements contain information that should, and does, affect stock prices. The questions that need to be answered are as follows:

1. How much of the earnings announcement is new information, and how much has been anticipated by the market—in other words, how much of the announcement is a "surprise"?
2. How quickly is the "surprise" portion of the announcement reflected in the price of the stock? Is it immediate, as would be expected in an efficient market, or is there a lag in the adjustment process? If a lag occurs, investors have a chance to realize excess returns by quickly acting on the publicly available earnings announcements.

To properly assess the earnings announcement issue, it is necessary to separate a particular earnings announcement into an expected part and an unexpected part, a dichotomy discussed in Chapter 12. The expected part is that portion anticipated by investors by the time of announcement and requiring no adjustment in stock prices, whereas the unexpected part is unanticipated by investors and requires an adjustment in price.

In 1968, Ray Ball and Philip Brown studied the impact of unexpected earnings announcements on stock prices using annual data.[25] Each earnings report was classified as either favorable or unfavorable, depending on

---

[25] P. Brown and R. Ball, "An Empirical Evaluation of Accounting Income Numbers," *Journal of Accounting Research,* Vol. 6 (Autumn 1968), pp. 159–178.

whether the earnings announced (reported earnings) exceeded that which had been predicted based on a simple forecast of previous earnings. Companies with favorable (unfavorable) earnings reports experienced positive (negative) risk-adjusted performance before the earnings were actually announced, indicating an ability by the market to anticipate forthcoming annual earnings. However, some portion of the earnings announcements was unanticipated, and prices continued to adjust with a lag after the announcement, not immediately, as expected in an efficient market. The authors concluded that only a small part of the earnings was unanticipated, and it is not clear that investors could have profited from acting on the publicly available announcements, given all costs.

Overall, the Ball and Brown study is usually taken as support for the efficient market hypothesis although, as noted, prices did continue to adjust after the announcement. This study used annual earnings, leaving quarterly earnings announcements as another possible source of information. It is this area that has proven to be of such interest in the question of market efficiency.

Latané, Tuttle, and Jones studied quarterly earnings reports in 1968 and found them to be positively correlated with subsequent short-term price movements, thereby indicating a lag in the adjustment of stock prices to the information in these reports.[26] Following several papers that examined the value of quarterly earnings in stock selection, Latané, Jones, and Rieke in 1974 developed the concept of standardized unexpected earnings (SUE) as a means of investigating the earnings surprises in quarterly data.[27] As explained in Chapter 12 SUE is defined as

$$\text{SUE} = \frac{\text{Actual quarterly earnings} - \text{Predicted quarterly earnings}}{\text{Standardization factor to adjust for size differences}}$$

$$= \frac{\text{Unexpected earnings}}{\text{Standard error of the estimate}}$$

The actual quarterly earnings is the earnings reported by the company and available on brokerage house wire services the same day as reported, or in *The Wall Street Journal* the following day. Predicted earnings for a particular company are estimated from historical earnings data before the earnings are reported. As each company's earnings are announced, the SUE can be calculated and acted on. Companies with high (low) unexpected earnings are expected to have a positive (negative) price response.

[26] See H. A. Latané, Donald L. Tuttle, and Charles P. Jones, "E/P Ratios vs. Changes in Earnings in Forecasting Future Price Changes," *Financial Analysts Journal*, January–February 1969, pp. 117–120, 123.

[27] For a discussion of much of this literature, see O. Joy and C. Jones, "Earnings Reports and Market Efficiencies: An Analysis of Contrary Evidence," *Journal of Financial Research*, Vol. 2 (Spring 1979), pp. 51–64.

Latané and Jones have documented the performance of SUE in a series of papers. SUE was shown to have a definite relationship with subsequent excess holding period returns. In a recent paper, the authors documented the precise response of stock prices to earnings announcements using a large sample of stocks (over 1400) for the 36 quarters covering mid-1971 to mid-1980.[28] Daily returns were used, so that the exact response of stock prices to quarterly earnings announcements could be documented before, on, and after the day the earnings were announced.

Figure 14–2 shows a similar analysis for an updated period through mid-1984 involving a sample size ranging from about 1700 companies per quarter to almost 2000 companies. SUEs are separated into 10 categories based on the size and sign of the unexpected earnings. Category 10 contains all SUEs > 4.0 while category 1 contains all SUEs ≤ −4.0; categories 5 and 6 contain the smallest unexpected earnings. Excess returns are calculated for each security as the difference between a security's return for each day and the market's return for that day. These excess returns are cumulated for the period beginning 63 days before the announcement date of earnings through 63 days following the announcement date (there are approximately 63 trading days in a quarter). As Figure 14–2 shows, the SUE categories follow a monotonic discrimination, with category 10 performing the best and category 1 performing the worst. Categories 5 and 6 show virtually no excess returns after the announcement date of earnings, as would be expected.

Figure 14–2 shows that while a substantial adjustment to the forthcoming earnings announcements occurs before the actual announcement, a substantial adjustment also occurs after the day of announcement. This is the unexplained part of the SUE puzzle. In an efficient market, prices should adjust quickly to earnings, rather than with a lag.

By the mid-1980s, considerable evidence had been presented about the relationship between unexpected earnings and subsequent stock returns. Although such evidence is not in any way conclusive, it cannot be easily dismissed. Different researchers, using different samples and different techniques, have examined the unexpected earnings issue and have found similar results.[29] It must be emphasized, however, that techniques such as SUE are not a guarantee of major success for investors. The relationships discussed are averages and do not necessarily reflect what any single investor would experience.

---

[28] See C. Jones, R. Rendleman, and H. Latané, "Stock Returns and SUEs during the 1970s," *The Journal of Portfolio Management* (Winter 1984), pp. 18–22.

[29] See, for example, C. M. Bidwell III, "A Test of Market Efficiency: SUE/PE," *The Journal of Portfolio Management* (Summer 1979), pp. 53–58; and O. M. Joy, R. H. Litzenberger, and R. W. McEnally, "The Adjustment of Stock Prices to Announcements of Unanticipated Changes in Quarterly Earnings," *Journal of Accounting Research* (Autumn 1977), pp. 207–225.

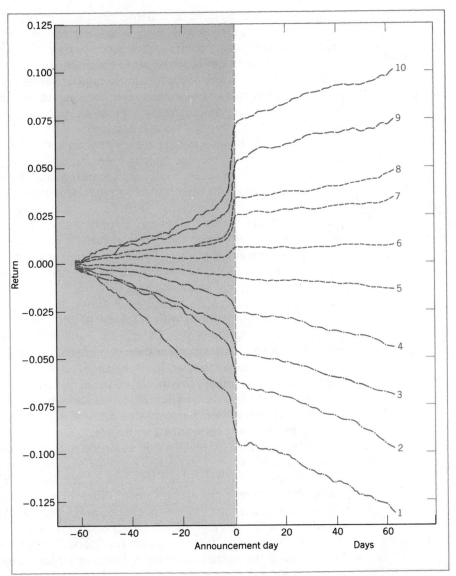

FIGURE 14–2 **Cumulative excess returns surrounding the announcement date of earnings for 10 SUE categories, mid-1975 to mid-1984.**

P/E Studies

One of the more enduring concepts in investments concerns the price/earnings (P/E) ratio discussed earlier in the valuation chapters. A number of investors believe that low P/E stocks will, on average, outperform high P/E stocks. The rationale for this is not explicit, but the belief persists.

Sanjoy Basu studied this issue by ranking stocks on their P/E ratios and comparing the results of the high P/E ratio group with those of the low P/E ratio group.[30] The stocks were assumed to be held for 12 months following purchase.

Since the P/E ratio is known information and presumably reflected in price, a relationship between the P/E ratio and subsequent returns should not exist if the market is efficient. The results of Basu's study indicated that the low P/E ratio stocks outperformed the high P/E ratio stocks. Furthermore, risk was not a factor; after various adjustments for risk, the low P/E stocks were still superior performers.

The implication of these results is that P/E ratios contain information not immediately discounted by the market. Publicly available information could be used to earn abnormal (i.e., risk-adjusted) returns, a finding that conflicts with the semistrong EMH. These results have attracted considerable attention because of their implications for the concept of market efficiency and because the P/E ratio is an easy, well-known strategy to use in selecting stocks. Subsequently, questions about the validity of the P/E ratio were raised by other academic researchers in studies of the firm size effect, which is discussed later as another anomaly.

In response to the questions raised, Basu conducted a study to reexamine the relationship between the P/E ratio, the size effect, and returns on NYSE stocks for the period 1963–1980.[31] He found that the stocks of low P/E firms had generally higher *risk-adjusted* returns than firms with high P/E ratios. This P/E ratio effect, furthermore, was significant even after differences in firm size were adjusted for. Controlling for differences in both risk and P/E ratios, Basu found that the size effect virtually disappeared.

In view of some research suggesting that the P/E effect is confined to low-beta risk securities, a recent study examined the P/E anomaly with respect to both total risk and systematic risk.[32] The results indicate that the P/E effect is not confined to low-beta risk securities. Regardless of the risk measure used, low-P/E securities provided significant positive excess returns across all risk levels.

The P/E ratio anomaly remains unexplained. Until it is refuted, however, it appears to offer investors a potential strategy for investing that may produce returns superior to many alternatives they may be using. And investing in low P/E stocks continues to be advocated by some well-known commentators. For example, as mentioned in Chapter 13, David Dreman recom-

---

[30] S. Basu, "Investment Performance of Common Stocks in Relation to Their Price–Earnings Ratios: A Test of the Efficient Market Hypothesis," *The Journal of Finance*, Vol. 32, No. 2 (June 1977), pp. 663–682.

[31] S. Basu, "The Relationship Between Earnings' Yield, Market Value and Return for NYSE Common Stocks: Further Evidence," *Journal of Financial Economics*, Vol. 12 (June 1983), pp. 129–156.

[32] See David Goodman and John Peavy, "The Risk Universal Nature of the P/E Effect," *The Journal of Portfolio Management* (Summer 1985), pp. 14–17.

TABLE 14–1   Annual Returns from P/E Quintiles, Mid-1963 to Mid-1985

P/E Group	Total Return	Appreciation	Dividend
Lowest	20.7%	15.4%	5.3
Second Lowest	15.7	10.2	5.5
Middle	10.7	6.0	4.7
Second Highest	10.4	6.7	3.7
Highest	10.4	8.2	2.2

Source: David Dreman, "A Strategy For All Seasons," *Forbes,* July 14, 1986, p. 118. Reprinted by permission.

mends that investors ignore professional investment advice and select stocks with low P/E ratios. His hypothesis is that low P/E stocks may be unwanted currently, but if they have strong finances, high yields, and good earnings records they almost always do well eventually.

In his articles in *Forbes,* Dreman periodically discusses some studies showing the results of selecting low P/E stocks. He recently reported on a study of almost 1500 stocks (on average) over the 22-year period 1963–1985. This time span included three major bull/bear markets and a wide range in the Dow Jones Industrial Average. As Table 14–1 shows, the lowest quintile of P/E ratio stocks far outperformed the other four quintiles, virtually doubling the highest P/E quintile. Results are measured annually based only on the P/E ratios. According to Dreman, $10,000 invested in the lowest quintile would have resulted in $630,042 compared to $88,169 for the highest P/E group (assuming annual switching).[33]

The Firm Size Effect

A third anomaly is the firm size effect, referred to earlier. In a well-publicized study, Rolf Banz found that the stocks of small NYSE firms earned higher *risk-adjusted* returns than the stocks of large NYSE firms (on average).[34] This "size effect" appears to have persisted for over 40 years. Mark Reinganum, using a sample of both NYSE and AMEX firms, also found abnormally large risk-adjusted returns for small firms.[35] Both of these researchers attributed the results to a misspecification of the CAPM rather than to a market inefficiency. That is, both Banz and Reinganum, in explaining persistent abnormal returns attributed to the size effect, were unwilling to reject the idea that the market could have inefficiencies of this type.

Additional research on the size effect indicates that "small" firms with

---

[33] See David Dreman, "A Strategy for All Seasons," *Forbes,* July 14, 1986, p. 118.

[34] R. Banz, "The Relationship between Returns and Market Value of Common Stocks," *Journal of Financial Economics,* Vol. 9 (March 1981), pp. 3–18.

[35] M. Reinganum, "Misspecification of Capital Asset Pricing: Empirical Anomalies Based on Earnings Yield and Market Values," *Journal of Financial Economics,* Vol. 9 (March 1981), pp. 19–46.

the largest abnormal returns tend to be those that have recently become small (or have recently declined in price), that either pay no dividend or have a high dividend yield, that have low prices, and that have low price–earnings ratios.[36] Keim found that roughly 50% of the return difference reported by Reinganum is concentrated in January.[37]

The January Effect

Several studies in the past have suggested that seasonality exists in the stock market. Recent evidence of stock return seasonality has grown out of studies of the size anomaly explained in the previous section. Keim studied the month-to-month stability of the size effect for all NYSE and AMEX firms with data for 1963 through 1979.[38] His findings again supported the existence of a significant size effect (a 30.5% small size premium). However, roughly half of this size effect occurred in January, and more than half of the excess January returns occurred during the first five trading days of that month. The first trading day of the year showed a high small-firm premium for every year of the period studied. The strong performance in January has become known as the **January effect**.[39]

A paper by Givoly and Ovadia examined and documented the high returns for stocks in January.[40] Their research suggests that the seasonal behavior of stock returns in January is related to tax-induced sales at year end. Prices of many stocks were temporarily depressed in December but recovered in January, contributing significantly to the high returns observed in January. Although the tax-loss selling hypothesis has been the most popular explanation offered to date for explaining the January effect, the evidence is inconsistent and other possibilities need to be examined.

A recent paper by Keim documented once again the abnormal returns for small firms in January. Keim also found a yield effect—the largest abnormal returns tended to accrue to those firms paying either no dividends or with high dividend yields.[41]

---

[36] See, for example, Donald B. Keim, "Dividend Yields and the January Effect," *The Journal of Portfolio Management* (Winter 1986), pp. 54–60. Keim finds that the largest abnormal returns accrue to smaller firms paying either no dividends or that have high dividend yields.

[37] These results, as well as a discussion of most of the anomalies, can be found in Donald B. Keim, "The CAPM and Equity Return Regularities," *Financial Analysts Journal* (May–June 1986), pp. 19–34.

[38] See Donald B. Keim, "Size-Related Anomalies and Stock Return Seasonality," *Journal of Financial Economics,* Vol. 12 (1983), pp. 13–32.

[39] See Richard Roll, "Vas ist das? The Turn of the Year Effect and the Return Premium of Small Firms," *Journal of Portfolio Management* (1983), pp. 18–28. Roll also found a turn-of-the-year effect with abnormal returns for small firms on the last trading day in December.

[40] See Dan Givoly and Arie Ovadia, "Year-End Tax-Induced Sales and Stock Market Seasonality," *The Journal of Finance* (March 1983), pp. 171–185.

[41] See Donald B. Keim, "Dividend Yields and the January Effect," *The Journal of Portfolio Management* (Winter 1986), pp. 54–60.

The Value Line Phenomenon

As discussed in Chapter 4, *The Value Line Investment Survey* is the largest, and perhaps best known, investment advisory service in the country. Value Line ranks each of the roughly 1700 stocks it covers from I (best) to V (worst) as to its "Timeliness"—probable relative price performance within the next 12 months. These timeliness ranks, which are updated each week, have been available since 1965. The performance of the five rankings categories has been spectacular.

The complete record of *Value Line* rankings for timeliness from 1965 through 1986 is shown in Table 14–2.

The first set of results assumes that equal amounts are invested in each stock in each grouping at the beginning of each year and held for 12 months without allowance for subsequent changes in ranking. The second set of results takes into account every change as it occurs. Such a strategy would lead to a prohibitive portfolio turnover rate. *Value Line* argues that most investors will reap benefits somewhere in between these two sets of results. It should be noted that all results exclude both commission costs and dividends.

Obviously, these results are impressive. The ranking system clearly discriminates in a monotonic order. Without allowing for changes in ranks, Group 3 stocks perform in an average way (using the average of the stocks covered by *Value Line*) while Groups 1 and 2 perform much better than either the average or the two market measures reported. On the other hand, shortselling Groups 4 and 5 would have been unsuccessful. Allowing for changes in ranks produces spectacular results, with Group 1 up some 11,800 percent and Group 5 down almost 100 percent.

If the market is efficient, how can these results be achieved? If investors know that *Value Line*'s rankings have been successful, how can the rankings

TABLE 14–2 Record of *Value Line* Rankings for Timeliness, 1965–1986, with and without Allowance for Changes in Ranks

Group	Without Allowance for Changes in Rank	With Allowance for Changes in Rank
1	+2071%	+11797%
2	+1103	+ 975
3	+ 495	+ 127
4	+ 166	− 48
5	+ 24	− 94
Average	+486%	
Dow Jones Industrials	+109%	
New York Stock Exchange Composite	+193%	

Source: "Selection and Opinion," *The Value Line Investment Survey*, January 23, 1987, p. 719. © 1987 Value Line, Inc. Reprinted by permission.

BOX 14–2 NEGLECTED STOCKS—ANOTHER ANOMALY?

The insider-trading scandal is big news on Wall Street, but many investors see it as another variation on an old theme: Professional investors are better-informed, whether legally or not, and that puts individuals at a disadvantage.

Now there's some good news for investors who don't want to quit the market or turn everything over to mutual funds: new academic studies suggest that you can beat the pros if you *don't* join them.

The investment strategies involve digging in areas neglected by the $820 billion of institutional investment in the stock market. There, in what Steven Carvell, a finance professor at Cornell University, refers to as "the shadows of Wall Street," the individual has a chance to beat the institutions in the information race.

"The kind of investment research we're proposing is like a flashlight," Prof. Carvell says. "It's completely useless in the spotlight, but in the shadows it can do a lot of good."

Winning Attributes

The studies found a variety of attributes among certain stocks that outperform the market, among them: low institutional investment, a low profile among analysts, and a relatively recent listing on an exchange. In practical terms, "companies that are neglected are more likely to be available at an attractive price than those that have already been shopped around to a hundred other people," says Robert Boddington of the investment-management firm Quest Advisory Corp.

An underlying principle regarding such "neglected" stocks is that investors tend to respond more negatively to uncertainty than to risk. "Psychologically, investors can deal with risk, which is a probability that can be measured," says Avner Arbel, another Cornell finance professor. "On the other hand, they have major difficulty handling uncertainty—which is the risk that the risk measure itself is wrong. Deficient information is what creates uncertainty."

Many if not most investors are turned off by a stock about which information is relatively unavailable or unreliable. That's especially true for institutions, whose fiduciary responsibility makes them less prone to act as entrepreneurial investors. Also, such stocks tend to be of smaller companies. This constrains institutions, which usually avoid low liquidity or ownership of as much as 5% of a company's stock, since that requires a public filing with the Securities and Exchange Commission.

As a result, individual investors have less competition from institutions for such stocks. The trick for the investor is to keep the uncertainties under control.

Studies have identified some ways an individual can screen for low-information stocks. For instance, recent work by two finance professors, Christopher Barry of Southern Methodist University and Stephen Brown of New York University, indicates that simply selecting newly listed stocks produces superior long-term gains. "The effect, which we have measured through the 50 years from 1931–1981, is consistent and very large," Mr. Brown says.

The study ranked stocks on the New York Stock Exchange into six groups according to how long they had been listed, and showed average monthly returns over the 50-year period ranged from 2.2% in the most newly listed group to 1.21% in the next newest group and minus 1.70% in the longest-listed group.

The rationale for the study was that newly listed stocks—after a brief adjustment period—are neglected and therefore discounted because there's little information about their performance record for analysts to consider.

"Another interesting thing about these stocks," says George Douglas, head of Drexel Burnham Lambert's quantitative research department, "is that they tend to represent emerging companies that are ambitious, successful and have graduated to the exchange, so they also have a growth bias."

Prof. Brown of NYU says that just buying stocks on the basis of a recent listing and small size isn't sufficient. That will help narrow the choices, but doesn't distinguish between undiscovered gems and stocks that deserve obscurity.

To protect against the bombs that might sink a portfolio, Prof. Brown makes these recommendations: Stocks that are new issues as well as new listings should not be considered until they have seasoned for six months. The candidates should also be subjected to some sort of financial test—for example, by sorting them according to price/earnings ratios. In addition, the stocks should be bought and held—not actively traded—for about a year.

Most important, Prof. Brown says, the investor should diversify his portfolio of these stocks by holding no fewer than about 20 of them. "You've got to have some degree of common sense," he says. "Looking at low information is *not* a substitute for looking at the financial fundamentals. There is substantial risk with this strategy, so you must apply it in a portfolio context."

While having to buy this many issues is a drawback to some investors, stocks in this category tend to be small and low-priced, which makes diversification more affordable.

Following this advice, an investor who bought 20 stocks last Dec. 31 that had been listed for less than a year, had market capitalization of $500 million or less, and had the lowest price/earnings ratio of this group would have done well. This exercise performed on Big Board new listings produced a gain of 32.71%, excluding dividends, compared with the NYSE composite index performance of 15.9%. The same exercise on the American Stock Exchange would have generated a 22.25% gain, more than triple the 6.8% gain in the exchange's index.

Finding New Listings

A monthly roster of new listings is available in the Standard & Poor's Stock Guide under "New Exchange Listings," for stocks that have moved from one exchange to another, and under "New Insertions," for stocks not previously listed.

Another group of academics including Profs. Arbel, Carvell and Paul Strebel of Switzerland's Imede Management Development Institute have focused on more specific evidence of institutional neglect. In one study, Mr. Arbel looked at stocks simply on the basis of whether they were covered by 10 or fewer Wall Street analysts and found that this group advanced by 40.2% in the year ended Oct. 31, compared with a gain of 28.3% in Standard & Poor's 400 index. "Given the conditions of the market, which favored Blue Chips, these results were surprising even to us," Prof. Arbel says.

Profs. Arbel and Carvell recommend that investors pool their professional insights and experience with investors who have backgrounds in other fields. By effectively acting as analysts this way, individuals looking at neglected stocks have a chance to "whittle the 20 top choices down to five or six real bargains," says Prof. Carvell. This approach, adds Mr. Gould of Lynch Jones & Ryan, "is the market-based translation of venture capitalism."

Investors trying such an approach must be prepared to live with a portfolio whose performance may be very volatile. "Any stock with comparatively high risk is more volatile," warns Prof. Barry of Southern Methodist. "The real question is whether the investor is prepared to bear that risk through the short term to get a higher average long-term return. The investor who can consciously take and live with that risk is acting in a sophisticated way."

Source: Barbara Donnelly, "In the Shadows: Neglected Stocks Offer Opportunities for Individuals," *The Wall Street Journal,* December 11, 1986, p. 35. Reprinted by permission of *The Wall Street Journal,* © Dow Jones & Company, Inc. 1986. All rights reserved.

continue to be successful over the coming year? Keep in mind that the rankings are based on known information that supposedly has been fully discounted in the market. The *Value Line* system has been completely described in its literature, making it duplicatable and verifiable. Apparently, it continues to work well.

Some Conclusions about Market Efficiency

Given all of the evidence about market efficiency discussed previously—the studies supporting it as well as the evidence of anomalies—what conclusions can be drawn? In truth, no definitive conclusion about market efficiency can be stated. The evidence in support of market efficiency is persuasive because of the large amount of research done over many years by numerous investigators; however, the evidence on anomalies has yet to be explained satisfactorily. And many technicians and fundamentalists are convinced that they can outperform the market, or at least provide more benefits than cost. Paradoxically, this belief helps to make the market efficient.

The paradox of efficient markets and active investors is that investors, in an attempt to uncover and use important information about security prices, help to make the market efficient. In other words, in the course of searching out undervalued and overvalued stocks, investors discover information and act on it as quickly as possible. If the information is favorable, the discoverers will buy immediately; if unfavorable, they will sell immediately. As investors scramble for information and attempt to be the first to act, they will make the market more efficient. If enough of this activity occurs, all information will be reflected in prices. Thus, the fact that a number of investors do not believe in the EMH results in actions that help to make the market efficient.

In the final analysis, it is probably best to accept the idea that the market is quite efficient, but not totally. Most of the research done to date suggests that information is received and acted on quickly, and generally the correct adjustments are made. To outperform the market, fundamental analysis beyond the norm must be done. The fundamental analysis that is routinely done every day is already reflected in stock prices. The marginal value of one more investor performing the same calculations already done by other investors is zero. And until more evidence to the contrary is forthcoming, technical analysis remains questionable, at best.

Simon Keane has argued that investors must choose between a belief in operational efficiency and operational inefficiency.[42] In an operationally efficient market some investors with the skill to detect a divergence between price and semistrong value earn economic rents. For the majority of investors, however, such opportunities are not available. An operationally inefficient market, on the other hand, contains inefficiencies that can be spotted by the average investor. The evidence to date suggests that investors face an operationally efficient market.[43]

Some anomalies do seem to exist, and since the late 1970s the flow of research reporting on anomalies has accelerated.[44] These anomalies require considerable work to document scientifically and do not represent a guarantee of investment riches; however, these anomalies appear to offer opportunities to astute investors. The reasons for the existence of these anomalies remain unsettled. The quantity and quality of the research in this area has undermined the extreme view that the market is so perfectly efficient that no opportunities for excess returns could possibly exist.

The controversy about market efficiency remains. Every investor is still faced with the choice between an active and passive investment strategy.

Summary

This chapter explains an alternative approach to the fundamental and technical approaches for selecting common stocks. If the stock market is efficient, investors should consider nontraditional approaches in their pursuit of the best portfolio performance.

An efficient market is defined as one in which the prices of securities fully reflect all known information quickly and accurately. The conditions that guarantee an efficient market can be shown to hold to a large extent: many

---

[42] See Simon Keane, "The Efficient Market Hypothesis on Trial," *Financial Analysts Journal* (March–April 1986), pp. 58–63. This paper presents an excellent discussion of the current efficient-market debate.

[43] For evidence that the market is not perfectly efficient and therefore offers investors investment opportunities, see Robert F. Vandell and Robert Panino, "A Purposeful Stride Down Wall Street," *The Journal of Portfolio Management*, Winter 1986, pp. 31–39.

[44] A special edition of the *Journal of Financial Economics* in 1978 was devoted to this contrary evidence.

investors are competing, information is widely available and generated more or less randomly, and investors react quickly to this information.

To assess market efficiency, three cumulative forms (or degrees) of efficiency are discussed: the weak form, the semistrong form, and the strong form. The weak form involves market data, whereas the semistrong and strong form involve the assimilation of all public and private information, respectively.

The weak-form evidence, whether statistical tests or trading rules, unanimously supports the hypothesis. In conducting these tests, it is important to make a fair test by adjusting for risk and all costs, checking consistency, and validating results out of sample.

Many tests of semistrong efficiency have been conducted, including among others, stock splits, money supply changes, accounting changes, dividend announcements, and reactions to other announcements. Although all of the studies do not agree, the majority support semistrong efficiency.

Strong-form evidence takes the form of tests of the performance of groups presumed to have "private" information and of the ability of professional managers to outperform the market. Insiders apparently are able to do well, although the decisions of the managers of mutual funds have not been found to add value.

Most knowledgeable observers accept weak-form efficiency, reject strong-form efficiency, and feel that the market is, to a large degree, semistrong efficient. This casts doubt on the value of technical analysis as well as conventional fundamental analysis. Although the EMH does not preclude investors from outperforming the market, it does suggest that it is quite difficult and that the investor must do more than the norm. Even if the market is efficient, money managers will still have activities to perform, including diversifying the portfolio, choosing and maintaining some degree of risk, and assessing taxes and transaction costs.

Several major "anomalies" that have appeared over the last several years have yet to be satisfactorily explained. These anomalies, which would not be expected in a totally efficient market, are as follows:

1. *Unexpected earnings, as represented by SUE*. The market appears to adjust with a lag to the earnings surprises contained in quarterly earnings. SUE has been shown to be a monotonic discriminator of subsequent short-term (e.g., three-month) stock returns.
2. *P/E ratios*. Low P/E ratio stocks appear to outperform high P/E ratio stocks over annual periods, even after adjustment for risk and size.
3. *The size effect*. Small firms have been shown to outperform large firms, on a risk-adjusted basis, over a period of many years.
4. *The January effect*. Much of the abnormal return for small firms occurs in the month of January, possibly because tax-induced sales in December temporarily depress prices, which then recover in January.
5. *Value Line's performance*. The Value Line rankings for timeliness

have performed extremely well over the period 1965–1986 and appear to offer the average investor a chance to outperform the averages.

In conclusion, investors must take heed of the EMH and its implications. Although it does not render all of their activities suspect, it does suggest certain courses of action that may be useless and others that may be more valuable. The market may not be totally efficient, but it is quite efficient.

Key Words

Efficient market	Semistrong form
Efficient market hypothesis (EMH)	Size effect
Filter rule	Strong form
January effect	Weak form
Market anomalies	

QUESTIONS AND PROBLEMS

1. What is meant by an efficient market?
2. Describe the three forms of market efficiency.
3. What are the conditions for an efficient market? How closely are they met in reality?
4. Why is a market that is weak-form efficient in direct opposition to technical analysis?
5. What is the purpose of semistrong market efficiency tests?
6. Describe two different ways to test for weak-form efficiency.
7. Distinguish between economic significance and statistical significance.
8. If the EMH is true, what are the implications to investors?
9. Could the performance of mutual fund managers also be a test of semistrong efficiency?
10. Describe the money management activities of a portfolio manager who believes that the market is efficient.
11. What are market anomalies? Describe four.
12. If all investors believe that the market is efficient, could that eventually lead to less efficiency in the market?
13. What is the relationship between SUE and fundamental analysis?

14. What other types of events or information could be used in semistrong form tests?
15. What are the benefits to society of an efficient market?
16. If the market moves in an upward trend over a period of years, would this be inconsistent with weak-form efficiency?
17. Do security analysts have a role in an efficient market?
18. Evaluate the following statement: "My mutual fund has outperformed the market for the last four years. How can the market be efficient?"
19. What are the necessary conditions for a scientific test of a technical analysis trading rule?
20. Are filter rules related to timing strategies or stock selection strategies? What alternative should a filter rule be compared with?
21. Assume that you analyze the activities of specialists on the NYSE and find that they are able to realize consistently above-average rates of return. What form of the EMH are you testing?
22. What are some possible explanations for the size anomaly?
23. Can technical analysis ever be completely invalidated?
24. How can data on corporate insiders be used to test both the semistrong and the strong forms of the EMH?
25. How can data on the performance of mutual funds be used to test both the semistrong and the strong forms of the EMH?
26. Assume that the price of a stock remains constant from time period 0 to time period 1, at which time a significant piece of information about the stock becomes available. Explain how you would expect to see this situation graphically if (a) the market is semistrong efficient, and (b) there is a lag in the adjustment of the price to this information.
27. How is the SUE concept related to technical analysis?
28. Calculate the SUE for a stock with actual quarterly earnings of $0.50 per share and expected quarterly earnings of $0.30 per share. The standard error of estimate is 0.05. Is this a good buy?
29. What is meant by an operationally efficient market?

Selected References

Arbel, Avner. "Generic Stocks: The Key to Market Anomalies." *The Journal of Portfolio Management*, Summer 1985, pp. 4–13.

Banz, Rolf. "The Relationship between Returns and Market Value of Common Stocks." *Journal of Financial Economics*, March 1981, pp. 3–18.

Basu, S. "Investment Performance of Common Stocks in Relation to Their Price–Earnings Ratios: A Test of the Efficient Market Hypothesis." *The Journal of Finance*, June 1977, pp. 663–682.

Basu, S. "The Relationship Between Earnings' Yield, Market Value and Return for NYSE Common Stocks: Further Evidence." *Journal of Financial Economics*, June 1983, pp. 129–156.

Bjerring, James H., Lakonishok, Joseph, and Vermaelen, Theo. "Stock Prices and Financial Analysts' Recommendations." *The Journal of Finance,* March 1983, pp. 187–204.

Brealey, Richard A. *An Introduction to Risk and Return from Common Stocks.* 2nd ed. Cambridge, Mass.: MIT Press, 1983.

Brown, Philip, and Ball, Ray. "An Empirical Evaluation of Accounting Income Numbers." *Journal of Accounting Research,* Autumn 1968, pp. 159–178.

Charest, G. "Split Information, Stock Returns, and Market Efficiency." *Journal of Financial Economics,* June–September 1978, pp. 256–296.

Fama, Eugene. "Efficient Capital Markets: A Review of Theory and Empirical Work." *The Journal of Finance,* May 1970, pp. 383–417.

Fama, Eugene. "The Behavior of Stock Market Prices." *The Journal of Finance,* January 1965, pp. 34–105.

Fama, Eugene, and Blume, Marshall. "Filter Rules and Stock-Market Trading." *The Journal of Business: A Supplement,* January 1969, pp. 2–21.

Fama, Eugene, Fisher, Lawrence, Jensen, Michael, and Roll, Richard. "The Adjustment of Stock Prices to New Information." *International Economics Review,* February 1969, pp. 2–21.

Finnerty, Joseph. "Insiders and Market Efficiency." *The Journal of Finance,* September 1976, pp. 205–215.

Foster, T. W., and Vickery, D. "The Information Content of Stock Dividend Announcements." *Accounting Review,* April 1978, pp. 360–370.

Givoly, Dan, and Ovadia, Arie. "Year-End Tax-Induced Sales and Stock Market Seasonality." *The Journal of Finance,* March 1983, pp. 171–185.

Goodman, David, and Peavy, John W. "The Risk Universal Nature of the P/E Effect." *The Journal of Portfolio Management,* Summer 1985, pp. 14–17.

Jaffe, Jeffrey. "Special Information and Insider Trading." *The Journal of Business,* July 1974, pp. 410–478.

Jensen, Michael. "The Performance of Mutual Funds in the Period 1945–1964." *The Journal of Finance,* May 1969, pp. 389–416.

Joy, O. Maurice, and Jones, Charles P. "Earnings Reports and Market Efficiencies: An Analysis of Contrary Evidence." *Journal of Financial Research,* Spring 1979, pp. 51–64.

Kaplan, Robert, and Roll, Richard. "Accounting Changes and Stock Prices." *Financial Analysts Journal,* January–February 1973, pp. 48–53.

Keane, Simon. "The Efficient Market Hypothesis on Trial." *Financial Analysts Journal,* March–April 1986, pp. 58–63.

Keim, Donald B. "Size-Related Anomalies and Stock Return Seasonality." *Journal of Financial Economics,* 1983, pp. 13–32.

Keim, Donald B. "The CAPM and Equity Return Regularities." *Financial Analysts Journal,* May–June 1986, pp. 19–34.

Latané, Henry, and Jones, Charles P. "Standardized Unexpected Earnings—A Progress Report." *The Journal of Finance,* December 1977, pp. 1457–1465.

Mains, Norman. "Risk, the Pricing of Capital Assets, and the Evaluation of Investment Portfolios: Comment." *The Journal of Business,* July 1977, pp. 371–384.

McDonald, John. "Objectives and Performance of Mutual Funds, 1960–1969." *Journal of Financial and Quantitative Analysis,* June 1974, pp. 311–333.

Reilly, Frank, and Drzycimski, Eugene. "Tests of Stock Market Efficiency Following Major World Events." *Journal of Business Research,* Summer 1973, pp. 57–72.

Reinganum, Mark. "Misspecification of Capital Asset Pricing: Empirical Anomalies Based on Earnings Yield and Market Values." *Journal of Financial Economics,* March 1981, pp. 19–46.

PART SIX

ADDITIONAL INVESTMENT OPPORTUNITIES

CHAPTER 15

OPTIONS

Rather than trade directly in common stocks, investors can purchase securities representing a claim—an option—on a particular stock. This option gives the holder the right to receive or deliver shares of stock under specified conditions. The option need not be exercised, and in many cases the option will not be worth exercising. An investor can simply buy and sell these equity-derivative securities (i.e., securities that derive all, or part, of their value from the equity of the same corporation). Gains or losses will depend on the difference between the purchase price and the sales price.

This chapter will discuss options, specifically puts and calls. Chapter 16 will discuss warrants and convertibles. All three are equity-derivative securities.[1]

Background

Options, which represent claims on an underlying common stock, are created by investors and sold to other investors, with the corporation whose common stock underlies these claims having no direct interest in the trans-

---

[1] Rights, another equity-derivative security, were briefly discussed in Chapter 2. They are not discussed further because of their minor importance to most investors.

action. The corporation is in no way responsible for the creation, termination, or execution of puts and calls.

A **call** is an option to buy a stated number of shares of a particular common stock at a specified price *anytime* before a specified expiration date. As an example, an IBM six-month call option at $120 per share gives the owner the right (an option) to purchase a specified number of shares of IBM at $120 per share from the writer (seller) of the option *anytime* during the six months before the specified expiration date.[2] Investors purchase calls if they expect the stock price to rise because the price of the call and the common stock will move together. Calls permit investors to speculate on a rise in the price of the underlying common stock without buying the stock itself.

A **put** is an option to sell a stated number of shares of a particular common stock at a specified price before a specified expiration date. If exercised, the shares are sold by the owner (buyer) of the put contract to a writer (seller) of this contract, who must, if called upon, take delivery of the shares and pay the specified price. For example, a writer (seller) of an IBM six-month put at $120 per share is obligated, under certain circumstances, to receive from the holder of this put a specified number of shares of IBM for which the writer will pay $120 per share. Investors will purchase a put if they expect the stock price to fall, because the value of the put will rise as the stock price declines. Puts allow investors to speculate on a decline in the stock price without selling short the common stock.

Why Puts and Calls?

An investor can always purchase a common stock if he or she is bullish about its prospects, or sell it short if bearish. Why, then, should we create these indirect claims on a stock as an alternative way to invest? Several reasons have been advanced, including the following:

1. In the case of calls, an investor can control (for a short period) a claim on the underlying common stock for a much smaller investment than required to buy the stock itself. In the case of puts, an investor can duplicate a short sale without a margin account and at a modest cost in relation to the price of the stock.
2. The investor's maximum loss is known in advance. If an option expires worthless, the most the investor can lose is the cost (price) of the option.
3. Options provide leverage—magnified gains (in percentage terms) in relation to buying the stock; furthermore, options can provide greater leverage than fully margined stock transactions.
4. Puts and calls expand the opportunity set available to investors, making available risk–return combinations that otherwise would not be

---

[2] Options that can be exercised anytime before expiration are known technically as American options. A European option, in contrast, can only be exercised at maturity.

possible or that improve the risk–return characteristics of a portfolio. For example, an investor can sell a stock short and buy a call, thereby decreasing the risk on the short sale for the life of the call.[3]

5. Options can reduce total portfolio transaction costs. While transaction costs at the single trade level may be higher for options, this need not be true for the total trades made for a portfolio.

6. Using index options, an investor can now participate in the overall movement of the market, or protect a portfolio against adverse market movements, with a single trading decision.

Understanding Options

Options Terminology

In order to understand puts and calls, one must understand the terms used in connection with them. Since 1973, when options trading on organized exchanges began, the following terms of put and call contracts have been standardized: the price at which the put or call can be exercised, the expiration date, and the number of shares (100) involved in each contract.[4] Our discussion applies specifically to options on the organized exchanges.[5] Important options terms include the following:

1. Exercise (Strike) Price. This is the per share price at which the common stock may be purchased (in the case of a call) or sold to a writer (in the case of a put). Most stocks in the options market have options available at several different exercise prices, thereby providing investors with a choice. For example, if IBM's market price is around $140–150, options may be available with the following strike prices: $125, $130, $135, $140, $145, $150, $155, $160, and $165.

Special terminology is used to describe the relationship between the exercise price of the option and the current stock price. If the price of the common stock exceeds the exercise price of a call, that call is said to be *in the money*. This means that the call has an immediate exercisable value. On the other hand, if the price of the common is less than the exercise price of a

---

[3] The majority of stocks do not have puts and calls available. Several hundred stocks constitute the active options market.

[4] It is important to remember throughout this discussion that the standard option contract is for 100 shares of the underlying common stock; therefore, when we speak of buying or selling *a* call or *a* put, we mean one contract representing an option on 100 shares of stock.

[5] Puts and calls existed for many years before these organized exchanges. They could be bought or sold in the over-the-counter market through brokers who were part of the Put and Call Dealers and Brokers Association. Members of this association endeavored to satisfy investor demands for particular options on a case-by-case basis. The terms of each individual contract (price, exercise date, etc.) had to be negotiated between buyer and seller. This was clearly a cumbersome, inefficient process.

call, it is said to be *out of the money*. Finally, *near the money* calls are those with exercise prices slightly greater than current market price.[6]

2. Expiration Date. This is the last date at which an option can be exercised.[7] All puts and calls are designated by the month of expiration, such as February-March-April or June-September-December. The farthest expiration date possible is the end of the farthest three-month interval—a maximum of nine months.[8]

3. Premium. This is the price paid by the option buyer to the writer (seller) of the option, whether put or call. The premium is stated on a per share basis for options on organized exchanges, and since the standard contract is on 100 shares, the premium represents hundreds of dollars. For example, an option premium may be stated as $3, but this represents $300, $15 represents $1500, and so on.

4. Naked versus Covered Options. A call option written against stock owned by the writer is said to be "covered." If a writer does not own the stock, a "naked" call option is involved since the writer may be required to deliver stock not owned if the call is exercised. A put writer who is short the stock is "covered," otherwise the put writer is "naked."

As a demonstration of this terminology, consider an excerpt from *The Wall Street Journal*'s "Listed Options Quotation" page as shown in Figure 15–1.[9] The most active options for the day for each of the five markets are indicated on the right side of the page. Let us consider the second option listed under the Philadelphia Exchange, that of "Bard," or C. D. Bard Company. Calls are shown first, followed by puts, and there are three expiration dates for each (in this example, February, March, and April). Four exercise prices are available for Bard—$35, $40, $45, and $50. Thus, an investor has a potential choice of 4 (exercise prices) × 3 (expiration dates) = 12 call options on this stock and 12 put options.[10]

Bard common stock closed at $43⅛ on the day shown in Figure 15–1. This means that the 35 and 40 call options were "in the money" because the stock price was greater than the exercise price, whereas the other two were out of the money. Notice that the premiums (market prices) increase as maturity increases; that is, premiums increase from the February contracts to the April contracts. Options are worth more the longer they have before expiration.

---

[6]These same definitions (in the money, out of the money, and near the money) also apply to puts, but in reverse.

[7]American-style options can be exercised anytime prior to expiration; European-style options can be exercised only at expiration.

[8]The exact expiration day is the Saturday following the third Friday of the exercise month.

[9]This excerpt shows only a few of the options traded, but all five markets that trade options—the Chicago Board Option Exchange, the American Stock Exchange, the Pacific Exchange, the Philadelphia Exchange, and the New York Exchange—are carried on this page and would be read in the same manner.

[10]The letter "s" indicates that options are unavailable for certain exercise prices and exercise dates; the "r" indicates that a particular option was not traded that day.

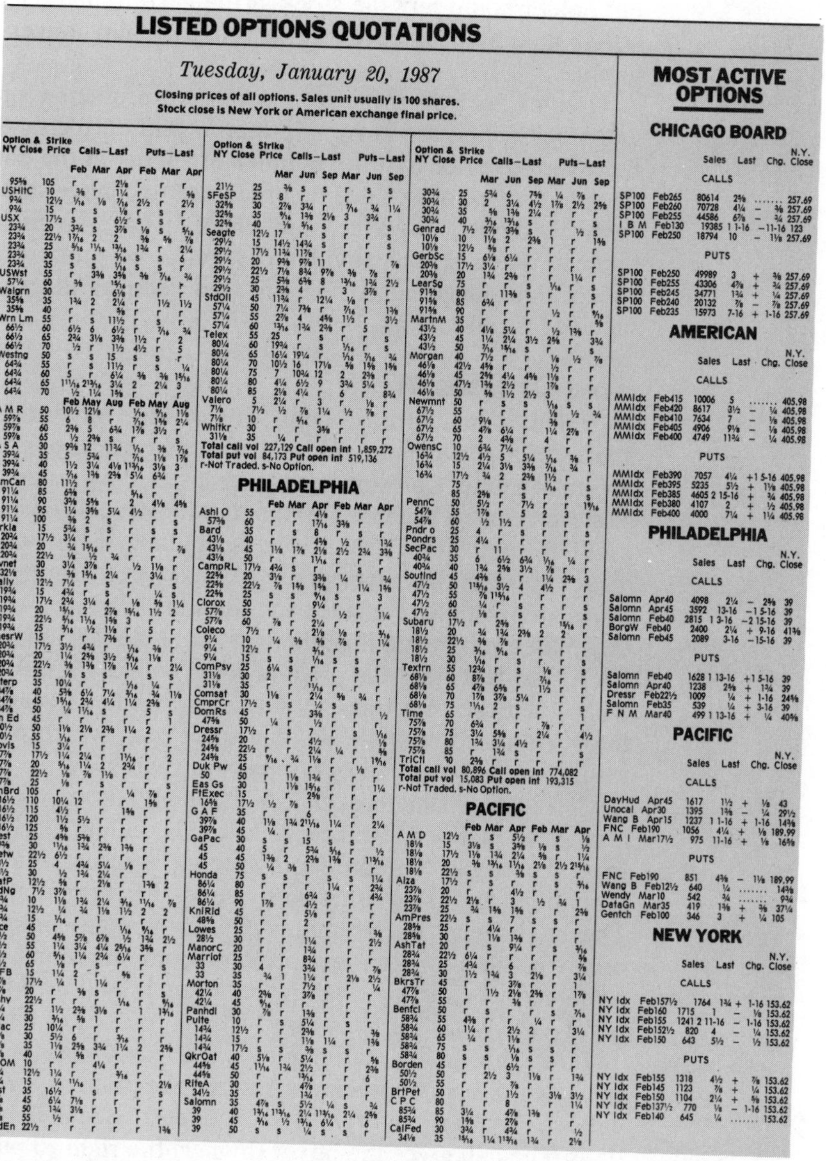

FIGURE 15–1 **An excerpt from the "Listed Options Quotations" page from** *The Wall Street Journal.*

Source: The Wall Street Journal, January 21, 1987, p. 42. Reprinted by permission of *The Wall Street Journal.* © Dow Jones & Company, Inc. 1987. All rights reserved.

As for Bard puts, the 45 and 50 puts are "in the money" because they are worth exercising on this particular date (ignoring transaction costs); that is, a put holder could buy the stock at the current market price and sell it to the writer at the specified exercise price. Again, longer maturities are worth more.

Options sold on these exchanges are protected against stock dividends and stock splits; therefore, if either is paid during the life of an option, both the exercise price and the number of shares in the contract are adjusted as necessary. Options traded on organized exchanges are not protected against cash dividends, however, and this can have significant effects on option values. When a cash dividend is paid, the stock price should decline to reflect this payment. Any event that reduces the stock price reduces the value of a call.

How Options Work

As noted, a standard call contract gives the buyer the right to purchase 100 shares of a particular stock at a specified exercise price anytime before the expiration date. Calls (and puts) are created by sellers who write a particular contract. Sellers are investors, either individuals or institutions, who seek to profit from their beliefs about the underlying stock's likely price performance, just as the buyer does.

As an example, consider an individual named Carl who owns 100 shares of XYZ common and is optimistic about XYZ's longer run prospects. However, Carl feels that the price of XYZ will be flat, or possibly decline somewhat, over the next three months. Carl wishes to earn a short-run return on the XYZ position while holding the stock, which can be accomplished by selling a (covered) call option on the shares.

Carl instructs his broker to write (sell) a three-month call option on XYZ at a strike price of $50. For writing this option, Carl will receive a premium from the buyer. The premium amount is a function of supply and demand conditions and is determined by several factors that we will examine later. The buyer pays the premium plus brokerage commissions, and the seller receives this premium less brokerage commissions. Let us assume, in this hypothetical example, that the premium is $4 (i.e., $400, since 100 shares are involved). What happens now? Three courses of action are possible.

First, the option may expire worthless three months from now because the stock did not appreciate. Assume the price of XYZ was $50.50 when this call was written, and that it subsequently declines to $48 by the expiration date. The call gives the buyer (owner) the right to purchase XYZ from Carl for $50, but this would make no sense when XYZ can be purchased on the open market at $48; therefore, the option will expire worthless. The buyer will lose the $400 investment, and Carl will gain the premium while continuing to own the XYZ shares.

Second, if XYZ appreciates, a call buyer could exercise the option and Carl could be called upon to meet this exercise. This means that the buyer pays Carl $5000 (the $50 exercise price multiplied by 100 shares) and receives 100 shares of XYZ. Assume the price has appreciated to $60 before expiration and the buyer exercises the option. The call buyer now owns 100 shares of XYZ worth $60 per share, for which the buyer paid only $50 per share (plus the $4 per share for the call option itself). An immediate sale of XYZ in the market would result in a $600 gross profit for the call owner (brokerage costs would have to be included to obtain a net profit figure).

Third, if XYZ appreciates, the value (price) of the call will also appreciate. The owner can simply sell the call in the secondary market to another investor who wishes to speculate on XYZ. Listed options are traded continuously on the five exchanges mentioned; therefore buyers call their broker and instruct him or her to sell. Most investors trading puts and calls do not exercise those that are valuable; instead, they simply sell them on the open market, just as they would the common stock if they owned it.[11] Puts work the same way as calls, except in reverse. Again, a writer creates a particular put contract by selling it for the premium that the buyer pays. The writer believes that the underlying common stock is likely to remain flat or appreciate, and the buyer believes it is likely to decline.

Note the obligation of a put writer (seller). Assume a writer sells a three-month XYZ put at $50 for a $4 premium, which the buyer of the put pays. Suppose the price of XYZ declines to $40 just before the expiration date. The put owner (buyer), who did not own XYZ previously, could instruct the broker to purchase 100 shares of XYZ in the market for $40. The buyer could then exercise the put, which means that a chosen writer must accept the 100 shares of XYZ and pay the put owner $50 per share, or $5000 total (although the current market price is only $40). The put buyer grosses $600 ($5000 received less $4000 cost of 100 shares less the $400 for the put). The put writer suffers an immediate paper loss. Brokerage costs have once again been omitted in the example.

As in the case of a call, two other courses of action are possible in addition to the exercise of the put as just described. First, the put may expire worthless because the price of the common did not decline or did not decline enough to justify exercising the put. Second, and far more likely, the put owner can sell the put in the secondary market for a profit (or a loss).

The Mechanics of Trading

Secondary markets   As noted, five option exchanges constitute the secondary market. These exchanges have made puts and calls a success by standardizing the exercise date and exercise price of contracts. One XYZ March 60 call option is identical to every other XYZ March 60 call option. These markets provide liquidity to investors, a very important requirement for

---

[11]One of the implications of the option pricing model to be considered later is that calls on stocks that do not pay a cash dividend should never be exercised before the expiration date. Calls on stocks paying a cash dividend might be exercised before the expiration date.

successful trading. Investors know that they can instruct their broker to buy or sell whenever they desire at a price set by the forces of supply and demand.

The same types of orders discussed in Chapter 3, in particular market and limit orders, are used in trading puts and calls.[12] Certificates representing ownership are not used for puts and calls; instead, transactions are handled as bookkeeping entries. Option trades settle on the next business day after the trade.

The secondary markets for puts and calls have worked well in the years since the Chicago Board Option Exchange (CBOE) started operations in 1973. Trading volume has been large, and the number of puts and calls available has expanded. One reason for the success of trading has been the clearing corporation.

The clearing corporation   The **options clearing corporation** (OCC) performs a number of important functions that contribute to the success of the secondary market for options. It functions as an intermediary between the brokers representing the buyers and the writers. Through their brokers, call writers contract with the OCC itself to deliver shares of the particular stock, and buyers of calls actually receive the right to purchase the shares from the OCC. This prevents the risk and problems that could occur as buyers attempted to force writers to honor their obligations. In effect, the OCC guarantees the performance of the contracts.

An investor wishing to exercise a call informs his or her broker, who in turn informs the OCC of the exercise. The OCC *randomly* selects a broker on whom it holds the same call contract, and the broker selects a customer who has written these calls to deliver the stock in accordance with the contract. Put contracts are handled in the same manner. Options writers chosen in this manner are said to be assigned an obligation or to have received an assignment notice.[13]

The OCC acts to cancel out the obligations of writers wishing to terminate their position. A call writer can terminate the obligation to deliver the stock anytime before the expiration date by making a "closing purchase transaction." The OCC offsets the outstanding call written with the call purchased in the closing transaction. A put writer can also close out a position at any time by making an offsetting transaction.

Brokerage commissions   All brokerage commissions are negotiable, as explained in Chapter 3. The major brokerage houses will typically charge more than discount brokers, who advertise that they may save an investor 50% or more on option commissions.

---

[12] Not all types of orders (for example, stop orders) are always valid on all exchanges that trade options.

[13] Assignment is virtually certain when an option expires in the money.

The following data will provide an idea of brokerage commissions on puts and calls using a discount brokerage service. The minimum option commission is $30 for one contract.[14] For option prices over $1, one (randomly selected) discount broker charges $30 for 1 to 3 contracts, $35 for 4 contracts, $40 for 5 contracts, and so on up to $65 for 10 contracts. Twenty contracts have a commission of $115, while for 30 contracts the cost is $165. These figures are only one example, and commissions vary between brokerage houses.[15]

Valuing Options

A General Framework

In this section we will examine the determinants of the value of a put or call. The value is the current market price, or premium, of the option.

The market value of a call option can be dichotomized in the following manner. If a call is in the money (the market price of the stock exceeds the exercise price for the call option) it has an immediate value equal to the difference in the two prices. This value will be designated the *intrinsic value* of the call; it could also be referred to as the option's minimum value, which in this case is positive. If the call is out of the money (the stock price is less than the exercise price) the intrinsic value is zero; in this case, the price of the option is based on its speculative appeal.

Puts, of course, work in reverse. If the market price of the stock is less than the exercise price of the put, the put is in the money and has an intrinsic value. Otherwise, it is out of the money and has a zero intrinsic value.

An option almost never declines below its intrinsic value. The reason is that market **arbitragers,** who constantly monitor option prices for discrepancies, would purchase the options and exercise them, thus earning riskless returns.[16]

Option prices almost always exceed intrinsic values; the amount of excess reflects the option's potential appreciation. Such excesses exist because buyers are willing to pay a price for potential future stock price movements. This part of the option's price reflects its time value.[17] Clearly, time has a positive value—the longer the time to expiration for the option, the more chance it has to appreciate in value. However, holding the stock price con-

---

[14]Some brokers charge less if the option price is less than $1; for example, $18 for the first contract.

[15]When an option is exercised, both the buyer of the stock (the exerciser) and the seller of the stock (who is assigned the obligation) must pay brokerage commissions.

[16]Arbitragers are speculators who seek to earn a return without assuming risk by constructing riskless hedges.

[17]The time value of a call can be calculated as the sum of the call price and the striking price less the stock price. If a call has no intrinsic value—that is, it is out of the money—its price and its time value are equal.

stant, options are a *wasting asset* whose value approaches intrinsic value as expiration approaches. In other words, as expiration approaches, the time value of the option declines to zero.

Determinants of Value

Fischer Black and Myron Scholes have developed a model for the valuation of call options that is widely accepted and used in the investments community.[18] The formula itself is mathematical and appears to be very complex. It can be programmed for calculators and computers, however, and numerous investors estimate the value of calls using the **Black–Scholes model.**

The Black–Scholes model uses five variables to value the call option of a *nondividend-paying stock*. These five variables, all but the last of which are directly observable in the market, are as follows:

1. The price of the underlying stock.
2. The exercise price of the option.
3. The time remaining to the expiration of the option.
4. The interest rate.
5. The volatility of the underlying stock price.

The first two variables are of obvious importance in valuing an option because, as noted before, they determine the option's intrinsic value—whether it is in the money or not. If it is out of the money, it has only a time value based on the speculative interest in the stock.

Time to expiration is also an important factor in the value of an option because, as noted, value increases with maturity, other things being equal. The relationship between time and value is not proportional, however. The time value of an option is greatest when the market price and the exercise price are equal. If the option is already in the money, a rise in the stock price will not result in the same percentage gain in the option price that would occur in the previous situation. And finally, for out-of-the-money options, part of the time remaining will be used for the price of the stock to reach the exercise price.

The interest rate affects option values because of the opportunity cost involved. Buying an option is a substitute to some degree for buying on margin, on which interest must be paid. The higher interest rates are, therefore, the more interest cost is saved by the use of options. This adds to the value of the option and results in a direct relationship between the value of a call option and interest rates in the market.

The last factor, and the only one not directly observable in the marketplace, is the volatility in the price of the underlying stock. Volatility is associated with risk, as discussed in Chapter 5. The greater the risk, the *higher* the price of a call option because of the increased potential for the

---

[18] F. Black and M. Scholes, "The Pricing of Options and Corporate Liabilities," *Journal of Political Economy*, Vol. 81 (May–June 1973), pp. 637–654.

stock to move up. Therefore, a positive relation exists between the volatility of the stock and the value of the call option.

The Black–Scholes option pricing formula can be expressed as[19]

$$P = CMP[N(d_1)] - EP[\text{antilog}(-rt)][N(d_2)] \qquad (15\text{–}1)$$

where

P = the market value of the call option.
CMP = current market price of the underlying common stock.
$N(d_1)$ = the cumulative density function of d_1.
EP = the exercise price of the option.
r = the continuously compounded riskless rate of interest on an annual basis.
t = the time remaining before the expiration date of the option, expressed as a fraction of a year.
$N(d_2)$ = the cumulative density function of d_2.

To find d_1 and d_2, it is necessary to solve these equations.

$$d_1 = \frac{\ln (CMP/EP) + (r + 0.5\sigma^2)t}{(\sigma[(t)^{1/2}])} \qquad (15\text{–}2)$$

$$d_2 = d_1 - (\sigma[(t)^{1/2}]) \qquad (15\text{–}3)$$

where

$\ln (CMP/EP)$ = the natural log of (CMP/EP)
σ = the standard deviation of the annual rate of return on the underlying common stock

The five variables previously listed are needed as inputs. Variables 1 through 4 are immediately available. Variable 5 is not, however, because what is needed is the variability expected to occur in the stock's rate of return. Although historical data on stock returns are typically used to estimate this standard deviation, variability does change over time. A formula user should try to incorporate expected changes in the variability when using historical data. To do this, the user should examine any likely changes in either the market's or the individual stock's volatility.

Variables 1 through 3 should be identical for a given stock for everyone using the Black–Scholes model. Variable 4 should be identical or very close among formula users, depending on the exact proxy used for the riskless rate of interest. It is variable 5 that will vary among users, providing different option values. Empirical studies have shown that estimates of the variance obtained from other than historical data are more valuable than the estimates based on historical data. Since the price of an option can be observed at any time, it is possible to solve the Black–Scholes formula for the implied standard deviation of the stock's return. Henry Latané and Richard Rendleman

---

[19]This model applies to nondividend-paying stocks.

found that better forecasts of the actual standard deviation could be obtained by preparing forecasts from the model itself.[20]

The following is an example of the Black–Scholes option pricing formula. Assume

$$CMP = \$40$$
$$EP = \$45$$
$$r = 0.10$$
$$t = 0.501 \text{ (183 days)}$$
$$\sigma = 0.45$$

STEP 1 Solve for d_1. (Round t to .5 for convenience.)

$$d_1 = \frac{ln\ (40/45) + [(0.10 + 0.5(0.45)^2]\ 0.5}{0.45\ [(0.5)^{1/2}]}$$

$$= \frac{-0.1178 + 0.1006}{0.3182}$$

$$= -0.054$$

STEP 2 Use a cumulative probability distribution table to find the value of $N(d_1)$.

$$N(d_1) = 0.4801$$

where $d_1 = -0.054$.

STEP 3 Find d_2.

$$d_2 = -0.054 - [0.45((0.5)^{1/2})]$$

$$= -0.372$$

STEP 4 Find $N(d_2)$.

$$N(d_2) \approx 0.3557$$

STEP 5 Solve for P.

$$P = CMP[0.4801] - EP[\text{antilog}\ (-(0.1)(0.5))][0.3557]$$

$$= 19.20 - 45(0.9512)(0.3557)$$

$$= 19.20 - 15.23$$

$$= \$3.97$$

The theoretical value of the option, according to the Black–Scholes formula, is $3.97. If the current market price of the option is greater than the theoretical value, it is overpriced; if less, it is underpriced.

---

[20] H. Latané and R. Rendleman, Jr., "Standard Deviations of Stock Price Ratios Implied in Option Prices," *The Journal of Finance*, May 1976, pp. 369–382.

Analyzing Basic Options Strategies

In this section we analyze some basic options strategies used by investors. We first consider the buyer's standpoint and then the writer's (seller of the option). Following these basic strategies, we consider more sophisticated approaches.

Buying Options

Many individual investors purchase calls and puts at some point in their investment program. Calls are more popular than puts, just as buying long is more popular than selling short. We will consider the purchase of a call and a put, followed by a consideration of both from the seller's (writer's) viewpoint.

Buying calls   Investors buy calls because they are bullish (optimistic) about the price of the underlying stock. They wish to have a claim on the stock that will allow them to profit if their expectations are correct. The use of calls minimizes the initial investment, specifies the maximum loss that can be suffered, and provides the potential for maximum leverage (the ratio of profit to dollars invested).[21]

Investors always have the alternative of purchasing the stock itself. In doing so, their profit or loss is a direct (linear) function of the price of the stock at any point in time. To see this, examine Figure 15–2, which shows the profit–loss relationship for a stock that can currently be purchased for $48. If the price drops to $40, the investor loses $8; if the price rises to $60, the investor gains $12. The profit or loss from buying a stock is directly tied to movements in its price, both up or down.

Alternatively, assume that at the current stock price of $48, a six-month call with an exercise price of $50 could be purchased for a premium of $4 (i.e., $400). If this call expires worthless, the maximum loss is the $400 premium (we will ignore brokerage costs in these examples). This is shown in Figure 15–2 by the profit–loss line for the call. Notice that up to the exercise price of $50, the loss to the investor is $4 (i.e., $400). The break-even point for the investor is the sum of the exercise price and the premium, or $50 + $4 = $54; therefore, the profit–loss line for the purchase of a call crosses the break-even line at $54. If the price of the stock rises above $54, the value of the call will increase with it at least point for point, as shown by the two parallel lines above the profit–loss line.

Figure 15–2 demonstrates why many investors purchase calls. Their loss is limited to the premium, no matter how much the price of the stock declines. For those investors interested in "taking a flyer," a call option may be a good alternative. As the stock price rises, the price of the call will keep pace, no matter how high the stock price rises.

---

[21] Of course, the leverage can be harmful, maximizing the losses.

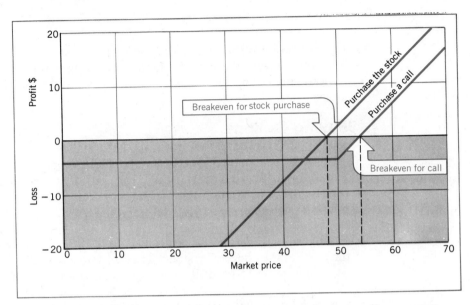

FIGURE 15–2 **The profit and loss possibilities from purchasing a call versus purchasing the underlying common stock.**

Now consider what calls can do for an investor via the leverage aspect. Assume an investor believes ABC common, priced at $48, will appreciate in the next six months. A six-month call with an exercise price of $50 is available on ABC for $4. The investor can either (ignoring commissions) buy 100 shares of ABC common for $4800 or buy 12 call contracts, representing 1200 shares of ABC, for $4800.

Should ABC advance to $57 before expiration, the gross profit would be $900 on the 100 shares of common and at least $12 \times \$300 = \$3600$ on the 12 call contracts.[22] The calls provide maximum leverage for speculative purposes. In our example, an investor in the calls could realize about four times the profit available on the stock itself for the same initial investment. However, it must *always* be remembered that the losses with the call could be large, or total. The high return potential is accompanied by large risk. Ask yourself what happens in the previous example if the stock is at $49 six months from now. Ignoring commissions, purchasing the stock would produce $100 in profit while the option strategy could result in a total loss because the calls are not worth exercising.[23]

Another potential reason for buying calls is to protect a short sale. An investor who has sold a stock short because of an expected drop in price can protect against an unexpected rise in price by purchasing a call on the shorted stock. If the stock price declines, the cost of the call option can be

[22] The break-even point is assumed to be the sum of the $50 exercise price and the $4 premium, or $54, and the intrinsic value of the call to be at least $7.

[23] As this became obvious, the calls could be sold before maturity to recover a small part of the investment.

viewed as insurance. If the stock price rises, the call can be exercised and the stock acquired and delivered to cover the short sale.

Buying puts   Investors buy puts when they are bearish (pessimistic) about the price of the underlying common stock. Since a put gives the owner the right to sell the underlying stock at the specified exercise price, a decline in price will allow the put owner to purchase the stock at a lower price and deliver it to the writer of the put at the higher exercise price.

When bearish about a particular stock, investors can sell a stock short. If they do this, their profit or loss will be a direct (linear) function of the price of the stock at any point in time, as shown in Figure 15–3. For expositional purposes, we will again use the example of a stock currently selling for $48. A short sale produces a downward-sloping line, which intersects the break-even line at $48. Below this price, the investor profits from a short sale at $48; above this line, the investor would lose—as the stock price rises, the potential loss increases.

Alternatively, assume that a six-month put with an exercise price of $50 could be purchased for a premium of $4. This put is currently in the money,

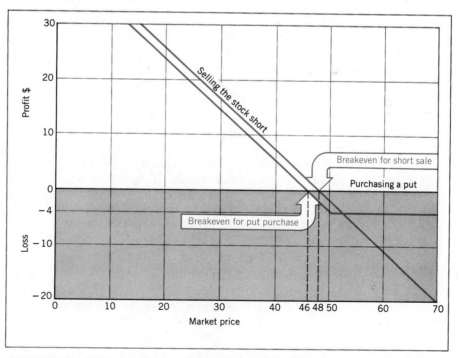

FIGURE 15–3   The profit and loss possibilities from buying a put versus selling short the underlying common stock.

and as the price of the stock declines it becomes more valuable. The break-even point is $50 − $4 = $46, and as the stock price declines below this level the value of the put keeps pace. If the price of the stock rises above $50, the loss from the put position can never exceed $4; the loss from selling short, however, continues to increase as the stock price rises. Just as with calls, put buyers are protected against potential losses. The most that can be lost with a put is its premium, or price. With short selling, the losses theoretically are unlimited because the stock price could rise to any level.

Put buyers, just as call buyers, can maximize the leverage potential involved in a transaction. In other words, put buying is a chance to earn big profits on a relatively small investment. Consider the following example. An investor believes the price of Delta Airlines will decline within the next six months (by July) from its current (January) price of about $42. A six-month put with an exercise price of $40 is available for $3. The investor, wishing to speculate based on the belief that the price will decline, could, for $2100, either (a) sell short 100 shares of Delta—a margin deposit (at 50%) would be required—or (b) buy seven put contracts at $3 each. Assume that the investor's judgment is correct and that Delta's price declines to $33 six months later. The profit, as a percentage of the money invested, would be (a) for selling short = $42 − $33 = $900/$2100 = 43% or (b) for buying puts = $400 × 7 = $2800/$2100 = 133%.[24]

Again, the purchase of puts provides leverage, which magnifies gains, but also magnifies losses. If Delta's price remained around $42 or rose, the puts would expire worthless and the total investment would be lost. The short seller is also losing in this case, but the position does not have to be closed out. This illustrates the great risk with options—because of their short maturity, the investor's expectations must be realized in a relatively short time.

Puts can be used to protect an investor's profit. Assume a stock owned by an investor has appreciated from $50 to $70. Perhaps the investor feels the stock price could appreciate even more, but there is concern over a market decline that may include this stock. In these circumstances, the investor could purchase a put with an exercise price of $70 and offset the lost profits should the stock price decline. This occurs when the investor exercises the put and delivers the stock already owned, receiving the exercise price of $70.

Writing Options

Both individuals and institutional investors write options. Most are written against stocks owned and held (covered), although "naked" options can be written. Let us consider why this would be done.

---

[24] The intrinsic value of the put would be $7 ($40 − $33). Subtracting out the premium of $3 leaves a profit of $4 (that is, $400) per contract.

Writing calls To write a call is to sell a call; that is, the call writer enters into a contract to sell a claim on a particular stock. If the writer owns the stock, he or she has sold a covered call; if the stock is not owned, he or she has sold a naked call.

The writer is obligated to deliver the stock at the stated exercise price if called on to do so when the holder of the call exercises it. The writer will receive the exercise price per share for the stock delivered, which could exceed the price originally paid by the writer for the stock. Continuing our previous example, assume that an investor had purchased 100 shares of this stock last year for $40 per share and this year, with the stock price at $48, writes a (covered) six-month call with an exercise price of $50. The writer receives a premium of $4. This situation is illustrated in Figure 15–4.

If called on to deliver his or her 100 shares, the investor will receive $50 per share, plus the $4 premium, for a gross profit of $14 per share. However, the investor gives up the additional potential gain if the price of this stock rises above $50—shown by the flat line to the right of $50 for the covered call position in Figure 15–4. If the price rises to $60 after the call is sold, for example, the investor will gross $14 per share but could have grossed $20 per share if no call had been written.

Writing a naked call is also illustrated (by the broken line) in Figure 15–4. If the call is not exercised, the writer profits by the amount of the premium,

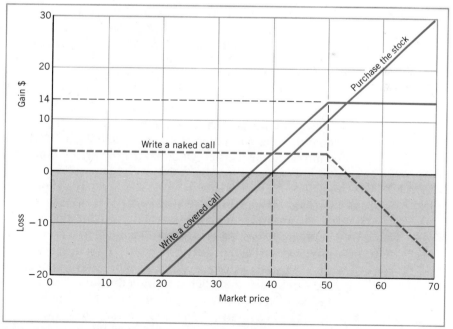

FIGURE 15–4 **The profit and loss possibilities from writing naked calls, covered calls, and purchasing the underlying common stock.**

$4; the naked writer's break-even point is $54. This position will be profitable if the price of the stock does not rise above this break-even point.

Notice that the potential gain for the naked writer is limited to $4. The potential loss, however, is large. If the price of the stock were to rise sharply, the writer could easily lose an amount in excess of what was received in premium income.

Why write a call? The call writer may be seeking the income from the premium. Writing calls against stocks owned is often considered to be a conservative strategy that supplements the dividend income on stocks held. If the calls expire unexercised, the call writer retains the premium and the stock. The premium also provides the covered writer with some downside protection in case the price of the stock declines. The annualized premium from writing six-month calls is approximately 15% of the stock price.

Writing covered calls is one form of a hedged position, which with simple strategies such as those discussed here involves puts or calls and the underlying stock. In a hedged position, options are used to protect the stock against unfavorable outcomes. The writing of covered calls is the most common hedge.

Remember that the writer of a call can terminate the contract at anytime before its expiration by purchasing a comparable call option. The clearing corporation cancels the position when this "closing purchase transaction" is made.

Writing puts Writers (sellers) of puts are seeking the premium income just as call writers are. The writer obligates him or herself to purchase a stock at the specified exercise price during the life of the put contract. If stock prices decline, the put buyer may purchase the stock and exercise the put by delivering the stock to the writer, who must pay the specified price.

Note that the put writer may be obligated to purchase a stock for, say, $50 a share when it is selling in the market for $40 a share. This represents an immediate paper loss (less the premium received for selling the put). Also note that the put writer can cancel the obligation by purchasing an identical contract in the market. Of course, if the price of the stock has declined since the put was written, the price of the put will have increased and the writer will have to repurchase at a price higher than the premium received when the put was written.

Figure 15–5 illustrates the position for the seller of a put. Using the previous figures, a six-month put is sold at an exercise price of $50 for a premium of $4. The seller of a naked put receives the premium and hopes that the stock price remains at or above the exercise price. As the price of the stock falls, the seller's position declines. The seller begins to lose money below the break-even point, which in this case is $50 − $4 = $46. Losses could be substantial if the price of the stock declines sharply. The price of the put will increase point for point as the stock price declines. Therefore, to

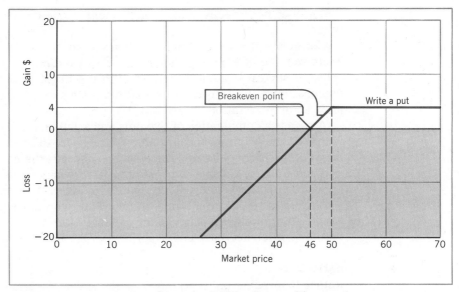

FIGURE 15–5 **The profit and loss possibilities from writing a put.**

close out this position, the put seller may have to repurchase the contract at a substantially higher price.

More Sophisticated Options Strategies

Puts and calls offer investors a number of opportunities beyond the simple strategies discussed in the previous section. We will briefly examine some combinations of options that can be written or purchased, and we will consider the use of spreads.

Combinations of Options

Options can be mixed together in numerous ways. The typical combinations are a straddle, a strip, and a strap. A **straddle** is a combination of a put and a call on the same stock with the same exercise date and exercise price. A purchaser of a straddle believes that the underlying stock price is highly volatile and may go either up or down. The buyer of the straddle can exercise each part separately, and therefore can profit from a large enough move either way. However, the price of the stock must rise or fall enough to equal the premium on both a put and a call.

Straddles can also be sold (written). As is always true about the two sides in an option contract, the seller believes that the underlying stock price will exhibit small volatility, but could go up or down. Like the purchaser, the writer does not forecast a likely movement in one direction rather than the other.

Consider a stock selling at $75 with a six-month straddle available with an exercise price of $75 and, for simplicity, call and put prices of $5 each. The seller of such a straddle is protected in the range of $65 to $85 (ignoring commissions). The buyers hope that the price exceeds one of these boundaries before expiration.

A *strip* is a combination of two puts and a call on the same security, again with the same expiration date and exercise price. In this case, the purchaser believes the probability of a price decline exceeds the probability of a price rise and therefore wants two puts (but also wants some protection in the opposite direction). The seller obviously believes the opposite.

A *strap* is similar to a strip but combines two calls with a put. Here, of course, the purchaser believes the probability of a price increase exceeds that for a price decrease and again, the writer expects the opposite.

Spreads

Rather than being only the buyer or the seller of various combinations of puts and calls, an investor can be both simultaneously by means of a spread. A **spread** is defined as the purchase and sale of an equivalent option varying in only one respect. Its purpose is to reduce risk in an option position, and it is a popular practice.

The two basic spreads are the *money spread* and the *time spread*. A money spread involves the purchase of a call option at one exercise price and the sale of the same maturity option, but with a different exercise price. For example, an investor could buy an IBM January 80 call and sell an IBM January 90 call.

A time spread involves the purchase and sale of options that are identical except for expiration dates. For example, an investor could buy an IBM January 90 call and sell an IBM April 90 call.

Investors use particular spread strategies depending on whether they are bullish or bearish. Assume you are bullish about IBM but wish to reduce the risk involved in options. IBM is selling for $84, with six-month call options available at exercise prices of $90 and $80 for $3 and $8 respectively. A bullish money spread would consist of buying the $80 call and selling the $90 call. Your net cost is now $5, which is the maximum you could lose if the calls expire worthless because the price of IBM dropped sharply. If IBM rises, you purchase the $90 call to offset the $90 call sold, resulting in a loss. However, your $80 call will be worth at least the price of the stock minus the exercise price of $80, and when this is netted against your loss on the $90 transaction you will have a net gain. In effect, you give up some potential profit (what could have been earned on the $80 call alone) to reduce your risk (by reducing your net cost) if the stock price declines.

An investor who was bearish about IBM could work out a similar spread to reduce the risk of an options transaction. Can you?

The Popularity of Options

Puts and calls on organized options exchanges have been available to investors since 1973. As we have seen, a number of strategies are available to investors using options, allowing many different possibilities in the way of risk reduction or return enhancement. What can we say about options as an investment alternative on the basis of this historical experience?

The creation of organized options exchanges has made puts and calls a viable investment alternative for many investors. The exchanges guarantee the performance of every option contract, all of whose key parameters are standardized. Most importantly, an active secondary market, which did not exist prior to 1973, is provided. Thus, investors are assured of being able to trade puts and calls on a continuous basis during the life of the option.

Puts and calls traded on organized exchanges have been a major success. Trading volume has expanded tremendously. By late 1986, total daily volume exceeded 900,000 contracts (roughly two-thirds of which were calls and one-third were puts). The CBOE has seen its market share decline somewhat as the new exchanges began trading. However, it still handles slightly more than 50% of all calls, and about 70% of all puts.

Puts and calls have been popular with individual investors since the beginning of CBOE trading. By the 1980s, however, options had proven themselves as a respectable investment alternative and had begun to attract institutional attention.[25] Changes in regulations occurred in 1980 that, in effect, encouraged institutional interest in options. Pension funds, insurance companies, and banks began to receive clearance for the trading of options, provided that such trading met the guidelines under which they normally operate.

Institutions have begun to hire "portfolio options strategists" to assist them in trading options. One use of options for institutions is to hedge their portfolios by writing calls against stocks in the portfolio that have appreciated significantly. The institutions doing this insure themselves against a decline in prices equal to the income earned from writing the calls; meanwhile, the holdings continue to pay dividends and represent long-term investments in the companies.

Option Pricing and Market Efficiency

The State of Option Pricing Models

Development of the Black–Scholes (BS) model was a very significant event and has had a major impact on all options investors, both directly or indirectly. This model has been the basis of extensive empirical investigations

---

[25] This discussion is based on "Money Management Begins to Accept Options as a Prudent Investment," *The Wall Street Journal*, September 22, 1980, p. 27.

into how options are priced. Other models have subsequently been developed. Since the BS model can be used to value options, providing investors with an estimate of the option's intrinsic value, the state of option pricing theory is important. Important advances in the theory of option pricing have been made since the seminal contribution of Black and Scholes. However, as of the early 1980s the available models did not completely explain the behavior of actual option prices. Although the numerous studies that have been conducted offer general support for the BS model, deficiencies remain. Furthermore, the results of these studies have not always been consistent. Given the number of empirical studies that have been done, it is not surprising that the results lack total agreement. For example, Fischer Black found that the BS model underpriced deep out-of-the-money call options (and overpriced deep in-the-money calls), whereas James MacBeth and Larry Merville reported biases that were exactly the opposite.[26] Gultekin et al. tested the BS model and found results in agreement with Black and exactly the opposite of MacBeth and Merville.[27]

A reasonable consensus of the options studies that have been conducted is desirable. Dan Galai, in a summary of the empirical tests of option-pricing models, concludes the following:[28]

1. The BS model works well for at-the-money options, although unexplained deviations still occur.
2. The biases noted previously for deep in- and deep out-of-the-money options do exist.
3. No other model consistently does better than the BS model in explaining actual option prices.

The deviations and biases that appear to remain in option pricing models may derive from several sources. Deviations of model prices from market prices appear to be significantly related to the extent to which options are in or out of the money. William Sterk has presented evidence suggesting that this in- and out-of-the-money bias depends on the magnitude of the dividend on the underlying stocks studied.[29] For out-of-the-money options, small dividend payers appear significantly underpriced and large payers, overpriced; this behavior is reversed for in-the-money options.

[26] See Fischer Black, "Fact and Fantasy in the Use of Options," *Financial Analysts Journal,* July–August 1975, pp. 36–72; J. MacBeth and L. J. Merville, "An Empirical Examination of the Black–Scholes Call Option Pricing Model," *The Journal of Finance,* December 1979, pp. 1173–1186 and MacBeth and Merville, "Tests of the Black–Scholes and Cox Call Option Valuation Models," *The Journal of Finance,* May 1980, pp. 285–301.

[27] See N. Gultekin, R. Rogalski, and S. Tinic, "Option Pricing Model Estimates: Some Empirical Results," *Financial Management,* Spring 1982, pp. 58–69.

[28] See Dan Galai, "A Survey of Empirical Tests of Option-Pricing Models," in Menachem Brenner, ed., *Option Pricing: Theory and Applications* (Lexington, Mass.: Lexington Books, 1983), pp. 45–80.

[29] See William E. Sterk, "Option Pricing: Dividends and the In- and Out-of-the-Money Bias," *Financial Management,* Winter 1983, pp. 47–53.

In summary, the best evidence to date, taken together, indicates that although some statistically significant biases may exist in the prices generated by the option pricing models, the validity of these models remains intact. What are the implications of this for market efficiency?

Market Efficiency and Investor Returns

The option pricing models can be used to test for the possibility of trading rules to exploit any economically viable biases in option prices. Continuing with his summary of the empirical tests of option-pricing models, Galai concludes that although actual prices do deviate from model predictions, the options market appears to be quite efficient; that is, traders do not appear able to consistently earn above-normal profits after commissions and taxes.[30] Galai believes that the studies indicate that nonexchange members are unable as well to consistently earn above-normal profits.

Stock Index Options and Interest Rate Options

The newest innovation in the options market is index options, specifically **stock index options** and **interest rate options.** The latter includes options traded on the American Exchange on Treasury notes, and on Treasury notes and bonds on the CBOE.[31]

As of early 1987, stock index options were available on the following broad market indexes—the S&P 100 Index, the S&P 500 Index, the New York Stock Exchange Index, the Major Market Index, the Value Line Index, the Financial News Composite Index, and the National OTC Index. Index options were also available on various industry subindexes, including the Technology Index, the Computer Technology Index, the Oil Index, and the Gold/Silver Index. In addition, index options were also available for an Institutional Index and a NYSE Beta Index.[32]

A potentially important development occurred in April 1986, when the S&P 500 Index option was converted to a European-style contract, meaning it cannot be exercised until the contract expires. The predictable exercise date appeals to institutional investors when they attempt to hedge their portfolios against losses in volatile markets. Hedgers using standard index options may find their hedges exercised before the contracts expire, thereby giving an edge to the European-style contracts. The Institutional Index is also European style.

Stock index options enable investors to trade on general stock market

---

[30] Galai, "A Survey of Empirical Tests," p. 69.

[31] Foreign currency options are available on the CBOE and on the Philadelphia Exchange.

[32] The Institutional Index is based on an index of 75 stocks most widely held by institutional investors. The Beta Index is a price-weighted index designed to track the performance of 100 of the most volatile stocks traded on the NYSE.

movements or industries in the same way that they can trade on individual stocks. Thus, an investor who is bullish on the market can buy a call on a market index, and an investor who is bearish on the overall market can buy a put. The investor need only make a market decision, not an industry or an individual stock decision.

Overall, stock index options are similar to the options listed on the options exchanges. As usual, the exercise price and the expiration date are uniformly established. Investors buy and sell them through their broker in the normal manner. The major difference in the two is that, unlike stock options that require the actual delivery of the stock upon exercise, buyers of index options receive cash from the seller upon exercise of the contract. The amount of cash settlement is equal to the difference between the closing price of the index and the strike price of the option.

Index option information is read in the same manner as for stock options. Figure 15–6 shows an example of the information carried in *The Wall Street Journal* for the S&P 500 index option.

As an example of the cash settlement procedure used for index options, assume that an investor holds a NYSE Index Option with a strike price of 135. This investor decides to exercise the option on a day that the NYSE Composite Index closes at 139.5. The investor will receive a cash payment from the assigned writer equal to $100 multiplied by the difference between the option's strike price and the closing value of the index, or

$$
\begin{array}{ll}
\text{NYSE Composite Index Close} & = \ 139.5 \\
\text{NYSE Index Option Strike Price} & = \ \underline{135.0} \\
& \quad 4.5 \times \$100 \ = \ \$450.
\end{array}
$$

Note the use of the $100 multiplier for the NYSE Index Option. The multiplier performs a function similar to the unit of trading (100 shares) for a stock option in that it determines the total dollar value of the cash settlement. Since options on different indexes may have different multipliers, it is important to know the multiplier for the stock index being used.

Strategies with Stock Index Options

The strategies with index options are similar to those for individual stock options. Investors expecting a market rise buy calls, and investors expecting a market decline buy puts. The maximum losses from these two strategies—the premiums—are known at the outset of the transaction. The potential gains can be large because of the leverage involved with options.

As an illustration of this strategy, consider the following example. In September, an investor expects the stock market to rise strongly over the next two to three months. This investor decides to purchase a NYSE Index November 130 call, which is currently selling for 3½. The NYSE Index closed at 129.5 on the day of purchase.

Assume that the market rises as expected by the investor to a mid-November level of 139.86 (an 8% increase). The investor could exercise the

Following is an example of S&P 500 index option prices as they appear in the financial tables of the *Wall Street Journal*.

S&P 500 INDEX

Strike Price	Calls—Last			Puts—Last		
	Jun	Jul	Sep	Jun	Jul	Sep
220	...	¼	...	...	...	...
225	...	...	17⅞	¹⁄₁₆	...	2¹³⁄₁₆
230	8⅞	10⅜	...	⁵⁄₁₆	1¹¹⁄₁₆	4¼
235	4½	7⅜	...	1¹⁄₁₆	2½	5⅞
240	2⅛	4⅜	8⅜	3⅜	5	8
245	⅞	2¹⁵⁄₁₆	4⅞	7⅝	8⅛	...
250	¼	1¹¹⁄₁₆	...	12⅛	...	...
255	¹⁄₁₆	¾	3¾	...	...	...

Total call volume 3,338   Total call open int. 51,270
Total put volume 3,741   Total put open int. 52,239
The index: High 240.08; Low 238.23. Close 239.58, −0.38

1. *expiration months.* SPX options trade in the two nearby months plus three months from the March-June-September-December cycle.

2. *last.* The option's last sale price (premium per share). Option premiums are expressed in terms of dollars and fractions per unit of the index. Each point represents $100. The minimum fraction is ¹⁄₁₆ ($6.25) for series trading below 3, and ⅛ ($12.50) for all other series.

3. *strike price.* The price at which the index may be bought or sold.

4. *volume.* Number of call and put options traded. Total volume is the sum of calls and puts.

5. *open interest.* The number of option contracts that were open at the end of the previous trading session. Each unit represents a buyer and a seller who still hold exercisable contracts. Total open interest is the sum of calls and puts.

6. *index values.* The day's high, low and closing index values, with the daily price change.

S&P 500 options are European-style options; they are exercised only at expiration. At expiration the value of an S&P 500 call is the amount by which the index exceeds the strike price. The value of a put is the amount the index is below the put's strike price. If the index closes below the strike price of an expiring call, or above the strike price of an expiring put, the option expires worthless.

Suppose, for example, that the index closes at 224.50 on the last trading day for September SPX options. A September 220 call would have an in-the-money value of 4.50— the closing index price of 224.50 minus the call strike price of 220, or $450 (4.50 × $100). A September 220 put under these same circumstances would expire worthless.

The principal difference between equity and index options is *cash settlement* upon exercise. The exercise of an equity option requires delivery of the underlying security. With S&P 500 index options, only cash changes hands. Exercise of an index option gives the holder the in-the-money cash difference between the exercise price multiplied by $100 and the closing index value multiplied by $100.

FIGURE 15–6 Understanding index option information.

Source: Reprinted from *A Basic Guide to SPX,* © 1986. Chicago Board Options Exchange Inc., by permission.

option and receive a cash settlement equal to the difference between the Index close (139.86) and the exercise price of 130, multiplied by $100, or[33]

$$
\begin{array}{r}
139.86 \text{ NYSE Index Close} \\
-130.00 \text{ Call Exercise Price} \\
\hline
9.86 \times \$100 = \$986
\end{array}
$$

The leverage offered by index options is illustrated in this example by the fact that an 8% rise in the Index leads to a 182% profit on the option position [($986 − $350)/$350] = 181.7%]. Obviously, leverage can, and often does, work against an investor. If the market declined or remained flat, the entire option premium of $350 could be lost. As with any option, however, the investor has a limited loss of known amount—the premium paid.

Investors can use stock index options to hedge their positions. For example, an investor who owns a diversified portfolio of stocks may be unwilling to liquidate his or her portfolio, but is concerned about a near-term market decline. Buying a put on a market index will provide some protection to the investor in the event of a market decline; in effect, the investor is purchasing a form of market insurance. The losses on the portfolio holdings will be partially offset by the gains on the put. If the market rises, the investor loses the premium paid but gains with the portfolio holdings. A problem arises, however, in that the portfolio holdings and the market index are unlikely to be a perfect match. The effectiveness of this hedge will depend upon the similarity between the two.

Assume an investor has a portfolio of NYSE common stocks currently worth $39,000. It is October and this investor is concerned about a market decline over the next couple of months. The NYSE Index is currently at 130, and a NYSE Index December 130 put is available for 3. In an attempt to protect the portfolio's profits against a market decline, the investor purchases three of these puts, which represent an aggregate exercise price of $39,000 (130 × 100 × 3 = $39,000).[34]

Assume that the market declines 10% by mid-December. If the NYSE Index is 117 at that point,

$$
\begin{array}{r}
\text{Put Exercise Price} = 130 \\
\text{NYSE Index Price} = 117 \\
\hline
13 \times \$100 \times 3 \text{ (puts)} = \$3900
\end{array}
$$

If the value of the investor's portfolio declines by exactly 10%, the loss on the portfolio of $3900 would be exactly offset by the total gain on the three puts contracts of $3900. It is important to note, however, that a particular portfolio's value may decline more or less than the overall market as repre-

---

[33] Before exercising, the investor should determine if a better price could be obtained by selling the option.

[34] The exercise value of an index option, like any stock option, is equal to 100 (shares) multiplied by the exercise price.

sented by one of the market indices such as the NYSE Composite Index. The value of a particular portfolio may decline less or more than the change in the index.

As before, if the option is held to expiration and a market decline (of a significant amount) does not occur, the investor will lose the entire premium paid for the put(s). In our example, the investor could lose the entire $900 paid for the three puts. This could be viewed as the cost of obtaining "market insurance."

Stock index options can be useful to institutional investors (or individuals) who do not have funds available immediately for investment but anticipate a market rise. Buying calls will allow such investors to take advantage of the rise in prices if it does occur. Of course, the premium could be lost if the anticipations are incorrect.

Investors can sell (write) index options, either to speculate or to hedge their positions. As we saw in the case of individual options, however, the risk can be large. If the seller is correct in his or her beliefs, the profit is limited to the amount of the premium; if incorrect, the seller faces potential losses far in excess of the premiums received from selling the options. It is impractical (or impossible) to write a completely covered stock index option because of the difficulty of owning a portfolio that exactly matches the index at all points in time. While the writer of an individual stock call option can deliver the stock if the option is exercised, the writer of a stock index call option that is exercised must settle in cash and cannot be certain that gains in the stock portfolio will *fully* offset losses on the index option.[35]

The Popularity of Stock Index Options

Stock index options appeal to speculators because of the leverage they offer. A change in the underlying index of less than 1% can result in a change in the value of the contract of 15% or more. Given the increased volatility in the financial markets in recent years, investors can experience rapid changes in the value of their positions.

Introduced in 1983, stock index options quickly became the fastest growing investment in the United States. Much of the initial volume was accounted for by professional speculators and trading firms. As familiarity with index options increased, individual investors assumed a larger role in this market.

Summary

Rather than buying common stocks, investors can, in some cases, purchase options or claims on stocks. Equity-derivative securities consist of puts and calls, created by investors, and warrants and convertible securities, created by corporations.

---

[35] Writers of index options are notified of their obligation to make a cash settlement on the business day following the day of exercise.

A call (put) is an option to buy (sell) 100 shares of a particular stock at a stated price anytime before a specified expiration date. The seller receives a premium for selling either of these options, and the buyer pays the premium. Most puts and calls are not exercised, but rather traded in the secondary markets. Advantages of options include a smaller investment than transacting in the stock itself, knowing the maximum loss in advance, leverage, and an expansion of the opportunity set available to investors.

Options have an intrinsic value ranging from $0 to the "in the money" value. Most sell for more than this, representing a premium. According to the Black–Scholes option valuation model, value is a function of the price of the stock, the exercise price of the option, time to maturity, the interest rate, and the volatility of the underlying stock.

Buyers of calls expect the underlying stock to perform in the opposite direction from the expectations of put buyers. Writers of each instrument have opposite expectations from the buyers. The basic strategies for options involve a call writer and a put buyer expecting the underlying stock price to decline, whereas the call buyer and the put writer expect it to rise. Options may also be used to hedge against a portfolio position by establishing an opposite position in options on that stock. More sophisticated options strategies include combinations of options, such as strips, straps, and straddles, and spreads, which include money spreads and time spreads.

Options have been popular with individual investors since the establishment of organized exchanges, and they are becoming more popular with institutional investors. The available empirical evidence seems to suggest that the options market is efficient, with trading rules unable to exploit any biases that exist in the Black–Scholes or other options pricing models.

Interest rate options and stock index options are available to investors. Stock index options are a popular innovation in the options area that allow investors to buy puts and calls on broad stock-market indices and industry subindices. In effect, these instruments allow investors to make only a market decision and/or to purchase a form of market insurance. The major distinction with these option contracts is that settlement is in cash.

Key Words

Arbitragers	Options clearing corporation
Black–Scholes model	Premium
Call	Put
Expiration date	Spread
Exercise (strike) price	Stock index options
Interest rate options	Straddle

QUESTIONS AND PROBLEMS

1. Distinguish between a put and a call and a warrant.
2. What are the potential advantages of puts and calls?
3. Explain the following terms used with puts and calls:
   a. Strike price.
   b. Naked option.
   c. Premium.
   d. Out-of-the-money option.
4. Who writes puts and calls? Why?
5. What role does the options clearing corporation play in the options market?
6. What is the relationship between option prices and their intrinsic values? Why?
7. What is meant by the time premium of an option?
8. Explain the factors used in the Black–Scholes option valuation model. What is the relationship between each factor and the value of the option?
9. Give three reasons why an investor might purchase a call.
10. Why do investors write calls? What are their obligations?
11. What is a straddle? When would an investor buy one?
12. What is a spread? What is its purpose?
13. Explain two types of spreads.
14. Why is the call or put writer's position considerably different from the buyer's position?
15. What is an index option? What index options are available?
16. What are the major differences between a stock option and an index option?
17. Explain how a put can be used to protect a particular position. A call.
18. How does writing a covered call differ from writing a naked call?
19. Summarize Galai's conclusions about the available empirical evidence on options.
20. What is the significance of the industry subindex stock index options?
21. Assume that you own a diversified portfolio of 50 stocks and fear a market decline over the next six months.
    a. How could you protect your portfolio during this period using stock index options?
    b. How effective would this hedge be?
    c. Other things being equal, if your portfolio consisted of 150 stocks, would the protection be more effective?
22. Assume that you expect interest rates to rise and that you wish to speculate on this expectation. How could interest rate options be used to do this?
23. The common stock of Teledyne trades on the NYSE. Teledyne has never paid a cash dividend. The stock is relatively risky. Assume that the beta for

Teledyne is 1.3. Assume that Teledyne closed at a price of $162. Hypothetical option quotes on Teledyne are as follows:

Strike Price	Calls			Puts		
	Apr	Jul	Oct	Apr	Jul	Oct
140	23½	s	s	⅜	s	s
150	16	21	25	1	3¾	r
160	8⅞	14	20	3	7	9
170	3	9	13¼	9	10	11
180	1¼	5¼	9	r	20	r

r = not traded; s = no option offered.

Based on the Teledyne data, answer the following questions:
a. Which calls are in the money?
b. Which puts are in the money?
c. Why are investors willing to pay 1¼ for the 180 call, but only 1 for the 150 put that is closer to the current market price?

24. Based on the Teledyne data answer the following:
a. Calculate the intrinsic value of the following calls:
   April 140
   October 170
b. Calculate the intrinsic value of the following puts:
   April 140
   October 170
c. Explain the reasons for the differences in intrinsic values between a and b.

25. Using the Teledyne data, answer the following:
a. What is the cost of 10 October 150 call contracts in total dollars? From the text, what is the commission? Total cost?
b. What is the cost of 20 October 160 put contracts in total dollars? What is the commission? Total cost?
c. On the following day, Teledyne closed at $164. Which of the options would you have expected to increase? Decrease?
d. The new quote on the October 150 call was 26. What would have been your one-day profit on the 10 contracts? What is the net profit (after commissions)?
e. The new quote on the October 160 put was 7½. What would have been your one-day profit on the 20 contracts? Net profit?
f. What is the most you could lose on these 20 contracts?

Selected References

Black, Fischer. "Fact and Fantasy in the Use of Options." *Financial Analysts Journal*, July–August 1975, pp. 36–72.

Black, Fischer and Scholes, Myron. "The Pricing of Options and Corporate Liabilities." *Journal of Political Economy*, May–June 1973, pp. 637–654.

Bookstaber, Richard. "The Use of Options in Performance Structuring." *The Journal of Portfolio Management,* Summer 1985, pp. 36–50.

Brennan, Michael and Schwartz, Edwardo. "The Valuation of American Put Options." *The Journal of Finance,* May 1976, pp. 449–462.

Brenner, Menachem, ed. *Option Pricing: Theory and Applications.* Lexington, Mass.: Lexington Books, 1983.

Clasing, H. *Dow Jones-Irwin Guide to Put and Call Options,* rev. ed. Homewood, Ill.: Dow Jones-Irwin, 1978.

Cleeton, C. *Strategies for the Option Trader.* New York: John Wiley, 1979.

Dimson, Elroy. "Instant Option Valuation." *Financial Analysts Journal,* May–June 1977, pp. 62–69.

Dimson, Elroy. "Option Valuation Nomograms." *Financial Analysts Journal,* November–December 1977, pp. 71–74.

Galai, Dan. "Tests of Market Efficiency of the Chicago Board Options Exchange." *Journal of Business,* April 1977, pp. 167–197.

Galai, Dan. "A Survey of Empirical Tests of Option-Pricing Models." In Menachem Brenner, ed. *Option Pricing: Theory and Applications.* Lexington, Mass.: Lexington Books, 1983.

Gastineau, Gary. *The Stock Options Manual,* 2nd ed. New York: McGraw-Hill, 1979.

Gultekin, N. Bulent, Rogalski, Richard J., and Tinic, Seha M. "Option Pricing Model Estimates: Some Empirical Results." *Financial Management,* Spring 1982, pp. 58–69.

Jarrow, Robert and Rudd, Andrew. *Option Pricing.* Homewood, Ill.: Richard D. Irwin, 1983.

Latané, Henry and Rendleman, Richard. "Standard Deviations of Stock Price Ratios Implied in Option Prices." *The Journal of Finance,* May 1976, pp. 369–381.

MacBeth, James and Merville, Larry. "An Empirical Examination of the Black–Scholes Call Option Pricing Model." *The Journal of Finance,* December 1979, pp. 1173–1186.

MacBeth, James and Merville, Larry. "Tests of the Black–Scholes and Cox Call Option Valuation Models." *The Journal of Finance,* May 1980, pp. 285–301.

Merton, Robert, Scholes, Myron, and Gladstein, M. "A Simulation of Returns and Risk of Alternative Option Portfolio Investment Strategies." *Journal of Business,* April 1978, pp. 183–242.

Nix, William E., and Nix, Susan. *Stock Index Futures and Options.* Homewood, Ill.: Dow Jones-Irwin, 1984.

Smith, Clifford. "Option Pricing: A Review." *Journal of Financial Economics,* January–March 1976, pp. 3–51.

Sterk, William E. "Option Pricing: Dividends and the In- and Out-of-the-Money Bias." *Financial Management,* Winter 1983, pp. 47–53.

Sterk, William E. "Comparative Performance of the Black–Scholes and Roll–Geske–Whaley Option Pricing Models." *Journal of Financial and Quantitative Analysis,* September 1983, pp. 345–354.

CHAPTER 16

WARRANTS AND CONVERTIBLE SECURITIES

Chapter 15 discussed one of the equity-derivative securities—options. This chapter continues that discussion by analyzing two other equity-derivative securities. As with options, these securities derive part or all of their value from the underlying common stock. Unlike options, however, which are created by investors, warrants and convertible securities are created by corporations. Although not as popular as options with many investors, these securities are viable investment alternatives.

Warrants

The definition of a warrant is very similar to that of the call option discussed in Chapter 15. A **warrant** is an option to purchase, within a specified time period, a stated number of shares of common stock at a specified price. The following are important differences between calls and warrants:

1. Warrants are issued by corporations, whereas puts and calls are created by investors (whether individuals or institutions).
2. Warrants typically have maturities of at least several years, whereas listed calls expire within nine months.
3. Warrant terms are not standardized—each warrant is unique.

Warrants are most often issued attached to bonds as a "sweetener," allowing the corporate issuer to obtain a lower interest rate (i.e., financing cost).[1] The warrants can be detached and sold separately. In effect, a purchaser of bonds with detachable warrants is buying a package of securities.

Warrants are sometimes issued in conjunction with an acquisition or reorganization. They may also be issued during a new stock sale as partial compensation to the underwriters, or as part of a common stock offering to investors.

The attractiveness of warrants to investors declined in recent years. The principal reason for this was the proliferation of alternative equity-derivative securities, including not only puts and calls but financial futures and futures options (both of which are explained in Chapter 17). By the early 1980s, however, the popularity of warrants was once again increasing, primarily in connection with bond issues. Larger and better capitalized companies, such as American Express and MCI Communications, were issuing warrants.

Characteristics of Warrants

A warrant provides the owner with an exercisable option on the underlying common stock of the issuer—that is, a claim on the equity. However, the warrant holder receives no dividends and has no voting rights.

All conditions of a warrant are specified at issuance. Although the issuer may set any expiration date, typically it is three to 10 years.[2] In a number of cases, the expiration date can be extended. Warrants often provide for a one-to-one ratio in conversion, allowing the holder to purchase a number of common shares equal to the number of warrants converted; however, any conversion rate can be specified by the company, and fractional shares may be involved.[3] The *exercise price* (the per share amount to be paid by the warrant holder on exercise) is also specified at issuance, and it always exceeds the market price of the stock at the time the warrant is issued.

As an example of warrant characteristics, consider Pier 1 Imports, Inc., a specialty retailer of imported home furnishings and related items.[4] Pier 1 issued a warrant on July 12, 1983 as part of a 20-year debenture offering (a good example of a sweetener). Each $1000 11.5% debenture carried 42 warrants with it, exercisable at $22 cash per share on a one-to-one basis. The expiration date for the warrants was set at July 15, 1988.

Some warrants contain provisions under which the corporate issuer can call the warrant or alter the expiration date if certain conditions transpire.

---

[1] This is particularly true of companies with small capitalizations.

[2] A few warrants are perpetual—they never expire.

[3] Warrant conversions are usually adjusted automatically for any stock dividends or splits.

[4] The original information for Pier 1 is taken from *The Value Line Convertible Survey, Part I: The Convertible Strategist,* Vol. 14, No. 35 (September 12, 1983), p. 118. This Value Line service, which is separate from the *Investment Survey* discussed in Chapter 4, is an excellent source of information on warrants, convertibles, and puts and calls.

For example, the Pier 1 warrants are callable anytime for $18. The expiration date can be accelerated by up to two years if the common closes at or above $40 for 10 consecutive trading days.

Why Buy Warrants?

Warrants offer investors a cheaper way to speculate on a particular common stock because the purchase of a given number of warrants is always cheaper than the purchase of a corresponding number of common stock shares. Therefore, investors can establish a given equity position for a considerably smaller capital investment through the use of warrants. Investors trade warrants on the exchanges and over the counter exactly as they would common stock; that is, they call their broker, usually trade in round lots, and pay normal brokerage commissions.[5] Most investors never exercise warrants but simply buy and sell them in pursuit of capital gains.

Investors are interested in warrants primarily because of their speculative appeal. Warrants provide leverage opportunities. Leverage produces larger percentage gains (and also losses) than the underlying common stock for given fluctuations in the price of the common.

Consider the Pier 1 Import warrants as an example. On one observation date after the warrant was trading, the common stock traded at $18.25 and the warrant traded at $5.75. Since an investor would have to pay $22 in order to exercise this warrant and receive a share of stock, no one would be willing to do so at that time. Nevertheless, investors were willing to pay $5.75 per warrant to speculate on future price movements. Assume, for example, the stock was to double in price to $36.50 per share (100% appreciation). The warrant at that point would be worth a minimum of $14.50 ($36.50 − the $22 exercise price). This would represent a gain of $8.75 per warrant, or 152% appreciation and, in fact, this warrant would probably sell for more than $14.50 because of increased investor interest, resulting in an even larger appreciation percentage relative to the common.

This example demonstrates the leverage potential possible from a warrant. Other things being equal, the warrant price will appreciate more *percentage-wise* than the common stock price for a given increase in the common. (Accordingly, if the stock price declines, the percentage decline of the warrant price will often be greater.)

In order to understand the relationships between the prices in this example, it is necessary to consider the valuation of warrants. As is true for every financial asset, a warrant has value because of an expected future return of some type. In the case of warrants, since no dividends are paid, the expected return must be realized in the form of capital appreciation, or price change. Warrant valuation, therefore, involves an understanding of the price range in which a warrant may trade.

---

[5] Prior to 1970, the NYSE had not permitted the trading of warrants for many years.

Valuing Warrants

Warrants fluctuate in price between a minimum and maximum value.[6] The *maximum value* is the price of the underlying common stock. The price of a warrant, which is a claim on the common stock, can never exceed the price of the stock itself because no return beyond the value of the stock is possible. In fact, most warrant prices never reach their maximum value because warrants are an expiring asset—their time value decreases as they approach maturity.

The *minimum value* or price for a warrant is the difference between the market price of the common and the warrant's exercise price, *if this spread is positive*. This difference must hold (at least approximately); otherwise, arbitragers would purchase the warrant, immediately exercise it, and sell the common stock received, thereby earning a profit. If the spread is negative (the exercise price exceeds the market price) the minimum price (MP) of the warrant is zero. Thus,

$$MP = \$0, \text{ if } CMP < EP$$

$$MP = (CMP - EP) \times N, \text{ if } CMP > EP \quad (16\text{--}1)$$

where

MP = minimum price of a warrant.
CMP = current market price of the stock.
EP = the exercise price of the warrant.
N = number of common shares received per warrant exercised.

Equation 16–1 is often referred to as the **theoretical (calculated) value of a warrant** because it produces the intrinsic value of a warrant. In actuality, warrants typically sell above this calculated value. The amount in excess of the formula value is referred to as the premium. The premium can be calculated by rearranging Equation 16–1 into 16–2.

$$\text{Premium} = \frac{\text{Market price}}{\text{of the warrant}} - \frac{\text{Minimum price}}{\text{of the warrant}} \quad (16\text{--}2)$$

Returning to the Pier 1 Imports warrants, the following calculations can be made, using the prices previously cited as an example.

Minimum price for Pier 1 warrants = $0 because CMP < EP

The minimum price would have to be considered zero because the current market price was less than the exercise price (obviously, the price cannot be negative).

The premium would be calculated as

Premium for Pier 1 warrants = $5.75 − $0 = $5.75

---

[6] For simplicity, this discussion assumes a one-to-one purchase ratio between the warrant and the common.

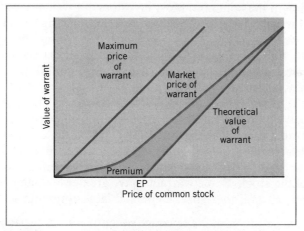

FIGURE 16–1 Relationships between the value of a warrant and the price of the underlying common stock (EP = Exercise price of the warrant).

On the observation date, the Pier 1 Imports warrant was selling for a premium of $5.75 above its minimum price. Investors were willing to pay this because the warrant was selling at slightly less than one-third the price of the common, the maximum loss was relatively small (i.e., $5.75 per warrant), and, as just shown, the potential return could be large because of the leverage involved.

Figure 16–1 shows the relationships that exist between the stock's price and the warrant's value: the minimum (theoretical) price as given by Equation 16–1, the maximum price of the warrant, and the premium. The minimum price line starts at EP, the exercise price of the warrant. The minimum price of the warrant rises (becomes positive) as the price of the stock exceeds the exercise price. Notice that as the price of the common stock continues to increase, the size of the premium decreases—a phenomenon that will be discussed later. Finally, note the line representing the maximum price for the warrant. Why is this drawn as a 45-degree angle?

The Speculative Value of a Warrant

What determines the premium investors will pay for a warrant, that is, its speculative value? Since investors typically purchase warrants in order to speculate on the underlying common stock, some obvious factors will affect the premium, or speculative potential, of the warrant. These include the following:

1. *Remaining warrant life.* Clearly, other things being equal, the larger the remaining life of a warrant, the more valuable it is. A warrant that currently is unattractive to exercise may become attractive six months, or two years, or eight years from now as a result of apprecia-

tion in the common. Most investors are well advised not to purchase a warrant with less than three years remaining to maturity.

2. *Price volatility of the common.* Other things being equal, the more volatile the price of the underlying common, the more likely the warrant is to appreciate during a given time period. Investors are willing to pay larger premiums for such a warrant.

3. *The dividend on the underlying common.* Since warrant holders receive no dividends, an inverse relationship exists between the warrant premium and the expected dividend on the common.

4. *The potential leverage of the warrant.* As previously explained, warrant prices rise (and decline) faster, in percentage terms, than the price of the stock. Some warrants have greater leverage possibilities than do others and, therefore, command larger premiums.

In connection with the leverage potential of the warrant, notice in Figure 16–1 that the premium becomes smaller as the price of the stock rises. Why? As the stock price increases, the leverage potential decreases; that is, the ability of the warrant to magnify percentage gains on the amount invested decreases as the price of the stock rises. Consider the following examples for the Pier 1 Imports warrant, assuming the same stock price of $18.25 and the same warrant price of $5.75 as previously used.

Stock price doubles from $18.25 to $36.50	100% gain
Theoretical value of warrant rises $5.75 to $14.50	152% gain
Stock price rises an additional 50% from $36.50 to $54.75	50% gain
Theoretical value of warrant rises from $14.50 to $32.75[7]	126% gain
Stock price rises an additional 25% from $54.75 to $68.44	25% gain
Theoretical value of market rises from $32.75 to $46.44	42% gain

Convertible Securities

A third form of equity-derivative securities is the convertible bond or convertible preferred stock, both of which permit the owner to convert the security into common stock under specified conditions. These **convertible securities** (''convertibles'') carry a claim on the common stock of the same

---

[7]$54.75 − 22 = $32.75 theoretical value; $32.75 − 14.50/14.50 = 126% gain.

issuer, which is exercisable at the owner's initiative (many convertible bonds cannot be converted for an initial period of 6 to 24 months). If the option is never exercised, the convertible bond remains in existence until its maturity date, whereas a convertible preferred could remain in existence forever since preferred stock has no maturity date.

Unlike puts and calls and warrants, convertible securities derive only part of their value from the option feature—that is, the claim on the underlying common stock. These securities are valuable in their own right, as either bonds or preferred stock. Puts and calls and warrants, on the other hand, are only as valuable as the underlying common stock. They have no value beyond their claim on the common stock.

Convertibles have increased in popularity in recent years because they offer a unique combination of equity and bond characteristics.

Terminology for Convertible Securities

Convertible securities, whether bonds or preferred stock, have a certain terminology.

1. **Conversion ratio.** The number of shares of common stock that a convertible holder receives on conversion, which is the process of tendering the convertible security to the corporation in exchange for common stock.[8]

2. **Conversion price.** The par value of the bond or preferred divided by the conversion ratio.[9]

$$\text{Conversion price} = \text{Par value} \div \text{Conversion ratio} \qquad (16\text{-}3)$$

3. **Conversion value.** The convertible's value based on the current price of the common stock. It is defined as

$$\text{Conversion value} = \text{Conversion ratio} \times \begin{array}{l} \text{Current price} \\ \text{of common} \end{array} \qquad (16\text{-}4)$$

4. **Conversion premium.** The dollar difference between the market price of the security and its conversion value.

$$\text{Conversion premium} = \begin{array}{l} \text{Market price} \\ \text{of convertible} \end{array} - \text{Conversion value} \qquad (16\text{-}5)$$

Convertible securities are, by construction, hybrid securities. They have some characteristics of debt or preferred stock and some characteristics of the common stock on which they represent an option. To value them, therefore, one must consider them in both contexts. This will be done first for convertible bonds and then for convertible preferred stock.

---

[8] Forced conversion results when the issuer initiates conversion by calling the bonds.

[9] It is obvious that the conversion privilege attached to a convertible can be expressed in either conversion ratio or conversion price terms. Both the conversion price and the conversion ratio are almost always protected against stock splits and dividends.

Convertible Bonds

Convertible bonds are issued by corporations as part of their capital-raising activities. Similar to a warrant, a convertible feature can be attached to a bond as a sweetener, thereby allowing the issuer to obtain a lower interest cost by offering investors a chance for future gains from the common stock. Convertibles are sometimes sold as temporary financing instruments with the expectation that over a period of months (or years) the bonds will be converted into common stock. The bonds are a cheaper source of financing to the issuer than the common stock, and their gradual conversion places less price pressure on the common stock. Finally, convertibles offer a corporation the opportunity to sell common stock at a higher price than the current market price. If the issuer feels that the stock price is temporarily depressed, convertible bonds can be sold at a 15 to 20% premium; that is, the price of the stock must rise by that amount before conversion is warranted.

Most bonds, whether convertible or not, are callable by the issuer. This results in additional concerns for the convertible bondholder.

Convertible bonds are typically issued as debentures. They are often subordinated to straight (nonconvertible) debentures, increasing their risk. Using S&P and Moody's bond ratings, most convertible bonds are one class below a straight debenture issue. Nevertheless, convertible bonds enjoy good marketability. Large issues on the New York Exchange are often actively traded in contrast to many nonconvertible issues of the same quality.

Analyzing Convertible Bonds

A convertible bond offers the purchaser a stream of interest payments and a return of principal at maturity. It also offers a promise of capital gains if the price of the stock rises sufficiently. To value a convertible bond, it is necessary to account for all of these elements. We will illustrate the convertible bond model graphically in order to have a framework for our analysis. We will then illustrate the components of value individually.

Graphic analysis of convertible bonds   Figure 16–2 shows the components of the convertible bond model. This diagram depicts the expected relationships for a typical convertible bond. The horizontal line from PV (par value) on the left to the maturity value (MV) on the right provides a reference point; any bond sold at par value would start out at PV, and all bonds will mature at their maturity value. If such a bond is callable, the call price will be above the par value in the early years because of the call premium; by maturity this price would converge to the maturity value.

Each convertible bond has an **investment value** (IV) or straight-debt value, which is the price at which a convertible would sell to equal the yield on a comparable nonconvertible. In other words, the investment value is the convertible's estimated value as a straight bond. By evaluating the coupons and the maturity value of the convertible at the going required rate of return

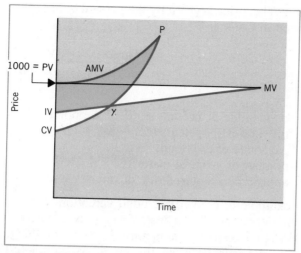

FIGURE 16–2 **Conceptual model for understanding convertible bonds.**

for a comparable straight bond, the beginning investment value can be determined. Remember that the straight—nonconvertible—bond has a higher market yield because it does not offer a speculative play on the common stock. The investment value is represented in Figure 16–2 by the line from IV to MV.

Each convertible has a conversion value at any point in time. The original conversion value (point CV) is established by multiplying together the conversion ratio and the price of the common stock at the time the convertible is issued. The conversion value curve in Figure 16–2 is then drawn on the assumption that the price of the stock will grow at some rate g. Obviously, this is an expected relationship and may not occur in this manner. Using this assumption, the conversion value rises above the par value as the price of the stock rises, tracing out the curve CV–P in Figure 16–2.

Finally, the convertible often sells at a premium; therefore, it is necessary to draw an actual market value (AMV) curve, which is shown in Figure 16–2 as PV–P. This curve eventually approaches the conversion value curve as the conversion value increases. This is attributable primarily to the fact that the convertible may be called, forcing conversion. If this occurs, the convertible holder can receive only the conversion value; therefore, investors are not likely to pay more than this for the convertible.

The shaded area in Figure 16–2 is the premium over conversion value, which declines as the market price of the convertible rises. This reflects the fact that the bond is callable.

Bond value   Every convertible bond has an investment value or straight debt value, which is the price at which the bond would sell with no conversion option. This price is given by the present value calculations for a bond, as explained in Chapter 7.

$$BV = \sum_{t=1}^{n} \frac{C_t}{(1 + r)^t} + \frac{FV}{(1 + r)^n} \tag{16-6}$$

where

  BV = bond value or present value of the bond.
  C = the interest payments (coupons).
  FV = par value of the bond.
  n = number of years to maturity.
  r = appropriate required rate of return.

As an example of convertible bond valuation, consider the 8.5s of 2008 convertible debenture of Hartmarx Corporation (formerly, Hart, Schaffner & Marx), a NYSE-listed manufacturer of men's clothing. According to *The Value Line Convertible Survey,* this bond, issued in late 1982, was convertible into 34.095 common shares, which is its conversion ratio.[10] The conversion price at that time was $29.33, or $1000/34.095.[11] At one observation point after its issuance, the common stock of Hartmarx was selling at 35½ while this debenture was selling at $1210. The conversion value of Hartmarx at that observation point was, therefore, 34.095 × $35.125 = $1197.59.

In the case of the Hartmarx bond, the expiration date was set at January 15, 2008.[12] Valuing this bond at the observation point just used (after the July 15 interest payment) meant that 24½ years remained to maturity, or 49 semiannual interest payments. Based on *The Value Line Convertible Survey*'s assigned investment grade value of 0 for this issue and the market rates in effect at that time, 12.2% was chosen as the applicable discount rate for a bond of this risk category.[13] Therefore, the bond or investment value for this Hartmarx convertible debenture was[14]

$$BV = \sum_{t=1}^{49} \frac{\$42.75}{(1 + 0.061)^t} + \frac{\$1000}{(1 + 0.061)^{49}}$$

$$= \$717.23$$

Of course, the bond value fluctuates over time as market interest rates change.

---

[10] *The Value Line Convertible Survey, Part I: The Convertible Strategist,* Vol. 14, No. 30 (August 8, 1983), p. 150.

[11] Many convertible bonds have a conversion price that increases over time.

[12] The Hartmarx debenture was not callable before January 15, 1985 (unless the common stock closed at $44 or more for 30 consecutive trading days).

[13] This information is available in each weekly issue.

[14] To solve this equation, the present value of the annuity must be found using the formula $1/[(1 - (1 + r)^n)/r]$. The present value factor for 49 periods can be found as $1/(1.061)^{49}$.

Conversion value   Every convertible bond has a conversion value, or the value of the common stock received upon conversion. At the time of issuance, a convertible bond has a conversion value equal to the market price of the common stock multiplied by the number of shares of stock that can be received by converting. As noted, the conversion price is usually set 15–20% above the current market price of the common so that conversion would not be worthwhile. Over time, if the price of the common stock grows, the conversion value should also grow at the same rate. This happened for the Hartmarx bond, which, as noted, had a conversion value of $1197.59.

Minimum (floor) value   Every convertible bond has a floor value, or minimum value. A convertible will always sell *for no less than* the larger of (a) its bond (investment) value or (b) its conversion value.

Even if the value of the conversion feature is zero with virtually no prospect of a change in this value, a convertible bond would have a minimum price of its investment or straight bond value—that is, its value as a nonconvertible debt instrument. If the price were to decline below this value, bond investors would buy it because its yield would be greater than alternative comparable bonds. The bond value for the Hartmarx debenture as of the valuation date was $717.23, the absolute minimum price for this bond as of that time.

In a similar manner, a convertible bond cannot sell below its conversion value; if it did, arbitragers would buy the bond, convert it into common stock and sell the shares, or simply establish an equity position at a cost lower than would otherwise be possible. Since the Hartmarx conversion value of $1197.59 was higher than its bond value, this was its minimum or floor value at the time of these calculations.

In Figure 16–2, the line IV–Y–P represents the minimum market value for the convertible bond. This minimum market value is made up of part of the investment value line (IV to Y) and part of the conversion value curve (Y to P). We can call this the effective market value floor.

Actual bond value (price)   Convertible bonds usually sell at prices above their minimum value which, as we have seen, is the higher of the bond value or the conversion value. This difference between the actual bond value and the effective market value floor is the premium.

The Hartmarx bond was selling at $1210 at the observation point with a conversion value of $1197.59. The dollar premium, therefore, was the difference, or $12.41. The reasons convertibles sell at premiums include the following:

1. The conversion option has a positive value; that is, the right to convert anytime during the life of the bond is valuable and investors are willing to pay for it. In effect, this is equivalent to owning a call on the stock, and calls command positive premiums.

2. A convertible bond offers investors downside protection, thereby decreasing their risk. If the price of the common declines sharply, resulting in a sharp decline in the conversion value, the convertible will still sell as a bond and will have a bond value determined by the present value of interest payments and principal. This dual minimum-price feature of convertibles reduces investors' risk and commands a premium in doing so.

The option pricing model   The key to valuing a convertible is to value its premium. To value convertible premiums, it is possible to use, at least in principle, the option pricing model explained in the previous section. Why? Because, in effect, a convertible security is a call option on the underlying common stock (a complex call, to be sure). As such, the premium should be amenable to interpretation using the option pricing model.

Although the model is difficult, at best, to apply directly, it can be used to indicate how certain factors will impact the premium. This will help investors to gauge their relative size.

Using the five variables in the Black–Scholes call option model from Chapter 15, the following relationships can be noted:

1. *The price of the underlying stock.* Clearly, a higher stock price is associated with a higher premium.
2. *The exercise price of the option.* The lower the effective exercise price (i.e., the higher the conversion ratio), the larger the premium should be, other things being equal.
3. *The time remaining to the expiration of the option.* In the case of convertibles, the option feature is available throughout the life of the security. Because most bonds are callable, however, the expected call date would be the effective expiration date. The longer the time to maturity, the higher the premium.
4. *The interest rate acts as an opportunity cost in affecting the value of a call.* The higher the interest rate, other things being equal, the higher the value of a call, and therefore the higher the convertible premium.
5. *The volatility of the underlying stock price.* The more volatility in stock price, the more likely the price is to rise, thereby involving the speculative appeal of convertibles and raising the premium.

Other factors to consider   In evaluating convertible bonds, certain details should be kept in mind in addition to the preceding factors.

1. When a convertible bond is converted, the holder loses the accrued interest from the last interest payment date. Furthermore, if a holder converts after the ex dividend date, the common stock dividend on the newly received common shares could be lost. Since the issuer can call the bonds and force conversion, these factors can be important. It is not unusual for issuers to choose a time favorable to themselves.

2. A bond is subject to call if the market price exceeds the call price. Investors who pay a premium over the conversion value in these circumstances run a risk of having the bond called as the company forces conversion.

Buying convertible bonds Why should investors consider convertible bonds? Are there disadvantages?

Convertible bonds offer investors a unique combination of an income stream from a fixed income security and a chance to participate in the price appreciation of the common stock. Convertibles offer downside protection in relation to owning the common stock, because regardless of what happens to the price of the common, the convertible bond will not decline below its value as a straight bond. They offer upside potential, because a convertible bond must always be worth at least its conversion as the price of the common stock rises.

The yield on a convertible bond usually exceeds that of the common stock, and interest payments have first order of priority.[15] Compared to common stock owners, convertible bondholders enjoy a yield advantage while awaiting appreciation in the stock price.

As for disadvantages, convertible bonds yield less than do straight bonds of similar risk and maturity. Investors must give up some yield to receive the conversion feature. Convertibles are callable, and thus in many cases the issuer can and will force conversion. When a convertible bond is called, the holder will choose the better alternative—accept the call price or convert into common stock. If a corporation calls a bond at, say, $1100 (face value of $1000 plus one year's interest of $100 for a call premium), and the conversion value is, say, $1200, the bondholders in effect are forced to convert. They give up their fixed-income security and the chance for future capital gains from the common stock.

For a good discussion of the pros and cons of convertibles, see Box 16–1.

Convertible Preferred Stock

A convertible preferred stock offers investors fixed quarterly dividends forever plus an option on the underlying common stock. This security is often issued in connection with mergers.

Convertible preferreds differ from convertible bonds in the following ways:

1. The conversion privilege does not expire.
2. The conversion rate does not change, as it often does with bonds.
3. Conversion can take place immediately upon issuance.

---

[15] In the case of Hartmarx, the yields at the observation point were 7% and 2.7% respectively, a 4.3% yield advantage for the convertible.

BOX 16–1 FENCE-SITTER BONDS

An optimist's scenario: long-term interest rates come down some more, and 30-year bonds priced to yield 6% become commonplace. A 3000 Dow arrives before the decade is out.

What do you do if you aren't so optimistic? If you fear a return of inflation that would kill bonds? Or a recession that would kill stocks? Buy a convertible bond, a cross between a stock and a bond.

Convertibles won't save you if stocks and bonds take a dive together, as they did in 1974. But converts do offer a hedge against a one-sided market fall, in which stocks or bonds do badly but not both.

These hybrid securities start their financial life as debt issues. In addition to drawing semiannual interest, each debenture can be converted into a certain number of shares of common stock. For example, each $1000 of the Automatic Data Processing 6½s of 2011 can be converted into 24 shares of ADP.

Putting a value on this security is a little tricky. Forget the conversion feature for a moment. A straight bond with a $1000 face value and a 6½% coupon, from a solid credit like ADP, is worth about $730, says Jack Levande, manager of a new convertible fund being set up at E.F. Hutton. That pure-bond value acts as a floor for the convertible, in case ADP stock falls sharply.

Now ignore the bond value and think of this security as just another way to buy 24 shares of ADP. Since ADP is currently trading at 43, the pure-stock value is $1032.

The convertible bond will cost you $1240—more than its pure-bond or pure-stock value—but the extra cost may be a good investment. You're better off than someone who owns just the stock, since the convert has that pure-bond value even if the stock sinks. In addition the bond's 5.3% current yield is much better than the stock's 1%.

The difference between the $1240 price of the bond and the $1032 value of the underlying stock is called the conversion premium. Here it is 20%.

At the same time, the convert holder is better off than someone who owns just a 6½% bond. If ADP stock takes off, the convertible will participate in most of the gain. In effect, the convert buyer has bought a straight bond for $730 and spent another $510 ($1240 minus $730) on a warrant for ADP stock.

Traditionally, the interest rate on a newly issued convertible runs about a third below what the issuer would pay on straight, nonconvertible debt. The conversion premium usually starts out at 25% or so.

It can get a little confusing, and properly valuing convertible securities requires computers larger than the average investor is likely to have at home. But plenty of convertible-debenture mutual funds are coming to market, from Fidelity and E.F. Hutton, for example. Established funds, such as those from Putnam, Value Line, Alliance and Vanguard, are growing rapidly.

A Kidder, Peabody index of the past ten years shows that the total return on converts has been within 98% of the return on stocks while the price volatility has been 25% less than that on stocks. But two cautions must be raised. One is that if interest rates rise and stock prices fall, anyone holding converts could suffer the worst of both worlds.

The other hazard is that most convertible issues can be called. When that happens, the conversion premium is erased. For example, a convertible trading at $1240 but convertible into only $1032 of stock is called at $1000. The holder is free to convert before the call deadline, but he still loses $208.

The best hedge is to buy a convert that pays substantially more than the common and determine how long it would take for the income advantage of the convert to wipe out the cost of the conversion pre-

mium. A debenture paying 6% while the underlying stock has a yield of 1%, for example, would be offsetting the premium at an annual rate of 5%.

Source: Ben Weberman, "Fence-Sitter Bonds," *Forbes*, February 9, 1987, p. 143. Reprinted by permission of *Forbes* magazine, February 9, 1987. © Forbes Inc., 1987.

As an example of a convertible preferred stock, consider the $3.75 B convertible preferred of Potlatch Corporation, which produces wood and paper products. It is convertible into 0.943 common shares and can be exchanged for the 7.5s 2011 convertible bonds at the company's option. At one observation point, the common was selling for 55 (providing a dividend yield of 2.8%) while the preferred was selling for $60.25.[16]

Analyzing Convertible Preferreds

A convertible preferred offers investors an infinite stream of quarterly dividends and a chance to participate in any appreciation in the common stock. Each of these elements for convertible preferreds must be accounted for and valued, exactly as they were in the case of convertible bonds.

Preferred stock value   As Appendix 7–A points out, a preferred stock is valued using a simple perpetuity formula.

$$P_{ps} = \frac{D}{k_{ps}} \qquad (16\text{--}7)$$

where

P_{ps} = the value of the preferred stock.
D = the fixed annual dividends.
k_{ps} = the appropriate required rate of return.

If k_{ps} rises, the value of the preferred will decline because D is permanently fixed and does not change. Thus, the value of a preferred stock changes as the required rate of return demanded by investors changes.

Reversing Equation 16–7, the required rate of return (yield) on the preferred is

$$k_{ps} = \frac{D}{P_{ps}} \qquad (16\text{--}8)$$

---

[16] All of the data for the Potlatch convertible preferred was available in *The Value Line Convertible Survey, Part I: The Convertible Strategist,* August 18, 1986, p. 142.

For Potlatch, the calculation is

$$k_{PO} = \frac{\$3.75}{\$60.25} = 6.2\%$$

Investors could purchase this convertible preferred stock, receive a 6.2% yield, and have an option on the common stock of Potlatch. What is this option worth?

Conversion value The conversion value of the Potlatch convertible preferred is

$$CV_{PO} = 0.943 \times \$55 = \$51.87$$

This convertible is selling at a typical premium over conversion value, which can be calculated as

$$\frac{\text{Premium over}}{\text{conversion value}} = \frac{\text{Market price of preferred} - \text{Conversion value}}{\text{Conversion value}}$$

$$= \frac{\$60.25 - \$51.87}{\$51.87} = 16.1\%$$

The percentage premium indicates the extent to which the common stock must appreciate before the preferred stockholder would enjoy capital gains. Thus, the common stock would have to appreciate 16% before the conversion value would be equal to the price of the preferred stock. Thereafter, if the common appreciated, the preferred would also, regardless of whether investors were willing to pay a premium for the preferred.

Buying Convertible Preferreds

Convertible preferreds, like any other security, have advantages and disadvantages. The preferred has priority over the common in payment of dividend and in case of liquidation while offering a claim on the underlying common stock, the value of which may appreciate over time. The dividend yield on a convertible preferred is almost always higher than that on the common stock, since preferreds are viewed by investors as fixed income securities. In the case of Potlatch, the yield on the preferred is more than twice that of the common. This return offers some downside protection on the price of the preferred stock, in relation to the common stock, because as stock prices decline the convertible preferred can trade on its merits as a preferred stock, offering a competitive return. *Value Line* estimated that the Potlatch preferred would share in only 50% of any decline in the common.

Disadvantages include a lower yield than a comparable straight (nonconvertible) preferred stock. Convertible preferreds, like any other preferreds, are affected by a rise in interest rates (required rate of return). Because the yield on a convertible preferred is lower than that on a comparable nonconvertible preferred, the impact on the price as a result of a rise in interest rates will be greater for the convertible. Finally, if the common stock price rises, the preferred will not rise as much. At the observation used previously, *Value Line* estimated that the Potlatch preferred would share 70% of any rise in the common.

Summary

Warrants are options to purchase common stock from corporations for a specified price and time, which is usually a period of years. Warrants offer leverage opportunities and require a smaller outlay than purchase of the stock. Percentagewise, warrants usually appreciate more than the stock price, both up and down.

Warrants have a minimum value, as calculated by the theoretical value formula, and a maximum value, which is the price of the stock. The amount above the minimum price at which a warrant sells is its premium. The premium is affected by the remaining warrant life, the price volatility of the common, any dividends, and the potential leverage of the warrant. The leverage decreases as the stock price increases.

Convertible securities consist of bonds and preferred stock, which are valuable in their own right. Convertible bonds are issued as debentures and are always worth at least their straight debt value. The bond may sell at its conversion value or the value of the common stock received on conversion. Convertibles usually sell above either of these values, the higher of which is the minimum, or floor, value. The amount above the minimum at which they sell is referred to as the premium. Investors are willing to pay a premium for the conversion option and the downside protection resulting from the straight debt value.

Convertible preferred stock is similar to bonds, but the conversion privilege never expires. This security has a minimum value—the value of a preferred stock paying a fixed dividend forever. In addition, it has a conversion value and it often sells at a premium over the conversion value. It offers investors downside protection, but a lower yield than a comparable nonconvertible preferred.

Key Words

Conversion premium	Investment value
Conversion price	Theoretical (calculated) value of
Conversion ratio	warrant
Conversion value	Warrant
Convertible securities	

QUESTIONS AND PROBLEMS

1. Why are warrants issued?
2. Why buy warrants?
3. What is the range of a warrant's price? Under what conditions will it approach either end of this range?
4. What is meant by the premium on a warrant? What factors affect this premium?
5. Explain the relationship between the leverage potential of a warrant and the price of the underlying stock.
6. Distinguish between the conversion ratio, the conversion price, and the conversion value.
7. Why do corporations issue convertible bonds?
8. What is meant by the floor value of a convertible bond?
9. Why do convertible bonds sell at premiums?
10. Explain the relationship between the factors in the Black–Scholes option model and the premium on convertible bonds.
11. What are the advantages of buying convertible bonds? What are the disadvantages?
12. How do convertible preferred stocks differ from convertible bonds?
13. What are the advantages of convertible preferreds? What are the disadvantages?
14. What does the percentage conversion premium on a convertible preferred stock indicate?
15. What risks are all convertible securities exposed to?
16. Explain what is meant by the theoretical value of a warrant.
17. Why might a corporation extend a warrant's expiration date?
18. Why does the market value of a convertible bond approach the conversion value as the conversion value increases?
19. The price of the Hartmarx common was about $26.50 when the convertible bond described in the chapter was issued. Determine the percentage conversion premium at that time if the bond was issued at par.
20. What are the basic differences between purchasing a warrant and purchasing the underlying common stock, and between a call and a warrant?
21. At a certain observation point, Pier 1 Imports common stock was trading at $15.875, with the warrant at $5.25. Exercise price remains at $22.
    a. Determine the theoretical value of the warrant at this point in time.
    b. Determine its premium.
    c. How would you justify the warrant's price at this point?
22. Golden Nugget had a warrant attached to their bond issue, the 8.38s of 1993. Assume a price quote on the bond of $745.00. The warrant expires on July 1,

1988. The price of the warrant is currently quoted at $4.13. The market price of the common stock is $11.25. The per-share exercise price is $18.00 and the conversion ratio is 1.0.

a. On the basis of this bond quote, is the current market interest rate greater or less than 8.38?

b. Using Equation 16–1, calculate the minimum price on this warrant.

c. Using Equation 16–2, calculate the premium.

d. The relationship between the value of the warrant and the price of common stock is shown in Figure 16–1. On that figure, the minimum price line starts at a common stock price of EP. For Golden Nugget, what is the value of EP?

e. For the market prices of Golden Nugget and for the market prices of the warrants shown here, calculate the minimum prices (Equation 16–1), and the premium values (Equation 16–2).

Stock Price	Minimum Value	Actual Warrant Price	Premium
$ 5.00		$ 1.50	
11.25		4.13	
12.50		5.00	
18.00		8.00	
20.00		9.00	
25.00		13.00	
35.00		22.00	
50.00		36.00	
70.00		54.00	

f. Use the values calculated in e to explain what will happen to the minimum value and to the premium as the stock price rises.

g. What should be expected regarding the value of the premiums:
  (1) As we approach July 1, 1988.
  (2) If the price of Golden Nugget should become quite stable around $15 per share.
  (3) If earnings of Golden Nugget become stable at $2.00 per share with a steady dividend payout ratio of 0.50.

23. Pan American World Airways has several convertible bond issues outstanding. One issue is the 15s of 1998. Upon issue of this bond it was specified that each $1000 par bond is convertible to stock at a conversion price of $5.50 per share. Assume that the quoted price on the bond is $1350. The closing price on Pan Am's common stock is $7.25.

a. Using Equation 16–3, calculate the conversion ratio. Explain what this means.

b. Using Equation 16–4, calculate the conversion value.

c. Using Equation 16–5, calculate the conversion premium.

d. Using Equation 16–6, assuming 14 years to the maturity date of the bond (t) and a required rate of return (r) of 12%, show that the bond value is $1199, using our computational formula (C = $150) of

$$\text{BV} = \frac{C}{r}\left[1 - \frac{1}{(1 + r)^t}\right] + \frac{\text{Par}}{(1 + r)^t}$$

    e. What is the actual bond value?

    f. What is the minimum price on the bond?

24. For the Pan Am convertible bond, the 15s of 98, assume that market interest rates rose, requiring the rate of return (r) to be 13%, while the price of Pan Am common stock fell to $6.50.

    a. What would happen to the market price of the bond?

    b. Calculate (1) the conversion value and (2) the minimum (floor) value.

    c. What do you expect to happen to the value of the premium?

25. Pan Am also has outstanding the convertible bond of 5.25s of 89. Assume this bond has five years to maturity at $1000 par value. The current market price of this bond is $700.00.

    a. Using a required rate of 14%, calculate the bond value (t = 5).

    b. The market price of Pan Am common stock is $7.00. The conversion ratio is 60.753. Calculate (1) the conversion price and (2) the conversion value.

    c. Explain why the bond is selling at such a deep discount, while the 15s of 98 are selling at a premium.

Selected References

Alexander, Gordon J., and Stover, Roger D. "Pricing in the New Issue Convertible Debt Market." *Financial Management,* Fall 1977, pp. 35–39.

Alexander, Gordon J., and Stover, Roger D. "The Effect of Forced Conversion on Common Stock Prices." *Financial Management,* Spring 1980, pp. 39–45.

Bierman, Harold, Jr. "Convertible Bonds as Investments." *Financial Analysts Journal,* March–April 1980, pp. 59–61.

Brennan, M. J., and Schwartz, E. S. "Convertible Bonds: Valuation and Optimal Strategies for Call and Conversion." *The Journal of Finance,* December 1977, pp. 1699–1715.

Brennan, M. J., and Schwartz, E. S., "The Case for Convertibles." *Chase Financial Quarterly,* Spring 1982, pp. 27–46.

Horrigan, James. "Some Hypotheses on the Valuation of Stock Warrants." *Journal of Business Finance and Accounting,* Summer 1974, pp. 239–247.

Ingersoll, Jonathan. "An Examination of Corporate Call Policies on Convertible Securities." *The Journal of Finance,* May 1977, pp. 463–478.

Jennings, Edward H. "An Estimate of Convertible Bond Premiums." *Journal of Financial and Quantitative Analysis,* January 1974, pp. 33–56.

Kassouf, Sheen. ''Warrant Price Behavior—1945 to 1964.'' *Financial Analysts Journal,* January–February 1968, pp. 123–126.

Leabo, Dick, and Rogalski, Richard. ''Warrant Price Movements and the Efficient Market Model.'' *The Journal of Finance,* March 1975, pp. 163–177.

Parkinson, Michael. ''Empirical Warrant–Stock Relationships.'' *The Journal of Business,* October 1972, pp. 563–569.

Ritchie, John C., Jr. ''Convertible Bonds and Warrants.'' In Frank J. Fabozzi and Irving M. Pollack, eds. *The Handbook of Fixed Income Securities,* Homewood, Ill.: Dow Jones-Irwin, 1983.

Rush, David F., and Melicher, Ronald W. ''An Empirical Examination of Factors which Influence Warrant Prices.'' *The Journal of Finance,* December 1974, pp. 1449–1466.

Walter, James E., and Que, Augustin V. ''The Valuation of Convertible Bonds.'' *The Journal of Finance,* June 1973, pp. 713–733.

CHAPTER 17

FINANCIAL FUTURES

One of the fastest growing areas in all of investments is the *futures markets*. New instruments in this area have proliferated, and techniques involving the use of futures, such as program trading, have captured wide media attention. Of particular importance to many investors is the wide range of **financial futures** now available. Investors should understand what financial futures are, how they can be used, and the wide variety of choices now available.

The major commodities traded in the United States can be classified into the following categories (as shown in *The Wall Street Journal,* mid-1987):[1]

GRAINS AND OILSEEDS: Wheat, corn, oats, soybeans, soybean oil, soybean meal, barley, flaxweed, rapeseed, and rye.

LIVESTOCK AND MEATS: Cattle (both live and feeders), pork bellies, and hogs.

---

[1] These commodities are traded on the following exchanges: Amex Commodities Corporation (ACC), Chicago Board of Trade (CBT), Chicago Mercantile Exchange (CME), Commodity Exchange, New York (CMX), International Monetary Market of the Chicago Mercantile Exchange (IMM), Kansas City Board of Trade (KCBT), New York Coffee, Sugar & Cocoa Exchange (CSCE), New York Cotton Exchange (CTN), New York Futures Exchange (NYFE), and the New York Mercantile Exchange (NYM).

FOODS AND FIBERS:	Cocoa, coffee, orange juice, sugar, cotton.
WOOD:	Lumber.
METALS:	Copper, gold, platinum, silver, and palladium.
OIL:	Gasoline, heating oil, crude oil, gas oil.
FINANCIAL:	Treasury bills, notes, and bonds, municipal bond index, stock indices, Eurodollars, foreign currencies, U.S. dollar index.

To most people, futures trading has traditionally meant trading futures contracts for commodities such as wheat, soybeans, and gold. Although the trading of such items on futures markets remains important, most investors seldom use such trading vehicles. To do so requires special interest or knowledge generally outside the range of most investors. For example, investors who trade in agricultural commodities ideally should understand such factors as agricultural markets, government stabilization policies, and the effects of weather on crops.

This chapter therefore focuses primarily on financial futures rather than the traditional commodities futures; however, the basic principles are the same for both. Indeed, money can be thought of simply as another commodity. Financial futures have become a particularly viable investment alternative for numerous investors and will almost certainly increase in popularity. Their development and growth is reminiscent of the options market, which became extremely popular with investors after the Chicago Board Options Exchange (CBOE's) debut in 1973.

What Are Futures Contracts?

Physical commodities are traded in cash markets. A *cash contract* calls for immediate delivery and is used by those who need a commodity now (e.g., food processors). In contrast, a **futures contract** is a commitment to buy or sell at a specified future settlement date a designated amount of a commodity. It is a legally binding contract by two parties to make or take delivery of the item some time in the future. The seller (sometimes called the short) of the futures contract agrees to make delivery, and the buyer (the long) of the contract agrees to take delivery, at a currently determined market price. It is extremely important to note that, unlike an options contract, *a futures contract involves a specific obligation to take or make delivery*.

Futures contracts are standardized, transferable agreements whose prices fluctuate constantly. As a legal contract, items such as quantity and price are spelled out precisely and cannot be changed during the life of the contract. Futures contracts are not securities, however, and are not regulated by the Securities and Exchange Commission. The Commodity Futures Trading Commission (CFTC), a federal regulatory agency, is responsible for regulating trading in all domestic futures markets.

Some Basic Terminology

A buyer assumes a *long position* and a seller assumes a *short position*. Selling short in futures trading means only that a contract not previously purchased is sold.

Contracts are traded on designated *futures exchanges,* which are voluntary, nonprofit associations. An important role in every futures transaction is played by the *clearinghouse,* which ensures the fulfillment of each futures contract by placing itself between the parties to each transaction. Buyers and sellers settle with the clearinghouse, not each other; that is, the clearinghouse, and not another investor, is actually on the other side of every transaction. The clearinghouse ensures that all payments are made as specified, and it stands ready to fulfill a contract if either buyer or seller defaults. It thereby helps to facilitate an orderly market in futures, because any buyer or seller can always close out a position and be assured of payment. A failure by the clearinghouse to perform would ruin the futures market.

Futures contracts can be settled by delivery or by offset. Delivery, or settlement of the contract, occurs in months that are designated by the various exchanges for each of the items traded. Delivery occurs in less than 2% of all transactions.[2] *Offset* is the typical method of settling a contract. Holders liquidate a position by arranging an offsetting transaction; that is, buyers sell their positions and sellers buy in their positions sometime prior to delivery. Thus, to eliminate a futures market position, we simply do the reverse of what we did (buy or sell) originally. It is important to remember that if a financial futures contract is not offset, it must be closed out by delivery of an approved cash instrument, or cash itself.

Each exchange establishes price fluctuation limits on the various types of contracts. Typically, for financial futures, a *minimum price change* is specified. In the case of Treasury bond futures contracts, for example, it is $\frac{1}{32}$ of a point, or $31.25 per contract. A *daily price limit* is in effect for all futures contracts except stock index futures. Again, in the case of Treasury bonds it is $\frac{64}{32}$ ($2000 per contract) above and below the previous day's settlement price.

Recall that in the case of stock transactions the term *margin* refers to the down payment in a transaction in which money is borrowed from the broker to finance the total cost. Futures margin, on the other hand, refers to the "good faith" (or earnest money) deposit made by the transactor to ensure the completion of the contract. It is not a down payment because ownership of the underlying item is not being transferred; in effect, it is a performance bond. Each exchange sets its own minimum *initial margin* requirements (in dollars); however, brokerage houses can, and most do, require a higher margin. The margin required for futures contracts, which is small in relation to the value of the contract itself, represents the *equity* of the transactor (either buyer or seller).

---

[2]Instruments that can be used in a delivery are explicitly identified in delivery manuals issued by the appropriate exchange.

TABLE 17-1 **Investor Accounts, Using Stock Index Futures, Marked to the Market**

	Buyer (Long)	Seller (Short)
Account after one day		
Original equity (Initial margin)	$3500	$3500
Day 1 mark to the market	(250)	250
Current equity	$3250	$3750
Account after two weeks		
Original equity (Initial margin)	$3500	$3500
Cumulative mark to the market	2125	(2125)
Current equity	$5625	$1375
Withdrawable excess equity	$2125	
Margin call		$2125

Source: Based on *Introducing New York Stock Exchange Index Futures,* New York Futures Exchange, p. 8. Reprinted by permission of the New York Futures Exchange, Inc. Copyright, 1984.

In addition to the initial margin requirement, each contract also requires a *maintenance margin* below which the investor's equity cannot drop. If the market price of a futures contract moves adversely to the owner's position, the equity declines. If the decline is substantial, bringing the equity below the maintenance margin, a *margin call* occurs requiring the transactor to deposit additional cash or close out the account. To understand precisely how this works, we must first understand how profits and losses from futures contracts are debited and credited daily to an investor's account.

All futures contracts are **marked to the market** daily; that is, all profits and losses on a contract are credited and debited to each investor's account every trading day. Those contract holders with a profit can withdraw the gains, while those with a loss will receive a margin call when the equity falls below the specified maintenance margin. Table 17-1 illustrates how accounts are marked to the market daily, and how a margin call can occur.

Consider an investor who buys a stock index futures contract for 75 (the pricing of these is explained later) and a second investor who sells (shorts) the same contract at the same price. Assume these contracts are on the NYSE Composite Index, where each point in the price is divided into 20 "ticks" worth $25 each.[3] For example, a price advance from 75 to 76, or one point, represents an advance of 20 ticks worth $25 each, or $500. Each investor puts up an initial margin of $3500. Table 17-1 traces each investor's account as it is marked to the market daily.[4]

---

[3] The NYSE Composite Index Futures Contract is quoted in the same manner as the index itself; for trading purposes, however, the contract is quoted in units called "ticks," each worth 0.05.

[4] This example is similar to an illustration in *Introducing New York Stock Exchange Index Futures* (New York Futures Exchange), p. 8. The level of the Index used here is for illustrative purposes only. I wish to thank the N.Y. Futures Exchange for their help with this example.

At the end of day one, the price of the contract has dropped to a settlement price of 74.5, a decrease of 10 ticks with a total value of $250. This amount is credited to the seller's account because the seller is short, and the price drops; conversely, $250 is debited to the buyer's account because the buyer is long, and the price moved adversely to this position. Table 17–1 shows that the current equity at the end of day 1 is $3250 for the buyer and $3750 for the seller.

Now assume that two weeks have passed, during which time each account has been marked to the market daily. The settlement price on this contract has reached 79.25. The *aggregate* change in market value for each investor is the difference between the current price and the initial price multiplied by $500, the value of one point in price, which in this example is

$$79.25 - 75 = 4.25 \times \$500 = \$2125$$

As shown in Table 17–1, this amount is currently credited to the buyer because the price moved in the direction the buyer expected; conversely, this same amount is currently debited to the seller who now is on the wrong side of the price movement. Therefore, starting with an initial equity of $3500, after two weeks the cumulative mark to the market is $2125. This results in a current equity of $5625 for the buyer and $1375 for the seller. The buyer has a withdrawable excess equity of $2125 because of the favorable price movement, while the seller has a margin call of $2125.[5]

Unique Characteristics of Futures Contracts

Transacting in futures contracts involves some features that differ from other securities such as stocks, or options. As previously noted, the whole concept of margin is different because a transfer of ownership of the underlying item is not involved. Because no credit is being extended, there is no interest expense on that part of the contract not covered by the margin as there is when stocks are purchased on margin.[6] Margin is the norm in futures trading, but not in stock trading. In fact, some stocks are not eligible for margin.

Most futures contracts have a daily price limit, as previously noted (stock index futures are the exception, having no daily price limits). Trading ceases for that day when this limit is reached.

With stocks, short selling can be done only on an "uptick"; with futures, however, there are no such price movement restrictions. Stock positions,

---

[5] If the investor's current equity drops below the maintenance level required (which in this case is $1500), he or she receives a margin call and must add enough money to bring the account back to the initial margin level.

[6] With futures, customers often receive interest on margin money deposited. A customer with a large enough requirement (roughly, $15,000 and over) can use Treasury bills as part of the margin.

short or long, can literally be held forever; however, futures positions must be closed out within a specified time, either by offsetting the position or by making or taking delivery.

Brokerage commissions on commodities contracts are paid on the basis of a completed contract (purchase and sale), rather than on each purchase and sale as in the case of stocks. As with options, no certificates exist for futures contracts.

Unlike stocks, there are no specialists on futures exchanges. Each futures contract is traded in a specific "pit" in an auction market process where every bid and offer compete without priority as to time or size. A system of "open outcry" is used, where any offer to buy or sell must be made to all traders in the pit.

The Specifics of Trading Financial Futures

The procedures for trading financial futures are the same as those for any other commodity with few exceptions. At maturity, stock index futures settle in cash because it would be impossible or impractical to deliver all the stocks in a particular index.[7] Unlike traditional futures contracts, stock index futures typically have no daily price limits (although they can be imposed).

Using Financial Futures

Financial futures provide investors more of an opportunity to "fine-tune" the risk–return characteristics of their portfolios. In recent years, this has become more important as interest rates have become much more volatile and as investors have sought new techniques to reduce the risk of equity positions. In fact, one can argue that the drastic changes that have occurred in the financial markets in the last 15–20 years have generated a genuine need for new financial instruments that allow market participants to deal with these changes.

Who uses futures, and for what? Traditionally, participants in the futures market have been classified as either hedgers or speculators. *Hedgers* buy or sell futures contracts in order to offset the risk in a cash position.[8] By taking a position opposite that of one already held, hedgers plan to reduce the risk of adverse price fluctuations. In fact, the real motivation for all futures

---

[7]What actually happens is that gains and losses on the last day of trading are credited and debited to the long and short positions in the same way—marked to the market—as was done for every other trading day of the contract. Therefore, not only is there no physical delivery of securities, but the buyer does not pay the full value of the contract at settlement.

[8]The cash position may currently exist (a cash hedge) or may be expected to exist in the future (an anticipatory hedge).

trading is to reduce price risk. A hedger is willing to forego some profit potential in exchange for having someone else assume part of the risk.

Hedging is not an automatic process. It requires more than simply taking a position. Hedgers must make timing decisions as to when to initiate and end the process. As conditions change, hedgers must adjust their hedge strategy.

One aspect of hedging that must be considered is "basis" risk. The **basis** is defined as the difference between the spot price of the commodity being hedged and the price of the futures contract used as a hedge; that is,

$$\text{Basis} = \text{Current Cash Price} - \text{Futures Price}^9$$

For example, if the S&P 500 Index settles at 200.75 while the S&P 500 Futures Stock Index closes at 200.30, the basis is 0.45. The basis is positive (negative) if cash prices are higher (lower) than prices in the futures market. The basis fluctuates in an unpredictable manner; basis risk, therefore, is the risk hedgers face as a result of unexpected changes in basis. Changes in the basis will affect the hedge position during its life. At maturity, the futures price and the cash price must be equal, resulting in a zero basis (transaction costs can cause discrepancies).

The significance of basis risk to investors is that risk cannot be entirely eliminated. Hedging a cash position will involve basis risk. Ultimately, the usefulness of financial futures is dependent on how well the cash price follows the futures price.

In contrast to hedgers, *speculators* buy or sell futures contracts in an attempt to earn a return. Speculators are willing to assume the risk of price fluctuations, hoping to profit from them. Some speculators are professionals who do this for a living and others are amateurs, ranging from the very sophisticated to the novice.

Speculators are very valuable to the proper functioning of the futures market, absorbing the excess demand or supply generated by hedgers. Speculators contribute to the liquidity of the market and reduce the variability in prices over time.

The futures markets serve a valuable economic purpose by allowing hedgers to shift risks to speculators; that is, the risk of price fluctuations is shifted from participants unwilling to assume such risk to those who are. Another economic function performed by futures markets is price discovery. Because the price of a futures contract reflects current expectations about values at some future date, transactors can establish current prices against later transactions.

We will divide the subsequent discussion of financial futures into the two major categories of contracts, interest rate futures and stock index futures, and discuss hedging and speculative activities within each category.

---

[9]Technically, a basis exists for each outstanding futures contract and can differ depending on the maturities of the contracts. Most references to basis refer to the nearby futures contract.

Interest Rate Futures

Bond prices are highly volatile, and investors are exposed to adverse price movements. Financial futures, in effect, allow bondholders and others who are affected by volatile interest rates to transfer the risk. In fact, one of the primary reasons for the growth in financial futures is that portfolio managers and investors are trying to protect themselves against adverse movements in interest rates. An investor concerned with protecting the value of fixed income securities must consider the possible impact of interest rates on the value of these securities.

Today's investors have the opportunity to consider several different **interest rate futures** contracts that are traded on two exchanges.[10] The International Monetary Market specializes in short-maturity instruments, including Treasury bills and Eurodollars. The Chicago Board of Trade specializes in long-maturity instruments, including Treasury notes, Treasury bonds, and GNMAs.

Table 17–2 describes some of the contracts on fixed income securities. Contracts are available on GNMA mortgages and U.S. Treasury bonds and notes in trading units of $100,000, and on Treasury bills in trading units of $1 million. The contracts for U.S. government securities are by far the most important.

Reading Quotes

As an illustration of the quotation (reporting) system for interest rate futures, Table 17–3 shows some hypothetical quotes for the Treasury bond contract on the CBT; these hypothetical quotes are intended only to illustrate relationships that typically exist. The value of the contract is $100,000, and the price quotations are percentages of par, with 32nds shown. One point is $1000; $1/32$ is worth $31.25. Thus, a price of $75^{16}/_{32}$ is equal to $75,500. Table 17–3 indicates that there are 10 different contract months for the Treasury bond contract, covering a period of more than two years.

In this illustration, the December futures contract opened at $74^{20}/_{32}$ of par, traded in a range of $74^{30}/_{32}$ to $74^{20}/_{32}$, and settled at $74^{25}/_{32}$, which translates into a yield of 11.816.[11] Notice that the change in price, $+^{8}/_{32}$, is opposite the change in yields, -0.042. In both cases, changes are measured from the previous day's respective variables. Finally, the open interest indicates contracts not offset by opposite transactions or delivery; that is, it measures the

---

[10] The Chicago Board of Trade (CBT) launched financial futures trading in 1975 by opening trading in Government National Mortgage Association (GNMA or Ginnie Mae) bonds. The concept accelerated in 1976 when the International Monetary Market started trading in Treasury bills. Treasury bond futures appeared in 1977.

[11] Futures prices on Treasury bonds are quoted with reference to an 8%, 20-year bond. Settlement prices are translated into a settlement yield to provide a reference point for interest rates.

TABLE 17-2 Characteristics of Interest Rate Futures Contracts

Contract	Where Traded[a]	Contract Size or Trading Unit	Minimum Fluctuations
Treasury bonds	CBT	$100,000 par value 8% coupon[b]	1/32 or $31.25
10-Year Treasury notes	CBT	$100,000 par value	1/32 or $31.25
Treasury bills	IMM	$1 million face value	1 basis point
GNMA	CBT	$100,000 principal balance with 8% coupon[c]	1/32 or $31.25

[a] CBT = Chicago Board of Trade; IMM = International Monetary Market.
[b] Bonds with other coupons are usable with price adjustments.
[c] Other coupons and principal amounts that are equivalent to $100,000, 8% can be used.

number of contracts outstanding. The open interest increases when an investor goes long a contract, and is reduced when the contract is liquidated.

Hedging with Interest Rate Futures

We now consider some examples of using interest rate futures to hedge positions. Obviously, other examples could be constructed involving various transactors, such as a corporation or financial institution, various financial instruments such as a portfolio of GNMAs or Treasury bills, and various scenarios under which the particular hedger is operating. Our objective is simply to illustrate the basic concepts.

TABLE 17-3 Hypothetical Quotes for One Day for the Various Maturities of the Treasury Bond Futures Contract

	Open	High	Low	Settle	Change	Yield Settle Change	Open Interest
Dec. 198X	74–20	74–30	74–20	74–25	+8	11.816−0.042	100,845
March 198X1	74–06	74–13	74–03	74–07	+8	11.911−0.041	24,566
June	73–28	73–31	73–21	73–25	+8	11.985−0.042	16,548
Sept.	73–13	73–16	73–09	73–13	+8	12.049−0.042	12,563
Dec.	72–32	73–06	72–30	73–03	+8	12.103−0.043	8,576
March 198X2	72–22	72–30	72–23	72–27	+8	12.146−0.042	7,283
June	72–15	72–23	72–16	72–20	+8	12.184−0.042	4,801
Sept.	72–12	72–17	72–10	72–14	+8	12.217−0.042	702
Dec.	—	—	—	72–09	+8	12.245−0.042	141
March 198X3	—	—	—	72–05	+8	12.267−0.042	58

TABLE 17–4   Illustration of Hedges Using Interest Rate Futures: A Short Hedge and a Long Hedge

Cash Market	Futures Market
Short Hedge	
June 1	June 1
Holds $1 million 11¾% Treasury bonds due 2005–10. Current market price: 117–23 (yield 9.89%)	Sells 10 T-bond futures contracts at a price of 83–06
September 1	September 1
Sells $1 million of 11¾% bonds at 104–12 (yield 11.24%)	Buys 10 T-bond futures contracts at 74–09
Loss: $133,437.50	Gain: $89,062.50
Weighted Long Hedge	
May 1	May 1
Wants to take advantage of prevailing yield level on 12¾% Treasury bonds priced at 94–08 (13.54% yield)	Buys 15 June bond futures contracts at 62–10
June 1	June 1
Buys $1 million of 12¾% Treasury bonds at 97–30 (13.02% yield)	Sells 15 June bond futures contracts at 64–24
Opportunity Loss: $36,875.00	Gain: $36,562.50

Source: U.S. Treasury Bond Futures, Chicago: Chicago Board of Trade, pp. 10 and 11. This information has been reproduced with the permission of the Chicago Board of Trade.

Short hedges   Suppose an investor has a bond portfolio and wishes to protect the value of his or her position.[12] For example, a pension fund manager holds $1 million of 11.75% Treasury bonds due 2005–10. The manager plans to sell the bonds three months from now (June 1), but wishes to protect the value of the bonds against a rise in interest rates.

To protect the position, the manager hedges by going short (selling) in the futures market. As illustrated in Table 17–4, the manager sells 10 September contracts (since each contract is worth $100,000) at a current price of 83–06. In this example, interest rates rise, producing a loss on the cash side (i.e., in the prices of the bonds held in the cash market) and a gain on the futures side (i.e., the manager can cover the short position at a lower price, which produces a profit). The futures position thus offsets 67% of the cash market loss.[13]

---

[12] This example is taken from *U.S. Treasury Bond Futures,* Chicago: Chicago Board of Trade, p. 10.

[13] The $89,062.50 gain is calculated as follows: the gain per contract is $83^{6}/_{32} - 74^{9}/_{32} = 8^{29}/_{32}$ or 8.90625 of par value. Multiplying the gain of 8.90625% by par value = $8,906.25 per contract, and for 10 contracts the total gain is $89,062.50.

The primary reason that the manager in this example offset only 67% of the cash market loss is that the T-bond contract is based on 8% coupon bonds, whereas the manager was holding 11.75% bonds. The dollar value of higher coupon bonds changes by a larger dollar amount than the dollar value of lower coupon bonds for any change in yields. One way to overcome this difference is to execute a "weighted" short hedge, adjusting the number of futures contracts used to hedge the cash position. With the example data in Table 17–4, selling 14 September contracts would offset 93.4% of the cash market loss.[14]

Long hedges An investor or portfolio manager with cash to invest can benefit from a long hedge. Assume, for example, that on May 1 a fund manager has $1 million to invest and thinks interest rates will decline over the next 30 days.[15] The manager wishes to lock in the prevailing long-term yield while taking advantage of *current* high short-term yields. The yield curve, which is now downward sloping (short-term rates exceed long-term rates), is expected to flatten. The 12.75% Treasury bond sells for 94–08, and 30-day CDs yield 16.5%.

One strategy is for the manager to buy 30-day CDs and bond futures contracts that will lock in the prevailing long-term bond yield for the 12.75% bonds. Using a *weighted* long hedge, the manager could buy 15 June bond futures contracts at 62–10. Assume that on June 1 interest rates have fallen, the bond's price is now 97–30 (a yield of 13.02%), and the futures price is 64–24. Table 17–4 shows the results of this transaction (the bottom half of the table).

The manager earned $13,750 on the CDs in one month, but gave up $11,128.77 on the 12.75% bonds that could have been purchased, resulting in a net gain of $2621.23. Adding this to the indicated gain on the futures position of $36,562.50 results in an effective cost on June 1 of $940,191.27 for the 12.75% bonds. This is equivalent to an effective yield of 13.6%, which is 6 basis points more than the yield of 13.54% on May 1.[16]

The importance of basis Note that risk cannot be eliminated completely from a hedge transaction such as the short hedge just illustrated because basis risk cannot be completely eliminated. Recall that basis is the difference between the price of the item being hedged and the price of the futures contract used to hedge it. The basis fluctuates over time and cannot be

---

[14] The market value of the 14 futures contracts changes from $1,164,625 to $1,039,937.50. The cash market values change from $1,177,187.50 to $1,043,750. Different Treasury bonds are related to the nominal 8% coupon, 15-year maturity bond used in the contract by means of a set of conversion factors that represent the relative values of the various deliverable bonds. The conversion factor for the 11¾% coupon bond used in this example, rounded off, is 1.40.

[15] This example is taken from *U.S. Treasury Bond Futures*, p. 11.

[16] In other words, the actual cost of the bonds on June 1 is $979,375 (97³⁰⁄₃₂% of $1 million). The combined profit of the futures gain and the CD return is $39,183.73 ($36,562.50 + $2,621.23). Subtracting this gain from the *actual* cost results in an effective cost of $940,191.27.

predicted precisely. Changes in the basis can affect the final results while the hedge is in effect; however, basis fluctuations are usually less volatile than price fluctuations.

A short hedge benefits from a strengthening basis (futures prices decline faster than cash prices or cash prices rise faster than futures prices). If the basis weakens, as in the short hedge example, the hedge loses some of its effectiveness.

Speculating with Interest Rate Futures

Investors may wish to speculate with interest rate futures as well as to hedge with them. To do this, investors make assessments of likely movements in interest rates and assume a futures position that corresponds with this assessment. If the investor anticipates a rise in interest rates, he or she will sell one (or more) interest rate futures because a rise in interest rates will drive down the prices of bonds and, therefore, the price of the futures contract. The investor sells a contract with the expectation of buying it back later at a lower price. Of course, a decline in interest rates will result in a loss for this investor.

Assume that in November a speculator thinks interest rates will rise over the next two weeks and wishes to profit from this expectation. The investor can sell one December Treasury bond futures contract at a price of, say, 90–20. Two weeks later the price of this contract has declined to 88–24 because of rising interest rates. This investor would have a gain of $1^{28}/_{32}$, or $1875 (each $^1/_{32}$ is worth $31.25), and could close out this position by buying an identical contract.

The usefulness of interest rate futures for pursuing such a strategy is significant. A speculator who wishes to assume a short position in bonds cannot do so readily in the cash market (either financially or mechanically). Interest rate futures provide the means to easily short bonds.

In a similar manner, investors can speculate on a decline in interest rates by purchasing interest rate futures. If the decline materializes, bond prices and the value of the futures contract will rise. Because of the leverage involved, the gains can be large; however, the losses can also be large if interest rates move in the wrong direction.

Stock Index Futures

Stock index futures trading was initiated in 1982 with several contracts quickly being created. Investors can trade futures contracts on the NYSE Composite, the S&P 500, and the *Value Line* Index.[17] The contract size for

---

[17] There is also a futures contract on the Major Market Index, which was designed by the American Stock Exchange to have a similar character to the Dow Jones Index. It has a value of $250 times the index.

each of these indexes is 500 times the index quote. Each is settled by cash on the settlement day.[18]

Stock index futures offer investors the opportunity to act on their investment opinions concerning the future direction of the market. They need not select individual stocks and it is easy to short the market. Furthermore, investors who are concerned about unfavorable short-term market prospects but remain bullish for the longer run can protect themselves in the interim by selling stock index futures.

Hedging with Stock Index Futures

Common stock investors hedge with financial futures for the same reasons that fixed-income investors use them. Investors, whether individuals or institutions, may hold a substantial stock portfolio that is subject to the risk of the overall market, that is, systematic risk. A futures contract enables the investor to transfer a part or all of the risk to those willing to assume it.

Chapter 8 pointed out the two types of risk inherent in common stocks: systematic risk and unsystematic risk. Diversification will eliminate most or all of the unsystematic risk in a portfolio, but not the systematic risk. Although an investor could adjust the beta of the portfolio in anticipation of a market rise or fall, this is not an ideal solution because of the changes in portfolio composition that might be required.

Investors can use financial futures on stock market indices to hedge against an overall market decline; that is, investors can hedge against systematic or market risk. By selling the appropriate number of contracts against a stock purchase, the investor protects against systematic risk while attempting to earn the unique part of a stock's return. In effect, stock index futures contracts give an investor the opportunity to protect his or her portfolio against market fluctuations.

Short hedges   Since so much common stock is held by investors, the short hedge is the natural type of contract for most investors. A short hedge can be implemented by selling a forward maturity of the contract. The purpose of this hedge is to offset (in total or in part) any losses on the stock portfolio with gains on the futures position; these losses may be realized or unrealized. To implement this defensive strategy, an investor would sell one or more index futures contracts. Ideally, the value of these contracts would equal the value of the stock portfolio.

Table 17–5 (top) illustrates the concept of a short hedge using the Standard & Poor's Index when it was at 173. Assume that an investor had a portfolio of stocks valued at $90,000 that he or she would like to protect against an anticipated market decline. By selling one S&P stock index future at 173, the investor has a short position of $86,500 because the value of the contract is $500 times the index quote. As the table illustrates, a decline in

---

[18]The final settlement price is set equal to the closing index on the maturity date.

TABLE 17–5 Examples of Short and Long Hedges Using Stock Index Futures

	Current Position	Pos. Following a 10% Market Drop	Change in Pos.
Short Hedge			
(Long position) dollar value of portfolio	$90,000	$81,000	$(9000)
(Short position) sell one S&P 500 futures[a] contract at 173	86,500	77,850	8650
Gain or loss from hedging			(350)

	Current Position	Position or Cost Following a 10% Market Rise	Change in Position or Cost of Position
Long Hedge			
Buy one S&P 500 futures contract at 173	$86,500	$95,150	$8650
Amount of money to be invested in stocks (cost of stock position)	75,000	82,500	(7500)
Gain or loss from hedging			1150

[a] Value of the futures contract is $500 × index.

the stock market of 10% results in a loss on the stock portfolio of $9000 and a gain on the futures position of $8650 (ignoring commissions). Thus, the investor almost makes up on the short side what is lost on the long side.

Long hedges The long hedger generally wishes to reduce the risk, while awaiting funds to invest, of having to pay more for an equity position when prices rise. Potential users of a long hedge include the following:

1. Institutions with a regular cash flow who use long hedges to improve the timing of their positions.
2. Institutions switching large positions who wish to hedge during the time it takes to complete the process. (This could also be a short hedge.)

Assume an investor with $75,000 to invest believes that the stock market will advance, but has been unable to select the stocks he or she wishes to hold. By purchasing one S&P 500 index future, the investor will gain if the market advances. As shown in Table 17–5, a 10% market advance will increase the value of the futures contract $8650. Even if the investor has to pay 10% more (on average) for stocks purchased after the advance, he or she still gains because the net hedge result is positive.

The importance of basis As with interest rate futures, basis is present with stock index futures. It represents the difference between the price of the stock index futures contract and the value of the underlying stock index. A daily examination of the "Futures Prices" page of *The Wall Street Journal* will show that each of the indices quoted under the respective futures contracts differs from the closing price of the contracts.

Futures prices are generally more volatile than the underlying indices and therefore diverge from them.[19] The index futures tend to lead the actual market indices. If investors are bullish, the futures are priced at a premium with greater maturities usually associated with greater premiums. If investors are bearish, the futures are normally priced at a discount, which may widen as maturity increases.

Excessively large discounts or premiums may signal a change in market direction. If the premium is unusually wide, it may signal a market decline. Speculators who follow such indicators would wish to go short. Conversely, an excessively wide discount could signal a market rally, suggesting to speculators that it is time to buy stock index futures.

Speculating with Stock Index Futures

In addition to the previous hedging strategies (and others not described), investors can speculate with stock index futures if they wish to profit from stock market volatility by judging and acting on the likely market trends.

We can refer to one group of speculators as "active traders." These individuals are willing to risk their capital on price changes they expect to occur in the futures contracts. Such individuals are often sophisticated investors who are seeking the opportunity for large gains and who understand the risk that they are assuming.

Strategies of active traders basically include long and short positions. Traders who expect the market to rise buy index futures. Because of the high leverage, the profit opportunities are great; however, the loss opportunities are equally as great. The same is true for traders expecting a market decline, who assume a short position by selling a stock index futures contract. Selling a contract is a convenient way to go short the entire market. It can be done anytime (no wait for an uptick as with stock short sales).

Another form of speculation involves *spreaders,* who establish both long and short positions at the same time. Their objective is to profit from changes in price relationships between two futures contracts. These would include the following:

1. The *intramarket spread,* also known as a calendar or time spread. This spread involves contracts for two different settlement months, such as buying a March contract and selling a June contract.
2. The *intermarket spread,* also known as a quality spread. This spread involves two different markets, such as buying a NYSE contract and selling a *Value Line* contract (both for the same month).

---

[19]This discussion is based on *The Merrill Lynch Guide to Stock Index Futures* (Merrill Lynch, Pierce, Fenner & Smith, 1983), p. 14.

Spreaders are interested in relative price as opposed to absolute price changes. If two different contracts appear to be out of line, the spreader hopes to profit by buying one contract and selling the other and waiting for the price difference to adjust. This adjustment may require the spread between the two contracts to widen in some cases and narrow in others.

Program Trading

A force of considerable magnitude has hit Wall Street. It is called **program trading** and it has captured much attention and generated considerable controversy. It leads to headlines attributing market plunges at least in part to program trading, as happened on September 12, 1986, when the Dow Jones Industrial Average fell almost 87 points.

Program trading involves the use of computer-generated orders to buy and sell securities based on arbitrage opportunities. The arbitrage occurs between common stocks on the one hand, and index futures and options on the other. Large institutional investors seek to exploit differences between the two sides. Specifically, when stock index futures prices rise substantially above the current value of the stock index itself (for example, the S&P 500), they sell the futures and buy the underlying stocks, typically in "baskets" of several million dollars. Because the futures price and the stock index value must be equal when the futures contract expires, these investors are seeking to "capture the premium" between the two, thereby earning an arbitrage profit. That is, they seek high risk-free returns by arbitraging the difference between the cash value of the underlying securities and the prices of the futures contracts on these securities. In effect, they have a hedged position and should profit regardless of what happens to stock prices. See Box 17–1 for a simple discussion of program trading.

BOX 17–1 OPPORTUNITY, THY NAME IS DISCREPANCY, OR, PROGRAM TRADING

It's 3:30 on the afternoon of Mar. 11, and the volume on the New York Stock Exchange is riding along at 166.1 million. Suddenly—frenzy. A billion-dollar trading binge convulses the stock market. Torrents of buy and sell orders rush in. And when the market closes, the Dow has jumped 43 points and volume has topped 187 million. Program trading has struck again.

What gives? Stanford professor of finance William Sharpe gives the following—very stripped down—explanation.

Imagine that three stocks form the S&P's 500, or the cash market. One trades every hour, and the other two trade every day or so. And then let's say that near the close of the day some information comes in indicating that the economy is set to fly.

This probably means all three stocks will look more valuable to investors. The more liquid stock trades immediately, and its price goes up to reflect the news. The prices of the two more illiquid stocks, however, stay the same. Thus, the S&P's goes up only slightly—less than the good news would seem to justify.

Meanwhile, traders are busy trading the S&P's Index futures, where transaction costs are cheaper than in the cash market. They are buying based on the expectation that the prices of the underlying stocks will shortly rise. This, of course, bids up the price of the futures.

Specifically, suppose our theoretical S&P's 500 was 100 before the good news. And let's say that after the news its value would be 108. But, because there are two illiquid stocks that haven't been bid up, the S&P's climbs only to 104. Busy buying in the futures, on the other hand, sends that index up to 110. Discrepancy! The index sells a good deal higher than the value of its component stocks. Program traders thrive on discrepancies.

The computer spots this discrepancy and figures that it can buy the actual stocks cheap. Thus, the discrepancy triggers trading programs to short the futures and buy the stock simultaneously.

When the program is activated, attempts to buy the stocks at the old prices drive the prices higher in the cash market, while selling in the futures market causes those prices to droop. Theoretically, at least, the buying and selling of stocks and futures will cause the two markets to reach equilibrium. Thus has program trading made the market more efficient.

In a given week program trading accounts for perhaps 20% of the turnover in stocks. But it is really the triple witching days—which occur four times a year, toward the end of the quarter, when ordinary stock options, S&P's Index futures and S&P's Index options expire at the same time—that unsettle investors. On these days computer-driven sell programs can roil the markets, causing big swings and tremendous volume. But Hans Stoll, a Vanderbilt University professor of finance, recently conducted a study for the exchanges that found that the triple witching hour has no more effect on a particular stock than a large block trade, which could occur at any time.

If you are the queasy type, best thing is to stay away from the markets at triple witching time. Otherwise, relax. The whole process is making investing better, not worse.

Source: Kerry Hannon, "Opportunity, Thy Name Is Discrepancy," *Forbes*, September 22, 1986, p. 156. Reprinted by permission of *Forbes* magazine, September 22, 1986. © Forbes Inc., 1986.

Normally, program traders and other speculators "unwind" their positions during the last trading hour of the day the futures expire. The so-called *triple witching hour* occurs when options, stock option indices, and futures contracts all expire at the same time. At this time, the futures premium goes to zero because, as noted, the futures price at expiration must equal the stock index value.

The headlines about program trading often reflect the results of rapid selling by the program traders. For whatever reason, traders decide to sell the futures. As the price falls, stock prices fall also. When the futures price drops below the price of the stock index, tremendous selling orders can be unleashed. These volume sell orders in stocks drive the futures prices even lower.

Futures Options

In Chapter 15 we discussed options (puts and calls) on common stocks. In this chapter we have discussed two types of futures contracts, interest rate futures and stock index futures. The latest innovation in financial instruments is a combination of the two, **futures options.** The development of this new instrument is a good example of the ever-changing financial markets in the United States, where new instruments are developed to provide investors with opportunities that did not previously exist.

Options, both puts and calls, are offered on both interest rate futures and stock index futures. Specifically, the following financial futures options were available in mid-1987:[20]

OPTIONS ON FOREIGN EXCHANGE FUTURES:	Pound, mark, franc, yen, Canadian dollar, sterling, and Eurodollars.
OPTIONS ON INTEREST RATE FUTURES:	Treasury bills, notes, bonds, and a municipal bond index.
OPTIONS ON STOCK INDEX FUTURES:	The S&P 500 Index (traded on the Chicago Mercantile Exchange) and the NYSE Composite Index (traded on the New York Futures Exchange).

Recall from Chapter 15 that an option provides the purchaser with the right, but not the *obligation,* to exercise the claim provided by the contract. An option on a futures contract gives its owner the right to assume a long or short position in the respective futures contract. If this right is exercised, the holder's position will be at the exercise (strike) price of the option that was purchased. For example, the exerciser of a call option buys the futures contract at the exercise price stated in the call option.

The key elements of an option contract on a particular futures contract are the exercise price and the premium. As in the case of stock options, premiums are determined in competitive markets. Each put and call option is either in the money or out of the money. With an in-the-money call option, the exercise price is less than the current price of the underlying futures contract (if the exercise price is greater than the current price, it is out of the money). For put options, the reverse is true.

Figure 17–1 shows the relationships between premiums on put and call futures options. The exercise (strike) price is on the horizontal axis. As the strike price rises above the current futures price, the premiums on calls

---

[20] Futures options are also available for several agricultural commodities, for copper, gold, and silver, for heating oil, crude oil and lumber, and for a U.S. dollar index.

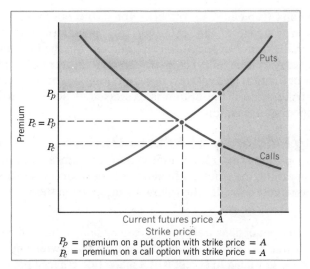

Current futures price A
Strike price
P_p = premium on a put option with strike price = A
P_c = premium on a call option with strike price = A

FIGURE 17–1 Relationship between premiums on put and call options on futures contracts.
Source: Michael T. Belongia and Thomas H. Gregory, "Are Options on Treasury Bond Futures Priced Efficiently?" *Review,* Federal Reserve Bank of St. Louis, January 1984, p. 8.

decline while the premiums on puts rise; if the strike price was below the current futures price, the reverse would be true.

Options on futures contracts can serve some of the same purposes as the futures contracts themselves. Specifically, both futures contracts and options can be used to transfer the risk of adverse price movements from hedgers to speculators. For example, a portfolio manager with bond holdings (a long position) who expects a rise in interest rates can hedge against the risk of the capital losses resulting from such a rise by selling futures contracts on Treasury bonds; alternatively, futures options on Treasury bonds could be used to hedge against this risk because the option's price will change in response to a change in the price of the underlying commodity.

A rise in interest rates is bearish (bond prices will fall); therefore, the portfolio manager would either buy a put or sell a call. The value of these options would rise as the price of the futures contract declined. On the other hand, an investor bullish on bond prices (i.e., one who expects interest rates to decline) would either buy a call or sell a put. In addition to these simple strategies, a number of spreading techniques can be used with options on Treasury bond futures.

The general appeal of options on futures contracts is the limited liability assumed by the purchaser. The purchaser, once the contract is bought, has no additional obligation as with a futures contract, which has to be settled by some means (typically, by offset). Nor is the purchaser subject to margin calls as in the case of futures. Even if a speculator in futures is ultimately correct in his or her expectations, margin calls in the interim can wipe out all the equity. A writer (seller) of an option on a futures contract, however, does have an obligation to assume a position (long or short) in the futures market at the strike price if the option is exercised.[21] Sellers must deposit margin when opening a position.

Pricing Efficiency of Futures Options

Futures options are a recent innovation; therefore, little evidence is available concerning the pricing efficiency of these options. This is an important issue, however; consider the following quote from the Federal Reserve Bank of St. Louis *Review*:

> In an efficient options market for Treasury bond futures, the risk of unexpected interest rate movements can be shifted from those with a high aversion to such risk to those willing to accept it at a market-determined premium. An inefficient market would price this risk incorrectly, producing "abnormal" returns to either purchasers or sellers of these options.[22]

A January 1984 article in the *Review* examined the pricing of options on Treasury bond futures. Based on data for October 1982 through April 1983, the authors concluded that "Treasury bond option prices are 'efficient' in the fundamental economic sense."[23] They were unable to find consistent arbitragable profit opportunities.

Summary

This chapter has discussed futures contracts—specifically, financial futures. A futures contract designates a specific amount of a particular item to be delivered at a specified date in the future and a currently determined market price. Futures contracts are negotiable, marketable instruments that represent legal contracts but not securities regulated by the SEC.

Buyers assume long positions and sellers assume short positions, which indicate only that a contract not previously purchased is sold. Most contracts are settled by offset, whereby a position is liquidated by an offsetting transaction. Margin, the norm in futures trading, is the "good faith" deposit made to ensure completion of the contract. Both initial margin and mainte-

---

[21] This discussion is based on Stanley W. Angrist, "It's Your Option," *Forbes,* February 28, 1983, p. 138.

[22] See "In This Issue . . . ," *Review,* Federal Reserve Bank of St. Louis, January 1984, p. 3.

[23] See Michael Belongia and Thomas Gregory, "Are Options on Treasury Bond Futures Priced Efficiently?" *Review,* Federal Reserve Bank of St. Louis, January 1984, pp. 5–13.

nance margin are involved. Deficiencies in margin result in margin calls. All futures contracts are marked to the market daily, meaning that all profits and losses are credited and debited to each investor's account daily.

Contracts are traded on designated futures exchanges, which set minimum price changes and may establish daily price limits. Positions must be closed out within a specified time. There are no certificates and no specialists to handle the trading.

Hedgers buy or sell futures contracts to offset the risk in some other position. Speculators buy or sell futures contracts in an attempt to earn a return and are valuable to the proper functioning of the market. The futures market performs a useful economic function in that it allows hedgers to shift risks to speculators.

Interest rate futures, one of the two principal types of financial futures, allow investors to hedge against, and speculate on, interest rate movements. Contracts are available on all Treasury securities as well as some instruments such as GNMAs.

Investors can, among other transactions, execute short hedges to protect bond positions and long hedges to lock in prevailing long-term bond yields. Speculators can use interest rate futures to speculate on likely movements in interest rates.

Stock index futures are available on the NYSE Composite Index, the S&P 500 Index, and the *Value Line* Index. Investors can use these contracts to hedge the systematic risk of common stocks, that is, broad market movements. Short hedges protect a stock position against a market decline, and long hedges protect against having to pay more for an equity position because prices rise before the investment can be made. Speculators seek to exploit their predictions of market movements. Spreaders establish both long and short positions at the same time in an attempt to profit from changes in price relationships between two futures contracts.

A new innovation is futures options, which give investors the right, but not the obligation, to exercise the claim provided by the contract. Their appeal is the leverage offered by futures combined with the limited liability assumed by the purchaser, who has no obligation and does not face margin calls. Puts and calls are available on both interest rate futures (Treasury bonds) and stock index futures (S&P 500 Index and the NYSE Composite Index).

Key Words

Basis	Interest rate futures
Financial futures	Marked to the market
Futures contract	Program trading
Futures options	Stock index futures

QUESTIONS AND PROBLEMS

1. Carefully describe a futures contract.
2. Explain how futures contracts are valued daily and how most contracts are settled.
3. Describe the role of the clearinghouses in futures trading.
4. What determines if an investor receives a margin call?
5. Describe the differences between trading in stocks and trading in futures contracts.
6. How do financial futures differ from other futures contracts?
7. Explain the differences between a hedger and a speculator.
8. What is meant by basis? When is the basis positive?
9. Given a futures contract on Treasury bonds, determine the dollar price of a contract quoted at 80–5, 90–24, and 69–2.
10. When might a portfolio manager with a bond position use a short hedge involving interest rate futures?
11. Is it possible to construct a perfect hedge? Why or why not?
12. What is the difference between a short hedge and a weighted short hedge using interest rate futures?
13. Why would an investor have preferences among the different stock index futures?
14. Which type of risk does stock index futures allow investors to hedge? Why would this be desirable?
15. Explain how a pension fund might use a long hedge with stock index futures.
16. When would an investor likely do the following?
    a. Buy a call on a stock index.
    b. Buy a put on an interest rate futures.
17. Specifically, how would expectations affect futures prices?
18. Assume that an investor buys one March NYSE Composite Index Futures contract on February 1 at 67.5. The position is closed out after five days. The prices on the four days after purchase were: 67.8, 68.1, 68, and 68.5. The initial margin is $3500.
    a. Calculate the current equity on each of the next four days.
    b. Calculate the excess equity for these four days.
    c. Calculate the final gain or loss for the week.
    d. Recalculate a, b, and c assuming that the investor had been short over this same period.
19. Given the information in Problem 18, assume that the investor holds until the contract expires. Ignore the four days after purchase and assume that on the next to last day of trading in March that the investor was long and the final settlement price on that date was 70.5. Calculate the cumulative profit.

20. With regard to futures options, fill in the following blanks with either "less than" or "greater than." The current futures price is 75.
    a. Put options with strike prices _____ 75 are in the money.
    b. Call options with strike prices _____ 75 are out of the money.
    c. Put options with strike prices _____ 75 are out of the money.
    d. Call options with strike prices _____ 75 are in the money.
21. Calculate the dollar gain or loss on Treasury bond futures contracts ($100,000) per contract for the following transactions. In each case the position is held six months before closing it out.
    a. Sell 10 T-bond contracts at a price of 82–80 and buy 10 at 76–12.
    b. Sell 10 T-bond contracts at a price of 80–14 and buy 10 at 77.
    c. Buy 15 T-bond contracts at 62–10 and sell 15 at 64–24.
    d. Sell one T-bond contract at 70–14 and buy one at 78–08.
22. Assume a portfolio manager holds $1 million of 8½% Treasury bonds due 1994–99. The current market price is 76–2 for a yield of 11.95%. The manager fears a rise in interest rates in the next three months and wishes to protect this position against such a rise by hedging in futures.
    a. Ignoring weighted hedges, what should the manager do?
    b. Assume T-bond futures contracts are available at 68, and the price three months later is 59–12. If the manager constructs the correct hedge, what is the gain or loss on this position?
    c. The price of the Treasury bonds three months later is 67–8. What is the gain or loss on this cash position?
    d. What is the net effect of this hedge?

Selected References

Asap, Michael R. "A Note on the Design of Commodity Option Contracts." *The Journal of Futures Markets,* Spring 1982, pp. 1–7.

Belongia, Michael T. and Gregory, Thomas H. "Are Options on Treasury Bond Futures Priced Efficiently?" *Review,* Federal Reserve Bank of St. Louis, January 1984, pp. 5–13.

Chicago Board of Trade, *U.S. Treasury Bond Futures.*

Figlewski, Stephen. *Hedging with Financial Futures for Institutional Investors: From Theory to Practice.* Cambridge, Massachusetts: Ballinger Publishing Company, 1986.

Gastineau, Gary L. "Futures and Options on Fixed Income Securities: Their Role in Fixed Income Portfolio Management." In Frank J. Fabozzi and Irving M. Pollack, eds. *The Handbook of Fixed Income Securities,* Homewood, Ill.: Dow Jones-Irwin, 1983, pp. 857–872.

Howard, Charles T. and D'Antonio, Louis J. "Treasury Bill Futures as a Hedging Tool: A Risk–Return Approach." *The Journal of Financial Research,* Spring 1986, pp. 25–39.

Kolb, Robert W. *Understanding Futures Markets*. Glenview, Illinois: Scott, Foresman and Company, 1985.

Loosigan, Allan M. "Financial Futures: Hedging Interest-Rate Risk." In Frank J. Fabozzi and Irving M. Pollack, eds. *The Handbook of Fixed Income Securities*. Homewood, Ill.: Dow Jones-Irwin, 1983, pp. 831–856.

Merrill Lynch, Pierce, Fenner & Smith. *The Merrill Lynch Guide to Stock Index Futures*. Merrill Lynch Futures, Inc., 1983.

Merrill Lynch, Pierce, Fenner & Smith. *The Merrill Lynch Guide to Hedging*. New York: Merrill Lynch Futures, Inc., 1978.

Moriarty, Eugene, Phillips, Susan, and Tosini, Paul. "A Comparison of Options and Futures in the Management of Portfolio Risk." *Financial Analysts Journal*, January–February 1981, pp. 61–67.

N.Y. Futures Exchange. *Introducing New York Stock Exchange Index Futures*. New York: New York Futures Exchange, 1982.

Niederhoffer, Victor and Zeckhauser, Richard. "Market Index Futures Contracts." *Financial Analysts Journal*, January–February 1980, pp. 49–55.

Niederhoffer, Victor and Zeckhauser, Richard. "The Performance of Market Index Futures Contracts." *Financial Analysts Journal*, January–February 1983, pp. 59–65.

Peters, Ed. "Index Futures and Index Funds: The New Investment Marriage." *Pension World*, April 1986, pp. 23–25.

Schwarz, Edward W., Hill, Joanne M., and Schneeweis, Thomas. *Financial Futures: Fundamentals, Strategies, and Applications*, Richard D. Irwin, 1986.

Smith, Courtney. *How to Make Money in Stock Index Futures*. New York: McGraw-Hill, 1985.

Trainer, Francis H., Jr. "The Uses of Treasury Bond Futures in Fixed-Income Portfolio Management." *Financial Analysts Journal*, January–February 1983, pp. 27–34.

Wolf, Avner. "Fundamentals of Commodity Options on Futures." *Journal of Futures Markets*, Winter 1982, pp. 391–408.

CHAPTER 18

INVESTMENT COMPANIES

In Chapter 2 we pointed out that an important alternative to investing directly in securities, indirect investing, is accomplished by the purchase of shares in investment companies, which offers investors a wide range of return–risk opportunities. Investors may be able to accomplish their objectives as well through indirect investing as through direct investing (i.e., doing it themselves); therefore, a thorough understanding of investment companies is essential for making intelligent decisions about investment programs.

Investment companies have suddenly become an extremely popular alternative with investors. The explosion in the number of funds available and the growth of their total assets is unprecedented. Consider the following figures:[1]

1. The total assets of all mutual funds (including money-market funds) in 1976 amounted to $51 billion. In 1986, the total assets of one mutual fund company, Fidelity Investments, was approximately $66 billion.
2. Mutual fund sales (excluding money-market funds) totaled $4 billion in 1976, $10 billion in 1980, and $40 billion in 1983. Following sales of $46

---

[1] Detailed figures on investment companies can be found in the *Mutual Fund Fact Book,* Investment Company Institute, 1775 K Street, Washington, D.C. 20036.

billion in 1984, sales more than doubled to $114 billion in 1985 and almost doubled again in 1986, reaching $216 billion.

3. There were 452 mutual funds of all types in existence at the end of 1976. By the end of 1986, the number approached 1850.

Some Basic Facts

In this section we will discuss the basic definition and nature of investment companies and outline the types of investment companies.

What Is an Investment Company?

A managed **investment company** can be defined as a financial service organization that sells shares in itself to the public and uses these funds to invest in a portfolio of securities such as money market instruments, stocks, and bonds.[2] Assume, for example, that an investment company called the Health Fund is formed to invest in the common stocks of health-related firms that are expected to benefit from the tremendous amount of money spent by Americans on health care. Health Fund might sell 20 million shares to the public for $10 a share, raising $200 million. Once the fund is started, it will invest in the common stocks of various companies in the health field industry, such as Pfizer Drugs, Abbott Labs, and Syntex. Health Fund now owns a portfolio of stocks, and, in turn, is owned by investors who purchased shares in it. These investors, if so disposed and financially able, could have constructed a similar portfolio directly by purchasing the same stocks bought by the Health Fund. By purchasing Health Fund, they own a percentage of its portfolio, and, in effect, they are stockholders in the companies owned by Health Fund. An investment company, therefore, is a **pure intermediary;** it performs a *basic* service—buying and selling securities—for its shareholders that they could perform for themselves.[3]

Investment companies are corporations usually formed by an investment adviser or manager who selects the board of trustees. The trustees, in turn, hire a separate management company to manage the fund. The management company is contracted by the investment company to perform necessary research and to manage the portfolio, as well as handle the administrative

---

[2] An alternative form of investment company is the Unit Investment Trust, an *unmanaged, fixed-income* security portfolio put together by a sponsor and handled by an independent trustee. Redeemable trust certificates representing claims against the assets of the trust are sold to investors at net asset value plus a small commission. All interest (or dividends) and principal repayments are distributed to the holders of the certificates.

The sponsor makes a secondary market in these certificates for those who wish to sell. The assets underlying a unit investment trust are almost always kept unchanged. In the case of fixed-income securities, the trust ceases to exist when the bonds mature.

[3] Note, however, that investment companies provide a variety of services for their shareholders, at least some of which cannot be performed as easily or conveniently by many investors.

chores, for which it receives a fee. For example, Fidelity Investments is a mutual fund company offering dozens of different funds to the public. FMR is a corporation that acts as investment adviser to the "Fidelity family of funds" as well as certain other funds that are generally offered to limited groups of investors. The stock of FMR is wholly owned by a holding company, FMR Corporation, which, in effect, is the Fidelity company.

Some funds use a sales force to reach investors, with shares available from brokers, insurance agents, and financial planners. An alternative form of distribution is direct selling, whereby the company uses advertising and direct mailing to appeal to investors. In 1986, 74 percent of all stock, bond, and income fund sales were made by those funds using a sales force.[4]

There are economies of scale in managing portfolios. Expenses rise as assets under management increase, but not at the same rate as revenues. Because investment managers can oversee various amounts of money with little additional costs, management companies seek to increase the size of the fund(s) being managed. Many operate several different funds simultaneously.

Investment companies are required by The Investment Company Act of 1940 to register with the SEC.[5] This act, which is a detailed regulatory statute, contains numerous provisions designed to protect shareholders.[6] Most states also regulate investment companies.

An important factor affecting investment company organization is the Internal Revenue Service classification of a *regulated* investment company. If a company meets the prescribed conditions and is so classified, it can elect to pay no federal taxes on any distributions of dividends, interest, and realized capital gains to its shareholders. The investment company acts as a *conduit*, "flowing through" these distributions to stockholders who pay their own marginal tax rates on them; in effect, fund shareholders are treated as if they held the securities in the fund's portfolio. After all, investment companies are pure intermediaries, and thus shareholders should pay the same taxes they would pay if they owned the shares directly. Meeting these conditions results in the following:[7]

---

[4] Equity funds had equal sales from direct marketing and sales forces. The majority of bond and income fund sales were made by sales forces.

[5] The 1940 act was amended in 1970. These amendments, among other things, prohibited the charging of excessive commissions to share purchasers and the payment of excessive fees to investment company advisers.

[6] Investment companies are also regulated under the Securities Acts of 1933, The Securities Exchange Act of 1934, and The Investment Advisors Act of 1940.

[7] To qualify as a regulated investment company, a fund must earn at least 90% of all income from security transactions and distribute at least 90% of all *interest and dividend income*. Furthermore, the fund must diversify its assets. For at least 50% of the portfolio, no more than 5% of the fund's assets can be invested in the securities of any one issuer, and a position in any one security cannot exceed 25% of the total market value of that security.

1. Dividends and interest are taxable to a fund only if retained; therefore, after operating costs are deducted, all such income is usually paid out.
2. Realized capital gains are taxable to a fund only if retained; if distributed to shareholders, they are taxable to them.

The Structure of Investment Companies

All investment companies begin by selling shares in themselves to the public. Some companies, however, continue to sell and redeem shares on an ongoing basis and others do not; in addition, some companies charge a sales fee and others do not. These two important distinctions are discussed in the following sections.

Open-end investment companies **Mutual funds,** which technically are **open-end investment companies,** continue to sell shares to investors after the initial sale that starts the fund. Owners of fund shares can sell them back to the company (redeem them) anytime they choose; the mutual fund is legally obligated to redeem them. Thus, the capitalization of an open-end investment company is continually changing as new investors buy additional shares and some existing shareholders cash in by selling their shares back to the company. Mutual funds are the dominant form of investment company.

Investors purchase new shares, and redeem their existing shares, at the **net asset value (NAV),** which is the value of a single share in the fund. The NAV of a fund is computed by calculating the total market value of the securities in the portfolio, subtracting any trade payables, and dividing by the number of mutual fund shares currently outstanding.[8] For example, if the total market value of the securities held by the previously mentioned Health Fund is $300 million on a day when 25 million shares of Health Fund are owned by shareholders, the NAV is $300/25 = $12 per share. The NAV is calculated daily, and new purchases and sales are made at the most recently calculated NAV.

Closed-end investment companies Unlike the mutual funds, **closed-end investment companies** usually sell no additional shares of their own stock after the initial public offering. Therefore, their capitalizations are fixed unless a new public offering is made. The shares of a closed-end fund trade in the secondary markets (e.g., on the exchanges) exactly like any other stock. To buy and sell, investors use their brokers, paying (receiving) the current price at which the shares are selling plus (less) brokerage commissions.[9]

---

[8]Total market value of the portfolio is equal to the product of each security's current market price multiplied by the number of shares of that security owned by the fund.

[9]A special type of closed-end fund is the dual-purpose fund. It differs from other investment companies in that it has a limited life, and sells two classes of shares to investors. At its inception, equal dollar amounts of income and capital shares are sold, with the proceeds used to purchase a portfolio of assets as usual. However, the *income shareholders* receive all interest

Because shares of closed-ends funds trade on exchanges, their prices are determined by the forces of supply and demand. Interestingly, however, the market price is seldom equal to the NAV of the closed-ends shares, which is calculated exactly as for the mutual funds. Historically, the market prices of closed-ends have ranged from roughly 5% to 20% below their NAVs. In this situation, the closed-end is said to be selling at a **discount**; if the market price exceeds the NAV, as it sometimes does for some closed-end funds, the fund is said to be selling at a **premium**. Although several studies have addressed the question of why these funds sell at discounts and premiums, no totally satisfactory explanation has been widely accepted by all market observers.[10]

As an illustration of the discount phenomenon, consider the following data for Super Fund, a hypothetical closed-end investment company.

	19X1	19X2	19X3	19X4	19X5
NAV	$16.24	11.33	12.85	13.76	12.00
Closing price	$12.38	9.50	9.88	11.25	10.62
Dividends	0.23	0.15	0.15	0.15	0.14
Cap. gains dis.	1.04	1.38	1.17	0.92	1.21
% Discount (rounded)	24	16	23	18	12

As we can see, the percentage discount from NAV for the five-year period ranged from 16 to 24%, with an average of 19%.[11]

By purchasing a fund at a discount, an investor is actually buying shares in a portfolio of securities at a price below their market value. Therefore, even if the value of the portfolio remains unchanged, an investor can gain or lose if the discount narrows or widens over time; that is, a difference exists between the portfolio's return and the shareholder's return. To see this, assume that an investor purchased shares in the Super Fund at year-end 19X2 and sold at year-end 19X3. Based on NAV, the portfolio return was

$$
\text{Portfolio return} = \frac{\text{Ending NAV} - \text{Beginning NAV} + \text{Dividends} + \text{Capital gains}}{\text{Beginning NAV}}
$$

$$
= \frac{\$12.85 - 11.33 + .15 + 1.17}{\$11.33}
$$

$$
= 25.1\%
$$

and dividends yielded by the assets, and at the termination date of the fund they receive a special redemption value. *Capital shareholders*, on the other hand, are entitled to all assets not received by the income shares; therefore, they receive everything remaining at the termination date. The life of dual-purpose funds ranges from 10 to 20 years. A new fund could be formed at that time, or the capital shares paid off by liquidating all remaining assets.

[10] See, for example, B. Malkiel, "The Valuation of Closed-End Investment Companies," *The Journal of Finance*, June 1977, pp. 847–856.

[11] The percentage discount can be calculated as

Percentage discount from NAV = [(NAV − Closing Price)/NAV] 100

The shareholder's return, however, is the HPY, calculated using closing prices

$$\text{Shareholder's return} = \frac{\$9.88 - 9.50 + .15 + 1.17}{\$9.50}$$

$$= 17.9\%$$

A shareholder would have realized 17.9% during 19X3 on an HPY basis, whereas the portfolio's performance was 25.1%. As we saw, the percentage discount widened in 19X3.

Load and no-load open-end investment companies Open-end investment companies can be subdivided into those that charge a sales fee (**load funds**) and those that do not (**no-load funds**). A load fund charges investors for the costs involved in selling the fund. This sales fee, added to the fund's NAV, has traditionally been a maximum of 8.5%. Thus, on a $1000 purchase, an investor could pay $85 "commission," acquiring only $915 in shares.[12] The load fee percentage usually declines with the size of the purchase. Typically, there is no redemption fee when the shares are redeemed, although in the early 1980s some funds began charging redemption fees in the 1 to 3% range. All of these fees must be stated in the **prospectus,** which is designed to describe a particular fund's objectives, policies, operations, and fees. Investors should carefully read a fund's prospectus before investing.

The load or sales charge goes to the marketing organization selling the shares, which could be the investment company itself, or brokers. The fee is split between the sales person and the company employing that person. The old adage in the investment company business is that "mutual funds shares are sold, not bought," meaning that the sales force aggressively sells the shares to investors.

In contrast to the load funds, no-load mutual funds are bought at net asset value directly from the fund itself. No sales fee is charged because there is no sales force to compensate. Investors must seek out these funds by responding to advertisements in the financial press, and purchase and redeem shares by mail, wire, or telephone.[13] Quite a few funds are said to be "low load" funds, with sales charges of 2–3%. It should be noted that a single investment company—for example, Fidelity Investments—may simultaneously offer both no-load funds and low-load funds.

A question that is often asked is, if the no-load funds charge no sales fee, how is the investment company compensated? The answer is that all funds, open-end and closed-end, load funds and no-load funds, charge the shareholders a **management fee.** This fee is paid out of the fund's income, derived

---

[12] Note that this is an effective charge of 9.3% ($85/$915).

[13] On any given day, the last few pages of *The Wall Street Journal* contain several ads for mutual funds.

TABLE 18–1   Percent Distribution of Total Net Assets by Type of Fund

	1976	1986
Equity Funds	67%* ⟶	21%*
Bond and Income Funds	26	38
Money Market Funds	7	32
Short-term Municipal Bond Funds	—	9
	100%	100%

*All percentages are rounded.

Source: Reprinted by permission of the Investment Company Institute, *1987 Mutual Fund Fact Book*, p. 12.

from the dividends, interest, and capital gains earned during the year. Typical annual management fees begin at 0.5% of the fund's total market value (in other words, 50 cents per year per $100 of assets under management).[14] Some funds reduce the fee as the fund's assets under management increase.

Types of Mutual Funds

There are two major types of mutual funds: money market funds (including short-term municipal bond funds) and equity, bond, and income funds, each of which is discussed later. The percent distribution of total net assets by type of fund has changed dramatically since the mid-1970s, as shown in Table 18–1. Whereas equity funds constituted about 67% of total mutual fund net assets in 1976, by 1986 this percentage had declined to only 21%. Money market funds grew from 7% of assets in 1976 to 32% in 1986, while bond-income funds grew from 26% to 38%. The new category of short-term municipal bond funds did not exist in 1976, but constituted 9% of all assets by 1986.

Money market funds   One of the major innovations in the investment company industry has been the creation, and subsequent phenomenal growth, of the money market funds. These funds were created in 1974, when interest rates were at record high levels; they grew tremendously in 1981–1982 when short-term interest rates were again at record levels. Investors sought to earn these high short-term rates but found that they generally could not do so directly.[15] However, this situation has changed with the deregulation of the thrift institutions, and competition has increased dramatically for investors' short-term savings. Banks can now offer money market deposit accounts (MMDAs), discussed in Chapter 2, that pay money market rates and

---

[14] The management fee for money market funds is less.

[15] Recall that the money market instruments discussed in Chapter 2 have large minimum investments, ranging from $10,000 for Treasury bills to a more typical $100,000 in the case of negotiable certificates of deposit and banker's acceptances.

are insured. Although their average current yield was less than that of the money market funds in 1984 and 1985, MMDAs have attracted record amounts of funds. As a result, while money market assets grew from $2 billion in 1974 to $207 billion by 1982, they totaled only about $240 billion by the end of 1986.

Money market funds are open-end investment companies that operate like a traditional mutual fund except that their portfolios consist of money market instruments such as Treasury bills, negotiable CDs, and prime commercial paper.[16] Some funds hold only bills, while others hold various mixtures. In 1986, commercial paper accounted for over 40% of the total assets held by these funds, with repurchase agreements and Treasury bills a distant second and third respectively. The average maturity of most of those portfolios is less than 40 days.

An alternative form of money market fund is the short-term *municipal bond fund,* also called a *tax-exempt money market fund*. These funds, available since 1979, invest in municipal securities with short maturities.

Investors in money market funds pay neither a sales charge nor a redemption charge, but do pay a management fee. Interest is earned and credited daily. The shares can be redeemed at any time by phone or wire. Many funds offer check-writing privileges for checks of $500 or more, with the investor earning interest until the check clears.[17]

Money market funds provide investors with a chance to earn the going rates in the money market while enjoying broad diversification and high liquidity. Although investors may assume little risk because of the diversification and quality of these instruments, money market funds are not insured. Banks and thrift institutions have emphasized this point in competing with money market funds for the savings of investors.

2) **Equity, bond, and income funds**[18]   The board of directors (trustees) of an investment company *must* specify the objective that the company will pursue in its investment policy. The companies try to follow a consistent investment policy, according to their specified objective.

Equity funds   There are five types of equity funds.

1. *Aggressive growth.*[19] Objective is maximum capital appreciation.
2. *Growth.* Objective is long-term growth of capital.

---

[16] Currently, three types of money market funds exist. General purpose funds are those with a varying mix of clients, both individuals and institutions. Broker–dealer funds, the largest of the three in terms of assets, are managed by brokerage firms and their clients are primarily individuals. Finally, institutional funds are designed exclusively for institutions such as banks and businesses.

[17] Shareholders have made only limited use of the check writing privilege, however, indicating that they regard money market funds primarily as a way to save.

[18] The Investment Company Institute uses this terminology.

[19] Aggressive growth funds may use techniques such as borrowing money to provide leverage, short selling, hedging, options, and warrants.

3. *Growth and income*. Objective is to provide both income and long-term growth.
4. *International.*
5. *Precious metals*.

The first three types of funds, as the names imply, stress common stocks either with greater than average risk (aggressive growth), with less risk (growth), or with equal emphasis on income and appreciation (some bonds may be held). Within the broad category of growth are a wide range of funds based on industry holdings, concepts, themes, or simply broad diversification.

Bond and income funds   Included within this category are the "balanced funds." As the name implies, balanced funds seek to balance the portfolio by not being restricted to one type of security. Stock (both common and preferred) and bonds are held, often in roughly equal proportions.[20] The objective is tilted toward income at the expense of capital appreciation.

With bond and income funds, the emphasis is on high current income and low risk. Investment holdings consist primarily of bonds, but policies vary among funds and investors should check each one individually. For example, some funds hold only high-quality corporates, whereas others hold several differently rated issues.

Bond and income funds include the following:

1. *Income funds*. These funds have a primary objective of high current income as opposed to growth of capital. Income funds invest in both stocks and bonds that pay higher dividends and interest.
2. *Taxable bond funds*. These funds hold only bonds, particularly corporate bonds. Some funds specialize in U.S. government securities and some in GNMAs. The primary objective is income rather than growth.
3. *Municipal bond funds*. Since 1976, investment companies have been able to offer portfolios of municipal bonds. These funds are designed to appeal to taxpayers in higher tax brackets. Some pay interest income monthly. Also included in this category are the single-state municipal bond funds, which limit their portfolios to the issues of only one state.
4. *Option/Income funds*. These relatively new funds, whose objective is high current return, invest in dividend-paying common stocks which have call options available. Return is a combination of dividends, premiums from expired call options, gains from securities sold when the calls are exercised, and regular capital gains.

Obtaining Information on Investment Companies

Because of their popularity and prominence in the investments world, and the fact that they are heavily regulated under the Investment Company Act

---

[20]Investors should check the statements (prospectus) issued by the fund to determine the exact ratio the fund is seeking.

of 1940, considerable information is available on investment companies. This information originates with the funds themselves, specialized services devoted to funds, and the popular press. We will discuss each of these information sources in turn.

Investment companies must file a registration statement with the SEC disclosing their investment policies, practices, and so on. In addition, they must make available to stockholders a prospectus that outlines in detail the fund's operations.[21]

Several organizations provide detailed data about investment companies. One of the best known is an annual publication by Wiesenberger Investment Companies Service entitled *Investment Companies,* which contains numerous statistics for over 500 mutual funds, including a history, investment objectives, sales charges, statistical history, and, for many funds, a 10-year performance analysis.[22] An example of this coverage is shown in Figure 18–1 for Affiliated Fund, Inc.

Forbes, a biweekly investment magazine, provides an annual rating of investment company performance. Several hundred funds are rated using the format shown in Figure 18–2. Both risk and return aspects are considered, and performance is related to up and down periods for the overall market. Letter ratings are assigned for both market conditions, ranging from A to D in an up market and A to F in a down market.[23] This gives investors some guidance in choosing a fund. If a market rise is expected, for example, the investor might select a fund that has done extremely well during such periods, regardless of its performance in a declining market. On the other hand, a risk averse investor might prefer a fund that has performed reasonably well in both good and bad markets.

A rapidly expanding source of information and investment advice are the mutual fund newsletters sold by individuals and companies to mutual fund shareholders. Some newsletters specialize in the funds for one company; for example, at least four cover only the funds of Fidelity. By 1986 at least 50 newsletters were being sold.

For daily results, investors usually consult *The Wall Street Journal,* which carries daily quotations on many open-end funds as well as a weekly listing on Monday. *Barron's,* a weekly financial newspaper, carries a comprehensive list of quotations, including yield and capital gains for the previous 12 months. *Barron's* also carries a list of closed-end funds with both the

---

[21] Complete information about operations is supplied to shareholders at least twice a year; most companies supply it four times a year.

[22] The Wiesenberger firm also publishes a quarterly update on the long-run performance of many funds, entitled *Management Results,* and a monthly report on short-run performance (plus dividends), entitled *Current Performance and Dividend Record.*

[23] In up markets, 12.5% of the funds rated by *Forbes* receive a rating of A +; the next 12.5% receive an A; the next 25% receive a B; and the next 25% a C; the bottom 25% receive a D. In down markets, a similar distribution is used with ratings ranging from A to F.

NAV and the current market price (and therefore the discount or premium), including quotes on the dual-purpose funds.

In order to show the types of information available in the financial press as well as illustrate some of the concepts we have discussed earlier in this chapter, consider the information shown in Table 18–2. Although the data are hypothetical, they simulate the actual data that can be observed in the financial press.

Consider first the kind of data to be seen daily in papers such as *The Wall Street Journal*. The top of Table 18–2 shows a small portion of the page on mutual funds, using as an example the family of funds run by an investment advisor operating under the corporate name National Funds Group. This company operates six funds, offering investors a wide choice of objectives. The net asset value of each of the funds is shown, along with the offer price, or the price at which National will sell investors shares of each fund. The difference in these two prices is the load fee, or sales charge. Notice that the high yield fund is a no load fund, and carries the "N.L." designation under the offer price. The NAV Change shows the change in the closing NAV from the previous day. There was no change in the NAV of the high yield fund from the previous day.

In the second half of the table, we see how our hypothetical funds performed for the week, as reported in *Barron's*. The 52-week high and low NAVs are shown, as well as the week's closing NAV. Dividend payments, including both income and capital gains, are for the latest 12 months.

Based on Table 18–2, the following observations can be made as a "typical" case. As we would expect, the aggressive frontiers fund, seeking maximum capital gains, has shown the widest fluctuation in NAV in the last 52 weeks. This fund holds volatile securities that rise and fall more than corresponding market movements. This fund and the other common stock fund (growth), along with the balanced fund, have paid shareholders both income and capital gains in the last 52 weeks. The growth fund has paid more in capital gains, whereas the balanced fund has paid more in income. The high-yield fund (a junk-bond fund), with the highest income payout, has paid only interest income, whereas the income fund, with the next highest payout, has paid both interest and dividends. The tax-free fund has paid a smaller amount of income, but is exempt from federal taxation.

Analyzing Mutual Funds

As noted, investors have a basic choice. They can design a portfolio of securities by doing their own analysis—with or without the aid of other parties such as brokers. Alternatively, they can simply invest in shares of an investment company, which will invest the funds on their behalf in an existing portfolio. This decision is an important one that confronts all investors, and should be considered carefully.

AFFILIATED FUND, INC.

Affiliated Fund was formed in 1934 as a diversified common stock open-end investment company. Its investments are supervised by Lord, Abbett & Co., which performs similar services for six other funds bearing the Lord Abbett name. Affiliated Fund's investment objective is long-term growth of capital and income, without excessive fluctuations in market value.

The portfolio usually consists principally of common stocks believed to be selling at the most reasonable prices in relation to value. Investments are in "large, seasoned companies that are expected to show above-average growth and that are in sound financial condition."

At the end of calendar 1985, the fund had 87% of its assets in common stocks, of which half was in five industry groups: electric light & power (15.4% of assets), electrical equipment & electronics (7.9%), communications (7.6%), automotive (7.5%) and oil & oil services & supplies (6.4%). The five largest individual common stock positions were General Motors (4.9% of assets), Eastman Kodak (3.4%), GTE (3.3%), Minnesota Mining (3.1%) and Southern Co. (2.7%). The rate of portfolio turnover in the latest fiscal year was 49.3% of average assets. Unrealized appreciation in the portfolio at the calendar year-end was 20.2% of total net assets.

Special Services: An open account arrangement serves for accumulation and for automatic dividend reinvestment. Income dividends are invested at the offering price. Regular investments of $50 or more may be made automatically through pre-authorized checks drawn against the investor's checking account. The withdrawal plan is available to accounts worth $10,000 or more at the current offering price. Monthly or quarterly payments may be either a specified amount or at an annual rate. Shareholders who have held 75% of their shares for 30 days or longer may exchange them at net asset value and without charge for those of other funds in the Lord Abbett group. A one-time privilege is available to redeeming shareholders who may reinvest redemption proceeds without charge in any of the Lord Abbett group funds within 30 days of redemption. Prototype corporate profit-sharing plans, Keogh Plans, 403(b) and 401(k) tax-sheltered plans, Individual Retirement Accounts (including payroll-deduction IRAs), and Simplified Employee Pension programs are available.

STATISTICAL HISTORY

	AT YEAR-ENDS								ANNUAL DATA				
			Net Asset				% of Assets in			Income	Capital Gains	Expense	Offering Price ($)	
	Total Net Assets	Number of Share-	Value Per Share	Offer-ing Price	Yield	Cash & Equiv-	Bonds & Pre-	Com-mon	Div-idends	Distribu-	Ratio		
Year	($)	holders	($)	($)	(%)	alent	ferreds	Stocks	($)	tion ($)	(%)	High	Low
1985	2,529,281,086	165,107	9.91	10.68	4.9	7	6	87	0.56	0.81	0.32	11.06	9.50
1984	2,095,833,599	155,799	8.98	9.68	5.2	3	5*	92	0.53	0.48	0.32	10.42	8.83
1983	2,061,615,155	152,121	9.41	10.15	4.7	4	5	91	0.52	0.82	0.33	11.26	9.13
1982	1,784,211,202	149,619	8.59	9.26	5.8	3	—	97	0.56	0.33**	0.36	9.48	7.28
1981	1,580,559,665	148,596	7.75	8.36	6.3	4	—	96	0.56	0.49	0.34	9.98	8.17
1980	1,719,544,589	150,677	8.78	9.47	5.0	8	—	92	0.51	0.71	0.38	10.37	7.77
1979	1,539,977,140	157,466	8.05	7.52	5.0	3	1*	96	0.45	0.44	0.41	9.37	7.57
1978	1,361,289,473	168,599	6.97	7.99	4.5	5	3*	92	0.39	0.31	0.42	8.86	7.22
1977	1,475,675,379	177,308	7.41	9.15	3.6	5	5*	90	0.37	0.15	0.41	9.13	7.76
1976	1,715,134,735	191,128	8.49	7.29	3.5	7	6*	87	0.34	0.22	0.41	9.19	7.35
1975	1,438,206,736	207,525	6.76	5.54	5.7	3	4*	93	0.26	0.12	0.49	7.94	5.68

*Includes a substantial proportion in convertible securities.   **Includes $0.03 short-term capital gains.

Directors: John M. McCarthy, Chmn.; Ronald P. Lynch, Pres.; Thomas F. Creamer; Stewart S. Dixon; Robert S. Driscoll; Paul M. Fye; John C. Jansing; Hansel B. Millican, Jr.; Thomas J. Neff.

Investment Adviser: Lord, Abbett & Co. Compensation to the Adviser is ½ of 1% annually on the first $200 million of net assets of the fund, ⅖ of 1% annu-ally on the next $300 million, ⅜ of 1% on the next $200 million, ¼ of 1% on the next $200 million, and ⅕ of 1% on assets in excess of $900 million; less $350,000.

Custodian: Morgan Guaranty Trust Company, New York, NY.

Transfer Agent: United Missouri Bank of Kansas City, N.A.

Shareholder Servicing Agent: DST, Inc., P.O. Box 1100, Kansas City, MO 64141.

Distributor: Lord, Abbett & Co., 63 Wall Street, New York, NY.

Sales Charge: Maximum is 7¼% of offering price; minimum is ½ of 1% at $4 million. Reduced charges begin at $5,000 and are applicable to initial and subsequent combined purchases of this fund and other funds in the Lord Abbett group on a permanent basis. Minimum is $25,000 for Statement of Intention. Minimum initial purchase is $250.

Distribution Plan: (12b-1) None.

Dividends: Income dividends are paid quarterly in the months of March, June, September and December. Capital gains, if any, are paid optionally in shares or cash in December.

Shareholder Reports: Issued quarterly. Fiscal year ends October 31. The current prospectus was effective in March.

Qualified for Sale: In all states, DC and PR.

Address: 63 Wall St., New York, NY 10005.

Telephone: (212) 425-8720.

An assumed investment of $10,000 in this fund, with capital gains accepted in shares and income dividends reinvested, is illustrated below. The explanation in the introduction to this section must be read in conjunction with this illustration.

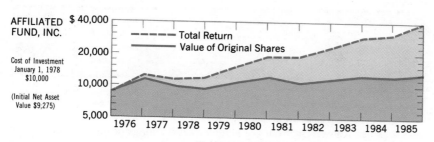

	1976	1977	1978	1979	1980	1981	1982	1983	1984	1985
Value of Shares Initially Acquired Through Investment of $10,000	$11,646	$10,165	$9,561	$11,043	$12,044	$10,631	$11,783	$12,908	$12,318	$13,594
Value of Shares Resulting From Reinvestment of Capital Gains and Income Dividends (Cumulative)	804	1,416	2,388	4,355	7,066	8,452	11,750	16,521	18,988	25,961*
Total Return	12,450	11,581	11,949	15,398	19,110	19,083	23,533	29,429	31,306	39,555

Dollar amounts of distributions reinvested:

	Capital Gains	Income Dividends
1976	$ 311	$ 473
1977	227	551
1978	502	621
1979	785	788
1980	1,414	996
1981	1,115	1,247
1982	856	1,416
1983	2,333	1,452
1984	1,564	1,693
1985	2,940	1,992
Total	$12,047	$11,229

Results Taking Capital Gains in SHARES and Income Dividends in CASH

Initial Investment At Offering Price, January 1, 1976	$10,000
Value as of 12/31/85 of Shares Initially Acquired	$13,594
Value of Shares Accepted as Capital Gains Distributions†	$ 9,836
Total Value, December 31, 1985	$23,430
Total Dividends PAID From Investment Income	$ 8,321

†Dollar Amount of these distributions at the time shares were acquired: $8,504

Results Taking All Dividends and Distributions in CASH

Initial Investment At Offering Price, January 1, 1976	$10,000
Total Value, December 31, 1985	$13,594
Distributions From Capital Gains	$ 6,530
Dividends From Investment Income	$ 6,570

FIGURE 18-1 **A Page from *Investment Companies* showing the coverage of Affiliated Fund, Inc.**

Source: Reprinted by permission from the Wiesenberger Investment Companies Service 1986 Edition. Copyright © 1986, Warren, Gorham & Lamont, Inc., 210 South Street, Boston, Mass. All Rights Reserved.

Performance in UP —markets—	in DOWN	Fund/distributor	Investment results Average annual total return 1976-86	Latest 12 months total return	return from income dividends	Total assets 6/30/86 (millions)	% change '86 vs '85	Maximum sales charge	Annual expenses per $100
		Standard & Poor's 500 stock average	14.7%	35.8%	3.2%				
		FORBES stock fund composite	16.7%	32.4%	2.2%				
C	D	ABT Growth & Income Trust/Leshner	14.2%	27.8%	5.6%	$123	5%	8.50%	$1.45‡
		ABT Investment-Emerging Growth/Leshner	—*	53.2	none	38	180	8.50	2.34‡
		ABT Investment-Security Income/Leshner	—*	12.9	1.4	19	–16	8.50	2.05‡
●D	●B	ABT Utility Income Fund/Leshner	—*	19.2	7.9	109	29	8.50	1.57‡
B	A	Acorn Fund/Acorn Fund	21.8	32.8	1.2	425	58	none	0.78
		Adam Investors/Conway	—*	28.3	3.8	14	88	none	2.53
D	B	Adams Express/closed end	15.8	36.0	3.0	522	29	NA	0.48
		Advantage Growth Fund/Advest	—*	—*	—*	14	—	4.00b	2.86‡
C	B	Affiliated Fund/Lord Abbett	15.8	32.3	4.8	3,125	30	7.25	0.32
B	C	Afuture Fund/Afuture	15.6	26.1	0.7	25	–6	none	1.60
		Alliance Convertible Fund/Alliance	—*	—*	—*	49	—	5.50	0.28‡
		Alliance Counterpoint Fund/Alliance	—*	41.1	1.6	38	101	none	1.41‡
		Alliance International Fund/Alliance	—*	93.5	0.1	139	94	8.50	1.24
		Alliance Technology Fund/Alliance	—*	40.6	none	153	14	8.50	1.13
C	B	Alpha Fund/Commodore	17.0	43.6	2.7	28	34	8.50	1.50

Total return is for 9/30/76 to 6/30/86. For all categories other than money markets, funds are added to this section when they exceed $5 million in net assets and deleted when they drop below $2 million. Stock and balanced funds are rated only if in operation since 11/30/80. ●Fund rated for two periods only; maximum allowable grade A. *Fund not in operation for full period. ‡Fund has 12b-1 plan (hidden load) pending or in force. b: Includes redemption fee that reverts to distributor. NA: Not applicable or not available.

FIGURE 18–2 **An excerpt from the annual *Forbes* ratings of mutual funds, *1986 Fund Ratings*, September 8, 1986, p. 112.**

Source: Excerpted by permission of *Forbes* magazine, September 8, 1986. © Forbes Inc., 1986.

Advantages and Disadvantages of Owning Mutual Fund Shares

Because of its importance, we will discuss in detail the benefits and costs of indirect investing through investment companies. By analyzing the cost and benefits, investors can decide whether to purchase securities directly or indirectly.

Choosing between direct and indirect investing is not always difficult. For example, an investor wishing to invest in money market instruments such as negotiable CDs or commercial paper may have no alternative because of the large minimum denominations that these securities carry. Also, an investor with less than $10,000 to invest cannot purchase even one Treasury bill. As another example, the alternatives are poor for many investors interested in corporate or municipal bonds if they wish to obtain the benefits of diversification and good liquidity (in case they need to sell before maturity). Unless they have considerable funds (at least $100,000) to invest and some knowledge about the bond markets, the unit investment trusts or a regular bond fund specializing in municipals or corporates are easily the most sensible way to invest.

TABLE 18–2 Data for One Hypothetical Family of Mutual Funds, the National Funds Group

The National Funds Group	NAV	Offer Price	NAV Change
Daily Data			
National income	6.12	6.55	+0.04
National growth	14.62	15.90	+0.06
National high yield	5.00	N.L.	—
National aggressive frontiers	8.16	8.90	+0.03
National tax free	9.14	9.60	−0.02
National balanced	8.45	9.14	+0.01

	52 Weeks				Income	
	High NAV	Low NAV	Close NAV	Week's Change	Divi- dends	Capital Gains
Weekly Data						
National income	7.02	5.98	6.10	+0.12	1.12	
National growth	18.36	11.82	14.70	+0.18	0.60	0.95
National high yield	6.12	4.62	5.02	+0.02	1.50	
National aggressive frontiers	22.14	4.82	8.03	+0.25	0.38	1.78
National tax free	9.38	9.00	9.12	−0.09	0.89	
National balanced	8.80	7.12	8.40	+0.06	0.90	0.50

When the choice between direct and indirect investing is not clear, it is important to weigh the potential benefits and costs of owning investment company shares.

The benefits include the following: (Also, see Box 18–1.)

- **Diversification** Perhaps the single greatest benefit of owning shares in an investment company is the instantaneous diversification conferred on the investor. As we shall see in Part Seven, one of the most important tenets of modern portfolio theory is the necessity to diversify one's holding among several assets in order to reduce risk. Investors may find this impossible to do with limited funds to invest, or expensive in terms of brokerage costs even with adequate funds. Most investment companies, on the other hand, are required by law to be diversified; specifically, the Investment Company Act of 1940 requires a *diversified* investment company to meet certain criteria with at least 75% of its assets, including no more than 5% of the total portfolio value invested in the securities of any one issuer.[24]

Overall, investment companies offer very substantial diversification. Some funds hold over 100 different securities, and sometimes as many as 200. On the other hand, other funds are not as well diversified. In particular,

---

[24]Investment companies may choose to be *nondiversified*, concentrating on narrow concepts such as one idea or one country or one industry.

those funds specializing in certain industries or commodities such as gold may be quite poorly diversified.

- **Variety of objectives**   A large number of investment companies are available with a wide variety of objectives. Investors can probably find one or more funds to meet their objectives. Funds specialize in stocks, bonds, and combinations thereof. With stocks, some are broadly diversified and others specialize in a particular industry, commodity, concept, or geographical area. With bonds, some funds are broadly diversified in Treasury securities, or corporates, or municipals.

  Thus, investors can typically <u>find funds to suit their investment outlook, tax situation, income needs, and risk preferences</u>. There is virtually a fund for everyone.

- **Services**   Investment companies offer a wide variety of services to their shareholders.

  1. *Record keeping*. The funds maintain and compile complete records of the shareholder's activity for a given year, including the dividends, interest, and capital gains received by the shareholder. This is a great convenience for income tax purposes.
  2. *Handling of securities*. Investment companies typically arrange for the physical custody of all securities in the portfolio. This includes the collection of all dividends and interest.
  3. *Fund swaps*. Increasingly, investors are taking advantage of the exchange privilege—the ability to switch their holdings among the family of funds being managed by a given investment advisor. The fees charged for purchase of shares are reduced, or even eliminated, for existing shareholders. Thus, shareholders may decide to switch from one fund emphasizing capital gains to another emphasizing maximum current income.
  4. *Accumulation and withdrawal plans*. Many funds permit the *automatic reinvestment* of all dividends into shares of the fund at net asset value.[25] Thus, investment income dividends and capital gains distributions can be reinvested automatically in additional shares. By 1982, almost 90% of the investment income dividends paid out by mutual funds was in the form of new shares—up considerably from the 54% of 10 years prior. In the case of net realized long-term capital gains, most funds offer an optional stock dividend that allows shareholders to receive stock at net asset value. As much as three-fourths of the paid-out

---

[25] It should be noted that some load funds reinvest investment income at the fund's offering price; however, no fund charges a load to reinvest capital gain distributions. The National Association of Securities Dealers has limited the maximum load chargeable on reinvested dividends to 7.5%.

capital gains is reinvested in this manner. Some funds also permit specified monthly withdrawals by the shareholder, based either on a fixed dollar amount or a fixed percentage of the shareholder's assets. A minimum investment amount is usually required to start a withdrawal plan.

5. *IRA and Keogh plans*. Many funds provide investors with a tax shelter through the use of Individual Retirement Accounts (IRAs) and Keogh plans for the self-employed. Liberalization of IRA regulations has enhanced the attractiveness of such alternatives.

The costs of investment companies include the following:

- **Load fee**   The most obvious cost of investment company ownership is the sales charge paid by owners of load fund shares. As noted before, this sales charge is substantial, averaging about 8.5% (an effective cost of 9.3%). Of course, these fees can be avoided if a comparable no-load fund can be found, which is often the case. Investors must also be alert for 12b-1 fees, which some funds are starting to impose. (See Box 18–2.)

- **Management fee**   Every fund charges an annual management fee, roughly 0.5% of asset market value, to compensate for the research and management costs incurred by the fund. This fee is deducted from the fund's earnings during the year.[26]

- **Administrative fees**   Operating expenses of the fund, including custodian, accounting, legal, and postage costs, must be paid by the shareholders. Such fees are deducted from the assets of the fund on an annual basis, and typically amount to less than 0.5% of asset value per year.[27]

- **Transaction costs**   Investment companies, like any investor, must pay transaction costs to buy and sell securities.[28] Investment companies have an advantage over individual investors, however, because of the large blocks they trade and their power to negotiate favorable commissions—available evidence suggests round-trip brokerage commission of about 0.5%. Obviously, brokerage commissions can be reduced by holding down portfolio turnover.[29] Some funds have relatively low turnover, while others turn over almost their entire portfolio regularly. By 1986 the average equity fund turnover was about 75%, up from 25% 10 years earlier.

---

[26]The management fee is usually the largest component of a fund's expenses. It covers salaries, office space and accessories, and the cost of portfolio management.

[27]Typically, total expenses for a fund are less than 1% of assets. For most funds, expenses cannot exceed 1 to 2% of average assets. If they do, management fees must be refunded.

[28]Brokerage costs are treated as capital items rather than expenses.

[29]The SEC defines turnover for investment companies as the lesser of sales or purchases dividend by average assets.

BOX 18–1 THE UNADVERTISED ADVANTAGES OF MUTUAL FUND INVESTMENTS

One of the best reasons for owning common stocks through mutual funds is almost never mentioned, let alone quantified.

It is the favorable impact lower management and transaction costs have on performance.

While most mutual fund sales literature promotes the value of the continuous supervision, expert management and relentless analysis you get for the usual one-half of 1 percent management fee, it is a fact that most studies of professional management fail to demonstrate that it can outperform investment selections made by throwing darts at the stock pages.

In fact, the advantage mutual funds have over individual investors is unrelated to investing skills: They have lower costs, and lower costs mean your long-term return probably will be superior in mutual funds.

Here's why:

Commission costs at major retail brokerage houses now take about 2 percent of each transaction, sometimes more. Since each sale is followed by a purchase, total commission costs for managing your own securities rise very quickly with turnover. Investors who hold an average stock three years, for instance, pay about 1.34 percent a year in commissions while investors who hold stocks for only a year pay 4 percent a year in commissions.

Now compare these costs with the annual cost of management and brokerage commissions at mutual funds. Typically, management fees and operating expenses absorb between 0.75 and 0.90 percent of fund assets per year. In addition, they pay brokerage commissions on their transactions but enjoy far lower commission rates than individuals. Although no industry figures are available, a sampling of records from major funds indicates commission expenses of about one-half of 1 percent—even with a portfolio turnover rate exceeding 100 percent.

Total expenses for a large mutual fund, in other words, will run about 1.25 percent a year.

As an individual, your portfolio turnover rate would have to be 30 percent a year, or less, to have the same low costs—a low turnover rate for most accounts.

What does this mean?

First, it means that professional management doesn't really cost anything. Management fees and associated fund expenses are recovered on the difference between retail and institutional commission rates. (Bank trust departments, by the way, have the same advantage.)

Second, it means that the more active your brokerage account, the more likely your total expenses are to exceed those of a mutual fund and reduce the long-term performance of your investments.

Suppose, for instance, that you held your stocks an average of 1.5 years. This would mean a 67 percent turnover rate (not far from many mutual funds) and an annual commission burden of 3.0 percent—1.75 percent more than the cost burden on a typical mutual fund.

How much does this affect performance?

A lot.

The table below shows the distribution of performance of 10,000 portfolios of 35 stocks picked at random by the computers at Media General Financial Services for an investment period of 10 years. As you can see, the distance between the median portfolio performance and the portfolios in the top 10 percent is only 2.1 percent. Similarly, one need only lose 2.1 percent to fall from a typical performance to the bottom 10 percent.

The Gap Between the Top and Bottom Is Small

Percentile Rank	Difference from Median
Top 10	plus 2.1 percent
Top 20	plus 1.4 percent
Top 30	plus 0.9 percent
Top 40	plus 0.4 percent
Median	plus 0.0 percent
Bottom 40	minus 0.4 percent
Bottom 30	minus 0.9 percent
Bottom 20	minus 1.4 percent
Bottom 10	minus 2.1 percent

In other words, if you as an amateur made the same selections as a professional and did it for 10 years, and both of you were only as good as a dart thrower, your per-formance still would be significantly worse than the professional's because his costs would be lower. If his performance was at the median of randomly selected portfolios, yours would be 1.75 percent lower, putting you somewhere between the bottom 10 and 20 percent of all portfolios.

There are two important messages here.

• For long-term investing no-load mutual funds offer a significant advantage for most people over traditional brokerage accounts.

• Since load funds place a cost burden that won't be equaled by a brokerage account for five to seven years, odds are the load fund investor will never overcome the initial cost disadvantage.

Source: Scott Burns "The Unadvertised Advantages of Mutual Fund Investments," *The Media General Financial Weekly,* August 30, 1982, p. 2. Scott Burns, Reprint Courtesy *Register & Tribune Syndicate, Inc.* and *The Media General Financial Weekly.*

A possible "hidden" transaction cost for investment companies is the price pressure caused by the trading of a large block; that is, buying or selling a large block may drive the price up or down beyond what would have occurred with a smaller number of shares. An additional transaction cost is the market maker's bid–ask spread (which applies to both listed and OTC stocks). These "hidden" transaction costs have been estimated at about 0.6%.[30]

• **Superfluous diversification** Adequate diversification is absolutely essential to the sound management of portfolios; however, some mutual funds may hold as many as 200 securities in their portfolios. This is more than adequate to reduce risk and it will tend to negate the positive effects of a few good performers in the portfolio. The fund's performance will tend to parallel the market averages, similar to an index fund, although it is attempting to out-perform such funds.

• **The active management cost** If securities markets are basically efficient, as suggested by the efficient market hypothesis, investment companies can

---

[30] See David Henry, "High Churnover," *Forbes,* March 10, 1986, p. 146.

BOX 18-2 BARK, WATCHDOGS!

Dwight Crane, professor of finance at Harvard Business School, moonlights as a mutual fund director, serving on the boards of all 15 E. F. Hutton mutual funds. For the latter service he will collect a sum that probably approaches his professor's salary: $62,900 a year if he attends all meetings, plus expenses and $500 per special meeting.

As an independent director, Crane's job, as the SEC defines it, is to defend shareholders' interests, helping keep fund profits high and fees low. So what have Crane and the other Hutton directors done to earn their keep? Crane declines to discuss the matter. But, it seems, they have not done a great deal. Excluding money market funds, the two largest Hutton funds are Investment Series Growth and Investment Series Government Securities. The growth fund last year had a 22% return, not nearly as good as the 28% gain of the average growth fund, according to Lipper Analytical Services. Contributing to the poor performance was a lot of overhead. Shareholders paid 1.77% of assets in annual expenses. That is a hefty fee. An investor could have bought any of the 23 stock funds on the FORBES honor roll and paid lower expenses. Government Securities did better, gaining 19% for 1985, while other bond funds returned 20%. But again, the performance was depressed by a 1.67% expense ratio.

The high fees would be understandable if these were little funds without economies of scale. But Hutton's Government Securities fund grew from $777 million to more than $3 billion during 1985, making it the sixth-largest bond fund at year-end.

Why are Hutton's funds so expensive? The culprit is 12b-1 fees. Named after a 1980 SEC regulation that authorizes them, 12b-1 plans permit the fund sponsor to dip into fund assets to pay the brokers who help sell the funds. Last year Hutton's Investment Series Growth charged 0.85% in 12b-1 fees and its Government Securities charged 0.90%.

Is that good for shareholders? In theory, maybe. The 12b-1 fees generate more fund sales, which means bigger funds, which supposedly benefits shareholders by producing economies of scale. This is what the fund industry, at least, argued in persuading the SEC to adopt rule 12b-1. The claim was also made that since a portfolio is much easier to manage with money flowing in then with money flowing out, investors might even enjoy higher returns.

There was one catch. The SEC said the 12b-1 fee could be taken out of shareholders' assets only when it was for their own good. And investors would rely on the integrity and conscience of a mutual fund's independent directors to halt the fee when it was no longer helping investors. A foolproof plan.

But the system has gone awry. Just look at the Dean Witter U.S. Government Securities Trust. At $9.6 billion, the fund is the second-largest publicly offered fund in the U.S. (not counting money markets), and the largest with a 12b-1 fee. The huge cash inflow obviously has not engendered higher returns: Last year the fund gained only 14%, vs. an average 20% gain for all bond funds. Does the fund have low overhead? Not at all. Last year expenses were 1.30% of average net assets, with 0.73% of that in 12b-1 fees. The average expense ratio at bond funds without 12b-1 fees recently was 0.89%.

Dean Witter charges U.S. Government Securities shareholders up to 0.75% annually for the 12b-1. The management fee starts at 0.50% and declines to 0.375% as assets grow beyond $5 billion. Investors are paying up to 0.75% a year for fund growth so they can save less than 0.125% a year—plus a few administrative costs—once the growth is achieved. Absurd.

The folks at Dean Witter look like sports compared with Kemper. Dean Witter has lowered its management fee twice as the fund has grown. Kemper's Investment Portfolio–Government Plus fund, now at $3.3 billion, has a 12b-1 fee of 1.25% and a flat management fee of 0.6%. If the management fee doesn't decline as the fund grows, where will the savings of size come from?

What do the directors who approve these 12b-1 fees say? Some plead that fund assets would fall to zero if brokers were not kept happy with these fees. The argument doesn't wash: Plenty of funds hold on to their investors because they do a good job for them year after year. Other funds retain investors because the latter tend to be passive and lazy about moving their money.

Whatever the SEC may choose to do about the 12b-1 monster, there is a simple lesson for investors. Stay away from funds with 12b-1 loads. And don't expect "independent" directors to look out for your interests.

Source: Laura R. Walbert, "Bark, Watchdogs!" *Forbes,* June 16, 1986, p. 174. Reprinted by permission of *Forbes* magazine, June 16, 1986. © Forbes Inc., 1986.

generate too much expense by unsuccessfully trying to time market moves or buy (sell) under (over) valued securities. And the evidence on mutual fund performance considered in Chapter 14 suggests that this is probably the case. Given the importance of this topic, we will consider it again.

Assessing Mutual Fund Performance

Measuring performance   Returns on mutual funds (or closed-end funds) can be calculated in the same manner as the holding period yields of Chapter 5. The total return during a particular period (both income and price appreciation) is related to the price at the beginning of the period. As an example, consider the hypothetical Wonder Fund, a diversified common stock fund that at year-end 19X7 has 97% of its assets in common stocks. Net asset value per share at year-end 19X6 and 19X7 are $7.75 and $8.59 respectively. During 19X7, $0.56 in income (dividends and interest) and $0.33 in capital gains are distributed to shareholders. Thus, total shareholder return on Wonder Fund in 19X7 is 22.3%, calculated as

$$\text{Shareholder total returns} = \frac{\$8.59 - \$7.75 + \$0.89}{\$7.75}$$

$$= 22.3\%$$

What can be said about the performance of Wonder Fund based on this information? The first comparison that is usually made is to the "market" during the same period. Assume that the S&P 500 Composite Index for 19X7 shows an HPY of 20.4%. Therefore, Wonder outperforms the market for that year. But is this enough information to conclude anything about this one company's performance? The answer is NO! Investors should ask several questions about a particular fund they own or are considering purchasing.

The first and most important question concerns the risk involved—did Wonder assume more risk than is represented in a market index such as the S&P 500? As we established in Chapter 1, the basis of investment decisions is that a risk–return trade-off is involved. Risk and expected return go together; therefore, if a particular fund assumes more risk than the market average, its return is expected to be larger.

As an illustration, consider HPY data for Wonder Fund and the S&P 500 for the years 19X0 through 19X9 (an investor can use annual results as calculated by Wiesenberger). Assume that the respective standard deviations of the annual returns for Wonder Fund and the market index are 19.69% and 20.94% and that the beta for the fund is 0.90. Therefore, Wonder shows less total risk (standard deviation) and less market risk (beta) than did the market index over this time period.

The second question that should be raised concerns performance over time. The fact that a fund performs well in one particular year is not reassuring for the longer run. Luck or short-term insights can play a role in performance. It is important to assess the consistency in performance over time. Assume that the mean return over this 10 year period for Wonder is 12.46%, whereas that for the S&P 500 was 8.45%. Furthermore, assume that except for 19X7, Wonder performed better than the market on an absolute basis for each year during 19X0 through 19X9. This analysis appears to suggest that Wonder has performed well.

Relative consistency of performance is also important. Assume that the *Forbes* ratings of performance in both up and down markets show that Wonder has a relative rating of C in both up and down markets. This indicates that the fund did not do as well as 50% of all the funds rated during up markets (it was in the third quartile); on the other hand, it did better than 50% of all funds in down markets (it was in the second quartile).[31] Thus on a relative ranking basis, Wonder is not a standout. In order to make the list of consistent performers over the period studied by *Forbes,* a fund had to achieve a ranking of B in both up and down markets—a feat usually accomplished by only a few funds.

A detailed breakdown of the dollar returns for investment companies can be seen in Wiesenberger's detailed data for each company. As Figure 18–1 shows, the results of an assumed investment of $10,000 are calculated for the most recent 10 years assuming capital gains are accepted in shares and income dividends are reinvested (results of taking all dividends and distributions in cash are also shown, as are results from taking capital gains in shares and income dividends in cash).

---

[31] In the *Forbes* ratings, a C in an up market represents the third quartile of Performance (A+ and A cover the first quartile, and B covers the second quartile); on the down side, A and B cover quartile one, C the second, D the third, and F the last.

A third area to question is ③expenses. A fund that performs well may have large expenses as it searches for undervalued securities or tries to time market movements. Assume that Wonder has annual expenses of $0.36 per $100 of average net assets. This figure, which includes both operating expenses and management fees, compares to an average of about $0.75 to 0.90. However, Wonder has a sales charge of 7.25% (with reduced charges beginning at $5000). This will clearly reduce the performance for an investor in the year of purchase. Of course, calculating shareholder returns over a longer period will diminish the relative impact of the sales charge; nevertheless, the load fee remains a significant item to consider. Furthermore, investors should check carefully for the imposition of 12b-1 fees.

The performance record   Chapter 14 discussed the performance of portfolio managers as one indication of market efficiency. Several studies of mutual fund performance were mentioned, most of which found that mutual funds do not outperform market averages on a risk-adjusted basis. A summary of these findings, together with those of other studies, suggests the following:[32]

1. Active portfolio management by mutual fund managers seems to produce positive results *gross* of fund expenses, but not *net* of fund expenses.
2. The risk of mutual funds is reasonably stable over time, and past risk levels can be used to predict future risk (obviously, by no means perfectly).
3. Consistency in fund performance typically has not been found. Although a few funds seem to perform well over a period of time, such results can be accounted for by the laws of probability. This issue, however, remains unsettled.

Thus, empirical studies of mutual fund performance suggest that active portfolio management does not increase shareholder welfare. For the typical mutual fund investor, this evidence suggests that mutual funds should not be purchased to obtain exceptional management performance.

One perspective on the performance of professional portfolio managers can be obtained by considering the following:

1. For the period 1981–1985, the Salomon Broad Bond Index outperformed 81% of professionally managed bond portfolios.[33]
2. Among mutual funds, the average general equity fund gained slightly more than 14% in 1986, while the S&P 500 Index exceeded 22% for the same period.[34]

---

[32] Other studies include J. McDonald, "Objectives and Performance of Mutual Funds, 1960–1969," *Journal of Financial and Quantitative Analysis,* June 1974, pp. 311–333.

[33] This information is collected by SEI Funds Evaluation Survey and reported in materials issued by The Vanguard Group as part of their material on the Vanguard Bond Market Fund.

[34] Through December 23, 1986. See Pamela Sebastian, "Mutual Fund Investors Advised to Expect Lower Returns in '87," *The Wall Street Journal,* January 2, 1987, p. 3B.

Investor Alternatives to Actively Managed Funds

One result of the overall poor performance of mutual funds has been the creation and growth of index funds. A special type of mutual fund, the **index fund,** is designed to parallel the movements of a stock market average or a bond index.

A stock-index fund may consist of all the stocks in a well-known market average such as the Standard & Poor 500 Composite Stock Index. No attempt is made to forecast market movements and act accordingly, or to select under- or overvalued securities. A bond-index fund is designed to match the performance of some well-known bond index, such as the Salomon Index. In either case, expenses are kept to a minimum, including research costs (security analysis), portfolio managers' fees, and brokerage commissions. Index funds can be run efficiently by a small staff.

Index funds have arisen in response to the growing body of evidence concerning the efficiency of the market, and have grown as the evidence of the inability of mutual funds to consistently, or even very often, outperform the market continues to accumulate. If the market is efficient, many of the activities normally engaged in by funds are suspect; that is, the benefits are not likely to exceed the costs. And, as previously indicated, the available evidence indicates that many investment companies have failed to match the performance of broad market indices.

Index funds grew rapidly in 1986, with stock-index funds estimated at roughly $150 billion by year-end. Bond-index funds totaled another $50 billion. Expenses and fees are considerably lower on these funds.

Summary

An investment company is a financial service organization that invests in a portfolio of securities on behalf of its own shareholders. It offers investors a way to invest indirectly by purchasing shares in the investment company which, in turn, invests in a portfolio of securities. Investment companies are, therefore, pure intermediaries.

Investment companies consist of open-end companies, popularly called mutual funds, and closed-end companies. The former continuously sells shares in itself to the public, and redeems them when its investors wish to sell. Closed-end funds, on the other hand, have a fixed number of shares of stock outstanding, and trade on exchanges like any other security. Mutual funds can be divided into load funds, which charge a sales fee to investors who purchase shares, and no-load funds, which do not. The average sales fee historically has been 8.50%. All funds charge their shareholders for the expenses involved, including a management fee.

Two major categories of investment companies are the money market funds and the equity, bond, and income funds. The former offer investors a chance to own money market instruments, which typically have large face values, that will earn current money market rates. Included in this category is the short-term municipal bond fund, which offers a tax-exempt return.

Equity, bond, and income funds invest primarily in stocks and bonds. They can be organized into common stock funds (which can be broken down into funds with different growth and income objectives as well as international funds and precious metals funds), balanced funds, income funds, option/income funds, and various types of bond funds.

Because they are closely regulated, investment companies must provide information to investors on a timely basis. Several services cover funds in detail, such as the Wiesenberger Service and *Forbes*. On a daily and weekly basis, sources such as *The Wall Street Journal* and *Barron's* are useful.

The potential benefits of owning investment company shares include diversification, an opportunity to choose from a variety of objectives, and a range of services such as record keeping, fund swaps, accumulation and withdrawal plans, and IRA and Keogh plans. The actual and potential costs include any load fee, the management fee, administrative fees, transaction costs, superfluous diversification, and active management cost. These benefits and costs must be evaluated by investors within a framework that considers their own situation and alternatives.

The question of fund performance remains unsettled. Considerable evidence suggests that the funds do not outperform the market when all relevant factors are considered. In assessing performance, shareholder returns should be measured using the HPY concept. Investors should also assess the risk, the consistency in performance over time, and the expenses involved. Index funds are increasing in popularity.

Key Words

Closed-end investment company	Net asset value (NAV)
Discount	No-load funds
Index funds	Open-end investment company
Investment company	Premium
Load funds	Prospectus
Management fee	Pure intermediary
Mutual funds	

QUESTIONS AND PROBLEMS

1. Explain what is meant by the term *pure intermediary*.
2. What is the difference between an open-end investment company and a closed-end investment company? A load fund and a no-load fund?

3. It has been said that many closed-end funds are "worth more dead than alive." What is meant by this expression?

4. Which investment companies charge a management fee, and what is its size, on average?

5. What does it mean for an investment company to be regulated?

6. List the benefits of a money market fund for investors. List the disadvantages. What alternative investment is a close substitute?

7. What is meant by an investment company's "objective"? List the various objectives pursued by equity, bond, and income funds.

8. How does a unit investment trust differ from an investment company?

9. What is meant by the statement that the portfolio manager's results differ from the shareholder's results for the closed-end investment company?

10. List the advantages offered by investment companies. What are the costs, both actual and potential?

11. Based on a consensus of the studies of mutual fund performance, what can be said about their returns and risk?

12. Examine the latest *Forbes* rating of mutual funds (August of each year). How many funds achieved a high rating in both up and down markets (B or better)?

13. List some reasons why an investor might prefer a closed-end fund to an open-end fund.

14. What do you think is the explanation for the fact that load funds dominate no-load funds in sales?

15. How is net asset value calculated for an investment company? How closely correlated could you expect changes in NAVs to be with changes in market indices?

16. What is meant by a "fund swap"?

17. How can risk measures be calculated for investment companies?

18. Using the following data for GoGrowth Fund, Inc., calculate the shareholder total returns for the years 19X2, 19X3, 19X4, and 19X5 (ignore the sales charge).

GoGrowth Fund

Year	Income Dividends ($)	Capital Gains Distribution ($)	NAV Per Share ($)
19X5	$0.56	$0.49	$7.75
19X4	0.51	0.71	8.78
19X3	0.45	0.44	8.05
19X2	0.39	0.31	6.97
19X1	0.37	0.15	7.41

19. a. GoGrowth began calendar year 19X7 with an NAV of $8.59 and ended the year with an NAV of $9.51. During the year it paid $0.51 in dividends

and distributed $0.82 in capital gains. Calculate GoGrowth's HPY for 19X7.

b. GoGrowth has a front-end load. Assume you purchased 100 shares at $8.59 on January 1, 19X7, and the load was 7.25%. For what amount did you write your check? How much do you have invested?

c. Calculate your 19X7 calendar-year HPY, net of your transaction cost.

d. The HPY on the S&P 500 for 19X7 was 22.4%. Compare your HPY on GoGrowth, both before and after transaction cost, with the market. Is this a fair comparison?

e. Assume that you had bought 100 shares of a no-load fund, and it had an HPY of 25%. Compare GoGrowth's HPY, both before and after transaction cost, with this fund. Is this a fair comparison?

20. Value Line has a family of no-load mutual funds. For each of their five funds, the relevant shareholder values are shown in the following table.

Fund	NAV 12-31-82 ($)	Dividends ($)	Capital Distribution ($)	NAV 12-30-83
Value Line Fund	$14.28	$0.55	$0.75	$12.87
Bond Fund	12.76	1.34	0.28	11.85
Income	7.01	0.56	0.14	6.77
Leveraged Growth	18.82	0.64	0.02	19.66
Special Situations	13.83	0.45	—	16.11

a. Calculate the calendar-year HPY for each fund. The HPY on the S&P 500 was 22.4%. Evaluate 1983's performance for each fund.

b. Compare each fund's HPY with the (net of transaction cost) HPY of GoGrowth.

c. In the text, different kinds of funds are described. From the names of these Value Line funds, can you identify the type of fund?

d. Based on c, try ranking these funds from highest risk to lowest risk.

21. A better comparison of fund performance is possible by looking at several years of HPYs. For the five Value Line funds, the annual HPYs are provided along with the HPY for the S&P 500. The mean, standard deviation, and beta are also provided. (All Value Line data courtesy of Wiesenberger Financial Services.)

a. On the basis of the standard deviation of the HPYs, and the betas, do the risks match with your rankings in 20 (d)?

b. Compare the 10-year results on average annual yield with the average for Affiliated in the text. How does Affiliated compare?

c. Compare the average HPY and the risk of each fund with the market. Do the results of the Income Fund surprise you?

d. For each fund, in how many years was the performance better than the market?

			Fund HPY%			
Year	Value Line	Bond Fund	Income	Leveraged Growth	Special Situation	S&P 500 HPY%
1973	10.5%	...	−15.9%	−48.2%	−45.7%	−14.5%
1974	−22.4	...	−16.1	−30.6	−29.2	−26.0
1975	39.2	...	41.7	59.1	47.0	36.9
1976	42.5	...	34.5	46.7	52.7	23.6
1977	9.5	...	1.8	51.1	12.3	− 7.2
1978	19.3	...	11.1	27.6	21.2	6.4
1979	44.0	...	27.6	26.2	43.5	18.2
1980	41.6	...	26.8	29.5	54.4	31.5
1981	2.4	...	16.2	15.9	− 2.3	− 4.8
1982	28.9	33.2	29.9	28.6	23.1	20.4
Mean	17.5	—	15.8	20.6	17.7	8.4
Standard deviation	27.1	—	20.3	34.5	34.6	20.9
Beta	1.2	—	.9	1.2	1.5	1.0

e. Which funds seemed to have better overall performance than the market? Generally, does it appear that mean returns above the market are associated with undertaking greater risk?

22. The following hypothetical values and prices are for publicly traded closed-end mutual funds.

Fund	Net Asset Value ($)	Stock Price ($)
Adams Express	$16.90	$15.85
Lehman	14.23	15.50
Tri-Continental	23.70	23.40

a. Calculate the discount or the premium.
b. Express these differences as a percentage of the NAV.
c. What reasons can you think of for these differences?
d. The Monday issue of *The Wall Street Journal* provides this information. Check the current quotes and determine what has happened to the NAV, the market price, and the difference for these three funds.

23. For the Super Fund data given in the text
a. Verify that the percentage discounts are as given.
b. Calculate the portfolio performance for each of the other four years. The closing NAV in 19X0 was $11.55.
c. Calculate stockholder's HPYs for each of the other four years. The closing price as of 19X0 was $8.25.
d. Compare the portfolio results with the shareholder's results. Compare

both with the HPYs for the S&P 500 as given in Chapter 5. What can you conclude?

24. Dual-purpose funds are typically initiated with an equal amount of income shares and capital shares. Assume a fund is initiated with $40 million, divided equally between the income shareholders and the capital shareholders.

    a. Show that the leverage ratio for income shareholders, and for capital shareholders, is 2.

    b. What would be your leverage ratio if you bought 10 shares of the income and 10 shares of the capital?

Selected References

Cranshaw, T. E. "The Evaluation of Investment Company Performance." *The Journal of Business,* October 1977, pp. 462–485.

Fielitz, Bruce. "Indirect vs. Direct Diversification." *Financial Management,* Winter 1974, pp. 54–62.

Friend, Irwin, Blume, Marshall, and Crockett, Jean. *Mutual Funds and Other Institutional Investors.* New York: McGraw-Hill, 1970.

Malkiel, Burton. "Valuation of Closed-End Investment Companies." *The Journal of Business,* June 1977.

McDonald, John. "Objectives and Performance of Mutual Funds, 1960–1969." *Journal of Financial and Quantitative Analysis,* June 1974, pp. 311–333.

Mutual Fund Fact Book. Washington, D.C., Investment Company Institute.

Sharpe, William. "Mutual Fund Performance." *The Journal of Business,* April 1968, pp. 119–138.

Treynor, Jack. "How to Rate Management of Investment Funds." *Harvard Business Review,* January–February 1965, pp. 63–75.

Wiesenberger Investment Company Service, Annual Editions. Boston: Warren, Gorham & Lamont.

Williamson, J. Peter. "Measuring Mutual Fund Performance." *Financial Analysts Journal,* December 1972, pp. 78–84.

PART SEVEN

PORTFOLIO MANAGEMENT

CHAPTER 19

PORTFOLIO THEORY

In earlier chapters we discussed the valuation and selection of common stocks using three approaches—fundamental, technical, and efficient markets. Various securities that investors can choose in a direct investing program have been analyzed, ranging from bonds to financial futures. Finally, the alternative of investing indirectly through investment companies was analyzed in the previous chapter.

For the remainder of this text our emphasis will shift to a consideration of portfolios rather than individual securities. The word *portfolio* simply means the combination of assets invested in and held by an investor, whether an individual or an institution. Technically, a portfolio encompasses the investor's entire set of assets, real and financial. In this text, however, we are concentrating on financial assets. Most people hold portfolios of assets (both real and financial), whether because of planning and knowledge or as a result of unrelated decisions.

The study of all aspects of portfolios can be designated **portfolio management.** This broad term encompasses the concepts of portfolio theory, a very important part of investments and the specific focus of this chapter. We will analyze the classic portfolio theory model developed by Markowitz. We will also learn how to simplify the process of obtaining inputs for this model by using the single index model. Finally, we will consider a new procedure for determining optimal portfolios, which vastly simplifies the calculations and provides a simple stock-screening device that portfolio managers and investors can use to make operational investment decisions.

The Markowitz Model

In the early 1950s, Harry Markowitz originated the basic portfolio model that underlies modern portfolio theory.[1] Before Markowitz, investors dealt loosely with the concepts of return and risk. Although they were familiar with the concept of risk, they usually did not quantify it. Investors have known intuitively for many years that it is smart to diversify, that is, not to "put all of your eggs in one basket." Markowitz, however, was the first to formally develop the concept of portfolio diversification. He showed quantitatively why, and how, portfolio diversification works to reduce the risk of a portfolio to an investor.

Markowitz sought to organize the existing thoughts and practices into a more formal framework and answer a basic question: Is the risk of a portfolio equal to the sum of the risks of the individual securities comprising it? Markowitz was the first to develop a specific measure of portfolio risk and to derive the expected return and risk for a portfolio. His model is based on the expected return and risk characteristics of securities, and is, in essence, a theoretical framework for analyzing risk–return choices.

Markowitz was also the first to derive the concept of an "efficient portfolio," a widely used term in portfolio theory. An **efficient portfolio** is defined as one that has the smallest portfolio risk for a given level of expected return, or the largest expected return for a given level of risk. Investors can identify efficient portfolios by specifying an expected portfolio return and minimizing the portfolio risk at this level of return. Alternatively, they can specify a portfolio risk level they are willing to assume and maximize the expected return on the portfolio for this level of risk.

Rational investors will seek efficient portfolios because these portfolios promise maximum expected return for a specified level of risk, or minimum risk for a specified expected return. Given their importance, we should know how they are determined. In order to determine an efficient set of portfolios, it is necessary to calculate the expected return and standard deviation of return for each portfolio. To do this, we need to understand the Markowitz model and the inputs needed for the model.

Markowitz made some basic assumptions in developing his model: investors (1) like return and dislike risk, (2) act rationally in making decisions, and (3) make decisions on the basis of maximizing their expected utility. Thus, investor utility is a function of expected return and risk, the two major

---

[1] See H. Markowitz. "Portfolio Selection." *Journal of Finance* 7 (March 1952), pp. 77–91; and *Portfolio Selection: Efficient Diversification of Investments*. New York: John Wiley, 1959.

parameters of investment decisions.[2] The model itself is based on equations for the expected return and risk of a portfolio. To solve these equations, some values are needed for the relevant variables. Before analyzing these inputs, however, we should clearly understand the types of data that are used to provide the inputs for the portfolio model.

Ex Post versus Ex Ante Calculations

Portfolios are built to be held over some future time period. Portfolio theory is concerned with *ex ante* events, meaning expected future events. If we wish to make portfolio decisions for the future, we must use ex ante values.[3] On the other hand, if we wish to evaluate portfolio performance for some previous period, we calculate the actual return and risk values for that period—*ex post* values.

Because we know the historical data, it is often convenient to use ex post values as proxies for the ex ante values needed in the portfolio model. In fact, historical data should be examined and used as a basis for estimating ex ante values; however, it is important to remember that portfolio models call for *ex ante* values which may, and often do, differ from the historical data. Investor expectations are crucial in determining security prices. When ex post data are used as a proxy for the required ex ante values, the assumption being made (either implicitly or explicitly) is that such realizations will be repeated in the future, which may or may not be true.

Inputs Needed

The Markowitz analysis generates efficient portfolios based on a set of inputs supplied by an investor (or security analyst).

1. The expected return, E(R), for every security being considered.
2. The standard deviation of returns, SD(R), as a measure of the risk of each security.
3. The covariance—a measure of relationships—between securities' rates of return.

We will discuss the first two of these now and the third after an initial consideration of portfolios. For purposes of illustrating portfolio concepts, we will use two companies, one real and one hypothetical: EG&G and General Fudge (GF). EG&G, as discussed in Chapter 12, is a technology-oriented company that grew rapidly in the 1970s and early 1980s. In recent years, investors in EG&G stock earned high Holding Period Yields (HPYs), as can be seen in the following data (in percentage form):[4]

---

[2]This assumption does not exclude other objectives, which do exist. Markowitz noted that there are "certain conceivable circumstances under which an investor would prefer a nonefficient portfolio." (*Portfolio Selection*, p. 281).

[3]Ex ante means "before the fact"; ex post means "after the fact."

[4]These data are taken from a recent 10-year period.

	19X0	19X1	19X2	19X3	19X4	19X5	19X6	19X7	19X8	19X9
EG&G	− 2.7	− 28.9	14.8	21.7	5.6	67.2	70.0	80.3	− 8.3	44.7
GF	−12.0	− 19.1	63.4	15.4	9.4	7.7	10.4	− 3.2	11.9	32.3
Market	−14.5	− 26.0	36.9	23.6	−7.2	6.4	18.2	31.5	− 4.8	20.4

Investors in EG&G also assumed substantial risk. The standard deviation of the 10 HPYs above is 37.3%, with three negative HPYs; the calculated beta is 1.21, indicating greater volatility than the market as a whole.[5] Given this performance record, EG&G could appeal to investors as a growth company with above-average expected return–risk possibilities.

GF, on the other hand, is a stable company with a much lower average HPY over the same period, 11.6%, and a standard deviation of HPYs of 23%, roughly two-thirds that of EG&G. The calculated beta is 0.78. As a general rule, stockholders gained less and lost less in any one year with GF than with EG&G. Thus, GF would seem to be a good contrast to the more volatile EG&G, which, as we shall see, is a key point when building portfolios.

We will discuss the first two inputs needed for the Markowitz model in the following two sections. Note that we will be discussing individual securities in these two sections.

Expected return on a security Investors buy stocks for their future returns; therefore, portfolio models must be formulated ex ante. Because the world is uncertain, security returns are really probability judgments. To calculate the expected return for a security, an investor needs an estimate of the realistically obtainable returns from the security plus the likelihood of occurrence (i.e., probabilities) for each possible return.[6]

As an example, assume that an investor is estimating the expected return for EG&G for a forthcoming time period. The investor must determine the possible returns and their associated probabilities. As a basis for doing this, it would be logical to examine prior stockholder returns; however, it is also necessary to incorporate expected conditions for the coming period. Examining the HPYs shown earlier, and modifying these figures for expected events, the investor might decide

There is a 40% chance of a very large HPY, say 60%.
There is a 20% chance of a better than market-average HPY, say 15%.
There is a 20% chance of a small HPY, say 5%.
There is a 20% chance of a negative HPY, say − 15%.

These probabilities sum to 1.0, as they must in a complete probability distribution, because they are exhaustive (we are assuming that all possible

---

[5] These betas are calculated later in the chapter from the 10 annual HPYs.

[6] As explained in Chapter 5, these are the two components of a probability distribution.

TABLE 19–1   Hypothetical Probability Distribution of Potential Returns for EG&G

(1) Potential Return (PR)	(2) Probability (P)	(3) (1) × (2)
Calculating the Expected Return for EG&G		
0.60	0.4	0.24
0.15	0.2	0.03
0.05	0.2	0.01
−0.15	0.2	−0.03
	1.0	$E(R_{EG\&G}) = 0.25 = 25\%$

(1) PR	(2) $ER_{EG\&G}$	(3) $PR - E(R_{EG\&G})$	(4) $[PR - E(R_{EG\&G})]^2$	(5) Probability	(6) (4) × (5)
Calculating the Variance and Standard Deviation of Expected Return for EG&G					
0.60	0.25	0.35	0.1225	0.4	0.049
0.15	0.25	−0.10	0.01	0.2	0.002
0.05	0.25	−0.20	0.04	0.2	0.008
−0.15	0.25	−0.40	0.16	0.2	0.032
				Variance =	0.091
				Standard deviation =	$\sqrt{0.091}$
				=	30.2%

events are expressed). The potential returns must ultimately reflect expectations of the future rather than be merely averages from the past. Because the future is uncertain, all investors will not agree on the potential returns and the associated probabilities.

Given the probability distribution of potential returns for a security, the expected return, E(R), can be calculated as the expected value of the probability distribution.[7]

$$E(R) = \sum_{k=1}^{m} (P_k) \, PR_k \qquad (19\text{–}1)$$

where

$E(R)$ = the expected return for any security.

PR_k = the potential return for the kth possibility.

P_k = the probability of occurrence of the kth possibility.

m = the number of possibilities.

The expected return for EG&G is calculated in Table 19–1 as

$$E(R_{EG\&G}) = 0.4(60\%) + 0.2(15\%) + 0.2(5\%) + 0.2(-15\%) = 25\%$$

---

[7]It is always assumed that $\Sigma_{k=1}^{m} P_k = 1$.

Risk of a security To measure the risk of any security we use the variance (or its square root, the standard deviation) of the expected returns. For discussion purposes, these two variables are assumed to be interchangeable. Statistically, the variance measures the dispersion of returns around its expected value. The greater the dispersion in returns, the greater the risk and the greater the variance or standard deviation. Therefore, variance is a logical and consistent measure of the risk of a security to an investor.

To calculate the expected variance or standard deviation for an individual security, the following equations can be used:

$$VAR(R) = \sigma^2 = \sum_{k=1}^{m} (PR_k - E(R))^2 \, P_k \qquad (19\text{--}2)$$

$$SD(R) = \sigma = \left[\sum_{k=1}^{m} (PR_k - E(R))^2 \, P_k \right]^{1/2} \qquad (19\text{--}3)$$

where VAR(R) is the variance of the return on any security and SD(R) is the standard deviation of the return, and all other terms are as previously defined.

As an illustration of these calculations, the lower portion of Table 19–1 shows the calculation of the variance and standard deviation for EG&G, based on the data in the top. The variance of the EG&G return is 0.091; taking the square root of this number, the standard deviation of the return is 30.2%.

Using the previous calculations, the expected return and the expected variance of return would be calculated for each individual security being considered for inclusion in a portfolio. For example, the same calculations would be made for General Fudge based on an estimated probability distribution for the next period. Assuming these inputs are now calculated, we can consider the portfolio's expected return and risk.

Portfolio Return

The expected return on any portfolio is easily calculated as a weighted average of the individual securities' expected returns. The weights used are the percentages of total investable funds invested in each security. The combined portfolio weights are assumed to sum to 100% of total investable funds. For example, with equal dollar amounts in three securities, the portfolio weights are 0.333, 0.333, and 0.333. Under the same conditions with a portfolio of five securities, each security would have a portfolio weight of 0.20.

The expected return of a portfolio can be calculated as

$$E(R_p) = \sum_{i=1}^{n} W_i \, E(R_i) \qquad (19\text{--}4)$$

where

$E(R_p)$ = the expected return on the portfolio.[8]
W_i = the percentage of investable funds placed in security i.
$E(R_i)$ = the expected return on security i.
n = number of securities.

As an example, consider a three-stock portfolio consisting of stocks G, H, and I with expected returns of 12%, 20%, and 17% respectively. Assume that 50% of investable funds is invested in security G, 30% in H, and 20% in I. The expected return on this portfolio is

$$E(R_p) = 0.5(12\%) + 0.3(20\%) + 0.2(17\%) = 15.4\%$$

Regardless of the number of assets held in a portfolio, or the percentage of total investable funds placed in each asset, the expected return on the portfolio is *always* a weighted average of the expected returns for individual assets in the portfolio. Intuitively, the expected return for a portfolio must fall between the highest and lowest expected returns for the individual securities making up the portfolio—exactly where is determined by the percentages of investable funds placed in each of the individual securities in the portfolio.

Portfolio Risk

The remaining computation in the basic portfolio model is that of the risk of the portfolio. In the Markowitz model, risk is measured by the variance (or standard deviation) of the portfolio's return, just as in the case of each individual security. It is at this point that the basis of modern portfolio theory emerges, which can be stated as

Although the expected return of a portfolio is a weighted average of the expected returns of the individual securities in the portfolio, the risk (as measured by the variance or standard deviation) is *not* a weighted average of the risk of the individual securities in the portfolio. Symbolically,

$$E(R_p) = \sum_{i=1}^{n} W_i \, E(R_i) \qquad (19\text{--}4)$$

but

$$VAR(R_p) \neq \sum_{i=1}^{n} W_i \, VAR(R_i) \qquad (19\text{--}5)$$

---

[8] For the remainder of this discussion, the subscript i is used to denote an individual security while p is used to denote a portfolio.

It is precisely because Equation 19–5 is an inequality that investors can reduce the risk of a portfolio beyond what it would be if risk were, in fact, simply a weighted average of the individual securities' risk. Portfolio risk depends not only on the weighted average of the risks of the individual securities in the portfolio, but also on the relationships, or covariances, among the returns on securities in the portfolio. Thus,

Portfolio risk is a function of each individual security's risk and the covariances between the returns on the individual securities. Stated in terms of variance, portfolio risk is

$$VAR(R_p) = \sum_{i=1}^{n} W_i^2\ VAR(R_i) + \sum_{i=1}^{n} \sum_{\substack{j=1 \\ i \neq j}}^{n} W_i W_j\ COV(R_i, R_j) \qquad (19\text{–}6)$$

where

$VAR(R_p)$ = the variance of the return on the portfolio.
$VAR(R_i)$ = the variance of return for security i.
$COV(R_i, R_j)$ = the covariance between the returns for securities i and j.
W_i = the percentage of investable funds invested in security i.

$\displaystyle\sum_{i=1}^{n} \sum_{j=1}^{n}$ = a double summation sign indicating that n^2 numbers are to be added together (i.e., all possible pairs of values for i and j).

The intuitive nature of portfolio risk can be seen by considering Equation 19–6. The first term on the right side of Equation 19–6 is the weighted individual security risks. The second term of the equation, the weighted relationships between securities' returns, can assume a positive value, a negative value, or a zero value, depending upon the exact relationships among the securities; therefore, this term can (1) add to the weighted individual security risks if the term is positive, (2) add nothing to the weighted individual security risks if the term has a value of zero, or (3) reduce the weighted individual security risks if the term has a negative value.

Clearly, then, the relationships among the returns on securities are a central part of portfolio theory. In our earlier discussion of the inputs needed for the Markowitz model, the third input listed was the covariance for each pair of securities' rates of return. We will now consider this input involving the relationships between securities in detail.

Covariance   The covariance is an absolute (as opposed to relative) measure of the degree of association between the returns for a pair of securities. **Covariance** is defined as the extent to which two variables covary (move together) over time. As is true throughout our discussion, the variables in question are the returns (HPYs) on two securities. The covariance can be

1. *Positive,* indicating that the returns on the two securities tend to move in the same direction at the same time; when one increases (decreases), the other tends to do the same.
2. *Negative,* indicating that the returns on the two securities tend to move inversely; when one increases (decreases), the other tends to decrease (increase).
3. *Zero,* indicating that the returns on two securities are independent and have no tendency to move in the same or opposite directions together.

The formula for calculating covariance is

$$COV(R_i, R_j) = E([PR_i - E(R_i)] [PR_j - E(R_j)])$$

$$= \sum_{k=1}^{m} P_k([PR_{ik} - E(R_i)] [PR_{jk} - E(R_j)])$$

$$= \frac{1}{m} \sum_{k=1}^{m} [PR_{ik} - E(R_i)] [PR_{jk} - E(R_j)] \qquad (19\text{--}7)$$

if all returns are equally likely to occur;
that is, $P_k = 1/m$ for each observation.

where

$COV(R_i, R_j) = $ the covariance between securities *i* and *j*.
$PR_i = $ the potential return on security *i*.
$E(R_i) = $ the expected value of the return on security *i*.
$P_k = $ the probability of each observation *k* where *k* represents an individual observation of PR_i and PR_j.
$m = $ the number of pairs of observations.

To illustrate the calculation of a covariance, Table 19–2 repeats the annual HPYs for EG&G and GF. We will use this ex post data to calculate a covariance between EG&G and GF, in effect assuming that each of the returns are equally likely to occur. However, it must be remembered that the model user should determine if the likely future covariations will be different from those of the past and, if so, should use the future expected covariances.

An examination of the HPYs for these two companies indicates that their movements are quite different. General Fudge sometimes has a large HPY while EG&G has a much lower one, with the reverse being also true. In two of the years, one stock's HPY was negative and the other was positive; furthermore, in the other eight years the HPYs had the same sign, but did not necessarily move in the same direction from the previous year.

The calculated covariance between these two stocks is 116.74—a low covariance, which is not surprising, given the differences in their HPY movements over this period. However, an investor cannot judge the size of this covariance in the abstract. The question is, how low is low—what is a

TABLE 19–2 Annual HPYs for EG&G and General Fudge, and Calculation of the Covariance between Them

	HPY% EG&G$_i$	HPY% GF$_j$	$R_i - E(R_i)$	$R_j - E(R_j)$	$[R_i - E(R_i)][R_j - E(R_j)]$
1973	−2.7	−12.0	−29.2	−23.6	689.12
1974	−28.9	−19.1	−55.4	−30.7	1700.78
1975	14.8	63.4	−11.7	51.8	−606.06
1976	21.7	15.4	−4.8	03.8	−18.24
1977	05.6	09.4	−20.9	−02.2	45.98
1978	67.2	07.7	40.7	−03.9	−158.73
1979	70.0	10.4	43.5	−01.2	−52.2
1980	80.3	−03.3	53.8	−14.9	−801.62
1981	−08.3	11.9	−34.8	0.3	−10.44
1982	44.8	32.3	18.3	20.7	378.81
					Σ = 1167.4
Mean	26.5	11.6		Covariance =	116.74
σ	37.3	23.3			

low (or high) covariance? To answer the question of the relative association between two securities' returns, we must refer to the correlation coefficient because it is bounded.

The correlation coefficient In order to account for the effect of the covariations between securities, which is done in the second term of Equation 19–6, it is necessary to estimate the correlation coefficient between each pair of securities, i and j. As used in portfolio theory, the **correlation coefficient** (r_{ij}) is a statistical measure of the extent to which the returns on any two securities are related; however, it denotes only association, not causation. It is a relative measure of association that is bounded by +1.0 and −1.0, with

r_{ij} = +1.0 = perfect positive correlation.
r_{ij} =   0.0 = no correlation.
r_{ij} = −1.0 = perfect negative (inverse) correlation.

Figure 19–1 illustrates these three cases for two securities. In the case of perfect positive correlation, the returns have a perfect direct linear relationship with each other. Knowing what the return on one security will do allows an investor to forecast perfectly what the other will do.

In the case of perfect negative correlation, the securities' returns have a perfect inverse linear relationship to each other; therefore, knowing the return on one security provides full knowledge about the return on the second security. When one security's return is high, the other is low.

With zero correlation, there is no relationship between the returns on the

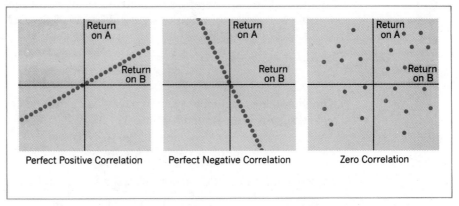

FIGURE 19–1 **Returns on two securities.** (a) perfect positive correlation; (b) perfect negative correlation; (c) no correlation.

two securities. A knowledge of the return on one security is of no value in predicting the return of the second security.

Combining securities with perfect positive correlation provides no reduction in portfolio risk. The risk of the resulting portfolio is simply a weighted average of the individual risks of the securities. As more securities are added under the condition of perfect positive correlation, portfolio risk remains a weighted average. There is no risk reduction.

Combining two securities with zero correlation (statistical independence) reduces the risk of the portfolio. If more securities with uncorrelated returns are added to the portfolio, significant risk reduction can be achieved. However, portfolio risk cannot be eliminated.

Finally, combining two securities with perfect negative correlation could eliminate risk altogether. This is the principle behind hedging strategies, some of which were discussed in Chapter 17.

In the real world, these extreme correlations are rare. Rather, securities typically have some positive correlation with each other. Thus, although risk can be reduced, it usually cannot be eliminated. Other things being equal, investors wish to find securities with the least positive correlation possible. Ideally they would like securities with negative correlation or low positive correlation but they generally will be faced with positively correlated security returns.

Relating the correlation coefficient and the covariance   The covariance and the correlation coefficient are linked in the following manner:

$$COV(R_i, R_j) = r_{ij} \, SD(R_i) \, SD(R_j) \qquad (19\text{–}8)$$

Equation 19–6 can therefore be restated to an equivalent expression, Equation 19–9, by substituting the right side of 19–8 for $COV(R_i,R_j)$ in 19–6.

$$VAR(R_p) = \sum_{i=1}^{n} W_i^2 VAR(R_i) + \sum_{i=1}^{n} \sum_{\substack{j=1 \\ i \neq j}}^{n} (W_i)(W_j)(r_{ij})\, SD(R_i)\, SD(R_j) \quad (19\text{–}9)$$

Knowing the covariance, we can easily calculate the correlation coefficient by rearranging Equation 19–8 into 19–10.

$$r_{ij} = \frac{COV(R_i,R_j)}{SD(R_i)SD(R_j)} \quad (19\text{–}10)$$

The correlation coefficient for EG&G and General Fudge is

$$r_{EG\&G,GF} = \frac{116.74}{(37.3)(23.3)} = 0.134 = 0.13$$

Thus, based on the historical data there is low positive correlation between EG&G and General Fudge. This is a good example of the types of securities that investors would like to combine in their portfolios, *given* a world of mostly positive correlation coefficients between the returns on securities.

Understanding Portfolio Risk

Having considered the correlation coefficient and the covariance as measures of the association between securities' returns, we are now in a position to better understand portfolio risk. We have said that to calculate portfolio risk, we must account for two factors (from Equation 19–6).

1. Weighted individual security risks (i.e., the variance of each individual security, weighted by the percentage of investable funds placed in each individual security).
2. Weighted relationships between securities (i.e., the covariation between the securities' returns, again weighted by the percentage of investable funds placed in each security).

We can now better understand Equation 19–6, or its equivalent, Equation 19–9. One of Markowitz's real contributions to portfolio theory is his insight about the relative importance of these two factors. As the number of securities held in a portfolio increases, the importance of each individual security's risk (variance) decreases, while the importance of the covariance relationships increases. In a portfolio of 500 securities, for example, the contribution of each security's own risk to the total portfolio risk will be extremely small; portfolio risk will consist almost entirely of the covariance risk between securities.

To see this, consider the first term in Equations 19–6 or 19–9.

$$\sum_{i=1}^{n} W_i^2 VAR(R_i)$$

Assume equal amounts are invested in each security. The proportions, or weights, will be $1/n$. Rewriting this term produces

$$\sum_{i=1}^{n} ((1/n)^2) \, VAR(R_i) = \frac{1}{n} \sum_{i=1}^{n} [VAR(R_i)/n]$$

The term in brackets represents an average variance for the stocks in the portfolio. As n becomes larger, this average variance becomes smaller, approaching zero for large values of n. Therefore, the risk of a well-diversified portfolio will be largely attributable to the impact of the second term in Equations 19–6 or 19–9.

We can rewrite Equation 19–6 into a shorter format.

$$VAR(R_p) = \sum_{i=1}^{n} \sum_{j=1}^{n} W_i W_j \, COV(R_i, R_j) \tag{19–11}$$

or

$$VAR(R_p) = \sum_{i=1}^{n} \sum_{j=1}^{n} W_i W_j \, r_{ij} \, SD(R_i) \, SD(R_j) \tag{19–12}$$

These equations account for both the variance and the covariances because when $i = j$, the variance is calculated; when $i \neq j$, the covariance is calculated.

To calculate portfolio risk using either (19–11) or (19–12), we need estimates of the variance for each security and estimates of the correlation coefficients or covariances. Both variances and correlation coefficients can be (and are) calculated using either ex post or ex ante data. If an analyst uses ex post data to calculate the correlation coefficient or the covariance and then uses these estimates in the Markowitz model, the implicit assumption is that the relationship that existed in the past will continue into the future. The same is true of the variances. If the historical variance is thought to be the best estimate of the expected variance, it should be used; however, it must be remembered that the variance and the correlation coefficient can change over time (and does).

After calculating (or estimating) the variances for each security and the covariances for every pair of securities, the portfolio risk can be calculated. The importance of the covariance (or correlation coefficient) can be seen in the following simple example for a portfolio of two securities. By focusing on only two securities, the impact of different covariances (or correlation coefficients) on the total risk of the portfolio can be easily seen.

The two-security case   The risk of a portfolio, as measured by the standard deviation of returns, for the case of two securities, X and Y, is

$$SD(R_p) = [W_X^2 VAR(R_X) + W_Y^2 VAR(R_Y)$$
$$+ 2(W_X)(W_Y)(r_{X,Y}) \, SD(R_X) \, SD(R_Y)]^{1/2} \tag{19–13}$$

In order to illustrate the two security case calculations, we will use the *historical data* for EG&G and GF. The mean annual HPYs for this period were 26.5% and 11.6% respectively, with standard deviations of 37.3% and 23.3%. As we saw earlier, the correlation coefficient between their returns is +0.13.

To see the effects of changing the correlation coefficient, assume that the weights are 0.5 each—50% of investable funds is to be placed in each security. With these data, the standard deviation, or risk, for this portfolio would be

$$SD(R_p) = [(0.5)^2(0.373)^2 + (0.5)^2(0.233)^2$$
$$+ 2(0.5)(0.5)(0.373)(0.233) \, r_{EG\&G,GF}]^{1/2}$$
$$= [0.0348 + 0.0136 + 0.0435 \, r_{EG\&G,GF}]^{1/2}$$

since $2(0.5)(0.5)(0.373)(0.233) = 0.0435$. The risk of the portfolio clearly depends heavily on the value of the third term, which in turn depends on the correlation coefficient between the returns for EG&G and GF. To assess the potential impact of this, consider the following cases: an r of +1, +0.5, +0.13, 0, −0.5, and −1.0. Calculating portfolio risk under each of these scenarios produces the following portfolio risks:

$$r = +1.0: \quad SD(R_p) = [0.0348 + 0.0136 + 0.0435(1)]^{1/2} \quad = 30.3\%$$
$$r = +0.5: \quad SD(R_p) = [0.0348 + 0.0136 + 0.0435(0.5)]^{1/2} \quad = 26.5\%$$
$$r = +0.13: SD(R_p) = [0.0348 + 0.0136 + 0.0435(0.13)]^{1/2} \quad = 23.2\%$$
$$r = \quad 0.0: \quad SD(R_p) = [0.0348 + 0.0136]^{1/2} \qquad\qquad\qquad = 22.0\%$$
$$r = -0.5: \quad SD(R_p) = [0.0348 + 0.0136 + 0.0435(-0.5)]^{1/2} = 16.3\%$$
$$r = -1.0: \quad SD(R_p) = [0.0348 + 0.0136 + 0.0435(-1.0)]^{1/2} = \quad 7.0\%$$

These calculations clearly show the impact on portfolio risk of combining securities with less than perfect positive correlation. The risk of the portfolio steadily decreases from 30.3% to 7% as the correlation coefficient declines from +1.0 to −1.0.

Conclusions about portfolio risk Our discussion of portfolio risk can be summarized in the following points:

1. The risk for a portfolio encompasses not only the individual security risks but also the covariances between all pairs of securities.
2. As previously shown in the two-security case, the importance of the covariance term can equal the combined importance of the individual securities' risks. Therefore, when adding a security to a portfolio, the average covariance between it and the other securities in the portfolio is more important than the security's own risk.
3. Three factors, not two, determine portfolio risk: individual variances, the covariances between securities, and the weights (percentage of investable funds) given to each security.[9]

---

[9] Both expected return and risk change as the weights change, whereas only the risk changes as the correlation coefficient changes.

Calculating Portfolio Return and Risk: An Example

Having considered both of the key parameters of the portfolio model, we now examine an example of building a portfolio using our two securities, EG&G and GF. Assume an investor is considering investing $20,000 in stocks. The investor has decided to buy either EG&G, GF, or a combination of the two. If a portfolio is to be held, the investor has decided to invest half of the funds in EG&G and the other half in GF. The investor believes that the expected return and risk estimates for EG&G in Table 19–1 are reasonable, and makes the following estimates for GF for the coming year based on a judgement that GF will enjoy an exceptionally good year: $E(R_{GF}) = 23\%$ and $SD(R_{GF}) = 25\%$. Note that $W_{EG\&G} = \$10,000/\$20,000 = 0.5$, and therefore $W_{GF} = 1.0 - W_{EG\&G} = 0.5$.

$$E(R_p) = 0.5(25\%) + 0.5(23\%) = 24\%$$
$$SD(R_p) = [(0.5)^2(0.30)^2 + (0.5)^2(0.25)^2 + 2(0.5)(0.5)(0.13)(0.30)(0.25)]^{1/2}$$
$$= [0.0225 + 0.0156 + 0.0049]^{1/2} = 20.7\%$$

By combining GF with EG&G, the investor builds a portfolio with a greater expected return and less risk than if GF was held alone. These beneficial portfolio effects are attributable to the low positive correlation between the returns on these two securities.

Notice that *having established the portfolio weights, W_1 and W_2, the calculation of the expected return on the portfolio is independent of the calculation of portfolio risk.* The expected return will not change if some other variable in the risk calculation changes. For example, assume that the correlation coefficient between EG&G and GF is -0.13 instead of $+0.13$. The expected return on the portfolio remains 24%. The risk would now be

$$SD(R_p) = [(0.5)^2(0.3)^2 + (0.5)^2(0.25)^2 + 2(0.5)(0.5)(-0.13)(0.30)(0.25)]^{1/2}$$
$$= 18.2\%$$

The risk of this portfolio declines because of the beneficial effects of combining negatively correlated stocks. Therefore, holding everything else constant, risk can be reduced without affecting expected return, if the correlation between securities can be reduced.

The two-security case can be generalized to the n security case. Portfolio risk can be reduced by combining assets with less than perfect positive correlation; furthermore, the smaller the positive correlation, the better. A good example of the benefits of diversification using classes of assets, rather than individual securities, can be seen in Box 19–1. A diversified portfolio of U.S. stocks, foreign stocks, bonds, real estate, and Treasury bills has outperformed both the stock market and the typical portfolio manager over a 20-year period.

Determining Efficient Portfolios

Having discussed the expected return and risk of portfolios in detail, we can now consider how the efficient portfolios of the Markowitz model are actually derived. Figure 19–2 illustrates the basic idea of an efficient set of

BOX 19–1 JOYS OF DIVERSIFICATION

Joys of Diversification: A Broad Portfolio Pays Off

Over the past two decades, a diversified investment index has outpaced the U.S. stock market and the typical portfolio manager. The index consists of five equally weighted parts: U.S. stocks, foreign stocks, U.S. corporate and government bonds, real estate and Treasury bills. This index has grown at a 10.2% compound rate since 1965, compared with 9.4% for the S&P 500-stock index and 7.9% for the median U.S. money manager invested in both stocks and bonds.

Most of the extra gains came from foreign equities and real estate, which raced ahead of U.S. stock for much of the 1970s and early 1980s. Analysts differ on whether this performance will continue. But they say diversified portfolios can be less volatile than all-equity accounts, because swings in different parts of broad portfolio often offset one another somewhat.

Individual investors could approximately duplicate the diversification index with a combination of Treasury bills, stocks of real estate investment trusts or limited partnerships in income-producing real estate, and mutual funds specializing in blue chip and overseas stocks and in fixed-income securities.

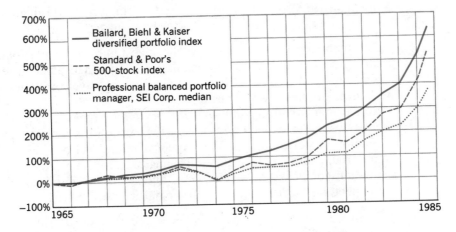

Source: The Wall Street Journal, September 29, 1986, p. 21. Reprinted by permission of *The Wall Street Journal,* © Dow Jones & Company, Inc., 1986. All Rights Reserved.

portfolios. First, note that the vertical axis is expected return and the horizontal axis is risk (as measured by the standard deviation). These are the standard axes in portfolio theory and this diagram will be applied throughout this discussion. It is very important to always keep in mind that portfolio theory is concerned with the returns anticipated for the future (i.e., the expected returns).

In Figure 19–2a, the expected returns and risks of a hypothetical group of securities have been plotted for the year 19X8. By combining these securities into various combinations, an infinite number of portfolio alternatives are possible. These possibilities are illustrated in Figure 19–2b, and include the entire shaded area, which represents the many combinations of expected return and risk obtainable by forming portfolios. In portfolio theory, this

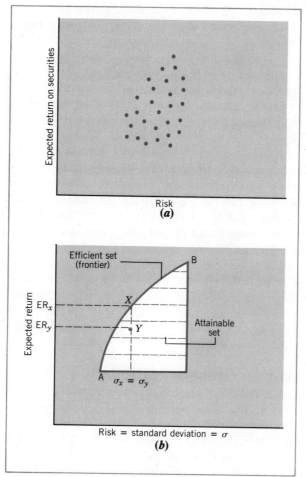

FIGURE 19–2 (*a*) **Expected returns and risk for a group of securities;** (*b*) **the efficient set of portfolios.**

area is referred to as the "attainable set" of portfolios—these portfolios are possible, but not necessarily preferable.

The curve AB represents the **efficient set (frontier)** of portfolios. This set dominates all interior portfolios (the remaining attainable set of portfolios) because it offers the largest expected return for a given amount of risk, or the smallest risk for a given expected return.[10] To see this, consider portfolio X on the efficient frontier and portfolio Y in the attainable set. Although both

---

[10]The dominance principle in portfolio theory states that at a given level of risk investors prefer the portfolio with the highest expected return, or that for a given level of expected return investors prefer the portfolio with the least risk. All other portfolios are then dominated.

have the same level of risk, X has a larger expected return; therefore, portfolio X dominates portfolio Y, and would be preferred by investors. The same type of comparisons could be made with other portfolios with the same result. The efficient set of portfolios is the optimal set of portfolios for investors.

Technically, the basic Markowitz model is solved by a complex technique called *quadratic programming*. Since the model is easily solved by computer, the details need not concern us. It is important to note, however, that the solution involves manipulating the portfolio weights, or percentages of investable funds to be invested in each security. In other words, having inputted the expected returns, standard deviations, and correlations for the securities being considered, this is the only variable that can be manipulated to solve the portfolio problem. Think of efficient portfolios as being derived in the following manner. The inputs are obtained and a level of desired expected return for a portfolio is specified; for example, 10%. Then, all combinations of securities that can be combined to form a portfolio with an expected return of 10% are determined, and the one with the smallest variance of return is selected as the efficient portfolio. Next, a level of portfolio expected return of 11%, for example, is specified, and the process is repeated. This continues until the feasible range of expected returns is processed. Of course, the problem could be solved by specifying levels of portfolio risk and choosing that portfolio with the largest expected return for the specified level of risk.

Selecting an Optimal Portfolio

Once the efficient set of portfolios is determined using the Markowitz model, investors must select the portfolio most appropriate for them from the full set. The Markowitz model does *not* specify one optimum portfolio. It generates the efficient frontier of portfolios, all of which, by definition, are optimal portfolios (for a given level of expected return or risk).

To select the expected return–risk combination that will satisfy an individual investor's personal preferences, indifference curves (which are assumed to be known for an investor) are used. These curves, shown in Figure 19-3 as a family of four curves, describe investor preferences; curve 1 is preferable to 2, which is preferable to 3, which is preferable to 4.[11]

The optimal portfolio for any investor occurs at the point of tangency between the investor's highest indifference curve and the efficient frontier. In Figure 19-3, this occurs at point 0. This portfolio maximizes investor utility because the indifference curves reflect investor utility preferences. Notice that curves U_2 and U_1 are unattainable and that U_3 is the highest

---

[11] Indifference curves are derived from utility analysis and represent the loci of equal utility in return–risk space. Although positively sloped in this analysis (because of the assumption that investors like larger returns and dislike risk), their exact shape depends upon investor preferences for taking risk.

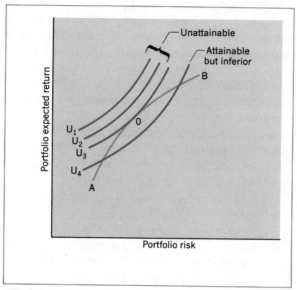

**FIGURE 19-3 Selecting the optimal portfolio on the
efficient frontier.**

indifference curve for this investor that is tangent to the efficient frontier. On
the other hand, U_4, though attainable, is inferior to U_3, which offers a higher
expected return for the same risk (and therefore more utility).

Note that on a practical basis, conservative investors would select portfolios on the left end of the efficient frontier AB because these portfolios
have less risk (and, of course, less expected return). Conversely, aggressive
investors would choose portfolios toward point B because these portfolios
offer higher expected returns (along with higher levels of risk).

The Single Index Model

The Markowitz model generates the correct solution to the portfolio problem; that is, given a set of inputs, the Markowitz efficient-set procedures
produce *the* optimal set of portfolios. It does so, however, at considerable
cost. The major problem with the Markowitz model is that it requires a full
set of covariances between the HPYs of all securities being considered.
There are $[n(n-1)]/2$ *unique* covariances for a set of n securities.[12] If an
analyst is considering 100 securities, it will be necessary to estimate
$[100(99)]/2 = 4950$ unique covariances. For 250 securities, the number is

---

[12] Although for n securities there are $n(n-1)$ total covariances, $COV_{ij} = COV_{ji}$; therefore,
there are only one half as many unique covariances.

[250(249)]/2 = 31,125 covariances. Obviously, estimating large numbers of covariances quickly becomes a major problem for model users. Since many institutional investors follow as many as 250 or 300 securities, the number of inputs required may become an impossibility. In fact, until the basic Markowitz model was simplified in terms of the covariance inputs, it remained primarily of academic interest.

In his original work, Markowitz suggested using an index to which securities are related as a means of generating covariances. William Sharpe, following Markowitz, developed the **single index model,** which relates returns on each security to the returns on a common index.[13] A broad market index of common stock returns is generally used for this purpose.[14]

The single index model can be stated as

$$R_{it} = a_i + b_iR_{Mt} + e_{it} \qquad (19\text{--}14)$$

where

R_{it} = the random return (HPY) on security i in period t.
R_{Mt} = the random return (HPY) on the market index in period t.
a_i = the constant return unique to security i.
b_i = measure of the sensitivity of the stock's return to the return on the market index.
e_{it} = the random residual error in period t, or the difference between the actual return for some period and the return expected given the market return.

To estimate the single index model, the HPYs for stock i can be regressed on the corresponding HPYs for the market index. Estimates will be obtained of a_i (the constant return on security i that is earned regardless of the level of market returns) and b_i (the beta coefficient that indicates the expected increase in a security's return for a 1% increase in market return).

The return on stock i in period t, conditional on a given market return in period t, is simply $a_i + b_iR_{Mt}$. The residual error, e_{it}, is the difference between the actual return for stock i in period t and its expected return. For any one period these error terms can be positive or negative. Over multiple periods the error term should average out to be zero.

To illustrate the calculation of the single index model, we will use the HPY data for EG&G and GF presented earlier in the chapter along with the HPYs for the S&P 500. Fitting a regression equation to each of these companies with the S&P 500 as the market index, the estimated equations are

$$R_{EG\&G} = 16.3 + 1.21R_{S\&P\,500}$$
$$R_{GF} = 5.1 + 0.78R_{S\&P\,500}$$

---

[13] W. Sharpe. "A Simplified Model for Portfolio Analysis." *Management Science* 9 (January 1963), pp. 277–293.

[14] There is no requirement that the index be a stock index. It could be any variable thought to be the dominant influence on stock returns.

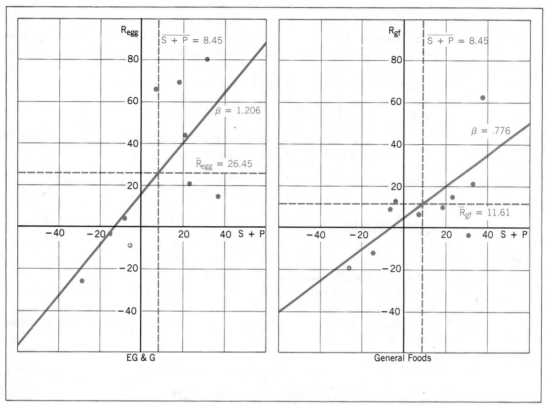

FIGURE 19–4 **Characteristic lines for EG&G and GF using annual HPYs.**

When the HPYs for each stock are plotted against the market index HPYs, and a regression line is fitted to these points, the *characteristic lines* shown in Figure 19–4 result. As can be seen, EG&G has a higher intercept (a_1) then GF (16.3 versus 5.1). This is the unique part of the return, that is, the return on each company when the market return is zero. EG&G's unique return is quite high.

The beta for EG&G is greater than 1.0 because this company's returns are more volatile than the market. On the other hand, GF's beta is considerably less than the market's beta of 1.0, indicating less volatility. This is shown in Figure 19–4 by the slopes of the characteristic lines with EG&G having the steeper slope.

The single index model assumes that the market index is unrelated to the residual error.[15] It is also assumed that securities are related only in their common response to the return on the market; that is, the residual errors for

---

[15] The use of regression analysis in estimating the single index model guarantees that these two variables will be uncorrelated.

security i are uncorrelated with those of security j. This is the key assumption of the single index model because it implies that stocks covary together only because of their common relationship to the market index. In other words, there are no influences on stocks beyond the market, such as industry effects.[16]

The single index model can be used in at least two ways.

1. To simplify the estimations for the inputs to the Markowitz variance–covariance model.
2. To solve the portfolio analysis problem directly; that is, to obtain the expected return and risk for portfolios.

Each of these will be considered in turn.

Using the Model to Estimate the Inputs

The single index model can be used to greatly simplify the estimations of the inputs needed for the basic Markowitz model. From the previous analysis, we know that, to generate the efficient set of portfolios, we need the expected return on each security, the variance of return on each security, and the covariances between each pair of securities.

Based on the single index model, the following equations can be used to obtain the inputs:

$$E(R_i) = a_i + b_i E(R_M) \qquad (19\text{--}15)$$

$$VAR(R_i) = b_i^2[VAR(R_M)] + VAR(e_i) \qquad (19\text{--}16)$$

$$COV(R_i, R_j) = b_i b_j VAR(R_M) \qquad (19\text{--}17)$$

To implement these equations, the user needs a_i, b_i, and $VAR(e_i)$. An expected return for the market index is also needed, as well as an estimate of its future variance. All of these variables may be estimated on the basis of historical data, by probability judgments about the future, or by a combination of the two.

To illustrate implementation of these equations, consider the two stocks previously used, EG&G and GF. The calculated a_i and b_i are 16.3 and 1.21 for EG&G, 5.1 and 0.78 for GF. Assume that the market has an expected return of 10%, with an expected standard deviation of 20% (variance of 400). The expected return for each security would be estimated as

$$\begin{aligned} \text{EG\&G} &= 16.3 + 1.21\,(10) = 28.4\% \\ \text{GF} &= 5.1 + 0.78\,(10) = 12.9\% \end{aligned}$$

---

[16] The use of regression analysis does not guarantee that this will be true. Instead, it is a specific simplifying assumption that, in fact, may or may not be true.

The variances and covariances could be calculated in a similar manner, using the $VAR(e_i)$ from an estimation of Equation 19–14. Notice that in the case of the covariance, the calculation reduces to the product of the two betas and the variance of the market. For these two companies, this would be

$$COV = (1.21)(0.78)(400) = 377.5$$

Here we see the critical assumption of the single index model—securities are related only in their common response to the market index. The residual error terms for stock i are uncorrelated with the residual error terms for stock j. All correlation between security returns is reflected in the "b" term. If, in fact this is not true, Equation 19–17 is incorrect.

Using the single index model for a sample of 250 securities, only 250 estimates of the b_i and the variance of the market index must be estimated to obtain the covariances needed. In contrast, the Markowitz model requires [250(249)]/2 unique covariance estimates. Clearly, the single index model greatly simplifies the problem of obtaining covariances.

The single index model requires $3n + 2$ total pieces of data to implement, where n is the number of securities being considered. For example, the 250 securities mentioned earlier would require $3n + 2 = 3(250) + 2 = 752$ estimates, consisting of 250 estimates of a_i, 250 estimates of b_i, 250 variances of the residual errors $VAR(e_i)$, 1 estimate of the expected return on the market index, and 1 estimate of the expected variance on the market index.

In contrast, the full variance–covariance model of Markowitz requires $[n(n + 3)]/2$ estimates for n securities. In the case of the 250 securities, $[250(253)]/2 = 31,625$ total pieces of data, or

$$
\begin{array}{l}
\ 250 \text{ expected returns} \\
+\ 250 \text{ variances} \\
+\ \dfrac{250(249)}{2} \text{ covariances} \\
\hline
=\ 31,625 \text{ total pieces of data}
\end{array}
$$

Using the Model for Portfolio Analysis

The single index model can be used to solve the portfolio problem directly; that is, the portfolio analysis problem can be reformulated in terms of expected return and variance on the market index. Rather than estimate the inputs for the Markowitz model, we can directly estimate the expected return and risk for a portfolio based on relationships involved with the single index model.

Since expected return on a portfolio is always a weighted average of the expected returns on individual securities, we can calculate $E(R_p)$ as a weighted average of the single index model's equation for the expected return on individual securities (Equation 19–15).

$$E(R_p) = \sum_{i=1}^{n} W_i(ER_i) = \sum_{i=1}^{n} W_iE[(a_i + b_iE(R_M)]$$

$$= \sum_{i=1}^{n} W_ia_i + \sum_{i=1}^{n} W_ib_iE(R_M) \qquad (19–18)$$

The characteristics of the single index model are such that

$$a_p = \sum_{i=1}^{n} W_ia_i \qquad (19–19)$$

$$b_p = \sum_{i=1}^{n} W_ib_i \qquad (19–20)$$

In other words, the portfolio a, a_p, is a weighted average of the individual security a_i's, and the portfolio b, b_p, is a weighted average of the individual security b_i's. Therefore, the expected return for a portfolio can be rewritten as

$$ER_p = a_p + b_pER_M \qquad (19–21)$$

As illustrated in Equation 19–16, the single index model partitions the risk of an individual security into two parts.

$$VAR(R_i) = b_i^2 VAR(R_M) + VAR(e_i)$$

To estimate directly the variance of a portfolio, we need a weighted average of these two parts. Taking advantage of Equation 19–20 for the beta of a portfolio, $VAR(R_p)$ becomes

$$VAR(R_p) = [b_p]^2 VAR(R_M) + \sum_{i=1}^{n} W_i^2 VAR(e_i) \qquad (19–22)$$

As a portfolio is diversified, the second term of Equation 19–22, the weighted unsystematic risk of the portfolio, declines drastically (this will be considered in more detail in the next chapter). The first term, the systematic risk of a portfolio, cannot be eliminated through diversification. Therefore, as the residual risk is reduced through diversification, for well-diversified portfolios the portfolio risk approaches

$$VAR(R_p) = [b_p]^2 VAR(R_M) \qquad (19–23)$$

and

$$SD(R_p) = b_p[SD(R_M)] \qquad (19–24)$$

Estimating Portfolio Return and Risk: An Example

As we did with the Markowitz model, we can estimate the portfolio expected return and risk for a two-stock portfolio consisting of EG&G and GF. Assume again that an investor has $20,000 to invest and plans to invest $10,000 in each stock; therefore, the weights in each will be 0.5. The expected return for the market is 10% with a standard deviation of 20%. Assume the following values for each stock:

	a	b	$VAR(e_i)$
EG&G	16	1.2	850
GF	5	0.8	310

Using Equation 19–18

$$E(R_p) = [0.5][16 + 1.2(10)] + [0.5][5 + 0.8(10)] = 20.5$$

Or, using Equations 19–19 and 19–20 to calculate the a and b for the portfolio, and Equation 19–21 to calculate $E(R_p)$,

$$E(R_p) = a_p + b_p E(R_M)$$
$$= 10.5 + 1.0(10) = 20.5$$

In calculating the risk of this portfolio, note that the weighted systematic risk is

$$[b_p]^2 VAR(R_M) = 1.0(400) = 400$$

whereas the weighted unsystematic risk is

$$[0.5]^2(850) + [0.5]^2(310) = 290$$

Therefore, total risk for the portfolio equals the sum of the two parts, or

$$VAR(R_p) = 400 + 290 = 690$$

and

$$SD(R_p) = [690]^{1/2} = 26.3\%$$

Multi-Index Models

As noted in the previous section, the single index model assumes that stock prices covary only because of common movement with one index, specifically that of the market. Some researchers have attempted to capture some nonmarket influences by constructing multi-index models. Probably the most obvious example of these potential nonmarket influences is the industry factor.[17] A multi-index model is of the form

$$E(R_i) = a_i + b_i R_M + c_i NF + e_i \qquad (19–25)$$

---

[17] In a well-known study, Benjamin King found a common movement among securities, beyond the market effect, associated with industries. See B. King. "Market and Industry Factors in Stock Price Behavior." *Journal of Business* 39 (January 1966), pp. 139–190.

where *NF* is the nonmarket factor and all other variables are as previously defined. Equation 19–25 could be expanded to include three, four, or more indices.

It seems logical that a multi-index model should perform better than a single index model because it uses more information about the interrelationships between stock returns. In effect, the multi-index model falls between the full variance–covariance method of Markowitz and Sharpe's single index model.

How well do these models perform? Given the large number of possible multi-index models, no conclusive statement is possible. However, one well-known study, by Kalman Cohen and Jerry Pogue, found that the single index model outperformed a multi-index model in that it produced more efficient portfolios.[18] This study, using industry classifications, found the single index model was not only simpler but led to lower expected risks.

It is worth noting that the multi-index model tested by Cohen and Pogue (and by Elton and Gruber) actually reproduced the *historical* correlations better than the single index model.[19] However, it did not perform better ex ante, which is the more important consideration because portfolios are built to be held for a future period of time.

Evaluation of the Single Index Model

The single index model is a valuable simplification of the full variance–covariance matrix needed for the Markowitz model. An obvious question to ask is how it performs in relation to the Markowitz model.

In his original paper developing the single index model, Sharpe found that two sets of efficient portfolios—one using the full Markowitz model and one his simplification—generated from a sample of stocks were very much alike.[20] A later study also found that the Sharpe model did no worse than the Markowitz model in all tests conducted, and in tests using shorter time periods it performed better.[21]

In summary, the single index model performs very well and is a major step forward in the evolution of portfolio theory. Furthermore, the use of the single index model makes possible an even more significant simplification in the determination of optimal portfolios, as explained in the next section.

---

[18] K. Cohen and J. Pogue. "An Empirical Evaluation of Alternative Portfolio Selection Models." *Journal of Business* 46 (April 1967), pp. 166–193.

[19] E. Elton and M. Gruber. "Estimating the Dependence Structure of Share Prices—Implications for Portfolio Selection." *Journal of Finance* 5 (December 1973), pp. 1203–1232.

[20] Sharpe, *op. cit.*

[21] G. Frankfurter, H. Phillips, and J. Seagle. "Performance of the Sharpe Portfolio Selection Model: A Comparison." *Journal of Financial and Quantitative Analysis* (June 1976), pp. 195–204.

Simple Techniques for Determining Optimum Portfolios

Based on the single index model, Edwin Elton, Martin Gruber, and Manfred Padberg (EGP) have developed procedures for determining optimal portfolios that are easy to implement compared to the techniques discussed earlier—the computations can even be made without the aid of a computer. Furthermore, the procedures indicate why a stock does or does not enter into an optimal portfolio.[22]

We will refer to this technique for determining the efficient frontier as the EGP technique. To implement it, the single index model must be accepted as the description of the comovement between securities. If this assumption is made, a single number can be used to measure the desirability of adding a stock to an optimal portfolio. This measure is the stock's **excess return to beta ratio,** defined as

$$\text{Excess return to beta} = \frac{E(R_i) - RF}{b_i} \qquad (19\text{--}26)$$

with all terms as previously defined.

In words, Equation 19–26 is the ratio of the extra return, beyond what is offered on a risk-free asset, to the stock's nondiversifiable (i.e., systematic) risk. The higher the ratio, the more desirable the stock for inclusion in a portfolio.

Using the expected returns for EG&G and GF estimated earlier from the single index model, the excess return to beta ratios would be (assuming a risk-free rate of 5%)

$$EG\&G = \frac{28.4 - 5}{1.21} = 19.3$$

$$GF = \frac{12.9 - 5}{0.78} = 10.1$$

To use the EGP technique, the following steps are performed. (This discussion will omit the formulas necessary to calculate certain variables, but Example V at the end of the chapter illustrates the calculations necessary to use this technique.)

1. Calculate the excess return to beta ratio for each stock being considered.
2. Rank all stocks on this ratio from highest to lowest.
3. Using a specified formula, calculate a cut-off point C*, which is based

---

[22] E. Elton, M. Gruber, and M. Padberg. "Optimal Portfolios from Simple Ranking Devices." *Journal of Portfolio Management* 3 (Spring 1978), pp. 15–19; ——. "Simple Criteria for Optimal Portfolio Selection: Tracing Out the Efficient Frontier." *Journal of Finance* 13 (March 1978), pp. 296–302.

on the characteristics of all stocks that belong in the optimum portfolio.

4. Knowing C*, select all stocks with an excess return to beta ratio above C*.

5. Using another formula, calculate the percentage of investable funds to invest in each security. The residual variance of each security plays a major part in this calculation.

EGP note that their technique produces results equivalent to those produced by the quadratic programming technique of the Markowitz model. Obviously, the calculations are much less complex and involved. Furthermore, additional stocks can be evaluated immediately by calculating this ratio. In fact, the attractiveness of stocks can be evaluated before the calculations for an optimal portfolio are initiated.

A Concluding Note

The single index model simplifies the calculations of the inputs needed in the Markowitz model. In addition, the model leads to the derivation of useful measures of risk that will be used in the next chapter to derive a theory of capital markets.

The Elton–Gruber–Padberg procedures greatly simplify the entire process of obtaining optimum portfolios. The calculations required are reduced enormously, although the final results are the same as would be produced using the more involved procedures. Perhaps more important, this procedure produces a very simple screening device (the excess return to beta ratio) that many portfolio managers and investors can readily use to evaluate securities to determine immediately if they warrant inclusion in the optimal portfolio, which was not previously possible.

Summary

This chapter has discussed the basics of portfolio theory, an important part of portfolio management. In earlier chapters we discussed the evaluation and use of securities on an individual basis, but here we were concerned with an investor's portfolio—the combination of assets invested in and held by an investor.

Basic portfolio theory originated with Harry Markowitz, based on the expected return and risk characteristics of securities. Investors seek efficient portfolios, defined as those with maximum return for a specified risk or minimum risk for a specified return. The efficient set (frontier) of portfolios can be calculated from equations for the expected return and risk for a portfolio.

The expected return for a portfolio is a weighted average of the individual securities' expected returns. Portfolio risk, however, is not a weighted average of individual security risks because it is necessary to account for the covariations between the returns on securities. Once determined, the weighted covariance term can be added to the weighted variance of the securities to determine portfolio risk.

To determine the covariations between securities' returns, it is necessary to calculate the covariance or the correlation coefficient. These variables can be positive, negative, or zero, but positive correlation is typical. Investors seek to reduce this positive correlation as much as possible.

Portfolio risk depends not only on the variances and covariances, but also on the weights for each security (as does the portfolio expected return). The weights are the variable to be manipulated in solving the Markowitz portfolio model. After generating the efficient set of portfolios, an investor chooses one based on the point of tangency between the efficient frontier and the investor's highest indifference curve.

The single index model greatly simplifies the calculations for the covariances in the Markowitz model by relating the return on each security to that of a market index. This model assumes that the only reason that stocks move together is because of a common relationship to the market. Using this model, the investor can determine the expected return, variance, and covariance for every security with only $3n + 2$ estimates.

The single index model appears to outperform multi-index models and to compare very favorably with the full variance–covariance model of Markowitz. Furthermore, this model makes it possible to greatly simplify the calculations involved in determining optimum portfolios by using the Elton–Gruber–Padberg techniques. With this approach, each security can be evaluated quickly and easily on the basis of its excess return to beta ratio. The efficient frontier can be determined using much simpler procedures than are involved with the full Markowitz model.

Key Words

Correlation coefficient	Excess return to beta ratio
Covariance	Portfolio management
Efficient portfolio	Single index model
Efficient set (frontier)	

QUESTIONS AND PROBLEMS

1. Evaluate this statement: With regard to portfolio risk, the whole is not equal to the sum of the parts.
2. What is meant by an efficient portfolio?

3. How is expected return for one security determined? For a portfolio?

4. Calculate the number of covariances needed for an evaluation of 500 securities using the Markowitz model. Also, calculate the total number of pieces of information needed.

5. Using the Sharpe model, how many covariances would be needed to evaluate 500 securities? How many total pieces of information?

6. How many, and which, factors determine portfolio risk?

7. The Markowitz approach is often referred to as a mean–variance approach. Why?

8. What is the key assumption underlying the single index model?

9. When, if ever, would a stock with a large risk (standard deviation) be desirable in building a portfolio?

10. What is the relationship between the market model, the single index model, and the characteristic line?

11. What is the relationship between the correlation coefficient and the covariance, both qualitatively and quantitatively?

12. Using the Markowitz analysis, how does an investor select an optimal portfolio?

13. What is the excess return to beta ratio? What are its advantages in relation to the Markowitz model?

14. Explain two different uses for the single index model.

15. Many investors have known for years that they should not "put all of their eggs in one basket." How does the Markowitz analysis shed light on this old principle?

16. What is a multi-index model? Give an example of one. If multi-index models are able to reproduce historical correlations better than the single index model, are they preferable?

17. Why do rational investors seek efficient portfolios?

18. How would the expected return for a portfolio of 500 securities be calculated?

19. Given a set of inputs, explain conceptually how efficient portfolios are determined.

20. Calculate the expected return and risk (standard deviation) for General Fudge for 198X, given the following information:

Probabilities:	0.15	0.20	0.40	0.10	0.15
Expected returns:	0.20	0.16	0.12	0.05	−0.05

21. Four securities have the following expected returns: A = 15%, B = 12%, C = 30%, and D = 22%. Calculate the expected returns for a portfolio consisting of all four securities under the following conditions:
   a. The portfolio weights are 25% each.
   b. The portfolio weights are 10% in A with the remainder equally divided among the other three stocks.
   c. The portfolio weights are 10% each in A and B and 40% each in C and D.

22. Assume the additional information provided below for the four stocks in Problem 21.

	SD(%)	Correlations with			
		A	B	C	D
A	10	1.0			
B	8	0.6	1.0		
C	20	0.2	−1.0	1.0	
D	16	0.5	0.3	0.8	1.0

a. Assuming equal weights for each stock, what are the standard deviations for the following portfolios?
   (1) A, B, and C.
   (2) B and C.
   (3) B and D.
   (4) C and D.
b. Calculate the standard deviation for a portfolio consisting of stocks B and C assuming the following weights: (1) 40% in B and 60% in C; (2) 60% in C and 40% in B.
c. In part a, which portfolio(s) would an investor prefer?

23. Provided in the following table is information on portfolios. Determine which of these portfolio(s) would constitute the efficient set.

Portfolio	Expected Return (%)	Standard Deviation (%)
1	10	20
2	12	24
3	8	16
4	6	12
5	9	21
6	20	40
7	18	36
8	8	15
9	11	19
10	12	22
11	14	26

24. Assume that the expected return on the market is 10% with a standard deviation of 20%. The following information is available for stocks A, B, and C.

	a	b	Residual Error or VAR(e_i)
A	3	1.4	300
B	1	0.7	500
C	20	1.0	200

Using the single index model, answer the following:
a. Calculate the expected return for each stock.
b. Calculate the variance and standard deviation for each stock.
c. Which of the three securities is the riskiest if 100% of an investor's wealth can be invested in only one security?
d. Under the same conditions as c, which security is more risky—B or C?
e. Which security is least risky when added to a well-diversified portfolio?

EXTENDED PROBLEMS, WITH EXAMPLES

I. **Example.** Excess return to beta. For EG&G and GF, the expected returns calculated from the single index model, on the assumption of an expected market return of 10%, are 28.4% for EG&G and 12.9% for GF. Assume an RF of 5%. The excess return to beta ratio for each stock is

$$EG\&G = \frac{(28.4 - 5)}{1.21} = 19.34$$

$$GF = \frac{(12.9 - 5)}{0.78} = 10.13$$

Problem. Using the alphas and betas for the following four corporations, and the same expected market return (10%) and risk-free yield (5%), calculate the excess return to beta for each of four corporations, and in combination with EG&G and GF, show the six corporations rank, from high to low, in the following order:

Corporation	Excess Return to Beta	Beta	Alpha
1. EG&G	19.34	1.21	16.30
2. GF	10.13	0.78	0.10
3. PepsiCo		1.01	0.96
4. IBM		1.06	0.55
5. NCNB		1.13	−1.50
6. EAL		1.62	−10.70

II. **Example.** Portfolio return and risk for the two-security case discussed in the chapter. Assume ex ante returns and standard deviations as follows:

	EG&G	GF
Return (%)	25	23
Standard deviation (%)	30	25
Covariance (%)		112.5

Using Equation 19–10, the correlation coefficient, r, is +0.15. We can now calculate expected portfolio returns and risk for different weights (W). We will now use intervals of 0.20, as shown here.

Proportion in		(1) Portfolio		(3) Standard
EG&G W_i	GF $W_j = (1 - W_i)$	Expected Returns (%)	(2) Variance	Deviation (%)
1.0	0.0	25.0	900	30.0
0.8	0.2	24.6	637	25.2
0.6	0.4	24.2	478	21.9
0.4	0.6	23.8	423	20.6
0.2	0.8	23.4	472	21.7
0.0	1.0	23.0	625	25.0

Problems

1. Using Equation 19–4, confirm the expected portfolio returns in column 1.
2. Using Equation 19–11, 19–12, or 19–13, confirm the expected portfolio variances in column 2.
3. Confirm the expected standard deviations in column 3.
4. On the basis of these data, determine the lowest risk portfolio.

Problem. HPY data are shown here for two different companies, along with the correlation coefficient and covariance. Using these ex post values in place of ex ante values, replicate the results shown in the previous example.

	PepsiCo	Eastern Air Lines (EAL)	
Mean HPY	9.5	3.0	r = 0.39
Variance	1001	2461	COV = 604

III. **Example.** Using the single index model to calculate expected portfolio returns and risk for the two-security case. Making slightly different assumptions from those in Problem I, with the alphas, betas, and the mean square nonsystematic errors for EG&G and General Fudge as follows:

	Alpha	Beta	Nonsystematic Errors	Expected Market Value
EG&G	16	1.2	850	Return = 10%
General Fudge	5	0.8	310	Standard deviation = 20%

Use these values for different portfolio weights to verify the numbers in columns 1 through 7 for $W_i = 0.8$.

$$\text{Alpha} = 16 W_i + 5 W_j = a_p.$$
$$\text{Beta} = 1.2 W_i + 0.8 W_j = b_p$$
$$\text{Expected return} = a_p + b_p (10) = R_p.$$
$$\text{Systematic risk} = 400b_p^2 = S.$$
$$\text{Nonsystematic risk} = 850 W_i^2 + 310W_j^2 = N.$$
$$\text{Variance} = \text{columns } 4 + 5.$$
$$\text{Standard deviation} = \text{square root of column 6.}$$

| Weights | | (1) | (2) | (3) | (4) | (5) | (6) | (7) Standard |
W_i	W_j	a_p	b_p	$R_p(\%)$	S	N	Variance	Deviation (%)
1.0	0.0	16.0	1.20	28.0	576	850.0	1426	37.8
0.8	0.2	13.8	1.12	25.0	502	556.4	1058	32.5
0.6	0.4	11.6	1.04	22.0	433	355.6	788	28.1
0.4	0.6	9.4	0.96	19.0	369	247.6	616	24.8
0.2	0.8	7.2	0.88	16.0	310	232.4	542	23.3
0.0	1.0	5.0	0.80	13.0	256	310.0	566	23.8

Problem. Using the same two corporations used in the previous problem (PepsiCo and EAL), replicate this example. Use the same values for the expected market return and the variance used in the preceding table and the following data:

	PepsiCo	EAL
Alpha	1.0	− 10.0
Beta	1.0	1.6
Ex ante nonsystematic risk	650.0	1500.0

IV. **Example.** Calculation of the characteristic line for EG&G. Let Y be the annual holding period yields for EG&G, and X the yields for the Standard & Poor's 500 (the values are shown in the text). The summary statistics are as follows:

$$n = 10$$
$$\Sigma Y = 264.5 \qquad \Sigma Y^2 = 19{,}503.65$$
$$\Sigma X = 84.5 \qquad \Sigma X^2 = 4{,}660.31$$
$$\Sigma XY = 6995.76$$

$$SS_y = \Sigma(Y - \bar{Y})^2 = \Sigma Y^2 - \frac{(\Sigma Y)^2}{n} = 12{,}507.625$$

$$SS_x = \Sigma(X - \bar{X})^2 = \Sigma X^2 - \frac{(\Sigma X)^2}{n} = 3946.285$$

$$SS_{xy} = \Sigma[(X - \bar{X})(Y - \bar{Y})] = \Sigma XY - \frac{(\Sigma X)(\Sigma Y)}{n} = 4760.735$$

$$\hat{\beta} = \frac{SS_{xy}}{SS_x} = 1.206384$$

$$\hat{a} = \bar{Y} - \hat{\beta}\bar{X} = 16.256$$

$$\hat{Y} = 16.256 + 1.206X$$

Analysis of Variance Source (Risk)	Sum of Squares	No. of Observations	Variance	
Total SS_y	= 12,507.625	$n - 1 = 9$	1389.736	= Total variance
Systematic $\beta^2 SS_x$	= 5,743.275	$n - 1 = 9$	638.142	= Systematic variance
Nonsystematic	= 6,764.350	$n - 1 = 9$	751.594	= Unsystematic variance

Problem. Let Y be the annual HPYs for General Fudge, and X the HPYs for the Standard & Poor's 500 (ΣX, ΣX^2, and the SS_x are the same as above.) Following are additional summary statistics:

$$\Sigma Y = 116.1 \qquad \Sigma Y^2 = 6217.13 \qquad \Sigma XY = 4042.23$$
$$SS_y = 4869.209 \qquad SS_{xy} = 3061.185$$

1. Show that the characteristic line for General Fudge is

$$\hat{Y} = 5.055 + 0.776X$$

2. Construct the analysis of variance table.

Problem. Annual data for four additional corporations are shown here for the same 10-year period. Again using Standard & Poor's 500 as the market index (X), and each of the corporations separately as Y, the summary statistics are as follows:

	PepsiCo	IBM	NCNB	EAL
ΣY	94.9	94.7	80.8	29.7
ΣY^2	9906.2	9776.6	10,667.3	22,236.3
SS_y	9005.6	8879.8	10,014.4	22,148.1
ΣXY	4785.2	4967.7	5,153.8	6,634.8
SS_{xy}	3938.3	4167.4	4,471.0	6,383.9

The ΣX, ΣX^2, and SS_x are the same as before.

1. Show that the characteristic lines for the companies are as follows:

	PepsiCo	IBM	NCNB	EAL
Alpha	1.057	0.550	−1.497	−10.702
Beta	1.009	1.056	1.133	1.618

2. If the ex post values in 1 can be expected to hold for the future and if the expected yield on the S&P 500 is 10%, show that the expected yields would be as follows:

	PepsiCo	IBM	NCNB	EAL
Expected Yield	11.047	11.110	9.833	5.478

V. **Example.** The determination of an optimum portfolio using the single index model. This example is highly simplified and designed to illustrate the principles of portfolio composition. Using the six corporations, and slightly different assumed ex ante values, first rank in descending order on the basis of excess returns to beta (shown in column 1 below). Continuing the assumption that the expected market yield is 10% and the risk-free yield is 5%, the values in the first five columns are assumed.

Ranked Corporation	(1) $(R_i - RF)$ b_i	(2) a_i	(3) b_i	(4) $(R_i - RF)$	(5) $VAR(e_i)$	(6) C_i	
1. EG&G	14.0%	9.8	1.2	16.8%	800	4.884	
2. GF	10.0	5.0	.8	8.0	400	6.949	
3. PepsiCo	8.0	3.0	1.0	8.0	640	7.172	
4. IBM	8.0	3.0	1.0	8.0	500	7.347	$C^* = 7.0$
5. NCNB	4.0	-2.2	1.2	4.8	800	6.705	
6. EAL	1.0	-9.4	1.6	1.6	1,600	5.949	

Using a tedious computational process, the cumulative C_i for the portfolio is calculated in column 6. For an investor with a cut-off point, $C^* = 7$, the optimum portfolio would include EG&G, GF, PepsiCo, and IBM, and NCNB and EAL would be excluded. This model further allows the computation of the appropriate portfolio weights using the formula

$$Z_i = \left[\frac{b_i}{VAR(e_i)}\right]\left[\frac{(R_i - RF)}{b_i} - C^*\right] = \left[\frac{\text{Column 3}}{\text{Column 5}}\right][\text{Column 1} - 7.0]$$

For the four securities to be included in the portfolio, the Z_i are as follows:

Security	Z_i	$W_i = Z_i/\Sigma Z_i$
EG&G	0.0105	0.52
GF	0.0060	0.30
PepsiCo	0.0015625	0.08
IBM	0.0020	0.10
	$\Sigma Z_i = 0.0200625$	$1.00 = \Sigma W_i$

and the $W_i = Z_i/\Sigma Z_i$.

Problem. Using the weights just calculated, show that the characteristic line for the portfolio is

$$R_p = a_p + b_pR_m = 7.136 + 1.044R_m$$

and with the assumed $\hat{\sigma}_m = 20$

$$\text{systematic risk} = 435.9744$$
$$\text{nonsystematic risk} = 261.4160$$
$$\text{total risk} = 697.3904$$

Note: There is still nonsystematic risk because the portfolio does not contain enough securities to completely eliminate it.

Selected References

Cohen, Kalman, and Pogue, Jerry. "An Empirical Evaluation of Alternative Portfolio Selection Models." *The Journal of Business,* April 1967, pp. 166–193.

Elton, Edwin J., and Gruber, Martin J. "Estimating the Dependence Structure of Share Prices—Implications for Portfolio Selection." *Journal of Finance,* December 1973, pp. 1203–1232.

Elton, Edwin J., and Gruber, Martin J. *Modern Portfolio Theory and Investment Analysis,* 3rd ed. New York: John Wiley, 1987.

Elton, Edwin J., and Gruber, Martin J. "Risk Reduction and Portfolio Size: An Analytical Solution." *The Journal of Business,* October 1977, pp. 415–437.

Elton, Edwin J., Gruber, Martin J., and Urich, Thomas. "Are Betas Best?" *Journal of Finance,* December 1978, pp. 1375–1384.

Elton, Edwin J., Gruber, Martin J., and Padberg, Manfred W. "Optimal Portfolios from Simple Ranking Devices." *Journal of Portfolio Management,* Spring 1978, pp. 15–19.

Elton, Edwin J., Gruber, Martin J., and Padberg, Manfred W. "Simple Criteria for Optimal Portfolio Selection: Tracing Out the Efficient Frontier." *Journal of Finance,* March 1978, pp. 296–302.

Elton, Edwin J., Gruber, Martin J., and Padberg, Manfred W. "Simple Criteria for Optimal Portfolio Selection." *Journal of Finance,* December 1976, pp. 1341–1357.

Evans, John, and Archer, Stephen. "Diversification and the Reduction of Dispersion: An Empirical Analysis." *Journal of Finance,* December 1968, pp. 761–767.

Frankfurter, George, and Phillips, Herbert. "Alpha–Beta Theory: A Word of Caution." *Journal of Portfolio Management,* Summer 1977, pp. 35–40.

Frankfurter, George, Phillips, Herbert, and Seagle, John. "Performance of the Sharpe Portfolio Selection Model: A Comparison." *Journal of Financial and Quantitative Analysis,* June 1976, pp. 195–204.

Frost, Peter A., and Savarino, James E. "Portfolio Size and Estimation Risk." *The Journal of Portfolio Management,* Summer 1986, pp. 60–64.

Joy, O. M., Panton, Don, Reilly, Frank, and Stanley, Martin. "Co-Movements of International Equity Markets," *The Financial Review,* 1976, pp. 1–20.

Klemkosky, Robert, and Martin, John. "The Effects of Market Risk on Portfolio Diversification." *Journal of Finance,* March 1975, pp. 147–153.

Markowitz, Harry. *Portfolio Selection: Efficient Diversification of Investments.* New York: John Wiley & Sons, Inc. 1959.

Markowitz, Harry. "Markowitz Revisited." *Financial Analysts Journal,* September–October 1976, pp. 47–52.

Martin, John, and Klemkosky, Robert. "The Effect of Homogeneous Stock Groupings on Portfolio Risk." *The Journal of Business,* July 1976, pp. 339–349.

Sharpe, William. *Portfolio Theory and Capital Markets.* New York: McGraw-Hill, 1970.

Thompson II, Donald. "Sources of Systematic Risk in Common Stocks." *The Journal of Business,* July 1978, pp. 173–188.

Wagner, W., and Lau, S. "The Effect of Diversification on Risk." *Financial Analysts Journal,* November–December 1971, pp. 48–53.

APPENDIX 19—A

INTERNATIONAL DIVERSIFICATION

Chapter 19 has demonstrated the importance of diversification in portfolio theory and management. Diversification reduces the risk of a portfolio, with the absolute amount of risk reduction dependent on the covariance relationships. In a fully diversified portfolio, a substantial portion of the total risk can be diversified away.

If diversifying a portfolio by choosing among U.S. securities reduces risk, what effect would diversifying among foreign securities have? In general, international diversification has a significantly beneficial effect because of the low covariances among the returns from securities of different countries. A study by Maurice Joy et al. of the relationships among major international equity markets showed that the correlations among the returns were low.[1] This is consistent with other studies that have found that international diversification could reduce the risk of portfolios from that existing in domestic portfolios; in other words, diversifications across countries produce less risk than intracountry diversification.

As an example of risk reduction with international diversification, consider the holding periods for a balanced portfolio of U.S. securities and four specialized portfolios of foreign securities, as shown in the following table. The U.S. securities are represented by one of the open-end funds indexed to

---

[1] See O. M. Joy, Don Panton, Frank Reilly, and Stanley Martin, "Co-Movements of International Equity Markets," *The Financial Review,* 1976, pp. 1–20.

609

the S&P 500 Index (like those of the American National Bank and Trust Company of Chicago, the Batterymarch Financial Management Corporations of Boston, or the Wells Fargo Investment Advisors). The foreign portfolios, with data from *Wiesenberger Investment Companies Service*, are represented by Japanese (Japan Fund), Canadian (Canadian Fund), European (Transatlantic Fund), and International (Putnam International Equities) funds.

Year	Holding Period Yields (%)				
	U.S.	Japan	Canada	Europe	International
1973	−14.5	−19.8	−1.7	−3.2	−25.7
1974	−26.0	− 5.1	−21.7	−12.2	−20.8
1975	36.9	41.9	10.7	32.4	35.1
1976	23.6	27.6	4.2	1.5	24.0
1977	−7.2	−2.3	−1.2	5.8	−1.0
1978	6.4	60.2	12.9	25.6	22.8
1979	18.2	−19.8	30.7	15.5	19.6
1980	31.5	32.2	20.5	49.2	25.5
1981	−4.8	19.4	−0.2	−14.6	−0.5
1982	20.4	1.4	7.2	−15.9	9.8
1983	22.3	28.7	25.2	33.0	27.9
Mean	9.7	15.0	7.9	10.6	10.6
SD	20.3	26.0	14.6	22.1	20.2

Source: Reprinted by permission from Wiesenberger Investment Companies Service, 1983 Edition Copyright © 1983, Warren, Gorham & Lamont Inc., 210 South Street, Boston, Mass. All Rights Reserved.

Using Equation 19–4, and either (19–11), (19–12) or (19–13), the combination of U.S. and Japanese securities, using various weightings for the two groups, would yield the following portfolio returns and risk (the covariance between U.S. and Japanese yields is 265.0):

Proportion in		(1)		
U.S.	Japan	Portfolio	(2)	(3)
W_i	W_j	Return (%)	Variance	SD(%)
1.0	0.0	9.70	412.09	20.30
0.9	0.1	10.23	388.25	19.70
0.8	0.2	10.76	375.58	19.38
0.7	0.3	11.29	374.06	19.34
0.6	0.4	11.82	383.71	19.58
0.5	0.5	12.35	404.52	20.11
0.4	0.6	12.88	436.50	20.89
0.3	0.7	13.41	479.63	21.90
0.2	0.8	13.94	533.92	23.11
0.1	0.9	14.47	599.38	24.48
0.0	1.0	15.00	676.00	26.00

In this example, even with a highly diversified portfolio of U.S. securities, the addition of Japanese securities to the portfolio can reduce the risk (and in this case, increase the portfolio return).

International diversification is not without its problems. An important factor affecting the attractiveness of diversifying internationally is changes in exchange rates, which can affect the investor's returns and risks (favorably or unfavorably). The studies of international diversification typically take this factor into account; for example, the Joy et al. study converted returns to dollars at prevailing exchange rates. However, these fluctuations have intensified in recent years. The important point about exchange rate fluctuations is that they introduce an element of uncertainty into the diversification process.

Problems

1. The covariance between U.S. and Canadian returns is 225. Calculate the portfolio average return, variance, and standard deviation for a portfolio of 30% U.S. securities and 70% Canadian securities.
2. The covariance between European securities and U.S. securities is 289. Make the same calculations as in Problem 1.
3. What is the lowest risk portfolio using Japanese securities? How does this risk compare with the Canadian and European cases just calculated?
4. Would you expect the covariance between the international portfolio and the U.S. portfolio to be higher or lower than the others?

CHAPTER 20

CAPITAL MARKET THEORY

This chapter is a natural sequel to the preceding, because capital market theory starts where Markowitz portfolio theory ends. **Capital market theory** describes the pricing of capital assets in the marketplace. Its objective is to provide a model that can be used to price risky assets.[1]

Portfolio theory is normative, describing how investors should act in selecting an optimal portfolio of securities. Capital market theory is positive, describing how assets are priced in a market of investors using the Markowitz portfolio model; that is, capital market theory is based on the concept of efficient diversification.

Assumptions of Capital Market Theory

Capital market theory builds on Markowitz portfolio theory. Each investor is assumed to diversify his or her portfolio according to the Markowitz model, choosing a location on the efficient frontier that matches his or her

---

[1]Much of this analysis is attributable to the work of William Sharpe. See W. Sharpe, "Capital Asset Prices: A Theory of Market Equilibrium under Conditions of Risk," *The Journal of Finance,* Vol. 19 (September 1964), pp. 425–442. Lintner and Mossin developed a similar analysis.

return–risk preferences. Because of the complexity of the real world, additional assumptions must be made.

1. All investors have identical probability distributions for future rates of return; they have identical (or homogeneous) expectations with respect to the three inputs of the portfolio model explained in the previous chapter: expected returns, the variance of returns, and the correlation matrix.
2. All investors have the same one-period time horizon.
3. All investors can borrow or lend money at the risk-free rate of return (designated RF in this text).
4. There are no transaction costs.
5. There are no personal income taxes—investors are indifferent between capital gains and dividends.
6. There is no inflation.
7. No single investor can affect the price of a stock through his or her buying and selling decisions.
8. Capital markets are in equilibrium.

Most, or all, of these assumptions appear unrealistic and disturb many individuals encountering capital market theory for the first time. However, the important issue is how well the theory predicts or describes reality and not how realistic its assumptions are. If capital market theory does a good job of explaining the returns on risky assets, it will be very useful and the assumptions made in deriving the theory will be of less importance.

It should be noted that most of these assumptions can be relaxed without significant effects on the capital pricing asset model (CAPM) or its implications; in other words, the CAPM is robust.[2] Although the results from such a relaxation of the assumptions may be less clear-cut and precise, no significant damage is done. Many of the conclusions of the basic model still hold.

Finally, it is worth noting that all of the assumptions are not necessarily unrealistic. For example, some institutional investors are tax exempt and their brokerage costs, as a percentage of the transaction, are quite small. Nor is it too unreasonable to assume that for the one-period horizon of the model, inflation may be fully anticipated and, therefore, not a major factor.

Introducing a Risk-Free Asset

The key to the development of capital market theory is the introduction of a risk-free asset into the analysis. Investors, in addition to the option of risky assets such as common stocks, always have the option of buying a riskless asset, which for our purposes can be proxied by short-term Treasury securi-

---

[2]For a discussion of changing these assumptions, see E. Elton and M. Gruber, *Modern Portfolio Theory and Investment Analysis,* 3rd ed. (New York: John Wiley, 1987), Chapter 11.

ties. A **risk-free asset** is defined as one with a certain expected return and a variance of return of zero. Since variance $= 0$, the risk-free rate in each period will be equal to its expected value. Furthermore, the covariance between the risk-free asset and any risky asset i will be zero, because

$$COV_{RF,i} = r_{RF,i} SD_i SD_{RF}$$
$$= r_{RF,i} SD_i (0)$$
$$= 0$$

where r denotes the correlation coefficient and SD denotes the respective standard deviation of asset i or the risk-free asset. Therefore, the risk-free asset will have no correlation with risky assets.

Although the introduction of a risk-free asset appears to be a simple step to take in the evolution of portfolio and capital market theory, it is a very significant step. It allows Markowitz portfolio theory to be extended in such a way that the efficient frontier is completely changed, which in turn leads to a general theory for pricing assets under uncertainty.

Combining Risk-Free and Risky Assets

Assume that the efficient frontier developed in the last chapter, as shown in Figure 20–1, has been derived by an investor. The arc AB delineates the efficient set of portfolios of risky assets (for simplicity, assume these are portfolios of common stocks). We now introduce a risk-free asset with return RF and SD $= 0$.

As shown in Figure 20–1, the return on the risk-free asset (RF) will plot on the vertical axis because the risk is zero. Investors can combine this riskless asset with the efficient set of portfolios on the efficient frontier. By drawing a line between RF and various risky portfolios on the efficient frontier, we can examine combinations of risk–return possibilities that did not exist previously. Consider an arbitrary point on the efficient frontier, risky portfolio X. An investor who combines the risk-free asset with portfolio X of risky assets would have a portfolio somewhere on the line RF–X (e.g., point Z). Assume this investor places W_{RF} of investable funds in the risk-free asset, and the remainder $(1 - W_{RF})$ in portfolio X. The expected return on this combined portfolio p would be[3]

$$ER_p = W_{RF}RF + (1 - W_{RF}) ER_X \qquad (20-1)$$

As always, the expected return of a portfolio is a weighted average of the individual assets' expected returns. Since portfolio X, consisting of risky assets, would always be assumed to have a larger *expected* return than the return on the risk-free asset (RF), the greater the percentage of an investor's

---

[3] For simplicity, we will drop the parentheses used in Chapter 19 to designate the expected return and standard deviation of return for an asset or portfolio and use only ER and SD, with appropriate subscripts, to designate the portfolio or asset being referenced.

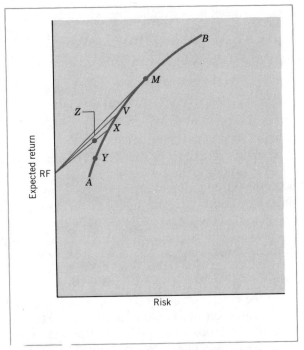

FIGURE 20–1 The Markowitz efficient frontier and the lending possibilities resulting from introducing a risk-free asset.

funds committed to X, $(1 - W_{RF})$, the larger the expected return on the portfolio.

The standard deviation of this portfolio is

$$SD_p = (1 - W_{RF}) SD_X \qquad (20\text{--}2)$$

because $SD_{RF} = 0$ and the correlation between RF and any risky portfolio is zero, eliminating the covariation term. Thus, the standard deviation of a portfolio combining the risk-free asset with a risky asset (portfolio) is simply the weighted standard deviation of the risky portfolio.

As an example, assume that portfolio X has an expected return of 15% with a standard deviation of 10%, and the risk-free security has an expected return of 7%. If half of investable funds is placed in each (i.e., $W_{RF} = 0.5$ and $1 - W_{RF} = 0.5$)

$$ER_p = 0.5(7\%) + 0.5(15\%) = 11\%$$

and

$$SD_p = (1.0 - 0.5)10\% = 5\%$$

An investor could change positions on the line RF–X by varying W_{RF}, and hence $1 - W_{RF}$. As more of the investable funds are placed in the risk-free asset, both the expected return and the risk of the portfolio decline.

It should be apparent that the segment of the efficient frontier below X (i.e., A to X) is now dominated by the line RF–X. For example, at point Z on the straight line, the investor has the same risk as portfolio Y on the Markowitz efficient frontier, but Z has a larger expected return.

Lending Possibilities

In Figure 20–1 a new line could be drawn between RF and the Markowitz efficient frontier above point X; for example, connecting RF to point V in the figure. Each successively higher line will dominate the preceding set of portfolios. This process ends when a line is drawn tangent to the efficient frontier, given a vertical intercept of RF. In Figure 20–1, this occurs at point M. The set of portfolio opportunities on this line (RF to M) dominates all portfolios below it. Point M, called the market portfolio, is very important in capital market theory and is discussed in the following paragraphs.

The straight line from RF to the efficient frontier at point M, RF–M, dominates all straight lines below it and contains the superior lending portfolios. Lending refers to the purchase of a riskless asset such as Treasury bills, because in doing so the investor is lending money to the issuer of the securities, the U.S. government. Through a combination of lending (investing funds at a rate of RF) and investing in a risky portfolio of securities, an investor has changed the opportunity set available from the Markowitz efficient frontier.

With the introduction of the possibility of lending (i.e., purchasing a risk-free asset) investors have several alternatives.

1. To invest 100% of investable funds in the riskless asset, providing an expected return of RF and zero risk.
2. To invest 100% of investable funds in risky asset portfolio M, offering ER_M, with its risk SD_M.
3. To invest in any combination of return and risk between these two points, obtained by varying the proportion W_{RF} invested in the riskless asset.

Each investor would choose a point on this line that corresponds to his or her risk preferences. Formally, this would be where the investor's highest indifference curve is tangent to the straight line. In practical terms, this means that the more conservative investors would be closer to the risk-free asset designated by the vertical intercept RF. More aggressive investors would be closer to, or on, point M, representing full investment in a portfolio of risky assets. This latter group, however, can go beyond point *M*, and it is to this possibility that we now turn.

Borrowing Possibilities

Recall from the assumptions of capital market theory that investors are able to borrow and lend at the risk-free rate RF. Borrowing additional investable funds and investing them together with the investor's own wealth allows investors to seek higher expected returns while assuming greater risk. These borrowed funds can be used to lever the portfolio position beyond point *M*, the point of tangency between the straight line emanating from RF and the efficient frontier *AB*. As in the lending discussion, point *M* represents 100% of an investor's wealth in the risky asset portfolio *M*. The straight line RF–*M* is now extended upward, as shown in Figure 20–2, and can be designated RF–*M*–*L*.

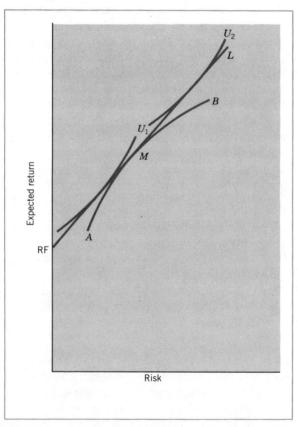

FIGURE 20–2 The efficient frontier when lending and borrowing possibilities are allowed.

What effects does borrowing have on the expected return and risk for a portfolio? These parameters can be calculated in the usual manner. It must be noted, however, that the proportions to be invested are now stated differently. Since the proportions to be invested in the alternatives are stated as percentages of an investor's total investable funds, various combinations must add up to 1.0 (i.e., 100%, representing an investor's total wealth). Therefore, the proportion to be borrowed at RF is stated as a negative figure,[4] so that

$$W_{RF} + (1 - W_{RF}) = 1.0 = 100\% \text{ of investor wealth} \quad (20\text{--}3)$$

As an example, assume an investor can borrow 100% of his or her investable wealth, which, together with the investable wealth itself, will be invested in risky asset portfolio M (i.e., 200% of investable wealth is invested in portfolio M). The $1 - W_{RF}$ weight must now equal 2.0 to represent the sum of original wealth plus borrowed funds. To obtain this result, the proportion of investable funds to be placed in the risk-free asset is negative— specifically, -1.0. Therefore, the proportion to be invested in portfolio M is $[1 - (-1)] = 2$. Overall, the combined weights are still equal to 1.0 since

$$W_{RF} + (1 - W_{RF}) = 1.0$$
$$-1 + [1 - (-1)] = 1.0$$

The expected return on the investor's portfolio p, consisting of investable wealth plus borrowed funds invested in portfolio M, is now

$$ER_p = W_{RF} \, RF + (1 - W_{RF}) \, ER_M$$
$$= -1(RF) + 2 \, ER_M$$

The expected return increases linearly as the borrowing increases. The standard deviation of this portfolio is

$$SD_p = (1 - W_{RF}) \, SD_M$$
$$= 2 \, SD_M$$

Risk will also increase as the amount of borrowing increases.

As an example of borrowing possibilities (i.e., leverage), consider the following example. Assume that the expected return on portfolio M is 20%, with $SD_M = 13\%$. The expected risk-free rate, RF, is still 7%, as in the previous example; however, it now represents the borrowing rate, or the rate at which the investor must pay interest on funds borrowed and invested in the risky asset M. The expected return on this portfolio would be

$$ER_p = -1(7\%) + 2(20\%)$$
$$= -7\% + 40\%$$
$$= 33\%$$

---

[4] Keep in mind that with lending, the investor earns a rate RF, whereas with borrowing, the investor pays the rate RF on the borrowed funds.

The standard deviation of this leveraged portfolio would be

$$SD_p = (1.0 - W_{RF}) SD_M$$
$$= (1.0 - (-1.0)) SD_M$$
$$= 2 SD_M$$
$$= 26\%$$

The Market Portfolio

Portfolio M in Figure 20–2 is called the **market portfolio** of risky securities. It is the highest point of tangency between RF and the efficient frontier. Every investor would want to be on the optimal line RF–M–L, and unless they invested 100% of their wealth in RF, would want to own portfolio M with some portion of their investable wealth or to invest their own wealth plus borrowed funds in portfolio M.

In equilibrium, all risky assets must be in portfolio M because all investors are assumed to hold the same risky portfolio. If they do, in equilibrium this portfolio must be the market portfolio consisting of all risky assets. All assets are included in portfolio M in proportion to their market value. For example, if the market value of IBM constitutes 2% of the market value of all risky assets, IBM will constitute 2% of the market value of portfolio M and, therefore, 2% of the market value of each investor's portfolio of risky assets.

In theory, the market portfolio should include all risky assets, both financial (bonds, options, futures, etc.) and real (gold, real estate, etc.), in their proper proportions.[5] Such a portfolio would be completely diversified. The market portfolio is a risky portfolio, and its risk will be designated SD_M.

Of course, the market portfolio is unobservable.[6] In practice, the market portfolio is often proxied by the portfolio of all common stocks, which, in turn, is proxied by a market index such as Standard & Poor's 500 Composite Index. Therefore, to facilitate this discussion, think of portfolio M as a broad-market index such as the S&P 500 Index.

The Separation Theorem

We have established that all investors will hold combinations of the risk-free asset (either lending or borrowing) and the market portfolio (M). By combining these two assets into various portfolios, investors can form efficient portfolios along line RF–M–L in Figure 20–2. Unlike the Markowitz analysis, it is not necessary to match an investor's utility curves with a particular

---

[5]The market portfolio contains all marketable assets in the proportions W_i, where

$$W_i = \frac{\text{Total value of the } i\text{th asset}}{\text{Total value of all assets in the market}}$$

[6]Market values and returns have been computed for a "world market wealth portfolio" consisting of stocks, bonds, cash, real estate, and metals. See Roger G. Ibbotson, Laurence B. Siegel, and Kathryn S. Love, "World Wealth: Market Values and Returns," *The Journal of Portfolio Management*, Fall 1985, pp. 4–23.

efficient portfolio, because only one efficient portfolio, portfolio M, is held by all investors. Rather, the investor uses utility curves to determine where along the new efficient frontier RF–M–L he or she should be; that is, how much of investable funds should be lent or borrowed at RF and how much should be invested in portfolio M. This decision process is known as the separation theorem.

The **separation theorem** states that the investment decision (i.e., which portfolio of risky assets to hold) is separate from the financing decision (i.e., how to allocate investable funds between the risk-free asset and the risky asset).[7] The risky portfolio M is optimal for every investor regardless of that investor's utility function; that is, M's optimality is determined separately from knowledge of any investor's risk–return preferences. All investors, by investing in the same portfolio of risky assets (M) and by either borrowing or lending at the rate RF, can achieve any point on the straight line RF–M–L in Figure 20–2. Each point on that line represents a different expected return–risk trade-off. An investor with utility curve U_1 will be at the lower end of the line, representing a combination of lending and investment in M. On the other hand, utility curve U_2 represents an investor borrowing at the rate RF to invest in risky assets—specifically, portfolio M.

The concept of the riskless asset–risky asset (portfolio) dichotomy is an important one in investments, with several different applications. As we have seen, using the two in combination allows investors to achieve any point on the expected return–risk trade-off that all investors face. Furthermore, some of the new techniques utilize the same two assets. For example, **portfolio insurance** is an asset allocation strategy that seeks to rebalance a portfolio between a risky component and a riskless component in order to keep the portfolio return from declining below some specified minimum return. See Box 20–1 for an explanation of portfolio insurance using the riskless and risky asset combination.

The New Efficient Frontier

The end result of introducing a riskless asset into the analysis is to create lending and borrowing possibilities and a set of expected return–risk possibilities that did not exist previously. As shown in Figure 20–2, the new frontier is a straight line tangent to the efficient frontier at point M and with a vertical intercept RF. Investors can be anywhere they choose on this line, depending on their risk–return preferences.

The introduction of the risk-free asset significantly changes the efficient frontier. Specifically, the following points emerge:

1. The new efficient frontier is no longer a curve, or arc, as in the Markowitz analysis. It is now linear.

---

[7]See J. Tobin, ''Liquidity Preference as Behavior Towards Risk,'' *Review of Economic Studies*, February 1958, pp. 65–87.

BOX 20–1 PORTFOLIO INSURANCE—COMBINING THE RISKY AND THE RISKLESS ASSETS

When a stampede of institutional sell orders sent the Dow Jones Industrial Average plunging 87 points last Sept. 11, a major part of the blame was put on something called "portfolio insurance."

To many individual investors, this new investment tactic—combining powerful computer programs and mammoth transactions in the stock and futures markets—seemed like one more mystifying example of the institutions' strength.

It may come as some surprise, then, to learn that portfolio insurance is really so simple that individual investors not only can understand it, but could also design their own insurance strategies and implement them using mutual funds.

Professional mumbo jumbo aside, portfolio insurance is nothing more than a graduated stop-loss strategy that sells stocks as the market declines and buys as it rallies. It isn't really insurance; the idea is to limit losses while still allowing investors to participate in the market's gains.

"It's just reinventing the wheel, just the same old stop-loss approach, which in itself is a revelation to most people," says Joseph Grundfest, a Securities and Exchange Commission member.

'Practical and Affordable'

Using a no-load mutual fund group that allows unlimited switching privileges "could make this practical and affordable for an individual," says Michael Granito, a managing director of J. P. Morgan Investment Management Inc. Otherwise, the transaction costs would be prohibitive.

But there is a cost to portfolio insurance, and it can be substantial. Because the tactic

The Cost of Insurance
Expected returns of one insured portfolio after a year under different market conditions:

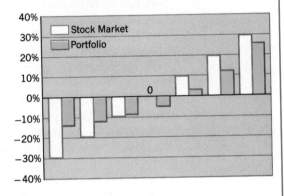

doesn't anticipate but only reacts to market moves, investors are always in the position of buying a little high and selling a little low. In a very jumpy market, the incremental losses caused by this "whipsaw effect" could sharply depress results even if stocks ended with a gain.

To understand how the strategy works, investors should think of a portfolio as containing a "risky" asset, such as an equity fund, and a "safe" asset, such as a money market fund. The basic approach is to shelter the investment in the safe asset when stocks decline and expose them to more risk as stocks rise. The portfolio-insurance trading plan will determine the "hedge ratio"—the portion of funds that should be in each asset at any given time to assure that the value of the total portfolio never falls below the minimum "insured" level, or floor.

The two key strategic choices for investors in designing a trading plan are the level of the floor and over what period of time they want the insurance to work. The higher the floor and the shorter the time span, the more conservative the strategy and the more it will cost.

Robert Ferguson, a vice president at Leland, O'Brien & Rubenstein, a Los Angeles-based investment-advisory firm that sells portfolio insurance to institutions, is using a three-year, no-loss trading plan with different Vanguard Group and Value Line Inc. mutual funds. By "no loss," he means that in the worse case his portfolio would be worth as much at the end of three years as it is at the beginning.

Thus, even if stocks drop so that the value of the total portfolio is down 10%–15% in the first year, Mr. Ferguson says, the value would be back to its starting level at the end of the third year. That's because the decline would cause him to switch his portfolio into money-market assets, which would earn enough in the remaining time to make up the loss.

The basic approach Mr. Ferguson uses works something like this: He starts with a 90%–10% mix of stocks to cash; when stock prices rise or fall 4% against Treasury bills, he alters the mix by 12%. If stocks went up 4%, he'd cap out at 100% invested; if they fell 4%, he'd lower his exposure from 90% to 78%, and so on.

"It's a simple rule like that," he says. "You take a starting mix, a trade barrier such as a 4% move, and set an amount to be moved from one asset to the other each time that barrier is crossed."

Fischer Black, a Goldman, Sachs & Co. partner who is a pioneer in portfolio-insurance theory, proposes an even simpler approach. "The version I like for individuals involves starting 100% invested, with an 80% floor," he says. "All you do is set trading points to sell half your stocks when the market declines half way to your floor; sell half of what's left in stocks when the value of the portfolio drops another quarter of the way to the floor; again, half of what's left when it's one-eighth of the way from the floor, and so on," he explains. "It's like a rabbit constantly jumping half way to its hole—mathematically, it will never get there."

If an investor wants a higher floor of, say, 90%, Mr. Black recommends starting with 50% already invested in the safe asset and using the same 80%-floor trading plan with the 50% that's in stocks. "An individual should never run a program like this with a floor higher than 80%; otherwise, if the market flips around, he'd stand to lose a lot on volatility," he cautions.

But nobody can eliminate the insidious effect of volatility. Consider what would happen under Mr. Black's strategy to a $100,000 portfolio if the market dropped 10%, then returned to its initial level.

Progressively Bigger Loss

At the low point, when the value of the portfolio fell to $90,000, the strategy would call for the investor to sell half the stocks—leaving $45,000 in money market funds and $45,000 in stocks. When stocks then rose 10%, the equity portion would be worth $49,500. The strategy would then call for shifting the $45,500 of money-market assets back into stocks. But the total portfolio would be worth only $94,500—a loss of 5.5% that wouldn't have been incurred if the investor had simply done nothing.

If the situation kept repeating itself, the investor would give up progressively more until virtually all of the portfolio was sheltered in the safe asset. The investor would then risk paying a very heavy cost in lost opportunity if the market rallied.

Even under normal conditions, volatility will nibble away at an investor's return.

For those put off by the complexities of these strategies, several mutual funds that intend to use portfolio insurance are currently in registration with the SEC. Mr. Ferguson predicts that fund groups will eventually develop customized automatic-switching services that will accomplish these same ends.

Source: Barbara Donnelly, "Portfolio Insurance Strategies Can Limit Investors' Losses, But Price May Be High," *The Wall Street Journal,* January 13, 1987, p. 31. Reprinted by permission of *The Wall Street Journal,* © Dow Jones & Company, Inc. 1987. All Rights Reserved.

2. Only one portfolio of *risky assets* is efficient. In the Markowitz analysis, many portfolios of risky assets are efficient.
3. Borrowing and lending possibilities, combined with the one efficient portfolio of risky assets, *M*, offer an investor whatever risk-expected return combination he or she seeks.

The straight line shown in Figure 20–2, which shows the optimal expected returns for any level of portfolio risk, has a special name in capital market theory, as discussed in the next section.

The Capital Market Line

The straight line shown in Figure 20–2 traces out the risk–return trade-off for efficient portfolios, which, as we have seen, is tangent to the Markowitz efficient frontier at point *M* and has a vertical intercept RF.

This straight line, usually referred to as the **capital market line (CML),** shows the conditions prevailing in the capital markets in terms of expected return and risk. It depicts the *equilibrium conditions* that prevail in the market for efficient portfolios consisting of the portfolio of risky assets or the risk-free asset, or both. All combinations of risky and risk-free portfolios are bounded by the CML, and all investors will end up with portfolios somewhere on the CML.

Consider the equation for the CML, which is shown as a straight line in Figure 20–3 without the now-dominated Markowitz frontier. We know that this line has an intercept of RF. If investors are to invest in risky assets, they must be compensated for this additional risk with a risk premium. The vertical distance between the risk-free rate and the CML at point *M* in Figure 20–3 is the amount of return expected for bearing the risk of the market portfolio; that is, the excess return above the risk-free rate. At that point, the amount of risk for the market portfolio is given by the horizontal dotted line between RF and SD_M. Therefore,

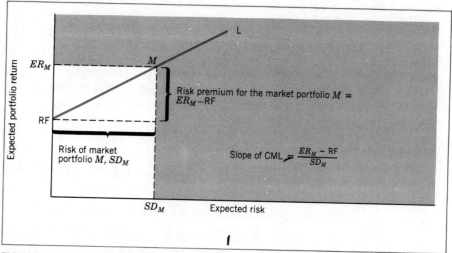

FIGURE 20–3   **The capital market line and the components of its slope.**

$$\frac{ER_M - RF}{SD_M} = \text{Slope of the CML} \qquad\qquad (20\text{--}4)$$

$$= \text{Expected return--risk trade-off for efficient portfolios}$$

The slope of the CML is the market price for risk for efficient portfolios. It indicates the additional return that the market demands for each percentage increase in a portfolio's risk—that is, in its standard deviation of return. Assume, for example, that the expected return on portfolio M is 13% with a standard deviation of 25%, and that RF is 7%. The slope of the CML would be

$$\frac{0.13 - 0.07}{0.25} = 0.24$$

The slope of the CML indicates the equilibrium price of risk in the market. In our example, a risk premium of 0.24 indicates that the market demands this amount of return for each percentage increase in a portfolio's risk.

We now know the intercept and slope of the CML. Since the CML is the trade-off between expected return and risk for efficient portfolios, and risk is being measured by the standard deviation, the equation for the CML is

$$ER_p = RF + \frac{ER_M - RF}{SD_M} SD_p \qquad\qquad (20\text{--}5)$$

where

ER_p = the expected return on any efficient portfolio on the CML.
RF = rate of return on the risk-free asset.

ER_M = the expected return on the market portfolio M.

SD_M = the standard deviation of the returns on the market portfolio.

SD_p = the standard deviation of the efficient portfolio being considered.

In effect, the expected return for any portfolio on the CML = (price necessary to induce investors to forgo consumption) + (market price of risk) times (amount of risk on the portfolio being considered).

Note that: RF is the price of forgone consumption,

$$\frac{ER_M - RF}{SD_M} \text{ is the market price of risk, and}$$

SD_p is the amount of risk being assumed on a particular portfolio.

The following points should be noted about the CML:

1. Only efficient portfolios consisting of RF and M lie on the CML. Portfolio M, the market portfolio of risky securities, contains all securities weighted by their respective market values—it is the optimum combination of risky securities. The risk-free asset has no risk. Therefore, all asset combinations on the CML are efficient portfolios consisting of M and RF.

2. The slope of the CML must always be upward because the price of risk must always be positive. Remember that the CML is formulated in a world of expected return, and risk-averse investors will not invest unless they *expect* to be compensated for the risk. The greater the risk, the greater the expected return.

3. On a historical basis, for some particular period of time such as a year or two, or four consecutive quarters, the CML can be downward sloping—that is, the return on RF exceeds the return on the market portfolio. This does not negate the validity of the CML, it merely indicates that returns actually realized differ from those that were expected. Obviously, investor expectations are not always realized (if they were, there would be no risk). Thus, although the CML must be upward sloping *ex ante* (before the fact), it can be, and sometimes is, downward sloping *ex post* (after the fact).

4. The CML can be used to determine the optimal expected returns associated with different portfolio risk levels. Therefore, the CML indicates the required return for each portfolio risk level.

The Security Market Line

The capital market line applies only to efficient portfolios. These portfolios contain only systematic risk and no residual (unsystematic) risk. What about individual securities or inefficient portfolios? Can this type of analysis be applied to them?

Conceptually, the same type of framework should be applicable for individual securities as for efficient portfolios. After all, the essence of investments is that expected return and risk go together, as explained in Chapter 5. An upward-sloping trade-off should exist between these two variables. The key question, however, is how to measure the risk of an individual security.

Two Sources of Risk

In the previous chapter, the single index model was used to simplify the Markowitz model by greatly reducing the number of covariances that must be calculated. This model was stated in Chapter 19 as

$$R_{it} = a_i + b_i R_{Mt} + e_{it} \qquad (20\text{--}6)$$

where

R_{it} = the random return on stock i during some period t.
R_{Mt} = the random return on the overall market during period t.
a_i = the unique part of stock i's return.
b_i = the measure of the expected increase in return for security i given a 1% increase in market return.
e_{it} = the random residual error in period t (i.e., the difference between the actual return in period t and the predicted return in period t).

Using this model, a security's return can be divided into a unique part and a market-related part. Similarly, a security's total risk, as measured by the standard deviation, can be attributed to two sources.

Taking the variance of Equation 20–6 results in

$$
\begin{aligned}
\text{VAR } R_i &= \text{VAR } [a_i + b_i R_M + e_i] \\
&= b_i^2[\text{VAR } R_M] + \text{VAR } e_i \\
&= \text{Systematic risk} + \text{Unsystematic risk} \qquad (20\text{--}7)
\end{aligned}
$$

As Equation 20–7 shows, the total risk of a security, as measured by the variance in the rate of return, can be decomposed into (1) systematic risk—that part of total risk associated with the variability in the overall market—and (2) unsystematic risk—that part of total risk not related to the variability in the overall market.

$$\text{Systematic risk} + \text{Unsystematic risk} = \text{Total risk}$$

The unsystematic risk portion of a security's variance in Equation 20–7 can be diversified away by holding a portfolio of securities. In effect, the unique part of the risk of each security is canceled out, leaving the portion that is attributable to the systematic variance arising from the market.

Figure 20–4 illustrates this concept of declining unsystematic risk in a portfolio of securities. As more securities are added, the unsystematic risk becomes smaller and smaller, and the total risk for the portfolio approaches its systematic risk. Since diversification cannot reduce systematic risk, total portfolio risk can be reduced no lower than the total risk of the market portfolio.

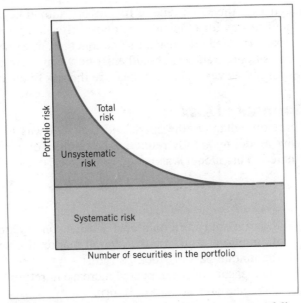

FIGURE 20–4 The effect of diversification on portfolio risk.

How many securities does it take to eliminate most or all of the unsystematic risk? In a well-known study, John Evans and Stephen Archer found that the total risk of a 15 stock portfolio was approximately the same as that for the market portfolio.[8] The added benefit of additional diversification declined sharply after 15 or 16 securities.

The Expected Return–Risk Relationship

What is important is each security's contribution to the total risk of the portfolio. If a portfolio is completely diversified, the only risk it has is systematic risk. Therefore, the contribution of any one security to the riskiness of a portfolio is its systematic risk.

We can relate each individual security to the risk of the portfolio through its covariance with the market portfolio, $COV_{i,M}$. However, it is more convenient to use a standardized measure of systematic risk, the beta coefficient, by taking advantage of the following relationship:

$$b_i = \frac{COV_{i,M}}{VAR\ R_M} = \frac{SD_i}{SD_M}\ r_{i,M} \qquad (20\text{--}8)$$

---

[8] See J. Evans and S. Archer, "Diversification and the Reduction of Dispersion: An Empirical Analysis," *The Journal of Finance*, Vol. 23 (December 1968), pp. 761–767.

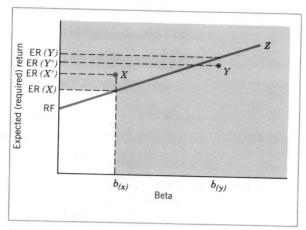

FIGURE 20–5   The security market line (SML).

To derive the expected return–risk relationship for one security, recognizing that the contribution of a security to the total risk of a diversified portfolio is its systematic risk, we simply reformulate the expected return–risk trade-off with beta (the measure of relative systematic risk) on the horizontal axis, as shown in Figure 20–5. The vertical axis remains the expected return, and the intercept of the trade-off on this vertical axis remains the risk-free rate of return, RF.

Note that the vertical axis is the expected, or required, return for an asset. In equilibrium, investors *require* a particular expected return before they will undertake the investment. In Chapter 5 we defined the required rate of return for a security as the minimum expected rate of return needed to induce an investor to purchase it; that is, given its risk, a security must offer some minimum expected return before a particular investor can be persuaded to purchase it. Thus, in discussing the security market line concept, we are simultaneously talking about the required and expected rate of return.

As we could (and should) expect, Figure 20–5 again demonstrates that if investors are to seek higher expected returns, they must assume a larger risk. The trade-off between *expected* return and risk must always be positive.[9]

The line RF–Z in Figure 20–5 is called the **security market line (SML)**. It depicts the trade-off between risk and required (expected) return for *all assets,* whether individual securities, inefficient portfolios, or efficient portfolios. The SML is the graph of the CAPM explained in Chapter 5. The equation for this relationship is

$$ER_i = RF + b_i[ER_M - RF] = SML = CAPM \qquad (20\text{–}9)$$

_____
[9]Again, this relationship may turn out to be negative ex post.

where

ER_i = the expected (required) rate of return for security i.

b_i = the beta or systematic risk for security i.

ER_M = the expected return on the aggregate market.

In Equation 20–9, the term $[ER_M - RF]$ is referred to as the market risk premium. It compensates for assuming risk because it is the expected return in excess of that available from buying the risk-free asset. The b_i for a security is calculated from Equation 20–8. Having calculated beta and estimated the market risk premium, the expected return for any security can be calculated from Equation 20–9.

Assume that the beta for EG&G is 1.20, as calculated from Equation 20–8. Also assume that RF is 0.10 and that the expected return on the market is 0.18. The expected return for EG&G can be calculated as

$$ER_{EG\&G} = 0.10 + 1.20[0.18 - 0.10]$$
$$= 19.6\%$$

EG&G's expected return would be 19.6%. Since its beta is larger than that of the market, its expected return should also be larger because the greater the risk assumed, the larger the *expected* return.

The CAPM is a simple but elegant statement about expected return and risk for any security or portfolio. It formalizes the basis of investments, which is that the greater the risk assumed, the greater the *expected* return should be. The CAPM states that an investor requires (expects) a return on a risky asset equal to the return on a risk-free asset plus a risk premium, and the greater the risk assumed, the greater the risk premium.

Over- and Undervalued Securities

The SML has important implications for security prices. In equilibrium, each security should lie on the SML because the expected return on the security should be that needed to compensate investors for the systematic risk.

What happens if investors determine that a security does not lie on the SML? In order to make this determination, they must employ a separate methodology to estimate the expected returns for securities. In other words, an SML can be fitted to a sample of securities to determine the expected (required) return–risk trade-off that exists. Knowing the beta for any stock, one can determine the required return from the SML. Then, estimating the expected return from, say, fundamental analysis, an investor can assess a security in relation to the SML and determine whether it is under- or overvalued.

In Figure 20–5, two securities are plotted around the SML. Security X has a high expected return derived from fundamental analysis and plots above the SML; security Y has a low expected return and plots below the SML. Which is undervalued?

Security X, plotting above the SML, is undervalued because it offers more expected return than investors require, given its level of systematic risk. Investors require a minimum expected return of ER_X, but security X, according to fundamental analysis, is offering ER_X. If investors recognize this, they will do the following:

Purchase security X, because it offers more return than required.
This demand will drive up the price of X, as more of it is purchased.
The return will be driven down, until it is at the level indicated by the SML.

Now consider security Y. This security, according to investors' fundamental analysis, does not offer enough expected return given its level of systematic risk. Investors require ER_Y for security Y, based on the SML, but Y offers only ER_Y. As investors recognize this, they will do the following:

Sell security Y (or perhaps sell Y short), because it offers less than the required return.
This increase in the supply of Y will drive down its price.
The return will be driven up for *new* buyers because any dividends paid are now relative to a lower price, as is any expected price appreciation.
The price will fall until the expected return rises enough to reach the SML and the security is once again in equilibrium.

Estimating the SML

In order to implement the SML approach described here, an investor needs estimates of the return on the risk-free asset, the expected return on the market index, and the beta for an individual security. How difficult are these to obtain?

The return on a risk-free asset, RF, should be the easiest of the three variables to obtain. In estimating RF, the investor can use the return on Treasury bills for the coming period (e.g., a year).

Estimating the market return is more difficult because the expected return for the market index is not observable. And, as noted in Chapter 10, several market indices could be used. Estimates of the market return could be derived from a study of previous market returns (such as the Standard & Poor's data in Table 5–1 and the Ibbotson–Sinquefield data referred to in Chapter 8). Alternatively, probability estimates of market returns could be made and the expected value calculated. This would provide an estimate of both the expected return and the standard deviation for the market.

Finally, it is necessary to estimate the betas for individual securities. This is a crucial part of the CAPM estimation process. The estimates of RF and the expected return on the market are the same for each security being evaluated. Only beta is unique, bringing together the investor's expectations of returns for the stock with those for the market. Beta is the only company-specific factor in the CAPM; therefore, risk is the only asset-specific forecast that must be made in the CAPM.

As noted, beta is usually estimated by fitting a characteristic line to the data (Equation 20–6). However, this is an estimate of the beta called for in the CAPM. The market proxy used in equations such as (20–6) may not fully reflect the market portfolio specified in the CAPM. Furthermore, several points should be kept in mind.

1. We are trying to estimate the future beta for a security, which may differ from the historical beta.
2. In theory, the independent variable R_M represents the total of all marketable assets in the economy. This is typically approximated with a stock market index, which, in turn, is an approximation of the return on all common stocks.
3. The characteristic line can be fitted over varying numbers of observations and time periods. There is no one correct period or number of observations for calculating beta. As a result, estimates of beta will vary. For example, *The Value Line Investment Survey* calculates betas from weekly rates of return for five years, whereas other analysts often use monthly rates of return over a comparable period.
4. The regression estimates of a and b are only estimates of the true a and b, and are subject to error. Thus, these estimates may not be equal to the true a and b.
5. As the fundamental variables (e.g., earnings, cash flow) of a company change, b should change; that is, the beta is not perfectly stationary over time. This issue is important enough to be considered separately.

The Accuracy of Beta Estimates

How much association is there between betas in different periods? Stated differently, are betas estimated by Equation 20–6 good estimates of future betas? This question has been closely examined in studies by Marshall Blume and Robert Levy.[10] Blume found that in comparing nonoverlapping seven-year periods for 1, 2, 4, 7, 10, 20, and so on stocks in a portfolio, the following observations could be made:

1. Betas estimated for individual securities are unstable; that is, they contain relatively little information about future betas.
2. Betas estimated for large portfolios are stable; that is, they contain much information about future betas.

In effect, a large portfolio (e.g., 50 stocks) provides stability because of the averaging effect. Although the betas of some stocks in the portfolio go up

---

[10] See M. Blume, "Betas and Their Regression Tendencies," *The Journal of Finance,* Vol. 10 (June 1975), pp. 785–795; and R. Levy, "On the Short-Term Stationarity of Beta Coefficients," *Financial Analysts Journal,* Vol. 27 (December 1971), pp. 55–62.

from period to period, others go down, and these two movements tend to cancel each other. Furthermore, the errors involved in estimating betas tend to cancel out in a portfolio. Therefore, estimates of portfolio betas show less change from period to period and are much more reliable than are the estimates for individual securities.

Tests of the CAPM

The conclusions of the CAPM are entirely sensible.

1. Return and risk are positively related—greater risk should carry greater return.
2. The relevant risk for a security is a measure of its effect on portfolio risk.

The question, therefore, is how well the theory works. After all, the assumptions on which capital market theory rest are, for the most part, unrealistic. In order to assess the validity of this or any other theory, empirical tests must be performed. If the CAPM is valid, and the market tends to balance out so that realized security returns average out to equal expected returns, empirical tests should find (over the long run)

$$\bar{R}_i = a_1 + a_2 b_i \qquad (20\text{--}10)$$

where

$\bar{R}_i$ = the average return on security i over some number of periods.
b_i = the estimated beta for security i.

When Equation 20–10 is estimated, a_1 should approximate the average risk-free rate during the periods studied, and a_2 should approximate the *average market* risk premium during the periods studied.

Extensive literature exists involving tests of capital market theory, in particular the CAPM. Although it is not possible to summarize the scope of this literature entirely, and reconcile findings from different studies that seem to be in disagreement, the following points represent a reasonable consensus of the empirical results:[11]

1. The SML appears to be linear; that is, the trade-off between expected (required) return and risk is an upward-sloping straight line.
2. The intercept term, a_1, is generally found to be higher than RF.
3. The slope of the CAPM, a_2, is generally found to be less steep than posited by the theory.
4. Although the evidence is mixed, no persuasive case has been made that unsystematic risk commands a risk premium—in other words, investors seem to be rewarded only for assuming systematic risk.

---

[11] For a discussion of empirical tests of the CAPM, see Elton and Gruber, *Modern Portfolio Theory.*

The major problem in testing capital market theory is that it is formulated on an ex ante basis but can be tested only on an ex post basis. We can never know investor expectations with certainty. Therefore, it should come as no surprise that tests of the model have produced conflicting results in some cases, and that the empirical results diverge from the predictions of the model. In fact, it is amazing that the empirical results support the basic CAPM as well as they do. Based on studies of many years of data, it appears that the stock market prices securities on the basis of a linear relationship between systematic risk and return with diversifiable (unsystematic) risk playing little or no part in the pricing mechanism.

The CAPM has not been proven empirically, nor will it be. In fact, Roll has argued that the CAPM is untestable because the market portfolio, which consists of all risky assets, is unobservable. In effect, Roll argues that tests of the CAPM are actually tests of the mean–variance efficiency of the market portfolio.[12] Nevertheless, the CAPM remains a logical way to view the expected return–risk trade-off.

Arbitrage Pricing Theory

The CAPM is not the only model of security pricing. An alternative model that has received attention is the **arbitrage pricing theory (APT)** developed by Stephen Ross.[13] According to APT, a security's value changes over time as a result of certain factors such as interest rates or industrial production. We can put these N factors together into a model for security returns in the following way:

$$R_i = a_i + b_{i1}F_1 + b_{i2}F_2 + \ldots b_{iN}F_N + e_i \qquad (20\text{--}11)$$

where

$\quad R_i =$ the actual return on security i.

$\quad a_i =$ the expected return for stock i if all factors have a value of zero.

$\quad b_i =$ the return sensitivity of the stock to factor i.

$\quad F_i =$ factors common to securities that affect their returns.

$\quad e_i =$ unique effect on stock i's return; that part of the return unrelated to the specified factors.

Equation 20–11 indicates that the actual return on a security is composed of its expected return and one or more factors (which can have a positive or a negative influence). Therefore, deviations of actual returns from expected returns are attributable to these factors affecting securities.

Equation 20–11 is called a **factor model,** the purpose of which is to express

---

[12] See R. Roll, "A Critique of the Asset Pricing Theory's Tests; Part I: On Past and Potential Testability of the Theory," *Journal of Financial Economics,* Vol. 4 (March 1977), pp. 129–176.

[13] This discussion is indebted to Elton and Gruber, *Modern Portfolio Theory.*

the behavior of security returns. Factor models describe the return-generating process for securities. The relevant factors should be identified by economic analysis of what affects security returns.

A factor model makes no statement about equilibrium. If we make it into an equilibrium model, we are saying something about *expected* returns across securities. Arbitrage pricing theory (APT) is an equilibrium theory of expected returns that requires a factor model such as Equation 20–11. As an equilibrium model, the e_i term in Equation 20–11 drops out, the Fs are the expected return per unit of sensitivity, and a_i is approximately equal to the risk-free rate (R_i becomes E_i, the expected return on a security).

What about the equilibrium returns that would be provided by securities under this more complex (relative to the CAPM) formulation. APT demonstrates that portfolios can be formed to eliminate arbitrage profits.[14] The a_i will be the same for all securities (and will approximate RF). The APT does not say anything about the size or the sign of the F_i's. Both the factor model and these values must be identified empirically.

APT is more general than the CAPM. If only one factor exists, the two models can be shown to be identical. The problem with APT is that the factors are not well specified, at least ex ante. To implement the APT model, we need to know the factors that account for the differences among security returns. In contrast, with the CAPM the factor that matters is the market portfolio, a concept that is well understood conceptually; however, as noted earlier, Roll has argued that the market portfolio is unobservable.

Most empirical work suggests that three to five factors influence security returns and are priced in the market. For example, one study identified three explanatory factors priced in the stock market—a general market index, price volatility of energy, and interest-rate sensitivity.[15] Because of the newness of APT, however, such results must be regarded as tentative. The question of how security prices and equilibrium returns are established—whether as described by the CAPM or APT or some other model—remains open.

Roll and Ross have argued that APT offers an approach to strategic portfolio planning.[16] The idea is to recognize that a few systematic factors affect long-term average returns. Investors should seek to identify the few factors affecting most assets in order to appreciate their influence on portfolio returns. Based on this knowledge, they should seek to structure the portfolio in such a way as to improve its design and performance.

---

[14] Arbitrage transactions occur when the prices of two perfect substitutes are not identical. Such transactions produce a risk-free profit with no commitment of capital.

[15] See Robert A. Pari and Son-Nan Chen, "An Empirical Test of the Arbitrage Pricing Theory," *The Journal of Financial Research,* Summer 1984, pp. 121–130.

[16] See Richard Roll and Stephen A. Ross, "The Arbitrage Pricing Theory Approach to Strategic Portfolio Planning," *Financial Analysts Journal,* May–June 1984.

Summary

This chapter, which builds on the portfolio theory of the previous chapter, is concerned with capital market theory, which describes the pricing of capital assets in the marketplace. Capital market theory is based on the concept of efficient diversification.

Capital market theory is derived from several assumptions that appear unrealistic. However, the important issue is the ability of the theory to predict. Relaxation of most of the assumptions does not change the major implications of capital market theory.

The key to the development of capital market theory is the introduction of a risk-free asset. Combining it with risky assets through borrowing and lending changes the efficient frontier from the arc of the Markowitz analysis to a straight line. This new efficient frontier has a vertical intercept of RF and is tangent to the old efficient frontier at point M, the market portfolio. In theory, this market-value-weighted portfolio should include all risky assets, although in practice it is typically proxied by a stock market index such as the Standard & Poor's 500.

The separation theorem states that the decision of which portfolio of risky assets to hold is separate from the decision of how much of an investor's funds should be allocated to the risk-free asset and how much to risky assets. All investors can achieve an optimal point on the new efficient frontier by investing in portfolio M and either borrowing or lending at the risk-free rate, RF.

The new efficient frontier is called the capital market line, and its slope indicates the equilibrium price of risk in the market. In effect, it is the expected return–risk trade-off for efficient portfolios. Ex ante, it must always be positive, although ex post it may be negative for certain periods.

Based on the separation of risk into its systematic and unsystematic components, the security market line (CAPM) can be constructed for individual securities (and portfolios). What is important is each security's contribution to the total risk of the portfolio, as measured by beta. Using beta as the measure of risk, the SML depicts the trade-off between required return and risk for securities. If the expected returns for securities can be estimated from security analysis and plotted against the SML, undervalued and over-valued securities can be identified.

Problems exist in estimating the SML, in particular estimating the betas for securities. The stability of beta is a concern, particularly for individual securities; however, portfolio betas tend to be more stable across time.

Tests of the CAPM are inconclusive. An ex ante model is being tested with ex post data. Although it has not been proven empirically, nor is it likely to be, its basic implications seem to be supported. Alternative theories of asset pricing, such as the arbitrage pricing theory, also exist but are unproved.

Key Words

Arbitrage pricing theory (APT)
Capital market line (CML)
Capital market theory
Factor model
Market portfolio

Portfolio insurance
Risk-free asset
Security market line (SML)
Separation theorem

QUESTIONS AND PROBLEMS

1. How do lending possibilities change the Markowitz model? Borrowing possibilities?
2. What are the implications of the separation theorem for the approach typically followed by most brokers in constructing portfolios for their clients?
3. In terms of their appearance of a graph, what is the difference between the CML and the SML?
4. What is the "market portfolio"?
5. What is the slope of the CML? What does it measure?
6. Why does the CML contain only efficient portfolios?
7. Based on your knowledge of b_i, write three equivalent expressions for the SML.
8. How can the SML be used to identify over- and undervalued securities?
9. What happens to the price and return of a security when investors recognize it as undervalued?
10. What are the difficulties involved in estimating a security's beta?
11. If individual security betas are unstable, can beta be a useful concept?
12. How can the CAPM be tested empirically? What are the expected results of regressing average returns on betas?
13. How many securities are required to diversify adequately?
14. With regard to mutual funds, what do you think is meant by the term *superfluous diversification?*
15. The CAPM provides required returns for individual securities or portfolios. What uses can you see for such a model?
16. What is the relationship between the CML and the Markowitz efficient frontier?

17. In Figure 20–2, how does an investor decide where to be on the new efficient frontier?

18. The CML can be described as representing a trade-off. What is this trade-off? Be specific.

19. Describe a diagram of the SML, including the axes and the intercept.
    a. Assume the risk-free rate shifts upward. Describe the new SML.
    b. Assume that the risk-free rate remains the same as before the change in a, but that investors become more pessimistic about the stock market. Describe the new SML.

20. The expected return for the market is 12% with a standard deviation of 20%. The expected risk-free rate is 8%. Information is available for five mutual funds, all assumed to be efficient, as follows:

Mutual Funds	SD (%)
Affiliated	14
Omega	16
Ivy	20
Value Line Fund	25
New Horizons	30

   a. Calculate the slope of the CML.
   b. Calculate the expected return on each of these portfolios.
   c. Rank the portfolios in increasing order of expected return.
   d. Do any of the portfolios have the same expected return as the market? Why?

21. Given the market data in Problem 20 and the following information for each of five stocks, do the following:

Stock	b_i	R_i (%)
1	0.9	12.0
2	1.3	13.0
3	0.5	11.0
4	1.1	12.5
5	1.0	12.0

   a. Calculate the expected return for each stock.
   b. With these expected returns and betas, think of a line connecting them. What is this line?
   c. Assume that an investor, using fundamental analysis, develops the estimates labeled R_i for these stocks. Determine which are undervalued and which, overvalued.
   d. What is the market's risk premium?

22. Given the following information:

Expected return for the market	12%
Standard deviation of market return	20%
Risk-free rate	8%
Correlation coefficient between	
Stock A and the market	0.8
Stock B and the market	0.6
Standard deviation for stock A	25%
Standard deviation for stock B	30%

   a. Calculate the beta for stock A and stock B.
   b. Calculate the required return for each stock.

23. Assume that RF is 7%, the estimated return on the market is 12%, and the standard deviation of the market's expected return is 20%. Calculate the expected return and risk (standard deviation) for the following portfolios:
   a. 60% of investable wealth in riskless assets, 40% in the market portfolio.
   b. 150% of investable wealth in the market portfolio.
   c. 100% of investable wealth in the market portfolio.

24. Assume that the risk-free rate is 7% and the expected market return is 13%. Show that the security market line, from Equation (20–9) is

$$ER_i = 7.0 + 6.0b$$

Assume that an investor has estimated the following values for six different corporations:

Corporation	b_i	$R_i(\%)$
GF	0.8	12
PepsiCo	0.9	13
IBM	1.0	14
NCNB	1.2	11
EG&G	1.2	20
EAL	1.5	10

Calculate the ER_i for each corporation using the SML and evaluate which securities are over- and which are undervalued.

25. On the assumption that RF is expected to be 5% and the expected market return is 13% with an expected standard deviation of 20%, what is the formula for the capital market line?

26. On the assumption that RF is expected to be 5% and the expected market return is 15% with an expected standard deviation of 14%, what is the formula for the security market line?

27. Using the annual data for the 10 years 1974–1983, the following ex post values are available for several mutual funds: (S&P 500 was used as the market)

$\bar{R}_p$ = average annual holding period yield.
SD_p = the standard deviation of the holding period yields.
a_p and b_p = the constant and slope of the characteristic line.

Mutual Fund	$\bar{R}_p$ (%)	SD_p (%)	a_p	b_p
A	15.5	19	4.4	0.9
B	14.5	22	1.8	1.0
C	21.0	18	12.4	0.7
D	17.0	27	3.0	1.2
E	13.2	24	3.1	0.8
F	22.0	24	9.4	1.0
G	20.5	23	9.0	0.9
H	24.5	27	9.3	1.2
I	9.3	18	−1.6	0.9
J	21.0	21	9.5	0.9
Overall market	12.0	20	0.0	1.0

a. On the basis of your CML in Problem 25, what are the values of the ER_p for the funds, assuming that the standard deviations will continue?

b. (1) On the basis of your SML in Problem 26, what are the values of the ER_p for the funds?

(2) Assume that a particular investor was certain that the ex post R_p in the first column were her expected yields. Which funds would that investor consider undervalued and which overvalued?

c. (1) For the ex post data, how many of the mutual fund portfolios had average annual holding period yields greater than the market?

(2) Using standard deviation as the risk measure, rank the funds from low risk to high risk. How many funds had greater risk than the market; how many had lesser risk?

(3) Using b_p as the risk measure, rank the funds from low risk to high risk. How many funds had greater risk; how many lower?

(4) Does the rank order of risk using ex post standard deviation agree with rank order using ex post b_p? Discuss ex post measurement of risk relative to *ex ante* risk.

d. Using the ex post values for return and risk, does it appear (on the average) that the higher risk funds achieved higher returns? Discuss this issue.

Selected References

Blume, Marshall E. "Betas and Their Regression Tendencies." *Journal of Finance,* June 1975, pp. 785–795.

Elton, Edwin and Gruber, Martin. *Modern Portfolio Theory and Portfolio Analysis,* 3rd ed. New York: John Wiley, 1987.

Elton, Edwin, Gruber, Martin J., and Urich, Thomas J. "Are Betas Best?" *Journal of Finance,* December 1978, pp. 1375–1384.

Fama, E. F. and MacBeth, J. D. "Risk, Return, and Equilibrium: Empirical Tests." *Journal of Political Economy,* May–June 1973, pp. 607–636.

Ibbotson, Roger G., Siegel, Laurence B., and Love, Kathryn S. "World Wealth: Market Values and Returns." *The Journal of Portfolio Management,* Fall 1985, pp. 4–23.

Jensen, Michael C., ed. *Studies in the Theory of Capital Markets.* New York: Praeger, 1972.

Lintner, John. "Security Prices, Risk, and Maximal Gains from Diversification." *The Journal of Finance,* December 1965, pp. 587–615.

Modigliani, Franco, and Pogue, Gerald A. "An Introduction to Risk and Returns." *Financial Analysts Journal,* March–April 1974, pp. 68–80; and May–June 1974, pp. 69–86.

Pari, Robert A. and Chen, Son-Nan. "An Empirical Test of the Arbitrage Pricing Theory." *The Journal of Financial Research,* Summer 1984, pp. 121–130.

Roll, Richard. "Ambiguity When Performance Is Measured by the Securities Market Line." *The Journal of Finance,* September 1978, pp. 1051–70.

Roll, Richard. "A Critique of the Assets Pricing Theory's Test." *Journal of Financial Economics,* March 1977, pp. 129–176.

Ross, Stephen. "The Arbitrage Theory of Capital Asset Pricing." *Journal of Economic Theory,* December 1976, pp. 341–360.

Ross, Stephen. "The Current Status of the Capital Asset Pricing Model." *The Journal of Finance,* June 1978, pp. 885–901.

Sharpe, William F. "Bonds versus Stocks: Some Lessons from Capital Market Theory." *Financial Analysts Journal,* November–December 1973, pp. 74–80.

Sharpe, William F. "Capital Asset Prices: A Theory of Market Equilibrium under Conditions of Risk." *The Journal of Finance,* September 1964, pp. 425–442.

Tobin, James. "Liquidity Preference as Behavior Toward Risk." *Review of Economic Studies,* February 1958, pp. 65–85.

CHAPTER 21

MEASURING PORTFOLIO PERFORMANCE

We have now discussed, in an organized and systematic manner, the major components of the investing process. After considering some background material, we studied bonds and stocks, and considered three approaches to common stock analysis with particular emphasis on the fundamental. We then considered other assets, such as options and futures, and the alternative of indirect investing. Finally, we have studied portfolio management and capital market theory.

One important issue remains—the "bottom line" of the investing process—evaluating the performance of a portfolio. In other words, we need to consider how well various portfolios performed. Every investor should be concerned with this issue because, after all, the objective of investing is to increase or at least protect financial wealth. If results are unsatisfactory, it must be determined so that changes can be made.

Evaluating portfolio performance is important regardless of whether an individual manages his or her own funds or invests indirectly through investment companies. Direct investing can be time-consuming with high opportunity costs. If the results are inadequate, why do it (unless the investor simply enjoys it)? On the other hand, if professional portfolio managers are employed, it is necessary to know how well they perform. If manager A consistently outperforms manager B, other things being equal, investors will want to be with A. Alternatively, if neither A nor B outperforms an index fund,

BOX 21–1 GAMES MONEY MANAGERS PLAY

You never meet a money manager who isn't in somebody's top quartile," says Bruce Hauptman, head of B. Hauptman & Associates, a firm that evaluates money managers for investors. "Trouble is, short of going in and scrutinizing the books yourself, a money manager's performance is whatever he chooses to tell you it is."

Why is this ludicrous situation allowed to exist? Good question. Unlike mutual funds, which are monitored by the Securities & Exchange Commission, there are no uniform standards for money managers. There are roughly 10,000 investment advisers in the U.S., of which perhaps half manage money as well as tell its owners what to do with it. Only those with more than $100 million under management have to submit quarterly reports to the SEC. But accountants contend those figures don't always reflect true performance because trades are not detailed.

The Financial Accounting Standards Board declines to address how to account for money manager performance. Two industry groups, the Bank Administration Institute and the Investment Counsel Association of America, have tackled the problem, but they have issued only recommendations, not rules.

The Bank Administration Institute and the Investment Counsel Association of America recommendations make it difficult to use obvious ploys like adjusting the start of the period measured so that money managers can produce the most favorable results—for example, beginning at the bottom of a bear market and ending in the top of a bull market.

Unfortunately, there are some important issues that neither the ICAA nor the BAI have addressed. At what point must money managers begin including a new portfolio in their results?

There are no guidelines on how to handle portfolios that were taken away during the year, either. Generally portfolios are dropped because they have performed poorly, points out Jeanne Gustafson, a senior manager with Peat, Marwick, Mitchell. So money managers can not only drop that portfolio but also restate prior years without it as well. Touche's practice is to prohibit this.

At present there are at least three different methods of calculating money managers' results: time-weighted (which eliminates the effect of cash contributions and withdrawals); dollar-weighted (which gives more weight to large, and generally slower growing, portfolios); or a combination of the two. The BAI and ICAA prefer time-weighting, since cash inflows and outflows are events over which the money manager has no control. But as long as there is no agreed-upon single standard, "a money manager can look at the different calculations and use whatever provides the best result," says Peter Dietz, research director at Frank Russell Co., a Tacoma, Wash. money manager evaluation service.

Perhaps the biggest problem is deciding which portfolios should be included in a money manager's performance average. Obviously, portfolios can have very different investment objectives. ICAA says that only portfolios over which the money manager has total discretion should be included. The problem here is that investment managers can define their investment objectives so narrowly that they end up including only their best performers.

As Dietz puts it, "A composite is what-ever a money manager wants it to be."

What is needed is for bodies like the FASB and SEC to set standards. A good first step would be adoption of the BAI and ICAA recommendations. The FASB should set down uniform rules accountants could follow, and the SEC should require such results to be audited.

Why do we have to wait until there's a crisis before we act in an area so clearly in the public's interest?

Source: Adapted from Lisa Gubernick, "Games Money Managers Play," *Forbes,* July 29, 1985, p. 134. Excerpted by permission of *Forbes* magazine, July 29 1985. © Forbes Inc., 1985.

other things being equal, investors may prefer neither. The important point is that performance has to be measured before intelligent decisions can be made, and this is not easy to do, as Box 21-1 illustrates.

In this chapter we will discuss what is involved in measuring portfolio performance. It is important to understand the issues in performance evaluation and the overall framework within which evaluation should be conducted. We will review the well-known measures of portfolio performance and the problems associated with them.

A Framework for Evaluating Portfolio Performance

Assume that in 1988, mutual fund X earned a total return of 20% for its shareholders. As a shareholder, you are trying to assess X's performance. What can you say?

Based on the preceding information and our discussion in Chapter 18 on investment company performance, you can legitimately say little or nothing. The primary reason for this is that investments is a two-dimensional process based on return and risk. These two factors are opposite sides of the same coin, and both must be evaluated if intelligent decisions are to be made. Therefore, knowing nothing about the risk of fund X, little can be said about its performance. After all, the managers of X may have taken twice the risk of comparable portfolios to achieve this 20% return.

Given the risk faced by all investors, it is totally inadequate to consider only the returns from various investment alternatives. Although all investors prefer higher returns, they are also risk averse. To evaluate portfolio performance properly, we must determine if the returns are large enough given the risk involved; that is, we must evaluate performance on a risk-adjusted basis.

The second reason that little can be said about the performance of fund X is that its 20% return, given its risk, is meaningful only when compared to some benchmark. Obviously, if the average fund or the market returned 25% in 1988, and fund X is average, its performance appears unfavorable. Therefore, it is necessary to make comparisons in performance measurement, and an important related issue is the benchmark to be used in evaluating the performance of a portfolio.

There are, of course, other important issues in evaluating the portfolio's performance. One of these involves evaluating the manager as opposed to the portfolio itself. It is essential to determine how well diversified the portfolio was during the period, because, as we have seen in the previous two chapters, diversification can reduce portfolio risk. If a manager assumes unsystematic risk, we will want to know if he or she earned an adequate return for doing so.

In evaluating the portfolio manager rather than the portfolio itself, an investor should consider the objectives set by the manager and any constraints under which he or she must operate. For example, if a fund's objective is to invest in small, speculative stocks, investors must expect the risk to be larger than the typical fund, with substantial swings in the annual realized returns. It is important to determine if the manager followed the stated objective. Similarly, if a portfolio manager is obligated to operate under certain constraints, these must be taken into account.

Measures of Portfolio Performance

It is now clear that in measuring portfolio performance, investors must consider both the realized return and the risk that was assumed. Therefore whatever measures or techniques are used, these parameters must be incorporated into the analysis.

When portfolio performance is evaluated, the total return to the investor is relevant. As discussed throughout this text, a proper measure of this total return is the holding period yield (HPY), which captures both the income component and the capital gains (or losses) component of return. Furthermore, as discussed, we know that two measures of risk are widely used in investments—standard deviation and beta.

Based on the concepts of capital market theory and the CAPM, and recognizing the necessity to incorporate both return and risk into the analysis, three researchers developed measures of portfolio performance in the 1960s. These measures are often referred to as the **composite (or risk-adjusted) measures of portfolio performance,** meaning that they incorporate both return and risk into the evaluation. These measures are often used today and are analyzed in the following section.

The Reward-to-Variability Measure

William Sharpe, whose contributions to portfolio theory have been previously encountered, introduced a composite measure of portfolio performance called the **reward-to-variability ratio (RVAR).**[1] Sharpe used it to rank the performance of 34 mutual funds over the period 1954–1963. This measure can be defined as

$$RVAR = \frac{\overline{HPY}_p - \overline{RF}}{SD_p}$$

$$= \frac{Excess\ return}{Risk} \qquad (21\text{–}1)$$

where

$\overline{HPY}_p$ = the average HPY for portfolio p during some period of time (we will use annual data).

$\overline{RF}$ = the average risk-free rate of return during the period.

SD_p = the standard deviation of return for portfolio p during the period.

$\overline{HPY}_p - \overline{RF}$ = excess return (risk premium) on portfolio p.

The numerator of Equation 21–1 measures the portfolio's excess return; that is, the return above the risk-free rate (RF could have been earned without assuming risk). This is also referred to as the *risk premium*. The denominator uses the standard deviation, which is a measure of the total risk or variability in the return of the portfolio. Together, these variables indicate the excess return per unit of total risk.

The higher the RVAR, the better the portfolio performance. Since this is an ordinal (relative) measure of portfolio performance, different portfolios can easily be ranked on this variable. Using only the Sharpe measure of portfolio performance, the portfolio with the highest RVAR would be judged best in terms of ex post performance.

As an example of calculating the Sharpe ratio, consider the data for three mutual funds for the years 1974 through 1982, as shown in Table 21–1. These funds were chosen randomly for illustrative purposes only.[2] Annual shareholder returns are shown, based on Wiesenberger data.[3]
Table 21–1 also shows the return on the Standard & Poor's 500 for those years, as well as the annual yields on Treasury bills as a proxy for RF.[4]

On the basis of these data, Sharpe's RVAR can be calculated as

$$New\ Horizons\ RVAR = \frac{17.1 - 8.6}{28.1} = 0.30$$

---

[1]W. Sharpe, "Mutual Fund Performance." *The Journal of Business* (January 1966), pp. 119–138.

[2]The use of these funds as *examples* in no way implies anything about their performance or operations.

[3]The calculation of total shareholder returns for a mutual fund, as well as the use of Wiesenberger data, was explained in Chapter 18.

[4]The annualized Treasury bill rate is taken from the *Economic Report of the President*.

TABLE 21-1 **Annual Shareholder Returns for Three Mutual Funds and HPYs for the S&P 500 and Treasury Bills, 1974–1982 (in percentages)**

	New Horizons	Affiliated	Ivy	S&P 500	RF
1974	−38.7	−16	−33	−26	7.9
1975	39.6	39.4	30	36.9	5.8
1976	11.1	34.3	18.2	23.6	5.0
1977	12.7	−6.9	−7.3	−7.2	5.3
1978	20.9	3.2	4.9	6.4	7.2
1979	35.5	28.9	30.9	18.2	10
1980	57.6	24.1	34.7	31.5	11.5
1981	−7.8	0.0	6.0	−4.8	14.1
1982	22.8	23.4	33.0	20.4	10.7
Mean	17.1	14.5	13.0	11	8.6
SD	28.1	19.7	22.8	20.5	—
Beta	1.20	0.92	1.04	1.00	—
R^2	0.77	0.90	0.87		

Source: Reprinted by permission from the *Wiesenberger Investment Companies Service,* 1983 Edition, Copyright © 1983. Warren, Gorham & Lamont, Inc., 210 South Street, Boston, Mass. All Rights Reserved.

$$\text{Affiliated RVAR} = \frac{14.5 - 8.6}{19.7} = 0.30$$

$$\text{Ivy Fund RVAR} = \frac{13.0 - 8.6}{22.8} = 0.19$$

$$\text{S\&P 500 RVAR} = \frac{11.0 - 8.6}{20.5} = 0.117$$

Based on these calculations, we see that all three funds outperformed the S&P 500 on an excess return–risk basis during the period 1974–1982 (when interest rates, and therefore RF, were unusually high by historical standards). New Horizons and Affiliated performed the same during this period on the basis of RVAR.

Sharpe's measure for these funds is illustrated graphically in Figure 21–1. The vertical axis is the return on the portfolio, and the horizontal axis is standard deviation of returns. The vertical intercept is RF. As Figure 21–1 shows, RVAR measures the slope of the line from RF to the portfolio being evaluated. The steeper the line, the higher the slope (RVAR), and the better the performance. Because of their better performance, Affiliated and New Horizons, with identical RVARs, have the higher slope, whereas Ivy's slope is lower.

Note in Figure 21–1 that we are drawing the capital market line (CML) when we plot the market's return against its standard deviation. Of course,

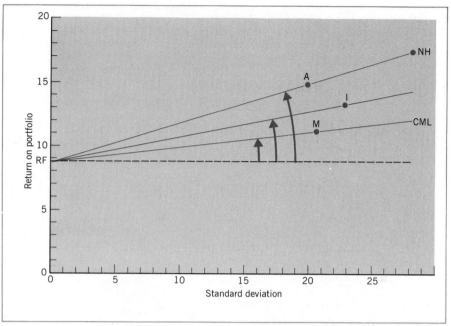

FIGURE 21–1 Sharpe's measure of performance (RVAR) for three mutual fund portfolios (A = Affiliated Fund; NH = New Horizons Fund; I = Ivy Fund).

this is the ex post and not the ex ante CML; therefore, it is not surprising that these portfolios lie off the ex post CML.

The Reward-to-Volatility Measure

At approximately the same time as Sharpe's measure was developed (the mid-1960s), Jack Treynor presented a similar measure called the **reward-to-volatility measure**.[5] Like Sharpe, Treynor sought to relate the return on a portfolio to its risk. Treynor, however, distinguished between total risk and systematic risk, implicitly assuming that portfolios are well diversified.

In measuring portfolio performance, Treynor introduced the concept of the characteristic line—used in earlier chapters to partition a security's return into its systematic and unsystematic components. It is used in a similar manner with portfolios, depicting the relationship between the returns on a portfolio and those of the market. The slope of the characteristic line measures the relative volatility of the fund's returns. As we know, the slope of this line is the beta coefficient, which is a measure of the volatility (or responsiveness) of the portfolio's returns to those of the market index.

---

[5]J. Treynor, "How to Rate Management of Investment Funds." *Harvard Business Review* (January–February, 1965), pp. 63–75.

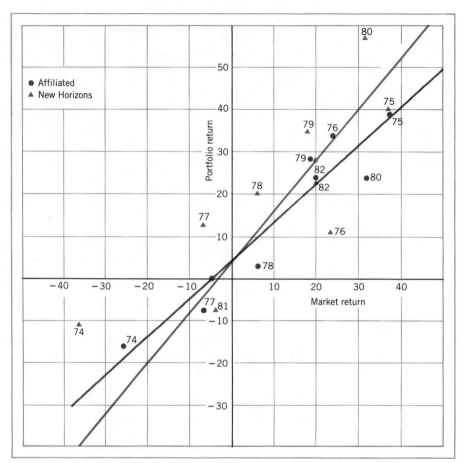

FIGURE 21–2 Characteristic lines for Affiliated and New Horizon, 1974–1982.

Figure 21–2 shows the characteristic lines for New Horizons and Affiliated, corresponding to the data in Table 21–1. As can be seen, New Horizons has the steeper characteristic line, reflecting a higher beta. These characteristic lines are estimated by regressing each fund's returns on the S&P 500 returns for 1974–1982, producing the following equations:

$$\text{New Horizons: } R_\text{p} = 3.84 + 1.20 \; R_{\text{S\&P}\,500}$$
$$\text{Affiliated: } R_\text{p} = 4.42 + 0.92 \; R_{\text{S\&P}\,500}$$

Treynor's measure relates the average excess return on the portfolio during some period (exactly the same variable as in the Sharpe measure) to its systematic risk as measured by the portfolio's beta. The reward-to-volatility (RVOL) is

$$RVOL = \frac{\overline{HPY}_p - \overline{RF}}{b_p}$$

$$= \frac{\text{Average excess return on portfolio } p}{\text{Systematic risk for portfolio } p} \qquad (21\text{--}2)$$

where all terms are as previously defined and b_p is the beta for portfolio p.

In this case, we are calculating the excess return per unit of systematic risk. As with RVAR, higher values of RVOL indicate better portfolio performance. Portfolios can be ranked on their RVOL, and assuming that the Treynor measure is a correct measure of portfolio performance, the best performing portfolio can be determined.

Using the data in Table 21–1, we can calculate RVOL for the same three portfolios illustrated. Using Equation 21–2

$$\text{New Horizons RVOL} = \frac{17.1 - 8.6}{1.20} = 7.1$$

$$\text{Affiliated RVOL} = \frac{14.5 - 8.6}{.92} = 6.4$$

$$\text{Ivy Fund RVOL} = \frac{13.0 - 8.6}{1.04} = 4.2$$

$$\text{S\&P 500 RVOL} = \frac{11.0 - 8.6}{1.00} = 2.4$$

These calculations indicate that all three funds outperformed the market on the basis of their excess return–systematic risk ratio. New Horizons, for example, had a higher beta than the other funds, but its higher return was sufficient to compensate (at least in these comparisons).

Figure 21–3 shows a plot of these funds in return–beta space. Again, lines are drawn from the RF to each fund's return–risk point with the steepest line representing the largest slope and the best performance; in other words, the steeper the slope, the better the performance.

As in Figure 21–1, plotting the market data produces the appropriate market line—in this case, the security market line (SML). All three funds plot above the ex post SML, suggesting better performance for the stated level of systematic risk than would be implied by the SML.

The use of RVOL, of course, implies that systematic risk is the proper measure of risk to use when evaluating portfolio performance (similarly, the use of RVAR implies that total risk is the proper measure to use when evaluating portfolios). As we learned in Chapters 19 and 20, systematic risk is a proper measure of risk to use when portfolios are perfectly diversified so that no unsystematic risk remains (the procedure for measuring the degree of diversification is explained in the following material).

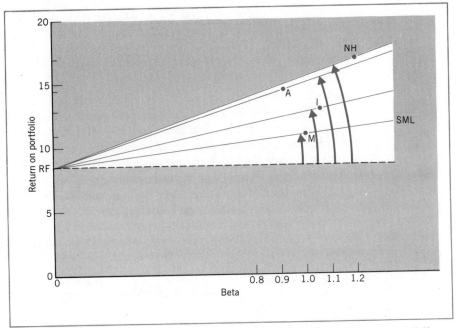

FIGURE 21–3 Treynor's measure of performance for three mutual fund portfolios (A = Affiliated Fund; NH = New Horizons Fund; I = Ivy Fund).

Comparing the Sharpe and Treynor Measures

Given their similarity, when should RVAR or RVOL be used, and why? Actually, given the assumptions underlying each measure, both can be said to be correct. Therefore, it is usually desirable to calculate both measures for a set of portfolios being evaluated.

The choice of which to use could depend upon the definition of risk. If an investor thinks it correct to use total risk, RVAR is appropriate; however, if the investor thinks that it is correct to use systematic risk, RVOL is appropriate.

What about the rankings of a set of portfolios using the two measures? Our earlier calculations provide the following rankings, where 1 represents the best performance:

	Sharpe	Treynor
New Horizons	1	1
Affiliated	1	2
Ivy	3	3

Why the difference in rankings? If the portfolios are fully diversified, the rankings will be identical. As the portfolios become less well diversified, the rankings will differ. This leads to the following conclusion about these two measures: RVAR takes into account how well diversified a portfolio was during the measurement period. Differences in rankings between the two measures result from a lack of complete diversification in the portfolio.

This analysis leads to an important observation about the Sharpe and Treynor measures. Investors who have all (or substantially all) of their assets in a portfolio of securities should rely more on the Sharpe measure because it assesses the portfolio's total return in relation to total risk, which includes any unsystematic risk assumed by the investor. However, for those investors whose portfolio constitutes but one (relatively) small part of their total assets, systematic risk may well be the relevant risk. In these circumstances, RVOL is appropriate because it considers only systematic risk.

The rankings of the three portfolios should lead us to expect that the New Horizons fund was not as well diversified as Affiliated. In order to determine this empirically, we must measure the degree of diversification in a portfolio.

Measuring Diversification

Portfolio diversification is typically measured by correlating the returns on the portfolio with the returns on the market index. This is accomplished as a part of the process of fitting a characteristic line, whereby the portfolio's returns are regressed against the market's returns. The square of the correlation coefficient produced as a part of the analysis—called the coefficient of determination, or R^2—is used to denote the degree of diversification. The **coefficient of determination** indicates the percentage of the variance in the portfolio's returns that are explained by the market's returns. If the fund is totally diversified, the R^2 will approach 1.0, indicating that the fund's returns are completely explained by the market's returns. The lower the coefficient of determination, the less the portfolio's returns are attributable to the market's returns. This indicates that other factors, which could have been diversified away, are being allowed to influence the portfolio's returns.

The R^2 figures in Table 21–1 indicate that New Horizons was indeed less diversified than was Affiliated, with an R^2 value of 0.77 compared to Affiliated's 0.90. This lower degree of diversification for New Horizons can be seen in Figure 21–2, which shows that the points around its characteristic line are more dispersed (spread out) than those of Affiliated. Therefore, New Horizons was exposed to more unsystematic risk than the other two funds, presumably because the portfolio managers expected to earn adequate returns to compensate for this risk.

Jensen's Differential Return Measure

A measure related to Treynor's RVOL is Michael Jensen's **differential return measure,** or **alpha** (we will refer to it simply as alpha); in fact, these two measures can produce, with proper adjustments, identical relative rankings of portfolio performance.[6] Jensen's measure of performance is based on the CAPM discussed in Chapter 20.[7] The expected return for any security (i) or portfolio (p) was given in Equation 20–9 of Chapter 20 as

$$ER_p = RF + b_p[ER_M - RF]$$

with all terms as previously defined.

Notice that Equation 20–9, which covers any ex ante period t, can be applied to ex post periods if investor's expectations are, on the average, fulfilled. Empirically, Equation 20–9 can be approximated as Equation 21–3.

$$R_{pt} = RF_t + b_p[R_{Mt} - RF_t] + E_{pt} \qquad (21\text{--}3)$$

where

R_{pt} = the return on portfolio p in period t.
RF_t = the risk-free rate in period t.
R_{Mt} = the return on the market in period t.
E_{pt} = a random error term for portfolio p in period t.
$[R_{Mt} - RF_t]$ = the market risk premium during period t.

Equation 21–3 relates the realized return on portfolio p during any period t to the sum of the risk-free rate and the portfolio's risk premium plus an error term. Given the market risk premium, the risk premium on portfolio p is a function of portfolio p's systematic risk—the larger its systematic risk, the larger the risk premium.

Equation 21–3 can be written in what is called the risk premium (or, alternatively, the excess return) form by moving RF to the left side and subtracting it from R_{pt}, as in 21–4

$$R_{pt} - RF_t = b_p[R_{Mt} - RF_t] + E_{pt} \qquad (21\text{--}4)$$

where

$R_{pt} - RF_t$ = the risk premium on portfolio p.

Equation 21–4 indicates that the risk premium on portfolio p is equal to the product of its beta and the market risk premium plus an error term. In other words, the risk premium on portfolio p should be proportional to the risk premium on the market portfolio if the CAPM model is correct and investor expectations were generally realized (in effect, if all assets and portfolios were in equilibrium).

A return proportional to the risk assumed is illustrated by Fund Y in Figure 21–4. This diagram illustrates an alternative form of the characteristic line discussed earlier, where portfolio returns are related to market returns.

---

[6] Jensen's alpha divided by beta is equivalent to Treynor's measure minus the average risk premium for the market portfolio for the period.

[7] M. Jensen, "The Performance of Mutual Funds in the Period 1945–1964." *The Journal of Finance* (May 1968), pp. 389–416.

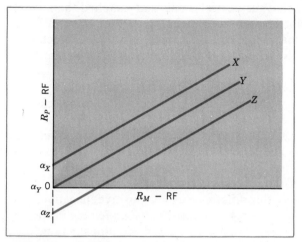

FIGURE 21–4 Jensen's measure of portfolio performance for three hypothetical funds.

In this case, the risk-free rate each period, RF_t, is subtracted from both the portfolio's return and the market's return.[8]

Equation 21–4 can be empirically tested by fitting a regression for some number of periods. Portfolio excess returns (risk premiums) are regressed against the excess returns (risk premiums) for the market. If managers earn a return proportional to the risk assumed, this relationship should hold; that is, there should be no intercept term (alpha) in the regression, which should go through the origin, as in the case of Fund Y in Figure 21–4.

Given these expected findings, Jensen argued that an intercept term, alpha, could be added to Equation 21–4 as a means of identifying superior or inferior portfolio performance. Therefore, Equation 21–4 becomes Equation 21–5.

$$R_{pt} - RF_t = a_p + b_p[R_{Mt} - RF_t] + E_{pt} \qquad (21\text{–}5)$$

The CAPM asserts that equilibrium conditions should result in a zero intercept term. Therefore, the alpha should measure the contribution of the portfolio manager since it represents the average incremental rate of return per period beyond the return attributable to the level of risk assumed. Specifically, (1) if alpha is significantly positive, this is evidence of superior performance (illustrated in Figure 21–4 with portfolio X, which has a positive intercept); (2) if alpha is significantly negative, this is evidence of inferior performance (illustrated in Figure 21–4 with portfolio Z, which has a negative intercept); (3) if alpha is insignificantly different from zero, this is

---

[8]This version is usually referred to as a characteristic line in risk premium or excess return form.

evidence that the portfolio manager matched the market on a risk-adjusted basis (as in the case of Fund Y).

Note that Equation 21–5 can be rearranged to better demonstrate what a_p really is. Rearranging terms, Equation 21–5 becomes

$$a_p = (\overline{R_p} - \overline{RF}) - [b_p(\overline{R_M} - \overline{RF})] \tag{21-6}$$

where the bars above the variables indicate averages for the period measured.

Equation 21–6 states that a_p is the difference between the actual excess return on portfolio p during some period and the risk premium on that portfolio that should have been earned, given its level of systematic risk and the use of the CAPM.

As noted, this difference can be positive, negative, or zero. It is important to recognize the role of *statistical significance* in the interpretation of Jensen's measure. Although the estimated alpha may be positive or negative, it may not be significantly different (statistically) from zero. If it is not, we would conclude that the manager of the portfolio being evaluated performed as expected; that is, the manager earned an average risk-adjusted return, neither more nor less than would be expected, given the risk assumed.

Jensen's performance measure can be estimated by regressing excess returns for the portfolio being evaluated against excess returns for the market (in effect, producing a characteristic line in excess return form). When this was done for the three mutual funds evaluated earlier, the following alphas were found:

Portfolio	Alpha	Standard Error	Significant?
New Horizons	5.64	4.88	No
Affiliated	3.67	2.21	No
Ivy	2.07	2.94	No

All three funds showed positive alphas, and reasonably high ones given the alphas typically observed for mutual funds. If significant, the 5.64 for New Horizons would indicate that this fund, *on the average,* earned an annual risk-adjusted rate of return that was more than 5% above the market average; in other words, New Horizons earned a positive return attributable to factors other than the market, presumably due to the ability of its managers. However, the standard errors for each fund indicate that the alphas are not significantly different from zero.[9] Therefore, we cannot conclude that

---

[9] A general rule of thumb is that a coefficient should be twice its standard error in order to be significant at the 5% level. Alternatively, t values can be examined in order to test the significance of the coefficients. For a reasonably large number of observations, and therefore degrees of freedom, t values of approximately 2.0 would indicate significance at the 5% level.

these three funds exhibited superior performance. As in any regression equation, the coefficients must be statistically significant for any conclusions to be drawn.

Superior and inferior portfolio performance can result from at least two sources. First, the portfolio manager may be able to select undervalued securities consistently enough to affect portfolio performance. Second, the manager may be able to time market turns, varying the portfolio's composition in accordance with the rise and fall of the market. Obviously, a manager with enough ability may be able to do both.

A computational advantage of the Jensen measure is that it permits the performance measure to be estimated simultaneously with the beta for a portfolio. That is, by estimating a characteristic line in risk premium form, estimates of both alpha and beta are obtained at the same time. However, unlike the Sharpe and Treynor measures, each period's returns must be used in the estimating process, rather than an average return for the entire period. Thus, if performance is being measured on an annual basis, the annual returns on RF, R_M, and R_p must be obtained.

Problems with Portfolio Measurement

Using the three composite performance measures just discussed to evaluate portfolios is not without problems. Investors should understand their limitations and be guided accordingly.

First, these measures are derived from capital market theory and the CAPM, and are therefore dependent on the assumptions involved with this theory, as discussed in Chapter 20. For example, if the Treasury bill rate is not a satisfactory proxy for the risk-free rate, or if investors cannot borrow and lend at the risk-free rate, this will have an impact upon these measures of performance.

An important assumption of capital market theory that directly affects the use of these performance measures is the assumption of a market portfolio that can be proxied by a market index. We have used the Standard & Poor's 500 Index as a market proxy, as is often done. However, there are potential problems.

Richard Roll has argued that beta is not a clear-cut measure of risk.[10] If the definition of the market portfolio is changed—for example, using the New York Stock Exchange Index instead of the S&P 500—the beta can change. This could, in turn, change the rankings of portfolios. Although a high correlation exists among most of the commonly used market proxies,

---

[10] See R. Roll, "Ambiguity When Performance Is Measured by the Securities Market Line." *The Journal of Finance,* Vol. 33 (September 1978), pp. 1051–1069; "Performance Evaluation and Benchmark Error I," *Journal of Portfolio Management,* Vol. 6 (Summer 1980), pp. 5–12, and Part II (Winter 1981), pp. 17–22.

this does not eliminate the problem—that some may be efficient but others are not. This relates to Roll's major point, mentioned in Chapter 20, that using a market portfolio other than the "true" market portfolio does not constitute a test of the CAPM; rather, it is a test only of whether or not the chosen market proxy is efficient.

According to Roll, no unambiguous test of the CAPM has yet been conducted. This should be kept in mind with performance measures based on the CAPM, such as the Treynor and Jensen measures.

Theoretically, each of the three performance measures discussed should be independent of its respective risk measure. However, a number of researchers over the years have found a relationship between them. In some cases the relationship was negative and in others it was positive. In fact, it can be shown that a fundamental relationship does exist between the composite performance measures and their associated risk measure.[11] Given an empirical CML, the relation between Sharpe's measure and the standard deviation can be instantly derived; similarly, given an empirical SML, the relationship between Jensen's and Treynor's performance measures and beta can be derived instantly. The only other variable needed to do these calculations is the mean market return for the period.

Summary

This chapter discusses the measurement and evaluation of portfolio performance, the bottom line of the investing process. It is an important aspect of interest to all investors and money managers.

The framework for evaluating portfolio performance consists of recognizing, and measuring, both the realized return and the risk of the portfolio being evaluated. Another important issue is what benchmark to use to compare a portfolio's performance. Finally, investors should note that an evaluation of the portfolio itself is not necessarily equivalent to an evaluation of the portfolio manager.

The most often used measures of portfolio performance are the composite measures of Sharpe, Treynor, and Jensen. All three incorporate return and risk together. The Sharpe and Treynor measures can be used to rank portfolio performance and indicate the relative positions of the portfolios being evaluated. Jensen's measure is an absolute measure of performance.

The Sharpe and Treynor measures both relate the excess return on a portfolio to a measure of its risk. Sharpe's RVAR uses standard deviation, whereas Treynor's RVOL uses beta. Since RVAR implicitly measures the lack of complete diversification in a portfolio and RVOL assumes complete diversification, portfolio rankings from the two measures can differ if portfolios are not well diversified. The Sharpe measure is more appropriate when

---

[11] See J. Wilson and C. Jones, "The Relationship between Performance and Risk: Whence the Bias?" *The Journal of Financial Research,* Vol. 4 (Summer 1981), pp. 109–117.

the portfolio constitutes a significant portion of an investor's wealth; the Treynor measure is more appropriate when the portfolio constitutes only a small part of that wealth.

Jensen's differential return measures the difference between what the portfolio was expected to earn, given its systematic risk, and what it actually did earn. By regressing the portfolio's excess return against that of the market index, alpha can be used to capture the superior or inferior performance of the portfolio manager. Based on capital market theory, alphas are expected to be zero; therefore, significantly positive or negative alphas are used to indicate corresponding performance.

These measures are not without their limitations and problems. If there are problems with capital market theory and the CAPM, such problems carry over to performance measurement. One problem in particular concerns the market portfolio, which can be measured only imprecisely. Failure to use the true ex ante market portfolio may result in different betas and different rankings for portfolios. Finally, a fundamental relationship exists between the composite performance measures and their associated risk measures. This relationship may be positive in some periods and negative in others.

Key Words

Coefficient of determination
Composite (risk-adjusted) measures
  of portfolio performance

Differential return measure (alpha)
Reward-to-variability ratio
Reward-to-volatility ratio

QUESTIONS AND PROBLEMS

1. Outline the framework for evaluating portfolio performance.
2. Why can the evaluation of a portfolio be different from the evaluation of a portfolio manager?
3. Explain how the three composite measures of performance are related to capital market theory and the CAPM.
4. What role does diversification play in the Sharpe and Treynor measures?
5. How can one construct a characteristic line for a portfolio? What does it show?
6. How can portfolio diversification be measured? On the average, what degree of diversification would you expect to find for a typical mutual fund?

7. For what type of mutual fund discussed in Chapter 18 could you expect to find complete diversification?
8. In general, when may an investor prefer to rely on the Sharpe measure? The Treynor measure?
9. Explain how Jensen's differential return measure is derived from the CAPM.
10. Why is the Jensen measure computationally efficient?
11. What role does statistical significance play in the Jensen measure?
12. How does Roll's questioning of the testing of the CAPM relate to the issue of performance measurement?
13. Illustrate how the choice of the wrong market index could affect the rankings of portfolios.
14. In theory, what would be the proper market index to use?
15. Explain why the steeper the angle, the better the performance in Figures 21–1 and 21–3.
16. If portfolios are evaluated using the Sharpe and Jensen measures, would the same rankings of performance be obtained?
17. The following data are available for five portfolios and the market for a recent 10-year period:

	Average Annual Return (%)	Standard Deviation (%)	b_p	R^2
1	14	21	1.15	0.70
2	16	24	1.1	0.98
3	26	30	1.3	0.96
4	17	25	0.9	0.92
5	10	18	0.45	0.60
S&P 500	12	20		
RF	6			

a. Rank these portfolios using the Sharpe measure.
b. Rank these portfolios using the Treynor measure.
c. Compare the rankings of portfolio 1 and 2. Are there any differences? How can you explain these differences?
d. Which of these portfolios outperformed the market?

18. Consider the five funds shown here.

	a	b	R^2
1	2.0	1.0	0.98
2	1.6[a]	1.1	0.95
3	3.5	0.9	0.90
4	1.2	0.8	0.80
5	0.9[a]	1.20	0.60

[a] Significant at 5% level.

    a.   Which fund's returns are best explained by the market's returns?

    b.   Which fund had the largest total risk?

    c.   Which fund had the lowest market risk? The highest?

    d.   Which fund(s), according to Jensen's alpha, outperformed the market?

19.   The following diagram shows characteristic lines in risk premium form for two portfolios. Assume that the alphas for each portfolio are statistically significant.

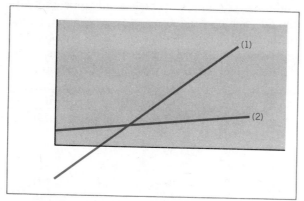

    a.   Label each axis.

    b.   Which fund has the larger beta?

    c.   Based on a visual inspection, which fund has the larger alpha?

    d.   Which fund outperformed the market?

20.   Annual holding period yields for the same nine years used in the chapter (1974–1982) are shown below for eight hypothetical mutual funds. The values were like those shown in Table 21–1, and the characteristic lines were calculated using annual market yields. The ex post values shown in the following table are:

Fund	(1) $\bar{R}_p$ (%)	(2) SD_p (%)	(3) a_p	(4) b_p	(5) R^2
A	17.0	20.0	7.53	0.88	0.82
B	19.0	17.8	11.70	0.65	0.57
C	12.3	25.0	3.12	0.83	0.47
D	20.0	24.5	9.00	1.00	0.72
E	15.0	17.4	6.15	0.79	0.88
F	19.0	18.0	10.11	0.83	0.89
G	8.6	19.0	−1.37	0.91	0.95
H	20.0	21.5	9.52	0.93	0.78

where

$\bar{R}_p$ = mean annual yield for each fund.

SD_p = standard deviation of the annual yields.

a_p = the constant of the characteristic line.

b_p = the slope.

Using 8.6% as the risk-free yield, answer the following problems:
a. Calculate Sharpe's RVAR for each of these 8 funds, and using the 3 additional funds used in the text, rank the 11 funds from high to low performance.
b. Calculate Treynor's RVOL for each fund and perform the same ranking as in a.
c. Using the R^2 in column 5, comment on the degree of diversification of the eight mutual funds. Which fund appears to be the most highly diversified? Which fund appears to be the least diversified?
d. The returns, standard deviations, and characteristic lines were recalculated using the annual Treasury bill rate, as in the text for Equation 21-4. The results are shown in the following table in excess yield form:

Fund	$\bar{R}_p$	SD_p	a_p	$SE(a)$	b_p	t Values
A	8.60	20.00	6.57	(3.53)	0.87	2.15
B	10.30	16.90	8.81	(4.78)	0.61	2.23
C	3.70	25.50	1.58	(7.37)	0.86	0.24
D	11.50	25.00	8.98	(5.23)	1.03	1.96
E	6.30	18.09	4.34	(2.51)	0.81	1.91
F	10.80	18.20	8.69	(2.40)	0.83	4.21
G	-0.02	19.80	-2.22	(1.65)	0.92	-1.49
H	11.30	23.40	8.88	(4.20)	0.95	2.40

In the column to the right of the a_p is the calculated standard error of alpha [$SE(a)$]. The critical value of t for 7 degrees of freedom (number of observations minus 2) for a two-tailed test at the 5% level is 2.365. With a large number of degrees of freedom (more observations), the critical value of t is close to 2.00. The calculated t values are shown in the last column of the table (t for a_p). If the absolute value in that column exceeds 2.365, that fund's alpha is significantly different from zero. On the basis of this test, which funds exhibit above, or below, average performance?
e. Compare the values of a and b calculated in excess yield form with those calculated initially. Can you suggest any generalizations about the relative magnitudes of the a or the b values?

Selected References

Cranshaw, T. E. "The Evaluation of Investment Performance." *The Journal of Business,* October 1977, pp. 462–485.

Fama, Eugene. "Components of Investment Performance." *The Journal of Finance,* June 1972, pp. 551–567.

Ferguson, Robert. "The Trouble with Performance Measurement," *Journal of Portfolio Management,* Spring 1986, pp. 4–9.

Friend, Irwin, and Blume, Marshall. "Measurement of Portfolio Performance Under Uncertainty." *American Economic Review,* September 1970, pp. 561–575.

Good, Walter. "Measuring Performance." *Financial Analysts Journal,* May–June 1983, pp. 19–23.

Hendriksson, R. D., and Merton, Robert. "On Market Timing and Investment Performance. II. Statistical Procedures for Evaluating Forecasting Skills." *The Journal of Business,* October, 1981.

Jensen, Michael C. "The Performance of Mutual Funds in the Period 1945–1964." *The Journal of Finance,* May 1968, pp. 389–416.

Jensen, Michael C. "Risks, The Pricing of Capital Assets, and the Evaluation of Investment Portfolios." *The Journal of Business,* April 1969, pp. 167–247.

Klemkosky, Robert. "The Bias in Composite Performance Measures." *Journal of Financial and Quantitative Analysis,* June 1973, pp. 505–514.

Pohlman, R., Ang, J., and Hollinger, R. "Performance and Timing: A Test of Hedge Funds." *Journal of Portfolio Management,* Spring 1978, pp. 69–72.

Roll, Richard. "Performance Evaluation and Benchmark Errors." *Journal of Portfolio Management,* Summer 1980, pp. 12–20.

Sharpe, W. F. "Mutual Fund Performance." *The Journal of Business,* January 1966, pp. 119–138.

Treynor, J. L. "How to Rate Management of Investment Funds." *Harvard Business Review,* January–February 1965, pp. 63–75.

Treynor, J. L., and Mazuy, M. "Can Mutual Funds Outguess the Market?" *Harvard Business Review,* July–August 1966, pp. 131–136.

Williamson, Peter. "Measurement of Forecasting of Mutual Fund Performance: Choosing an Investment Strategy." *Financial Analysts Journal,* November–December 1972, pp. 78–84.

Williamson, Peter. "Performance Measurement." Edward Altman (ed.), *The Financial Handbook.* New York: John Wiley, 1980.

Wilson, Jack, and Jones, Charles. "The Relationship Between Performance and Risk: Whence the Bias?" *The Journal of Financial Research,* Summer 1981, pp. 109–117.

INTEREST TABLES

TABLE A–1 Compound (Future) Value Factors for $1 Compounded at R Percent for N Periods

N	R = 1%	2%	3%	4%	5%	6%	7%	8%	9%	10%	11%	12%	13%
1	1.01	1.02	1.03	1.04	1.05	1.06	1.07	1.08	1.09	1.1	1.11	1.12	1.13
2	1.02	1.04	1.061	1.082	1.103	1.124	1.145	1.166	1.188	1.21	1.232	1.254	1.277
3	1.03	1.061	1.093	1.125	1.158	1.191	1.225	1.26	1.295	1.331	1.368	1.405	1.443
4	1.041	1.082	1.126	1.17	1.216	1.262	1.311	1.36	1.412	1.464	1.518	1.574	1.63
5	1.051	1.104	1.159	1.217	1.276	1.338	1.403	1.469	1.539	1.611	1.685	1.762	1.842
6	1.062	1.126	1.194	1.265	1.34	1.419	1.501	1.587	1.677	1.772	1.87	1.974	2.082
7	1.072	1.149	1.23	1.316	1.407	1.504	1.606	1.714	1.828	1.949	2.076	2.211	2.353
8	1.083	1.172	1.267	1.369	1.477	1.594	1.718	1.851	1.993	2.144	2.305	2.476	2.658
9	1.094	1.195	1.305	1.423	1.551	1.689	1.838	1.999	2.172	2.358	2.558	2.773	3.004
10	1.105	1.219	1.344	1.48	1.629	1.791	1.967	2.159	2.367	2.594	2.839	3.106	3.395
11	1.116	1.243	1.384	1.539	1.71	1.898	2.105	2.332	2.58	2.853	3.152	3.479	3.836
12	1.127	1.268	1.426	1.601	1.796	2.012	2.252	2.518	2.813	3.138	3.498	3.896	4.335
13	1.138	1.294	1.469	1.665	1.886	2.133	2.41	2.72	3.066	3.452	3.883	4.363	4.898
14	1.149	1.319	1.513	1.732	1.98	2.261	2.579	2.937	3.342	3.797	4.31	4.887	5.535
15	1.161	1.346	1.558	1.801	2.079	2.397	2.759	3.172	3.642	4.177	4.785	5.474	6.254
16	1.173	1.373	1.605	1.873	2.183	2.54	2.952	3.426	3.97	4.595	5.311	6.13	7.067
17	1.184	1.4	1.653	1.948	2.292	2.693	3.159	3.7	4.328	5.054	5.895	6.866	7.986
18	1.196	1.428	1.702	2.026	2.407	2.854	3.38	3.996	4.717	5.56	6.544	7.69	9.024
19	1.208	1.457	1.754	2.107	2.527	3.026	3.617	4.316	5.142	6.116	7.263	8.613	10.197
20	1.22	1.486	1.806	2.191	2.653	3.207	3.87	4.661	5.604	6.727	8.062	9.646	11.523
21	1.232	1.516	1.86	2.279	2.786	3.4	4.141	5.034	6.109	7.4	8.949	10.804	13.021
22	1.245	1.546	1.916	2.37	2.925	3.604	4.43	5.437	6.659	8.14	9.934	12.1	14.714
23	1.257	1.577	1.974	2.465	3.072	3.82	4.741	5.871	7.258	8.954	11.026	13.552	16.627
24	1.27	1.608	2.033	2.563	3.225	4.049	5.072	6.341	7.911	9.85	12.239	15.179	18.788
25	1.282	1.641	2.094	2.666	3.386	4.292	5.427	6.848	8.623	10.835	13.585	17	21.231
30	1.348	1.811	2.427	3.243	4.322	5.743	7.612	10.063	13.268	17.449	22.892	29.96	39.116
35	1.417	2	2.814	3.946	5.516	7.686	10.677	14.785	20.414	28.102	38.575	52.8	72.069
40	1.489	2.208	3.262	4.801	7.04	10.286	14.974	21.725	31.409	45.259	65.001	93.051	132.782
45	1.565	2.438	3.782	5.841	8.985	13.765	21.002	31.92	48.327	72.89	109.53	163.98	244.641
50	1.645	2.692	4.384	7.107	11.467	18.42	29.457	46.902	74.358	117.39	184.56	289.00	450.736

TABLE A–1 Compound (Future) Value Factors for $1 Compounded at R Percent for N Periods

N	|R =| 14%	15%	16%	18%	20%	22%	24%	25%	30%	35%	40%	45%	50%
1	1.14	1.15	1.16	1.18	1.2	1.22	1.24	1.25	1.3	1.35	1.4	1.45	1.5
2	1.3	1.323	1.346	1.392	1.44	1.488	1.538	1.563	1.69	1.823	1.96	2.103	2.25
3	1.482	1.521	1.561	1.643	1.728	1.816	1.907	1.953	2.197	2.46	2.744	3.049	3.375
4	1.689	1.749	1.811	1.939	2.074	2.215	2.364	2.441	2.856	3.322	3.842	4.421	5.063
5	1.925	2.011	2.1	2.288	2.488	2.703	2.932	3.052	3.713	4.484	5.378	6.41	7.594
6	2.195	2.313	2.436	2.7	2.986	3.297	3.635	3.815	4.827	6.053	7.53	9.294	11.391
7	2.502	2.66	2.826	3.185	3.583	4.023	4.508	4.768	6.275	8.172	10.541	13.476	17.086
8	2.853	3.059	3.278	3.759	4.3	4.908	5.59	5.96	8.157	11.032	14.758	19.541	25.629
9	3.252	3.518	3.803	4.435	5.16	5.987	6.931	7.451	10.604	14.894	20.661	28.334	38.443
10	3.707	4.046	4.411	5.234	6.192	7.305	8.594	9.313	13.786	20.107	28.925	41.085	57.665
11	4.226	4.652	5.117	6.176	7.43	8.912	10.657	11.642	17.922	27.144	40.496	59.573	86.498
12	4.818	5.35	5.936	7.288	8.916	10.872	13.215	14.552	23.298	36.644	56.694	86.381	129.746
13	5.492	6.153	6.886	8.599	10.699	13.264	16.386	18.19	30.288	49.47	79.371	125.25	194.62
14	6.261	7.076	7.988	10.147	12.839	16.182	20.319	22.737	39.374	66.784	111.12	181.61	291.929
15	7.138	8.137	9.266	11.974	15.407	19.742	25.196	28.422	51.186	90.158	155.56	263.34	437.894
16	8.137	9.358	10.748	14.129	18.488	24.086	31.243	35.527	66.542	121.71	217.79	381.84	656.841
17	9.276	10.761	12.468	16.672	22.186	29.384	38.741	44.409	86.504	164.31	304.91	553.67	985.261
18	10.575	12.375	14.463	19.673	26.623	35.849	48.039	55.511	112.45	221.82	426.87	802.83	1477.892
19	12.056	14.232	16.777	23.214	31.948	43.736	59.568	69.389	146.19	299.46	597.63	1164.1	2216.838
20	13.743	16.367	19.461	27.393	38.338	53.358	73.864	86.736	190.05	404.27	836.68	1687.9	3325.257
21	15.668	18.822	22.574	32.324	46.005	65.096	91.592	108.42	247.06	545.76	1171.3	2447.5	4987.885
22	17.861	21.645	26.186	38.142	55.206	79.418	113.57	135.52	321.18	736.78	1639.8	3548.9	7481.828
23	20.362	24.891	30.376	45.008	66.247	96.889	140.83	169.40	417.53	994.66	2295.8	5145.9	11222.74
24	23.212	28.625	35.236	53.109	79.497	118.20	174.63	211.75	542.80	1342.7	3214.2	7461.6	16834.11
25	26.462	32.919	40.874	62.669	95.396	144.21	216.54	264.69	705.64	1812.7	4499.8	10819.	25251.17
30	50.95	66.212	85.85	143.37	237.37	389.75	634.82	807.79	2619.9	8128.5	24201.	69348.	191751.1
35	98.1	133.17	180.31	327.99	590.66	1053.4	1861.0	2465.1	9727.8	36448.	130161	444508	
40	188.88	267.86	378.72	750.37	1469.7	2847.0	5455.9	7523.1	36118.	163437	700037		
45	363.67	538.76	795.44	1716.6	3657.2	7694.7	15994.	22958.	134106	732857			
50	700.23	1083.6	1670.7	3927.3	9100.4	20796.	46890.	70064.	497929				

TABLE A–2 Present Value Factors (at R Percent) for $1 Received at the End of N Periods

R =

N	1%	2%	3%	4%	5%	6%	7%	8%	9%	10%	11%	12%	13%
1	.990	.980	.971	.962	.952	.943	.935	.926	.917	.909	.901	.893	.885
2	.980	.961	.943	.925	.907	.890	.873	.857	.842	.826	.812	.797	.783
3	.971	.942	.915	.889	.864	.840	.816	.794	.772	.751	.731	.712	.693
4	.961	.924	.888	.855	.823	.792	.763	.735	.708	.683	.659	.636	.613
5	.951	.906	.863	.822	.784	.747	.713	.681	.650	.621	.593	.567	.543
6	.942	.888	.837	.790	.746	.705	.666	.630	.596	.564	.535	.507	.480
7	.933	.871	.813	.760	.711	.665	.623	.583	.547	.513	.482	.452	.425
8	.923	.853	.789	.731	.677	.627	.582	.540	.502	.467	.434	.404	.376
9	.914	.837	.766	.703	.645	.592	.544	.500	.460	.424	.391	.361	.333
10	.905	.820	.744	.676	.614	.558	.508	.463	.422	.386	.352	.322	.295
11	.896	.804	.722	.650	.585	.527	.475	.429	.388	.350	.317	.287	.261
12	.887	.788	.701	.625	.557	.497	.444	.397	.356	.319	.286	.257	.231
13	.879	.773	.681	.601	.530	.469	.415	.368	.326	.290	.258	.229	.204
14	.870	.758	.661	.577	.505	.442	.388	.340	.299	.263	.232	.205	.181
15	.861	.743	.642	.555	.481	.417	.362	.315	.275	.239	.209	.183	.160
16	.853	.728	.623	.534	.458	.394	.339	.292	.252	.218	.188	.163	.141
17	.844	.714	.605	.513	.436	.371	.317	.270	.231	.198	.170	.146	.125
18	.836	.700	.587	.494	.416	.350	.296	.250	.212	.180	.153	.130	.111
19	.828	.686	.570	.475	.396	.331	.277	.232	.194	.164	.138	.116	.098
20	.820	.673	.554	.456	.377	.312	.258	.215	.178	.149	.124	.104	.087
21	.811	.660	.538	.439	.359	.294	.242	.199	.164	.135	.112	.093	.077
22	.803	.647	.522	.422	.342	.278	.226	.184	.150	.123	.101	.083	.068
23	.795	.634	.507	.406	.326	.262	.211	.170	.138	.112	.091	.074	.060
24	.788	.622	.492	.390	.310	.247	.197	.158	.126	.102	.082	.066	.053
25	.780	.610	.478	.375	.295	.233	.184	.146	.116	.092	.074	.059	.047
30	.742	.552	.412	.308	.231	.174	.131	.099	.075	.057	.044	.033	.026
35	.706	.500	.355	.253	.181	.130	.094	.068	.049	.036	.026	.019	.014
40	.672	.453	.307	.208	.142	.097	.067	.046	.032	.022	.015	.011	.008
45	.639	.410	.264	.171	.111	.073	.048	.031	.021	.014	.009	.006	.004
50	.608	.372	.228	.141	.087	.054	.034	.021	.013	.009	.005	.003	.002

TABLE A–2 Present Value Factors (at R Percent) for $1 Received at the End of N Periods

N	14%	15%	16%	18%	20%	22%	24%	25%	30%	35%	40%	45%	50%
1	.877	.870	.862	.847	.833	.820	.806	.800	.769	.741	.714	.690	.667
2	.769	.756	.743	.718	.694	.672	.650	.640	.592	.549	.510	.476	.444
3	.675	.658	.641	.609	.579	.551	.524	.512	.455	.406	.364	.328	.296
4	.592	.572	.552	.516	.482	.451	.423	.410	.350	.301	.260	.226	.198
5	.519	.497	.476	.437	.402	.370	.341	.328	.269	.223	.186	.156	.132
6	.456	.432	.410	.370	.335	.303	.275	.262	.207	.165	.133	.108	.088
7	.400	.376	.354	.314	.279	.249	.222	.210	.159	.122	.095	.074	.059
8	.351	.327	.305	.266	.233	.204	.179	.168	.123	.091	.068	.051	.039
9	.308	.284	.263	.225	.194	.167	.144	.134	.094	.067	.048	.035	.026
10	.270	.247	.227	.191	.162	.137	.116	.107	.073	.050	.035	.024	.017
11	.237	.215	.195	.162	.135	.112	.094	.086	.056	.037	.025	.017	.012
12	.208	.187	.168	.137	.112	.092	.076	.069	.043	.027	.018	.012	.008
13	.182	.163	.145	.116	.093	.075	.061	.055	.033	.020	.013	.008	.005
14	.160	.141	.125	.099	.078	.062	.049	.044	.025	.015	.009	.006	.003
15	.140	.123	.108	.084	.065	.051	.040	.035	.020	.011	.006	.004	.002
16	.123	.107	.093	.071	.054	.042	.032	.028	.015	.008	.005	.003	.002
17	.108	.093	.080	.060	.045	.034	.026	.023	.012	.006	.003	.002	.002
18	.095	.081	.069	.051	.038	.028	.021	.018	.009	.005	.003	.002	.001
19	.083	.070	.060	.043	.031	.023	.017	.014	.007	.005	.002	.001	.001
20	.073	.061	.051	.037	.026	.019	.014	.012	.005	.003	.002	.001	.001
21	.064	.053	.044	.031	.022	.015	.011	.009	.004	.002	.001	.001	
22	.056	.046	.038	.026	.018	.013	.009	.007	.003	.002	.001	.001	
23	.049	.040	.033	.022	.015	.010	.007	.006	.002	.001	.001		
24	.043	.035	.028	.019	.013	.008	.006	.005	.002	.001			
25	.038	.030	.024	.016	.010	.007	.005	.005	.001	.001			
30	.020	.015	.012	.007	.004	.003	.002	.004	.001				
35	.010	.008	.006	.003	.002	.001	.001	.001					
40	.005	.004	.003	.001	.001								
45	.003	.002	.001	.001									
50	.001	.001	.001										

TABLE A–3 Compound Sum Annuity Factors for $1 Compounded at R Percent for N Periods

N	1%	2%	3%	4%	5%	6%	7%	8%	9%	10%	11%	12%	13%
1	1	1	1	1	1	1	1	1	1	1	1	1	1
2	2.01	2.02	2.03	2.04	2.05	2.06	2.07	2.08	2.09	2.1	2.11	2.12	2.13
3	3.03	3.06	3.091	3.122	3.152	3.184	3.215	3.246	3.278	3.31	3.342	3.374	3.407
4	4.06	4.122	4.184	4.246	4.31	4.375	4.44	4.506	4.573	4.641	4.71	4.779	4.85
5	5.101	5.204	5.309	5.416	5.526	5.637	5.751	5.867	5.985	6.105	6.228	6.353	6.48
6	6.152	6.308	6.468	6.633	6.802	6.975	7.153	7.336	7.523	7.716	7.913	8.115	8.323
7	7.214	7.434	7.662	7.898	8.142	8.394	8.654	8.923	9.2	9.487	9.783	10.089	10.405
8	8.286	8.583	8.892	9.214	9.549	9.897	10.26	10.637	11.028	11.436	11.859	12.3	12.757
9	9.369	9.755	10.159	10.583	11.027	11.491	11.978	12.488	13.021	13.579	14.164	14.776	15.416
10	10.462	10.95	11.464	12.006	12.578	13.181	13.816	14.487	15.193	15.937	16.722	17.549	18.42
11	11.567	12.169	12.808	13.486	14.207	14.972	15.784	16.645	17.56	18.531	19.561	20.655	21.814
12	12.683	13.412	14.192	15.026	15.917	16.87	17.888	18.977	20.141	21.384	22.713	24.133	25.65
13	13.809	14.68	15.618	16.627	17.713	18.882	20.141	21.495	22.953	24.523	26.212	28.029	29.985
14	14.947	15.974	17.086	18.292	19.599	21.015	22.55	24.215	26.019	27.975	30.095	32.393	34.883
15	16.097	17.293	18.599	20.024	21.579	23.276	25.129	27.152	29.361	31.772	34.405	37.28	40.417
16	17.258	18.639	20.157	21.825	23.657	25.673	27.888	30.324	33.003	35.95	39.19	42.753	46.672
17	18.43	20.012	21.762	23.698	25.84	28.213	30.84	33.75	36.974	40.545	44.501	48.884	53.739
18	19.615	21.412	23.414	25.645	28.132	30.906	33.999	37.45	41.301	45.599	50.396	55.75	61.725
19	20.811	22.841	25.117	27.671	30.539	33.76	37.379	41.446	46.018	51.159	56.939	63.44	70.749
20	22.019	24.297	26.87	29.778	33.066	36.786	40.995	45.762	51.16	57.275	64.203	72.052	80.947
21	23.239	25.783	28.676	31.969	35.719	39.993	44.865	50.423	56.765	64.002	72.265	81.699	92.47
22	24.472	27.299	30.537	34.248	38.505	43.392	49.006	55.457	62.873	71.403	81.214	92.503	105.491
23	25.716	28.845	32.453	36.618	41.43	46.996	53.436	60.893	69.532	79.543	91.148	104.60	120.205
24	26.973	30.422	34.426	39.083	44.502	50.816	58.177	66.765	76.79	88.497	102.17	118.15	136.831
25	28.243	32.03	36.459	41.646	47.727	54.865	63.249	73.106	84.701	98.347	114.41	133.33	155.62
30	34.785	40.568	47.575	56.085	66.439	79.058	94.461	113.28	136.30	164.49	199.02	241.33	293.199
35	41.66	49.994	60.462	73.652	90.32	111.43	138.23	172.31	215.71	271.02	341.59	431.66	546.681
40	48.886	60.402	75.401	95.026	120.8	154.76	199.63	259.05	337.88	442.59	581.82	767.09	1013.704
45	56.481	71.893	92.72	121.02	159.7	212.74	285.74	386.50	525.85	718.90	986.63	1358.2	1874.165
50	64.463	84.579	112.79	152.66	209.34	290.33	406.52	573.77	815.08	1163.9	1668.7	2400.0	3459.507

R =

TABLE A–3 Compound Sum Annuity Factors for $1 Compounded at R Percent for N Periods

R =

N	14%	15%	16%	18%	20%	22%	24%	25%	30%	35%	40%	45%	50%
1	1	1	1	1	1	1	1	1	1	1	1	1	1
2	2.14	2.15	2.16	2.18	2.2	2.22	2.24	2.25	2.3	2.35	2.4	2.45	2.5
3	3.44	3.472	3.506	3.572	3.64	3.708	3.778	3.813	3.99	4.172	4.36	4.552	4.75
4	4.921	4.993	5.066	5.215	5.368	5.524	5.684	5.766	6.187	6.633	7.104	7.601	8.125
5	6.61	6.742	6.877	7.154	7.442	7.74	8.048	8.207	9.043	9.954	10.946	12.022	13.188
6	8.536	8.754	8.977	9.442	9.93	10.442	10.98	11.259	12.756	14.438	16.324	18.431	20.781
7	10.73	11.067	11.414	12.142	12.916	13.74	14.615	15.073	17.583	20.492	23.853	27.725	32.172
8	13.233	13.727	14.24	15.327	16.499	17.762	19.123	19.842	23.858	28.664	34.395	41.202	49.258
9	16.085	16.786	17.519	19.086	20.799	22.67	24.712	25.802	32.015	39.696	49.153	60.743	74.887
10	19.337	20.304	21.321	23.521	25.959	28.657	31.643	33.253	42.619	54.59	69.814	89.077	113.33
11	23.045	24.349	25.733	28.755	32.15	35.962	40.238	42.566	56.405	74.697	98.739	130.16	170.995
12	27.271	29.002	30.85	34.931	39.581	44.874	50.895	54.208	74.327	101.84	139.23	189.73	257.493
13	32.089	34.352	36.786	42.219	48.497	55.746	64.11	68.76	97.625	138.48	195.92	276.11	387.239
14	37.581	40.505	43.672	50.818	59.196	69.01	80.496	86.949	127.91	187.95	275.3	401.36	581.859
15	43.842	47.58	51.66	60.965	72.035	85.192	100.81	109.68	167.28	254.73	386.42	582.98	873.788
16	50.98	55.717	60.925	72.939	87.442	104.93	126.01	138.10	218.47	344.89	541.98	846.32	1311.682
17	59.118	65.075	71.673	87.068	105.93	129.02	157.25	173.63	285.01	466.61	759.78	1228.1	1968.523
18	68.394	75.836	84.141	103.74	128.11	158.40	195.99	218.04	371.51	630.92	1064.6	1781.8	2953.784
19	78.969	88.212	98.603	123.41	154.74	194.25	244.03	273.55	483.97	852.74	1491.5	2584.6	4431.676
20	91.025	102.44	115.38	146.62	186.68	237.98	303.60	342.94	630.16	1152.2	2089.2	3748.7	6648.513
21	104.76	118.81	134.84	174.02	225.02	291.34	377.46	429.68	820.21	1556.4	2925.8	5436.7	9973.77
22	120.43	137.63	157.41	206.34	271.03	356.44	469.05	538.10	1067.2	2102.2	4097.2	7884.2	14961.65
23	138.29	159.27	183.60	244.48	326.23	435.86	582.63	673.62	1388.4	2839.0	5737.1	11433.	22443.48
24	158.65	184.16	213.97	289.49	392.48	532.75	723.46	843.03	1806.0	3833.7	8032.9	16579.	33666.22
25	181.87	212.79	249.21	342.60	471.98	650.95	898.09	1054.7	2348.8	5176.5	11247.	24040.	50500.34
30	356.78	434.74	530.31	790.94	1181.8	1767.0	2640.9	3227.1	8729.9	23221.	60501.	154106	383500.1
35	693.57	881.17	1120.7	1816.6	2948.3	4783.6	7750.2	9856.7	32422.	104136	325400	987794	
40	1342.0	1779.0	2360.7	4163.2	7343.8	12936.	22728.	30088.	120392	466960			
45	2590.5	3585.1	4965.2	9531.5	18281.	34971.	66640.	91831.	447019				
50	4994.5	7217.7	10435.	21813.	45497.	94525.	195372	280255					

TABLE A–4 Present Value Annuity Factors (at R Percent Per Period) for $1 Received Per Period for Each of N Periods

R =

N	1%	2%	3%	4%	5%	6%	7%	8%	9%	10%	11%	12%	13%
1	0.990	0.980	0.971	0.962	0.952	0.943	0.935	0.926	0.917	0.909	0.901	0.893	0.885
2	1.970	1.942	1.913	1.886	1.859	1.833	1.808	1.783	1.759	1.736	1.713	1.690	1.668
3	2.941	2.884	2.829	2.775	2.723	2.673	2.624	2.577	2.531	2.487	2.444	2.402	2.361
4	3.902	3.808	3.717	3.630	3.546	3.465	3.387	3.312	3.240	3.170	3.102	3.037	2.974
5	4.853	4.713	4.580	4.452	4.329	4.212	4.100	3.993	3.890	3.791	3.696	3.605	3.517
6	5.795	5.601	5.417	5.242	5.076	4.917	4.767	4.623	4.486	4.355	4.231	4.111	3.998
7	6.728	6.472	6.230	6.002	5.786	5.582	5.389	5.206	5.033	4.868	4.712	4.564	4.423
8	7.652	7.325	7.020	6.733	6.463	6.210	5.971	5.747	5.535	5.335	5.146	4.968	4.799
9	8.566	8.162	7.786	7.435	7.108	6.802	6.515	6.247	5.995	5.759	5.537	5.328	5.132
10	9.471	8.983	8.530	8.111	7.722	7.360	7.024	6.710	6.418	6.145	5.889	5.650	5.426
11	10.368	9.787	9.253	8.760	8.306	7.887	7.499	7.139	6.805	6.495	6.207	5.938	5.687
12	11.255	10.575	9.954	9.385	8.863	8.384	7.943	7.536	7.161	6.814	6.492	6.194	5.918
13	12.134	11.348	10.635	9.986	9.394	8.853	8.358	7.904	7.487	7.103	6.750	6.424	6.122
14	13.004	12.106	11.296	10.563	9.899	9.295	8.745	8.244	7.786	7.367	6.982	6.628	6.302
15	13.865	12.849	11.938	11.118	10.380	9.712	9.108	8.559	8.061	7.606	7.191	6.811	6.462
16	14.718	13.578	12.561	11.652	10.838	10.106	9.447	8.851	8.313	7.824	7.379	6.974	6.604
17	15.562	14.292	13.166	12.166	11.274	10.477	9.763	9.122	8.544	8.022	7.549	7.120	6.729
18	16.398	14.992	13.754	12.659	11.690	10.828	10.059	9.372	8.756	8.201	7.702	7.250	6.840
19	17.226	15.678	14.324	13.134	12.085	11.158	10.336	9.604	8.950	8.365	7.839	7.366	6.938
20	18.046	16.351	14.877	13.590	12.462	11.470	10.594	9.818	9.129	8.514	7.963	7.469	7.025
21	18.857	17.011	15.415	14.029	12.821	11.764	10.836	10.017	9.292	8.649	8.075	7.562	7.102
22	19.660	17.658	15.937	14.451	13.163	12.042	11.061	10.201	9.442	8.772	8.176	7.645	7.170
23	20.456	18.292	16.444	14.857	13.489	12.303	11.272	10.371	9.580	8.883	8.266	7.718	7.230
24	21.243	18.914	16.936	15.247	13.799	12.550	11.469	10.529	9.707	8.985	8.348	7.784	7.283
25	22.023	19.523	17.413	15.622	14.094	12.783	11.654	10.675	9.823	9.077	8.422	7.843	7.330
30	25.808	22.396	19.600	17.292	15.372	13.765	12.409	11.258	10.274	9.427	8.694	8.055	7.496
35	29.409	24.999	21.487	18.665	16.374	14.498	12.948	11.655	10.567	9.644	8.855	8.176	7.586
40	32.835	27.355	23.115	19.793	17.159	15.046	13.332	11.925	10.757	9.779	8.951	8.244	7.634
45	36.095	29.490	24.519	20.720	17.774	15.456	13.606	12.108	10.881	9.863	9.008	8.283	7.661
50	39.196	31.424	25.730	21.482	18.256	15.762	13.801	12.233	10.962	9.915	9.042	8.304	7.675

TABLE A-4 Present Value Annuity Factors (at R Percent Per Period) for $1 Received Per Period for Each of N Periods

N	14%	15%	16%	18%	20%	22%	24%	25%	30%	35%	40%	45%	50%
1	0.877	0.870	0.862	0.847	0.833	0.820	0.806	0.800	0.769	0.741	0.714	0.690	0.667
2	1.647	1.626	1.605	1.566	1.528	1.492	1.457	1.440	1.361	1.289	1.224	1.165	1.111
3	2.322	2.283	2.246	2.174	2.106	2.042	1.981	1.952	1.816	1.696	1.589	1.493	1.407
4	2.914	2.855	2.798	2.690	2.589	2.494	2.404	2.362	2.166	1.997	1.849	1.720	1.605
5	3.433	3.352	3.274	3.127	2.991	2.864	2.745	2.689	2.436	2.220	2.035	1.876	1.737
6	3.889	3.784	3.685	3.498	3.326	3.167	3.020	2.951	2.643	2.385	2.168	1.983	1.824
7	4.288	4.160	4.039	3.812	3.605	3.416	3.242	3.161	2.802	2.508	2.263	2.057	1.883
8	4.639	4.487	4.344	4.078	3.837	3.619	3.421	3.329	2.925	2.598	2.331	2.109	1.922
9	4.946	4.772	4.607	4.303	4.031	3.786	3.566	3.463	3.019	2.665	2.379	2.144	1.948
10	5.216	5.019	4.833	4.494	4.192	3.923	3.682	3.571	3.092	2.715	2.414	2.168	1.965
11	5.453	5.234	5.029	4.656	4.327	4.035	3.776	3.656	3.147	2.752	2.438	2.185	1.977
12	5.660	5.421	5.197	4.793	4.439	4.127	3.851	3.725	3.190	2.779	2.456	2.196	1.985
13	5.842	5.583	5.342	4.910	4.533	4.203	3.912	3.780	3.223	2.799	2.469	2.204	1.990
14	6.002	5.724	5.468	5.008	4.611	4.265	3.962	3.824	3.249	2.814	2.478	2.210	1.993
15	6.142	5.847	5.575	5.092	4.675	4.315	4.001	3.859	3.268	2.825	2.484	2.214	1.995
16	6.265	5.954	5.668	5.162	4.730	4.357	4.033	3.887	3.283	2.834	2.489	2.216	1.997
17	6.373	6.047	5.749	5.222	4.775	4.391	4.059	3.910	3.295	2.840	2.492	2.218	1.998
18	6.467	6.128	5.818	5.273	4.812	4.419	4.080	3.928	3.304	2.844	2.494	2.219	1.999
19	6.550	6.198	5.877	5.316	4.843	4.442	4.097	3.942	3.311	2.848	2.496	2.220	1.999
20	6.623	6.259	5.929	5.353	4.870	4.460	4.110	3.954	3.316	2.850	2.497	2.221	1.999
21	6.687	6.312	5.973	5.384	4.891	4.476	4.121	3.963	3.320	2.852	2.498	2.221	1.999
22	6.743	6.359	6.011	5.410	4.909	4.488	4.130	3.970	3.323	2.853	2.498	2.222	2.000
23	6.792	6.399	6.044	5.432	4.925	4.499	4.137	3.976	3.325	2.854	2.499	2.222	2.000
24	6.835	6.434	6.073	5.451	4.937	4.507	4.143	3.981	3.327	2.855	2.499	2.222	2.000
25	6.873	6.464	6.097	5.467	4.948	4.514	4.147	3.985	3.329	2.856	2.499	2.222	2.000
30	7.003	6.566	6.177	5.517	4.979	4.534	4.160	3.995	3.332	2.857	2.500	2.222	2.000
35	7.070	6.617	6.215	5.539	4.992	4.541	4.164	3.998	3.333	2.857	2.500	2.222	2.000
40	7.105	6.642	6.233	5.548	4.997	4.544	4.166	3.999	3.333	2.857	2.500	2.222	2.000
45	7.123	6.654	6.242	5.552	4.999	4.545	4.166	4.000	3.333	2.857	2.500	2.222	2.000
50	7.133	6.661	6.246	5.554	4.999	4.545	4.167	4.000	3.333	2.857	2.500	2.222	2.000

R =

GLOSSARY

A

Accrued Interest   Interest that has accrued on a bond since the payment of the last coupon. The purchaser of a bond pays the accrued interest plus the market price.

Active Management Strategy   Bond strategies designed to provide additional returns by trading in bonds.

Allocationally Efficient   A market that allocates resources to the most productive uses.

Arbitrage Pricing Theory   An equilibrium theory of expected returns for securities involving few assumptions about investor preferences. It does require a factor model.

Arbitragers   Investors who seek discrepancies in security prices in an attempt to earn riskless returns.

Ask Price   The price at which the specialist or dealer offers to sell shares.

Auction Market   A securities market such as the New York Stock Exchange where the prices of securities are determined by the actions of buyers and sellers transacting at a specified location.

B

Bar Chart   Probably the most popular chart in technical analysis. It is plotted with price on the vertical axis and time on the horizontal axis and shows each day's price movements.

Basis   With futures contracts, the difference between the price of the item being hedged (the cash contract) and the price of the futures contract used to hedge it.

Bear Market   A period of time (usually months) during which measures of the stock market decline.

Beta   A measure of volatility, or relative systematic risk, for stock or portfolio returns. Typically found by regressing stock (or portfolio) returns on a market proxy such as the S&P 500.

Bid Price   The price at which the specialist or dealer offers to buy shares.

Black–Scholes Model   A widely used model for the valuation of call options.

Blocks   Transactions involving at least 10,000 shares.

Blue Chip Stocks   Stocks of the highest quality, with long records of earnings and dividends—well known, stable, mature companies.

Bond   Long-term debt instrument representing a contractual obligation on the part of the issuer to pay interest and repay principal.

Bond Ratings   Letters (e.g., AAA, AA, etc.) assigned to bonds to express their relative probability of default. Widely recognized ratings are done by Standard & Poor's and Moody's.

Bond Swaps   An active bond management strategy involving the purchase and sale of bonds in an attempt to improve the rate of return on the bond portfolio. There are several different types of bond swaps.

Book Value   The value of a corporation's equity as shown on the books (i.e., balance sheet).

Broker   An intermediary who represents buyers or sellers in securities transactions and receives a commission. The broker acts in the best interest of the customer.

Bull Market   A period of time (usually months) during which measures of the stock market rise.

Business Cycle   Reflects movements in aggregate economic activity.

Business Risk   The risk of a company suffering losses, or profits less than expected, for some time period because of adverse circumstances in that company's particular line of activity.

C

Call   An option to buy stock at a stated price within a specified period of nine months or less.

Call Feature   Gives the issuer the right to call in a security and retire it by paying off the obligation.

Capital Asset Pricing Model (CAPM)   Relates the required rate of return for any security with the risk for that security as measured by beta.

Capital Gain   The amount by which the sale price of a security exceeds the purchase price.

Capital Loss   The amount by which the sale price of a capital asset is less than its purchase price.

Capital Market   The market for long-term securities such as bonds and stocks.

Capital Market Theory Describes the pricing of capital assets in the marketplace.

Cash Account The most common type of brokerage account in which a customer may make only cash transactions.

Certificates of Deposit (1) If negotiable, a marketable short-term deposit liability of the issuer that pays principal (a minimum of $100,000) plus interest at maturity; (2) if nonnegotiable, savings certificates with varying maturities and interest rates.

Charting The classical technical analysis technique of charting security price trends in order to detect patterns in price movements.

Closed-End Investment Company An investment company with a fixed capitalization whose shares trade on exchanges and OTC.

Coefficient of Determination The square of the correlation coefficient, measuring the percentage of the variance in the dependent variable that is accounted for by the independent variable.

Commission Brokers A broker who executes public orders to buy and sell securities.

Composite Indices of Economic Activity A series of leading, coincident, and lagging indicators of economic activity that help to assess the status of the business cycle.

Constant Growth Model A version of the dividend valuation model which assumes that dividends are expected to grow at a constant rate over time. It can be used to solve for the current price of a stock.

Contrary Opinion The idea of trading opposite those investors who supposedly always lose—to go against the crowd.

Conversion Premium With convertible securities, the dollar difference between the market price of the security and its conversion value.

Conversion Price The par value of a bond or preferred stock divided by the conversion ratio.

Conversion Ratio The number of shares of common stock that the owner of a convertible security receives upon conversion.

Conversion Value A convertible security's value based on the current price of the common stock.

Convertible Securities Bonds or preferred stock that are convertible, at the holder's option, into shares of common stock of the same corporation.

Corporate Bonds Long-term debt securities of various types sold by corporations.

Correlation Coefficient A statistical measure of the extent to which two variables are associated. This coefficient ranges from $+1.0$ (perfect positive correlation) to -1.0 (perfect negative or inverse correlation), with 0.0 being no correlation.

Coupon Bond Coupon refers to the periodic interest payments paid by the issuer to the bondholders. Most bonds are coupon bonds.

Covariance An absolute measure of the extent to which two variables tend to co-vary, or move together.

Current Yield The yield on a security resulting from dividing the interest payment or dividend by the current market price.

Cyclical Industries Industries that usually do well when the economy prospers and are likely to be hurt when it falters.

D

Dealer   An individual (firm) who buys and sells securities for his or her own account. Dealers in OTC securities profit by the spread between the bid and ask prices.

Debenture   An unsecured bond, backed by the general credit of a company.

Defensive Industries   Industries least affected by recessions and economic adversity.

Differential Return (Alpha)   Jensen's measure of portfolio performance. It is the difference between what the portfolio actually earned and what it was expected to earn given its level of systematic risk.

Discount   The amount by which a bond or preferred stock sells below its par or face value. For closed-end investment companies, the amount by which the net asset value exceeds the current market price.

Discount Broker   Brokerage firms offering execution services at prices typically less than full-line brokerage firms.

Dividends   The only cash payments regularly made by corporations to their stockholders.

Dividend Valuation Model   A widely used model to value common stocks. The model states that the current price of a stock is equal to the discounted value of all future dividends.

Dow Jones Industrial Average (DJIA)   A price-weighted series of 30 leading industrial stocks, used as a measure of stock market activity.

Dow Theory   The oldest theory of technical analysis, based on three types of price movements—primary, secondary, and daily.

Duration   A measure of a bond's lifetime, stated in years, that accounts for the entire pattern (both size and timing) of the cash flows over the life of the bond.

E

E/P Ratio   A capitalization rate used to capitalize earnings—the reciprocal of the P/E ratio.

Earnings Multiplier   The P/E ratio approach, which states that the price of a stock is equal to the product of its earnings and a multiplier.

Efficient Market   A market in which the prices of securities fully reflect all known information quickly and, on average, accurately.

Efficient Market Hypothesis (EMH)   The idea that securities markets are efficient, with the prices of securities reflecting their economic values. This hypothesis is typically broken into the weak, semistrong, and strong forms.

Efficient Portfolio   A portfolio which has the largest expected return for a given level of risk or the smallest risk for a given level of expected return.

Efficient Set (Frontier)   The set of portfolios generated by the Markowitz portfolio model. These portfolios have the maximum expected return for a given level of risk, or the minimum risk for a given level of expected return.

Equity-Derivative Securities   Securities that derive their value in whole or in part by having a claim on the underlying common stock. Examples include options, warrants, and convertibles.

Equity Risk Premium   The difference between the return on common stocks and the return on riskless assets (Treasury bills). It is the additional compensation, over and above the riskless rate of return, for assuming the risk of common stocks.

Equity Securities   The nondebt securities of a corporation representing the ownership interest. Includes both preferred and common stock.

Ex Ante   Before the fact—what is expected to occur.

Ex Post   After the fact—what has occurred.

Excess Return to Beta Ratio   Measures the desirability of adding a stock to an optimal portfolio. The higher this ratio, the more desirable the stock for inclusion in a portfolio.

Exercise (Strike) Price   The per-share price at which the common stock may be purchased (in the case of a call) or sold to a writer (in the case of a put).

Expectations Theory   One theory of the term structure of interest rates. It states that the long-term rate of interest is equal to an average of the short-term rates that are expected to prevail over the long-term period.

Expected Return   The ex ante return expected by investors over some future holding period. The expected return often differs from the realized return.

Expected Value   The weighted average return of a probability distribution, given the likely outcomes and their associated probabilities.

Expiration Date   With options, the last date at which an option can be exercised.

F

Factor Model   Used to depict the behavior of security prices by identifying major factors in the economy that affect large numbers of securities.

Federal Agency Securities   Securities issued by federal credit agencies. Federal agency securities are fully guaranteed whereas government-sponsored agency securities are not.

Filter Rule   A well-known technical trading rule specifying a breakpoint for an individual stock or market average. Trades are made when the price change is greater than this filter.

Financial Assets   Pieces of paper evidencing a claim on some issuer.

Financial Futures   Futures contracts on financial assets such as Treasury bonds, CDs, and stock indices.

Financial Risk   Risk arising from the use of debt in financing the assets of a firm.

Financial Statements   The major financial data provided by a corporation, primarily the balance sheet and the income statement.

Fixed-Income Securities   Securities with specified payment dates and amounts, primarily bonds and preferred stock.

Fourth Market   A communications network linking large institutional investors.

Fundamental Analysis   The idea that a security has an intrinsic value at any time which is a function of underlying economic variables. By analyzing these variables, intrinsic value can be estimated.

Futures Contracts   Agreements providing for the future exchange of a particular asset at a currently determined market price.

Futures Options   Option contracts (both puts and calls) on both interest futures and stock index futures.

Future Value   Also referred to as compound value. The terminal value of a beginning amount of money compounded at some interest rate for some period of time.

G

Generally Accepted Accounting Principles (GAAPs)   A standard set of rules developed by the accounting profession for the preparation of financial statements.

Geometric Mean   The nth root of the product of n numbers. It is used as a measure of the compound rate of return over time.

GNMA Pass-Through Certificates   A federal agency security that monthly passes through the principal and interest payments on the underlying mortgages to the bondholder as the mortgages are repaid.

Gross National Product   The market value of all goods and services produced during some time period.

Growth Industries   Industries whose earnings are expected to be significantly above the average of all industries.

H

Hedgers   Investors who attempt to minimize the risk of financial loss from adverse price changes by assuming futures positions opposite to cash positions.

Holding Period Return (HPR)   The total return from an investment for a given period of time, including both yield and capital gain or loss. HPRs are stated on the basis of 1.0, which represents no gain or loss.

Holding Period Yield (HPY)   The total return from an investment for a given period of time, including both yield and capital gain or loss. HPY is stated in percent form.

I

Immunization   The strategy of immunizing (protecting) a portfolio against interest rate risk by canceling out its two components, price risk and reinvestment rate risk.

Index Funds   Mutual funds holding portfolios that attempt to duplicate a market average such as the S&P 500.

Indirect Investing   The buying and selling of the shares of investment companies which, in turn, hold portfolios of securities. This is an investor alternative to direct investing.

Individual Retirement Accounts (IRAs)   Tax-sheltered accounts available to all income earners. IRA funds can be invested in a wide range of assets.

Industry Life Cycle   The evolvement of industries through stages, including the pioneering, expansion, and stabilization stages.

Institutional Investors   Pension funds, investment companies, bank trust departments, life insurance companies, and so forth, all of whom manage large portfolios of securities.

Interest Rate Futures   Futures contracts on fixed-income securities such as Treasury bills and bonds, CDs, and GNMA mortgages.

Interest Rate Options   Option contracts on fixed-income securities such as Treasury bonds.

Interest Rate Risk   The change in the price of a security resulting from a change in market interest rates.

Interest Sensitive Industries   Industries particularly sensitive to expectations about changes in interest rates.

Intermarket Trading System   A form of a central routing system, consisting of a network of terminals linking together several stock exchanges.

Intrinsic Value   The economic value of an asset.

Investment   The commitment of funds to one or more assets that will be held over some future time period.

Investments   The study of the investment process.

Investment Bankers   Firms specializing in the sale of new securities to the public, typically by underwriting the issue.

Investment Company   A financial service organization that sells shares in itself to the public and uses these funds to invest in a portfolio of securities.

Investment Value   The straight-debt value of a convertible bond.

J

Junk Bond   Bonds that carry ratings of BB or lower, with correspondingly higher yields. The junk bond market is perhaps better referred to as the "high-yield debt market."

L

Leverage   The magnification of gains and losses in earnings resulting from the use of fixed-cost financing.

Limit Order   An order to buy or sell at a specified (or better) price.

Liquidity   The ease with which an asset can be bought or sold quickly with relatively small price changes.

Liquidity Preference Theory   One of the theories of the term structure of interest rates. It states that interest rates reflect the sum of current and expected short rates, as in the expectations theory, plus liquidity (risk) premiums.

Load Funds   Mutual funds with a sales charge, typically 8½%.

M

M1   The basic measure of money supply, consisting of currency, demand deposits and other checkable deposits.

M2   M1 plus savings and small time deposits plus money market deposit accounts plus shares in money market funds.

M3 M2 plus large time deposits.

Management Fee The fee charged by all investment companies for managing the portfolio. A typical fee is 0.5% of the net assets.

Margin That part of a transaction's value that a customer must pay to initiate the transaction, with the other part being borrowed from the broker. The initial margin is set by the Federal Reserve System. The maintenance margin is the amount, established by brokers and exchanges, below which the actual margin cannot go.

Margin Account An account that permits margin trading, requiring $2000 to open.

Margin Call A demand from the broker for additional cash or securities as a result of the actual margin declining below the maintenance margin.

Marginal Tax Rate The tax rate on the last dollar of income.

Marked to the Market The daily process of debiting and crediting gains and losses resulting from changes in futures prices.

Market Anomalies Techniques or strategies that appear to be contrary to an efficient market. These anomalies include SUE, the low P/E strategy, the size effect, and the seasonal effect.

Market Average An arithmetic average of the prices for the sample of securities being used.

Market Data Primarily, stock price and volume data.

Market Index Measures the current price behavior of the sample in relation to a base period established for a previous time.

Market Model Relates the return on each stock to the return on the market, using a linear relationship with intercept and slope.

Market Order An order to buy or sell at the best price when the order reaches the trading floor.

Market Portfolio The portfolio of all risky assets, with each asset weighted by the ratio of its market value to the market value of all risky assets.

Market Risk Premium The difference between the expected return for the market and the risk-free rate of return.

Market Segmentation Theory One of three hypotheses for explaining the term structure of interest rates. It states that rates on securities with different maturities are effectively determined by the conditions that prevail in the different maturity segments of the market.

Market Value The market value of one share of stock is the current market price; for the corporation, it equals market price per share multiplied by the number of shares outstanding.

Marketable Securities Financial assets that are easily and inexpensively traded between investors.

Money Market The market for short-term, highly liquid, low-risk assets such as Treasury bills and negotiable CDs.

Money Market Deposit Accounts Accounts at banks and thrift institutions with no interest rate ceilings.

Money Market Mutual Fund A mutual fund that invests in money market instruments.

Mortgage-Backed Securities Securities representing an investment in an underlying pool of mortgages.

Municipal Securities Securities issued by political entities other than the federal government and its agencies, such as states and cities and airport authorities.

Mutual Funds The popular name for open-end investment companies. A mutual fund continually sells and redeems its own shares.

N

NASDAQ The automated quotation system for the OTC market, showing current bid–ask prices for thousands of stocks.

NASDAQ National Market System A combination of the competing market makers in OTC stocks and the up-to-the-minute reporting of trades using data almost identical to that shown for the NYSE and AMEX.

National Association of Securities Dealers (NASD) A self-regulating body of brokers and dealers overseeing OTC practices.

National Market System The market system for U.S. securities called for, but left undefined, by the Securities Acts Amendments of 1975.

Negotiable Title can be transferred from one owner to another.

Negotiated Market A market involving dealers, such as the OTC.

Net Asset Value (NAV) The per share value of an investment company, based on its portfolio. It is equal to the market value of the portfolio held by the company divided by the number of its shares outstanding.

No Load Funds Mutual funds that do not have a sales charge (load fee).

NYSE Rule 390 States that members must obtain NYSE permission before transacting off the exchange in a listed stock (unless exempted specifically by the exchange).

O

Odd-Lot Theory The idea that small investors who often transact in odd lots (i.e., less than 100 shares) are unsophisticated and usually wrong in their actions.

Open-End Investment Company An investment company whose capitalization constantly changes as new shares are sold and outstanding shares are redeemed.

Operationally Efficient A market with the lowest possible prices for transaction services.

Over-the-Counter (OTC) Market A network of securities dealers for the trading of securities not on the exchanges.

P

P/E Ratio The ratio of stock price to earnings, using historical, current or estimated data. This ratio is also referred to as the multiplier.

Par Value The value assigned to a security when it is issued. For bonds and preferred stock, par value is equivalent to face value. For common stocks, par value is arbitrary and of little importance.

Passive Management Strategy A bond management strategy whereby investors do not actively seek out trading possibilities in an attempt to outperform the market.

Payout Ratio   The ratio of dividends to earnings.

Point-and-Figure Chart   A technical analysis chart that shows only significant price changes and does not show volume.

Portfolio   The securities held by an investor taken as a group.

Portfolio Insurance   An asset management technique designed to provide a portfolio with a lower limit on value while permitting it to benefit from rising security prices. The basic concept involves the purchase of a "protective put" on the portfolio, with the balance of the funds invested in the underlying assets.

Portfolio Management   The second step in the investment decision process, involving the management of a group of assets (i.e., a portfolio) as a unit.

Preferred Stock   An equity security with an intermediate claim (between the bondholders and the stockholders) on a firm's assets and earnings. Dividends are specified, but can be omitted.

Premium   The amount by which a bond or preferred stock exceeds its par or face value. For closed-end investment companies, the amount by which the current market price exceeds the net asset value. In the case of options, the price paid by the option buyer to the seller of the option.

Price Risk   That part of interest rate risk involving the inverse relationship between bond prices and required rates of return.

Primary Market   The market for new issues of securities, typically involving investment bankers.

Private Placement   The sale of an issue of securities to an institutional investor.

Program Trading   Involves the use of computer-generated orders to buy and sell securities based on arbitrage opportunities between common stocks and index futures and options.

Prospectus   Provides information about an initial public offering of securities to potential buyers.

Pure Intermediary   An organization providing services for its clientele that they could provide for themselves (e.g., investment companies).

Put   An option to sell a specified number of shares of stock at a specified price within a nine-month period.

R

Real Assets   Physical assets, such as gold or real estate.

Real Rate of Interest   The marginal physical productivity of capital, or the opportunity cost of foregoing consumption. It is the basic component of market interest rates.

Realized Yield   The return actually earned on a bond as opposed to the yield to maturity, which is a promised yield.

Reinvestment Rate Risk   That part of interest rate risk resulting from uncertainty about the rate at which future interest coupons can be reinvested.

Relative Strength   A technical analysis technique involving the ratio of a stock's price to a market index or other index. These ratios are plotted across time to form a graph of relative prices.

Required Rate of Return   The minimum expected return on an asset that an investor requires before investing.

Restricted Account   A margin account where the actual margin is between the initial margin and the maintenance margin. Additional margin purchases are prohibited.

Retention Rate   1.0 minus the payout ratio.

Return on Assets (ROA)   A fundamental measure of firm profitability, equal to net income divided by total assets.

Return on Equity (ROE)   The rate of return on stockholders equity, equal to net income divided by equity.

Reward-to-Variability Ratio   Sharpe's measure of portfolio performance. It is the ratio of excess portfolio return (i.e., return minus the risk-free rate) to risk as measured by the standard deviation.

Reward-to-Volatility Ratio   Treynor's measure of portfolio performance. It is the ratio of excess portfolio return (i.e., return minus the risk-free rate) to risk as measured by beta.

Rights   A short-term (weeks) option permitting the holder to purchase from the corporation a specified number of shares of a new issue of common stock at a specified subscription price.

Risk   The chance that the actual return on an investment will be different from the expected return.

Risk-Averse Investor   An investor who will not assume a given level of risk unless there is an expectation of adequate compensation for having done so.

Risk-Free Asset   An asset with a certain expected return and a variance of return of zero.

Risk-Free Rate of Return   The return on a riskless asset, often proxied by the rate of return on Treasury securities.

Risk Premium   The additional compensation demanded by investors, above the risk-free rate of return, for assuming risk—the larger the risk, the larger the risk premium.

S

Secondary Market   The market where previously issued securities are traded, including both the organized exchanges and the OTC.

Securities and Exchange Commission (SEC)   A federal government agency established by the Securities Exchange Act of 1934 to protect investors.

Security Analysis   The first part of the investment decision process, involving the valuation and analysis of individual securities.

Security Market Line   An alternative name for the CAPM (see Capital Asset Pricing Model).

Semistrong Form   That part of the Efficient Market Hypothesis which states that prices reflect all publicly available information.

Separation Theorem   The idea that the investment decision (which portfolio of risky assets to hold) is separate from the financing decision (how to allocate investable funds between the risk-free asset and the risky asset).

Serial Bonds   Bonds that mature at specified stated intervals.

Shelf Rule   Permits qualified companies to file a short form registration and "place on the shelf" securities to be sold over time under favorable conditions.

Short Interest Ratio   A technical analysis indicator used primarily in aggregate market analysis. It is calculated as the ratio of total shares sold short to average daily trading volume.

Short Sale   The sale of a stock not owned in order to take advantage of an expected decline in the price of the stock. If the decline occurs, the stock can be purchased and the short position closed.

Single Index Model   A model that relates returns on each security to the returns on a market index.

Specialist   A member of an organized exchange who is charged with maintaining an orderly market in one or more stocks by buying or selling for his or her own account. The specialist also acts as a broker's broker, executing limit orders for brokers.

Spread   The purchase and sale of an equivalent option varying in only one respect, such as time or maturity.

Standard Deviation   A measure of the dispersion of outcomes around the mean (or expected value), used to measure total risk. It is the square root of the variance.

Standard Industrial Classification (SIC) System   A system based on Census data used to classify industries on the basis of what the firms produce.

Standard & Poor's Stock Price Indices   Market value indices of stock market activity, with a base of 10 (1941–1943). The S&P 500 Composite Index is a broad and well-known measure of market activity.

Standardized Unexpected Earnings (SUE)   A variable used in the selection of common stocks. It is calculated by subtracting expected earnings from actual earnings and dividing the result by the standard error of the regression equation used to estimate the expected earnings.

Stock Dividend   A payment by the corporation in shares of stock rather than cash.

Stock Index Futures   Futures contracts on stock indices, including the S&P 500, the NYSE Index, and The Value Line Index.

Stock Index Options   Option contracts on a stock market index such as the S&P 500.

Stock Split   The issuance by a corporation of a larger number of shares of stock in proportion to the existing shares outstanding. A split changes the book value and the par value.

Stop Order   An order specifying a certain price at which a market order takes effect.

Straddle   A combination of a put and a call on the same stock with the same exercise date and exercise price.

Street Name   When customers' securities are held by a brokerage firm in its name. Customers often leave securities with their brokers for safekeeping.

Strong Form   That part of the Efficient Market Hypothesis that states that prices reflect all information, public and private.

Super NOW Account   An unrestricted checking account paying money-market rates.

Syndicate   Several investment bankers involved in an underwriting.

Syndicated Offering   The sale of a new issue of securities through investment bankers.

Systematic Risk   Also called market risk or nondiversifiable risk. It is risk attributable to factors affecting all investments.

T

Technical Analysis   The methodology of forecasting fluctuations in the prices of securities, whether individual securities or the market as a whole.

Term Structure of Interest Rates   Refers to the relationship between time to maturity and yields for a particular category of bonds.

Term to Maturity   The remaining life of a bond.

Theoretical (Calculated) Value of a Warrant   A formula value for a warrant which produces its intrinsic value. Warrants typically sell above this value.

TIGRs (Tigers)   Fixed-income receipts sold at discount (by Merrill Lynch) and backed by U.S. Treasury bonds.

Third Market   An OTC market for exchange-listed securities.

Treasury Bill   A short-term money market instrument sold at discount by the U.S. government.

Treasury Bond   Long-term bonds sold by the U.S. government.

U

Unbundle   The separation of brokerage charges so that customers pay only for those services desired, such as execution services.

Underwriting   The process by which investment bankers purchase an issue of securities from an issuer and resell them to the public.

Unlisted Security   A security not listed on one of the exchanges.

Unsystematic Risk   Also called nonmarket risk or diversifiable risk. It is risk attributable to factors unique to the security.

V

Variability   Dispersion in the likely outcomes.

Volatility   Fluctuations in a security's or portfolio's return.

W

Warrant   A corporate-created option to purchase a stated number of common shares at a specified price within a specified time (typically several years).

Weak Form   That part of the Efficient Market Hypothesis that states that prices reflect all price and volume data.

Wealth   The sum of current income and the present value of all future income.

Y

Yield Curve   A graphical depiction of the relationship between yields and time for bonds that are identical except for maturity.

Yield Spreads   The relationships between bond yields and the particular features on various bonds such as quality, callability, and taxes.

Yield to Call   A better measure than yield to maturity for bonds likely to be called, using as the time element the end of the deferred call period rather than term to maturity.

Yield to Maturity   The indicated (promised) compounded rate of return an investor will receive from a bond purchased at the current market price and held to maturity.

Z

Zero Coupon Bond   A bond sold with no coupons. It is purchased at a discount and redeemed for face value at maturity.

SUBJECT INDEX